LANGUAGE PROBLEMS
OF DEVELOPING NATIONS

Joshua A. Fishman
Charles A. Ferguson
Jyotirindra Das Gupta

Editors

JOHN WILEY & SONS, INC.
New York • London • Sydney • Toronto

Library of Congress Catalog Card Number: 68–30910
SBN 471 26160 2
Printed in the United States of America

CONTRIBUTORS

Joshua A. Fishman	Yeshiva University, New York	Sociology, Sociolinguistics
Jyotirindra Das Gupta	Political Science Department, University of California, Berkeley	Political science
Charles A. Ferguson	Committee on Linguistics, Stanford University, California	Linguistics, Sociolinguistics
Heinz Kloss	Forschungsstelle für Nationalitaten und Sprachenfragen, Marburg, Germany	Sociology
Dankwart Rustow	Columbia University, New York	Political science
A. Tabouret-Keller	Institut de Psychologie, Université de Strasbourg, Strasbourg, France	Social psychology
Pierre Alexandre	Ecole Pratique der Hautes Etudes, Paris	Applied linguistics
Charles F. Gallagher	American Universities Field Staff, New York	Sociology
John J. Gumperz	Department of Anthropology, University of California, Berkeley	Social anthropology, Sociolinguistics
Björn Jernudd	Linguistics Section, Monash University, Clayton, Victoria, Australia	Linguistics
Ali A. Mazrui	Department of Political Science, Makerere University College, Kampala, Uganda	Sociology

John N. Paden	Program of African Studies, Northwestern University, Evanston, Illinois	Political science
Pierre L. van den Berghe	Department of Sociology, University of Washington, Seattle	Political sociology
Robert G. Armstrong	Institute of African Studies, University of Ibadan, Nigeria	African linguistics
Haim Blanc	Linguistics Department, Hebrew University of Jerusalem, Israel	Linguistics
Einar Haugen	Department of Germanic Languages and Literature, Harvard University, Cambridge, Massachusetts	Linguistics, Sociolinguistics
Jiri V. Neustupný	Department of Modern Languages, Monash University, Clayton, Victoria, Australia	Linguistics
Edgar Polomé	Center for Asian Studies, University of Texas, Austin	Linguistics
Albert Valdman	Department of Linguistics, Indiana University, Bloomington	Applied linguistics
W. H. Whiteley	The University College, Dar es Salaam, Tanzania	Linguistics
Stephen A. Wurm	Australian National University, Canberra	Linguistics
Petr Zima	Department of Linguistics, University of Ghana, Legon	African linguistics
John B. Bowers	Institute of Education, London University, London	Applied linguistics
Donald H. Burns	Summer Institute of Linguistics, Ministry of Public Education of Peru, Lima	Applied linguistics
R. B. Le Page	Department of Language, University of York, England	Applied linguistics
Herbert Passin	Columbia University, New York	Sociology
Clifford H. Prator	Department of English, University of California, Los Angeles	Applied Linguistics

| Joan Rubin | Department of Anthropology, George Washington University, Washington, D.C. | Anthropological linguistics |
| Lyndon Harries | Department of African Languages and Literature, University of Wisconsin, Madison | African literature |

PREFACE

Most of the essays presented in this book were papers prepared for a conference on the language problems of the developing nations at Airlie House, Warrenton, Virginia, November 1–3, 1966. This conference was one of several organized and sponsored by the Committee on Sociolinguistics of the Social Science Research Council in its efforts to promote interdisciplinary research and training in the relatively new field to which its attention is directed.

Although a number of the papers presented at this conference have since been published in various scholarly journals and books, it seemed highly desirable to bring all of them together in one volume. The number of disciplines involved would otherwise tend to scatter them to journals appearing in all parts of the world and in various languages as well. Thus it was felt that a single volume including most of these papers (a few were dropped for various reasons, primarily, the rapid changes in the language situations in some areas) would elicit the attention of a larger number of students and specialists from a variety of backgrounds. The problems dealt with in this book are of great practical and theoretical complexity and will long continue to require the dedication of large numbers of highly trained and broadly oriented individuals, both in and outside university circles. One of the goals of this collection is to foster interest in such training and orientation.

The theoretical issues related to the language problems of the developing nations are hardly less complicated than the applied questions faced by governments, school systems, mass media, and industrial developers throughout much of Africa, Asia, Latin America, and the Pacific islands. The birth and rebirth of nations, peoples, and languages do not constitute traditional topics of inquiry for sociologists, political scientists, and linguists anywhere. Least of all do they constitute traditional topics for American specialists in the social, behavioral, and linguistic disciplines. Yet these phenomena are not only provocative but basic to an understanding of social change, national integration, and language development —areas of study that are at the very heart of several major branches of American higher education.

It is a sad fact of American academic life—one that speaks volumes about our contact with the world as well as about our ability to enrich both it and science as a result of such contact—that there is still no institution in the United States in which students can be adequately trained for either theoretical or applied involvement in the language problems of developing nations. At a time when the major part of the human race is entrapped by such problems, most American linguists continue to be only marginally interested in language development (language policy, graphization, standardization, modernization, planning), and most sociologists and political scientists are just becoming aware of language as an aspect of societal and national functioning. At the same time sociolinguistics itself is still a very fragile flower, cultivated only at a handful of universities, and focused primarily on microphenomena at the level of the speech act in face-to-face interaction.

All of the preceding considerations constitute rationale enough for this book. It is intended to be of particular interest to social scientists who are not familiar with technical linguistics, although a modicum of such material could not be avoided and was even thought to be desirable as an antidote for those who are still wont to equate the analysis of a language with the perusal of a dictionary. It is for such social scientists—and they represent the vast majority in their respective disciplines—that this book seeks to provide ample examples of the diverse societal and national functions of language varieties, examples of the changes in these functions as the roles and statuses of their speakers change, and examples of the changes in the language varieties per se that accompany their changed uses and users. Language is not only a powerful *lever* in social, cultural, and national development but it is a constant ingredient of such development and, in its realization as speech or writing, a powerful *indicator* of interaction networks, social situations, role-relationships, domains of aggregative activity, dominant value clusters, and national missions or symbols. The language problems of the developing nations can thus provide sociologists and political scientists with new opportunities to look into some of their *current* disciplinary preoccupations, as well as new opportunities to tackle a host of more novel theoretical concerns.

Linguists and specialists in adult literacy and in second-language learning should also find much that is of value in the essays presented here. For them the language problems of the developing nations represent an opportunity to view language in much broader perspective. Societal and national perspectives on language clarify the fact—otherwise easily overlooked—that languages do not really exist except as part of a matrix of language varieties, language behaviors, and behaviors toward language. Any attempt to describe "a language" without recognizing its actual matrix position and any attempt to influence language learning or literacy without questioning what they signify for the language-and-behavior matrix of the prospective learners is to preserve or protect one's own ignorance in connection with those very matters toward which one's expertise should be directed.

The time is certainly approaching when American social science and American linguistics will not only work together without embarrassment but their joint endeavors will be addressed to important questions rather than merely neat ones. It is a goal of this book to hasten that time, for it is our view that few areas are more fruitful or urgent with respect to interdisciplinary attention than the language problems of the developing nations. For their contributions to this volume—and therefore to the several long- and short-term goals it has set for itself—we are deeply indebted to the participants in the original Airlie House Conference, to three other authors who have permitted us to reprint their papers so that this book might attain better topical and geographic balance, to the members of the Committee on Sociolinguistics of the Social Science Research Council, who encouraged us to plan the conference and this volume of its proceedings, to Elbridge Sibley, S.S.R.C. Staff Representative to the Committee, who never ceased to be helpful and stimulating in the many years of the Committee's dependence on him, and to William Gum of John Wiley and Sons for his constant good cheer and good faith.

JOSHUA A. FISHMAN
CHARLES A. FERGUSON
JYOTIRINDRA DAS GUPTA

New York, New York
May 1968

CONTENTS

LANGUAGE PROBLEMS
OF DEVELOPING NATIONS

I

Introduction

Joshua A. Fishman

SOCIOLINGUISTICS AND THE LANGUAGE PROBLEMS OF THE DEVELOPING COUNTRIES

WHAT IS SOCIOLINGUISTICS, AND WHY?

Interest in the sociology of language can be traced back quite far, certainly to the French, German, Italian, and British masters of eighteenth- and nineteenth-century sociology and social philosophy. A more sensitive search, however, that is, one that was responsive to more fragmentary indications of interest, would easily take us much further back as well as to more distant parts of the globe. Medieval, renaissance, and reformation Christendom, early and later Islam, the Talmudic and Responsa periods in Judaism, ancient Greece and Rome, Persia and India and China as well, all produced thinkers, some of whose concerns were recognizably sociolinguistic. Nevertheless, modern sociolinguistics of the past 10 years is not the direct heir of any of these or other older substantive traditions but, rather, is most accurately viewed as a byproduct of very recent and still ongoing developments in its two parent disciplines, linguistics and sociology.

I think it is only fair to admit that the stronger and clearer interest has come from linguistics, both as a result of its recently more sophisticated synchronic (i.e., nonhistorical) concerns as well as a result of its growing (and growingly comfortable) response to applied demands.

Many more linguists have come to be concerned with variations that were formerly set aside as purportedly unsystematic and of little scientific account. These have increasingly been discovered not to be "free" or unsystematic at all but, rather, to correspond to *intragroup* (speech community) norms relating to face-to-face interactional ("situational") or higher order language behavior contexts (Ervin-Tripp, 1964; Fischer, 1958; Gumperz, 1964; Hymes, 1962; Labov, 1964). Linguistics has discovered (or rediscovered for synchronic purposes) the principle of co-territoriality: one and the same population usually controls several fully systematic varieties (whether registers, dialects, or languages) and these varieties may come to influence *each other* quite systematically as well (Blanc, 1964;

3

Ferguson, 1959; Ferguson and Gumperz, 1960; Gumperz, 1966; Haugen, 1966; Kachru, 1965).

The foregoing discovery makes many linguists even better prepared to struggle with literacy problems, problems of nonstandard ("dialect") speakers, problems of societal second-language learning, and problems of language planning and language policy than they might otherwise be, for each of these, in turn, is illuminated by the realization that speech communities possess a *repertoire* of varieties, each of which may have and retain its separate, accepted and systematic purpose(s), even while the repertoire as a whole can be expanded in order to cope with new interests, opportunities, or concerns of the entire community or of certain of its networks.

Sociology too has contributed to and benefited from the new sociolinguistics. Initially, interest was greatest among a number of sociologists preoccupied with the relationship between transformations in *intragroup identification* on the one hand and *intergroup relations* on the other. As human aggregates come to view *themselves* differently (i.e., as their consciousness of kind changes in content and in saliency) their relations with their neighbors change as well. These concomitant changes, equally (although far from identically) noticeable among international civil servants and other extraterritorial elites (Useem, 1967), among impoverished and dislocated urban populations of recent rural origin (Fishman, 1964), among populations moving from limited (tribal) to larger (national) identifications (Fishman, 1965b), among working class populations struggling against the economic and cultural domination of those in control of technology and High Culture (Lieberson, 1965), among delinquent or pariah groups seeking self-dignity as well as differentiation from society (Savitz, 1966), all have highly visible counterparts in the languages and in the language-related views and behaviors of the populations involved. Thus some sociologists have become sensitively aware of language as a *clue* to societal change and development and, furthermore, aware of language as an *area or object* of societal change and development per se (Bernstein, 1958; Bidwell, 1962; Das Gupta and Gumperz, 1968; Fishman, 1965a; Fishman, 1967; Gallagher, 1964; Grimshaw, 1966; Harrison, 1960; Hunt, 1966; Paden, 1968; Passin, 1963; van den Berghe, 1968; Zima, 1968).

More recently another branch of the sociological fraternity has demonstrated even more central interest in language; it is concerned with small network interaction in general and with the foundations of everyday life and the detailed understandings on which such life is based. Since most human utterances are ambiguous and incomplete, to say the least, what contextual and linguistic regularities are utilized to arrive at the high proportion of meaningful and consensual interpretations that nevertheless obtains? This branch of sociological sociolinguistics is still in its infancy, but it is developing with great theoretical and methodological thrust (Garfinkel, 1964; Lennard, 1960; Rose, 1964; Sacks, 1963; Schegloff, 1967) and will be heard of increasingly over the coming years. Whether or not this microprocess wing will ultimately be organically relatable to the macroprocess (and macrostructure) wing mentioned earlier remains to be seen.

It should be obvious by now that sociolinguistics as a whole (the study of the relationship *between* the linguistic repertoire and its range, compartmentalization, access, and fluidity, on the one hand, *and* the social role repertoire and its range, compartmentalization, access, and fluidity *within* speech communities, on the other hand) is by no means exclusively concerned with the language problems of the developing countries. What follows therefore is by no means an impartial review of sociolinguistics as a whole; rather it is an attempt to focus only on one corner of it.

This attempt should not be begun, however, without stressing the fact that among those who refer to themselves as sociolinguists there is considerable conviction that their field is now making and will continue to make important contributions to both parent fields. Nevertheless, the foregoing division into linguists and sociologists, and, even more, the division into linguistic and sociological interests, is somewhat arbitrary and is likely to become even more so. As time goes by a few sociolinguists are tending to define themselves as *such* rather than as primarily linguists or sociologists. The topics to which they have devoted their attention reveal increasing dependence upon or influence from the "other" discipline, that is, from the field or fields other than the ones in which they obtained their own initial training. It is not clear how far this trend will go. There are certainly many traditional forces in academic life that will tend to keep it from going very far for very many. Nevertheless, there is widespread agreement within sociolinguistics that the true promise of the field will be realized only if one or another way is found to foster truly interdisciplinary work and thought.

On the other hand, there is considerable awareness that the field as a whole faces serious problems of training, theoretical systemization, empirical verification, and applied implementation. Although this essay attempts to focus only on sociolinguistics and the language problems of developing nations it is hoped that in so doing some of the broader implications and more general problems of sociolinguistics will also be touched upon.

THE LANGUAGE COMPONENT OF THE PROBLEMS
OF DEVELOPING NATIONS

The problems of developing nations differ largely in degree rather than in kind from those of most other nations, for few if any nations are completely stabilized, unified, and legitimized. Precisely because the developing nations are at an earlier stage in development, however, the problems and processes of nationhood are more apparent in such nations and their transformations more discernible to the researcher. As a result the developing nations ("new nations") have come to be of great interest to those sociolinguists who are interested in the transformations of group identity in general as well as to those interested in societal (governmental and other) impact on language-related behavior and on language itself.

A widespread problem of new nations is that their political boundaries correspond rather imperfectly to any pre-existing ethnic-cultural unity. If this was true of the new nations of Eastern Europe after the conclusion of World War I—even though they had behind them decades if not centuries of nationalistic, ethnic-cultural activity, which led to a high degree of cultural consolidation and integration *before* the achievement of nationhood (Rustow, 1968)—how much truer is it of the new nations of Africa where political independence has commonly been achieved far in *advance* of such unification around a common set of "national" behaviors and myths? In the absence of a common, nationwide, ethnic and cultural identity new nations proceed to plan and create such an identity through national symbols that can lead to common mobilization and involvement above, beyond, and at the expense of pre-existing ethnic-cultural particularities (Almond and Verba, 1963; Bell and Oxaal, 1964; Bidwell, 1962; Fallers, 1961; Geertz, 1963; Hunt, 1966; Marriott, 1963; Moscos and Bell, 1965; Whitely, 1957). It is at this point that a national language is frequently invoked (along with a national flag, a national ruler, a national mission, etc.) as a unifying symbol. It is also at this point that the local counterparts of these national symbols may be reactively developed among populations that never ideologized them before (Greenberg, 1965; Harrison, 1960; Rustow, 1968). Thus language may and has become a symbol of supralocal ethnic-cultural identification, that is, of ethnic-cultural identification at the nationality level (therefore: nationalism), just as it may and has become a symbol of contranational ethnic-cultural identification on the part of smaller groups who, resisting fusion into the larger nationality, develop a localized nationality consciousness of their own (Haugen, 1959).

It is in this process of conscious integration (and, in counterreaction, of conscious differentiation) that hitherto local languages or languages of restricted populations or functions become elevated to national, unifying symbols (e.g., Swahili, Hindustani), are frequently rendered more differentiated from languages or varieties with which they have long been in contact (e.g., Afrikaans versus Dutch, Hindi versus Urdu, Landsmaal versus Riksmaal, Yiddish versus German, Ukrainian versus Russian, Macedonian versus Bulgarian, etc.; for the general case see Kloss, 1952; Read, 1964), and are related to national heroes, national values, national missions, and ultimately to the sacredness of the state and of the moral order. Thus the ideologization of languages, which enables them to play desired roles in symbolic mobilization and unification, also leads to the development of these languages per se into fitting instruments of government, technology, and High Culture (Auty, 1953; Guxman, 1967; Nahirny and Fishman, 1965; Weinreich, 1953; Whitely, 1968; Wurm, 1966).

Thus we come to the second large cluster of problems of developing nations, those that revolve about efficiency and instrumentality more than about authenticity. Successful nationalisms finally create a sense of ethnic-cultural unity and of involvement or commitment within the geographic limits of their nations, but that takes time and, frequently, also force (as exemplified by the lack of full ethnic-cultural unity in such well-established polities as Great Britain, France, Spain, etc.). Until such unity is established (and certainly if such organic unity is not—or is no longer— sought, as in Belgium, Switzerland, India) the nation must continue to function, must continue to protect itself from external and internal opponents, and must continue to meet the needs of its citizenry with respect to the facilitation of communication and the conduct of commerce, industry, education, and all other organized societal pursuits.

Once again then, this time in the pursuit of the efficiency of *"nationism,"* new nations must face language problems (Fishman, 1968). The need for a broader ethnic-cultural unity may well point to the long-term espousal of a given language as *the* national language. Nevertheless, the immediate operational needs of the country may well necessitate the short-term recognition of another or of multiple languages, which leads away from the long-range goal of creating a new, supralocal authenticity. Thus some nations have hit upon the expediency of recognizing several local languages as permissible for early education (i.e., grades one to three or even six), whereas the preferred national language is retained for intermediate education and a nonindigenous language of international significance is retained (at least temporarily) for governmental activity and higher education (Armstrong, 1968; Friedrich, 1962; Gallagher, 1964; LePage, 1964; Passin, 1963; Ramos, 1961; Whitely, 1968). If such a pattern promotes or retains sufficient stability, language policies can subsequently be set into motion to continually develop the preferred language, enabling it to successively displace the language of wider communication above it (e.g., the increasing displacement of English in the Philippines and in India) and, eventually, the languages of narrower communication below it. Such displacement not only requires careful educational, political and social planning (for it fosters the co-occurrence of identities which may become resistant to displacement or to containment) but requires concomitant language planning of a very careful and concerted sort. Thus a successful language policy focused on *nationism* ultimately also helps form the new *nationalism,* just as surely as a successful language policy focused on nationalism also helps form and maintain the new nation.

The preceding sketch of the language component in the growth of nationalism on the one hand and in the growth of nationism on the other is a highly theoretical reconstruction based more on hunches, extrapolations, and partial observations than on systematic and comparative study. The truth of the matter is that sociolinguistics has not (yet) been closely or directly involved in the vast amount of recent (and ongoing) sociological, economic, political science, educational, and other scholarly work on the developing nations. Very few of the area-studies centers specializing in Africa, Asia, or Latin America have attracted scholars devoted to sociolinguistics, and even where this has been done, very little interest has been shown in the transformations of society-and-language per se as distinguished from "sociolinguistically oriented" but otherwise quite definitely linguistic pursuits. The major recent volumes on developing nations have devoted little attention to language (for a welcome exception see Passin, 1963). The few recent volumes on language problems of developing nations have been singularly innocent of social science expertise (Anon., 1963; Anon., 1965; Anon., 1966; LePage, 1964; Spencer, 1963). As a result, although much is suspected and roughly understood concerning the role of language in nationalism (Deutsch, 1953) and in nationism, all too little is known with certainty and indeed very little is known that can be clearly used as the basis of policy.

All this is most unfortunate, for not only are the new nations beset by problems that are clearly language-related, but the earliest stages of these problems are the most fleeting and the ones most difficult to reconstruct by means of archival or laboratory analysis. Furthermore, although the new nations are submerged in a churning sea of social change, there is very little language-related research under way on the transmutations and elaborations of ethnicity, on the development of identification with the broader nationality and the broader nation, on the resurgence of tradition in certain behaviors (e.g., in dress, naming practices, and religious observances) together with the growth of modernity in the occupational, educational, and governmental spheres, on the impact of previously available Great Traditions upon the acceptance of more modern and broader identifications, on the restructuring of traditional value hierarchies as distinguished from their disintegration, on the bicultural counterparts to diglossia, and so on.

All of the foregoing topics are clearly language-related, but they cannot be studied as such by most *sociolinguists* today (not to mention most sociologists or most linguists). Topics such as these require the close collaboration and integration of disciplines that are still too rarely in serious contact with each other. Optimally they require much more than multidisciplinary research; they require the preparation of researchers who are themselves interdisciplinary and therefore can approach questions in this area in terms of a total problem-orientation rather than in terms of vested disciplinary interests and skills. Problems such as the preceding truly require sociolinguists rather than merely "sociolinguistically oriented" sociologists or linguists.

THE SOCIAL COMPONENT OF THE PROBLEMS OF DEVELOPING LANGUAGES

The developing languages (i.e., languages undergoing greatest and most rapid change in societal functions and therefore most exposed to substantial planned and unplanned change) and the developing countries do not stand in a completely isomorphic relationship to each other. In addition, the developing languages do not reveal problems or processes that are really discontinuous with those of other more accepted or better established languages. Nevertheless, the developing nations do tend to present the best and most numerous laboratories for the study of developing languages and must be of interest to the sociolinguist for that reason alone. Languages undergo development when their functions undergo real or anticipatory expansion as a result of the expanded role repertoires (once more, real or anticipatory) of those for whom these languages have become too symbolic of group membership and of group goals to be easily displaced. Such expansion and symbolic elaboration of language functions has, in recent years, occurred most frequently in the developing nations.

Both nationism and nationalism are concerned with language choice (selection) but in quite different ways. For the nationalist, language represents the continuity of a Great Tradition with all of its symbolic elaborations in terms of ideologized values and goals. Language selection therefore represents a triumph over other, purportedly lesser traditions and goals. Nationalisms do not need to ponder language choice since each nationalism is seemingly irrevocably and seemingly naturally committed in this connection. Thus nationalisms pursue language reinforcement and maintenance rather than selection per se. For the nationist, however, language choice is a matter of calculated effectiveness, of communicational ease, of operational efficiency (Fishman, 1966b). Rival languages are considered in terms of what they can contribute to the functional strength of the nation. The nationist may conclude that the fewer the languages the better, and the less the opposition to them the better. Thus language choice may well come as the resultant of these two frequently contradictory considerations. Nationism has more initial degrees of freedom with respect to language choice than does nationalism. However, nationism too tends to fence itself in on the language question since even initial nationistic solutions set into motion forces that soon engender inflexible language maintenance and reinforcement goals of their own.

Whether language selection evolves primarily from nationalistic or from nationistic considerations, or, as is more common, from a combination of both, the engineering of consent or acceptance is needed. Without such acceptance language selection may be resisted or sabotaged. The vehicles of engineered acceptance are many: language censuses (often rigged); subsidized schools for children and classes for adults; free publications and audio-visual materials; language societies with national, regional, and local branches; examinations and contests yielding honorific or more tangible rewards; translation institutes for converting world literature into the selected language, etc. (see, e.g., Anon., 1965; Anon., 1966; Das Gupta and Gumperz, 1968; Haugen, 1966b).

Many of the examples mentioned imply that in the process of winning friends and influencing people on behalf of a particular language the language itself is usually enriched (or at least altered) in one way or another. This is indeed the case and a case well worth studying for far too little is known about it.

Western languages, even those that have considerable international prominence, are constantly undergoing elaboration (in response to the growing and changing technological, scientific, and cultural pursuits of certain networks of users of these languages). Similarly, Western languages are constantly undergoing recodification, through dictionaries, grammars, and usage handbooks by means of which multifocal elaboration efforts are evaluated and consolidated (Guxman, 1968b). Such processes of elaboration and codification are even more necessary (and noticeable) in those new nations in which an indigenous language has been selected for some function above and beyond those with which it has hitherto been associated. Inevitably, official, semi-official, and unofficial agencies, institutes, and societies arise that prepare and distribute orthographies, word lists, and grammars (as well as related teaching and learning materials). These frequently reveal serious disagreement (or elicit such) in view of different postures that are adopted with respect to a few basic issues (Berry, 1958; Ferguson, 1968; Garvin, 1959; Heyd, 1954; Lunt, 1959; Mills, 1956; Pietrzyk, 1965; Ray, 1963).

Where the language being elaborated or codified has lacked a generally accepted standard variety, elaboration/codification efforts may initially disagree as to which variety should be selected for attention. Selections for elaboration, codification are normally guided by such considerations as number of speakers (although at times a case is made for a variety spoken by relatively few on the grounds that it is not involved in the bitter traditional rivalries to which more widespread varieties have become exposed), past association with a Great Tradition, current association with major social trends (urbanization, Christianization, etc.), greater purity in the sense of fewer influences from varieties or languages considered undesirable or, conversely, greater similarity to other highly regarded varieties or languages, and, finally, a middle-ground position vis-à-vis overly pure and overly indistinguishable varieties. Depending on the initial selection based upon considerations (and value-laden positions) such as those just mentioned, the endproducts of subsequent elaboration/ codification efforts can obviously differ widely in orthography, phonology, lexicon, and grammar.

Considering the number of instances in which the selection, elaboration, and codification of developing languages have occurred during the past century, we have surprisingly few complete case studies of these processes, even fewer that relate them to the ongoing societal developments with which they co-occurred (there *are* a few, e.g., Clough, 1930; Haugen, 1966a), and fewer yet that attempt to do so on a comparative or contrastive basis so that generalizable parameters can be formulated and their relative significance estimated (perhaps only Guxman, 1968a, and Haugen, 1966b). Although we have many lists of new words (and new forms) in language X we know almost nothing of how language academies operate, how governments review and implement the recommendations of such academies, how language societies popularize and defend the recommendations and decisions of academies and governments, or of how rival academies and societies confront each other and seek to influence governments and populations in accord with their own preferences. We are particularly limited with respect to any systematic social theory-guided approach to why certain selective, elaborative, and codificatory attempts succeed (i.e., why they are accepted by the desired target populations), whereas others fail (Morag, 1959).

Very little work on questions dealing with the *social* component of the problems of developing languages is currently being conducted in the United States (but note Ferguson, 1962; Ferguson, 1968; Haugen, 1966a). The current centers for the study of exotic, critical, or less commonly taught languages (most of these being developing languages according to our definition) have not turned their attention to matters such as these. A study of the social component of developing languages requires more than linguistic sophistication embellished by societal curiosity or sensitivity. It requires thorough familiarity with theories of social change and social innovation and social research methodology. Given such familiarity, the developing nations represent an indispensable and truly intriguing array of field-work locations for a new breed of genuine sociolinguists, some of whom may ultimately become attached to one or another center for the study of less commonly taught languages (or language and area center), provided such centers undertook to expand their currently limited appreciation of the relationship between societal development and language development.

POSSIBLE CONTRIBUTIONS TO OTHER TOPIC AREAS

There are a number of implications of sociolinguistic research in general and particularly of that on the language problems of developing nations for other language-related topics. Language teaching should some day be ready to give up its attachment to the myth of fully separate and unvarying languages, and when it does it will find the sociolinguistic concern with situationally and functionally defined varieties extremely useful. Native-language as well as foreign-language teaching should benefit from the concept of a speech community with its repertoire of varieties, which would define communicative appropriateness not linguistically alone but also in terms of appropriate interlocutors, situations, interactions, and emphases. Contact between sociolinguistics and language instruction is just beginning (Gumperz, 1965, 1967; Stewart, 1964) and should become stronger with the passage of time.

The rapidly expanding concern with language problems of disadvantaged speakers of nonstandard varieties represents another area of growing interaction with sociolinguistics. The language of lower-class urban Negroes and Puerto Ricans in the United States has already begun to be viewed as revealing several varieties, along a scale of intimacy-distance, differing noticeably in the extent to which they are effortlessly mastered during and after adolescence (Labov, 1966a; Stewart, 1965). Some of these varieties have already been found to command intragroup loyalty so that the impediments between them and the activization of more standard varieties are not only structural but functional as well and fully ideologized to boot (Labov, 1965; Fishman, 1965). The educator's task in connection with the verbal repertoire of the disadvantaged has been stated to be repertoire expansion accompanied by role expansion (Bernstein, 1966; Friedman and Hannerz, 1966; Gordon, 1966; Labov, 1966b). In general, the problems of disadvantaged populations might helpfully be seen in broader perspective if they were considered against the background of coterritorial language differences more generally and of planned language shift in particular. The long experience of other countries in coping with home-school dialect differences of a major sort (e.g., in England, Germany, Italy) may be illuminating if only to more clearly indicate the difference between those cases and the American Negro case. All in all, there have been ample signs of the potential value of sociolinguistics for the study of the language problems of developing populations in the United States as well as those abroad (The Urban Language Study, the work of Labov, the Conference convened by the NCTE [Shuy, 1965], the conferences convened by Yeshiva University's Project Beacon [Gordon, 1966]).

CONCLUSIONS

The language problems of developing nations present sociolinguistics with a virtually inexhaustible and untouched field for the exploration of its central hypotheses and concerns. The problems themselves require interdisciplinary, comparative study as well as both theoretical and applied attention. The intensity of these problems, their difficulty of solution, and their centrality to several major interests of sociologists, linguists, and political scientists as well as sociolinguists, argue for devoting greater attention to them in the years ahead. It is the purpose of this book to indicate some of the areas to which such attention might well be directed.

REFERENCES

Almond, G. A., and S. Verba. 1963. *The Civic Culture*. Princeton, N.J.: Princeton University Press.

Anon. 1963. *Multilingualism*. London: Commonwealth Conference on the Teaching of English as a Second Language (CCTA).

Anon. 1965. *The Restoration of the Irish Language*. Dublin: The Government of Ireland.

Anon. 1966. *White Paper on the Restoration of The Irish Language: Progress Report for the Period ended 31 March, 1966*. Dublin: Department of Finance, Government of Ireland.

Armstrong, Robert G. 1966. Language Policy in West Africa. This volume.

Auty, R. 1953. The Evolution of Literary Slovak. *Trans. Philol. Soc.* (London), 143–60.

Bell, Wendell, and I. Oxaal. 1964. *Decisions of Nationhood*. Denver, Co.: Social Science Foundation (University of Denver).

Bernstein, Basil. 1958. Some Sociological Determinants of Perception. *British J. of Soc.*, 9, 159–174.

Bernstein, Basil. 1966. Elaborated and Restricted Codes: An Outline. *Sociological Inquiry*, 254–261.

Berry, Jack. 1958. The Making of Alphabets. In *Proceedings of the Eighth International Congress of Linguists*. Oslo: Oslo University Press, 752–764.

Bidwell, Charles E. 1962. Language, Dialect and Nationality in Yugoslavia. *Human Relations*, 15, 217–225.

Blanc, Haim. 1964. *Communal Dialects in Baghdad*. Cambridge, Mass.: Harvard University Press.

Bright, William (ed.). 1966. *Sociolinguistics*. The Hague: Mouton.

Clough, Shepard B. 1930. *A History of the Flemish Movement in Belgium*. New York: Smith.

Das Gupta, J., and John J. Gumperz. 1968. Language, Communication, and Control in North India. This volume.

Deutsch, Karl. 1953. *Nationalism and Social Communication*. Cambridge, Mass.: M.I.T. Press.

Ervin-Tripp, Susan M. 1964. An Analysis of the Interaction between Language, Topic and Speaker. *Amer. Anthropol.* 66(6), part 2, 86–102.

Fallers, L. A. 1961. Ideology and Culture in Uganda Nationalism. *Amer. Anthropol.* **63**, 677–686.

Ferguson, Charles A. 1959. Diglossia, *Word*, **15**, 325–40.

Ferguson, Charles A. 1963. The Language Factor in National Development. *Anthrop. Lings.*, **4** (1), 23–27.

Ferguson, Charles A. 1966. National Sociolinguistic Profile Formulas. In Bright, 1966, 309–324a.

Ferguson, Charles A. 1968. St. Stefan of Perm and Applied Linguistics. This volume.

Ferguson, Charles A., and John J. Gumperz (eds.). 1960. Linguistic Diversity in South Asia. *IJAL* (Indiana University) Publication 13, **26**(3).

Fischer, John L. 1958. Social Influences on the Choice of a Linguistic Variant. *Word*, **14**, 47–56.

Fishman, Joshua A. 1964. Language Maintenance and Language Shift as Fields of Inquiry. *Linguistics*, **9**, 32–70.

Fishman, Joshua A. 1965a. Who Speaks What Language to Whom and When? *Linguistique*, **2**, 67–88.

Fishman, Joshua A. 1965b. Varieties of Ethnicity and Language Consciousness. *Monograph Series on Languages and Linguistics* (Georgetown University), **18**, 69–79.

Fishman, Joshua A. et al. 1966a. *Language Loyalty in the United States.* The Hague: Mouton.

Fishman, Joshua A. 1966b. Some Contrasts between Linguistically Homogeneous and Linguistically Heterogeneous Politics. *Sociological Inquiry*, **36**, 146–158. (Also: This volume).

Fishman, Joshua A. 1967. Bilingualism with and without Diglossia; Diglossia with and without Bilingualism. *J. Soc. Issues*, **23**(2), 29–38.

Fishman, Joshua A. 1968. Nationality-Nationalism and Nation-Nationism. This volume.

Friedman, Anita, and Ulf Hannerz. 1966. Language Development and Socialization: The Social Context. Progress Report, Urban Language Study. Washington, D.C., Center for Applied Linguistics (mimeo).

Friedrich, Paul. 1962. Language and Politics in India. *Daedalus* (Summer), 543–559.

Gallagher, Charles F. 1964. North African Problems and Prospects. Part III: Language and Identity. *American Universities Field Staff, North Africa Series*, **10**(5).

Garfinkel, Harold. 1964. Studies of the Routine Grounds of Everyday Activities. *Social Problems*, **11**, 225–250; reprinted in his *Studies in Ethnomethodology*, Englewood Cliffs, N.J.: Prentice-Hall, 1967 (Chapter 2).

Garvin, Paul. 1959. The Standard Language Problem: Concepts and Methods. *Anthrop. Lings.* **1**(2), 28–31.

Geertz, C. 1963. The Integrative Revolution. In C. Geertz (ed.), *Old Societies and New States*. New York: Free Press, 105–157.

Gordon, Edmund W. (ed.). 1966. *Summary of the Proceedings of the First Working Conference on Language Development in Disadvantaged Children, October 20–22, 1965.* New York: Yeshiva University.

Greenberg, Joseph H. 1965. Urbanism, Migration and Language. In Hilda Kuper (ed.), *Urbanization and Migration in West Africa*. Berkeley and Los Angeles: University of California Press, 50–59.

Grimshaw, Allen D. 1966. Directions for Research in Sociolinguistics: Suggestions of a Non-Linguist Sociologist. *Sociological Inquiry*, **36**, 319–332.

Gumperz, John J. 1964. Linguistic and Social Interaction in Two Communities. *Amer. Anthropol.*, **66**(6), Part 2, 137–153.

Gumperz, John J. 1965. Linguistic Repertoires, Grammars and Second Language Instruction. *Monograph Series on Languages and Linguistics*, **18**, 81–90.

Gumperz, John J. 1966. On the Ethnology of Linguistic Change. In Bright, 1966, 27–49.

Gumperz, John J. 1967. On the Linguistic Correlates of Bilingual Communication. *J. Soc. Issues,* **23**(2), 48–57.

Guxman, M. 1968a. *Voprosy formirovanija i razvitija nacional'nyx jazykov.* English translation being prepared by The Center for Applied Linguistics, Washington, D.C.

Guxman, M. 1968b. Some General Regularities in the Formation and Development of National Languages. In Guxman, *1968a,* 295–307.

Harrison, Selig S. 1960. *India: The Most Dangerous Decades.* Princeton, N.J.: Princeton University Press.

Haugen, Einar. 1961. Language Planning in Modern Norway. *Scandinavian Studies,* **33**, 68–81. [Originally, with textual examples added, in *Anthrop. Lings.,* 1(3), 8–21 (1959).]

Haugen, Einar. 1966a. *Language Conflict and Language Planning: The Case of Modern Norwegian.* Cambridge, Mass.: Harvard University Press.

Haugen, Einar. 1966b. Linguistics and Language Planning. In Bright, 1966, 50–71.

Heyd, Uriel. 1954. *Language Reform in Modern Turkey.* Jerusalem: The Israel Oriental Society.

Hunt, Chester L. 1966. Language Choice in a Multilingual Society. *Sociological Inquiry,* **36**, 240–253.

Hymes, Dell H. 1962. The Ethnography of Speaking. In T. Gladwin and W. C. Sturtevant (eds.), *Anthropology and Human Behavior.* Washington, D.C.: Anthropological Society of Washington, 13–53.

Kachru, Braj B. 1965. Indian English: A Study in Contextualization. In C. E. Barell et al. (eds.), *In Memory of J. R. Firth.* London: Longmans, 1965

Kloss, Heinz. 1952. Der linguistische und der sociologische Sprachbegriff: Abstandsprachen und Ausbausprachen. In his *Die Entwicklung neuer germanischer Kultursprachen.* Munich: Pohl, 15–37.

Labov, William. 1964. Phonological Indices to Social Stratification. *Amer. Anthropol.* **66**(6), part 2, 164–176.

Labov, William. 1966a. *The Social Stratification of English in New York City.* Washington, D.C.: Center for Applied Linguistics.

Labov, William. 1966b. The Effect of Social Mobility on Linguistic Behavior. *Sociological Inquiry,* **36**, 186–203.

Labov, William, et al. 1965. *A Preliminary Study of the Structure of English Used by Negro and Puerto Rican Speakers in New York City* (Cooperative Research Project 3091). New York: Columbia University.

Lennard, Henry L. 1960. *Anatomy of Psychotherapy.* New York: Columbia University Press.

LePage, R. B. 1964. *The National Language Question.* London: Oxford University Press.

Lieberson, Stanley. 1965. Bilingualism in Montreal: A Demographic Analysis. *Am. J. Soc.* **71**, 10–25.

Lunt, Horace G. 1959. The Creation of Standard Macedonian: Some Facts and Attitudes. *Anthrop. Lings.* 1(5), 19–26.

Marriott, M. 1963. Cultural Policy in the New States. In C. Geertz (ed.), *Old Societies and New States.* New York: Free Press, 27–56.

Mills, H. C. 1956. Language Reform in China. *Far Eastern Quarterly,* **15**, 517–540.

Morag, Shelomo. 1959. Planned and Unplanned Development in Modern Hebrew. *Lingua,* **8**, 247–263.

Moscos, Charles C., Jr., and Wendell Bell. 1965. Cultural Unity and Diversity in New States. *Teachers College Record,* **66**, 679–694.

Nahirny, Vladimir, and Joshua A. Fishman. 1965. American Immigrant Groups: Ethnic Identification and the Problem of Generations. *Sociological Review,* **13**, 311–326.

Paden, John N. 1968. Language Problems of National Integration in Nigeria: The Special Position of Hausa. This volume.

Passin, Herbert. 1963. Writer and Journalist in the Transitional Society. In Lucien W. Pye (ed.), *Communications and Political Development*. Princeton, N.J.: Princeton University Press, 83–123. Also: This volume.

Pietrzyk, Alfred. 1965. Problems in Language Planning: The Case of Hindi. In B. N. Varma (ed.), *Contemporary India*. London: Asia Publishing House, 247–270.

Ramos, Maximo. 1961. *Language Policy in Certain Newly Independent States*. Paesay City (Philippines): Philippine Center for Language Study.

Ray, Punya Sloka. 1963. *Language Standardization: Studies in Prescriptive Linguistics*. The Hague: Mouton.

Read, Allen Walker. 1964. The Splitting and Coalescing of Widespread Languages. In *Proceedings of the IXth International Congress of Linguists*. The Hague: Mouton, 1129–34.

Rose, Edward, et al. 1964, 1965, 1966. *Small Languages* (three volumes). Boulder: Bureau of Sociological Research, University of Colorado.

Rustow, Dankwart A. 1968. Language, Modernization and Nationhood; An Attempt at Typology. This volume.

Sacks, Harvey. 1963. On Sociological Description. *Berkeley Journal of Sociology*, **8**, 1–16.

Savitz, Leonard. 1966. Unpublished studies of the language of juvenile delinquent gangs. Philadelphia: Temple University.

Schegloff, Emanuel. 1968. Sequencing in Conversational Openings. In H. Garfinkel and H. Sacks (eds.), *Contributions in Ethnomethodology*. Bloomington: Indiana University Press.

Shuy, Roger W. (ed.). 1965. *Social Dialects and Language Learning*. Champaign: NCTE.

Spencer, J. (ed.). 1963. *Language in Africa*. London and New York: Cambridge University Press.

Stewart, William A. 1964. *Non-Standard Speech and the Teaching of English*. Washington, D.C.: Center for Applied Linguistics.

Stewart, William A. 1965. Sociolinguistic Factors Affecting English Teaching. In Shuy, 1965, 10–18.

Useem, John, and Ruth H. Useem. 1967. The Interfaces of a Bi-National Third Culture: A Study of the American Community in India. *J. Social Issues*, **23**, 130–143.

van den Berghe, Pierre L. 1968. Language and "Nationalism" in South Africa. This volume.

Weinreich, Uriel. 1953. *Languages in Contact*. New York: Linguistic Circle. Second Printing: The Hague: Mouton, 1963.

Whitely, W. H. 1957. Language and Politics in East Africa. *Tanganyika Notes and Records*, **47** & **48**, 159–173 (September).

Whitely, W. H. 1968. Ideal and Reality in National Language Policy: A Case Study from Tanzania. This volume.

Wiggins, W. Howard. 1960. *Ceylon: Dilemmas of a New Nation*. Princeton, N.J.: Princeton University Press, 241–270.

Wurm, S. A. 1966. Papua-New Guinea Nationhood: The Problem of a National Language. *Journal of the Papua and New Guinea Society*, 1, 7–19. Also: This volume.

Zima, Petr. 1968. Hausa in West Africa: Remarks on Contemporary Role and Functions. This volume.

Jyotirindra Das Gupta

LANGUAGE DIVERSITY AND NATIONAL DEVELOPMENT

Problems of language policy involve certain salient questions regarding the nature of the policy-making authority as well as the context of the policy-making processes. The importance of the national political authority in solving problems of language policy is readily recognized. But this recognition of the role of the national authority is relatively recent, for the very concept of national authority is a product of political modernization which began in sixteenth-century Europe [1].

This does not imply that the political authority was of no consequence to the processes of language development before this period. Although conscious thinking about language questions was primarily carried on by the intelligentsia, the one of language for political communication had occasionally assumed salience when the empire-builders of the universal states needed a medium of transaction across diverse language groups. In this process some empire-builders tried to impose their own mother tongues, or in certain cases they favored another language already current in their empire as a commonly comprehensible language [2]. The language question was usually solved in accordance with the political prudence of the patrimonial ruler and it rarely took into account the sentiments and opinions of the ruled people [3]. In general, the growth of languages as vehicles of consciously organized social communication was facilitated as much by its political promotion as by liturgical and theological promotion. Political promotion was mainly confined to administrative promotion sponsored by the pragmatic needs of imperial communication. Before the rise of the modern state, imperial linguistic need was naturally limited to the communicational network of the notables. The people in general were outside this network.

All this radically changed with the rise of the national political communities. These communities arose as a result of a fundamental democratization of the social foundation of politics [4]. The idea of a national community was inconceivable in the absence of positive linkages between the general population and the political authority. These linkages were established through representational systems of participation brought in the wake of general modernization involving educational, economic, and social transformation. These processes converted the hitherto unpoliticized population into conscious members of the political community [5]. It was natural that with this consciousness of membership would follow the development of popular languages in order to build a communicational bridge for the community. The classical languages were usually inadequate for performing such popular communicational functions. In addition, these languages, by successfully bridging the elite drawn from diverse language communities, had proved to be useless for promoting the separate identific pride of particular national communities. The task of national development thus inevitably meant that the political authorities had to act as conscious agencies for national language promotion and development.

The early cases of political modernization and national development in Europe were by and large based on fairly homogeneous language communities. Their problem was mostly one of developing a standard language out of a welter of variations among related codes. In other words, the question of encountering a multilingual situation did not plague these early developmental efforts. In this sense, problems of language policy were less concerned with conflict resolution among multiple languages than with the problems of standardization of one identific and functionally efficient language for the community.

Even when conflict resolution assumed salience—as in the cases of the later phase of European nationalism—the national political communities were largely favored by the maturing effects of modernization in several sectors of social life before the politicization of language divisions.

The language problems of the developing nations have not had the vantage point of the European processes of modernization. In these nations modernization itself is of a different character by virtue of the fact that it is externally introduced rather than internally induced [6]. The long-drawn succession of developmental sequences, which brought different social problems to prominence at different times in European history, is largely absent in contemporary Asia and Africa. In these areas the challenge of modernization requires the telescoping of several stages of development into one single stage. In addition, few countries belonging to these areas had escaped the imposition of artificial colonial boundaries whereby diverse cultures, languages, religions, and social forms were lumped together under colonially convenient administrations [7].

The logic of colonial convenience was obviously unconcerned with the logic of cultural, linguistic, or social congruence of the artificially juxtaposed groups. And yet many of the new nations are continuations of these artificially administered units. It is not surprising that many leaders of these new nations are found to rely less on natural factors than on the political art of holding diverse units together in a national community.

It is this art that is usually referred to when one suggests the concept of nation-building. The idea of nation-building implies an underlying mechanistic or architectural model. In the actual process of nation-building, however, the freedom of the political architects is partially limited by the historical fact that nations are only partly products of deliberate design, whereas in large part they are the results of organismic growth processes [8]. The concepts of nation-building and national growth, when taken alone, can only account for selective partial aspects of developing a nation. In contrast, Karl Deutsch suggests a more comprehensive concept of national development, which seeks to unite a limited but significant degree of combinatorial freedom. It is reminiscent of the mechanistic and voluntaristic aspects of the "nation-building" concept, but it has the awareness of internal and external interdependence in both space and time—this concept characterizes the organismic image and tends to stress the influence of the past, the environment, and the vast, complex, and slow-changing aspects of the actions and expectations of millions of people [9]. These aspects of freedom and constraint taken together are likely to be useful in considering the capabilities of the national political authorities in handling the fundamental issues of national development.

One of these fundamental issues is related to the problem of the opposition between primordial group loyalty and the civic loyalty to the nation. Most new nations are based on a plurality of segmental groups. The natural tie of the people to their segmental groups is often valued more highly than their civil ties with the nation. This segmental attachment is sometimes referred to as primordial attachment to one's given or assumed-to-be-given order of social existence. These given orders of existence include religious community, language community, and other such communities based on congruities of faith, speech, blood, custom, etc. [10].

However, the dichotomy between primordiality and civility is less than useful if it is studied in a static context. The origin of a social cleavage is perhaps less important than what happens to this cleavage in the transitional process of national development. Compared to a traditional society, in a modernizing transitional society the dynamic factors of political mobilization often radically transform the nature of the segmental groups even when they retain their old appearance. Hence the structural order of existence of these groups should be studied in the light of their probable (and often actual) functional fluidity and adaptation [11]. The given order of segmental division by itself does not tell us much about the patterning of the social groups' participation in politics and its consequence on national development. These, to a large extent, depend on the definition of political interest of such groups, the nature of organizational mediation, the style of leadership, the nature of the political system in which the groups act, and the methods of action which have been found in practice to gratify the demands of the conflict groups [12].

In general, social divisions are of consequence in national development to the extent that they are manifested as political divisions. In considering political divisions, we have to take into account various kinds as well as characteristics of such divisions [13]. Thus political divisions insofar as they are in the form of policy disagreements are not likely to create any problem for national development. They may be problematic only when they are related to cultural divergence or segmental cleavage. In such cases it is important to note the extensiveness and the intensity of the political divisions. When specific divisions are cumulatively related to other divisions, they gain in extensiveness. Thus a specific disagreement on language policy may be related to language diversity in the country concerned, and in some cases the boundary of the language community may coincide with the cultural, racial, religious, and party cleavages. Here the affective involvement of the actors concerned may be extremely high. Such an extreme reinforcement of divisions and affective involvement may lead to a cumulative convergence of extensiveness and intensity of the linguistic cleavage leading to a crisis, but this is only a possibility and not a necessary consequence of language division.

It is important to recognize the complex variety of political divisions and their variable alignments in order to assess their impact on national integration. Moreover, the divisions themselves have to be balanced against the positive factors of cohesion. Political cohesion is often described as a result of a relative lack of political division, but it can exist despite divisions and often because of political divisions [14]. Given the divided social base of most new states, it is not likely that cohesion will result from lack of political division. Rather, in such states the other two processes of cohesion are likely to be of greater importance. This is a way of saying that in the analysis of national development it is necessary first to assume that political divisions do not necessarily hinder political integration. Second, there is reason to assume that political conflicts among social groups may prove to be factors of positive sociation offering integrational possibilities [15]. Third, it may be assumed that even if such conflicts are not moderated by their mutually cross-cutting nature [16], and even when they are not mutually balanced, there may exist parallel cohesive norms and institutions that may contribute to political integration. It is in the context of these assumptions that one can appreciate the positive roles played by the political institutions and by certain overarching [17] norms in mitigating the effects of political divisions.

At this stage it may be useful to distinguish political integration from national integration. Political integration can be regarded as the minimal cohesion necessary for the coordination of political groups through institutionalized procedures of the political community. The concept of political community may be used to identify one particular aspect of a political system, as one of a number of basic political objects toward which support may be extended or from which it may be withdrawn [18]. David Easton uses this term to refer to a common political enterprise which may be based on different degrees and kinds of cohesion. The primary cohesive tie binding this common enterprise arises from a political division of labor. This primary tie may or may not be reinforced by affective solidarity [19] on the part of the community.

The use of the concept of political community in this particular sense has an important bearing on the understanding of national development in the new states based on heterogeneous societies. This is because such a use enables us to conceive of a political community independent of the question of natural solidarity of the members of the community. Moreover, by postulating this conceptual framework it is possible to gain an insight into the sequences of national development. In other words, the question of political integration of a nation can be considered separately from the questions of social, cultural, and other forms of integration subsumed under the general category of national integration. Such a separation may sensitize us to the point that in the initial phases of national development "a sense of belonging together politically, may normally follow rather than precede the emergence of a political community" [20].

This implies that a national political community does not require for its existence a precondition of sentimental solidarity. Most writings on national development in Europe have focused attention on the necessity of such a precondition. The sequence of the growth of the classical cases of national development in Europe, however, should not be rationalized as a norm for all societies and all times. In fact, a reversal of the sequence of these classical cases of national development may be more relevant for the practice and the understanding of national development in especially the new states based on plural social divisions. If, in England and France, sentimental solidarity preceded the foundation of the modern nation-state, in the multiethnic, multilingual, and multireligious new states the political development of the nation is likely to precede and is expected to promote national loyalty and cohesion.

Yet many writers, tied as they are to the classical European models, have constantly reiterated the need for the elimination of social divisions as the precondition for the success of national cohesion. Their works are marked by the presumption that the success of national development requires a certain degree of social homogenization. What is more, they suggest that given this need national development in the new states can be achieved only by a forcible amalgamation of the divisive social groups under authoritarian political management. Thus it has been pointed out that the prime requirement of the new states is authoritarian rule and that autocracy is intrinsic in the enterprise of consolidating a nation [21].

The experience of the new nations seems to suggest that there may be some truth in the preceding suggestions. In many of these new nations the departure of the colonial rulers signaled the end of the era of negative nationalism. Initially, the first phase of positive nation-building was accompanied by a relatively high degree of political participation. With this participation followed a plethora of new demands on the political community without a corresponding rise in structured support for this community. This tended to destabilize the new political communities [22]. Many of these demands were based on competitive strivings of the politically mobilized primordial social groups. This fact and the very unmanageability of the proliferation of demands generated a feeling among many political leaders as well as writers that only a suppression of these demands and the elimination of social cleavages can build the basis of stable national development.

These reactions seem to be based on the conviction that the only decision-system that is appropriate for the task of national development is one that follows the rule of amalgamation [23]. The idea of amalgamation is appealing to the technologically oriented rationalistic modernizers because it puts a premium on the imposition of their own ideology of social homogenization and elite control. Basically this implies a pyramidal structure of authority where the men at the top are supposed to have an advance knowledge of what the people below actually need and how to satisfy these needs [24]. It is the task of the pyramidal authority to seek the amalgamation of the units of random aggressiveness into a smooth solidary system. Given the perception of this task, it is no wonder that the participative decision-making systems of the democratic type is widely assumed to be incapable of ensuring national development in the new states [25]. However, the amalgamative model of decision-making may not be as effective in the long run as it may appear to be initially. It should be noted that under this system of decision making, the crucial responsibility of coordination is appropriated by an agency which is external to the components of the system. On the other hand, in the pluralistic system of coordination, the responsibility is located in the very components of the system by avoiding the function of a third-party command [26]. In the pluralistic system decisional responsibility is widely dispersed. It is this dispersal that facilitates the development of the communications equipment as well as the capability of the units. It thereby increases the chance of political coordination through voluntary representation [27]. It provides for not merely the developing art of making demands but at the same time it seeks to institutionalize the representational procedures into coordinated systems [28]. In other words, it seeks to bring the demands into the open and to accommodate such demands through institutional bargaining, negotiation, and compromise rather than suppressing these demands.

In this sense the pluralistic decision-systems do not seek to eliminate diversity by imposing social homogenization and amalgamation. It accepts the identific requirements of the various social groups and at the same time seeks to bring them together into a coordinated political community. Thus it contributes to the linking of diverse social groups into a common enterprise through the processes of group competition and conflict. Such a voluntary system of institutionalized coordination may ultimately contribute more to national development than its amalgamative alternative.

Decisions regarding language policy will vary with the system of decision making that undertakes it. When a new state faces the problem of competing languages, one response may be to suppress this competition and to impose one over the others. If the language situation is one where such competition involves minimal political challenges, such a policy may somehow succeed. But in many new states this is not the case. In Indonesia, despite a great diversity of languages, it was possible to impose the language of a small minority as the national language because the political competition of the regional languages for national status was low [29]. In India and Pakistan, given the high degree of competition among several major languages, a policy of imposition will create more problems than it will solve [30]. The political reconciliation of the language demands, however, has not been found to be impossible in these situations. In fact, whenever such solutions have been attempted, they have resulted in certain additional gains for the political community by strengthening the ties of the masses to the political community. This implies that the coordination of language demands may lead to a significant penetration effect involving new linkages between the hitherto unpoliticized people and the political center of the nation. It is this penetration of the center of political authority to the periphery of popular politics which is likely to deepen the supportive base of the national political community and thus contribute to long-range national development.

Problems of language policy rarely troubled the colonial rulers because of the lack of interest on the part of the authority for creating linkages between the center and the periphery. The creation of national political authority signaled, of necessity, the beginning of participative national communities. This naturally involved the politicization of selective group loyalties, including language loyalty, but not all language loyalties assumed derisive salience. Out of the language loyalties that did, many have been adjusted by a policy of accommodation through representational political systems [31]. Policies of imposition have mostly been of tempo-

rary value. Imposition in most cases has purchased political discipline at
the cost of the alienation of social groups from the political authority.
In doing this what is usually gained in point of temporary stability is
generally lost in point of political integration.

Given our conception of national development, it seems that the degree of freedom of technologically oriented national language policies
has to be measured against the degree of constraint that is offered by the
political factors. For purposes of national development, the political
divisions based on language assume variable salience in different national
situations. In most cases, however, the greater the institutional capacity
revealed by the political community to handle such divisions through
pluralistic coordination, the greater the prospects of national development in the long run. This institutional capacity cannot be built by
denying or deriding the existence of the language divisions in a multilingual society. Insofar as these divisions assume political importance,
they have to be considered as reflections of legitimate group interests.
These interests have to be processed through open institutional channels
and procedures. In this process the interested groups themselves will
learn the art of negotiation and compromise, thus yielding a possibility
of a political solution of language problems and thereby strengthening
the institutional basis of national development.

NOTES

1. For a general discussion of the evolution of national authority in the context of
   modernization in Europe see Karl W. Deutsch, *Nationalism and Social Communication*, Cambridge: M.I.T. Press, 1966, esp. Chapter 2.
2. The language policies of the universal states are discussed in Arnold J. Toynbee,
   A Study of History, London: Oxford University Press, 1954, Vol. 7, pp. 239–255.
3. A useful typology of the forms of political domination based on ruler-subject
   relations can be found in the works of Max Weber. For an analysis of the Weberian
   typology see Reinhard Bendix, *Max Weber*, London: Heinemann, 1960, Part 3.
   See especially pp. 334–359 for a discussion of patrimonialism.
4. The notion of fundamental democratization refers to the extension of popular
   participation and of public space. It has no necessary relation to any particular
   form of political democratization. See Karl Mannheim, *Man and Society in an
   Age of Reconstruction*, London: Routledge, 1940.
5. These processes are discussed in detail in Reinhard Bendix, *Nation-Building and
   Citizenship*, New York: Wiley, 1964, esp. pp. 74–104.
6. For a discussion of this point, see John W. Hall, "Changing Conceptions of the
   Modernization of Japan," in Marius B. Jansen (ed.), *Changing Japanese Attitudes
   Toward Modernization*, Princeton, N.J.: Princeton University Press, 1965, pp. 34 ff.
7. For an analysis of the impact of colonial boundaries, see John H. Kantsky, "Nationalism," in Kantsky (ed.), *Political Change in Underdeveloped Countries:
   Nationalism and Communism*, New York: Wiley, 1962, pp. 38 ff.
8. These points are discussed in detail by Karl W. Deutsch in Karl W. Deutsch and
   William J. Foltz (eds.), *Nation-Building*, New York: Atherton Press, 1963, pp. 2–3.

9. *Ibid.*, p. 3.
10. This point has been extensively discussed by Clifford Geertz, "The Integrative Revolution, Primordial Sentiments and Civil Politics in the New States" in Geertz (ed.), *Old Societies and New States,* New York: Free Press, 1963, pp. 109 ff.
11. See, for instance, the account of the Indian situation in Richard D. Lambert, "Some Consequences of Segmentation in India," *Economic Development and Cultural Change,* 12(4), 416–424 (July 1964).
12. For a distinction between groups and "conflict groups," see Ralf Dahrendorf, *Class and Class Conflict in Industrial Society,* Stanford, Cal.: Stanford University Press, 1965, esp. pp. 179 ff. (paperback).
13. This classification of political divisions is adapted from Harry Eckstein, *Division and Cohesion in Democracy, A Study of Norway,* Princeton, N.J.: Princeton University Press, 1966, pp. 33–36.
14. *Ibid.*, p. 69.
15. For an analysis of conflict as a process of sociation and integration see George Simmel, *Conflict and the Web of Group Affiliations,* New York: Free Press, 1964, Part 1, Chapter 1 (paperback), and Lewis Coser, *The Functions of Social Conflict,* New York: Free Press, 1964, esp. Chapters 7 and 8 (paperback).
16. On the moderating possibility of cross-cutting cleavages, see *ibid.*, pp. 72–80, and S. M. Lipset, *Political Man,* New York: Doubleday, 1963, pp. 76–82 (paperback).
17. For one view suggesting this point, see Gabriel A. Almond and Sidney Verba, *The Civic Culture,* Princeton, N J : Princeton University Press, 1963, pp. 490–493.
18. See David Easton, *A Systems Analysis of Political Life,* New York: Wiley, 1965, p. **176.**
19. *Ibid.*, p. 177.
20. *Ibid.*, p. 188.
21. For clear statements to this effect, see Rupert Emerson, *From Empire to Nation,* Cambridge, Mass.: Harvard University Press, 1960, pp. 289–290. For the idea that autocracy "is intrinsic to a development situation," see David E. Apter in Harry Eckstein and David E. Apter (eds.), *Comparative Politics,* New York: Free Press, 1963, p. 649. For the idea that the chances of political integration are maximized to the extent the political system "is authoritarian, consensual, identific and paternal," see Claude Ake, "Political Integration and Political Stability," *World Politics,* 19(3), 486 (August 1967).
22. For a detailed treatment of this aspect, see, for example, Myron Weiner, "Political Integration and Political Development" in J. L. Finkle and R. W. Gable (eds.), *Political Development and Social Change,* New York: Wiley, 1966, pp. 551–562.
23. The amalgamative and the pluralistic models of decision making and their consequences on integration are discussed in detail in Karl W. Deutsch, "Communication Theory and Political Integration" in P. E. Jacob and J. V. Toscano (eds.), *The Integration of Political Communities,* Philadelphia, Pa.: Lippincott, 1964, pp. 58–61.
24. For an analysis of this point see S. N. Eisenstadt, "The Problems of Emerging Bureaucracies in Developing Areas and New States" in B. F. Hoselitz and D. Moore (eds.), *Industrialization and Society,* Paris: UNESCO, esp. p. 168.
25. See, for instance, Selig S. Harrison, *India, The Most Dangerous Decades,* Madras: Oxford University Press, 1960, p. 10 *et passim.*
26. The idea of a third-party command ensuring coordination is a constant theme in Western political theory. The legacy of Hobbes seems to persist stubbornly even in contemporary writings.
27. The term representation is used here in the wider sense developed in detail in Reinhard Bendix, *Nation-Building and Citizenship, op. cit.,* pp. 83–94 and 131–136.
28. The crucial relation between institutionalization of representation and political development is discussed in Samuel P. Huntington, "Political Development and Polit-

ical Decay," *World Politics,* 17(3), 386–430 (April 1965), and Alfred Diamant, "Political Development: Approaches to Theory and Strategy" in John D. Montgomery and William J. Siffin (eds.), *Approaches to Development, Politics, Administration and Change,* New York: McGraw-Hill, 1966, pp. 15–48.

29. For details, see Takdir Alisjahbana, *Indonesian Language and Literature: Two Essays,* New Haven, Conn.: Yale University, South East Asia Studies, 1962, pp. 1–22.

30. For an outline of language situations in these two countries, see Ram Gopal, *Linguistic Affairs of India,* Bombay: Asia Publishing House, 1966, and Donald N. Wilber, *Pakistan, Its People, Its Society, Its Culture,* New Haven, Conn.: HRAF Press, 1964, pp. 71–83.

31. Representational political systems may or may not be of liberal democratic forms, although they may incorporate various degrees of the democratic norms and institutions.

Charles A. Ferguson

LANGUAGE DEVELOPMENT

Discussions of language problems of developing countries cover a wide range of problems such as national multilingualism, language education policies, and languages as symbols of group identity. Many of these issues can be dealt with by the conceptual frameworks used in the study of social organization, political systems, or economic processes. Some questions, however, relate to the state of a language itself, as shown by observations that such and such a language is "backward" or "inadequate" or that a particular language needs "purifying," "reforming," "modernizing," or some other forms of improvement. This kind of issue is closer to the conceptual framework of linguistics, although not commonly dealt with by professional linguists, and it may be useful to offer a linguistic perspective on it.

LINGUISTIC STRUCTURE

The traditional twofold task of linguistics is to make statements that hold true for all languages everywhere and at all times (a general theory of language) and to make statements about particular varieties of language under particular conditions (characterization of languages, e.g., grammars, language histories, etc.). In either case linguists have been concerned with what kinds of sequences are "pronounceable" in a given language (or in all languages), what kinds of sequences are grammatically possible in a given language (or in general), and what kinds of sequences are meaningful in a language (or in general). Although the range of possible variation remains within the definite limits of the general characteristics of languages, now commonly called "language universals" (Greenberg, 1966a, 1966b; Uspenskij, 1965), there is an astonishing diversity of possible structures as exemplified by the thousands of different languages now in existence and the several hundred for which there is historical documentation. Accordingly, it has often been tempting to regard one kind of linguistic (phonological-grammatical-semantic) structure as being in some way superior to or more advanced than others. As time has passed, however, linguists have increasingly become convinced that there is no simple scale of superiority in structure and no simple evolutionary line along which known linguistic structures could be placed. In this fundamental sense there is as yet no convincing evidence that the total structure of one language is better than that of another in that it is easier to acquire (as a first language), less ambiguous, more efficient for cognitive processes, or more economical of effort in oral use, let alone more "logical," "expressive," or the like (Ray, 1963, Ch. 10).

The three great world languages—Russian, Chinese, and English—differ greatly in structure. Russian has a relatively stable vowel system, a pervasive feature of palatalization, and a complex inflectional morphology. Chinese has a phonology and lexicon largely based on the syllable, it has distinctive tone, and it has almost no morphological machinery. English has a very variable vowel system and is somewhere between the other two in morphological complexity. There is at present no known way to rate the respective structures of the three languages as wholes.[1]

The assumption is now standard in linguistics that all known languages apparently constitute roughly the same kind of symbolic behavior system, in spite of this great variety, and that there are at the present time no "primitive" languages exemplifying the type of earlier stage in language behavior that must have existed hundreds of thousands of years ago (Hymes, 1961, 75–76).

FEATURES OF DEVELOPMENT

If judgments of backwardness or limited development of a language cannot be made on the basis of linguistic structure, how can they be made? The view adopted here is that there are at least three dimensions relevant for measuring language development: graphization—reduction to writing; standardization—the development of a norm which overrides regional and social dialects; and, for want of a better term, modernization —the development of intertranslatability with other languages in a range of topics and forms of discourse characteristic of industrialized, secularized, structurally differentiated, "modern" societies.

---

[1] This does not, of course, exclude the possibility that particular features of particular languages may be rated as more regular, easier to acquire, etc. For example, the representation of the grammatico-semantic category of number (singular-plural) is very complex and irregular in Russian, much simpler in English, and very simple and relatively unimportant in Chinese. It is reasonable to assume—and there is some confirmatory evidence—that children learning these languages acquire the notion of plurality at roughly the same ages but that it takes the Russian child longest to attain full mastery of the plural inflection, the English-learning child less time, and the Chinese child least. There is no way to weight this isolated phenomenon against the total structure of the language. Children seem to master the basic structures of their languages at roughly the same age, no matter what language they are acquiring.

Hymes (1961) offers a more comprehensive approach for evolutionary study of language; here we follow a more limited approach comparable to developmental studies in political sociology or economics rather than the evolutionary approach of anthropology. Ferguson (1962) uses two dimensions: (a) "utilization in writing," which combines graphization and modernization, and (b) standardization. Haugen (1966) offers a four-way matrix of development form-function-society-language giving (a) selection of norm, (b) codification, (c) elaboration of function, (d) acceptance; of these, elaboration corresponds roughly to modernization, and the other three are aspects of standardization. Fishman (1968) emphasizes that the processes of language development are not single events but involve repeated elaboration and recodification. Sjoberg (1964) offers a suggestive but oversimplified matching of stages of language development with preliterate, preindustrialized civilized, transitional, and industrialized nations.

Graphization

The regular use of writing in a speech community, like such other innovations as the use of a steel knife in a stone-age society, has repercussions throughout the culture and social organization. The relative permanence of written records makes possible the transmission of more material from generation to generation; the transportability of written records makes possible communication with a larger number of people; and the immediate fixing in written form makes possible more complex sequential thought on the part of individuals. In this essay, however, we are concerned with the effect of writing on the development of language itself.

The first point to be made is that *the use of writing adds another variety of language to the community's repertory.* The vocabulary, grammatical structure, and even the phonological structure of the language as used in writing begin immediately, as it were, to have a life of their own. Linguists like to point out that speech is primary and writing secondary and that written language is always in some sense a representation of speech. Although this is true in a general way, and is worth repeated emphasis to correct widespread misconceptions, the fact is that writing almost never reflects speech in an exact way, written language frequently develops characteristics not found in the corresponding spoken language, and it may change along lines quite different from changes in the spoken language. After the spread of writing, varieties of the spoken language can no longer be described *in vacuo;* they will interact with the written form to a greater or lesser degree, and the linguistic analyst must note spelling pronunciations, lexical displacements, and grammatical fluctuations which originate in or are reinforced by written usage.

It is remarkable that communities, as they begin the regular use of writing, generally do not feel that ordinary, everyday speech is appropriate for written use. Sometimes this may be because the community already makes use of a classical language, but sometimes it merely transfers to the new medium some of the attitudes already present in the community toward the language of higher levels of discourse such as formal speeches, religious rituals, and the like. It may be assumed that all speech communities show linguistic differentiation along a casual/noncasual dimension (Voegelin, 1960), and many communities will regard the new use of writing as far along toward the noncasual end, only much later coming to recognize the value of written representation of casual speech. Two well-described examples of this tendency may be found in the beginnings of modern Bengali prose and the early use of modern English as a regular means of written communication (Das, 1966, pp. 17–22; Jones, 1953, Ch. I).

It is sometimes asserted that the existence of a written variety inhibits language change, thus constituting an important influence for uniformity through time comparable to the kind of regional and social uniformity implicit in standardization. Evidence on this point is conflicting and the question merits systematic study (cf. Zengel, 1962).

The second point to be made is that *the use of writing leads to the folk belief that the written language is the "real" language and speech is a corruption of it*. This attitude seems to be nearly universal in communities which have attained the regular use of writing. It is only the occasional perceptive observer, or in more recent times the professional linguist, who sees the relationship in other terms. To the extent that after the passage of time the written form of the language proves to be the more conservative, the spoken may be regarded with some justification as derived from it, but the picture is invariably more complicated than this, since isolated relic areas may be less innovative than the written language, or the original dialect base of the written language may have been a highly divergent variety of the language.

The importance of this folk belief for language development lies in the way it limits the kind of conscious intervention in the form of language planning that the community will conceive of or accept. Much time and effort is often spent on questions of orthography and language reform, in the tacit assumption that changes in the written language will be followed automatically by changes in speech. Some reforming zeal is also expended on bringing pronunciation in line with existing written norms. Insofar as these various efforts are part of a standardization process which responds to the communicative needs of the speech community, they may result in actual change, especially if they do not conflict with the basic phonological and grammatical structure of the language, but often the efforts fail, at least in part because the beliefs do not correspond to the realities of the written-spoken relationship.

Standardization

Language standardization is the process of one variety of a language becoming widely accepted throughout the speech community as a supradialectal norm—the "best" form of the language—rated above regional and social dialects, although these may be felt appropriate in some domains. The process of standardization in language is often mentioned in works on general linguistics and many books on the history of particular languages deal with the process, but general treatments of standardization are rare (cf. Kloss, 1952, Ch. I; Guxman, 1960; Ray, 1963). The concept of standardization also includes the notions of increasing uniformity of the norm itself and explicit codification of the norm. It is sometimes extended also to include such notions as the introduction of writing, the expansion of lexicon, and even the choice of one language instead of another as an official or national language, but it will not be understood in these senses here.

Various aspects of the process of standardization can be documented for scores of languages in the past and it is in progress in many languages today. While standardization is recognized as a dimension in language development as viewed here, there are a good number of instances where a language has been highly standardized and has then regressed to a state of dialect diversity without a standard and may even have been restandardized on a different basis later. This is especially clear with languages with a very long written history such as Egyptian, but other cases are also well-known (Pulgram, 1958, Ch. 23). Such regressions, comparable to returning from a high level of technology to a lower one, are known in other aspects of cultural evolution and do not invalidate the developmental viewpoint.

Although at this point in history there can be no certainty about the nature of the final achievement of standardization as a stage in language development, it seems possible to interpret the various forms of standardization as moving toward an ideal state when the language "has a single, widely accepted norm which is felt to be appropriate with only minor modification or varieties for all purposes for which the language is used" (Ferguson, 1962, p. 10). If this interpretation is followed, a number of special types of language standardization can be viewed as way-stations in the developmental process. Examples of these special types include diglossia, where the supradialectal norm is not used for ordinary conversation, as in Arabic and Tamil (Ferguson, 1959), and multimodal standardization, where competing supradialectal norms exist, as in Eastern and Western Armenian (Garibian, 1960), Hindi-Urdu (Gumperz and Naim, 1960), Norwegian Bokmål-Nynorsk (Haugen and Chapman, 1964, pp. 365–366).

The process of language standardization is not well understood and needs both case studies and attempts at generalization so that some testable hypotheses can be advanced, but at least two points can be made on the basis of present knowledge. First, *there are many paths of standardization and a number of sociolinguistic variables* to be investigated in connection with the different paths. Second, in most of the well-known cases of language standardization in Europe since the Renaissance, a number of features keep recurring, although they are not all present in each case:

1. The basis of the standard was the speech of an educated middle class in an important urban center.

2. The standardizing language was displacing another language from its position as normal written medium.

3. One writer or a small number of writers served as acknowledged models for literary use of the standardizing language.

4. The standardizing language served as a symbol of either religious or national identity.

Some of these features are also evident in language standardization in other parts of the world and at other times, but the examination of other cases would probably require adding some features to the list.

Modernization

The modernization of a language may be thought of as the process of its becoming the equal of other developed languages as a medium of communication; it is in a sense the process of joining the world community of increasingly intertranslatable languages recognized as appropriate vehicles of modern forms of discourse. This view of modernization —and indeed the very term itself—should not disguise the fact that this process is not really new or "modern": it is essentially the same process that English went through in the fifteenth century or Hungarian in the nineteenth when the language was extended to cover topics and to appear in a range of forms of discourse for which it was not previously used, including nonliterary prose and oral communication such as lectures and professional consultation. Two important forms of discourse in contemporary modernization are the news and feature stories of the press and radio.

The process of modernization thus has two aspects: (a) *the expansion of the lexicon* of the language by new words and expressions and (b) *the development of new styles and forms of discourse*. The second aspect has less often been discussed than lexical expansion and would repay study. Interestingly enough the new forms of discourse that must be developed seem in themselves to be less distinctive for the speech community than the more literary forms (oral or written) preceding them. Thus the poetic structures (meter, rhyme, assonance, allusion, stanza-form, etc.) of a given language may be highly distinctive and difficult to transfer to other languages, whereas the structures of nonliterary prose (paragraphing, ordered sequences, transitions, summaries, cross-references, etc.) tend to be universal and highly translatable.

Lexical expansion is required in order to treat new topics, and this seems to take place most effectively when the tempo of change is not too fast, the practitioners who need the vocabulary are involved in its creation, and there are sufficient lines of communication among the users of the new terminology to achieve consistency. In this area, too, there has been little systematic study. The efforts of language planners generally focus on the production of glossaries and dictionaries of new technical terms and on disputes about the proper form of new words, when the critical question seems to be that of assuring the consistent use of such forms by the appropriate sectors of the population. When the lexical expansion of modernization actually takes place, it may not be at all in accord with the carefully prepared glossaries of the planners. Probably the use of new terms and expressions in such places as secondary school textbooks, professional papers, and conversation among specialists is far more important than the publication of extensive lists of words. Case studies of rapid lexical expansion in recent times should be made to determine the factors accounting for success in cases like Japanese and Hungarian and relative lack of success in cases like Hindi and Arabic.

On the issue of the source of new vocabulary and the methods of word creation, one important point seems to be that a *technical vocabulary can be equally effective whether it comes from the language's own processes of word formation or from extensive borrowing from another language.* The issue of purism can be a critical one in the sense that feelings may be strong and disagreements sharp, but it seems almost totally irrelevant to the final success of the lexical expansion process. Of the two examples cited, Hungarian followed almost exclusively the path of internal creation, whereas Japanese used extensive borrowing from English as well. This issue is important for social psychological research in finding the factors involved in the attitudes adopted, and it has a kind of importance for linguistic research in that it may involve changes in word structure and the distribution of sounds, but it seems of less importance for understanding the process of language development itself (cf. Ray, 1963, pp. 36–44 and references).

SUMMARY

Among the many language aspects of national development that could be the object of study and measurement, it is possible to isolate the question of the degree of development of a particular language. Language development in this sense is viewed here as having three conceptually distinct components: (a) graphization, the use of writing; (b) standardization, the use of a supradialectal norm; and (c) modernization, the development of vocabulary and forms of discourse.

Graphization adds to the language a new variety, which in relation to the spoken varieties tends to be slower to change, is generally regarded by the users as more fundamental, and can serve as a better means of standardization and modernization.

Standardization brings to a language the kind of integration and uniformity needed for large-scale communication, but there are various paths of standardization, and analysis of these and the relevant social variables is needed.

Modernization provides the language with the specialized subvocabularies and forms of discourse corresponding to the highly differentiated functions the language must fulfill in a modern society.

Finally, all three components of language development can be the object of language planning (Haugen, 1966, and references) although the factors making for success and failure in such planning are not clear.

REFERENCES

Das, Susirkumar. 1966. *Early Bengali Prose*. Calcutta: Bookland.

Ferguson, Charles A. 1959. Diglossia. *Word*, 15:325–340.

Ferguson, Charles A. 1962. The Language Factor in National Development. *Anthro. Ling.*, 4(1), 23–27. Reprinted in F. A. Rice (ed.), *Study of the Role of Second Languages*, Washington, Center for Applied Linguistics, 1962, pp. 8–14.

Fishman, Joshua A. 1968. Sociolinguistics and the Language Problems of the Developing Countries. This volume.

Garibian, A. S. 1960. Ob armjanskom nacional'nom literaturnom jazyke. In M. M. Guxman (ed.), *Voprosy formirovanija i razvitija nacional'nyx jazykov*, Moscow 1960, pp. 50–61.

Garvin, Paul, and Madeleine Mathiot. 1960. The Urbanization of the Guarani Language —A Problem in Language and Culture. In A. F. C. Wallace (ed.), *Men and Cultures*, Philadelphia: University of Pennsylvania Press, pp. 783–790.

Guxman, M. M. (ed.). 1960. *Voprosy formirovanija i razvitija nacional'nyx jazykov.* Moscow.

Greenberg, Joseph H. 1966a. Language Universals. In T. A. Sebeok (ed.), *Current Trends in Linguistics III*. The Hague: Mouton, pp. 60–112. (Reprinted separately with slight revisions by Mouton.)

Greenberg, Joseph H. (ed.). 1966b. *Universals of Language*, 2nd ed. Cambridge: MIT Press.

Gumperz, John J., and C. M. Naim. 1960. Formal and Informal Standards in the Hindi Regional Language Area. In C. A. Ferguson and J. J. Gumperz (eds.), *Linguistic Diversity in South Asia, Int. J. Amer. Ling.*, 26(3), Pt. III (Bloomington, Ind.).

Haugen, Einar. 1966. Dialect, Language, Nation. *Amer. Anthro.*, 68, 922–935.

Haugen, Einar, and Kenneth G. Chapman. 1964. *Spoken Norwegian*, rev. ed. New York: Holt, Rinehart and Winston.

Hymes, Dell H. 1961. Functions of Speech: An Evolutionary Approach. In F. Gruber (ed.), *Anthropology and Education,* Philadelphia: University of Pennsylvania Press, pp. 55–83.

Jones, R. F. 1953. *The Triumph of English.* Stanford, Cal.: Stanford University Press. (Repr. paper 1966.)

Kloss, Heinz. 1952. *Die Entwicklung neuer germanischer Kultursprachen von 1800 bis 1850.* Munich: Pohl.

Pulgram, Ernst. 1958. *The Tongues of Italy; Prehistory and History.* Cambridge, Mass.: Harvard University Press.

Ray, Punya Sloka. 1963. *Language Standardization.* The Hague: Mouton.

Sjoberg, Andree F. 1964. Writing, Speech, and Society: Some Changing Relationships, in *Proc. 9th Intl. Cong. Ling.* The Hague: Mouton, pp. 892–898.

Uspenskij, B. 1965. *Strukturnaja tipologija jazykov.* Moscow.

Voegelin, C. F. 1960. Casual and Noncasual Utterances within Unified Style. In T. A. Sebeok (ed.), *Style in Language,* 57–68. Cambridge: MIT Press, pp. 57–68.

Zengel, Marjorie Smith. 1962. Literacy as a Factor in Language Change, *Amer. Anthro* **64,** 132–139.

II

Language and
National Development

Joshua A. Fishman

NATIONALITY-NATIONALISM AND NATION-NATIONISM

The relationship between language and nationalism is a central topic for all those concerned with the language problems of the developing nations. The term nationalism proves to be a particularly troublesome one, however, because it pertains simultaneously to nation and to nationality, two concepts that require rather more careful differentiation than they have usually received.

I suggest that the word nation be reconsidered as a politico-geographic entity (otherwise referred to as country, polity, state) such as might qualify for membership in the United Nations. A nation may present no high degree of sociocultural unity, and, indeed, nations vary greatly in the extent to which they possess such unity within their borders. Those who choose to ignore this often confuse the separate questions of political community and sociological community—each having very definite language needs that frequently go unrecognized by the others.

"Nationality," on the other hand, might best be reconsidered as a sociocultural entity that may have no corresponding politico-geographic realization. Its discriminanda are essentially at the level of authenticity and solidarity of group behaviors and group values, rather than at the level of governmental, politico-geographical realizations and implementations. The advantage of separating these two kinds of national integration (both terminologically and conceptually) is that such separation provides greater insight into *why* social solidarity is not a precondition for the existence of a national political community and into *how* a national political community can attain such solidarity in successive steps.

"Nation" signifies something different for Americans, Englishmen, Frenchmen, and Eastern Europeans, not to mention Africans and Asians. I have selected a meaning of the term for elaboration here that is closer to the everyday American than to other meanings. The traditional distinction drawn between nation and state in political science is not unrelated to the distinction I seek to make, but it fails to reflect in the labels selected the developmental relationship between the two entities.[1] The further fact that much of modern political science proceeds comfortably *without* the notion of nationalism merely means that it is not deeply concerned with the ideological-emotional components of attachment to nationality and to nations. This lack of concern may indicate an unconscious American intellectual bias, which is all the more unfortunate because of the aura of objectivity in which it is cloaked.

The reason for the widespread confusion concerning the meaning of nationalism in many Western tongues is quite simply that the past several centuries (and particularly the past five decades) have witnessed the successful acquisition on the part of many *nationalities* of their own politico-geographic entities, or *nations*.[2] The driving or organizing dynamic in this nationality-into-nation process has been referred to as *nationalism*. The trio (nationality, nationalism, and nation) would not be so troublesome to us today if the process of nationality-into-nation had stopped at the boundaries of the nationalities purportedly involved, that is, if all nations had initially been or remained *single-nationality nations*. However, history is no great respecter of terminology and nations have constantly gone on to absorb and consolidate territories peopled by quite different nationalities, and this process (which is essentially past the nationality-into-nation stage) has also been referred to as "nationalism."

Finally, to make matters even more troublesome, the processes by which nationalities *themselves* were formed, out of prior (indeed primordial) tradition-bound ethnic groups, has also been referred to as *nationalism*.[3] Thus the term utilized to designate the nationality-into-nation process has also been *extended backward* to refer to a formative, dynamic period coming *before* the nationality-into-nation transition at the same time that it has been *extended forward* to refer to a formative, dynamic period coming *after* the nationality-into-nation transition.

Obviously, the term nationalism has been given too great a burden to carry, without sufficient clarity as to what the *underlying* phenomenon is that ties all of these uses together. If *this* could be clarified, then the role of language in each of these stages or kinds of nationalism might also become clearer.

It seems to me that we have here two separate but relatable continua (nationality and nation), each capable of successive transmutations and cumulative symbolic elaborations of their pre-existing stages.

THE SUCCESSIVE STAGES OF SOCIOCULTURAL INTEGRATION: NATIONALISMS

At the sociocultural level it is the *transition between ethnic group and nationality* that is initially crucial to our immediate purpose (although prior transitions occurred along the band-to-clan stages). As a result of symbolic elaboration the daily rounds of life that constitute traditional

ethnicity (including ways of speaking, dressing, harvesting, cooking, cele-
brating, worshipping, etc.) come to be viewed not as minimally ideologized (which is not to say unrationalized), localized, and particularized
"innocent" acts but, rather, as expressions of common history, common
values, common missions, longings, goals, etc.[4]

This awareness of basic or *underlying unity* in the presence of and in
preference to seemingly *disparate appearances* may come in the face of
common superordinate threat, or after conquest of one group by another
or, at times, by intermarriage and peaceful diffusion and assimilation.
What is crucial, however, is the *ideologized transformation,* the more
inclusive (or exclusive) and conscious point of view, that has been erected
over behaviors that had hitherto existed on a more localized, traditionalized, and routinized scale. This process of transformation from fragmentary and tradition-bound ethnicity to unifying and ideologized nationality may well be called nationalism.[5] If it is so called, however, it
should be referred to as nationalism$_a$ ("sub *a*") in recognition of the fact
that it is only the first of many transformations of sociocultural integration yet to come.[6] Certainly many developing countries are witnessing
exactly *this* kind of transformation from ethnicity to nationality among
certain population segments at this very time. Language, too, comes to be
viewed differently in this process, as the actual range of varieties in the
nationality-conscious-speech community expands and as distinctions between locals, nationals, and marginals obtain. By way of contrast much of
Western Europe has gone through several successive transmutations: first
from ethnicity to nationality, then from nationality to larger nationality,
and, in some cases, from larger nationality to even more inclusive nationality—each transmutation bringing with it characteristic changes in
repertoire-range and attitudes.[7] This consideration, however, brings us to
another dimension—the politico-geographic base on which these sociocultural transmutations of ethnicity and nationality are realized.

THE SUCCESSIVE STAGES OF POLITICO-GEOGRAPHICAL INTEGRATION: NATIONISMS

The unifying and ideologizing dynamism of nationalism bombards and
transmutes not only human populations viewed as territorially abstracted
sociocultural aggregates but also the very territories that these populations inhabit. Hills and rivers and woods cease to be merely familiar; they
become ideologically significant (shrines, birthplaces, battlefields, com-
memorative sites, ancestral grounds, etc.). However, the unification and
transmutation of these two systems—the sociocultural and the politico-
territorial—do not always or even usually proceed apace. On occasion,
populations that are already socioculturally integrated on the basis of
common nationality seek coextensive, self-determined, political bound-

aries. On other occasions the fortunes of war or diplomacy or economic ascendency result in common political boundaries for populations whose common nationality develops later. If we go back far enough in the history of *Western Europe* we find *nationality* sentiments *pressuring* for appropriate political boundaries (i.e., nationalism forming the state), rather than merely nationalism *catching up with* political boundaries and then creating greater nationalities to match these boundaries (i.e., the nation forming nationalism).[8] Thus the sociocultural nationality and the politico-geographic nation are rarely in phase with each other. Rather, one is (or is seen to be) frequently out of phase with the other and there is often considerable pressure "to catch up," with concomitant impact *on* language (repertoires) and exploitation *of* language symbols.

I would hope we might agree to no longer call *both* of these "catching up" processes by the *same* name. Where the political boundaries are most salient and most efforts are directed toward maintaining or strengthening them, regardless of the immediate sociocultural character of the populations they embrace—indeed, wherever politico-geographic momentum and consolidation are in advance of sociocultural momentum and consolidation—we might prefer a term such as *nationism*[9] (or "political integration") to that old standby, nationalism. Whenever the boundary of the nation, however, is more ideologized than that of the nationality

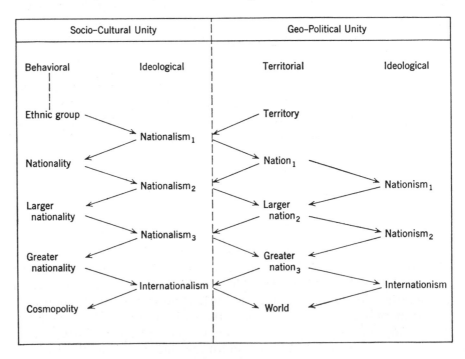

Figure 1. Nationalism and nationism.

we may also begin to find pressure building up for "authentic" cultural unification or intensification. These are the nationalistic consequences of nationism.

THE DIFFERING LANGUAGE PROBLEMS
OF NATIONALISM AND NATIONISM

It seems only reasonable to conclude that language problems (or at least those language problems that are emphasized) will *differ,* depending on which of these pressures, nationalism or nationism, is stochastically paramount. Among those for whom *nationalism* is clearly paramount, that is, where populations are actively pursuing the sociocultural unification that befits those whose common nationality is manifest, the choice of a national language is not in question since it is usually already a prominently ideologized symbol. The major language problems of nationalism are language maintenance, reinforcement, and enrichment (including both codification and elaboration) in order to foster the nationalistic (the vertical or ethnically single) unity, priority, or superiority of the sociocultural aggregate. Note, however, that some of these (nationalistic) language actions have indirect implications for *nationism* as well, since such matters as the use of intricate writing systems, or the rejection of westernisms, or the rejection of the legitimacy of specialized registers per se have necessary consequences for the conduct of the politico-geographic nation and the institutions under its control (government, schools, technological, industrial, and agricultural planning, etc.).[10]

Conversely, among those for whom *nationism* is stochastically paramount *other* kinds of language problems come to the fore. The geographic boundaries are far in advance of sociocultural unity. Thus problems of horizontal integration, such as quick language choice and widespread literary language use, become crucial to the nation's functional existence per se. Language policy based on nationism, however, has direct implications for nationalism (i.e., for sociocultural unity) in the new nation. The language(s) selected may foster or long delay isomorphism (or catching up) between nationism and nationalism; it may strengthen or weaken the potential for sociocultural unity of the several populations within common politico-geographic boundaries,[11] and so on.

As a result, there are both *direct* and *indirect* ties between language and nationism as well as between language and nationalism. However, language and nationalism represents a more ideologized historical interaction (in terms of mass ideology) since nationalism so commonly elaborates upon language as one of its markers of symbolic unity and identity. This is partially a byproduct of the much *longer* and more intimate relationship between language and sociocultural pattern that enters into nationalism and *its* view that *a* particular language is a uniquely appropriate link between speakers and their sociocultural pattern. It is nationalism that views self-identity, group-identity, and self-identity through group-identity as impossible (unthinkable) without a *particular* language rather than merely without a common language. For nationism, language questions are initially not questions of authenticity (identity) but of efficiency (cohesion). Only after efficiency seems likely can attention be divided between it and the search for as unified a version of national authenticity as is feasible. Nevertheless, such feelings of authenticity can come in the future, as they have in the past, on a purely or largely exoglossic base.

All nations apportion attention and resources between the claims of authenticity (sociocultural integration) on the one hand and the claims of efficiency (political integration) on the other.[12] The new nations are merely at an earlier, more formative stage in connection with both and, as a result, must orient themselves toward local multilingualisms and official exoglossia at a time when older nations are withdrawing increasingly from that once commonplace pattern.[13]

NATIONAL INTEGRATION AND MULTILINGUISTISM

The distinctions made here between sociocultural integration (nationalism) and political integration (nationism) and the successive transitions of both should enable us to examine the internal, intranational consequences of multilinguistism in the developing nation as well as some of its external, international consequences.

Our Western, post-Versailles intellectual heritage has caused many contemporary sociologists to be all too ready to assume that cultural and linguistic *differences* automatically tend toward demands for nation-formation and language *recognition* [12]. The postwar African experience is therefore a puzzle to many sociologists and political scientists, and even the Indian experience, though seemingly more "natural," puzzles those who know that India has many, many times as many languages as those that have either received or demanded political recognition. This puzzlement brings to light three points.

1. Not all language differences that exist are noted, let alone ideologized. By this I mean that linguists recognize language differences (whether in phonology, morphology, or syntax) that millions of native-speakers consciously or unconsciously ignore. Thus Wolff has reported several instances in which West African groups speaking distinct, and at times unrelated, languages ignore the differences between them, at times reciprocally and at times unilaterally [12]. Wolff claims that mutual intelligibility is largely a function of intergroup attitudes. Polomé [10] has reported similar data for the Swahili region of Central and East Africa; Wurm has much the same to say for New Guinea [13]; Haugen comments on such developments at various times in different Scandinavian contexts [7]; and similar phenomena have long been known to students of Southeast Asia.[14] The general point here is that differences do *not* need to be divisive. *Divisiveness is an ideologized position* and it can magnify minor differences; indeed, it can manufacture differences in languages as in other matters almost as easily as it can capitalize on more obvious differences. Similarly, *unification is also an ideologized position* and it can minimize seemingly major differences or ignore them entirely, whether these be in the realm of language, religion, culture, race, or any other basis of differentiation.

2. *Conscious and even ideologized language differences need not be divisive,* whether at the national or at the international level. Thus the pattern of national diglossia has its international counterparts as well.

In the diglossia situation a single society recognizes two or more languages as its own, with each having its own *functionally exclusive* domains [3].[15] Most of Europe is still marked by such diglossia if we recognize differences between dialectal varieties (utilized when one is among family and friends) and the national standard (the language of school, government and "high" culture). In former days, European elites were marked by a diglossia pattern in which (Parisian) French functioned as an international status symbol that alternated with one's own national standard and local dialect in accord with the demands of particular role-relationships, interactional patterns, and domains of discourse [5]. Today English is often the diglossia key to "elitemanship" as were Latin, Provençal, Danish, Salish, and other regional languages for certain parts of Europe in the past [4].

In non-European settings, particularly in the new nations of Africa and Asia, diglossia is extremely widespread and therefore language statistics or nation-and-language typologies that slight this fact are somewhat to very misleading. On occasion, it is a traditional diglossia in which two or more languages have long-established, functionally separate roots in the same society (e.g., classical and vernacular Arabic in Egypt and Syria, Sanskrit and Hindi in parts of India, Spanish and Guarani in Paraguay, tribal languages and Hausa and Arabic in Northern Nigeria).[16] Diglossia of a more modern sort exists throughout most of sub-Saharan Africa, Asia, and Latin America and involves English, French, or Spanish together with one or more indigenous languages. Such diglossia, combined with other factors to be mentioned, basically accounts for the lack of language divisiveness in the political integration of most of modern Africa. Instead of trying to cope with hundreds of local languages as instruments of government, education, industrialization, etc., most African states have decided to assign all of them equally to their respective home, family, and neighborhood domains and to utilize a single, major European language (usually English or French) for all more formal, statusful, and specialized domains.[17] This approach tends to minimize internal linguistic divisiveness since it does not place any indigenous language at an undue advantage as *the* language of nationhood.

3. *Most "new nations" of Africa (and Asia) are not yet ethnic nations,* which tends to reinforce the diglossic approach. They are not yet sociocultural units as a result of the long and painful common struggle of a population to unite across local differences, to create heroes and histories, songs and dramas, in order to attain certain common goals. African languages have rarely become symbolic of the quest for nationhood because from the very first nationhood normally implied a supra-ethnic, supra-local entity, whereas almost all indigenous languages remained entirely local and therefore prenational or non-national or even antinational in implication.[18] As a result the indigenous African and the imported European languages are more easily retained in functionally noncompetitive spheres, thus avoiding a confrontation between them.

Can such separation last? Is it not inevitable that urbanization and industrialization[19] will bring to the fore large indigenous populations who seek roles in the spheres of government and economy without knowing the "proper" language for such roles. Will language conflict not ensue as Woloff and Sango and countless other languages of urbanizing Africans become connected with nationalistic (ethnically cohesive, unifying, and expansive) movements that oppose domination by the narrow population segment that controls French or English?

THE SPECIAL NEED FOR DIGLOSSIA
IN THE CURRENT QUEST FOR NATIONISM

This *may* come to pass but it is not inevitable.[20] The experience of the Arab world is exactly that of entering planned mobilization with diglossia far from abandoned. Indeed, in continents so long accustomed to superposed languages, both foreign and indigenous, there are several factors that should minimize the displacement of diglossia.

1. As distinct from conditions that existed in pre-Versailles days, new languages now become politically consolidated and recognized primarily on the basis of their utility and actual use in the domains of science and technology [9]. Belletristic and even governmental use are no longer signs that languages have "arrived" as fitting vehicles for elitist use. This state of affairs is merely a reflection of the changed position of technology vis-à-vis literature as a source of status mobility for nations and interest groups.

2. Technology is basically nonethnic and uniformizing throughout the world. It leads linguistically to but one, two, or three world "technology" languages and to essentially similar life-styles regardless of language. This is in sharp contrast to the basically heterogeneous and diversifying role

of the languages of belletristics prior to World War I. The purpose and the function of those languages was to render their speakers maximally different in terms of cultural values and world views.

3. The uniformizing requirements and consequences of technology are such that for many years to come many monolingual nations in control of "old languages" will need to resort to diglossian compromises in various technological and educational domains. This trend should be much stronger than the countertrend, namely, the abandonment of diglossia on behalf of *new* national standard languages with undisputed hegemony in all domains of national expression. Such diglossian compromises may mean the end of *forced* language assimilation in the domain of family and friends, but they may also mean the end of the exclusivistic sway of a single language in all domains of national life. Both of these factors when viewed in long-term perspective should lead to a diminution of *internal* linguistic strife and thus to a dimunition of purely or basically linguistic strife in international affairs as well.

Having appeared on the world scene as nonethnic nations at a time when the struggle for existence is particularly fierce, I predict that many of the "new nations" will long need to emphasize *nationism* (rather than *nationalism*) and diglossia involving a LWC (language of wider communication) rather than monoglossia. In the successful nations a wider diglossic nationalism will ultimately develop, so that feelings of national identity *will* correspond approximately to their wider geographical borders.[21] In the unsuccessful nations a narrower diglossic-nationalism will develop corresponding to smaller regions that are already defined in terms of sociocultural unity. Neither Pan-Africanism nor Negritude nor communism nor Islam nor democracy nor Christianity is likely soon to replace the nation as the unit of efficient, rational management of administrative affairs, or the nationality as the unit of authenticity toward which nations and subnations will be attracted. The language problems of each stage and kind of national integration (i.e., of nationalism) will be a reflection of the unfinished business of each.

NOTES

1. For many good examples of modern and fruitful discussions of political integration and the political system see David Easton's *A System Analysis of Political Life* (New York, Wiley, 1965, esp. Ch. 11) and his earlier essay "An Approach to the Analysis of Political Systems," *World Politics*, 9, 383–400 (1956–1957).
2. van den Berghe (this volume) defines nationalism as either "a political movement" or "a process of growing self-consciousness based on a feeling of common ethnicity," thus confusing a byproduct with the core of the phenomenon in question.
3. See my "Varieties of Ethnicity and Varieties of Language Consciousness" [4] for an elaboration of nationalism so defined.

4. Deutsch's conviction that such elaborations usually occur during periods of intense modernization ignores the elaborative role of traditionalization. Reorientation rather than its stimulus is the crucial factor.

5. Both van den Berghe and Mazrui (in this volume) have commented on religion as a factor in nationalism. In addition, van den Berghe considers racism as foreign to nationalism per se. Actually, both religion and racism are very common unifying threads, particularly in the fabric of early nationalism. *Ultimately,* the successive transmutations of religious, racial and class ideologies are antinationalistic, although many do not pass beyond their nationalistic phase.

6. This early (but not earliest) variety of sociocultural integration has received fairly extensive attention from Deutsch [2] to C. Geertz [6], although generally subsumed under the label "national integration," which masks the distinction between political and sociocultural integration that I wish to stress.

7. The sociocultural consolidation of the English (both as a result of opposing the Normans and as a result of fusion with them) is one unification and transformation that stands in a reciprocal relationship with the politico-geographical nation "England." Great Britain, the United Kingdom, and the British Commonwealth of Nations are successive transformations toward life at an ever-larger scale. Each is another step away from the original ethnic base, each is ideologized at a more abstract level, but each ultimately is associated with certain recurring traditionalized affiliative behaviors. Similar transmutations from nationalism$_a$ to nationalism$_b$ to nationalism$_e$ may be encountered in the history of France, Spain, Germany, etc. After a certain point, of course, internationalism or cosmopolitanism appears to be more appropriate than nationalism for the process under consideration.

8. Rustow (in this volume) considers the latter typical of post-dynastic states of Western Europe, the countries of overseas immigration, and the post-colonial states. He considers the former process (nationalism creating the state) typical of the "linguistic states of Central and East Europe and the Middle East." Van den Berghe describes Afrikaner nationalism as being of this type (nationality into nation) as well (this volume). Although I do not quarrel with these characterizations, I wish to point out that they may be no more than accurate but static characterizations of stages in an inherently cyclical and unstable process.

   I am quite convinced that Tabouret-Keller's reference (this volume) to the "coincidence between national and linguistic" frontiers in Western Europe is, at best, accurate only for a very restricted period in history, since there have been in Western Europe, as elsewhere, not only ample cases of "forward developing" out-of-phase instances between nationalities and their nations but also instances of regressive development in which nationalities crumbled and returned to more primitive stages of ethnic consciousness or lack of consciousness.

9. Van den Berghe speaks of "territorialism" (this volume), but in most concrete instances I believe "nationism" to be the more fruitful designation because of its cognate relationship to nationalism and because of its ideologized implication.

10. Alexandre (this volume) is absolutely right in pointing out that language characteristics transform political programs as are Gumperz and Das Gupta (this volume) in their reiteration that without proper language specialization (technical enrichment) *and* its widespread popularization the availability of a common language does not improve national functioning.

11. It must be realized that all nations—particularly new ones—are concerned with nationism and nationalism simultaneously. As a result, Alexandre's claim (in this volume) that "an independent African government must develop precisely horizontal channels to promote any kind of nationwide feeling of common purposes and interests" is probably an exaggeration since no national apparatus can function

without vertical specialization in language as in roles. Rustow's perceptive statement (this volume) that "the closer interaction and interdependence of the modern age tend to pose sharply latent questions of identity and unity" applies to both nationalistic and nationistic entities. If the reformulations presented in this essay are of value it will be because they attempt to define identity and unity (both types of solidarity) in more incremental fashion, closer to the level of social process and social interaction, to the end that *their measurement in human behavior* per se (rather than their use as categories or descriptive labels alone) becomes a more feasible task.

12. Tabouret-Keller (this volume) is certainly correct in her diachronic comparison between Africa today and Europe of a century or more ago.

13. Since much of my critique has been by way of "exaggeration for the purposes of clarity" let me briefly sketch an actual case to indicate how the interplay between nationism and nationalism has unfolded in the past eighty years of Jewish history. Political Zionism was initially only one sector of the total nationalistic fervor that gripped Eastern European Jewry in the latter part of the nineteenth century. In its early stages it was perhaps more concerned with "people building" than with "nation building," both of these terms being coined almost immediately. Its nemesis, the "Jewish Labor Bund of Russia, Lithuania, and Poland," was frequently more popular (until World War II) and concentrated entirely on "people building" *(arbet af di erter, döizm)* within a socialist-autonomist framework. Both organizations derived some of their appeal from more traditional nationalist sentiments carried by Jewish beliefs and practices through the centuries. Between them at both extremes there arose a veritable host of splinter parties that sought to combine nationism, nationalism, socialism, and traditionalism in differing degrees.

Thus certain early Zionist thinkers disclaimed interest in a political entity, believing that only a cultural center *(mercaz rukhni*—Akhad Ha'am) was needed. Whereas the Bund was primarily Yiddishist, the Zionist movement was primarily Hebraist. Between the two there were several programs favoring Yiddish *and* Hebrew, albeit in differing degrees, and with differing priorities and long-term commitments. Competing versions of national history, national school systems, national literatures, and national destiny were devised and cultivated in Eastern Europe, up to 1939. None of these were *actually* nation building (since the nation was both elsewhere and iffy) and therefore positions with respect to language choice and language acceptance were far less pressing than were the constant efforts on behalf of language codification and language elaborations.

Not so in Palestine proper where "nation building" was a more urgent pursuit although "people building" was rarely lost sight of entirely. (Of course, even Palestine itself had a rival as the national homeland since some Zionists favored accepting the Crown's offer of Uganda and, when defeated, established a Territorialist movement which is still in existence today—although the forthcoming "Sociolinguistic Survey of East Africa" need not now expect to run into many of its adherents in Uganda.) Language choice was long a very hot issue in Palestine with both German and Yiddish attracting very considerable support, German before World War I and the Yiddish between the two wars. The conflict between the adherents of Yiddish and the adherents of Hebrew is referred to as "the language conflict" *(riv halashonot*—*riv haloshoynes)*. There were also serious but less fiery discussions of diglossic solutions: Hebrew *and* Yiddish, Hebrew *and* English, Hebrew *and* Arabic, etc.

With the creation of the State enormous attention was given to the rapid acceptance of Hebrew by both new settlers and older inhabitants who had not yet learned it. (However, while immigrants were learning Hebrew in Ulpanim many native-born Israelis were learning Yiddish and other Jewish communalects via service in the armed forces and in the temporary settlement camps.) With the relaxation of nation building efforts per se in more recent years, renewed attention has been given to people building, particularly in the hope that the young will become more appreciative of and knowledgeable about a wider definition of Jewish nationality than that which is evident within the minuscule boundaries of Israeli time and space. Those with a far different concept of Jewish nationality than the one recognized by the State are still pressing for alternative linguistic realizations.

14. Of course, the opposite also obtains under certain circumstances. There are many instances where linguistic differences are exceedingly marginal, indeed, where they are no greater than the minor dialectal differences existing *within* certain well-recognized national standards, but where these differences are emphasized and cultivated. Several such "cultivated" differences exist in the Western World today (see Kloss [9] for the best discussion of such *"ausbau"* languages in the Germanic area) and are treated as seemingly autonomous languages (Czech and Slovak, Serbian and Croatian, Macedonian and Bulgarian, Russian and Byelorussian), whereas their parallels in the new nations are still rather few (Hindi-Urdu being the prime example). If the cultivation of minor differences is pursued in the new nations, a major possibility is the fractionization of English (East African, West African, Indian, etc.) that might be fostered thereby.

15. Tabouret-Keller (this volume) mentions that the absence of socioeconomic and sociocultural competition between two language groups leads to a remarkable stability of the "(bi) language pattern," but she fails to note that this is a *necessary* precondition of the stable intragroup bilingualism that diglossia typifies.

16. It is important to distinguish between (a) diglossia, which normally implies a *societally based* and *culturally valued functional differentiation* between languages and (b) bilingualism, which carries no such implication. Thus Switzerland, Belgium, and Canada may well be bilingual *countries* in which the proportions of bilinguals are rather small and unilateral, precisely because they are *not* diglossia settings (except for German, Swiss-German diglossia) in which a single, unified population views two or more languages as its own for particular purposes. For further details see my "Bilingualism with and without diglossia; Diglossia with and without Bilingualism," *Journal of Social Issues,* **23** (2), 29–38 (1967).

17. In several instances the result has been that a native speech-community finds itself divided into two segments due to differences in the national diglossia (or triglossia) pattern to which different parts of the community have been attached. Thus Hausa speakers in Nigeria are developing English-Hausa-Arabic triglossia and those in Niger, French-Hausa-Arabic triglossia. If this split is ideologized it may lead to demands for a Pan-Hausa State, with or without a superposed European language. A similar situation exists with respect to Swahili speakers in the Congo and in Tanzania. It is not apparent to me why Alexandre claims that such divisions of a language group between two nations is injurious to the development of each (this volume). No such injury seems to have visited upon the English or French speaking nations of the world.

18. It should be recognized that where the boundaries of ethnicity and nationhood correspond fairly closely indigenous languages have been symbolically elaborated into national languages. Alexandre, Mazrui and Paden all make this point, although in quite different ways. Alexandre and Mazrui show how colonial languages were the instruments of Westernization, education, national liberation, and even such postnationalistic ideologies as Pan-Africanism and Negritude. Paden demonstrates how a regionally consolidated superposed language can be a base for national power and yet never transcend its local roles.

19. Although we must be grateful to Tabouret-Keller (in this volume) for raising the

question of language maintenance and language shift and for pointing to industrialization and urbanization as facilitators of shift, some may find her presentation lacking with respect to social process analyses. Categories such as urban-rural, older-younger, male-female, etc., do not explain the dynamics of culture change which carry language shift along with them.

20. The slow spread of national standards in Europe is well illustrated by Tabouret-Keller. This volume.

21. Alexandre's view that "for an African the valuation of English or French is cultural not national" (this volume) and a similar position by Tabouret-Keller (this volume) are contradicted by Mazrui and by the historical experience of most other (even if only transitionally) exoglossic nations in world history.

REFERENCES

1. Deutsch, Karl W. 1942. The Trend of European Nationalism; The Language Aspect *Amer. Pol. Sci. Rev.*, **36**, 533–541.

2. Deutsch, Karl W. 1953. *Nationalism and Social Communication; An Inquiry into the Foundations of Nationality.* Cambridge and New York: Technology Press of MIT and Wiley.

3. Ferguson, Charles A. 1959. Diglossia. *Word*, **15**, 325–340.

4. Fishman, Joshua A. 1966. Varieties of Ethnicity and Varieties of Language Consciousness. *Georgetown Univ. Monog. No. 18, Languages and Linguistics*, pp. 69–79. Also see my application of these concepts to Ukrainian language maintenance and shift in my *Language Loyalty in the United States,* The Hague: Mouton, 1966.

5. Fishman, Joshua A. 1965. Who Speaks What Language to Whom about What? *La Linguistique*, **2**, 67–88.

6. Geertz, Clifford. 1963. *Old Societies and New States.* New York: Free Press.

7. Haugen, E. 1966. Semicommunication: The Language Gap in Scandinavia. *Sociological Inquiry*, **36**, 280–297.

8. Hymes, Dell. 1962. The Ethnography of Speaking. In *Anthropology and Human Behavior,* Washington, Anthrop. Soc. of Wash., pp. 13–53. Also see his Functions of Speech: An Evolutionary Approach, in F. C. Gruber (ed.), *Anthropology and Education.* Philadelphia: University of Pennsylvania Press, 1959, pp. 50–66. BMRS: A-124.

9. Kloss, Heinz. 1952. Der linguistische und der sociologische Sprachbegriff: Abstandsprachen und ausbausprachen, in his *Die Entwicklung neuer germanischer Kultursprachen,* Munich: Pohl, pp. 15–37.

10. Polomé, Edgar. 1963. Cultural Languages and Contact Vernaculars in The Republic of the Congo. *Texas Studies in Literature and Language,* **4**, 499–511.

11. Stewart, Wm. A. 1962. An Outline of Linguistic Typology for Describing Multilingualism. In F. A. Rice (ed.), *Study of the Role of Second Languages,* Washington, D.C.: CALMLA, pp. 15–25.

12. Wolff, Hans. 1959. Intelligibility and Inter-Ethnic Attitudes. *Anthrop. Ling.,* **1**(3), 34–41.

13. Wurm, S. A., and D. C. Laycock. 1961/62. The Question of Language and Dialect in New Guinea. *Oceania,* **32**, 128–143.

Joshua A. Fishman

SOME CONTRASTS BETWEEN LINGUISTICALLY HOMOGENEOUS AND LINGUISTICALLY HETEROGENEOUS POLITIES

INTRODUCTION

In recent years the absence of exhaustive international data on language behavior has been bemoaned by a growing number of specialists. While some would seek to assemble such data as quickly as possible and others would hope to attain somewhat greater conceptual and methodological refinement before embarking on such massive undertaking, most would agree that only worldwide-and-diachronic data can hope to answer many of the questions posed by the interaction of linguistics and the social-behavioral sciences. Certainly, students of the language problems of developing nations would have a great deal to gain from the availability of systematic data of this kind.

Specialists in language behavior have not been the only ones, by any means, with an interest in worldwide comparative data. The Yale Human Relations Area Files (an outgrowth of Yale's earlier Cross-Cultural Sur-

I wish to express my thanks to the following members of the Seminar on Elites and Ideologies of the Center for Advanced Study in the Behavioral Sciences, Stanford, California, 1963–1964, for their assistance and encouragement, as well as for their critical reading of a preliminary draft: Juan Linz (Columbia University), Charles Moskos (University of Michigan), and Sidney Verba (Stanford University). I am also indebted to Heins Kloss (Forschungsstelle für Nationalitäten und Sprachenfragen, Marburg), Robert B. Textor (Stanford University), Stanley Lieberson (University of Washington), and Arthur S. Banks (Indiana University) for their suggestions in connection with the preparation of the version that was originally published in *Sociological Inquiry*, Vol. 36.2 (Spring, 1966), pp. 146–158 (reprinted here by permission of the editor, *Sociological Inquiry*). For their critical assistance in the preparation of the current (somewhat revised) version I owe a debt of gratitude to J. Das Gupta and Ralph Retzloff (University of California, Berkeley).

vey) are deservedly well known[1] and have proved to be valuable in conjunction with a large number of anthropological studies. Unfortunately, the language data in these files have not proved to be of great interest to scholars in other fields, primarily because the data pertain largely to primitive peoples and, secondly, because they are not available in a form that makes immediate data processing possible. More recently political scientists, economists, and sociologists have undertaken to compile "cross-polity" files. Their interest in such files has undoubtedly been strengthened by the appearance of several score new African and Asian nations since the conclusion of the Second World War. Interest in "nation building" and in various comparisons between old nations and new nations (e.g., in connection with economic development, social ideology, political organization, cultural modernization, social change, etc.) is now at an all-time high and is yielding both practical and theoretical dividends.

Two preliminary reports of "cross-polity" files have recently appeared.[2] In both instances data on linguistic homogeneity are included among the many indices that are provided for a large number of countries.[3] Data on linguistic homogeneity are of interest to political scientists, economists, and sociologists primarily as an aid in identifying cultural homogeneity or heterogeneity. The above-mentioned reports are organized so as to make it possible for investigators to compare individual polities or groups of polities with each other in order to discover their "profiles" across many indices of recognized interest and importance. In addition, the reports should enable investigators to gauge the interaction between various social, economic, political, and cultural factors across polities. Both of the "cross-polity" reports referred to here content themselves with indicating the statistical relationships between many indices across all of the polities for which pertinent information was available to their compilers. The relationships obtaining between individual indices or between groups of indices are neither commented

[1] George P. Murdock *et al., Outline of Cultural Materials,* Third Revised Edition, New Haven: Human Relations Area Files, 1950. Also note Murdock, *Outline of World Cultures,* New Haven: Human Relations Area Files, 1954.
[2] Arthur S. Banks and Robert B. Textor, *A Cross Polity Survey,* Cambridge: M.I.T. Press, 1965; Bruce M. Russett, *et al., Handbook of Basic Political and Social Data for Cross National Comparisons,* New Haven: Yale University (mimeographed), 1963. Also note Howard R. Alker, Jr. and Bruce M. Russett, *Relationships between Paired Indices of Political and Economic Development,* New Haven: Yale University (mimeographed), 1964. The more final publication resulting from these last two mimeographed reports (Bruce M. Russett and H. R. Alker, Jr., K. W. Deutsch, H. D. Lasswell, *World Handbook of Political and Social Indicators,* New Haven, Yale Univ. Press, 1964 was not yet available when this paper was originally prepared.
[3] Banks and Textor deal only with politically independent polities. Alker and Russett provide data on colonies as well as on independent nations.

upon nor integrated in these reports. The reports are intended to serve as basic reference (i.e., as dictionaries or directories) by means of which other investigators can select, interrelate, and explicate the particular topics of concern to them.

The purpose of this paper is threefold: (1) to integrate and briefly review the strongest (and presumably the most reliable) relationships which are reported between linguistic homogeneity and other characteristics of polities throughout the world; (2) to subject some of the reported findings to further analysis by controlling particular variables; and, on the basis of the foregoing (3) to comment upon the worldwide file approach to the study of language behavior. Our basic procedure will be to follow the lead of one of the two reports referred to, that by Banks and Textor. Their approach is to contrast those polities in which a single language is "natively spoken" by 85 per cent or more of the population and in which no significant linguistic minority is present, on the one hand, with those polities that are more linguistically heterogeneous, in that a significant linguistic minority *is* present among the remaining 15 per cent of the population, or in that no single language is natively spoken by 85 per cent or more of the population, on the other hand.[4]

[4] This dichotomous definition of linguistic homogeneity-heterogeneity is neither explained nor defended by Banks and Textor. It may be open to serious question, not only because of the arbitrariness of the 85 per cent cut off but (primarily) because of the functional ambiguity of the term "native speaker." Russett and Alker attempt a somewhat more refined definition, distinguishing between childhood mother tongue, language currently or usually spoken in the home, and (other) language(s) "spoken." Both compilers are dependent on official statistics (many of which have been charged with inaccuracy and tendentiousness), although Banks and Textor also seem to have employed "expert opinion" whenever official statistics were unavailable or unacceptable. The greater refinement attempted by Russett and Alker becomes functionally inapplicable when they turn to correlating "speakers of dominant language as a per cent of population" with other indices. Since they lack all three linguistic statistics for most polities they are forced to select the "best" single statistic available in each case. The difficulties involved become painfully apparent when we note that most of the correlations supported by Russett and Alker are based upon less than half of all polities and when we note that Banks and Textor include among their homogeneous polities a few that do *not* meet the 85 per cent cut off according to the statistics reported by Russett and Alker. Although the current writer does not claim special competence in judging most of the other indices utilized by these two reports it seems that quite similar problems obtain in connection with many of them, e.g., (a) vague, inadequate or completely absent definitions of the *topical indices* or categories employed and (b) inexact, incomplete, unavailable or noncomparable data with respect to these indices in the case of many polities. Faced by these problems, the two reports have adopted quite different solutions. Russett and Alker have limited themselves to reporting Pearsonian correlations on far fewer and on far less "interesting" indices for a small number of polities. Banks and Textor have gone to the opposite extreme by reporting double dichotomy ("fourfold") chi squares on many more and on far more interesting judgmental indices for a larger number of polities. Nevertheless, the language findings reported by both compilers frequently seem to make sense and to hold together. They are intended to be

THE ORGANIZATION OF REPORTED RELATIONSHIPS
AND DIFFERENCE

Demographic Variables[5]

Linguistically homogeneous polities tend to be smaller in area (i.e., below 75,000 square miles), to have a higher population density (i.e., above 100/square mile), to have a lower proportion of agricultural population (i.e., less than 66 per cent), and to be more highly urbanized (all of the foregoing figures are cutoffs in 2 x 2 tables). The latter characteristic is reported by both compilations: Russett and Alker utilize the percentage of the population in localities of 20,000 population or more; Banks and Textor define as "highly urbanized" those polities in which 20 per cent or more of the population resides in cities of 20,000 or more *and* in which 12.5 per cent resides in cities of 100,000 or more. Linguistically heterogeneous states tend in the *opposite direction* in connection with all of these variables, i.e., they tend to be larger, of lower population density, of a higher proportion of agricultural population, and to be of a lower degree of urbanization. Related to the above characteristics are three others reported by Russett and Alker, namely that linguistically homogeneous polities have a higher life expectancy for females, a lower death rate, and a lower infant death rate.

Economic Variables

Banks and Textor report that linguistically homogeneous polities tend to have at least a "medium" per capita gross national product (at least 300 U.S. dollars per year) and that they tend to have "developed" or "intermediate" economic status (i.e., at least stable and nearly self-sustaining economic growth). Linguistically heterogeneous polities tend in the *opposite direction* with respect to both of these variables; i.e., they tend to have "low" or "very low" per capita gross national product and to

preliminary findings, and are here considered as such, pending their future revision and refinement.

Table 1 indicates the Banks and Textor linguistic homogeneity classification for 114 polities. The following polities classified as linguistically heterogeneous by Banks and Textor appear to be at least 85 per cent homogeneous in the Russett and Alker data: Equador, Finland, Panama, Rumania, Syria, Turkey. The People's Republic of China is classified as "ambiguous" by Banks and Textor and is unlisted by Russett and Alker.

[5] Both compilers report probability values in connection with the particular statistics of relationships that they employ. In both cases they indicate that these values might better be considered as rough guides or cutoffs for separating stronger from weaker relationships rather than in the usual sense of testing the null hypothesis. All relationships mentioned in this paper have a chance probability value of .15 or less. In a large majority of cases the .05 level is satisfied.

be "economically underdeveloped" or "very underdeveloped." Russett and Alker substantiate these differences by reporting acceptably high correlations between linguistic homogeneity and (1) revenues of general and central government, and of social security and public enterprises, as a percentage of gross national product; (2) per capita gross national product in 1957 U.S. dollars, and (3) wage and salary earners as a percentage of the working-age population. Finally, Banks and Textor report that although *all* polities tend to have other than "low" or "very low" international financial status (i.e., a U.N. assessment of .25 per cent or higher) the linguistically homogeneous polities show this tendency to a much greater degree than do those that are linguistically heterogeneous.

Educational Variables

Russett and Alker report an acceptably high correlation between linguistic homogeneity and "students enrolled in higher education per 100,000 population" as well as "primary and secondary school pupils as a percentage of the population aged 15–64." These are the only indices pertaining directly to differences in formal education between linguistically homogeneous and heterogeneous states. Indirect evidence on this score is derived from literacy data. Both compilations indicate that literacy and newspaper circulation rates are higher in the linguistically homogeneous polities. Indirectly related to economic development, education, and several aspects of cultural style are the following characteristics of linguistically homogeneous populations reported by Russett and Alker: more items of domestic mail per capita, more radios per 1,000 population, larger average annual increase in radios per 1,000 population, more cinema attendance per capita, and more television sets per 1,000 population.

Religious Variables

Both compilations indicate a strong relationship between linguistic homogeneity and the predominance of Christians in the population. Going beyond this, Banks and Textor report that linguistically homogeneous polities also tend to be religiously homogeneous (regardless of the specific religion involved), whereas the opposite is true of linguistically heterogeneous polities. Finally, although most polities have literate predominant religions, this characterization is particularly true of linguistically homogeneous polities.

Historical Variables[6]

Linguistically homogeneous polities tend to be those that achieved independence before 1914, that are historically Western or that have be-

[6] From this point on, all variables are those reported by Banks and Textor only.

come significantly Westernized, that were formerly dependencies of Spain (rather than of Britain or France) among those once under colonial rule, and those whose stage of political modernization is "advanced" or "mid-transitional" (rather than "early transitional" or "pretransitional"). While most polities are historically non-Western this is much less so in the case of linguistically homogeneous polities. While most non-Western polities that have become significantly Westernized did so through colonial status, such Westernization occurred most frequently by far among the linguistically homogeneous polities.

Ideological Variables

Linguistically homogeneous polities tend to be those whose ideological orientation is *other than* "developmental" (i.e., not having development as a national goal) and whose ideological orientation is "conventional" (i.e., using conventionalized procedures for legitimization of new or changed power relationships).[7] While most polities have a "non-mobilizational system style" (i.e., not using political mobilization to meet compelling problems of national emergency), this is particularly true of linguistically homogeneous polities.

Political-Governmental Variables

Linguistically homogeneous polities tend to be those that are constitutional or totalitarian (rather than authoritarian), those in which governmental stability is "generally present" (rather than "moderately present" or "absent"), those in which the representative nature of the regime is "polyarchic" (a broadly representative system rather than one that is "limited," "pseudo-," or "non-polyarchic"), those in which "autonomous groups" are fully tolerated in politics (rather than partially or not at all tolerated), and those in which political enculturation (the *absence* of communalism, factionalism, sectionalism, or political nonassimilation) is "high" or "medium." Linguistically heterogeneous polities tend in the opposite direction in each of these instances.

Interest Articulation Variables

Linguistically homogeneous polities tend to be those in which political interests are articulated, demands are presented to other political structures at least to some extent by associational groups which specialize in this function rather than by institutional groups performing other functions (such as legislative blocks, officer cliques, clergy, skill groups), or nonassociational groups (those based on kinship, lineage, ethnicity, region, religion, status, or class membership), or anomic groups (spontane-

---

[7] Other ideological orientations recognized by Banks and Textor (besides developmental and conventional) are "doctrinal," "situational," and "traditional."

ous structures such as riots, mobs, or demonstrations). The linguistically homogeneous polity is also less likely than its counterparts to have frequent articulation of interests by anomic groups and more likely to display "moderate" or "significant" articulation by political parties.

Interest Aggregation Variables

While most polities are characterized as revealing "less than significant" interest aggregation by the executive branch of government (the extent to which the executive impedes the independent activity or availability of other branches of government), this is particularly true of the linguistically homogeneous variables. Such polities, on the other hand, tend to be those with more than "negligible" interest aggregation by the legislature, whereas linguistically heterogeneous polities tend in the opposite direction—that is, their legislatures tend to be of the "rubber stamp" variety of totalitarian and traditional regimes.

Party System Variables

There are no party system variables which qualitatively distinguish homogeneous polities from linguistically heterogeneous polities. On the other hand, several significant *intensity* differences do obtain. Thus, whereas most polities are characterized as being of "other than a one party system," linguistically homogeneous states are particularly characterizable in this fashion. Furthermore, whereas most polities tend toward "other than a two party system" and toward party systems based upon "other than class oriented or multi-ideological distinctions" such characterizations are least applicable to linguistically homogeneous politics.

Political Leadership Variables

Linguistically homogeneous polities tend to be those in which "personalismo" ("the tendency to follow or oppose for . . . individual or family reasons rather than for reasons of political idea, program or party") is "negligible" rather than "moderate" or "pronounced." While *most* polities are described as revealing "negligible leadership charisma" (leadership charisma exists where leaders are considered to have qualities beyond those possessed by most human beings), this is particularly true of linguistically homogeneous polities.

Horizontal Power Distribution Variables

Linguistically homogeneous polities tend to be those that reveal more than "negligible" horizontal power distribution (effective and functionally autonomous legislative, executive, and judicial "branches"), legislatures that are "fully" or "partially" effective (rather than "largely" or "wholly ineffective"), bicameral (rather than unicameral) legislatures, and "strong" (rather than "dominant") executives. The contrary characteristics tend to be true for linguistically heterogeneous polities.

Bureaucracy, Police and Legal System Variables

No qualitative differences between linguistically homogeneous and heterogeneous polities are reported in this topic area. On the other hand, several *intensity* differences are noted. Thus, while most polities are described as having a semimodern rather than a "post-colonial transitional" bureaucracy, this is particularly true of the linguistically homogeneous polities. Finally, while most polities are described as having legal systems other than under either civil law or common law, and as having politically active police, both of these characteristics tend to be less true for linguistically homogeneous polities.

SUMMARY OF REPORTED RELATIONSHIPS
AND DIFFERENCES

One cannot help but come away from this recitation of findings with the decided impression that linguistic homogeneity is currently related to many more of the "good" and "desirable" characteristics of polities than is linguistic heterogeneity. Linguistically homogeneous polities are usually economically more developed, educationally more advanced, politically more modernized, and ideologically-politically more tranquil and stable. They more frequently reveal orderly, libertarian, and secular forms of interest articulation and aggregation, greater division of governmental powers, and less attraction toward personalismo and charisma. All in all, linguistic homogeneity characterizes the state in which primordial ties and passions are more likely to be under control, cultural-religious homogeneity and enlightenment are advanced, more modern forms of heterogeneity via associational, institutional, and political groups are fostered, and in which the good life is economically within the reach of a greater proportion of the populace. If there is any fly in this ointment it is that some polities have been in such a hurry to approach these desirable endpoints that they have felt a need for more "decisive" authoritarian guidance in order to do so.

In general we find here the well-known relationships between industrialization, urbanization, modernization, Westernization, Christianization, and homogenization that have been explicated by modern political philosophy, history, and sociology during the past century. In most instances linguistic (and more generally, cultural) homogeneity has been interpreted as a consequence of the other processes and characteristics enumerated above. Linguistic and cultural parochialism and particularism have usually been interpreted as giving ground as man becomes ever more at home with the delights and complexities of society on a larger and presumably higher scale. However, the cohesiveness of so many of the distinctions between linguistically homogeneous and heterogeneous polities prompts the question as to whether causal forces may not have been at work *in the opposite direction as well*. Is it possible that an appreciable level of linguistic (and other cultural) homogeneity may have facilitated the "Westernization" of the West? [8] This question (or more probably, this suspicion) must be in the minds of many planners in currently underdeveloped nations. It may require an exceptional concern (by force or by choice) for linguistic heterogeneity to fly in the face of the obviously greater competitive efficiency of linguistic homogeneity. It remains to be seen whether linguistically and culturally heterogeneous Africa and Asia can move significantly forward into the "modern world" without either bringing about or being helped along by degrees of homogeneity as great as those recorded in Western experience.

CONTROLLING THE ECONOMIC FACTOR

Since so many of the reported differences between linguistically homogeneous and heterogeneous polities also appear to be differences between rich and poor polities, it is appropriate to inquire as to which one of these two variables (linguistic homogeneity or wealth) is of greater importance. It is also appropriate to ask the related question: whether the noted differences between linguistically homogeneous and heterogeneous polities still obtain when the economic factor is held constant or partialled out. One way to investigate this last question is to compare linguistically homogeneous and heterogeneous polities of similar wealth or economic development. The former question (as to which variable is of greater importance) can be answered quite directly from the Banks and Textor data. The latter question (whether controlling for economic wealth eliminates the differences noted between linguistically homogeneous and heterogeneous polities) requires secondary analyses utilizing the basic data cards which these investigators make available to all interested parties.[9]

Banks and Textor provide several indices of economic development. Of these, "per capita gross national product" seems to be the most objective and is available for the largest number of polities. When we contrast this variable (dichotomized so as to distinguish between polities with medium to very high per capita gross national product, on the one hand,

[8] My impression is that the preindustrial 17th century "West" was more culturally heterogeneous than it is today but that it was, nevertheless, more homogeneous than underdeveloped Africa or Asia of today. A careful analysis based upon early records might enable a more confident apportionment of the causal variance in this connection.
[9] This is equally the case with respect to the Russett and Alker data. In each case a minor fee is charged for the cards and code sheets.

and those with very low to low standing on the other) [10] with linguistic homogeneity-heterogeneity we easily discern that the former is far more strongly related to most of the other previously mentioned variables than is the latter. Thus, whether we look at the constitutionality of the re-

TABLE 1. *Arrangement of Polities by Linguistic Homogeneity-Heterogeneity and Per Capita Gross National Product*

Gross National Product	Linguistic Factor	
	Homogeneous	*Heterogeneous*
Very High, Medium	Australia, France, Luxembourg, New Zealand, Norway, Sweden, United Kingdom, United States, Austria, Denmark, East Germany, German F.R., Iceland, Ireland, Italy, Netherlands, Venezuela, Argentina, Chile, Cuba, Greece, Hungary, Jamaica, Japan, Lebanon, Poland, Uruguay.	Belgium, Canada, Switzerland, Finland, Czechoslovakia, Israel, USSR, Bulgaria, Rumania, Spain, Trinidad, Cyprus, Malaya, South Africa, Yugoslavia.
Number	27	15
Low, Very Low	Albania, Brazil, Colombia, Costa Rica, Dominican Republic, El Salvador, Honduras, Mexico, Nicaragua, Portugal, Saudi Arabia, Tunisia, United Arab Republic, Burundi, Haiti, Jordan, Korea N., Korean Rep., Libya, Malagasy, Rwanda, Somalia, Yemen.	Panama, Syria, Turkey, Algeria, Ecuador, Guatemala, Iraq, Peru, Philippines, North Vietnam, Republic of Vietnam, Afghanistan, Bolivia, Burma, Cameroun, Central African Rep., Ceylon, Chad, Congo (Bra.), Congo (Leo.), Dahomey, Ethiopia, Gabon, Ghana, Guinea, India, Indonesia, Iran, Ivory Coast, Laos, Mali, Liberia, Mauritania, Morocco, Nepal, Niger, Nigeria, Pakistan, Senegal, Sierra Leone, Sudan, Tanganyika, Togo, Uganda, Upper Volta.
Number	25	47

gime; at its governmental (polyarchic) stability; at whether it has a competitive electoral system, freedom of political opposition for autonomous groups, personalismo, leadership charisma, or horizontal power distribution; at the current status of the legislature; at the interventive role of

[10] Table 1 indicates the position of 114 polities with respect to the cross-tabulations of per capita gross national product (dichotomized) and linguistic homogeneity (dichotomized), based upon the indices of Banks and Textor.

the police; or what have you—we find far greater differences between polities with higher and lower per capita gross national product than between linguistically homogeneous and heterogeneous polities. Indeed, there are only two variables for which the reverse holds true; political enculturation and (most particularly) sectionalism.

TABLE 2. *Political Enculturation and Sectionalism Related to Per Capita Gross National Product and Linguistic Homogeneity-Heterogeneity*

	Per Capita G.N.P.		Linguistic Factor	
Related to	*Very High, Medium* %	*Low, Very Low* %	*Homo- geneous* %	*Hetero- geneous* %
Political Enculturation				
High, Medium	74	46	73	44
Low	26	54	27	56
TOTAL (n)*	100 (32)	100 (61)	100 (40)	100 (55)
χ^2	5.68		6.70	
P	0.11		.007	
Sectionalism				
Negligible	55	37	67	25
Moderate, Extreme	45	63	33	75
TOTAL (n)	100 (40)	100 (68)	100 (48)	100 (59)
χ^2	2.71		6.64	
P	.074		.001	

* Missing data account for variable numbers of cases.

In connection with these two variables we find that linguistically homogeneous and linguistically heterogeneous polities differ from each other as much as or more than do polities with higher and lower per capita gross national product. Thus, it would appear that exaggerated sectionalism and (to a lesser degree) the presence of significant, politically nonassimilated minorities in extreme opposition come closer to being major correlates (both as preservers and as consequence) of linguistic heterogeneity than any of the many other variables we have examined.

Granted that per capita gross national product is a more powerful differentiating factor between polities than is linguistic homogeneity per se, we now ask whether the aforementioned differences between linguistically homogeneous and heterogeneous polities are modified appreciably when differences in per capita gross national product are taken into account. On the basis of secondary analyses of the Banks and Textor cards[11] it would seem that the best answer to this question is as follows:

[11] I am indebted to John Gilbert, then staff statistician at the C.A.S.B.S., for the computations and analyses on which this discussion is based.

most differences between linguistically heterogeneous and linguistically homogeneous polities become greatly attenuated but remain recognizable when differences in per capita gross national product are controlled. The articulation of interest by anomic groups may be taken as a case in point. Initially, before controlling for per capita gross national product, 61 per cent of all linguistically homogeneous and 18 per cent of all linguistically heterogeneous polities were characterized by "infrequent or very infrequent articulation by anomic groups." Thus we have an initial difference of 43 per cent. After controlling per capita gross national product we find that this initial difference is decreased. It fell to only 23 per cent among polities with higher per capita gross national product and to only 34 per cent among polities with lower per capita gross national product. Nevertheless, within each level of gross national product the original direction of the difference between linguistically homogeneous and linguistically heterogeneous polities was maintained, with the latter being more subject to frequent interest articulation by anomic groups than the former.

The present example reveals yet another widespread consequence of controlling economic development. Though the economic and linguistic factors were additive in their negative association with the frequency of articulation of interests by anomic groups, such association with the former was more pronounced when the latter was used as control than was association with the latter when the former was held constant. Where gross national product and linguistic homogeneity were both high, 81 per cent of the polities were characterized by infrequent articulation of interests by anomic groups. Where the economic factor alone was high, this figure only dropped to 58 per cent, but where homogeneity alone was high it was reduced to 40 per cent. Finally, where both were low, only seven per cent of the polities had such an unappreciable rate of anomic articulation of interests. This sort of finding, which applies equally well to almost all of the other variables that were examined earlier, is a direct reflection of the greater potency of economic differences in contrast to linguistic differences. It strongly suggests that the simultaneous pursuit of the advantages of higher economic status coupled with the protection or maintenance of valued cultural-linguistic differences is not a will-o'-the-wisp. The major advantages of higher economic status that are most likely to elude those maintenance-oriented linguistically heterogeneous polities which advance economically, however, were found to be the two that have already been pointed out: high political enculturation and low sectionalism. These were the only two variables for which controlling the level of economic development resulted in no diminution of the differences originally encountered between linguistically homogeneous and heterogeneous polities.

CAVEATS

Since the findings reported here are based so largely on data that require considerable refinement, it might be best to conclude neither by belaboring that point nor by emphasizing the yields of such data. Rather than engage in either, it might be more appropriate to close with a number of observations that have been prompted by this inquiry but which may be applicable to *all* worldwide cross-unit files, regardless of the reliability of their data:

1. All units (in this case, polities) are given equal weight regardless of their "importance" as sources of influence or as models for emulation. Similarly, all indices are given equal weight in discussion regardless of their centrality in human affairs.

2. The relationships between variables are necessarily greatly influenced by the number and diversity of units that exist (or are recognized) at a particular time. The appearance of several score underdeveloped polities since the end of the Second World War may well bring about quite different relationships between variables (as well as different variables *per se*) than would have been the case before the war or even earlier. If this is (and, with the further appearance of additional "new nations," if it continues to be) the case then the *reasons* for the changed relationships that obtain require every bit as much attention as do the relationships per se. Such attention will hardly be forthcoming unless a time-dimension is added to worldwide cross-unit files.

3. Even when the indices themselves become much improved (and much work is currently underway toward that very goal) it may be difficult (or even more difficult) to keep in mind the fact that the correlations between indices are *invariably low* (particularly in terms of possible *causal* variance).[12]

4. The existence of many non-"significant" relationships is easily lost sight of, despite sincere attempts to the contrary. Thus, the foregoing discussion of differences between linguistically homogeneous and hetero-

[12] The question of causal variance is always a complicated one in scientific research, particularly in work based upon correlational evidence that is independent of the investigator's control over the variables involved. This difficulty in connection with cross-polity data has already received explicit attention in such publications as: Hayward R. Alker, Jr., "Causal Inference and Political Analysis," in *Mathematical Applications in Political Science, II,* Dallas, Southern Methodist University, 1966; Hayward R. Alker, Jr., "Research Possibilities Using Aggregate Political and Social Data," in *Comparing Nations* (Stein Rokkan, ed.), The Hague, Mouton, 1966; Hayward R. Alker, Jr., *Mathematics and Politics,* New York: Macmillan, 1965 (Chapter 6: Correlation and Causation).

geneous polities masks the fact that barely a third of the indices presented
by either source revealed significant relationships. Among the variables
coded by Banks and Textor that appear to be substantially unrelated to
linguistic homogeneity or heterogeneity are a number that are quite
important in modern affairs: population growth rate, freedom of the
press, racial homogeneity, interest aggregation by political parties, stability of party system, eliteness of political leadership, vertical power
distribution (federalism-centralism), legislative-executive structure, political participation by the military, and communism or noncommunism.
Similarly, many important indices advanced by Russett and Alker reveal
no relationship to linguistic homogeneity, e.g., expenditures on defense
as percentage of G.N.P., votes in national elections as a percentage of
voting age population, deaths from domestic group violence per 1,000,000
population, foreign trade as a percentage of G.N.P., etc.

5. The files focus studies upon the variables that they include and dis-
tract investigators from defining and refining other variables that may
be potentially more important. The two files examined in this paper
would seem to be lacking in a number of respects, e.g., they present no
data on natural resources (either in terms of endowment or accessibility)
or on inter-polity relations, or on intra-polity complexities although such
data are (or are becoming) available.[13]

6. The limitations of the two data-pools referred to in this paper and
the limitations of aggregate social and political data more generally are
coming to be widely recognized. Nevertheless such data will doubtlessly
continue to be of concern and of value to many social scientists including
some of those with interests in the intersection between language and
national development. Thus, it behooves us to give some attention to
how language data might be more usefully and insightfully recorded in
the future expansions and revisions that cross-polity (and intra-polity)
data files are likely to undergo.

At this time there are three cross-polity language files at varying stages
of completeness.[14] These should not only be consulted to obtain access

[13] Norton Ginsburg, *Atlas of Economic Development*, Chicago: University of Chicago
Press, 1961; Frederick Harbison and Charles A. Myers, *Education, Manpower and Economic Growth*, New York: McGraw-Hill, 1964.

In the mimeographed code book accompanying the Banks and Textor data cards a
variable is reported that was not included in their published reference, namely, frequency of foreign conflict. This variable shows no significant relationship to either
linguistic homogeneity-heterogeneity or to per capita G.N.P.

For some recent exemplary work on intra-polity differences, see *Comparing Nations*,
Part 3 (R. L. Merrit and S. Rokkan, eds.), New Haven and London: Yale Univ. Press,
1966.

[14] The files are maintained by The Center for Applied Linguistics, Washington, D.C.;
Forschungsstelle für Nationalitäten und Sprachenfragen, Marburg/Lahn; International
Center for Research on Bilingualism, Laval University, Quebec City, Quebec.

to their latest figures (which are likely to be more accurate and more recent than those otherwise easily available) but also to become familiar with the "national profiles" or "national formulas" that they have developed for describing the language situation in a country.[15] The initial goal of such familiarity might well be not so much to adopt any of these "profiles" or "formulas" per se, nor to integrate them with other cross-polity files with wider sociological and political science appeal. Rather, the initial goal of the interaction hereby recommended might better be to consider some of the parameters that are recognized by the linguistic cross-polity, files for these are likely to entail new dimensions of awareness for social scientists who have not heretofore thought deeply about language in connection with political or sociocultural integration.

Among specific recommendations regarding language parameters that deserve incorporation into the future cross-polity (or intra-polity) files of social scientists, I would initially advance the following:

a. *Language other than mother tongues.* The widespread availability of a lingua franca or "contact" language (which may, on occasion, be almost no one's mother tongue), such as Hausa, Pidgin English, Koranic Arabic, may be of far greater social and political significance than the diversity of mother tongues per se. Certainly, mother tongue diversity is of vastly different significance in the *presence* of a widely used lingua franca as compared to its significance in the *absence* of such. The one person—one language fallacy must be set aside as soon as possible in future studies.

b. *Characteristics other than demographic.* Both of the files referred to in the present paper limit themselves to only one characteristic of language behavior, namely, the (relative) number of speakers (or claimants). However, the mainstay of sociolinguistic work—whether on the language problems of developing nations or more generally—depends on other designations or characterizations, e.g., the societal functions of particular languages, the legal status or political position of particular languages, etc. Thus, rather than merely ask whether a polity is linguistically homogeneous, most sociolinguists would much rather ask whether the functions of the available languages are competitive or complementary, whether they are at developmentally similar or dissimilar stages, whether they are equally recognized by law. Sociolinguistics is primarily concerned with the societal function and position of languages and these are not usually determinable from demographic information alone.

c. *Variation in use rather than designation.* Related to both of the foregoing points is this third one, namely, that most individuals possess a *repertoire of languages* or varieties which they then put to use in a

---

[15] Note the "formula" suggested by Kloss (in this volume) and his references to earlier "formulas" devised by William Stewart and Charles A. Ferguson.

repertoire of roles and interactions. Most sociolinguists would welcome information on the *range* and *compartmentalization of the language repertoires* of speech communities *within* polities, in addition to information characterizing the polity as a whole or a language as a whole. Thus, the ultimate goal of sociolinguistic description is to indicate *who* uses (speaks, writes, etc.) *what* variety (pure, mixed, etc.) of *what* languages (developmental type, recognition type) with *whom* (role-relationship) and *when* (situations, contexts). This model assumes (and, indeed, reveals) widespread and stable societal multilingualism[16] (or multidialectalism), with some segments of every speech community (these segments being definable in terms of education, contact with diversified social networks, etc.) having more diversified and more discontinuous (i.e., noninterpenetrating) repertoires than others. It is difficult, but not impossible, to transfer this primary interest in variability and range to the national level of description, which is usually concerned only with designation. When this transfer is accomplished, if only in part, sociolinguistic interest in cross-polity and intra-polity data pools will expand considerably.

[16] See my "Bilingualism With and Without Diglossia; Diglossia With and Without Bilingualism," *Journal of Social Issues,* **23** (No. 2), 29–38 (1967).

Heinz Kloss

NOTES CONCERNING
A LANGUAGE-NATION TYPOLOGY

It is customary to say that a state with a single official language is a nation-state; the singleness of the language seems to indicate that we are dealing with a nation undivided, that is, with a clearly dominant ethnic group which constitutes an undisputed majority of the inhabitants.

Similarly, we are inclined to call "multinational" any country that has two (or more) official languages [1]. Here the linguistic duality is assumed to correspond to a similar "side-by-side" existence of two ethnic communities.

Now let us take some examples. English is the only national official language of

A. Great Britain   where it is the mother tongue of the bulk of the inhabitants,

B. Liberia   where it is the mother tongue of 5 per cent of the inhabitants,

C. Ghana   where it is almost nobody's mother tongue (expatriates excluded) but is an imported "othertongue."

Obviously what we are dealing with in example C is not a nation-state in the accepted sense of the term. It is at best a "nationism-state," a country whose inhabitants are striving for some measure of nationhood not yet warranted by today's linguistic facts. We are dealing in B with a country that can support its claim to being a nation-state by pointing to a core group of native speakers of the national language. But only category A meets our expectations of what constitutes a genuine nation-state.

Matters are equally confusing with countries that are officially bilingual: Somalia (Italian and English), India (Hindi and English), Eire (Irish and English), Canada (English and French). In each case English is paired with another language. The similarity seems striking. But as we look into the cases we find

A. Somalia   with a single dominant ethnic group making use, for na-
              tional official purposes, of two imported "othertongues,"
B. India   with a multiplicity of ethnic communities having agreed on
              national official use of one indigenous (Hindi) and one
              imported language,
C. Eire   with a single ethnic group consisting of two (overlapping)
              speech communities,
D. Canada   with two major ethnic communities, each speaking its own
              language.

Here only category D conforms fully to our traditional image of a multinational state. Eire and Somalia are both basically mono-ethnic countries. In India the two national languages do not represent the two
largest indigenous speech communities. Countries like Ghana or Somalia
have to make use, for governmental purposes, of nonindigenous languages because the indigenous languages are not yet fully developed for
written use in a modernized, mobilized society.

Thus we have to take into account a number of factors such as demar-
cations between ethnic and speech communities, numerical strength of
speech communities, developmental status of the languages in question.

These illustrations may be sufficient to indicate that a good deal of
conceptual (and terminological) clarification is needed to avoid gross
misstatements and misjudgments. On the following pages a skeletal survey is offered to those who seek sociolinguistic problems of foreign countries in more sophisticated and more conceptually organized perspective.

FOUR SETS OF VARIABLES

Variables Here Discussed

The relationship between language and nation is determined by a
great number of variables. Of these, four are singled out for discussion
in the present article:

1. The type of state the country in question is, or purports to be, with
regard to the language, or languages, serving its government for national
official purposes.

2. The developmental status of a specific language spoken within the
boundaries of the state in question.

Two other sets of variables refer to the members of the speech community sharing the language mentioned under (2) as a mother tongue and
living within the boundaries of the state mentioned under (1):

3. The juridical status of the speech community.
4. Its relative numerical strength [2].

Other Variables

The discussion will thus emphasize the relationship between state and language and speech community. It therefore largely skips those aspects that have to do with the type and degree of individual bilingualism. In a former article [3] I discussed, or at least mentioned, such other variables as the number of languages used by individuals, the type and degree of individual bilingualism, personal and impersonal bilingualism, population segments involved, and the prestige of the languages in question [4]. William A. Stewart, in a paper on linguistic typology [5] has isolated such features as the use of a language (*other than an official one*) as a medium of wider communication or as an educational, literary, religious, or technical language—uses which are outside the scope of this essay.

NATION-STATE AND MULTINATIONAL STATE

Basic Definitions

We may call a country a nation-state when it is dominated by a single ethnic group which either actually represents the nation at large, or, although forming only a section of the population, has made its mother tongue (or tongues) the national official language (or languages). We may call a state multinational either if two or three indigenous languages spoken natively by as many different ethnic groups are recognized as national official, or if four or more languages, all of them spoken natively by sizeable groups among the citizenry, are considered co-equal, though for practical reasons (as stated later) only one or two of them have been recognized as national official. Both nation-states and multinational states may be either endoglossic or exoglossic.

We may call a country endoglossic when the national official language(s) is spoken natively by a sizeable segment of the population (hereafter called an "indigenous language"). We may call a country exoglossic when the national official language has been brought in from abroad, and its few native speakers do not form the majority of the inhabitants in any district or major locality [6] (hereafter called "imported language").

A country may be all-exoglossic, using none of the indigenous languages for the purposes of national government [7], or it may be part-exoglossic, granting the status of a national official language also to one or several indigenous rival tongues.

Part-exoglossic states occur chiefly in Asia, where we find the use of English combined with Hindi (India), Tagalog (Philippines), Malay (Malaysia), etc. By definition, a part-exoglossic country is at the same time part-endoglossic; we are dealing with a partnership between an imported and an indigenous tongue (or tongues). Psychologically the role of the indigenous language is generally more significant than the role of the language brought in from abroad. Part-exoglossic nations share with fully endoglossic nations the pride in an indigenous language that is felt to symbolize nationhood. In other words, part-exoglossic nations are more similar to endoglossic than to exoglossic nations in their feelings and their relevant actions and reactions with regard to national language problems. For most purposes it will be advisable to group the part-exoglossic with the endoglossic countries.

Currently, exoglossic countries are usually former colonies which, after shaking off the alien yoke, have decided to retain the alien language. But in former centuries the exoglossic state was a rather common feature. In Europe, Latin, French, and, for shorter periods, German have been employed by nations to whom they were by no means native. Even now we have in Luxemburg an exoglossic country where the vernacular is a German dialect but the leading official tongue is French.

The Endoglossic Nation-State

At least three major subdivisions of endoglossic nation-state are discernible.

Genuine Nation-State and Section-Based Nation-State. The dominant ethnic group:

1. Forms the bulk of the population—let us say at least 70–80 per cent; in this case we may speak of a *genuine nation-state.*

or

2. Forms less than 70–80 per cent (sometimes, like the 5 per cent Americo-Liberians, a tiny fraction) but considers either itself (as a group) or its language, or both, as symbols and safeguards of the nation's at-large identity. Nation-states belonging to this second category may be called *section-based*—because members of the ethnic group claiming a privileged status for themselves or their languages are not sufficiently numerous to automatically represent the nation as a whole.

Of section-based nation-states we have two fundamentally different varieties. In a majority of cases the ethnic group speaking the dominant language has formerly subjugated the other ethnic groups. Some examples are the Amhara in Ethiopia, the Afro-Americans now ruling Liberia, and the Spaniards whose tongue dominates public life in Bolivia. These groups have defeated and conquered those ethnic groups who to this very day have preserved their own languages and who still form the majority of the population [8]. In these instances we may speak of *subjection-based nation-states* [9].

But there are countries where the voluntary consensus of the major speech communities concerned has accorded to a language spoken by far less than 70 per cent, perhaps not even by a majority, the status of a national official tongue. Cases in point are Tanzania, Indonesia, and the Philippines. It certainly is no accident that in these three countries the selected language is closely akin to all or most of the other major languages of the country. People who see no chance to have their mother tongue acquire high national status are much more willing to yield to a language they feel to be related to their own than to one they feel to be completely foreign to their mother tongue in substance, structure, and spirit. Thus we frequently see nations speaking Romance languages promoting the cause of French instead of their own tongue [10], and in India communities speaking Indo-Aryan tongues seem to put up with the prominent status of Hindi somewhat more readily than do those speaking Dravidian languages.

Unfragmented and Fragmented Nation-States. The unfragmented nation-state (in German *Ganznationalstaat*) comprises the bulk (at least 70–80 per cent) of the members of a certain speech community or ethnic nationality living on the same continent and inhabiting a contiguous area. Thus Denmark and Portugal comprise nearly all of the Danish- and Portuguese-speaking inhabitants of Europe, Australia all of the English-speaking inhabitants of the fifth continent, France a huge majority of the members of the French speech community living in Europe.

Fragmented nation-states existing in our time include most of the Spanish-American and Arab speaking countries [11]. In the past, that is, in the epoch preceding the unification of Italy and Germany, the various monarchies on Italian and German soil were good examples of fragmented nation-states. Frequently authors using the term "nation-state" actually think in terms of the unfragmented ethnic nationality; thus the occurrence of fragmented nation-states is often overlooked or ignored.

Dominant Groups with One or Two Inherited Indigenous Languages. As a rule, all members of the dominant ethnic group will use the same language in daily conversation, be it Swedish in Sweden or Portuguese in Brazil. Yet there are a few instances of dominant groups who are split up linguistically. Thus, for example, the Norwegians, who undoubtedly constitute a single ethnic community, make use of two standard languages called Riksmaal (or Bokmaal) and Nynorsk (or Landsmaal). Similarly, the mother tongue of some of the inhabitants of Eire still (or anew) is Irish, whereas a majority are native English speakers. Yet it would be foolish to dub the two respective segments of the Irish and the Norwegian peoples two nations and to call Norway and Eire binational. It would be almost equally misleading to call the two nations in question bilingual, a term usually implying that the average citizen is able to speak two languages. Perhaps it might be appropriate to speak of two-tongued nations (or even of two-pronged nations—which would evoke the image of a fork Y).

On the other hand, both Belgium and Holland are not only bilingual but bi-ethnic countries, the two languages spoken by the populace (Dutch and French in Belgium, Dutch and Frisian in Holland) being the tools of two different ethnic groups. However, while the Belgian nation is not only bilingual and bi-ethnic but even bicultural, the same cannot be said with certainty of the inhabitants of Holland, the Dutch and the Frisians being closely akin not only linguistically but also in tradition and outlook [12].

The Exoglossic Nation-State

The exoglossic nation-state, according to the definition previously given, is dominated by a single ethnic group but has as its national official language not the one spoken natively by the members of the dominant group but one imported from abroad.

The exoglossic nation-state may be either unfragmented or fragmented, and the members of the dominant group may either share the same mother tongue or be linguistically divided. We run into difficulties of definition if we try to conceive of an exoglossic nation-state which is section-based, that is, where the dominant group does not exceed 70 per cent of the citizenry. It would seem to be definitionally necessary that in order to be called a nation-state—a country politically dominated *and* culturally impregnated by a single ethnic group—the latter must:

1. Form a considerable majority (70 per cent and above)—as in Somalia.
or
2. Be "endoglossic" by having made its own language the tool of governmental activities—as in Ethiopia.

The exoglossic nation-state may make use of one imported language —as does Haiti, or of two—as does Somalia.

The Endoglossic Multinational State

Of paramount importance is the distinction between multinational states that are just *plurilingual* (i.e., bilingual or trilingual) and those that are truly *multilingual* (i.e., using more than three languages). The importance of this distinction lies in the fact that full equality of several languages seems impossible where more than three languages are involved [13]. The business of running a country's government would become hopelessly entangled were ten languages to be put on a fully equal footing. In truly multilingual countries one or two languages— usually one—have to be given the status of *prima inter pares*—German in Imperial Austria, Hindi in India, Urdu and Bengali in Pakistan. It goes almost without saying that a multilingual country, being compelled to accord a privileged status to one or two of its leading languages, is much more exposed to internal tensions than a bilingual or trilingual one.

The *fragmented multinational state* (in German *Teilnationalitäten-staat*) consists largely of fragments of larger speech communities. Belgium comprises parts of the French, the Dutch, and the German speech area. In Switzerland fringe groups of the German, French, and Italian speech communities live in harmony.

The *unfragmented multinational state* (in German *Ganznationali-tätenstaat*) comprises largely entire speech communities inhabiting a contiguous area on the same continent or island. India is primarily (in spite of the halved Bengali-speaking community and some other exceptions) an unfragmented multinational state; the same holds for the Soviet Union.

Finally there occurs a hybrid phenomenon, the multinational state comprising some speech communities en bloc as well as sizeable fragments of others. The former Austria-Hungary was a good example of what can be called the *part-fragmented multinational state*.

Another important distinction bears on the degree of language corpus distance (intrinsic distance) between the various languages considered "national" by the country involved. There are instances where they are recognizably akin—as in Yugoslavia, where Serbocroatian, Slovenian, and Macedonian all belong to the same subgroup of Slavic languages. On the other hand, we find in India a sharp borderline separating the Northern (so-called Indo-Aryan) from the Dravidian languages. It would seem that close linguistic kinship facilitates collaboration and mutual understanding between the leading ethnic nationalities, whereas fundamental linguistic distance tends to make for mutual distrust and to be an obstacle (though not an unsurmountable one) to a national feeling of belonging together. (In German we speak of *homoiophone Nationalitätenstaaten* and *heterophone Nationalitätenstaaten*.)

The Exoglossic Multinational State

The term "national" as contained in multinational implies the living-together of ethnic units which are not just tribes speaking at best recently alphabetized but as yet unstandardized vernaculars. It implies a federation of ethnic groups which constitute "nationalities" in the modern (and we may add in the European) sense of the word.

Probably the most clear-cut way of delimiting the exoglossic multinational country from other multilingual countries is to define it as a state where the only recognized tool for *national* official purposes is an imported language but where indigenous tongues are recognized as *regional* official languages. One example is Uganda where English is the

TABLE 1

		Illustrations	
Type of Country	Name of Country	Mother Tongue(s) and Foreign Language(s) Involved and Percentage of Inhabitants Speaking Mother Tongues M = Mother Tongue (Indigenous Tongue) F = Foreign Tongue (Imported Tongue)	National Officia Language(s) (NOL) or Regional Official Languages (ROL)
Endoglossic genuine nation-state, subtype I	Denmark	$M\,1$ = Danish (98%)	NOL: $M\,1$
Endoglossic genuine nation-state, subtype II	Eire	$M\,1$ = English (97%) $M\,2$ = Irish (3%)	NOL: $M\,1$, $M\,2$
Endoglossic section-based nation-state, subtype I (subjection-based nation-state)	Ethiopia	$M\,1$ = Galla (44%) $M\,2$ = Amharic (32%) $M\,3$ = Tigrinya (7%)	NOL: $M\,2$
Endoglossic section-based nation-state, subtype II (consensus-based nation-state)	Philippines	$M\,1$ = Visayan (40%) $M\,2$ = Tagalog (20%) $M\,3$ = Jlokano (10%) ($F\,1$ = English)	NOL: $M\,2$ (+ $F\,1$)
Exoglossic genuine nation-state, subtype I	Haiti	$M\,1$ = Créole (98%) $F\,1$ = French	NOL: $F\,1$
Exoglossic genuine nation-state, subtype II	Somalia	$M\,1$ = Somali (90%) $F\,1$ = English $F\,2$ = Italian	NOL: $F\,1$, $F\,2$
Endoglossic multinational state, subtype I: plurilingual state	Belgium	$M\,1$ = Dutch (54%) $M\,2$ = French (44%)	NOL: $M\,1$, $M\,2$
Endoglossic multinational state, subtype II: multilingual state	India	$M\,1$ = Hindi (38%) ($F\,1$ = English) $M\,2$–12 = the "national constitutional" languages other than Hindi	NOL: $M\,1$ (+ $F\,1$) ROL: $M\,2$ − 13
Exoglossic multinational state	Uganda	$F\,1$ = English $M\,1$ = Luganda (38%) $M\,3$ = Nyoro (11%) $M\,3$ = Teso (9%)	NOL: $F\,1$ ROL: $M\,1$–3
Exoglossic multitribal state	Guinea	$F\,1$ = French	NOL: $F\,1$

sole national official language but where Luganda, Nyoro, and Teso are also admitted for regional official purposes.

Exoglossic Multitribal Countries

Most exoglossic multilingual countries, however, fall under the heading *exoglossic multitribal countries*. It is easy to see why this term might be called a misnomer: The foreign language has been enthroned for the very purpose of overcoming tribal loyalties, so the terms "exoglossic" and "tribal" refer to radically divergent dimensions: one to hoped-for nationhood, the other to backward-harking tribalism. Yet the coexistence, for the time being, of the language tugged in from abroad ("exo . . .") and the various, frequently rather vigorous tribes, is the most salient criterion of these emerging nations, and so we may put up with the contradictory designation exoglossic multitribal state.

Tabulation

Table 1 [14] may serve to illustrate my analysis.

TYPOLOGY OF LANGUAGES ACCORDING TO STAGES OF DEVELOPMENT

We now consider a second set of variables—one that is especially significant from a sociolinguistic point of view. In describing the second, third, and fourth sets of variables I shall, for brevity, use the invented name "Hurdu" for the language involved instead of using clumsy circumlocutions such as "the language in question."

In using the term "developmental status" I assign to "development" a specific, very restricted meaning which closely corresponds to "elaboration" and to the German word *Ausbau* as used in the compound *Ausbausprache* (a term I coined in my book *Die Entwicklung neuer germanischer Kultursprachen*) [15]. I sketched briefly the steps by which spoken vernaculars or dialects can be made over or reshaped into standard languages. I also set forth that centuries ago it was chiefly through accomplishments in the domain of *imagination,* for example, poetry, that a language attained a high status, whereas in our times it is not as a tool of imagination but as a tool of *information* that a language becomes prestigious. Therefore it is prose, mostly non-narrative prose, which has to be fashioned in order to give a language prestige in the eyes of those who speak it, and to make it fit for interlingual competition.

On the basis of its developmental status, of its *ausbau,* Hurdu may belong to one of the following groups:

1. It is a fully modernized *mature standard language* [16] through which all modern branches including the sciences and technology may be taught at secondary-school and college level institutions of learning.

2. Hurdu is a *small-group standard language* [17], which means that because of the smallness of the speech community it is doomed to remain forever excluded from broad domains of modern civilization—for example, from research—unless it be strictly group-oriented, thus dealing with the speech community or the territory it inhabits. This is the case of Faroese with its mere 40,000 native speakers, and it seems likely that all speech communities numbering less than 200,000 fall under this category.

3. It is an *archaic standard language,* the flowering of which took place within some pre-occidental and pre-industrial civilization. Great poetry and deep-searching religious and philosophical treatises may have been written in it, but it may as yet be unfit for the teaching of modern biology or modern physics.

4. Hurdu is a *young standard* language, which has been standardized in very recent time, and its remolding is still in the earliest stage. It may be used in writing for mass education (fundamental education) and community development, as well as for religious and for political (e.g., Marxian) indoctrination. Although it may be used in the first three primary grades of the public schools, most stages of advanced education are reserved to some other language or languages.

5. Hurdu is an *unstandardized alphabetized language* [18], which, in most instances, has been reduced to writing only recently [19] but the standardization of which has not yet been accomplished. Its use in writing extends to pretty much the same domains as that of the semi-elaborated young standard languages.

6. Finally, we still have a considerable number of languages that are never, or only at rare intervals, used in writing and which we therefore may call *preliterate languages.*

What is frequently referred to as a *vernacular language* seems to be vaguely coterminous with categories 5 and 6. It would seem advisable that this term be given a sharply circumscribed meaning. UNESCO usage has tended—probably under the influence of legalistic thinking —to define vernacular languages by a juridical criterion alone. As a result, any nationalism or imperialism running amuck may relegate a mature standard language to the status of a mere vernacular by ousting it from its present "national official" position.

These categories are dynamic and not static ones. All over the world we observe efforts to make preliterate languages over into neoliterate ones and to reshape young as well as archaic standard languages to make them fit for most or all necessities of modern civilization.

JURIDICAL TYPOLOGY

Let us now turn to the third and fourth sets of variables, those defining the juridical status and the statistical rank order of the speech communities living together under one single state.

With regard to juridical status we may distinguish five major possibilities [20]:

1. Hurdu—to stick to this label—is an official language of the country in question.

2. Hurdu is recognized as a regional official language in one of the component states, or in some province or district.

3. Without being among the official tongues of the country or of one of its regions, Hurdu is promoted by governmental, municipal, and other public authorities; this promotion may mean that it is admitted, and even used, in the public schools, that it is represented in public libraries, that newspapers printed in Hurdu receive public advertisements, that some governmental reports, laws or proclamations are translated into Hurdu at the expense of the state, etc.

4. Hurdu is in no way promoted by the state or other public corporations, but neither is its use or its cultivation restricted. Religious bodies may cultivate it, clubs may conduct their affairs in Hurdu, it may be used in public gatherings as well as over the telephone and on the air, movie houses may present Hurdu films, and what is most important, nonpublic schools may teach it and even teach in it.

5. Hurdu is not tolerated but proscribed. This means that Hurdu speakers are not permitted to use it in their communal life, in their religious congregations or in their secular clubs, nor may they do any printing in it, let alone to cultivate it in schools. Even its use among members of Hurdu-speaking families may be restricted to the four walls of their homes, it conceivably being dangerous to use it in the streets or over the telephone.

It will readily be seen that each of these five categories allows for numerous subdivisions, which it would take a special article to describe. For the purpose of tabulation, I shall create only one subcategory by separating those cases where Hurdu is the *only* official language from those where it is one among several coequal national official tongues. In this way we arrive at six variables; Hurdu may be

1. The only national official language.
2. A coequal national official language.
3. A regional official language.

4. Promoted.
5. Tolerated.
6. Proscribed.

With regard to (1), it may be desirable to examine the term "national official language" somewhat more closely. We may have to replace this unitary term by a conceptual trichotomy comprising

1. The "national language," which may be a mere vernacular but one that carries prestige as a symbol of national identity.
2. The official language (at the central government level), which may be a locally non-ethnic imported instrument (French in Guinea).
3. The working language(s).

A country's single national official language has both prestige and functional utilitarian value. A mere "national language" carries prestige in spite of its restricted functional value (Sango in Central African Republic). A mere working language (English in Ceylon) fulfills most of the functions of a national official language without enjoying its prestige.
    Of mere "working languages," [21] we have two types:

1. In the U.N., English, French, Spanish, Russian, and Chinese are official languages, but only the two first-named are working languages.
2. In the Consultative Assembly of the Council of Europe English and French are the only official languages, but in addition other languages may be (and have been) recognized as working languages.

In part-exoglossic states the tendency may be *either* (a) to call the indigenous language *national,* the imported language *official,* or (b) to call the indigenous language *official* while the imported tongue, although probably more viable for transacting governmental business, has to put up with the lowly status of a *working* language. It seems that the second solution has been preferred in some Asian countries.
    It will be remembered that the juridical status listed previously—the recognition of several coequal national languages—may cover at least five different situations: (a) the co-occurrence in the nation of two national languages within one ethnic group, (b) the coexistence, within the nation-state, of one indigenous and one imported language, (c) the co-existence, within a multinational state, of two (or three) indigenous national official tongues spoken natively by two (or three) ethnic groups, (d) the pairing off of one indigenous and one imported national official language in a multinational state, (e) the joint rule of two coequal imported tongues.

STATISTICAL RANK ORDER

We now turn to the question of statistical rank order. Here our categories have to be even more arbitrary than with regard to juridical status. The following classification seems reasonable:

I. "Hurdu" is spoken natively by at least 90 per cent of the native inhabitants.

II. Hurdu is the mother tongue of 70–89 per cent of the native population.

III. It is the mother tongue of 40–69 per cent.

IV. It is the mother tongue of 20–39 per cent.

V. It is the mother tongue of 3–19 per cent.

VI. Less than 3 per cent speak it natively.

Special problems may and often do arise if a language is the mother tongue of very few native-born inhabitants but of a considerable number of immigrants, many of whom may not even be naturalized citizens. This may be disregarded in the present context.

COMBINED TABULATIONS

We try to combine in Table 2 the last two sets of variables:

1. One indicating numerical strength of a speech community.
2. One indicating juridical status of a speech community.

TABLE 2

	Relative Numerical Strength						
VI	Below 3%	VI_1	VI_2	VI_3	VI_4	VI_5	VI_6
V	3–19%	V_1	V_2	V_3	V_4	V_5	V_6
IV	20–39%	IV_1	IV_2	IV_3	IV_4	IV_5	IV_6
III	40–69%	III_1	III_2	III_3	III_4	III_5	III_6
II	70–89%	II_1	II_2	II_3	II_4	II_5	II_6
I	90–100%	I_1	I_2	I_3	I_4	I_5	I_6
	Juridical Status	Sole official language	One among several official languages	Regional official language	Promoted	Tolerated	Proscribed
		1	2	3	4	5	6

For the purpose of providing clarifying examples, we now simply define the position of certain languages, and countries, within this tabulation.

I_1. Icelandic is the only national official language of the free state of Iceland. Also practically all Icelanders living in Europe are inhabitants of Iceland, where they form more than 91 per cent of the population. Iceland is a genuine unfragmented nation-state.

IV_1. Amharic is the only national official language in Ethiopia. Nearly all speakers of Amharic are inhabitants of Ethiopia. They therefore consider Ethiopia their nation-state. Actually, however, the speakers of Amharic form just 32 per cent of the population of Ethiopia. The speakers of Gallah, for example, are more numerous (44 per cent) than those of Amharic; yet their language falls under the category of proscribed languages (III_6). Ethiopia, therefore, although legally a nation-state, is statistically a multinational state, with several languages being entitled to a status of co-equality.

The status of Finnish in Finland forms a contrast to that of Amharic in Ethiopia. It is the mother tongue of 93 per cent of the population, the remainder being largely Swedish-speaking. Finland also comprises the near-totality of Finnish-speakers living in Europe. Statistically and sociologically, therefore, Finland may be called a nation-state. Juridically, however, Finland is a multinational state (*Nationalitätenstaat*), both Finnish and Swedish being recognized as national official languages. Here we have an instance where a speech community renounces those privileges that might be considered due to it on the grounds of numerical strength.

We may complete this way of tabulating languages by introducing symbols for the types of languages in question as follows:

A. A mature standard language (stlg).
B. A (fully developed) small group stlg.
C. An archaic stlg.
D. A young stlg.
E. An unstandardized alphabetized language.
F. A preliterate language.

This leads to the configurations of Table 3.

This way of characterizing the status of language may be elaborated. By writing

$$D \rightarrow A$$

we indicate that a young standard language (like Bahasa Indonesia) is on its way to become a mature standard language; writing

$$5 \rightarrow 4$$

indicates that a language hitherto just tolerated is beginning to be promoted by the government.

TABLE 3

Language	Country	Symbols	Explanation (*stlg = standard language*)
Luganda	Uganda	D IV 3	Young stlg; in the 20–39% group; regional official
Somali	Somalia	E I 4	Unstandardized alphabetized vernacular; in the 90–100% group; promoted
Tamil	India	C V 3	Archaic stlg; in the 3–19% group; regional official
Gallah	Ethiopia	F III 6	Preliterate language; in the 40–69% group; proscribed
French	Guinea	A VI 1	Mature stlg, imported; sole national official language

We may say that wherever we have the combination

$$A + VI + 1$$

we are dealing with an all-exoglossic state; wherever we find the combinations

$$A \text{ (or B)} + I \text{ (or II)} + 1$$

we are dealing with a genuine nation-state; wherever we find the combinations

$$A \text{ (or B)} + III \text{ (or IV)} + 1$$

we are dealing with a section-based nation-state, etc. In this way we may arrive at permanent language status formulas.

The next step is linking these almost algebraic formulas with Charles Ferguson's proposed "Sociolinguistic Profile Formulas," which in turn make use of spadework done by William A. Stewart [22]. My language categories E (unstandardized but alphabetized) and F (preliterate) taken together are coterminous with vernaculars as defined by both these authors. The national official language of an exoglossic nation is what Ferguson calls [23] a "language of special status" (Lspec). My 20 per cent cutoff is not too far removed from Ferguson's 25 per cent cutoff separating "major language" (Lmaj) from minor ones (Lmin).

SOME PROBLEMS PECULIAR
TO THE DEVELOPING NATIONS

It would have served no purpose to isolate the language problems of the developing nations to create a specific typology adapted solely to their peculiar problems. Within the framework of a general typology sketched thus far in this essay, it is possible to discover a number of phenomena and problems that are more or less peculiar to the Third World.

A majority of the young standard languages as well as of the neo-alphabetized and preliterate languages are to be found in the developing countries, chiefly in Africa and Oceania. Outside this area we find a sizeable number of vernaculars among the North American Indians and in the Soviet Union [24]; to the Soviet Union goes the credit of having done much for their unfolding.

Archaic standard languages are restricted almost exclusively to Asia.

The language configuration among the developing nations is characterized by the predominance, in oral usage, of variants of:

1. Mature standard languages in Latin America.
2. Archaic standard languages in Asia.
3. Vernaculars in Africa and Oceania.

The all-exoglossic nation is a corollary to the predominance of vernaculars and young standard languages considered unfit for the serious business of governing a nation. It is therefore almost wholly confined to Africa.

The part-exoglossic nation is a corollary to the occurrence of archaic or young standard languages, which are considered to be as yet only partly adequate tools for the official transactions of government. Part-exoglossic nations are frequent in Asia.

The usefulness of the distinctions and categories introduced in this essay will, it is hoped, not be lost upon the reader. No longer will he be tempted to overstate similarities between developing nations such as Somalia, Honduras, and Ethiopia. Instead, he will first inquire whether or not these countries are exoglossic or endoglossic, fragmented or unfragmented, section-based or genuine nation-states, and whether the languages they use are archaic, young, or mature standard languages—or unstandardized and perhaps even preliterate. Nor will he quickly conclude that multitribal exoglossic countries of the Guinea or Niger type can be classed with traditional nation-states. He may, in short, have become aware of the phenomena and pitfalls, the co-occurrences and cross-occurrences characteristic of the field of language-nation relationship. As a result he may be able to judge, and to handle, in a more realistic, less generalizing fashion, present-day phenomena bound up with the impact of language and ethnicity on national and international problems, especially among the developing nations.

NOTES

1. Cp. the definition given by the Belgian Arille Carlier, Vice President of the Federal Union of European Nationalities (F.U.E.N.): "Wer sich für die Nationalitätenlehre interessiert, weiss, was unter dem Begriff Nationalstaat zu verstehen ist: der Staat, der seine Einheitlichkeit dem Gebrauch einer einzigen Sprache verdankt, Beispiel: Portugal. Ein Staat, der zwei oder mehr Sprachen offiziell anerkennt, ist ein Na-

tionalitätenstaat, Beispiel: die Schweiz und Belgien" (quoted from *Der Wegweiser,* Eupen, Vol. 3, No. 3, p. 8, 1963).

2. Strength in absolute numbers, which is certainly not irrelevant, usually is less important than relative strength.

3. "Types of Multilingual Communities: A Discussion of Ten Variables," *Sociological Inquiry* 36, 135–145 (1966).

4. The following variables mentioned in my 1966 article are taken up again in the present article:

Variable	Number in 1966 Article	Present Section
Types of speech communities	I	"The Endoglossic Multinational"
Legal status	IV	"Juridical Typology"
Degree of language corpus distance	IX	"The Endoglossic Multinational State"

5. Wm. A. Stewart, "An Outline of Linguistic Typology for Describing Multilingualism," in F. A. Rice (ed.), *Study of the Role of Second Languages in Asia, Africa, and Latin America,* Washington; CAL-MLA, 1962, pp. 15–25 (see esp. p. 21).

6. The terms endoglossic and exoglossic I owe to professors E. Haugen and J. A. Fishman, respectively.

7. In a few instances, *two* imported languages are used: French and English in Cameroon, English and Italian in Somalia.

8. Plausible though none-too-reliable figures are: Ethiopia— Amharic 32%, Gallah 44%, Tigrinya 7%; Philippines—Tagalog 20%, Visayan 40%, Ilokano 10%.

9. One is even tempted to speak of "spurious nation-states."

10. Compare the fact that Portugal has insisted on French becoming one of the official languages of the EFTA though no French-speaking nation adheres to this loose federation.

11. Albert Hourani, *A Vision of History. Near Eastern and Other Essays,* Beirut, 1961, p. 104: "The Near East is now divided into nation-states."

12. See the remarks on "Bilingualism and Mono-Culturalism" by E. G. Lewis (rapporteur) in: *Report on an International Seminar on Bilingualism, Aberystwyth, Wales . . . ,* London, 1965, p. 154.

13. On this problem see Kloss in *Sociological Inquiry,* 36, 136 (Spring 1966).

14. I have disregarded the part-exoglossic states which, as set forth previously, may be grouped with the endoglossic states for most purposes.

15. H. Kloss; *Die Entwicklung . . . ,* Munich, 1952, p. 17.

16. Abbreviation for "mature large-group standard language."

17. Abbreviation for "mature small-group standard language."

18. On the difference between alphabetization and standardization see Paul Garvin in D. Hymes (ed.), *Language in Culture and Society,* New York, 1964, p. 521.

19. There are exceptions: Swiss Romansh is an unstandardized language whose alphabetization goes back to the Reformation period.

20. Cp. Kloss in *Sociological Inquiry,* 36, 142–143 (1966).

21. On "working languages" see A. Ostrower, *Language, Laws, and Diplomacy,* Philadelphia, Penn., 1965, Vol. I, pp. 407–430. See also *ibid.,* p. 380.

22. Charles A. Ferguson," National Sociolinguistic Profile Formulas," in Wm. Bright (ed.), *Sociolinguistics,* Proceedings of the UCLA Sociolinguistics Conference, 1964. The Hague, Paris 1966, pp. 309–315 (discussion, pp. 315–323).

23. Ferguson, 1960, pp. 310–311.

24. Isolated examples from other areas are Ainu, Eskimo, Lappish.

Dankwart A. Rustow

LANGUAGE, MODERNIZATION, AND NATIONHOOD—
AN ATTEMPT AT TYPOLOGY

Modernization typically involves a wholesale territorial reorganization of states—a redefinition, that is to say, of the geographic units within which the political process takes place. The modern state must be a territorial state and it must reconcile the imperatives of largeness for division of labor with the imperatives of smallness for mutual trust. The more intensive communication in modernizing societies puts a premium on linguistic unity and distinctiveness: nation-states have been most securely founded where all nationals speak the same language, and preferably a language all their own. Yet in fact most of the postcolonial states that formed in the nineteenth and twentieth centuries either shared a language with their neighbors or included a variety of linguistic communities; hence they have been committed to the search for identity on a different basis. (For relevant statistical data, see Tables 1–4.)

Only a few countries have maintained continuous geographic identity from traditional to modern times; everywhere else there have been extensive realignments. The Holy Roman, Habsburg, and Ottoman empires and the European colonial realms in Asia and Africa proved too disparate and unwieldy to permit effective modernization. At the opposite end of the scale, the petty principalities of Germany and Italy, the nomadic tribes of the Middle East, and the village communities of the African rain forest proved too small. In all these areas large empires and small parochial communities have yielded to nations or would-be nations of intermediate size.

This transition from dynastic or colonial empires to modern nation-states is often complicated by a reversal of attitudes toward linguistic diversity. Empires have seen a major danger in ethnic loyalties and

This essay is adapted from my book *A World of Nations: Problems of Political Modernization* (Washington, D.C.: Brookings Institution, 1967), pp. 49–58, 62–71, and 284–88.

combatted them in a variety of ways. The older nation-states of Europe have found in ethnic loyalty and linguistic unity their securest foundation, and hence they have striven for compactness and neat distinction.

A number of related factors contribute to the ethnic mélange of the empires. First, the imperial rulers preserve or accentuate ethnic distinctions or even create them where none exist. At times they may be following the cynical precept of *divide et impera;* at other times they may be acting from an unconscious instinct of self-preservation or from some positive concept of imperial mission. The Habsburg and Ottoman emperors, locked for three centuries in mortal combat, settled loyal populations in enclaves along either side of the shifting frontier: Germans in the Banat and Transylvania, Muslims in Bosnia and the Dobruja. When the British announced their support of Zionist policies of Jewish settlement they promised vaguely "that nothing shall be done which may prejudice the civil and religious rights of existing non-Jewish communities in Palestine"—disregarding the plain fact that 87 per cent of all Palestinians at the time were Arabs and 77 per cent belonged to a single Sunni-Muslim community. To the north, the French in 1920 doubled the size of Lebanon to transform a solidly Christian-Arab territory into one almost evenly split between Christians and Muslims; in predominantly Sunni-Muslim Syria they gave autonomy to Druzes and Shiis. Later, French officials in combatting Arab nationalism in Algeria spoke invariably of the "peoples" of Algeria and studiously avoided calling any of them Arabs.

Second, in staffing their military and civil services, the imperial rulers rely by preference on immigrants from outside the realm or small minority groups within. The rolls of the Habsburg public service were replete with French, Italian, Spanish, and Irish names. The early Ottomans recruited their ruling class from Balkan Christians converted to Islam and from Caucasian immigrants. The British recruited their Indian army from Sikhs, Gurkhas, and Muslims; their Iraqi levies from the tiny Assyrian-Christian minority.

Third, in many parts of the globe an ethnic division of labor grew up in traditional times, and this often reinforced the divisiveness of imperial rule. The cultural patterns of subsistence agriculture are not easily reconciled with the requirements of commerce. Hence long-distance trade (and later banking and industry) became the monopoly of geographically more mobile groups clearly distinct in language, religion, and customs from their agricultural customers: Chinese in Southeast Asia; Indians and Arab Muslims in East Africa; Syrian Christians in West Africa; Parsis in Bombay; Greeks, Armenians, Jews, and Levantines in the Near East. A slightly different economic-political pattern led to the wholesale importation of Africans as plantation workers in the tropical and subtropical parts of America. In British Guinea, when emancipated Negroes flocked to the towns, East Indians were imported to take their places on the plantations; a century later, Guiana, bitterly divided between Africans and East Indians, became the scene of smoldering communal tensions verging on civil war. In Malaya, Chinese workers were brought to work in the rubber plantations and tin mines, and their descendants today constitute an even half of the population.

The minority groups of warriors, administrators, traders, or agricultural workers that lent stability to the imperial tapestry disrupt the warp and woof of emerging nationality. The Germans in the Danubian basin, once a mainstay of Habsburg rule, became subversive *irredenta* in the successor states. In Turkey, early in this century, the Armenians were massacred and the Greeks transferred in a forced population exchange. Newly independent Iraq in 1933 wreaked a terrible vengeance on its Assyrian minority. More recently Nasser has expropriated Greeks and Copts and Sukarno tried to wrest the interisland trade from the Chinese. Everywhere the loyal instruments of empire and the prosperous practitioners of trade face the perils of expulsion, expropriation, or extermination. Where empires found their strength in checkerboard diversity, new nation-states dread the prospect of Balkanization.

Mazzini's dream of humanity composed of national states based on solid and distinct communities of language has been only most imperfectly realized in the past, and there is little prospect that it will become true in the near future. In order to assess the relationship of modern states to language groups, it is helpful first to survey the main patterns of state formation in the modern world and then the most significant types of linguistic constellation in the resulting political entities.

The methods of modern state formation have varied a great deal from century to century and from continent to continent. Five distinct patterns may broadly be distinguished: (a) Postimperial states; (b) the postdynastic states of Western Europe; (c) the linguistic states of Central and Eastern Europe and the Middle East; (d) the countries of overseas immigration; and (e) the postcolonial countries of Asia, Africa, and Latin America. Each category involves some necessary oversimplification; some countries (e.g., Thailand, Afghanistan) do not fit neatly into the classification; and some others will be referred to under two different headings [e.g., the Arab countries under (c) and (e) and Argentina and Brazil under (d) and (e)]. These minor distortions and asymmetries, however, seem well worth the gain in over-all clarity.

1. *Post-Imperial States.* These are large traditional states that have preserved their geographic identity into the modern period. The outstanding case is Japan—an archipelago clearly set off by the sea from the Asian mainland. Except for the diminutive group of Ainu aborigines in the North, the islands have been inhabited since prehistoric times by a

people with a distinct language and a culture that (despite the lavish borrowings from China in traditional and Europe and America in modern times) is equally distinct. The two other examples are Russia and China, where totalitarian Communist regimes in bloody civil wars reestablished political unity within the traditional borders of the Romanov and Manchu empires and revived the imperial policies of administrative centralization and linguistic assimilation.

2. *The Postdynastic States of Western Europe.* In Western Europe, most of the nation-states that emerged in the eighteenth and nineteenth centuries coincided with linguistic communities, but these communities had themselves been shaped earlier by warfare and inheritance among dynastic rulers. Great Britain emerged as a "United Kingdom" after Welsh Tudors and Scottish Stuarts claimed in turn the heritage of Norman England. The French kings at Paris over many centuries extended their rule to Gascony, Brittany, Provence, Burgundy, and other outlying provinces and thus made the dialect of the Ile de France the common language of the realm. Spain owes its territorial identity to successive dynastic unions among the Christian rulers of Castile, Leon, Navarra, Aragon—the last and most famous one concluded between Ferdinand and Isabella in 1469—and to their centuries-long conquests from Arab Muslims. Portugal, once given as a fief by a king of Castile to his son-in-law, happened to produce a more durable line of princes and, largely as a result, remained distinct: in the north the language boundary today still follows the feudal frontier of 1095. Similarly, Dutch developed as a language distinct from German after the United Provinces won their independence in 1568–1681. Throughout Western Europe therefore linguistic nationality reflected earlier political structures. In Scandinavia, the division among Norway, Sweden, and Denmark follows the natural configuration of mountains and seas: here geographic, political, and linguistic identity reinforced each other.

There are three well-known exceptions to the rule of linguistic nationality in Western and Northern Europe: Belgium, divided about evenly between Flemings and Walloons since its independence in 1830; Finland, where a rapidly growing Finnish population has confronted a stationary Swedish minority long dominant in the towns and in commercial life; and Switzerland, where a majority of German-speaking Swiss live side by side with smaller groups of French-, Italian-, and Romansch-speaking fellow citizens. Switzerland in particular has confounded those theorists who have mistakenly included a common language in their definition of nationhood. Its remote location athwart the strategic Alpine passes, a strong tradition of cantonal self-rule, and a political evolution (by no means free from conflict and turbulence) of nearly seven centuries all contributed to shaping and preserving a sense of Swiss national identity. Hence Switzerland has become a model of that rare political accomplishment: a viable multilingual nation-state.

3. *The Linguistic States of Central and East Europe and the Middle East.* Further to the East the Western European sequence of political and linguistic evolution toward nationhood was reversed. The poetry of Dante and Petrarch and Luther's Bible translation shaped an Italian and a German cultural identity that transcended the kaleidoscopic array of petty states. In the Danubian and Balkan countries there was an upsurge of vernacular literatures in the late eighteenth and nineteenth centuries; in the Middle East, modern Arabic and Turkish literature began to flourish toward the turn of the twentieth century. It was this literary-national resurgence that heralded the ultimate doom of the Habsburg and Ottoman empires and contributed to the downfall of the Tsars. In all these countries, from Finland to Greece and from Italy to Syria, poets and writers played the role of early shapers of national identity that kings and ministers had played in France and Britain: the political careers of the poet Namik Kemal in Turkey, the pianist Paderewski in Poland, and of the philosopher Masaryk in Czechoslovakia furnish vivid illustrations. For some of these awakening nations, notably Poland and Hungary, memories of political independence provided a source of inspiration.

When it came to translating the romantic yearnings of poets, writers, and artists into practical policies of state formation, rival factions fought for sharply divergent territorial solutions. In the nineteenth century partisans of Prussia's "Little Germany" clashed with advocates of a "Greater Germany" including Austria and with bitter-end supporters of the existing principalities in "duodecimo size." In the Ottoman Empire the principle of linguistic nationality itself was slow to win out over dynastic and religious loyalties. Even after the modernizing revolution of 1908, the so-called Young Turks still wavered among multinational Ottomanism, Pan-Islam, Pan-Turkism, and Turkish nationalism; only the disastrous defeat of 1918 persuaded their Kemalist successors to accept the narrower boundaries of the later Turkish Republic. The Arabs, freed from foreign mandates and military occupation after World War II, set to quarreling over conflicting schemes for unity: Greater Syria, Fertile Crescent, Nile Valley, Maghrib, and visions of an inclusive Arab state from Morocco to Uman. In the Balkan, Danubian, and Baltic areas border conflicts after the First and Second World Wars, plebiscites, precarious minority guarantees, and tenuous federal experiments all testified to the difficulty of finding, as Arnold Toynbee disdainfully put it, "the criterion of Nationality in the shibboleth of Language" [1].

4. *Countries of Overseas Immigration.* An important variant of the Western European pattern occurs in countries that began as overseas

colonies of European powers and were subsequently populated by immigrant settlers—the United States, Australia, New Zealand, Argentina,
Brazil, and (with some additional variations on the common theme)
Canada and Israel. Here too linguistic identity grew up later within
boundaries politically drawn—in this case by colonial conquest. In most
of these countries the small indigenous population died out or severely
diminished during the colonial period; the earliest settlers imposed their
language and culture; and successive waves of immigrants were assimilated, even though a majority of them might come from other countries.
(In the United States immigrants from Great Britain and Ireland have
constituted only 20.7 per cent of the total since 1820; in Argentina, Italian
immigrants over the last century have vastly outnumbered those of Spanish descent.) Canada, large portions of which changed hands between
France and Britain in the colonial period, faces in Quebec a problem of
linguistic conflict not unlike that between Flemings and Walloons in
Belgium; but in its Western provinces, the process of assimilation to
English has proceeded with the same dynamic force as in the United
States. In Israel the dominant social and cultural structure was created
during the Palestine mandate period by Zionist immigrants from Eastern
Europe who decided to revive Hebrew as a unifying national language;
and to this Hebrew-speaking culture, successive waves of Jewish immigrants from Europe and the Middle East have been rapidly assimilated
after independence. The resident Arab majority of the Israeli parts of
Palestine fled or were expelled in the war of 1948; today less than 10
per cent of the population form an unassimilable Arab-Muslim and Arab-
Christian minority. "Assimilation in language or culture," Karl W.
Deutsch has pointed out, "involved the learning of many new habits,
and the unlearning of many old ones—habits, in both cases, which often
interlock and reinforce each other. Such learning as a rule is slow; its
changes are counted in decades and generations" [2]. In immigrant
countries, one may add, the new settlers who flee from oppression and
come in search of new opportunity can compress this rehabituation into
a few years or at most a single generation.

5. *The Postcolonial States of Asia, Africa, and Latin America.* In most
of the underdeveloped countries of Asia, Africa, and Latin America the
principle of linguistic nationality has fared far worse than in Western
Europe, in East-Central Europe, or in the immigrant countries. These
continents do include sizeable linguistic communities, notably the 100
million speakers of Spanish in Latin America, the 70 million Arabs in
the Middle East and North Africa, and the various ancient language
groups of the Indian subcontinent. In the inaccessible and long-isolated
tropical regions of Africa, by contrast, most language groups are of diminutive size—only one, the Hausa, numbers as many as 13 million, and

only five others between 3 and 6 million speakers. South and southeast Asia is the only region where there are solid and distinct language communities of an intermediate size on the European scale.

Colonial boundaries have usually determined the geographic identity of successor states. In contrast to East-Central Europe, that is to say, political rather than linguistic factors were paramount; but in contrast to Western Europe the earlier political structures were erected by alien rather than indigenous rulers. Almost everywhere, the resulting borders have been sharply at variance with linguistic lines. Time and again, the solid linguistic regions have been subdivided, whereas unrelated languages have been grouped together. Spanish-speaking America today consists of 18 sovereign states, and Arabic is spoken by the entire population or by sizeable majorities in 20 territories [3]. Elsewhere in Asia and Africa, some three dozen states have been formed since 1945; more than half of these, as Table 1 indicates, do not have a linguistic majority, and only in a handful do 30 per cent or more speak the same national tongue. (Ironically, two of the latter, Korea and Vietnam, are today divided between bitterly opposing Communist and anti-Communist regimes.) In most Asian and African states languages pose not a minority problem but a majority problem; by necessity of their ethnic composition, they are committed to the arduous path of multilingual nationality.

The detailed patterns of postcolonial boundaries deserve closer examination. In most areas the departing colonial rulers had a decisive voice in determining the identity of the postcolonial states—although in a few cases they were unable to enforce federation or prevent partition. The British in the 1930s separated Burma and Ceylon from India, and in 1947 yielded to demands for partition between Hindu and Muslim areas. Yet both India and Pakistan are multilingual, and through their armies and civil services in effect are heirs to a grand imperial legacy. In India the diverse language groups won their campaigns for formation of linguistic states soon after independence but have not launched any serious secession movements. The boundaries among the Arab countries, except in Palestine, still follow precisely the imperialist partition of the Ottoman Empire between 1830 and 1920. The French in 1958–1960 took a course opposite to that of the British in India: separate independence was conferred upon 14 states in what had once been French West Africa and French Equatorial Africa; the administrative cadres left behind, moreover, were diminutive; and the *Rassemblement Démocratique Africain,* which had embraced both regions, quickly broke apart into autonomous state units. In Spanish America a large colonial empire became fragmented mainly through the decentralization of the independence movement; most of the boundaries that emerged in the early nineteenth century followed those of the Presidencias, Captaincies, and Audiencias of the colonial period. In the Congo the departing Belgians bequeathed a

TABLE 1. *Linguistic Unity and Diversity of Countries*[a]

Country and Source	Mother Tongue of Largest Group	Per Cent of Population	Mother Tongue of Second Largest Group	Per Cent of Population
Europe				
Germany (B)	German	100		
Norway (B)	Norwegian	100		
Portugal (C)	Portuguese	100		
Austria (C)	German	99	Serbo-Croatian	0
Italy (C, F)	Italian	99	German	1
Greece (B)	Greek	98	Turkish	2
Sweden (C)	Swedish	98	Finnish	1
United Kingdom (E)	English	98	Welsh	1
Denmark (C)	Danish	97	Faroese	1
Hungary (A)	Hungarian	97	German	1
Iceland (C)	Icelandic	97	Danish	1
Ireland (F)	English	97	Gaelic	3
Albania (C)	Albanian	95	Greek	2
Malta (C)	Maltese	95	English	2
Netherlands (C)	Dutch-Flemish	95	Frisian	4
Luxembourg (C)	German	93	Italian	2
Finland (A)	Finnish	92	Swedish	7
Poland (B)	Polish	88	German	8
Bulgaria (C)	Bulgarian	86	Turkish	9
France (C)	French	86	German	4
Romania (A)	Romanian	86	Hungarian	10
Spain (C)	Spanish	73	Catalan	17
Yugoslavia (B)[b]	Serbo-Croatian	73	Slovene	9
Switzerland (A)	German	69	French	18
Czechoslovakia (C)	Czech	67	Slovak	27
U.S.S.R. (A)	Russian	59	Ukrainian	16
Belgium (B)[c]	Dutch-Flemish	50	French	44

Sources. In selecting language names for the table, the following sources have been consulted: Center for Applied Linguistics, various mimeographed materials: A. Meillet and Marcel Cohen, *Les langues du monde*, 2d ed., 2 vols. (Paris: H. Champion, 1952); International African Institute, *Handbook of African Languages*, 6 vols. (London: Oxford University Press, 1952–1966); Joseph H. Greenberg, "The Languages of Africa," *International Journal of American Linguistics*, Vol. 29, No. 1 (January 1963).

The letters following the country names indicate the following sources: (A) *Demographic Yearbook* 1963 (United Nations, 1964); (B) *Demographic Yearbook* 1956 (United Nations, 1957); (C) S. I. Bruk, ed., *Chislennost' i Rasselenie Naradov Mira* (Moscow: Izdatel'stvo Akademii Nauk S.S.S.R., Institut Etnografii, 1962); (D) Janet Roberts, "Sociocultural Change and Communications Problems," in Frank A. Rice, ed., *Study of the Role of Second Languages in Asia, Africa, and Latin America* (Center for Applied Linguistics, 1962), pp. 112–20; (E) Siegfried H. Muller, *The World's Living Languages* (Frederick Ungar, 1964); (F) estimate supplied by Dr. Heinz Kloss, Forschungsstelle für Nationalitäten-und Sprachenfragen, Marburg/Lahn, West Germany.

[a] *Countries.* The table includes all countries that at the end of 1966 were independent and had populations over 100,000 or were dependent and had populations over one million.

Language names: There is no general agreement, especially with regard to Tropical Africa, whether a given form of speech is a dialect, a language, or a group of languages. There is often equal uncertainty about the name by which a language or group is to be called. In the table, hyphens join alternate names for the same language (or for dialects in a dialect cluster), for example, Dutch-Flemish, Malinke-Bambara-Dyula. Names of language groups are given in parentheses (a) after a language name when the group name is more widely known, and (b) instead of a language name when the source does not give separate figures for each language in the group.

Percentages. Percentages have been calculated from absolute figures in the sources above. Where the classification or nomenclature in the source differed from that in the table, the necessary adjustments were made. Where censuses reported in sources A or B list bilinguals separately, these have been added to the speakers of the non-official languages, for example, to the Indian languages of Middle and South America. But see note (c).

[b] Alternate estimates, source C: Thailand, Thai-Lao, 74; (Chinese), 18. Yugoslavia, Serbo-Croatian, 65; Slovene, 9.

[c] Flemish-French bilinguals in Belgium and Sinhalese-Tamil bilinguals in Ceylon have been divided evenly between the two groups. Data for Algeria have been adjusted to account for the departure of French speakers since 1962.

TABLE 1 (*Continued*)

Country aud Source	Mother Tongue of Largest Group	Per Cent of Population	Mother Tongue of Second Largest Group	Per Cent of Population
East and South Asia				
Korea (C)	Korean	100		
Maldive Islands (C)	Sinhalese	100		
Japan (C)	Japanese	99	Korean	1
Bhutan (C)	Bhutanese-Bhotia	98		
Thailand (A)[b]	Thai-Lao	91	(Chinese)	4
Hong Kong (E)	Cantonese	88		
Vietnam (N and S) (C)	Vietnamese	85	Thai-Lao	4
Cambodia (C)	Cambodian-Khmer	84	Vietnamese	7
China (Mainland) (C, D)	Mandarin	81	Wu	8
Mongolia (C)	Mongolian-Khalkha	78	(Oirat)	8
Taiwan (A)	Fukienese-Taiwanese	78	Mandarin	18
Singapore (B)	(Chinese)	75	Indonesian-Malay	14
Burma (C)	Burmese	71	(Karen)	9
Laos (C)	Thai-Lao	69	Mon	11
Ceylon (B)[o]	Sinhalese	67	Tamil	29
Pakistan (A)	Bengali	56	Punjabi	30
Nepal (C, F)	Nepali	49	Hindi-Urdu	28
Indonesia (C)	Javanese	45	Sundanese	15
Malaysia (A)	Indonesian-Malay	43	(Chinese)	36
India (B)	Hindi-Urdu, Punjabi	42	Telugu	9
Philippines (A)	Cebuano-Visayan	24	Tagalog	21
Oceania				
Australia (C)	English	91	Italian	1
New Zealand (C)	English	91	Maori	7
New Guinea (C)	(Papuan)	69	(Melanesian)	30
Middle East and Northern Africa				
United Arab Republic (C)	Arabic	98	Nubian	1
Jordan (C)	Arabic	98	Circassian	1
Yemen (C)	Arabic	98	(African Languages)	1
Saudi Arabia (C)	Arabic	96	(African Languages)	1
Somalia (C)	Somali	95	Arabic	2
Tunisia (C)	Arabic	93	French	2
Lebanon (C)	Arabic	92	Armenian	5
Turkey (A)	Turkish	90	Kurdish	7
Muscat and Oman (C)	Arabic	89	Baluchi	4
Libya (C)	Arabic	88	(Berber)	6
Algeria (D)[o]	Arabic	87	(Berber)	12
Syria (C)	Arabic	87	Kurdish	6
Kuwait (C)	Arabic	85	Persian-Tajik	9
Mauritania (C)	Arabic	82	Fulani	12
Iraq (A)	Arabic	79	Kurdish	16
Cyprus (A)	Greek	77	Turkish	18
Iran (D)	Persian-Tajik	69	Azerbaijani	12
Israel (A)	Hebrew	66	Arabic	16
Morocco (C)	Arabic	65	Tamazight and Shilha (Berber)	12 each
Afghanistan (C)	Pashto	53	Persian-Tajik	31
Ethiopia (C)	Amharic	49	Galla	23
Sudan (C)	Arabic	48	Dinka (Nilotic)	12
Tropical and Southern Africa				
Lesotho (C)	Sotho	99	Zulu-Xhosa	1
Madagascar (C)	Malagasy	97	French	2
Rwanda (E)	Rwanda	90		

TABLE 1 (*Continued*)

Country and Source	Mother Tongue of Largest Group	Per Cent of Population	Mother Tongue of Second Largest Group	Per Cent of Population
Botswana (C)	Tswana	69	Shona	9
Rhodesia (C)	Shona	65	Zulu-Xhosa	15
Dahomey (C)	Ewe-Fon	58	Gurma-Somba	13
Upper Volta (C)	Mossi	54	Lobi, Bobo, Dogon	13
Sierra Leone (C)	Temne, Bulom, Limba	52	Mende	34
Mozambique (C)	Makua	51	Tsonga	24
Congo (Brazzaville) (C)	Kongo	50	Teke	25
Central African Rep. (C)	Banda	47	Gbaya	27
Gambia (C)	Malinke-Bambara-Dyula	46	Fulani	19
Ghana (A)	(Akan)	44	Mossi, Dagomba	16
Niger (C)	Hausa	43	Songhai	18
Senegal (C)	Wolof	42	Fulani	24
Togo (C)	Ewe-Fon	41	Tem-Kabre	22
Mali (C)	Malinke-Bambara-Dyula	40	Fulani and Senufo	14 each
South Africa (C)	Zulu-Xhosa	40	Afrikaans	21
Guinea (C)	Fulani	39	Malinke-Bambara-Dyula	26
Angola (C)	Umbundu	36	Kimbundu	24
Malawi (D)	Nyanja	36	Nguru and Yao	14 each
Chad (C)	Arabic	33	(Bongo-Bagirmi)	25
Zambia (C)	Bemba	33	Tonga	15
Gabon (C)	Kele, Njabi	31	Fang	30
Liberia (D)	Kru-Bassa	30	Kpelle	25
Kenya (C)d	Kikuyu	29	Luhya	19
Burundi (E)	Rundi	28	Swahili	17
Uganda (C)	Ganda	28	Nyoro, Nyankore, Hororo	17
Ivory Coast (C)	Anyi-Baule	24	Bete	18
Nigeria (C)	Hausa	21	Ibo	18
Cameroon (C)	Fang	19	Bamileke	18
Congo (Kinshasa) (C)d	Rwanda	17	Luba Lulua	17
Tanzania (C)d	Nyamwezi-Sukuma	17	Hehe	7
The Americas				
Haiti (C)	French	99	Spanish	1
Barbados (C)	English	98	Spanish	1
Brazil (B)	Portuguese	98	German	1
Cuba (C)	Spanish	98		
Dominican Republic (B)	Spanish	98	French	1
Jamaica (C)	English	98	Spanish	1
Colombia (C)	Spanish	97	Chibcha	1
Costa Rica (B)	Spanish	97	English	2
Trinidad (C)	English	97	Hindi-Urdu	2
Nicaragua (B)	Spanish	96	Mosquito	3
Uruguay (C)	Spanish	94	Italian	2
Venezuela (C)	Spanish	94	Italian	1
Honduras (C)	Spanish	93	Mosquito	3
Chile (C)	Spanish	92	Araucanian	4
Panama (B)	Spanish	92	English	8
Paraguay (F)	Guarani	88	Spanish	6
Ecuador (B)	Spanish	86	Quechua	13
El Salvador (C)	Spanish	86	Nahuatl-Pipil	4
United States (including Puerto Rico) (E)	English	86	Spanish	3
Argentina (C)	Spanish	84	Italian	5
Mexico (C)	Spanish	81	Aztec	2
Canada (A)	English	58	French	29
Guatemala (C)	Spanish	55	Quiche	14
Peru (C)	Quechua	47	Spanish	45
Guyana (C)	English	45	Hindi-Urdu	45
Bolivia (B)	Quechua	37	Spanish	36

d In addition, 50% in Tanzania, 15% in Congo (Kinshasa), and 11% in Kenya speak Swahili as a second language.

most precarious unity to the succeeding regime, though some of them actively fostered the abortive Katanga secession movement of Moise Tshombe in 1960–1962. Throughout Tropical Africa the newly proclaimed states—whether large as Nigeria or the Congo, or small as Niger or Sierra Leone—comprise a multitude of small languages. Ironically, almost each of the few large African communities is divided among several postcolonial countries.

The territorial identities established upon independence tend to endure into the future. Any boundary, no matter how arbitrary its origin, tends to engender its own vested interests, which tend to perpetuate it. An extreme case is Transjordan, whose formation was decided upon by Winston Churchill, then Colonial Secretary, on a Sunday afternoon stroll through Jerusalem in 1922; a generation later, King Husein and a small group of military officers and civilian administrators were valiantly fighting against great odds, but so far with remarkable success, to preserve the reality of that idea in a slightly enlarged Jordanian kingdom. In Latin America the number of states has remained the same since the breakup of the federations of Gran Colombia in 1829 and of Central America in 1839 [4]. In the more recently emancipated countries, schemes for unity and federation have had some success in Malaysia, but have failed in the West Indies, in West Africa (the shortlived Mali-Senegal, Guinea-Ghana, and Ghana-Guinea-Mali schemes), in Rhodesia-Nyasaland, in East Africa, and among the Arabs. Elsewhere, only the smallest of the Asian and African ex-colonies (e.g., Spanish Morocco; British Togoland, Cameroons, and Somaliland, Dutch Guinea, and Goa) have been joined to their larger neighbors—whether by agreement, plebiscite, or force. It seems safe to predict that boundaries that have become fixed during one or more decades after independence will be impossible to remove by political negotiation and agreement alone.

The linguistic constellations that have resulted within these various states may be grouped into six categories which cut across, rather than coincide with, the state and boundary formation patterns just surveyed. In identifying the major linguistic patterns, it is important to keep in mind not only the number and size of the linguistic communities in a given country, but also the degree of relatedness and distinction among these languages and, above all, whether one or several of them have a substantial literary tradition. As with state formation, it is possible for one country to show characteristics of several categories.

1. *A Distinct Language Predominant throughout the Country.* This is the situation in most European countries; in Japan, Korea, Mongolia, Vietnam, Turkey, and Malagasy; and in the countries settled by European overseas immigration. Here linguistic unity provides a secure foundation for nationality. The problems that remain are likely to be of manageable scope. For some languages, such as Mongolian and Malagasy, a

diversified vocabulary for modern technology and social organization still has to be developed. For some others there has been the task of eliminating vocabulary elements felt to be alien and to be reflecting a prenational, imperial past—such as Japanese words from Korean, or Arabic ones from Turkish. In the immigrant countries, educational and social policies must be geared to the task of rapid cultural assimilation of newcomers. In some countries, finally, the political status of the small remaining linguistic minorities must be clarified—the major choices being assimilation, emigration, or boundary revisions for *irredentas*.

2. *A Single Language Predominant in Several Neighboring Countries.* This is the situation among the Spanish-speaking countries of Latin America and the Arab countries of the Middle East and North Africa. The movements for wider unity or federation at the time of independence, as we have seen, have encountered major difficulties. Yet there has been a freer interchange of political leadership personnel and greater hospitality for political exiles within each of these groups of countries than anywhere else. To cite just a few examples, Che Guevara, the Cuban Communist, is a native of Argentina; one of the main speechwriters for President Paz Estenssoro of Bolivia is the son of an Ecuadorian diplomat; Cecil Hourani, long a political adviser to President Bourguiba of Tunisia, is of Lebanese origin; and 'Abd al-Rahman 'Azzam Pasha, Egyptian ex-secretary of the Arab League, later became an adviser to the royal Saudi government. Latin American countries have regularly given asylum in their embassies to political leaders on the losing side in any given internal upheaval. And Nasser at one time or other has supported exile movements in opposition to the government of almost every other Arab country. Clearly, despite the existing political divisions, there is an underlying feeling of political community within each of these two groups of states that somewhat blurs the dividing line between internal and external politics. If in Latin America the present hesitant efforts at economic coordination should in the future produce a full-blown movement of functional integration on the European model, the ease of communication in a single language may lead to quicker growth of sentiments of common loyalty. Perhaps among the Arab states, too, functional integration will be found to provide a safer path to unity than the recent practice of *faits accomplis* by subversion, coup, or military intervention.

3. *A Variety of Closely Related Languages, One of Which Serves as an Official Language.* This is the situation in Indonesia, where several languages of the Western Malayo-Polynesian family are spoken. One of these, Bahasa Indonesia, traditionally has been the language of commerce and now has been adopted and developed as the official language of government and education. (Except for differences in spelling, reflect-

ing the Dutch and English colonial heritages, Bahasa Indonesia is almost identical with Malay, the majority language of Malaya and Malaysia.) In the Philippines the situation is somewhat similar, although Tagalog (the official language) faces serious competition as a literary language from English and even Spanish.

In Tanzania, the majority speaks some type of Bantu language, but none of these languages is spoken by as many as one-fifth of the population. However, roughly half of all Tanzanians speak Swahili—a language with a Bantu base and strong Arabic influences, which has long been the lingua franca of trade and was promoted for official uses by the German colonial regime before the First World War. Its connection with Arabic gives Swahili access to a far richer vocabulary than is available to other Bantu tongues, and it therefore is the likeliest of all African languages to offer serious competition to the former colonial language as a national medium of communication in the future. The countries just named—Indonesia, the Philippines, and Tanzania—all face a similar problem of linguistic unification and development of a modern vocabulary. There is some prospect, however, that linguistic identity will follow upon political identity, somewhat as it did in Western Europe.

4. *A Variety of Unrelated Languages of Which Only One Has a Substantial Literary Tradition.* In these situations the literary language tends to win out as the national language, even if it is spoken only by a bare majority or a mere minority. The most striking examples are Morocco (where the majority speaks Arabic and the minority a variety of Berber tongues), Peru (where Spanish competes with Quechua, the ancestral language of the Incas, which spread as a second official language in the South American Andes under Spanish rule), Bolivia (where the majority speaks Quechua or Aymara, the indigenous language of the high plateau), Burma (where the Burmese of the Irrawaddy Valley confronts Karen and other languages of the "hill tribes"). Other examples are Mexico, Guatemala, and Ecuador among the Spanish-American and Algeria and the Sudan among the Arabic countries. As the Berber tribesman or the Quechua-speaking villager moves from the mountains to the city, acquires an education, or otherwise rises on the social ladder, he becomes Arabized or Hispanized.

There are several further variants of this basic situation. In predominantly Arabic Iraq, the assimilation of the Kurdish mountaineers has been delayed through heavy-handed policies of repression by successive governments in Baghdad. In Paraguay the majority language, Guarani, has been elevated to the status of second official language; but, if the official statistics can be trusted, a majority of the population is bilingual in Spanish and Guarani, and eventual assimilation to Spanish therefore seems likely.

TABLE 2. *Widespread Languages*

Languages	Spoken by Largest Group in:		Spoken by Second Largest Group in:	
Spanish	Cuba	98%	Peru	45%
	Dominican Republic	98	Bolivia	37
	Colombia	97	Paraguay	6
	Costa Rica	97	United States	3
	Nicaragua	96	Barbados	1
	Uruguay	94	Haiti	1
	Venezuela	94	Jamaica	1
	Honduras	93		
	Chile	92		
	Panama	92		
	Ecuador	86		
	El Salvador	86		
	Argentina	84		
	Mexico	81		
	Spain	73		
	Guatemala	55		
Arabic	United Arab Rep.	98	Israel	16
	Jordan	98	Somalia	2
	Yemen	98		
	Saudi Arabia	96		
	Tunisia	93		
	Lebanon	92		
	Muscat and Oman	89		
	Libya	88		
	Algeria	87		
	Syria	87		
	Kuwait	85		
	Mauritania	82		
	Iraq	92		
	Morocco	65		
	Sudan	48		
	Chad	33		
English	Barbados	98	Panama	8
	Jamaica	98	Costa Rica	2
	United Kingdom	98	Malta	2
	Trinidad	97		
	Australia	92		
	New Zealand	91		
	United States	86		
	Canada	58		
	Guyana	45		
German	Germany	100	Poland	8
	Austria	99	France	4
	Luxembourg	93	Brazil	1
	Switzerland	69	Hungary	1

TABLE 2 (*Continued*)

Languages	Spoken by Largest Group in:		Spoken by Second Largest Group in:	
French	Haiti	99	Belgium	44
	France	86	Canada	29
			Switzerland	18
			Madagascar	2
			Tunisia	2
			Dominican Rep.	1
Italian	Italy	99	Argentina	5
			Hungary	2
			Luxembourg	2
			Australia	1
			Venezuela	1
Fulani	Guinea	39	Senegal	24
			Gambia	19
			Mali	14
			Mauritania	12
Hindi-Urdu	India	42	Guyana	45
			Nepal	28
			Trinidad	2
Turkish	Turkey	90	Cyprus	18
			Bulgaria	9
			Greece	2
Greek	Greece	98	Albania	2
	Cyprus	77		
Kurdish			Iraq	16
			Turkey	7
			Syria	6
Malinke-Bambara-Dyula	Gambia	96	Guinea	26
	Mali	40		
Persian-Tajik	Iran	69	Afghanistan	31
			Kuwait	9
Quechua	Peru	47	Ecuador	13
	Bolivia	37		
Thai-Lao	Thailand	91	Vietnam	4
	Laos	69		
Zulu-Xhosa	South Africa	40	Rhodesia	15
			Lesotho	1

Note. The table lists all languages the speakers of which are the largest or second largest group in three or more countries, that is, all languages that appear at least three times on Table 1. Note that the groups listed are not necessarily the largest groups among the speakers of a particular language. For example, Persian-Tajik speakers in the Soviet Union, where they are the sixteenth largest group, greatly outnumber those in Kuwait, where they are the second largest.

TABLE 3. *Linguistic Unity and Diversity, by World Region*

| | Number of Countries by Per Cent of Population Speaking Main Language | | | | | | | | | |
Region	90–100	80–89	70–79	60–69	50–59	40–49	30–39	20–29	10–19	Total 10–100%
Europe	17	4	2	2	2	—	—	—	—	27
East and South Asia	5	3	4	3	1	4	—	1	—	21
Oceania[a]	2	—	—	—	—	—	—	—	—	2
Middle East and Northern Africa	8	6	2	3	1	2	—	—	—	22
Tropical and Southern Africa	3	—	—	2	5	8	7	5	3	33
The Americas	15	6	—	—	2	2	1	—	—	26
World Total	50	19	8	10	11	16	8	6	3	131

Source. Table 1.

[a] Not including New Guinea, for which no breakdown by individual languages was available.

5. *A Variety of Unrelated Languages without Literary Tradition.* This is the typical situation in Tropical Africa. The multiplicity of indigenous languages and their lack of literary evolution have thus far prevented any serious challenge to French or English as the dominant language of higher education and of politics. In former French West Africa a substantial body of poetry in French has grown up. Some of the indigenous African languages are used in the primary schools and as a second official language. But since in most countries linguistic unity can only be established if a majority take up a foreign tongue, it seems more advantageous to place increasing reliance on English and French. For a Tiv of Northern Nigeria Hausa is as difficult to learn as English, but English provides far wider access to the modern world. Hence the pressure in favor of English or French can be expected to come especially from the smaller language groups in each country.

6. *A Variety of Unrelated Languages Each with its Own Literary Tradition.* This is the situation in India, Pakistan, Ceylon, Malaysia, and Cyprus. In India the situation is attenuated by the multiplicity of languages, by the unifying factor of Hindu religion, and by the continued use of English as the language of government and higher education. Although the Indian constitution accepted English as the official language only for a 10-year transition period, this delay has been extended. Understandably, the shift to Hindi is opposed with particular tenacity by the Dravidian language groups (Telugu, Tamil) in the South who

TABLE 4. *Linguistic States*[a]

Language Spoken (1)	Country (2)	Per Cent Population in Country Who Speak Language (3)	Per Cent of Speakers of Language Who Live in Country (4)
Europe			
Albanian	Albania	95	69
Bulgarian	Bulgaria	86	93
Czech	Czechoslovakia	67	91
Danish[b]	Denmark	97	89
Finnish	Finland	92	85
French[c]	France	86	70
German[c]	Germany (W and E)	100	75
Greek[c]	Greece	98	83
Hungarian[b]	Hungary	97	91
Icelandic	Iceland	97	93
Italian[b]	Italy	99	84
Maltese	Malta	95	93
Norwegian	Norway	100	78
Polish	Poland	88	83
Romanian	Romania	86	85
Serbo-Croatian	Yugoslavia	73	96
Swedish	Sweden	98	81
East and South Asia			
Bhutanese-Bhotia	Bhutan	98	83
Burmese	Burma	71	99
Cambodian-Khmer	Cambodia	84	84
Japanese	Japan	99	99
Korean[b]	Korea (S and N)	100	95
Mandarin[b]	China (Mainland)	81	99
Mongolian-Khalkha	Mongolia	78	100
Sinhalese[d]	Ceylon	67	99
Thai-Lao[c]	Thailand	91	94
Vietnamese[b]	Vietnam (N and S)	85	98
Middle East and Northern Africa			
Persian-Tajik[b]	Iran	69	82
Turkish	Turkey	90	96
Tropical and Southern Africa			
Malagasy	Madagascar	97	100
The Americas			
Portuguese[d]	Brazil	87	86

Sources. Column 3 from Table 1; column 4 calculated from source C, Table 1, pp. 418–50. Note that this source tends to underestimate the proportion of speakers of European languages resident in their home country, since overseas emigrants and some of their descendants are often attributed to their native or ancestral language. Figures for Persian and Mandarin in column 4 calculated from estimates by Center for Applied Linguistics.

[a] The table includes all those groups who constitute two-thirds or more of their country's population as well as two-thirds or more of the speakers of their language—that is, all language-country pairs for which the figure in each column is 67 per cent or more.

[b] This language also is spoken by the second largest group in one or more other countries. See Table 1.

[c] This language is spoken by the largest or second largest group in one or more other countries. See Table 1.

[d] This language is spoken by the largest group in one or more other countries. See Table 1.

fear that it would further accentuate the preponderance of candidates from Uttar Pradesh in the civil service. In Ceylon, in Malaya, and on Cyprus, linguistic and religious divisions coincide, and the contrast is mainly between two solid groups. This clearly is the most explosive situation. In Malaysia, Prime Minister Abdul Rahman succeeded in preserving a Malay-speaking majority by including not only Singapore but also the three former British territories on Borneo in his federation. Moreover, Abdul Rahman himself and the dominant United Malays National Organization (UMNO) have been conducting a circumspect and conciliatory policy designed to bridge the gap between Malays and Chinese-best, symbolized perhaps by his adoption of two Chinese children into his family. In Ceylon, by contrast, the Tamil Hindus were in danger of being reduced to second-class citizenship after the "Sinhalese Only" campaign of the Sri Lanka Freedom Party in 1956 and as a result of the upsurge of militant Buddhist sentiment. On Cyprus, ethnic conflict between Greeks and Turks broke out into the open late in 1963 after only two years of operation of a precariously balanced constitution.

In the preceding discussion language has been singled out as one of the key factors in the growth of national unity and identity. It should be kept in mind that it is only one of the important factors in this context. Religious differences, the contrast between settled population and nomads, and similar social, cultural, and economic factors can be of equally crucial importance.

Nor is the language situation itself ever static. Herder, Mazzini, and other romantics assumed that language is the most indelible characteristic of peoples; hence it seemed logical to make language the guiding criterion for the drawing of just boundaries—a principle that the peacemakers of 1919 tried to transfer to diplomatic practice. In fact, language is a variable, dependent on political factors. The revival of Gaelic in the late nineteenth century was the consequence, not the cause, of Irish discontent with British rule. The landsmaal movement in Norway emphasized the non-Danish elements of the vernacular to reinforce the earlier political separation from Denmark. Literary Romanian since the nineteenth century has emphasized the Latin as against the Slavic elements of common speech, and modern literary Greek was patterned on Byzantine and classical models—in each case reflecting the search for historical antecedents that we found to be characteristic of early nationalisms.

Generally, the closer social interaction and interdependence of the modern age tend to pose sharply latent questions of identity and unity. When no one can read or write, it makes little difference in what language they are illiterate; the introduction of universal education, however, makes the choice of a language of instruction imperative—and this will have inexorable consequences in directing the further quest for identity. As Karl Deutsch has shown, intense feelings of nationalism usually arise first during a period of intensive modernization (or "social mobilization"). To estimate, therefore, whether future national identity will be based in Bolivia on Spanish or Quechua or Aymara, in the Philippines on Tagalog, English, Spanish, or the various local languages, it is essential to determine at what rates traditional people are being "mobilized" into each of these groups [5]. And the contrasting situations in Morocco and Iraq, in Malaysia and Ceylon show that government policy will be a major factor in solving or exacerbating existing problems of unity and disunity.

NOTES

1. Arnold J. Toynbee, *A Study of History* (London: Oxford University Press, 1934–1954), viii, p. 536.
2. Karl W. Deutsch, *Nationalism and Social Communication* (New York: Wiley, 1953), p. 99.
3. This number includes the 13 present members of the Arab League (from East to West: Morocco, Algeria, Tunisia, Libya, Egypt, Sudan, Lebanon, Syria, Jordan, Iraq, Kuwait, Saudi Arabia, and Yemen), Mauritania, Chad, and the still dependent areas of the Arabian coast (Bahrayn, Qatar, Trucial Shaykhdoms, Masqat and Uman, and the Federation of South Arabia).
4. Except for the separation of Panama from Colombia, enforced by the United States in 1903, and various attempts at Central American federation between 1842 and 1898.
5. Deutsch, *Nationalism and Social Communication, op. cit.*

A. Tabouret-Keller

SOCIOLOGICAL FACTORS OF LANGUAGE MAINTENANCE AND LANGUAGE SHIFT: A METHODOLOGICAL APPROACH BASED ON EUROPEAN AND AFRICAN EXAMPLES

Two specialists in the study of bilingual situations, the American authors Weinreich [1] and Haugen [2], did not fail to stress that, whenever two or more languages coexist in one population, the distribution of the use of each corresponds to divisions other than those of linguistic origin. For Weinreich, "in any concrete contact situation, the division between mother-tongue groups is usually congruent with one or more other divisions of a nonlinguistic nature" (p. 89). These nonlinguistic divisions are reflected in the status of the second language. They may correspond to geographic areas, indigenous groups, immigrant groups, cultural or ethnic groups, religion, race, sex, age, social status, occupation, rural or urban habitat. Haugen too underlines divisions along social lines, particularly concerning the status of the Norwegian language in America [3]. More recently Fishman, in his nationwide study of language maintenance and language shift among immigrant groups in the United States [4], made an attempt to define language maintenance and language shift as a field of inquiry [5]. The study of this field "is concerned with the relationship between change or stability in habitual language use, on the one hand, and ongoing psychological, social or cultural processes, on the other hand, when populations differing in language are in contact with each other" (p. 32).

The questions that have guided my research are very limited in comparison to the broad array of questions meriting examination. These questions are:

1. In what sociological context does the need for acquiring and using a second or even a third language arise?
2. Is it possible to discern, among these sociological conditions, factors speeding up the shift from a given linguistic situation (unilingual or bi-

lingual) to another (bilingual or plurilingual) or factors checking this shift, that is, maintaining the given situation?

The research I have carried out in Europe on bilingual situations that developed into unilingualism or trilingualism or on stabilized bilingual situations has shown that such factors may be isolated [6]. The problem raised here is determining how similar the sociological factors of language shift met with in Africa are to those isolated in Europe or determining how far they differ.

Because of the complexity of the problems thus raised, research must be based on a substructure that reveals both linguistic and sociological facts: such a substructure will be geographic and demographic. It will allow us to differentiate two main sorts of situation: (a) the establishment of a second—possibly a third—language among a population located on the very area of its first learned language; and (b) the establishment of a second—possibly a third—language among groups settling in the geographic area of another mother-tongue. Both situations may be observed today in Europe as well as in Africa. Actually, these situations are not always distinguished, and often they make up the two aspects of one and the same reality. In the former case the adoption of a second language reflects a change in the entire existing social structure; the latter case, the arrival of new population groups, is in itself a sociological fact that remolds the existing language relations: a new social group, the immigrants, will use the language of its adoptive country in a particular way.

LANGUAGE SHIFT AMONG SEDENTARY POPULATIONS

One basic difference between Europe and Africa is connected with the fact that in Europe we may study the consequences of the past, whereas in Africa new situations are just arising and we can only try to predict their consequences. The numerous bilingual regions to be found in Europe give evidence of an evolution in social and language relations that has been going on for decades, even centuries. This has sometimes resulted in bilingualism or trilingualism in which the language relations are fairly well stabilized; two examples are the French province of Alsace and the different plurilingual provinces of Switzerland. Here the development of bilingualism corresponds to the gradual growth of national languages beside the spoken languages, dialects or patois. The knowledge of these national languages has spread especially since attendance at school became compulsory. Since the beginniing of this century some of these cases of bilingualism have developed into unilingualism, as in the case of some French provinces such as Languedoc, where knowledge and use of patois is tending to disappear.

In Africa we may witness the beginnings of a general plurilingualization. However, let us first define certain differences, and above all remember that the concepts of "national language" and "official language" do not mean the same thing. The unification of the larger European states was carried out as a result of national aspirations [7]. Unity of language ranked first among the apparent aspirations. Coincidence between national and linguistic frontiers was favorable to the establishment of national languages and to the extension of their use. In the different African states the "official languages" are European tongues, mainly English and French. Hence they can hardly act as catalysts of national unity as European national languages have done. For an African the motivation for using English or French is cultural, not directly national.

There is another difference between the circumstances of the establishment of national languages in Europe and official languages in Africa. In Europe national languages have spread very slowly. Thus in France four centuries elapsed between Francis I's edict at Villers-Cotterets (1539) in which it was decided that henceforth judgments and ordinances were to be promulgated in French, and the present time, when we may claim that every French citizen is able to read and write the national language —which does not mean, however, that it is either his first learned language or his everyday tongue. In Africa the diffusion of an official language may profit initially by new conditions which were absent in Europe during past centuries. These conditions include such wide means of diffusion as the press, radio, television, cinema; there are also parliamentary systems that demand, to a greater or lesser extent, the cooperation of the average citizen, in the affair of the state, first of all by voting. This possible participation develops the need for information about current events. It is precisely from the time when all these conditions were achieved in European states—let us say within the last century—that the linguistic situation progressed most speedily, particularly in the knowledge of the national tongue, which in many provinces is a second language more or less remote from the first learned language. The mere realization of these new conditions, however, was not sufficient to bring about a change in the relation between the local and national languages. Knowledge and use of the national language do not spread simultaneously. Since elementary education became compulsory, knowledge has stood statistically ahead of everyday spoken use. It is no longer possible to do without the knowledge of written French; it is possible to have only a few opportunities for its practice. At this point we meet with sociological determinism. Indeed, the factor that most fundamentally influences the evolution of speech configurations is the social necessity for the spoken use of a second language. This social necessity is different in urban and rural surroundings.

Sociological Factors of Language Shift in Urban Surroundings

Europe. We must consider two cases, depending on whether or not a town lies on a language border. In a town lying on a language border, the two language groups living in the same urban district may or may not be in economic and cultural competition.

In Switzerland both Fribourg and Bienne lie on the border between French and German language areas. In Fribourg most inhabitants are French-speaking and in Bienne they are German-speaking. In both cases the knowledge of the other language is ensured by elementary schools (since the second language is compulsory from the sixth school year onwards), whereas basic socialization is acquired in the mother-tongue. Actual use of the second language by adults depends for every person on the necessity of practicing it in professional use and, more generally, on the individual level of professional and cultural aspirations. The absence of socioeconomic and sociocultural competition between both language groups leads to a remarkable stability in the proportion of people speaking either language.

The capital of Belgium, Brussels, lies near the language border between the Flemish (Dutch) and Walloon (French) areas. The two languages in contact are fighting for the rank of first language both in socioeconomic and in sociocultural terms. Up to the years 1955–1960 French was the winner for two reasons: the French-speaking South of Belgium was mainly industrial and imported labor, whereas the Flemish North was mainly agricultural and possessed a surplus of labor; moreover, the prestige of French as a medium of culture and technical knowledge was superior to that of Dutch. In the last 10 years important changes have taken place. Although the Southern coal industry has rapidly declined, new industrial units have tended to be established in the Northern areas due to the following factors: situation of the main harbors, better network of roads, greater cheap labor resources in Brussels. The Flemish population is dominant demographically (Flemish: 55%, Walloon: 33%), therefore also politically. However, French retains its cultural and social weight. It remains the language of classes that are socioeconomically dominant. This cultural and social weight of French plus a preponderant Walloon immigration determine the linguistic situation in Brussels where a Fleming still must be bilingual, but a Walloon need not be.

In Belgium as well as in Switzerland two language groups border—even overlap. More frequent, however, is the situation of towns that did not develop in the area of a single language group, but where the national evolution imposed the knowledge of a second or a third tongue. In Strasbourg (France), in a historical context of two world wars and two periods of German occupation, the configuration including the Alsatian dialect (the mother-tongue), German, the culture language corresponding to this dialect, and French, the national and school language, has changed in favor of French. The dialect has not been given up as a mother-tongue, but the population has become bilingual (dialect-French). In towns the knowledge and use of French as a second language is favored, but even there the dialect as a mother-tongue has not disappeared, nor even receded, as it remains the most widespread means of communication. The distribution and use of both languages in contact varies according to the districts of the town (living in blocks of tenements fosters bilingualism), the social and professional divisions (French unilingualism being limited to the use of the upper classes), age (only very old people and children under six remain dialectal unilingualists), place of language use (home, place of work, shops, etc.). The influence of these different factors accumulates. The situation has become more complicated within the last years due to the strengthening of German. Previously, German tended to be confined to written texts; nowadays the spoken form is heard on the frequently selected programs of German television. The understanding of German is thus promoted, although its use is not stimulated. It is too early yet to draw a conclusion from this new state of affairs. On the whole the socioeconomic necessities are in favor of the Alsatian-French bilingualism.

Africa. I have not yet encountered any case of a town lying on a language border where this border has been maintained for centuries between the two population groups of the same aggregation. Yet there may exist some fairly ancient town that has not sprung up within the last 50 years, as most African towns have. The arrival in towns of large numbers of people coming from the bush is similar to what happened in European cities during the nineteenth century, when the rapid growth of industry caused a desertion of rural areas, particularly by the poorest. Both in Africa and in Europe the development of towns by the arrival of rural people promoted the growth of a common language within every state. In Europe the national languages were thus favored; in Africa some local languages are gradually making their way and beginning to predominate as privileged means of communication.

In Senegal, the Wolof language is progressively asserting itself as the most frequent communication tongue in towns. "Wolof has never been an administrative language, this part having been assumed for more than a century by French. But as the idiom in industrial towns (Thies, Rufisque) and ports (Dakar, St. Louis) it has become the medium of a new form of civilization. . . . For Serers farmers as well as for a good half of the Senegalese population, Wolof has become a second language and even the main language of all those who have left their native rural districts" [8]. The largest towns have developed in the Wolof language area, but the use of Wolof has increased also in towns outside of this area. Let us take the example of the administrative region of Casamance [9] to the south of the river Gambie. The two towns of Velingara and Kolda lie in a predominantly Peul language area: 22 per cent of all elementary school pupils (meaning pupils up to the sixth school year) at Velingara and 13 per cent at Kolda speak Wolof at home as their mother-tongue. But far more can speak it: 47.8 per cent at Velingara and 27.2 per cent at Kolda. Now in the rural areas around these towns hardly 2 per cent of the children speak Wolof as their mother-tongue, and only 7 per cent in the province of Velingara and 5 per cent in Kolda can speak it at all (E.S. 150–59).

TABLE 1

Wolof	Velingara (%)		Kolda (%)	
	Town	Country	Town	Country
Spoken at home	22	2	13	1.9
Spoken as first or second language	47.8	7	27.2	5

Several factors play a part in the spread of Wolof: whereas in the whole of Senegal there are more marriages between Wolof men and women of other ethnolinguistic groups than between Wolof women and men of other ethnolinguistic groups (with the exception of the town of Podor, where the proportion is slightly reversed), the inquiry into the language spoken at home by the children shows that it is not the father or mother who gives his or her language to the child, but the Wolof-speaking party. Wolof still seems to be preferred by the population in general, even though the campaign in its favor, which started when Senegal became independent, has now been interrupted. The prestige of St. Louis, a Wolof-speaking town, has continued for several centuries, and the Wolof tongue now profits by the fascination of the people of the bush for towns in general and for the capital in particular. In Dakar, Wolof is the mother-tongue of 72 per cent of the families and is spoken by 98 per cent of all first-grade students [10] (E.S. 33–48); in 50 per cent of the families both parents are Wolof-speaking and the children rarely speak a second African language (E.S. 33); almost all the other children are bilingual and have Wolof for their second spoken language.

Sociological Factors of Language Change in Rural Areas

Rural surroundings are usually marked by the stability of language configurations. In the French province of Alsace, for instance, the situation of the Alsatian dialect, the mother-tongue of a large majority of the population, has remained practically unchanged for the past 10 centuries [11]. Since 1945 the dialect has been maintained just as steadily as a language of everyday use but knowledge of French as a vehicle for mass media (press, cinema, radio) is progressing, and Alsatian-French bilingualism, still imperfect in the period between the two world wars, is developing into a more highly structured bilingualism in which the dialect dominates as the spoken language and French as the written language. Developments of this kind are to be found in Luxembourg as well as in the various Swiss provinces where the languages spoken usually do not have a written form and are significantly different from the official written language. In all these cases the population continues speaking its own vernacular, but the spread of schooling and modern means of communications have contributed to the establishment of a sound knowledge of a second language, which is mainly used in its written form.

This kind of development, however, is not general. In certain cases a situation that had been bilingual for a long time moved swiftly toward unilingualism. Such was the case in the regions of the Midi, in France. Research in the course of the last 10 years [12], particularly in the district of Toulouse, has brought to light how certain sociological factors determined the linguistic changes.

The spread of French, which for so many centuries had been a second and not a customary language, corresponds to the transformation of the original bilingual situation (Languedocien-French) into a situation of French unilingualism. The factors that accelerated the linguistic change in favor of French unilingualism were industrialization of the area, development of its mass communication network, and proximity of the rural aggregates to these networks. These main factors have actually brought about changes in the proportions of agricultural and industrial workers, and they have greatly increased the daily migration to places of work (16 to 74 per cent of the active population within a radius of 40 to 50 kilometers around the big industrial areas); in addition, there has been great immigration of foreign workers and their families.

In a given area, the villages that have maintained the same proportion between the languages spoken, and have continued to use local languages, are always small (less than 500 inhabitants), there is a predominance of farmers (more than 60 per cent), the place of employment is always on the spot (for more than 85 per cent of the active population), and immigration is of no account (less than 4 per cent of the population). (See Figure 1.)

The industrialization of an area and the consequent daily migration do not change the existing linguistic configurations in every case. For example, 30,000 people (whose homes are spread over an area of 50 kilometers around the town) come to work in Strasbourg (France) every day: this phenomenon is not accompanied by any notable linguistic shifts in the countryside.

The factor that allows us to explain the evolution toward unilingual-

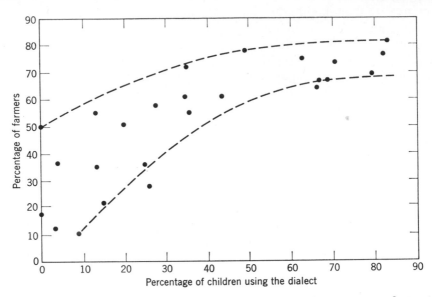

Figure 1. The variations of the percentage of farmers in the active population in relation to the percentage of children using the dialect. Each point represents a village.

ism in the region of Toulouse and the stability of the use of Alsatian dialect in the district around Strasbourg is the degree of wealth of the rural areas in question. In the region of Toulouse the soil has never been rich and its yield has been declining for the last 50 years, since other richer areas have been able to offer the same type of production at lower prices. The professional urge for industrial or administrative posts is accompanied by a linguistic urge in favor of French, this being even more important for women than for men, as, in poor country districts, it is their lot which is the less favorable [13]. On the other hand, in the region of Strasbourg the countryside is rich but divided up into small plots, according to the customary inheritance system of individual ownership. Under such conditions it is economically rewarding to hang on to a small estate while having a regular income from some industrial or administrative job. Any change in economic status is undesirable, as is any change in one's way of life, which would be brought about by departure to town. The socioeconomic motivation for using French is clearly not so strong, and the stability of the dialect should not be endangered for the moment.

In Africa the kinds of linguistic changes mentioned have not as yet taken place; linguistic homogeneity in the countryside remains intact even in a region as overrun by urban phenomena as Le Cap Vert (the narrow area around Dakar). In Dakar itself 49 per cent of the pupils in the pre-elementary grade come from families where both parents are

Wolof speaking; in the corresponding area of Cap Vert this is 63 per cent; then again at Dakar 70 per cent of the children use Wolof as their first language, whereas in the corresponding region 84 per cent do. Stability of the linguistic situations is a general rule in the rural zones. We can suppose that in Africa, too, it will be maintained for a great length of time.

LANGUAGE SHIFT AMONG MIGRANTS

All migrations into a differently speaking area have this in common: they cannot avoid acquiring a more or less thorough knowledge of the language of the country of their adoption. But we also notice their need to keep up at least language-links with the land of their origin.

In Europe migration from the countryside to industrial and urban areas was especially evident in the nineteenth century; in Africa this is actually happening now. In Europe it has given way to daily migration: the development of the transport network makes it possible to live in a village and have a professional occupation in a relatively distant industrial or urban zone. The language consequences of this type of migration have already been mentioned and I need not go into them again. The rural migrations to towns during the last century have hardly left any traces. In big cities, such as Paris, certain professions still remain occupied by natives of a particular province; for instance, the coal merchant business belongs to the Auvergnats, the chimney sweeps are Savoyards. Nowadays these groups tend to lose their cohesion—they are no longer recognizable by the patois of their original district.

At the moment another kind of migration is to be encountered in Europe: the search for work by groups of people outside of their native country. The most important groups of immigrants are of Italian, Portuguese, Spanish, Greek, Turkish, or North African origin. To their difficulties inherent in the social status of immigrants—integration into a new social order, into new economic conditions, into a new way of life—must be added the difficulty of acquiring a new language. In the Belgian Borinage, where the children of Italian immigrants must follow the pattern of French teaching in local schools, their backwardness at school is serious [14]. The causes of this backwardness are due to various factors: (a) the economic and cultural poverty of the Italian home (the children's parents themselves hardly know how to read and write); (b) their relative poverty and insecurity in the country of adoption, in this case Belgium; (c) the inability of the schools to cope with the respective needs of this child population, which should have special classes with qualified teachers and a distinct syllabus at their disposal. As long as their fathers remain in unskilled employment they will do poorly in the language of the country of their adoption; the mothers of such families only pick up a few essentials of the language in their day-to-day contacts with shop-keepers. Moreover, when such groups of emigrants are housed in lodgings reserved for Italians only and located out of town, the opportunities for learning the second language are very limited. This situation is not only peculiar to the Belgian Borinage, it is also to be found, for example, in the Parisian suburbs for Portuguese or African people.

The expansion of African towns is based on the inflow of rural populations, like that of many European towns, but it is also based on the arrival of populations from distant territories and of different ethnic groups. The East-to-West movement from Mali, the western parts of Senegal, and the northwestern parts of Guinea to Senegal and Gambia is one of the main migratory flows in West Africa. The number of migrants may be estimated at 75,000 yearly. Most of them are young; few are over 35 [15]. In Dakar-Ville seven languages are spoken in the homes of more than 1 per cent of children in the pre-elementary grade. A comparison of the languages spoken in the homes at Dakar-Ville (city), Greater Dakar, and Dakar-suburbs [16] shows that the suburbs are, linguistically speaking, the least uniform of the three districts considered (E.S. 29–45). Several factors are evident: the suburbs form the zone of expansion of the town and are peopled mainly by new arrivals (even when part of the suburbs has a residential character); only 36.8 per cent of the homes are purely Wolof speaking as compared with 49 per cent in Dakar-city; the proportion of homes where Wolof is not the first language is 37 per cent compared with 27 per cent in the town; and the proportion of mixed marriages between a Wolof party and a party belonging to another ethnolinguistic group is 14.4 per cent, whereas in town this proportion is only 10 per cent.

The most important feature, however, is the increase of Wolof in Senegal. In a town of the interior like Kaolac, bordering on a Serer area, Wolof is the first language in 73 per cent of the homes of the pupils attending the pre-elementary grades. "Instead of being marked by its hinterland, the town imposes its own linguistic structure, which is, in this case, Wolof. This is an urban linguistic phenomenon which deserves mentioning" (E.S. 82–83).

Even professional groups traditionally composed of nationals of distinctive ethnolinguistic origin are now acquiring Wolof; thus the sole occupation of the Moors and Lebanese is business on a small scale at Thies, where there is no Moorish or Lebanese quarter. In Serer or Toucouleur quarters business transactions are carried on by Moors in Wolof.

CONCLUSION

In Europe, as in Africa, the principal factors in linguistic shift (the transition from a unilingual or bilingual situation to a bilingual or multilingual situation) are linked with the expansion of compulsory, primary-school education, with urban phenomena, and with the transformation of the social and economic conditions of everyday life. The principal factors safeguarding the stability of a linguistic situation are linked with the rural way of life insofar as rural life assures living conditions that are not too precarious. A strictly synchronic comparison, limited to the present day, of the manner in which linguistic shifts are brought about in Africa and in Europe shows more differences than similarities: the great number of languages spoken in Africa may still seem to be the dominant factor in a situation in which it is difficult for European languages to take root as a possible means of communication within an entire state. In Europe, on the other hand, bilingualisms are either well established or already developing toward unilingualism. In a country such as Germany, where an enormous variety of patois were spoken 50 years ago, a leveling process arose in favor of a spoken form of German derived from literary German (which does not correspond to any of the local vernaculars; only the intonation is kept). A similar leveling process is making itself felt in France.

A diachronic comparison, on the other hand, would reveal more analogies than differences, provided we compare the present transformations in Africa with the transformations that began toward the end of the nineteenth century in Europe. The statistical data we now have at our disposal allow us to state that the sociological factors involved in either case, which speed up or check the linguistic shifts, are the same. It is not yet possible to verify whether the various mass media, from which Europe did not benefit during the last century, will influence (by way of a speeding up) the spread of European languages as the principal medium of scientific and technical knowledge, and the diffusion of certain African tongues as the support of communications between the different linguistic groups of a single state. At any rate, we may presume this to be so.

NOTES

1. Weinreich, U., *Languages in Contact* (New York: Linguistic Circle of New York, 1953).
2. Haugen, E., *Bilingualism in the Americas: A Bibliography and Research Guide* (publication no. 26 of the American Dialect Society, University of Alabama Press, 1956).
3. Haugen, E., *The Norwegian Language in America*, 2 vols. (Philadelphia, University of Pennsylvania Press, 1953).
4. Fishman, J. A., et al., *Language Loyalty in the United States* (The Hague: Mouton, 1966); Fishman, J. A., Language Maintenance and Language Shift: The American Immigrant Case within a General Theoretical Perspective. *Sociologus, Journal for Empirical Social Psychology and Ethnic Research*, 16(1), 19–39 (1965).

5. Fishman, J. A., Language Maintenance and Language Shift as a Field of Inquiry. A Definition of the Field and Suggestions for Its Further Development, *in Language Loyalty in the United States, op. cit.*

6. See, for example, Tabouret-Keller, A., Problèmes socio-linguistiques liés à l'acquisition d'une deuxième langue, *in: Aspects psychopedagogiques de l'enseignement du français comme langue étrangère* (Ecole Normale Supérieure Saint-Cloud, 1962), pp. 20–25.

7. We need not here examine the economic and political backgrounds of these aspirations.

8. Manessy, G., Les langues négro-africaines de grande extension et l'unification linguistique de l'Afrique Noire, *L'homme*, IV(3), 71–86 (1964) (See pp. 76–77.)

9. The data used here have been provided by the inquiries carried out by the Dakar Centre of Applied Linguistics (C.L.A.D.). References to E.S. are all taken from Vol. XI of the publications of the C.L.A.D.: *Enquête sur les langues parlées au Sénégal par les élèves de l'enseignement primaire. Etude statistique 1965,* by F. Wioland.

10. These children, aged from six to seven, are taught to speak French, in which language they will learn to read and write in the following year. The pre-elementary standard is an additional school-year.

11. Levy, P., *Histoire linguistique d'Alsace et de Lorraine,* 2 vols. (Fasc. 47, Paris: Publications de la Faculté des Lettres de Strasbourg, 1929).

12. Tabouret-Keller, A., *Contribution à l'étude sociologique des bilinguismes* (The Hague: Mouton, 1964, Proc. 9. International Congrès linguists, pp. 612–619).

13. Tabouret-Keller, A., Observations succintes sur le caractère sociologique de certains faits de bilinguisme, *Bulletin de la Faculté des Lettres et Sciences Humaines de Toulouse,* XI(4) (1962); (Via Domitia IX, 1–13).

14. This aspect has been closely studied by S. De Coster and E. Derume, *Retard pedagogique et situation sociale dans la région du Centre et au Borinage* (Université Libre de Bruxelles, 1962). See also Tabouret-Keller, A., Incidences psychologiques du bilinguisme, Ministère de l'Education Nationale et de la Culture, Bruxelles, *Journées d'Etudes,* **25,** 95–109 (1962).

15. Berg, E. J., The Economics of the Migrant Labor System, *in Urbanization and Migration in West Africa,* H. Kuper, ed. [Berkeley: University of California Press, 1965 (see pp. 161–162)].

16. Here the suburbs of Dakar are meant and not the administrative district Dakar-Banlieue, which includes a number of typically nonurban villages.

Pierre Alexandre

SOME LINGUISTIC PROBLEMS OF NATION-BUILDING IN NEGRO AFRICA

What, exactly, is a nation? Three generations ago most political thinkers would have more or less agreed with Maurice Barrès's criteria of a
community of people bound by a common language, a common origin,
and common customs, living on a common territory. Today, after two
world wars and several revolutions, French authors are stressing, as criteria of nationhood, a consciousness of unity or community and the will
to live together. These new criteria and the older ones are by no means
exclusive, but rather complementary. To put it in another way, the older
criteria may be considered to an extent preconditions of the new: it is
necessary, or at least useful, to have lived together to wish to live together. And it is useful, if not quite absolutely necessary, to communicate
easily to be able to form a conscious, or near-conscious, community of
purpose.

The colonial tide submerged and in some cases destroyed a number
of African communities—most of them rather small—which answered
Barrès's criteria (and which, in fact, would have been called "nations"
rather than "tribes" by seventeenth-century authors). Then it receded
under the impetus of a "nationalism" (which, in most cases, had little
relationship with the submerged "nations") and the victorious "nationalists" inherited new states whose populations had had no other common
purpose than the wish to oust their foreign rulers. They did meet one
requirement of the nineteenth-century theoreticians: the territorial one.
As for community of purpose and the will to live and work together
these still have to be built, with or without a common language.

That the linguistic situation of Negro Africa is very complicated is a
well known fact. How complicated, nobody can tell for sure, because nobody, not even the professional linguists, knows exactly how many languages are spoken in Africa, and not even, in most cases, how many
languages are spoken by how many people in any given country [1]. And
at this point politics already interferes: a project of linguistic geography

submitted to WALS in 1963 was dropped because it was felt that many African governments would oppose it for political reasons.

There is, of course, an all-too-easy way out of this difficulty: that is, to consider that independent Africa is divided in two parts, the French-speaking and English-speaking countries. Yet, even if Sudan and Ethiopia are omitted, this is a dangerous oversimplification, since, according to the most reliable estimates, probably less than 10 per cent of the population of Africa south of the Sahara is possessed of any degree of proficiency in either French or English. The French phrase *"Afrique d'expression anglaise/française"* is less of a misnomer, provided it be remembered at all times that it is only a very small portion of this more or less vague entity, Africa, which expresses itself at all in the languages of the former colonial powers.

French and English nevertheless remain the two most important languages in the political field, with Arabic coming third, possibly followed by Swahili. It may be suggested seriously that if there is such a thing as "Africa," it is to a very large extent a colonial invention. A consequence of this is that French and English, the former colonial languages, have been the chief languages of the struggle for decolonization, and remain now the chief languages of Pan-Africanism. In other words these colonial languages, although they are not vernaculars, must still be considered African, and indeed are considered as such by many of the people who use them (a rather anecdotal, and at the same time practical example is the opposition of African Ministers of Education to the proposed reform of spelling-rules in France) [2].

I shall mention only in passing the international aspect of the African language situation at its two levels. First there is the need for communicating with countries outside Africa; this problem is about the same in Africa as in all countries where so-called "rare" or "small" languages are spoken. The answer is that the small group of specialists in charge of foreign relations in various fields learn to speak a world language or use interpreters. Things are, however, less simple at the other level—inter-African communication. There is always, of course, the possibility of using French or English, or even, in a few cases, Arabic. But the situation is complicated by the fact that some vernaculars are spoken in contiguous countries with a different "colonial" language (e.g., Zande: Sudan-Central, African Republic, Congo-K.; Kongo: Congo-B., Congo-K., Angola; Hausa: Niger, Nigeria; Ewe: Togo, Ghana). In most cases this is likely to create political problems rather than solve them. A community of vernaculars across a border often tends to hinder nation-building on one or both sides of this border, and it seems that, at the present time, any hindrance of this kind reacts in turn in an unfavorable way upon most attempts toward regional or general regroupings either political or economical.

In considering nation-building, my initial assumption is that it is to take place within the present borders of the existing states, that is, within the former colonial borders, some of which are quite recent and most of which take little or no account of the actual boundaries between tribes and languages (cf. preceding examples). Generally the language situation in those states can be summed up as follows:

1. In all of them (with the possible exceptions of Rwanda and Burundi) there are a variety of African languages.

2. All of them are still using the former colonial language—sometimes together with one or more vernaculars or a lingua franca—either as "official" or "national" language, which means they use it for transacting the most important government business.

If we look more closely at local situations, we find many variations of these two generalities [3]:

1. There are extreme cases of linguistic homogeneity (Rwanda—90 per cent kinya-Rwanda) and heterogeneity (Cameroun—about 100 languages or strongly differentiated dialects for less than 5 million people) and "medium" cases such as:

a. Tanzania: about 80 per cent of the people speaking closely related Bantu languages; one dominant lingua franca (Swahili).

b. Mali: about 70 per cent of the people speaking related Mande languages; Bambara in process of becoming prestige language.

c. Sénégal: Wolof, spoken as native language by about 45 per cent of population, is becoming the prestige language.

d. Guinée: only four really important languages (Fulani or Pular, Maninka, Susu, Kpelle).

Another differentiating factor is the extent to which the vernaculars were used by the colonial power and are still used by independent governments:

a. Almost nonexistent in former French colonies where there were no official or standard spellings of vernaculars, since their use in school was prohibited.

b. Important in former British and Belgian colonies where some of the vernaculars were used in primary education.

2. Here the important factor is the proportion of the population able to use the "colonial" language. In West Africa this proportion is in reverse ratio to the distance from the Coast; a secondary factor is the influence of Islam. On the whole, European education—and the ability to speak French or English—developed more quickly in the coastal districts of the coastal territories. At the same time it was more easily accepted in

non-Moslem tribes where Christian missions and their school-system had a freer hand and did not meet with the competition of Koranic schools.

In viewing Africa as a whole, it can be said that linguistic problems as such played a very minor part in the political struggle for independence, especially in comparison with historical European precedents. It would therefore be interesting to find out whether the differentiating factors previously mentioned accounted for any significant differences in the various chains of events leading to decolonization. Obviously, linguistic heterogeneity is linked with cultural heterogeneity and could have been expected to be a serious obstacle in the way of the nationalist leaders. It could also have been expected that a territory with a high proportion of educated people, with direct access to European political thought, would have been able to organize more easily and efficiently. The reported facts do not seem to support either of these views. My impression is that there may be some kind of optimal élite/mass ratio, élite being here arbitrarily synonymous with French/English-speaking group. Too small an élite (e.g., Tchad) would cause difficulties of organization and mobilization; too large an élite (Sénégal) would cause division between the potential leaders. This is only an impression, lacking systematic substantiating comparisons. One thing, at any rate, is sure—the common sharing of a European language (hence, to some extent, European culture) has created a new nontribal or supratribal group, which, at least in the former French colonies, has frequently become a kind of oligarchy or class, because of its monopoly of this very special and powerful intellectual instrument or tool. The situation is probably slightly different in the former British colonies, in which such modernizing institutions as the Native Authorities used the vernaculars, thus allowing individuals without a knowledge of English to gain a degree of political and administrative sophistication and to wield a measure of power unparalleled in the French colonial system and the postcolonial systems issuing from it.

My next assumption is that nation-building essentially consists of creating or strengthening within the borders of a country a collective sentiment of belonging together, irrespective of individual or subgroup differences. A secondary assumption is that in modern Africa modernization for development is both an aim of, and a way to nation-building. Third, it is also assumed that every person or group engaged in modern politics wants to gain or retain power in order to further nation-building; this last assumption applies as well to some dissenting or irredentist bodies as long as they do not pursue a throwback to traditional, precolonial, non-national political structures [4].

Language is important, even essential, in nation-building insofar as the whole process can be considered as a problem of communication. This problem already existed in colonial times, since the European administrators had to communicate with the native populations. But a colonial government needed only, or chiefly, what we term vertical channels of communication: it was not trying to build up a nationwide network of crosswise, intergroup links; in some cases it actually tried to prevent the formation of such a network. Conversely, a national independent African government must develop precisely this type of crosswise, horizontal channels if it seeks to promote any kind of nationwide feeling of common purposes and interests.

It is very seldom that any local language can be chosen to implement this purpose without the risk of generating political problems even more serious than those resulting from the lack of linguistic homogeneity. I can think of but four cases: two where an overwhelming majority of the population already speaks the new national languages (Rwanda and Burundi, which are, anyway, in a special position as former precolonial kingdoms), and two where the new official (or national) language is a very widespread, nontribal lingua franca (Tanzania with Swahili, and the Central African Republic with Sango). In all other countries where a local language has been chosen—be it that of a small majority or that of a strong minority—there have been troubles on a pattern quite familiar in other parts of the world. On the other hand, the retention as a national language of either French or English (or of both, as in the Cameroun federation) has been severely criticized (in French and English) on nationalistic grounds. In this respect also we are on comparatively familiar ground. I think that it is therefore useless to review once more those relatively well-known problems, and that I would rather concentrate on more peculiar (though by no means strictly specific) aspects of the African situation. This I shall do at three different levels: technical innovations in nonpolitical matters, new or modernized institutions, and ideologies.

I mention technical innovation more as a reminder than anything else. It is, of course, linked with development, which is primarily a government concern. Finding names to explain new techniques of production or to introduce new tools is not likely to raise many serious political issues. It belongs, in fact, to the administrative rather than to the political domain. Nevertheless, African and expatriate technicians all too often forget the necessity of explaining their gadgets and knacks in terms understandable by the very people who are supposed to benefit from them. The best laid plans of experts and ministers are apt to fail when explained in kiBongo-Bongo to the waPongo-Pongo, and *this* may have serious political consequences.

New political institutions can, of course, be looked at as just another case of technical innovation. There is, however, an important difference between them and most newfangled imports: *there were* political institutions in Africa before the white men came. Every single society had a proper terminology for its own institutions, and, even if these institutions have been destroyed or deeply modified during the colonial and post-colonial periods, the corresponding terminology generally survives to this day [5]. Now the leaders of the new states are quite often faced with a treble choice when they are attempting to introduce and explain new institutions.

1. They may borrow a term from a non-African language, sometimes adapting its pronunciation, for example, *falsidang* (Ewondo and Bulu, Cameroun, from French *président*) or *raisi* (Swahili, Tanzania, from Arabic).

2. They may coin a new term, summing up or defining the new institution: "*nda ya minloman,*" literally "house of the sent-out-persons" for *chambre des députés* (Fang).

3. They may use the name of an old institution as an equivalent for a new one; *tõ*, literally "work-group raised among the members of an age-set" for "local section of the National Youth Movement" (Maninka, Bambara in Mali).

The first solution can be a good one, given enough time; it happened during the colonial era with such European loan-words as D.C. (Swahili: *disi*), commandant (Maninka: *kumadã*), tax (Bulu: *toya*), government (Ewondo: *gomna*). But the time factor is all-important and, in many cases, the urgency is or seems to be too great to allow for the delays demanded by this kind of naturalization. Moreover, accidents may happen: in the Cameroonese cocoa districts *coopérative* (the official marketing-board) has, as *kubiratif,* become a serious insult, meaning crook or scoundrel. Now the foreign expert who is supposed to rebuild the cooperative system is desperately trying to find a new word. There is also the case of S. M. Apithy, former representative of Dahomey in the French parliament, whose name, for phonetic reasons, became synonymous with *député,* so that *voter pour un député* or *élire un député* came out in translation as "vote for Apithy" or "return Apithy." When he lost the voters' favor another term for M.P. had to be introduced. On the other hand, a loan-word has the big advantage of being, so to speak, neutral, nontribal, and also, despite phonetic limitations, understandable or recognizable all over the country.

The third solution—borrowing from the vernaculars—has one main advantage: the term is already known and need not be taught over a period of months or years. There are, however, many dangers. First there are as many terms as there are languages and they are not mutually understandable. Then, and this is very important, the native terms have a previous semantic load, which may modify out of recognition the image of the new institution. Thus the use of Swahili *chama* (association, group) for "party" certainly does not connote the same picture of an

M.P.'s role as Bulu *nsamba,* originally "raiding party, armed trade caravan" same modern translation)—which, by the way, has been previously used for "school grade, form." Discrepancies of this kind occur not only between the original (French or English) name of the modern or modernized institution and its rendering in any given language but also between various renderings in different languages within the same country. Thus "alderman" or "town-district councillor" has often been rendered by the terms meaning tribal or village elder in various languages. The trouble is that such "elders" have quite different roles and positions in, say, a city-state and a segmentary society (e.g., Yoruba or Ewe versus Tiv or Kabre). To take a last example from Swahili, *kupiga kura,* literally "cast lots" for "to vote" is (or is it?) a somewhat misleading translation or description of a regular electoral procedure. To sum up, there is a serious risk of compounded misunderstandings with this method: "vertical" misunderstanding between the originators of the modern institution and the ordinary citizen, "horizontal" between citizens of different tribes. This is certainly no way to build national consensus.

The solution of using explanatory phrases would seem to avoid vertical misunderstandings and to limit horizontal ones. To be really explanatory, however, these phrases are generally cumbersome and intricate. Very likely a process of abbreviation will take place after a time (how long a time?). Meanwhile the main difficulties remain those inherent in any kind of translation [6].

Institutions, even if they are quite new and foreign, remain nevertheless concrete to a degree, allowing for a measure of actual experience and experiments which help people to understand more or less how they work. Ideologies are quite different in this respect. Traditional societies used to explain and justify their own institutions through myths; modern and modernizing ones used ideologies to achieve the same effect. Although it can be maintained that there is a contact zone between them, myth and ideology are quite different modes of conceptualization, or quite different languages. Translation from one into the other—either way—is in most cases next to impossible, and perhaps not very desirable.

As far as I know, there is but a single example of a modern African ideology created and expressed originally in an African language: J. K. Nyerere's *ujamaa.* All the other brands of African socialism, as well as Nkrumahian consciencism (or was it conscientialism?) and Senghor's *négritude,* were conceived, and written down, and broadcast either in French or in English. All these ideologies are supposed to shape up the behavior and even the thinking of all citizens in every country with a single party system. Yet I do not think that any of their fundamental creeds and formulations can be precisely and entirely translated in any African language I know [7]. It may well be that this is only a transient situation and that evolution under political pressure will transform those languages and enable them some day to express fully and exactly these ideologies. It is even more likely that the process will be a reciprocal one and that linguistic pressures will also transform the ideologies. For the time being there is no possibility of real communication between the political élite who formulate in all cases the ideology, and in most cases the policies, and the masses who are supposed to live by and implement them.

Marxism offers especially good examples because of its very stylized phraseology and vocabulary, and also because, as in Guinée, it has inspired many theoreticians of African socialism. I have made [8] some experiments of double translation of Sekou Touré's speeches and writings (from French into several African languages and back), always with the same results: the very special meaningful Marxist phraseology (e.g., such neo-Pickwickian adverbs as "historically," "objectively") just does not come through. The purely ideological texts become at times quite nonsensical. The only way out for the translator is to keep in his translation a very high proportion of French lexemes—and then the text becomes meaningless for the uneducated African. In more factual communiqués or policy reports there is an almost total loss of nuances and the translation, reduced, as W. H. Whiteley [9] observed, to "the larger issues," is either quite edulcorated or far more brutal than the original.

One of the results is a kind of divorce between the élite and the masses, who, in many cases, just cannot understand the real "whys" of a policy, or understand them only in part; thus their reactions may come as a surprise even for the leaders. Hence, as a secondary result, a discrepancy between official declarations and actual behavior, which can seriously complicate international relations: foreign observers tend to explain discrepancies of this kind by a willful duplicity of the leaders, when it is really a result of imperfect communication.

At the time of this writing, the general situation appears on the whole as a strong social dichotomy between a small élite group with a practical monopoly of the intellectual instruments of wider politics at the national and international levels, and a majority of people who can deal only with what is left of traditional (tribal) politics and the more concrete and practical sector of modern affairs at the local level. To a large extent the single, authoritarian party becomes a kind of necessity, since a majority of the people just *cannot* yet form a valid, well-informed opinion. It would be wrong to argue that differences in education end up in a similar situation in modern, unilingual, industrial nations, because in this case the difference between the élite and the masses is quantitative rather than qualitative. The promotion of any vernacular to the status of national language brings, at best, a very partial answer as long as its state of evolution does not enable its speakers to break the monopoly of the élite group whose tools of conceptualization remain non-African. A more effective answer to the problem would be, of course, the creation of really African ideologies, conceptualized and expressed in vernaculars; some religious syncretisms seem to indicate that it can be done. There is no proof as yet that any ideology of this type could be really efficient in nation-building with or without modernization. The historical example of Negro-African Islam in the Western Sudanic empires, with its effects on such languages as Hausa and Fulani, indicate, however, that it has been done in the past.

NOTES

1. See J. Greenberg, *Languages of Africa* (The Hague, 1963); and the IAI *Handbook of African Languages, passim.*
2. See also protests by African nationalist students in France against the article by P. F. Lacroix advocating the use of African languages in elementary schools, *Le Monde* (August 1965). *Contra* the resolution of the Rome Congress of Negro Artists and Intellectuals, *Présence Africaine,* pp. 24–25 and 27–28 (1959).
3. P. Alexandre, "Problèmes linguistiques des Etats négro-africains à l'heure de l'Indépendance," *Cahiers d'Etudes Africaines* II–II(6), (1961); also *Language in Africa,* J. Spencer, ed., 1963, esp. Chapters II and IV and Conference Reports (XII).
4. I. Wallerstein, "Ethnicity and National Integration, in West Africa," *C.E.A.,* I–III (3), (1960); B. Weinstein, "Social Communication Methodology in the Study of Nation-Building," *C.E.A.,* IV–IV(16), (1964).
5. It is probably easier to have people invent or adapt a name for something totally new (as automobile or airplane) than for an improvement or modification of something already well-known (a new variety of millet or goat). This may apply to institutions as well.
6. When I had to advise a national radio corporation on news broadcasts, in 1962, I suggested a combination of the explanatory method with the other two: explaining at least once in each broadcast both the loan-words and the revamped African terms used by the announcer.
7. Languages with a strong proportion of Arabic loan-words and a long tradition of writing in the *ajami* script seem more pliable; this is due, of course, to the influence of Islam. I cannot elaborate on this point, yet is it not possible to imagine an evolution of some important languages—say Wolof, or Ewe—with French or English loan-words (and notions!) in a similar position?
8. P. Alexandre, "Sur les possibilités expressives des langues africaines en matière de terminologie politique," *L'Afrique et l'Asie,* 56–IV (1961) (see esp. the appendices).
9. W. H. Whiteley, "Political Concepts and Connotations, Observations on the Use of Some Political Terms in Swahili," *St. Anthony's Papers 10 (African Affairs 1),* London, 1961.

Charles F. Gallagher

NORTH AFRICAN PROBLEMS AND PROSPECTS: LANGUAGE AND IDENTITY

"Qui ten la lengo ten la claou"
—Mistral

Decisions regarding linguistic identification and the teaching of a common, working tongue are of vital importance in the struggle to shape the future of the countries of North Africa, and also serve as an indication of their present character. In the modern world people are often known for their words as much as for their deeds. So it is with the Arabs, who base their identity in large measure upon the use of a common tongue. Equally true of the French is the belief that language will play a predominant role in the cultural orientation of a man or of a nation.

Today in the Maghrib language serves both as this kind of symbol—of affinities and aspirations, as direction and identification—and as a tool for reordering, re-creating, and seeking propitious ground in which to put down renewed roots. Both opportunities and dangers abound amid the prospects aroused by an educational and cultural drive which combines elements of birth and rebirth. There is the chance to unbar the gates to modernism and progress on the one hand, and to rediscover an intellectual attic filled with ancestral treasures on the other. Either act may in its turn impose new norms of self-assessment and understanding leading to even greater adventures of the unknown for the collective soul. These chances and perils are expressed in the traditional Arab antithesis of the *qadim* and the *jadid,* the Old and the New; in the tension between the Secular and the Godly, between the Self and the

Reprinted from, "North African Problems and Prospects, Part III: Language and Identity," Charles F. Gallagher, *AUFS Reports, North Africa Series,* Vol. X, No. 5, June 1964. Reprinted by permission of the American Universities Field Staff, Inc.

Other; and most markedly in the need to resolve the boundary lines between the Symbolic and the Utilitarian, which now tend to mark off the areas in which, respectively, revelation and reason dominate. This search for the proper tongue is perhaps the true North African dilemma, the problem which distills the essence of all other problems facing the area, beyond that of mere peasant existence.

The outstanding expression of the linguistic dilemma is the split between official dogma and observable reality. The three countries of the Maghrib: Tunisia, Morocco, and Algeria [1], are by self-proclamation Islamic in spirit and Arabic in language. The Tunisian Constitution in its preamble declares the "Will of this people . . . to remain faithful to the teachings of Islam, to the unity of the Greater Maghrib, to belong to the Arab family . . . ," and Article 1 establishes Arabic as the language of the state. Likewise, the preamble of the Moroccan Constitution defines the Kingdom as a "sovereign Muslim state, whose official language is Arabic," but significantly separates language from other areas by making no mention of Arabism as a concurrent social or political phenomenon. The Algerian Constitution, adopted in September 1963, after describing Algeria as an "Integral part of the Arab Maghrib, of the Arab World, and of Africa" in Article 2, continues in Article 5 to state that "Arabic is the national and official language of the state." By provisions of Article 73, however, "French can be used provisionally along with Arabic." In all three cases Islam is described as the state religion, a statement with as many repercussions in the language field as elsewhere [2]. To the bustling graduate student arriving in the area from the United States to work in political science or economics, these official statements would be a clear indication of the language training needed to carry out successful research, just as they would serve to reassure a businessman from the Levant that he would have no difficulty from the communications point of view in opening a branch office in Casablanca, or as they would console religious authorities visiting from Saudi Arabia to know that they would be understood by the urban masses of Algeria. How wrong they all would be emerges from a glance at the actualities underlying these pronouncements.

Today one can observe the leading figures and high officials of the Algerian Republic using French overwhelmingly as their means of communication with the Algerian people. In spring 1964 President Ben Bella called for the revision of the military clauses of the Evian agreements in French before a National Assembly (significantly not using the earphones available for simultaneous translation) which in August 1963 had called for "the use of Arabic in all administrations at the same level as French" and recommended "the translation of the Official Journal into Arabic." The late Foreign Minister, Mohammed Khemisti, was unable to speak directly to President Nasser in Cairo because they had no common language. A distinguished American scholar of Arabic vainly suggested to President Bourguiba during an interview in French that they might switch to Arabic. Journalists at press conferences held by the King of Morocco must be able to follow the monarch's impeccable French, but they need not know a word of Arabic. Considering only the question of external communication (internal exchange between North Africans will be discussed later), the scholar, visitor, or tourist will find French spoken everywhere throughout the administrations in Maghrib countries, and used as a *de facto* working language, not only at state functions and receptions, but to the point where the Post Office (in Morocco, for example) has refused to accept telegrams written in Arabic and most government offices insist that bilingual forms be filled out in French by preference. The foreigner will note that French is the overwhelmingly used language of entertainment in cinemas, theaters, and cabarets, and is widely, but far from exclusively, employed as the vehicle for information communication. The most widely read newspapers in North Africa are French-language journals [3], and radio newscast bulletins in French which use directly incoming European-language cables are more up-to-date and reliable than their Arabic translations. To illustrate the dangers to the unwary by paraphrasing Simeon Potter [4] on the nonunderstanding of American English in London before World War II, a foreigner in Algiers today who knew only Arabic might well die of a heart attack in the street before he could find a pharmacy, explain what specific medicine he required, and make himself understood.

The fact that independent North African states came into being burdened—if that word may be used, for in the long run the benefit may prevail—by these linguistic vagaries is not accidental, in the strict sense, nor can more than a small part of the problem be attributed to Machiavellian maneuvers by colonialism. It is rather the direct result of history at its extremes in time, space, and men: North Africa received too few Arab speakers, spread out too far from their original homelands, and strung over too many centuries, while it was blanketed in the colonial period by too many Europeans in too intense a concentration.

Upon a permeable but finally ineradicable Berber substratum which has left about 20% of the entire area Berber-speaking today, the Arab invasions poured out over some six centuries a series of diverse groupings: perhaps 150,000 soldiers in the first waves of the 7th and 8th centuries, plus the merchants, functionaries, women and hangers-on around them, and a doubtful 200,000 in the Hilalian invasions of the 11th and 12th centuries. A further infusion came in the later Middle Ages in the mass migration of Andalusian Moriscos from the towns and *huertas* of Spain. In between, trickling arrivals of individuals and smaller groups, usually from the Arab centers in the East or Spain, came to the cities of the Maghrib, leaving large parts of the countryside untouched. And, finally, came centuries of much reduced intercourse tantamount to isolation. North Africa, accordingly, has never been "Arab" in race or blood—although we should shy away from any attempt to use the word "Arab" on other than a culturo-linguistic basis. Eventually the heterogeneity of the immigration and its insufficient quantity produced what might be expected: in the long-established traditional cities, like Tunis and Fez, an often distinguished urban *bourgeoisie* speaking a dialectal but rich Arabic and possessing some literacy; in those parts of the countryside settled early and open to urban influence, like the Jbala in Northern Morocco, an older, city-type speech; in the mountains, dialects influenced by Berber, particularly in consonantal degradation and dentalization; in the Orient, others reflecting more or less clearly their Bedouin ancestry (some of these, as is true everywhere in language refuge-areas, of exceptional purity-in-archaism). There are Berberophone pockets of some size in the more rugged regions, and a heavy infiltration of Berber in most rural speech, having to do particularly with the names of flora and fauna, tools and utensils, toponymy, and a special vocabulary fitted to the settled agriculture of the area.

The potential of the French language as a force toward homogeneity was never fully invoked either. For over 130 years, from 1830–1962, North Africa was inundated, consciously and unconsciously, with a more massive dose of metropolitan culture than that bestowed on any comparable subject area. The French conquest had several powerful means at its disposal. First, there were the sheer numbers of the colonization. It is interesting to reflect that in 1931 the 1,400,000 Europeans [5] in a total population of 14 million represented probably as large a minority as the Arabs had some seven centuries earlier. Their political and economic power positions were much the same, but the communications facilities of the latter-day conquerors were infinitely superior. Moreover, France appeared with a will to impose itself, centered in terms of assumed cultural, and therefore linguistic, superiority as much as or more than in other domains. A methodical policy of deracination and deculturization was followed in Algeria in the 19th century, was repeated to a lesser extent in Morocco over a shorter period, and carried out most slightly in Tunisia. Finally, this policy was carried forward with the certitude of the morally right (and the victorious), and was in devious ways abetted by the semicomplicity of the vanquished to whom one of the most expressive symbols of power became the magic new language.

Despite the French conception of themselves as fulfilling a *mission civilisatrice,* there was little energy expended in forcing French thought and language down the throats of recalcitrant Arab millions in the Maghrib. The minuscule number of North Africans receiving a modern, French education in 1939 (about 100,000), and the obstacles often put in their way, testified to the rigidity of a traditional policy of educating and assimilating a small elite. For the masses, indifference and disdain were the keynotes, and the main effort, if any can be said to have been deliberately made, was to destroy the colonized by a complete denigration of their fundamental values. Algerian peasants were often physically forced off their lands in the 19th century and turned into little more than scavengers for scraps; the natural cultural counterpart of this was the conviction that they needed no more of a native vocabulary than that suitable for gathering nuts and berries (or esparto grass), and just enough French to obey commands. Only much later, with the coming of modern industrial fringe activity, was it thought necessary to teach them the rudiments of a technical lexicon so as to let them occupy the essential bottom rungs of the new hierarchy.

While a generalized, low-level knowledge of French inevitably came to be widely spread among these masses, the colonial ruling group had from the start a healthy fear of contact between the culturally dispossessed *indigène* and classical Arabic [6]. Distant and dead as that might seem to the non-literate North African at the turn of this century, both because of desuetude and systematic discouragement by the colonial authorities, it represented a threat to *colon* supremacy vaguely but deeply felt by the settler community. The vicissitudes undergone by a young Maghribi rising through the French educational system were on the whole nothing compared to those suffered by him if he chose to vest himself with a fully Muslim-Arab education, especially if he compounded this by trying to wed the prestige of this tradition to the forbidden realms of political action [7].

In the end—which began to take shape with the awakening of the 1930's—North Africans of the previous generation started to understand that both these "exotic" languages were weapons to be used in separate ways. French was increasingly learned by young modernists as a means of combatting the Other, the enemy on his own terrain, and for ferreting out his secrets. The study of classical Arabic, meanwhile, became a way of preserving one's identity and of restoring to the Self a dignity which had fallen away through oppression and neglect over decades and centuries. Religious schools everywhere, and groups like the *ulama* in Algeria, encouraged young men along this path wherever they were politically free to do so, but their efforts were limited by official restraints which increased as World War II approached.

After the war, French policy turned in the direction of opening up education (always in French) on a much wider scale, and by the mid-1950's, when independence for at least part of the Maghrib had become certain, a still small but much more respectable number of North Africans than that of ten years before was receiving a full or modified form of French-inspired teaching. Moreover, by this time French had clearly

been established as the lingua franca of the three countries, both on an
administrative and literary basis, and as an external, vulgate tongue for
communication in all cases between natives and non-natives. Its dominant position was unstable, however, because it represented domination
and humiliation as well as access to the outside world of modern thought.
It was written and spoken well by only a tiny minority of the indigenous
population and there clung to it an odor of foreign impurity. It was an
infidel in the Muslim household faced with a potential rival of great
prestige and emotional attraction. To an observer in 1955–56, specu-
lating on the linguistic future of North Africa was fascinating but difficult—just as it is today.

The linguistic realities of today, after nearly ten years of independent
orientation in Morocco and Tunisia and a short two years in Algeria,
are very different from those of a decade ago and in some ways surprising. They can be summed up *grosso modo* as regards quantity in the
table below with the comments that follow:

TABLE 1 [8]

		Approximate Number of Persons Normally Using or Having a Knowledge of:				
		Dialectal Arabic	*Berber*	*Classical Arabic*	*French*	
Country	*Estimated 1964 Population*	*(speaking)*	*(speaking)*	*(reading)*	*(speaking)*	*(reading)*
Morocco	13,000,000	11,000,000	4,000,000	1,000,000	4,000,000	800,000
Algeria	11,500,000	10,000,000	2,500,000	300,000	6,000,000	1,000,000
Tunisia	4,500,000	4,500,000	—	700,000	2,000,000	700,000
Total	29,000,000	25,500,000	6,500,000	2,000,000	12,000,000	2,500,000

(Totals do not tally horizontally, of course, because many individuals fall into several
categories.)

As can be seen, dialectal Arabic is the common tongue of North Africa,
spoken by everyone except a portion of the Berberophones, mostly
women, who are little in contact with the outside world. The dialects
in North Africa are, by and large, mutually intelligible with little effort
(the writer has observed Moroccans with a very limited classical background functioning without problems in Tunisia a few weeks after their
arrival there) and they could be considered one. Technically they should
be subdivided into at least two subdialects of a group which extends
roughly from Tripolitania westward. The dialect is not written under
normal circumstances, although French colonial policy sometimes attempted this in order to avoid using classical Arabic. (A few outdated
railway carriages in Morocco still have bilingual notices which use

vulgar Arabic written in the 1920's.) One immediately apparent difficulty is that the verbal bond between North Africans is made up by a richly expressive and lively spoken tongue which is, particularly from the standpoint of vocabulary, quite inadequate to the needs of modern, technical civilization.

The estimates given for classical Arabic presuppose the ability to read and understand tolerably well a local newspaper. The number of those speaking a degree of the classical, or what the speakers themselves consider some facsimile of it, would be very different; so, too, would the number of those able to understand and repeat with reasonable accuracy the content of a radio news broadcast. Widespread inculcation of classical Arabic, on a very limited and rote-learned basis, has been achieved by religious teaching and memorization of Koranic passages. Thus, nearly every male in the area knows a fair number of set phrases and passages which permit him, depending on individual ability, to extend this understanding to other spheres. The knowledge in such cases almost always remains passively conceived, however. Two socially important notations should be made with regard to classical Arabic: first, that it is used by two kinds of elites, one a traditional and religious group, the other a modern, educated group which includes much of the administrative hierarchy; second, that the age-curve is significantly low—that is, there is a steadily rising percentage of young North Africans becoming fluent in it. Ten years ago there were far fewer than 500,000—and this is probably a very generous estimate—who could read an Arabic-language newspaper in North Africa. Today there are four times as many, and from 200,000 to 250,000 join them each year.

Like vulgar Arabic, Berber is only a spoken language; occasionally but rarely, as in Kabylia, one may see it written in Roman letters. Several facts stand out about the Berber dialects: (1) They are confined to specific geographical areas in Morocco and Algeria, all in the mountains; (2) They seem to be gradually losing ground but at an extremely slow pace; (3) There is some mutual intelligibility (Kabyles and Riffians claim to be able to understand each other; and (4) Most adult male Berber-speakers are forced to learn another language—Arabic or French —for their dealings with out-groups, so that about half of all Berberophones are at least bilingual. Official policy in both Morocco and Algeria toward Berber as a language has been complicated by the political overtones in Berber areas. Flurries of self-interest approaching a form of separatism have occurred and caused problems. Still, aside from occasional misunderstandings, administrative tendencies have been to leave the language as is without encouraging it—but pointedly rejecting the previous French-colonial policy of distinguishing Berber speakers from those of Arabic. Government radios broadcast several hours a day in Berber dialects and the central administrations have become more careful in appointing regional officials who can be understood by the population.

Taken as a whole, some general conclusions which can be drawn from the above figures are:

1. North Africa is still very much an illiterate area. Literacy seems to vary from about 10% to 20%, with important variations between city and country as well as between men and women.

2. With 29 million individuals producing 44 million speakers of one or another language, there is a high degree of bilingualism and some trilingualism.

3. There is an important diglossia between the primary spoken language (dialectal Arabic) and the standard written form of that language (classical Arabic). In fact, the sharpness of the difference—much greater than for comparable dialects in the Middle East vis-à-vis the classical— may help explain why a mélange akin to the "third language" of the Arab East has not really developed in North Africa. However, the brief time span in which classical has been taught, and the much wider use of French, may be equally inhibiting factors.

4. Only one of the three spoken tongues is written as such.

5. The secondary spoken language (French) is a vehicle of literacy for more individuals than the written form of the primary spoken language.

*   *   *   *

This linguistic structure appears to have become solidified in the Maghrib in recent years through the instrument of generally similar educational policies. Morocco and Tunisia adopted their present educational systems soon after independence (in 1958 in both instances), and Algeria, although still operating somewhat *ad hoc,* seemingly intends to follow much the same path. The basic principles guiding the governments of the Maghrib in educational matters are these: (1) Full, public education for all nationals, as opposed to the formation of an intellectual elite, is felt necessary—every child has a right to education; (2) It is considered that Arabic culture and the Arabic language have been neglected in favor of an approach uniquely stressing European civilization and its values; and (3) It is recognized how difficult it would be to attack the problem of mass education rapidly while simultaneously shifting the whole emphasis of instruction as well as substituting one language for another. The importance of the third principle was reinforced by the disaster suffered by Morocco in 1956–57 through an overhasty Arabization of curriculum and methods. In consequence, the 1958 reforms in that country, and in Tunisia, were impregnated with a spirit of moderation and gradualism. The basic aim laid down was to nationalize instruction by unifying the complex system of school types which previously existed, by progressively Arabizing the course content, and by using Arabic as the vehicle of instruction [9]. In practice, the compromise adopted was to institute a functional bilingualism in the educational system. Thus, the beginning student was given preparatory instruction in classical Arabic, following which he was to use both Arabic and French as languages of instruction on an equal or nearly equal basis (15 hours for each in Morocco, a slight excess of Arabic in Tunisia) during the remaining years of elementary schooling. In the secondary schools in both countries, French predominates (20 out of 33 hours in Morocco), often more in reality than on paper. In Algeria during the first year of independence seven out of 30 hours were given in Arabic; this was increased to ten hours during the current 1963–64 school year.

As to how well the North African governments have been able to carry out the twofold task of extending education and Arabizing, the first part at least is statistically demonstrable:

TABLE 2. *Primary School Attendance in North Africa*

	1955–1956 (excluding Europeans)		1962–1963	
	Number	*Percentage of School Age Children*	*Number*	*Percentage of School Age Children*
Morocco	307,000[a]	18	1,020,000	43
Algeria	272,000	18	940,000[b]	43
Tunisia	224,000	26	527,000	55

[a] As of November 1956.
[b] As of the end of the school year. Not all were enrolled at the beginning owing to internal upheaval.

In examining the more subtle but crucial second part of the problem—Arabization—two questions come to mind. Can Arabization become effective according to schedule under present circumstances? As a corollary, do the governments concerned mean what they say about making it work?

The first question has two distinct aspects, one dealing with the material and personnel problems involved, the other with the problems inherent in the language itself. Before all else, and assuming that purely budgetary questions have been taken care of (in itself a great assumption), strenuous requirements in textbooks and teachers must be met. So far, Tunisia has made the best showing on all scores, by establishing its own educational office for printing textbooks and setting up the most coherent system of teacher training. Morocco is following suit and now

prints texts which are translations from other Arab sources or from
Western languages, but complaints are heard about the quality of the
translations. The dimensions of the problem of finding and training an
adequate number of teachers in Arabic, and of borrowing them from
abroad in French, can be seen in Table 3:

TABLE 3

	Number of Teachers Available in North Africa (1963)		Contribution of French Nationals Under Co-operation Programs	
	French or Bilingual	Arabic	Total	Teaching in Cultural and University Missions
Morocco	14,000	13,000	8,196	1,867
Algeria	21,000	3,800	14,872	3,700
Tunisia	4,500	6,000	2,293	1,112

In none of the countries is the number of Arabic-language instructors
sufficient for thoroughgoing Arabization, and all three are still very
dependent on French nationals, especially in secondary and specialized
education. Algeria is in the worst position by far, particularly in the
matter of teacher-training facilities. The figures strongly suggest that the
near-million Algerian children in school cannot possibly be receiving
ten hours' instruction in Arabic each week, although in 1964 history
and civics in primary school were scheduled to be taught entirely in
Arabic. Nor do numbers alone tell the whole story. Algeria faces the
same problems of poor teacher quality encountered by its neighbors
nearly a decade ago. In most country schools there is recourse to monitors whose intellectual horizons are at times only slightly less limited
than their pupils'. The situation in the two ex-protectorates is infinitely
better now than it was some years back [10], but it is still agreed that
a one-to-one correlation cannot be made in terms of "instruction value"
between the average local product and a teacher imported from France.
Of course, not all Arabic-language instructors are North Africans.
Tunisia uses no Middle Eastern teachers except those on special as-
signments or visiting lecturers at the University, but Algeria has been
bolstered by over 1,000 incoming Arabic teachers and Morocco had
more than 500 in 1964, mostly Egyptians whom it expelled in the fall of
1963 when the United Arab Republic supported Algeria during the border clashes. Another weakness in the program is clear from this: the degree to which North Africa is dependent on outside sources and the
political considerations which may intrude. The Bizerte crisis led to a
massive departure of French teachers from Tunisia in 1961, and such
events as the Moroccan-Egyptian rupture play havoc with the orderly

attainment of objectives. Now the main danger comes in Algeria where many French teachers, dissatisfied because of new fiscal burdens added to many other material and psychological problems, plan not to renew their contracts in 1964–65. A look at the preceding table shows what a blow to Algerian educational progress the loss of a sizable number of these teachers would be.

As to the ability of Arabic itself to cope with the demands of industrial and scientific civilization, few subjects raise stronger emotions among Arabs, including North Africans. Since so much of the Arab Renaissance of today has been intimately bound up with the repolishing of a language which itself was, and still is, closely interlocked with a sacred area of religious culture and history, this is understandable. If the subject is raised, there is usually a heated defense of the genius of the tongue and those special qualities which it has shown in history and which none will deny: the creation of a great literature in poetry and prose, the ability to stir men's hearts at the most profound levels of response, a mastery of evocatively nuanced imagery and phrasing, a rigorously formal framework of construction, and many others. Its more objective defenders are less certain of its qualities of preciseness—the very richness of vocabulary presents problems and has been contrasted by opponents of Arabic with the clarity of French—and inventiveness, and of its ability to translate with exactitude the batteries of modern terminology being spewed out by the West. The retort of the defense is that on the historical record Arabic showed itself capable of translating and transmitting Greek thought, and showed great inventiveness in such fields as mathematics and medicine.

Despite a tendency to public apologetics, not all North Africans are convinced that Arabic is suitable, however. The Algerian weekly organ of the FLN (National Liberation Front Party), *El Moudjahid,* explaining that the literacy campaign in Algeria would be conducted bilingually (in fact much more work was done in French), remarked on the "more functional character" of French [11]. The former director of the Bureau of Arabization in Rabat noted that "conversation between bilingualists is automatically in French as soon as the subject of conversation reaches a certain level and becomes technical" [12]. Several prominent Moroccan officials have confided to this writer that they consider Arabic technically useless in their work, and the director of one important autonomous office in Rabat thinks all teaching in Arabic should be abolished. The present head of the Bureau of Arabization described the language as "underdeveloped" and "not ready to play a role in technical matters." To cite such opinions is not to imply that they form a majority; but they do represent a considerable—and, in this writer's judgment, growing— minority which questions whether Arabic can indeed do the job alone, and thus whether Arabization is the answer.

Objectively viewed, Arabic faces some grave problems if it is to adapt itself to the efficient transmission of technical information. It is burdened with an inadequate and ossified script which needs overhauling and simplification. The present-day hesitancy of the language (which has not been true at all times in the past) to borrow directly is a sign of weakness. The inability to prefix and suffix easily and to build combining forms is a serious handicap in a world whose vocabulary is being enlarged every day with compound constructs. But, above all, as Vincent Monteil has pointed out in his admirable summary of modern Arabic, "the fundamental question is that of setting up a unified scientific and technical terminology" [13]. Here, the political anarchy of the Arab countries seems reflected in what Pellat called the "semantic anarchy of this language which hesitates to fix itself." Today, as the result of disparate efforts by academies in Cairo and Damascus and by intellectuals working on their own, terminology is not unified to the point where serious scientific work can be exchanged in Arabic with the certainty of exact comprehension. Another part of the problem, that of scientific translations, is steadily getting more acute as new vocabulary is formed in the West at ever-increasing rates. It is enough to point out that, even in fairly static sciences like zoology and botany, Arabic has no standard binominal scientific classification, and the terminology of social sciences like anthropology and sociology is so imprecise as to make translation of little value [14]. On the other hand, the performances of Syria and Egypt in recent decades, while technically difficult to judge in terms of the long-range effects of Arabization—one doesn't know what would have happened in other circumstances—prove that an Arab country can function using Arabic almost exclusively in all fields of endeavor without running up against insurmountable problems.

The reform of modern Arabic is a problem which concerns all Arabs, but primarily those of the Middle East who are closer to the spiritual nexus of their culture and who took the lead in resuscitating and revivifying their language in the last century. A quite subjective impression derived from many North African intellectuals is that they are somewhat detached from this issue in the sense that they feel themselves to be "secondhand" in any case, condemned to have ideas and the symbols which express them passed on to them from either the Middle East or from France, from one or the other "mainline" culture. This is a fairly common attitude, difficult to pin down, and not limited to the question of language. One senses almost that here, as in many domains, some North Africans see the future in terms of observing and comparing the performances of the Arab East and the Occident (which means, in effect, France) with the notion of accepting specific items that look promising, from whichever source. This tendency to look upon culture as a kind of *joteya,* a secondhand bazaar where bargains (and short cuts) can be found, is disturbing, and it is allied, at least in this writer's mind, with that elusive quality described elsewhere, which pervades what is a basically non-idea-producing society.

If one wishes to follow the progress of Arabization, a visit to the Bureau of Arabization in Rabat is instructive. The Bureau is busy translating, co-ordinating, preparing lexicons, and drawing up lists. It is working on a lexicon of tourism (Arabic-French-English) of 700 words, and on a sports lexicon of 1,000 words. It keeps in touch with special congresses held in Arab countries (like the one on medicine in Alexandria) and records and collates the vocabularies used at them. A year ago it began to study primary-school texts used in various Arab and European countries. From this effort it has now extracted a 7,500 word vocabulary as used in French schoolbooks. This list will be circulated to committees set up in the Ministry of Education in each Arab country, which will then start preparing new Arab texts with terms which are to be both exact translations of the French terms and standard in all Arab countries. At the same time, the Bureau is undertaking a census of French administrative terms for which a similar procedure will be followed.

The results so far are disappointing to the director, who is a learned and sympathetic man. There have been great delays in countries responding. Inter-Arab political problems intervene and on several occasions have caused communications to be broken off. Moreover, he volunteered that the Arabs "were not serious" and refused to work hard at this task. In Morocco, he put much of the blame on the Ministry of Education, which had not shown enough initiative. It had issued a circular "urging" the use of Bureau terminology in schoolrooms, but in fact practically none of the sciences were taught in Arabic and secondary instruction was still almost exclusively in French. In an interview, conducted entirely in French, he explained that he was bilingual: he thought in French but spoke Arabic. This is the contrary of the claim made recently by President Ben Bella to the effect that although he spoke in French he thought in Arabic.

The question as to how serious some governments are about Arabization is partially answered here. There is very little frank discission of the pros and cons of the subject in North Africa [15], and responsibility for some of the embarrassing operational results connected with it is usually covertly passed to another office. Conversations with Ministry of Education officials produce the same type of generalities as those uttered in all high places, but the blame is put elsewhere. Few seem to be true believers themselves, and it is worth noting that most ministry personnel in these countries, like the people working in the Bureau, are bilingual. This may create personality problems for them as individuals, but it also creates a personality type, one which tends to oppose or look askance at monolinguals, meaning in practice Arabophones. Sometimes this attitude stems from the fact that the bilingual individual is not completely sure of himself in either of his languages; sometimes it is the linguistic professional who, in the end, is more interested in making lexicons than in seeing society progress; and sometimes the bilingual expert likes to be in the position of dividing and ruling. Thus many bilinguals in key positions—and most people in these positions in the Maghrib are bilingual—profit from the present state of affairs, they do not want to upset their apple cart, they have no real interest in seeing (any) one language predominate, and consciously or not they tend to brake progress. All in all, it is hard to avoid concluding that if a *de facto* bilingualism seems to be becoming institutionalized it is due in large measure to bureaucratic inertia combined with personal status advantages [16].

*   *   *   *   *

Because an effective bilingualism appears to be taking root among ever larger segments of the North African population, it might be useful to look briefly at the way it functions, how it affects the individual in his environment, and to assay its advantages and disadvantages.

The subject can perhaps best be illustrated by tracing the steps in an average educational career. The child who has already learned his dialect as a maternal language and possesses the vocabulary of the family, the home, and the immediate community of daily life around him, enters school at six or seven and studies classical Arabic for two years. The languages have the same background and a good deal of similar vocabulary, but the complex grammatical apparatus of the classical language and the problems of its script are beyond this age group at this time. A voluntary effort is usually made because of the prestige of the written language, but there is an undeniable strain [17]. At eight or nine the child is introduced to French—just at the time when classical Arabic is catching hold—and plunged into using this as the vehicle for learning mathematics and natural sciences, while he applies his classical Arabic to the study of geography, history, civics, and such. The most common complaint of teachers and observers at this juncture is that neither language has been satisfactorily learned at the end of the elementary period. The total number of hours given in French, for example, varies from 1,600–1,800, compared to the more than 4,000 hours considered necessary by French pedagogues for full mastery of the language. Nevertheless, some authorities argue that the child graduating with this modicum of double culture is better fitted for living and working at a modest level in his country, all uncertainties of the near future blindly weighed, than he would be under any other system feasible at this point.

Some teachers insist that intellectual and personal difficulties deepen early in the secondary cycle. The low level of most actual Maghrib primary instruction, and the high level of traditional French secondary instruction (fairly well kept up by the transfusion of so many French teachers at higher levels) creates a gap often hard to bridge for the North African student whose basic language foundation is shaky. He often feels insecure linguistically, at times extends this to the whole intellectual field, and occasionally compounds his difficulties by splitting his personality into two parts, justifying his failure to keep up with the "Cartesian" world (for that is what usually escapes him) by taking refuge in a literary mysticism which rejects the "practical" and scientific attitude. Equally poignant in human terms, of course, is the case of the student who fully takes to a Western education and comes to disdain his own cultural background and reject his family. In all cases the pitfalls facing the secondary student are manifold. He must be proficient in French if he wishes to continue his studies abroad at the university level. The equivalence of *baccalauréats* between North Africa and France is a salvation rope for solid higher learning and material success, but it means a stiff examination in which the student must show a very considerable mastery of the other side of his double culture [18]. Although most students strongly prefer to study abroad if possible, many must remain in their own countries; and even in the Maghrib itself there is a preponderance of French-language instruction at university level. In 1962–63 at the Law Faculty in Rabat, 1,790 students followed courses in French and 1,193 in Arabic, while all courses in the Faculties of Medicine and Science were given in French. In Tunisia, 64 French nationals and 59 Tunisians, many of them bilingual, were teaching at the university in Tunis in that same year.

The bachelor's degree or the university *licence* leads to careers in which government service predominates. It may be stated flatly that in Morocco and Tunisia today the non-French-speaking candidate has no chance of getting a good government job and advancing himself in any ministry except Justice, Religious Affairs, or in specialized functions in the Interior (police work) or Education. High-level posts in key ministries like Foreign Affairs, Commerce and Industry, Planning, Public Health, Defense (except in Algeria), and Agriculture, as well as in the many specialized offices dealing with production and technical matters, are virtually closed to the monolingual Arabophone, not to mention jobs in important commercial or industrial enterprises in private business. In sum, from the third year of primary school on, there is an unrelenting pressure forcing the individual to adapt himself to a double set of goals, both of which ideally should be equally striven for. If the student cannot compete on both levels, he may withdraw from one sector of the battle at the cost of mortgaging his future in one way or another, or he may be led to drop out altogether as soon as possible, a problem now beginning to preoccupy some education specialists in the region.

Since one of the most valid objectives of a bilingual, bicultural formation is to avoid splitting youth into two groups, one deracinated in terms
of its own civilization and the other withdrawn into its cultural cocoon,
it is necessary to insist on the phenomenon, easily observable among
many students, that the split may occur within the individual as well as
within society as a whole [19]. The personality division may take many
forms, too, from benign to malignant. Many bilingual individuals in
North Africa—the most successfully adjusted ones—do use their second
language much as a Scandinavian uses English, or as a Zurich banker
visiting Geneva speaks French; it is merely a division of communication
for the convenience of the situation and the person spoken to. Others
vary their language according to the social situation, using it like a code
either to communicate with special in-groups or deliberately not to communicate with certain out-groups. One example of this is the tendency
of bilingual North African officials to address each other in Arabic in
front of technical advisers for whom they reserve French; the latter thus
have access to only part of the communication. There are infinite
variations, however, and the weapon can be directed as effectively against
Arabic-speaking monolinguals, and often is. In such interaction the
fluent bilingual experiences a sense of power and mobility. When he
amuses himself with friends in French, his bantering attitude, indeed
his whole character, is quite distinct from that expressed by his more
robust joking in Arabic. His normally authoritarian attitude toward his
wife and children at home in Arabic changes publicly under the influence of Western convention and the use of French in a *salon de thé*.
Most of all, traditional male attitudes toward women are wrenched about
in the new circumstances. It is fascinating to see how a completely new
etiquette has had to be improvised in a country like Tunisia to deal with
the social (and professional) situations involving men and women
shifting back and forth between two language worlds. (Mohammed
Khemisti's secretary, an *évoluée* Algerian lady married to a French con-
sultant, observed when she accompanied the late Algerian Foreign
Minister to Rabat early in 1963 that Moroccan men usually ignored her
and refused to rise or shake hands, until the quality of her French impressed them sufficiently to make them revise their opinions. It was not
rudeness in her opinion, rather a compartmentalization of behavior triggered by language.) The bilingual also often reflects his sense of subtle
class and other differences in the language vehicle he selects; his choice
may reveal some of his deeper inner value judgments about what, or who,
is modern, aristocratic, pious, properly oriented politically, or the opposite.

In most cases, though, the bilingual individual operates at a cost to
himself. Within the wide spectrum of all those that fall inside the definition, there are few who can move freely and without trauma between

two quite disparate views of life. These fortunate ones, who constitute a socio-intellectual asset of the highest worth to their countries, reap the true and substantial advantages of a double culture: an easier mastery of technical problems, a sense of universalistic belonging, and an understanding heightened by a comparative scale. But the great majority of the others too often represent an unstable compound which at times breaks down into insoluble constituents. In large measure these are individuals who are uncertain about some of the most basic values of their lives—and for this who can blame them?—just as their own society as a whole is unsure. It has been said that the man who cannot make up his mind is greedy; the biculture of North Africa, and a common type it is now producing, is—with reason—just that. This culture wants to be supremely rational and delightfully unpredictable at one blow. It values the mantle of tradition but delights in experimenting with the exciting and the untried. And, at the heart of the matter, one part of it, frightened of the future it seems to be heading toward, fervently wants to keep the Sacred it has long known and venerated, while another part, discouraged by this very past, seeks to put Caesar and God on the same level and separate them decisively.

Here we enter the most sensitive domain of the language question, in which foreigners should tread warily. For language is ultimately more than mere communication, and the pull it exerts is more than that ex plicit in its manipulability, usefulness, and aesthetic style. Language is the verbalization of the shared beliefs, fraternal bonds, communal historical ties, and the joint expectations of a people. It is only a mirror of existential reality, however, and, accordingly, as the beliefs and expectations are strong and fully shared, or slight and in the process of weakening, these truths will be reflected in the thinking, writing, and general creativity of the times.

For North Africa, the major historical frame in which these shared beliefs and experiences have been assembled has been the Community of Islam. This has been elaborated most satisfactorily for a great peasant majority by an ensemble of folk cultures, assimilated to and forming part of Islam, and by a folk language adequately expressing it. This culture is still buoyant and vibrant in many regions, untouched seriously by outside influences, and to the extent that it is, the folk language and the self-view of it as a means of expression, is undisturbed. For an elite and smaller group, the elaboration was that of a firmly set traditional urban civilization, which, while employing a language much akin to the language of the peasantry, leaned heavily on its access to a great historical heritage through the keeping alive of the classical written language as an implement in the service of God, his knowledge and science. Unlike the rural masses, the traditional elite has been shaken from its complacency by recent history, and its apologetics cover the language prob-

lem as only one of the aspects of a civilization in which many of its
more active and restless members no longer wholeheartedly believe, a
civilization which some of them have in fact completely abandoned.
Evidence for this abounds in the political literature, belles-lettres, and
experimental theater, and in the flowering of the hitherto restricted representational fine arts of sculpture and painting. It is too much to say
that the Maghrib is in a Golden Age of intellectual effervescence—although the change from half a century ago is remarkable—but new ideas
and new forms are spreading everywhere outside the traditional paths,
and often in opposition to them.

As far as language is directly concerned, the one point that should
be noted is the existence of, at least, a one-way crosslinkage of religious
and linguistic disuse: Less Arabic does not always mean a weakening of
religious practice or faith, but religious disobservance or disbelief will
always mean less Arabic, usually in ascending order as the passive disobservance turns into more active disbelief. Naturally, there are found
in North Africa, as in all Muslim areas, many variations on "modernism,"
within or without Islam in a formal sense. This is not the subject under
discussion here, but something can be noted. Many individuals are seeking in diverse ways a large accommodation with a revitalized faith which
will enable them to solder together the best of their own tradition and
the most useful from other sources of inspiration. Some, however, are
frankly not seeking this. The extreme left and a considerable group
around it in all three countries are at best indifferent to the place of
religion in their vision of the new state. They are correspondingly interested in language (unlike *Al Alam*) only for its social efficiency, or in
temporarily using it for ulterior political purposes. Where the left is
potent and numerous, as in Algeria where the best test seems likely to
come, it looks inevitable that the conflicting pull toward secularism and
the counterreaction stimulated among those who resist it will someday
lead to a showdown. When President Ben Bella says, as he did recently
at Ghardaia, that "there are some men who still hesitate to associate
their efforts for the realization of our socialist objectives, proclaiming
that this policy is contrary to Islam," [20] he has been forced to protest
too much precisely because he is trapped between these two forces.

In the end, the most searching questions raised in this field are un-
answerable, but they merit reflection. Can a foreign language representing an impersonal, secular, unbelieving way of life coexist with one
fundamentally opposed to it in ethic, provided that the crosslinkage of
the latter with its religious foundation remains as reasonably strong as
it is today? Or, since the movement of individuals between traditional-
ist and modernist groups (of one or another kind) is, at this point in
history, moving in only one direction and accelerating, are we to expect
a modulation or weakening of religion which will have repercussions on

the linguistic future of the area? Summing everything up, the final question—which should perhaps have been the first—is one which many North Africans in positions of the greatest responsibility hesitate to put to themselves: Who are we? And, by hesitating, they prolong the crisis. Everything revolves around this query: the alternatives for political development, the chances of building true nation-states, and the issues of co-operation within the Maghrib, or outside it in the Arab World; the problems relative to joining the European Economic Community in some form of association, plus the crucial issue of the steady emigration which is forming a European subproletariat; the issue of regional associations of all kinds, and notably the recent, burning flirtation with Africanism which has been an attempt to suggest an answer. To come full circle, the whisper of an answer may come as suggested in the first paragraph of this piece. They will know what they are and who they are only as they think it, formulate it, and express it, and by expressing it become the product of whatever their will permits and their imagination refuses to limit. The rebate on the price being paid by North Africa in its present dilemma is that it is potentially as open-ended a society as exists on this planet. The hidden dividend for suffering through a crisis of identity is that there is a valid choice. Not until North Africans make it will we have our answer.

NOTES

1. Because its linguistic and cultural development has been so different, no mention is made here of Libya. No real problem of bilingualism or Arabization exists there; the underlying reasons for this fact and the policy of the Libyan government, however, are interesting in themselves.
2. A different categorization of the North African states, and one useful in exhibiting French views on the question of cultural penetration and influence, appears in one of the few official French statements which discuss the cultural orientation of various countries to France. This is a report on *La Politique de Coopération avec les Pays en Voie de Développement* (the so-called Jeanneney Report) published 1964. In Annex 12, p. 201, countries are divided into four categories according to "the importance of the French language in the countries considered." These are:
   (A) A first group of countries having its own national language and a sufficiently structured and adequate teaching system. Example, Latin America.
   (B) Some other countries where formerly there was strong implantation of French teaching and where our language was widely spread, but where a national educational system in the language of the country predominates . . . . Examples, Lebanon, Cambodia, Laos, Vietnam.
   (C) A third group of countries characterized by the existence of a double system, national and French (with a well-stocked Cultural Mission), a heavy integration of our agents in the national system, an extremely vast diffusion of our language in the administrative structure, and the existence of an important French minority.

(D) A last group where our language has the character of a national language
. . . . Example, Black Africa.

3. E.g., *Jeune Afrique* and *La Presse* in Tunis. *La Dépêche* in Algiers had an estimated circulation of 95,000 before it was closed down last autumn. Estimates on Moroccan papers vary widely, but it is generally agreed that *Le Petit Marocain* distances the field.

4. Cf. Simeon Potter, *Our Language* (London: Penguin Books, 1954).

5. Not all the Europeans were French, of course, and a small minority did not speak the language; but French was the language of the European community in French-held territories in North Africa. (This does not include Spanish Morocco.)

6. A gross but useful simplification for nonspecialists would be to suggest that the relationship between classical Arabic and the North African dialect(s) resembles that between Latin and Spanish (or, in the Moroccan extreme, Portuguese). The general directions of changes in morphology and syntax over more than a millennium have been similar in both cases as well (reduction of verb endings, elimination of cases, etc.).

7. There were important differences in what was allowed, where, and when. What was impossible in Algeria, and usually difficult in Morocco, might be permitted in Tunisia, as the example of the Khalduniya, among others, shows.

8. The estimates in this table are highly approximate. They have been arrived at, except in the case of Algeria, by taking as a base the number of graduates at the primary level, presumably literate, from national schools before and after bilingual instruction was introduced, plus graduates from private schools, free schools, religious institutions, and the cultural missions. Another breakdown might be:

TOTAL NUMBER OF LITERATES (Estimated)

	Tunisia	Morocco	Algeria
Arabic only	300,000	400,000	100,000
Bilingual	500,000	700,000	300,000
French only	100,000	100,000	900,000
Total	900,000	1,200,000	1,300,000
	20%	10%	12%

9. For a thorough discussion of this subject, cf. David C. Gordon, *North Africa's French Legacy, 1954–1962* (Cambridge: Harvard University Press, 1962), especially, Chapter VIII "Arabization and Modernization." Some interesting general comments on the subject by a leading Algerian nationalist, Mostefa Lacheraf, are presented in "Réflexions Sociologiques sur le Nationalisme et la Culture en Algérie," *Les Temps Modernes* (March 1964).

10. See *Morocco Goes Back to School* (CFG-10-'58) by Charles F. Gallagher, American Universities Field Staff, September 1958.

11. *El Moudjahid* (Algiers), June 22, 1963.

12. As quoted in Gordon, *op. cit.,* note 9, p. 115.

13. Cf. Vincent Monteil, *L'Arabe Moderne* (Paris: C. Klincksieck, 1960).

14. On the question of Latin terminology in the sciences, cf. Monteil, *op. cit.,* note 13, pp. 177–181; on the social sciences, pp. 204–205.

15. Just as this paper was being finished, a National Conference on Education began in Rabat (April 1964). The general tone at the beginning confirmed that the subject of Arabization in all its implications would not and could not be discussed with frankness, but some interesting overtones came out. In his detailed opening remarks, King Hassan II made an impressive and reasoned appeal for the application of

common sense to all educational questions. Sounding like a distressed parent in any country, he commented on what he considered the insufficiency of a 30-hour school week (and noted that he had studied 50 hours a week for eight years in higher education), on the problems of technical instruction, on the place of teachers in the national life, etc. Without making any direct reference to Arabization, and passing over Arabism in total silence, he stated:

"We must organize our culture and our instruction as seems necessary, and reform what must be reformed, in order to turn it into an instrument capable of shaping our children, who hope, thanks to it, to become citizens of their country, and of their continent which does not speak Arabic. We live in a continent which speaks English and French. [In fact, the total population of those countries which considered themselves Arabic-speaking in Africa is about 70 million out of a total African population of about 230 million.]

"Our country, which has transmitted the beams of culture, has no intention of living shut in on itself or of preventing our culture from spreading. We have the will to restitute to our present the prestige of our past. If we make our children citizens living in a Muslim country but also children equipped to live in a great ensemble speaking French and English, we will be armed to face our difficulties and our choices. We will have made our teaching an homogeneous teaching, preparing us to be citizens of our country, of the African continent, and of the world."

The Minister of Education followed this address with an exposé of the problems facing Moroccan education and raised the possibility that the government may be considering abandoning the present primary system for one which divides the student body into two groups and reintroduces an elitist concept based on bilingualism. Developments along this line would be extremely important.

16. Commenting in a revealing way on the opening of the Conference on Education in Rabat, and on the state of education in Morocco, was Rabat's *Al Alam* (April 13, 1964), organ of the Istiqlal Party and spokesman for a large, conservative, usually traditionally oriented group of the urban middle classes and rural notables:

"It is truly stifling to speak seven years [sic] after independence of the Moroccanization or the Arabization of anything whatever; still less of the school, which should have been transformed into a school with Moroccanized teachers and with a language and spirit Arabized from the first hours of our independence . . . .

". . . We have inherited as the backwash of colonialism a language of instruction and programs of foreign study. We have kept them like something sacred which cannot be touched. In fact, under the banner of independence, we follow out a course which colonialism could not dream of applying as strictly . . . .

"If we persevere in this path, before ten years French will have become the first language of the country, spoken in the plains and in the mountains, and used in the schools, the administration, the factories, and—why not?—the mosques, too. Arabic will be relegated to second place, known only by those interested in ancient civilization, and in questions of the Orient, that is, by those who are called 'orientalists.' "

17. The November 1962 issue of *Esprit*, entitled "Le Français, Langue Vivante," was entirely given over to the question of French linguistic and cultural penetration overseas. Part III, "Le Débat avec L'Autre," pp. 753–794, contains much valuable testimony by French experts and teachers working in North Africa. The section has a piece by Selim Abou on "Bilinguisme au Liban" (Bilingualism in Lebanon), which the author also treats exhaustively from every point of view (much of it pertinent to and with references to North Africa) in his *Bilinguisme Arabe-Français au Liban* (Paris: Presses Universitaires de France, 1962).

18. A recent reform in the Algerian *baccalauréat* system instituted a separate "Algerian" examination, with a higher coefficient for Arabic, alongside the "French" examination. Unless agreement is reached between governments for an *équivalence* for the new examination, this will pose new problems for many students in Algeria who will feel it necessary to take both examinations.

19. Not always, however. A more optimistic view of adaptability is taken by Blondel and Decorsiere in "Une possibilité d'Enrichissement," *Esprit, op. cit.*, note 17, especially pp. 790–791.

20. *Le Monde* (Paris) March 25, 1964.

Jyotirindra Das Gupta and John J. Gumperz

LANGUAGE, COMMUNICATION AND CONTROL IN NORTH INDIA

Since linguists have only recently turned from grammatical analysis to consider the role of language in society, the study of modernization has been left largely to social scientists, who can hardly be expected to deal with linguistic questions. Yet language problems are known to plague developing societies. In postindependence India, for example, national language, the linguistic states issue, problems of script and minority group claims for linguistic autonomy have long played a dominant part in public life. So far, however, such problems tend to be treated primarily as cultural or political issues. Few if any attempts have been made to examine their relation to mass communication, social mobility, social control, and other aspects of socioeconomic development [1].

Karl Deutsch's early writings suggest that language and literacy are important measures of socioeconomic change, along with other indices such as the rise of political consciousness and the development of marketing systems [2]. But his suggestions have not been followed up systematically. Studies in communication, even when they refer to language, tend to focus on values, attitudes, and ideologies—on the content of what is transmitted—without attempting any systematic analysis of the structure of the verbal channels by which messages are propagated [3].

This essay explores the problem by examining the linguistic policies and practices of twentieth-century language societies in the North Indian state of Uttar Pradesh. We shall attempt to demonstrate the close interdependence between communication and political processes by showing how the policies and activities of these interest groups both affect internal communication channels and are in turn affected by them.

Work on this paper was in part supported by grants from the National Science Foundation and from the Institute of International Studies, University of California, Berkeley. We are grateful to Miss Patricia Calkins and Dr. Om Talwar for comments and assistance.

By making use of the concepts of mobilization and technical special-ization, two distinct processes involved in modernization, we are able to treat specific phenomena being studied as indices of a more general process of change. Social mobilization has been described by Deutsch as the process by which hitherto isolated sectors of the population are drawn into fuller participation in public life through the opening of channels of communication capable of transmitting information from centers of political control, economic power, and innovation to outlying areas [4]. The relatively more intensive communication among individuals of such a mobilized population implies the creation of widely circulating mass media, increased literacy, and a general educational system to sustain both.

The concomitants of technical specialization, on the other hand, have been discussed by Keller [5]. She argues that technology and knowledge in industrialized society have become so diversified and complicated that no single individual can hope to make all relevant decisions; hence the emergence of strategic elites, groups of experts, whose power depends only on their specialized skill. These strategic elites differ from tradi-tional upper-class ruling groups in that they are recruited on the basis of their performance in their speciality, rather than upon any criterion of family or social background. Although Keller does not state this directly, it seems evident that implicit in the concept of strategic elites is the existence of a mobilized population, where social barriers limiting the individual's participation in public affairs are minimized. However, the particular requirements of many of the technical specialities supporting strategic elites tend to limit members' contacts to others with similar skills; once membership in an elite group is obtained, members are rela-tively cut off from other technical elites and from the general public.

The two processes, mobilization and technical specialization, are thus complementary. Modernization serves at once to broaden popular par-ticipation in public life and to increase its technological and communi-cative complexity. In both modernized and traditional societies, the individual's ability to understand all the details of his environment is limited, but whereas in traditional societies the barriers are largely social, in modern ones they are (at least, in principle) technical—that is, directly connected with the task performed.

Our discussion is based on the premise that social organization is more directly reflected in the language distance—the grammatical and lexical distinctions among the languages, dialects, and speech styles—of the com-munity linguistic repertoire [6] than in the structure of a single language. This approach leads us to predict that whenever interaction among speakers is restricted by social or ecological boundaries, preexisting lan-guage differences are reinforced. With the breakdown of such barriers through modernization, or other social change, language differences would be expected to decrease.

The Czech linguist Havranek calls attention to important implications of this approach to verbal communication systems [7]. He observes that because of the widespread use of classical literary languages like Greek and Latin in ancient and medieval times, writings produced in one region could be read and appreciated throughout the contemporary civilized world. Such linguistic uniformity was possible, he argues, only because literary skills were the preserve of a small, exclusive literary elite, which had little or no direct contact with vernacular-speaking local populations. Communicability over large areas was thus achieved at the expense of serious gaps in internal communication. The rise of national consciousness and the broadening of political and economic participation during the last several centuries have generated pressure tending to remove such intrasocietal language barriers.

Following this argument to its logical conclusion, we may suppose that the ideal language situation is one where, to use Ferguson's terms, a single accepted norm of pronunciation, grammar, and vocabulary is used for all levels of speaking and writing [8]. Such a system would be well suited for the transmission of objective information. Members would have access to literary resources and could otherwise participate in the full range of available occupations and activities with a minimum of vocabular learning, and without having to master pronunciation and grammatical rules not acquired as part of their home background.

Such a system would be limited in other ways. Wherever language variation is regularly associated with speakers' home background or certain role performances, its very occurrence encodes important social information. A native's ability to diagnose pronunciation differences and choice of word and sentence structure gives him information about his interlocutors' social identities, their attitudes, and the probable content of their message. In small, homogeneous, closed groups where actors know each other intimately, and where the range of possible discussion topics is limited, this information is largely redundant. Such communities in fact tend to show a minimum of speech diversity. In complex and industrial societies, however, speakers deal with individuals of widely varying cultural background, whose attitudes and values differ from their own. They frequently know little about their interlocutors. Here clues derived from speech performances serve an important function in evaluating what is said, in singling out some items as more important than others, and in generally facilitating the processing of information.

Aside from differences in social background, the communication of technical specialists such as lawyers, physicians, and scientists, is a further source of language variants. Members of these groups communicate more intensively with each other than with outsiders in the area of their specialty, and thus they tend to generate their own terminological conventions. Knowledge of these conventions becomes part of the skills required for admission to the group. For members themselves, technical parlance serves as a shorthand way of alluding to a whole body of shared knowledge. It eliminates the need for unnecessary elaboration and explanation, speeds up communication within the group, and facilitates development of the specialty. However, the greater the number of technical terms, the greater the communication difficulties for the lay public.

Whereas linguistic diversity thus serves necessary functions in large speech communities, this diversity need not take the form of languages grammatically distinct from local idioms as did Greek and Latin in ancient and medieval Europe. Command over the grammatical intricacies of an otherwise foreign language is obviously unrelated to the performance of most technical and literary tasks, when special styles of one's own language will suffice. Wherever such command is a requirement for recruitment to elite positions, or even more important, wherever it is made a precondition for access to communication media, barriers to mobilization can be quite as restrictive as purely ascriptive barriers of kin and family background. The development of modern standard languages can thus be viewed as a direct consequence of the increasing pressures for democratization and greater popular participation in public life in recent times.

Although the standard languages of modernized nation-states are never identical with the spoken idiom, they tend to be similar enough for easy switching from formal or technical speech styles to informal language. The technological requirements of mass communication, and especially those of mass distribution, require that spelling, morphology, and syntax be uniform. There must be generally accepted rules of codification defining what is acceptable grammar and writing, and these must be set down in readily available dictionaries and grammars.

But communicative efficiency requires only that diversity be controlled; it need not be eliminated. Since codification rules apply only to formal modes of communication, they need not apply to all styles of the standard language. Minor differences in accent do not affect communicability; on the contrary, they serve as carriers of social information.

Technical terminologies and the special communicative conventions of strategic elites, on the other hand, pose serious communication problems. For example, very few laymen in the United States can expect to understand the *Journal of the American Chemical Society* or the full meaning of the official text of a new law, although both follow the codification rules of standard English. But in the United States, as in other modernized societies, there exist secondary communication media such as *Scientific American, Popular Mechanics,* and *Time.* These media make a specialty of translating technical terminologies into a language intelligible to the layman. The styles they employ represent a linguistic bridge between strategic elites and the rest of the mobilized population. Internal diversity is functionally related to the requirements of technical tasks and is controlled by codification so that everyone has direct access to as much information as he can utilize without having to rely on others.

Although the Indian situation is in many ways more complex, the general trend toward a decrease in dysfunctional diversity, accompanied by an increase in functional diversity, follows the same pattern as in Western societies. Initially, internal diversity was even greater than in ancient Europe. Long before the trend toward westernization began, most regions in India exhibited concurrent use of three literary languages, each having its own distinct function. Sanskrit was used mainly for Hindu religious and high literary purposes; Persian as the dominant medium of administration; and the regional languages such as Marathi, Bengali and also the precursors of Modern Hindi, Khari Boli and Braj Bhasa, served as additional literary media. All these literary languages, furthermore, were grammatically distinct from the many often mutually unintelligible local dialects used in informal interaction. A third group of spoken trade or bazaar languages was used for rather limited transactional purposes among the various local communities in market relations and festival situations. To complicate the picture even further, many commercial or artisan castes maintained their own special parlances often marked by special secret script, which served to protect their activities from outsiders.

Since they were regularly employed in what on other grounds must be considered a single social system, all these language varieties formed a single communication system. But where modernized communication systems are fluid, marked largely by gradual transitions in phonology and lexicon, the traditional Indian system was segmented into a limited set of discrete subdomains, each set off from the others by sharp grammatical and sometimes even script distinctions, as well as by lexical and phonological features. The barriers of ethnic origin, caste, and occupation characterizing Indian society were thus reflected by compartmentalization of verbal interaction into distinct communicative spheres.

The implications of such a communication system for social mobility and participation have already been mentioned. Deep barriers of language served to cut off the ordinary resident from much of the information he needed to conduct his daily affairs. Since land records, money lenders' accounts, administrative regulations, and even the religious texts he needed for his ceremonials were often kept in different languages, he had to rely on the personal mediation of others for access. The system thus favored the formation of a large number of mediating groups whose literary skills were their main stock in trade.

Individuals wishing to enter linguistically marked occupations found their tasks made more difficult by the fact that they had to learn not only the relevant technical skills and the appropriate terminologies but also a whole new set of grammatical rules and the stylistic norms associated with them. In the absence of a public education system, this training could be acquired only through personal apprenticeship; education was not a right but a privilege, depending on personal relationships with teachers and on the parents' social standing in the community. The lack of explicit and generally available codification rules, moreover, left the teachers themselves as the sole guardians of what constituted closed communities, whose literary skills were their main assets. Self-interest led them to make every attempt to preserve these assets for their own kind. Since each group served as guardian and judge of the authenticity of its own style, it could by manipulation of standards of correctness erect almost insurmountable access barriers to the technical skills it controlled.

The introduction of English as the official language in the early nineteenth century led to the disappearance of Persian and reduced the social importance of Sanskrit. But for a long time the pattern of internal linguistic barriers remained as before. Historical records from the early days of English occupation in fact give evidence of certain dominant caste groups' attempts to capitalize on their control of English in much the same way that their ancestors had controlled previous literary languages [9].

English education, however, was public, open to all who had the financial means. This, combined with the fact that the growing governmental bureaucracy opened up more and more opportunities for those with literary skills, soon led to the development of new groups of literati who were outside of the system of traditional occupational ties [10]. Under the influence of these new groups, new vernacular prose styles modeled on English were developed. Gradually, as these were adopted as the official media in the lower rungs of administration, they began to gain more general acceptance and to displace previous literary languages and special craft idioms. In what is now known as the Hindi area there were two such developing vernaculars, Hindi and Urdu. In the initial stages of their development they differed primarily in script. The grammatical and lexical base was largely the same. It derived from Hindustani, which had been current as a bazaar language throughout Northern India since Mogul times.

The extension of the communication system, liberalization of the access barriers, along with the improved educational facilities materially increased the size of the mobilized population, providing a base for the spread of nationalism with its demand for further linguistic reforms. With the gradual entry of the masses to the extended political and social scene there arose a general agreement among nationalists that English would eventually have to go [11]. The language of the foreign conqueror could hardly serve as a symbol for the new Indian nation.

Hindustani and its derivatives, Hindi-Urdu, were, to be sure, widely used but they lacked the literary prestige and respectability of English. It was felt therefore that these new idioms needed to be changed so as to more closely reflect the genius of the nation—the native literary traditions —and to become the intellectual equal of English.

This goal lent itself to a number of different interpretations, in accordance with the special interests of its advocates. The leaders of the predominantly westernized Muslim elite came largely from Western Uttar Pradesh where Persian influence had been strongest. This led them to introduce a large number of Persian borrowings into what they considered acceptable Urdu. A rival group of Hindi intellectuals, on the other hand, was based in Eastern Uttar Pradesh and Bihar where Sanskrit learning had remained strongly rooted [12]. Their language reforms leaned heavily on Sanskrit. Each of these groups identified language with their community, invoking and glorifying the history of their respective religious and cultural background, and in this way each tended to drift away from the other. As the Hindu-Muslim conflict grew, literary Hindi and Urdu began to grow more and more distinct, not only from each other but also from the spoken everyday idiom of the urban middle classes. Rising social mobilization and political consciousness were thus accompanied by a widening rift between these two groups and, within each group, between the elite and the yet unmobilized masses.

It was Gandhi, the initiator of the first all-India-based political mass movement, who realized the dangers to mobilization that were inherent in the political particularism of the new Hindu and Muslim elites. He accused both the "Hindi Pandits of Prayag" and the "Urdu Maulvis of Aligarh" of exaggerating the mutual differences between Hindi and Urdu, pointing out that much of what they rejected as mixed forms was in fact commonly employed throughout North India. He felt that a common language for India should build on popular usage and convention and not on literary injunctions of the Pandits and their political defenders. Gandhi's emphasis on basing linguistic reform on the common elements of popular speech was intended to emphasize three points: unity of the national movement, social and political mobilization of the masses, and the linking of the masses to the successively higher levels of social and political authority [13].

The intended, as well as the unintended, consequences of the struggle waged over the question of language reform can be better appreciated if we consider the group processes involved in language politics in India during the late nineteenth and twentieth centuries. The first organized association devoted to the cause of propagation of Hindi was established in Banaras as the Nagari Pracharani Sabha (1893). It began as a literary association but was soon converted into a political promoter of the cause of Hindi [14]. In 1910 a more exclusively politically oriented association, the Hindi Sahitya Sammelan (HSS), was established at Allahabad by the Hindi-oriented leaders of the Indian National Congress [15]. During the earlier years of its existence Gandhi and the Gandhian leaders of Indian National Congress partially succeeded in getting this organization to work for popularizing the idea of a commonly comprehensible national written language as a means of breaking through the barriers of communication between the elite and the masses and bridging the linguistic gulf separating the various regions of India.

Linguistic consensus among the nationalists was short-lived. With the broadening of the base of the national movement, and with the widening mobilization of the masses in the late 1920s, the Hindu-Muslim conflict began to intensify again. Within the Congress Party there rose a new group of political leaders who revived the concern for the purity of Hindi. They resisted what they called Gandhi's efforts to conciliate the Muslim demands for Urdu. In their search for symbols of identity these leaders increasingly identified Hindi with Hindu and Sanskrit culture and returned to the policy of magnifying and sometimes manufacturing divergences between Hindi and Urdu. Frequently, Urdu was branded as an alien language imported by former invaders. In 1935 control over the Hindi Sahitya Sammelan passed into the hands of this newer group of leaders and ultimately Gandhi, Nehru, and other proponents of "broader Hindi" or Hindustani had to resign from the Sammelan.

In 1942 Gandhi and his followers founded the Hindustani Prachar Sabha in order to promote the Hindustani form of Hindi. But this new organization did not succeed in influencing the course of the Hindi movement in North India. It should be noted, however, that the Gandhian efforts were eminently successful in South India. Already in 1918 Gandhi had founded the Dakshina Bharat Hindi Prachar Sabha in Madras for propagating Hindi in South India. This organization had always worked in close cooperation with the Hindi Sahitya Sammelan. After the split in the Sammelan, it remained aligned more with the Hindustani Prachar Sabha than with the Sammelan [16]. These organizations continued with their efforts to implement Gandhi's policy for a common Indian language. Their Hindi was as close as possible to the urban colloquial style current in Western Uttar Pradesh, Delhi, or in the Eastern Punjab (i.e., the area where Hindi originated and where it is commonly spoken by the middle classes, both Muslim and Hindu, and a high proportion of the lower classes), drawing for its technical terms on whatever seemed most popularly accepted, whether Persian, Sanskrit, or English. It could be written in either the Urdu or Nagari script, and both were taught in their schools. In line with the Gandhian policy of basic education they emphasized rural literacy programs as an integral part of village development through many centers. In addition, a number of highly influential centers for the propagation of Hindi in non-Hindi speaking areas of the South were created.

Whereas Hindi is the most commonly accepted spoken language in Western Uttar Pradesh, the traditional centers of literary learning are largely located in Eastern Uttar Pradesh. Here, the spoken medium of home and friendship groups are such local dialects as Avadhi and Bhojpuri, which are grammatically quite different from Hindi. Hindi is learned as a second language by the Hindu middle classes. Urban Muslim middle classes speak local dialects and learn literary Urdu [17]. Because of the attitude to Hindi as a language of scholarship, the utilitarian policies and lack of literary sophistication found little support here, and instead urban literati tended to align themselves with the HSS.

The HSS spread its organizational roots throughout most of North India, but unlike the Gandhians, its educational efforts were directed primarily toward those who were already somewhat literate in Hindi. It succeeded in gathering around it the most important Hindi scholars, literary critics, and philologists, as well as some of the most active and productive writers in the Hindi language, many of whom came from Eastern Uttar Pradesh. A new school of Hindi writing developed, including such famous critics as Ram Chandra Shukla, such prose writers as Hazari Prasad Dwivedi, and such poets as Maithili Sharan Gupta, who through their writings succeeded in giving literary respectability to the new Hindi [18]. Although the works of these writers never achieved the popular success and the wide popular distribution of modern Bengali or Marathi authors, they nevertheless were highly successful in rallying around them the younger Hindi literary elite. There was, in many cases, no formal connection between this group of writers and the HSS, but it was the frequently highly Sanskritized style of these writers which the HSS employed and attempted to promulgate.

One of the most significant organizational achievements of the HSS was the establishment of a network of examination centers for secondary and college diplomas and degrees. Before independence, these Hindi training and examination centers, as well as the Gandhian basic education centers, competed directly with government-sponsored educational institutions. After independence, these competing systems were recognized and directly aided by the Uttar Pradesh and the national state government [19].

These educational centers have been unique sources of support for the HSS organization. Financially they provide substantial funds through training and examination fees. Structurally the HSS acquired a regular, routinized bureaucracy supervising its educational and literary activities in North India and outside. Even before independence few voluntary associations in India working with a political purpose could match the resources of the HSS [20].

The importance of the HSS educational activities and its vast scale of operation are, however, significant on another level. Thousands of teacher-publicists or "pracharaks" working through the vast network of educational centers have proved to be effective instruments for codifying the literary Hindi that is learned by the students. This control mechanism is important because it has tended to standardize Hindi in accordance with the HSS leaders' norm of Sanskritized Hindi. The concerted efforts of the examination centers at the base and the Hindi literary elite at the top have tended to remake Hindi in the image of the Eastern Uttar Pradesh literary language at the expense of many colloquial forms generally accepted in the West.

The fact that most Hindi literary scholars are imbued with attitudes toward literary language similar to those of the HSS has had a profound effect on the Indian government's language planning efforts. Under the official government policy Hindi is eventually to become the national language [21] of India. While English continues to play an important part, more and more the official business both at the state and national level is being transacted in Hindi. In implementing its task of developing Hindi, almost every ministry at the state and national level has set up official committees charged with the task of creating legal and technical terminologies suitable for the new functions the language is filling.

The Board of Scientific Terminology was constituted in 1950. It was assigned the task of preparing 350,000 new terms in Hindi; by 1963, 290,000 were already in [22]. For fields other than science, another committee has the responsibility of coining new terms. Various standard manuals are being prepared for different subjects. Glossaries, dictionaries, and encyclopedias are being prepared either directly by official committees, or by private organizations with official patronage [23]. In 1956 the work of creating an encyclopedia in Hindi was entrusted to the Nagari Pracharani Sabha, a voluntary association for the promotion of Hindi. In ten years it has produced six volumes.

The stated official policy in regard to newly introduced terms is that they be commonly intelligible. But since Gandhians have paid little attention to the technical aspects of language planning, government language committee staffs have had to be drawn primarily from the ranks of Hindi scholarship, with the result that these terminologies, as well as the official writings in Hindi, are in effect quite close to the literary style advocated by the HSS.

Once pressed into service, the Hindi scholars were quick to bring their basic conviction to bear on the task of language planning. One respected Hindi expert has articulated some of these convictions in clear terms [24]. He begins with the premise that the development of Hindi is dependent on the creation of a vocabulary that is consistent with the genius [25] of the Indian languages. According to him, this is a way of rescuing India from the denationalizing effect of alien languages [26]. These ideas imply that the development of Hindi is dependent on a conscious policy of Sanskritization. This would be a way of purifying Hindi by purging it of the influence of English and Urdu.

In this sense, the Hindi scholars have interpreted the task of language development as being synonymous with increasing classicalization [27]. But classicalization implies that the literary language diverges sharply from the common speeches, thus causing an increasing separation between the media of elite communication and mass comprehension. Evidently, the Hindi scholars are less concerned with standardizing the language for popular use than for retaining its purity from the contamination of the outside influences. Hence the policy of elitist sanctity has been of greater salience to their conception of language planning than the policy of extension of mass communication.

This conception of language planning to a certain extent has been facilitated by the ambiguity in the constitutional provision concerning the style of official Hindi. This provision pays homage to the "genius" of Hindi, but at the same time it requires the reflection of "composite culture" in official Hindi [28]. It is not clear whether "composite culture" refers to a reconciliation of culture conflict based on religion or on resolving the dichotomy between elite and mass culture or both of them taken together. A leading coalition of factions within the Congress and some other parties maintained that official Hindi should be of sufficient common comprehension and therefore should be based on composite culture. On the other hand, the Hindi interest associations and generally the Hindi literary elite emphasized the genius of Hindi, which they identified with classical Sanskritic language and tradition. By virtue of political influence and actual influence on language planning, however, the Hindi scholars and associations have successfully impressed their views on official Hindi as well as the general new Hindi style.

Here are some examples of the new literary style. Items 1 and 2 are taken from signboards intended for the public. Item 3 is from the text of the Indian Constitution as given in the Government of India, Ministry of Law, Manual of Election Law [29]. In each case *a* gives the official text, *b* the English translation, and *c* an approximate equivalent in the colloquial educated style.

Item 1
    a. dhuumrpaan varjint hai
    b. smoking prohibited
    c. sigret piinaa manaa hai
Item 2
    a. binaa aagyãã praveeš nišeedh
    b. entrance prohibited without permission
    c. binaa aagyãã andar jaanaa manaa hai

Item 3

    a. raastrapati kaa nirvacin eek aisee nirvaacik gan kee sadasy
       karēēgee jisjmēē

    b. the president's election will be done by electors chosen to include

    c. raastrapati kaa cunaaoo eek aisee cunee huwee sadasy karēēgee
       jisjmēē

    a. (k)sansad-kee doonõõ sadnõõ-kee nirvaacit sadasy tathaa

    b. (a) the elected members of both houses of parliament and

    c. (k)sansad kii doonõõ sabhaaoo kee cunee huwee sadasy aur

    a. (kh) raajyõõ kii vidhaan sabhaaõõ-kee nirvaacit sadasy hõõgee

    b. (b) the elected members of the lower houses of state legislatures
       will be

    c. (kh) raajyõõ kii vidhaan sabhaaõõ-kee cunee huwee

On the surface the official language seems to differ from the colloquial
style largely in vocabulary. Colloquial terms like *manaa* (prohibited) are
replaced by *varjit* or *niseedh, nirvaacin* replaces *cunaaoo* (election) and
so on. Such innovations are common in most complex societies and can
be justified partly for technical reasons. Many new official terms (all borrowed from Sanskrit) such as *sadasy* (member), *raastrapati* (president),
udyoog (industry) are in fact becoming more and more commonly accepted in everyday Hindi speech. But the substitution of *tathaa* for the
colloquial *aur* serves no such technical function. This is one of a series
of literary-colloquial alternates which affect a large proportion of the
commonly used Hindi conjunctions, post-positions (post-positions correspond in Hindi to prepositions in English), number terms, and other
grammatically important function words. Other examples include *yadi*
for *agar* (if), *kintu* for *magar* (but), *atah* for *isliyee* (therefore), *saabit* for
saath (with), *pratharm* for *pahlaa* (first). Such grammatical variation is
more commonly found in traditional literary languages than in modern
standard languages.

    A number of new grammatical features are being introduced into the
literary language, along with the lexical borrowings. *Varjit* (prohibited)
is derived from the norm *varjan* by addition of the participial suffix *-it*.
This suffix also occurs in other Sanskrit borrowings such as *prakaasit*
(published) and *staapit* (established). The suffix *-ik* in *nirvaacik* or
audyoogik (industrial, from *udyoog*, industry) is one of a group of new
derivative suffixes that are beginning to be more and more frequent. They
differ from the other derivational rules in that they affect only words
borrowed from Sanskrit and they may require certain vowel alternations
such as the change of initial *u-* to *au-* in *audyoogik;* these rules were common Sanskrit but are not found in the modern vernacular. In syntax,
furthermore, the literary style tends toward new norm constructions such

as *pravees* (entrance), where colloquial Hindi would simply use a verbal derivative such as *andar jaanaa* (literally "going inside").

Other important innovations are beginning to affect the sound system. The final consonant clusters *-mr, -jy, -sy* in *dhuumr, raajy, sadasy,* the final short vowels *-i* and *-u* in *raastrapati* and *kintu* do not occur in colloquial speech. Words like *raajy* were used in their colloquial *raaj* in early Hindi writings. The *-y* seems to have been added around 1900 as part of the general trend toward Sanskritization.

It seems evident that the new grammatical differences between colloquial and literary Hindi resulting from recent language reform materially add to the ordinary speaker's task of learning literary Hindi. Many of the new rules are irregular in that they affect only certain parts of the vocabulary. Others affect deeply ingrained pronunciation patterns. Considerable exposure time is required before such rules can be mastered. Many native-speakers of Hindi, including some educated persons, feel uneasy about their control of literary Hindi. On the other hand, those who have been exposed to the present form of literary Hindi as part of their family background have considerable advantage in the educational system. New barriers to mobilization are being created, providing an opportunity for elite particularism to assert itself.

The work of the language planners has aroused considerable public dissatisfaction. Newspapers periodically carry articles that are highly critical of the new Hindi. At one point even Nehru exclaimed in Parliament that the Hindi broadcasts of his own speeches were incomprehensible to him [30]. But since linguistic scholarship in Hindi continues to be under the influence of the Hindi elite, and of those sympathetic to its aims, any effort to stem the present trends involves more than simply a policy decision. Present language-training programs will have to be reexamined in light of the need for mobilization and socioeconomic development.

Even in the absence of government efforts for change, however, the present language elite as represented by the HSS leaders and their allies, though dominant in the Hindi area and to some extent within the Congress Party language policy makers, cannot take their dominance for granted. Historically their power has depended on the fact that their interests were identical with those of the political groups in power. The pattern of dominance achieved so far, however, must be maintained against substantial opposition both within and outside the ruling party. Because of the relatively fluid nature of the faction system represented by the structure of the Congress Party, the Hindi elite must constantly guard its political resources. Only in this way can it maintain its strategic position in language planning on a national scale.

The structure of politics in which modern elites operate in India compels them to seek the aid of other groups. Hindi elites cannot achieve their aims without the support from the wider, uneducated, Hindi-speaking masses including those who themselves would have difficulty in using Sanskritized literary styles. In addition, the Hindi elite must build coalitions against the supporters of English and in doing so it must recruit support of non-Hindi associations.

As the struggle over language continues, attitudes toward language purity are increasingly affected by the necessity for political compromise. In their efforts to gain mass circulation and general acceptance by new Hindi speakers, recently created literary journals as well as a significant number of younger prose writers are beginning to reject overly Sanskritized literary styles. Thus the logic of mass politics under democracy may once more lead to a decrease in the dysfunctional grammatical differences between colloquial and literary Hindi and create more tolerance for deviant accents. To the extent that the Hindi elite is ready to push the case of Hindi political dominance its efforts should have the unintended consequences of reducing internal communication barriers and facilitating social mobilization and linguistic modernization.

NOTES

1. For some exceptions to this see Frank A. Rice (ed.), *Study of the Role of Second Languages*, Washington, D.C.: Center for Applied Linguistics, 1962; John J. Gumperz, "Linguistic and Social Interaction in Two Communities" in J. J. Gumperz and Dell Hymes, "The Ethnography of Communication," *Amer. Anthropol.*, 1964.
2. See Karl W. Deutsch, *Nationalism and Social Communication*, Cambridge: MIT Press, 1966.
3. For instance, see Lucian W. Pye (ed.), *Communication and Political Development*, Princeton, N.J.: Princeton University Press, 1963; or Richard R. Fagen, *Politics and Communication*, Boston, Mass.: Little, Brown, 1966.
4. See Karl W. Deutsch, "Social Mobilization and Political Development," *Amer. Pol. Sci. Rev.*, 55(3), 494 (September 1961).
5. See Suzanne Keller, *Beyond the Ruling Class, Strategic Elites in Modern Society*, New York: Knopf, 1963.
6. John J. Gumperz, *op. cit.*
7. B. Havranek, "Zum Problem Norm in der Heutigen Sprachwessenschaft und Sprachkultur," International Congress of Linguists, 4th *Actes . . .* Copenhagen, 1936, pp. 151–157.
8. Charles A. Ferguson in Frank A. Rice (ed.), *Study of the Role of Second Languages*, Washington, D.C.: Center for Applied Linguistics, 1962, p. 4.
9. R. E. Frykenberg, "Traditional Processes of Power in South India: An Historical Analysis of Local Influence," *Indian Ec. Soc. Hist. Rev.* 1, 122–142 (1963).
10. Ellen McDonald, *Social Mobilization and Vernacular Publishing in 19th Century Maharashtra*, 1967, 28 pp. (mimeo).
11. For a representative collection of views of the nationalist leaders see Z. A. Ahmad (ed.), *National Language for India*, Allehabad: Kitabistan, 1941. See especially P. D. Tandon's advocacy of Hindi: "I believe that political freedom cannot come

out of cultural slavery to the English language and things English. I have therefore always stood strongly . . . for the exclusion of English from our national . . .
work. *India's real self must assert itself through her own languages and particularly through Hindi . . .*" p. 93. (Emphasis added.)

12. For accounts of the Hindu and Muslim efforts to emphasize the difference between
Hindu and Urdu, see Aziz Ahmad, *Studies in Islamic Culture in the Indian Envi-
ronment,* London: Oxford University Press, 1964, especially pp. 239–262; and Ram
Gopal, *Linguistic Affairs of India,* Bombay: Asia Publishing House, 1966, especially
Chapters 4 and 8.

13. For Gandhi's views see M. K. Gandhi, *Thoughts on National Language,* Ahmeda-
bad: Navajivan, 1956.

14. For an account of the origin of this organization, see *Hirak Jayanti Granth,*
Benaras: Nagari Pracharani Sabha, Sambat 2011, p. 3 (in Hindi).

15. On the development of the HSS, see Kantilal Joshi in *Rajat Jayanti Granth,*
Wardha: Rashtradhasha Prachar Samiti, 1962, pp. 581 ff. (in Hindi).

16. Gandhi also founded in 1936 the Rashtradhasha Prachar Samiti, Wardha, for promoting Hindi in the non-Hindi areas not covered by the scope of the Madras Sabha.
For accounts of these organizations see Kantilal Joshi's chapter, *ibid.,* pp. 592 ff.

17. See John J. Gumperz, "Language Problems in the Rural Development of North
India," *The Journal of Asian Studies,* 16(2), 251–259 (February 1957).

18. For a brief discussion of the impact of these writers on the new Hindi, see
R. A. Dwivedi, *A Critical Survey of Hindi Literature,* Delhi: Motilel Banarsi Dass,
1966, especially pp. 164–216.

19. In 1962 the HSS and in 1964 the DBH PS were recognized by the state as Institutions of National Importance.

20. The financial and other resources of the major Hindi associations are indicated in
their annual reports.

21. This means primarily official language of the Union but Hindi is also being made
a general link language for nonofficial purposes. See *Report of the Education Commission, 1964–66, Education and National Development,* New Delhi: Ministry of
Education, Government of India, 1966, pp. 13–16.

22. The Board was later replaced by the Standing Commission for Scientific and Technical Terminology.

23. For samples of the official efforts see *A Consolidated Glossary of Technical Terms,*
(English-Hindi), Delhi: Central Hindi Directorate, Ministry of Education, Government of India, 1962; and on translation problems, plans, and programs, *The Art of
Translation,* New Delhi: Ministry of Scientific Research and Cultural Affairs, 1962.
On the problem of translating legal works see M. C. Sharma, *Rendering of Laws in
Hindi—Its Problems,* New Delhi: Ministry of Law, Government of India, 1964. The
private efforts have been conspicuously led by Dr. Raghu Vira. His ideas on language planning are summarized in his *India's National Language,* New Delhi: International Academy of Indian Culture, 1965 (in English and Hindi).

24. The reference here is to Dr. Raghu Vira. See *ibid.*

25. His attempt to develop Hindi "in consonance with the genius of Indian languages"
is discussed in *ibid.,* p. 221.

26. As he points out, "Our languages will again go into the lap of mother Sanskrit,
when she was free. We shall have again our own words." *Ibid.,* p. 207.

27. For a valuable discussion of standardization with special reference to major Indian
languages, see P. S. Ray, *Language Standardization,* The Hague: Mouton, 1963,
especially pp. 125 ff.

28. For instance, Art. 351 states: "It shall be the duty of the Union to promote the
spread of Hindi language, to develop it so that it may serve as a medium of expression for all the elements of the composite culture of India, and to secure its enrich-

ment by assimilating without interference with its genius, the forms, style, and expressions used in *Hindustani* and in the other languages of India specified in the Eighth Schedule and by drawing, wherever necessary or desirable, for its vocabulary, *primarily on Sanskrit* and secondarily on other languages."

29. Ministry of Law, Government of India, *Manual of Election Law,* rev. second ed., Delhi: Manager of Publications, Government of India, 1961.
30. See *National Herald,* April 5, 1958; and G. C. Awasthy, *Broadcasting in India,* Bombay: Allied Publishers, 1965, p. 132.

Björn Jernudd

LINGUISTIC INTEGRATION AND NATIONAL DEVELOPMENT: A CASE STUDY OF THE JEBEL MARRA AREA, SUDAN

PROBLEM

A language choice is essential in any planned development: if governmental activities and future UN campaigns are to be efficient in the area studied, either Arabic must be promoted or the native language must be used. The language in the Sudan, according to Government policy, should be and officially is Arabic [1]. This leads to the following questions: How widespread is the knowledge of Arabic? When is it accepted in use? How can it be promoted among the For of the Jebel Marra?

GENERAL INFORMATION ON THE WESTERN DISTRICT

The material used in this essay comes from a half-year's field study carried out in the Western District of the Province of Darfur, Sudan, January to May 1965 [2]. Figures given here refer to the period March to April 1965.

The For tribe inhabits mainly the Western District. Occupying the same area are nomadic Arab and Fellata groups. The towns of the District have a mixed population, Zalingei being mainly For. Neighboring tribes other than Arabs are: to the north, Zaghawa and Tama; to the east, Birgit (entirely Arabic-speaking); and to the west and southwest, Dagu, Senjar, and Masalit.

The Jebel Marra For inhabit what is considered the heartland of the tribe: the mountain itself. There we find conservative villages, whose inhabitants have little contact with members of any other tribe, whereas on the surrounding lowlands (the Lowland For) contact with nomads is more frequent. Approximately 25,000 persons live in the mountain region with a subsistence economy based on hoe agriculture of dry and irrigated lands.

The For are Muslim and the official, educational, religious, and wider communication language is Arabic.

The For language is unintelligible to non-For speakers of any other language. It is not written [3, 4]. Greenberg classifies the language as Nilo-Saharan, forming a language family of its own [5]. The dialects of For, according to my principal informants in the foothills of the mountain (in Nyertete) [6], are shown on Map 1. These dialects (except possibly the

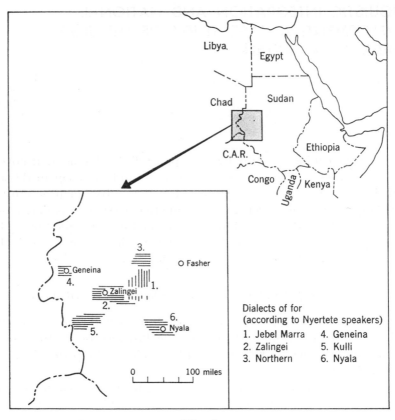

Map 1

northern dialect) cause no intelligibility difficulties. The Jebel Marra speakers form a separate dialect group (number 1 on the map).

The Sudan Government activities that involve frequent contact with the population are chiefly education and health services. New road-building also requires local labor. Tax collection and minor court matters are the responsibilities of and are carried on through the tribal chiefs (sheikhs, omdas, and shartais).

For some years the United Nations has been studying the area in cooperation with the Sudanese Government to provide a basis for economic development. The practical phase of this project has not yet begun; the work now is mainly exploratory. This study has had an impact on the society by recruiting local labor and improving the roads.

METHOD AND SOURCES OF DATA

To obtain information I spent two months in Nyertete (interviewing the population) and surveyed Golo and the Turra-Daja area in the mountain interior. I further interviewed the population in Fugo Kafir, near Guldo (Map 2). I participated in the village life, observed language use,

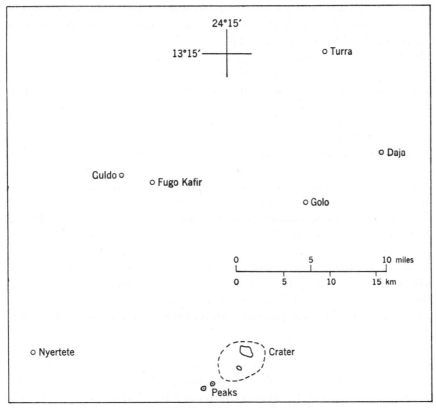

Jebel Marra (area studied)

Map 2

and elicited information informally whenever appropriate and possible to do so.

The Turra-Daja and Golo informants enumerated the inhabitants of their villages: name, job, marital status, and knowledge of Arabic as none, some, or good. It is obvious what "none" means, but the distinction between "some" versus "good" is most probably not the same for all informants. I will therefore give the "some" and "good" data but use only the "none" versus "some + good" distinction in the analysis.

In Nyertete and Fugo Kafir my informants ranked the Arabic skills of the villagers on a 10-point scale: 10 meaning fluent local colloquial Arabic, around 5 meaning a working knowledge of Arabic, sufficient for the marketplace and simple conversations, 1 and 2 meaning a very small command of Arabic, limited to the most basic needs of asking for food and water and the most common goods in the market. However, the ranking as such is much more interesting than the meaning of the numerical values. (I would assign points 2 to 4, perhaps 5, to the "some" category above). The rankings in all cases refer to spoken, not written, skills. The total performance as an Arabic user (speaker and hearer, i.e. communication partner) underlies the estimates.

In Nyertete the ranking of Arabic knowledge was made by my two principal resident informants. My own observations do not contradict their estimates, nor does informal checking with other informants. Their independent rankings show a correlation of +0.8.

Literacy information was collected only in Nyertete, through interviews. I asked the men to read a passage from the Koran (selected from the extracts sold in the market); their achievement was ranked as (1) good, (2) able to read, or (3) unable to read. (I use only (1) + (2) versus (3) here.) Recognition of key words in the Koran stimulating passages learned by heart may have influenced the validity of the test. I consistently tried to check this influence by demanding reading in the middle of paragraphs and of particular words. The same procedure and ranking applies to the reading of an "ordinary" Arabic text: I showed informants a sentence copied from a school textbook (I had a selection of sentences) written in clear handwriting and having a most ordinary content, and asked them to read. To write, I asked them to write their names and to write what I said (local pronunciation of the same sentences). I checked the results with my principal informants.

These principal informants were For men in their twenties, with eight years' schooling. The two Nyertete informants are native to that area and appointed by the project. The third informant was born and has his parents in Fugo Kafir. He also accompanied me during the surveying of the Turra villages. I consider information from the three principal informants reliable.

The enumeration of Golo and the Turra-Daja area was made by informants recommended by the local chiefs. I have no check on the reliability of the local informants.

Nyertete was selected to serve as an example of a developing village; it is a traditional small village being expanded because of farming developments that require hired labor. Because of Nyertete's special character as a village offering paid jobs and its foothills position, it has attracted more people from other tribes [7] than is usual in a For settlement. The presence of these "outsiders" (only the Arabs who have married For women and settled in the village can be considered fully accepted residents by the For natives) appears to promote Arabic skills. I consider here only For tribesmen, unless otherwise stated.

Fugo Kafir represents a traditional village close to a larger market, Guldo. Turra constitutes a traditional village in an isolated For region with little contact with the lowlands and other tribes, and Golo, halfway between Turra and Guldo, represents a mountain village with a large market.

KNOWLEDGE OF SPOKEN ARABIC: DATA

Turra-Daja Area

The result of the enumeration for the male population (349 males) indicates that approximately 60 per cent cannot speak Arabic, 30 per cent know "some" Arabic, and only 10 per cent have a "good" knowledge of Arabic; thus 40 per cent know at least "some" Arabic.

In one large village, Sollo, the informant distributed the men over an age scale that made possible a correlation between the knowledge of Arabic and relative age. The table below [8] shows that the knowledge of Arabic is considerably higher in the lower age group, although only half of them have any knowledge at all.

Arabic

Yes	No	Age (relative)
22	18	−25
9	26	26+

Number of men in Sollo according to age and Arabic knowledge. A chi²-test shows a significance between 0.02 and 0.01.

Local concentrations of better-than-average Arabic knowledge are noticeable in a hospital-school settlement and in Turra Gami, an administrative village.

Among the women the knowledge of Arabic is negligible. From a total of 470 enumerated women only 2 per cent know Arabic.

Golo

Slightly more than half of the men do not know Arabic. An informant gave one-third of the men the mark "good." He may have been giving high estimates.

The women know slightly more Arabic than in Turra-Daja. Approximately 4 per cent (of 117 females) know "some" Arabic.

Fugo Kafir

Among the men 11 do not know any Arabic and 37 (or 75 per cent) know at least "some" Arabic.

My principal informant estimated the Arabic knowledge on a 10 point scale:

Arabic mark:	0	1	2	3	4	5	6	7	8	9	10
Number of men:	11	4	3	5	5	4	3	1	1	4	7

Those men who know Arabic either know it well or have only a "market" knowledge. Six of the eleven men knowing Arabic very well (marks 9 and 10) had been to school.

There are young men without any knowledge of Arabic. The table below suggests that young men know more Arabic than do old men, but a chi²-test does not give a significant result.

Arabic

0–5	6–10	Age (relative)
6	8	−35
16	8	36+

Number of men in Fugo Kafir according to age and Arabic skills. (Not included are 10 men whose ages are not known to me. They know no Arabic.) A chi²-test shows a significance between 0.30 and 0.20.

Among the women approximately 17 per cent (of 48) know "some" Arabic.

The interviews showed that most men had learned their Arabic through contact with Arabs when "buying and selling" in the market and in the cattle camps. Seven of Fugo Kafir's men had been to the Khartoum area and Gezira, giving this stay as explanation of their Arabic knowledge.

Nyertete

In Nyertete the Arabic knowledge among the For is considerably higher than in the previous places. Only two men do not know Arabic at all. Half of the men know it better than 5, half 5 or less. For comparison, subjective overall estimates, given by Lowland For informants, indicate that we would expect half of the men there to be reasonably good speakers of Arabic. The Nyertete situation is slightly better than this. Mark 5 includes the largest group of speakers:

Arabic mark:	0	1	2	3	4	5	6	7	8	9	10
Number of men:	2	2	7	3	6	18	16	7	3	3	8

An inspection of age and Arabic knowledge shows:

Arabic

0–5	6–10	Age (relative)
12	22	−35
20	10	36+

Number of men in Nyertete according to age and Arabic knowledge. A chi²-test shows a significance at the 0.02 level.

The table below shows the extent of Arabic skills among For men who have been to the Gezira to work (only those born on the mountain and having no education).

Arabic		
0–5	6–10	Gezira
7	10	yes
15	4	no

Number of men in Nyertete according to Arabic skill and Gezira stay. A chi²-test shows a significance at the 0.05 level.

Twenty-five men have been at least to the subgrade school. Their Arabic is generally "very good" both in speech and writing. The former pupils' attitudes toward Arabic are highly positive. They make up the group that uses Arabic the most.

The men can be divided into three major occupational categories: the farmers, the paid labor (projects), and the service group (merchants, tailors, tribal leaders). Members of the service group know Arabic, not always well, but they have at least a "reasonable" knowledge (5 and above). The tribal leaders need to know Arabic since they have jurisdiction over a territory with Arabic nomads and are required to report to the local administration in Zalingei, in the official language of Arabic.

There is a marked difference in Arabic skills between farmers and project workers. The project workers know more Arabic than the farmers do:

Arabic		
0–5	6–10	Group
18	5	farmers
13	21	project labor

Number of men in Nyertete according to occupational group and Arabic skills. A chi²-test shows a significance on the 0.01 level.

The data in this table are best explained by the fact that those who went to school (and consequently know Arabic quite well) work in the project and not as farmers. If we remove the schooled group, the difference between farmers and laborers is no longer statistically significant.

The project developments in Nyertete are so recent that any Arabic effect on the workers would not be noticeable anyway. Inside the projects Arabic and English are used among higher ranks and For and Arabic in the lower ranks (among the manual workers) [9].

The women, predictably, show a small knowledge of Arabic. They cluster around marks 2 and 3:

Arabic mark:	0	1	2	3	4	5	6	7	8	9	10
Number of women:	3	7	23	25	14	9	8	2	1	—	—

KNOWLEDGE OF SPOKEN ARABIC: INTERPRETATION

Region: Less Arabic Is Known in the Mountain than in the Foothills

The Nyertete market dominates an area within a radius of 3 miles and has an influence area of about 13 miles [10]. Arabic and Fellata nomads are regular visitors: every market day (Sundays and Wednesdays, which are the smaller) an average of one-quarter of the women attending are Arab or Fellata. Between one-quarter and one-third are local For women, and the other For women, one-half of the total, come from the surrounding territory. Market day is a major social occasion. The linguistic effect of the intertribal communication must be significant.

Also, the population migrates outward, to other local and larger markets. They visit relatives in neighboring villages. These visits sometimes extend over a day's walking distance. In one month (my question referred to April) about 25 per cent both of the men and the women of Nyertete had been at least 18 miles away. In addition, 25 per cent of the men had been to places situated much farther away (Zalingei, Kas, Nyala, and Geneina), although only two of the women had traveled that far (Zalingei).

The migration patterns and the larger number of Arabic nomads and settlers suggest an explanation of the general increase in Arabic knowledge as we move toward the lowlands. The contact with Arabic speakers is naturally higher in these areas than in the mountain. For instance, Fugo Kafir is close to the Guldo market and has regular contact with cattle herding Arabic nomads, while Nyertete in addition has a small but permanent Arabic population, not to speak of the frequency of Arabic usage because of the development projects.

The better knowledge of Arabic in the Nyertete service group than among farmers partly demonstrates the same facts: middle-man jobs mean much contact with suppliers outside of Nyertete and Arabic customers in Nyertete.

It is not only the contact in the District with Arabic speakers, however, that accounts for the knowledge of Arabic: some men, as shown by Nyertete and Fugo Kafir data, go to Gezira and Khartoum to work for a number of years. The man takes home not only wealth, but also a knowledge of Arabic. These migrants have a positive attitude toward Arabic: they use the language as a sign of distinction and experience.

Sex: Women Generally Do Not Know Arabic

The lesser mobility of the women and to a certain extent their more restricted social intercourse in the market may partly explain their lack of Arabic knowledge.

This is particularly the case in the interior of the mountain area. There are no Arabic nomads there. The opportunities for the women to use Arabic in the market are therefore almost nil. Moreover, the frequent, short-distance visits do not bring them into contact with Arabs.

Age: Young People Know More Arabic than Old People

The mountain census suggested a higher proportion of Arabic skills among younger men—this is definitely the case in Nyertete. There are, however, still some young men who know little Arabic. We may conclude that a change is taking place in the mountain: Arabic is gaining, although far from all learn it.

Note that a For does not learn Arabic as a native language. Usually he first comes into more frequent contact with Arabic during his Koranic school years, when a boy, or when visiting the cattle camps. Of course, in the market he cannot avoid hearing the language and may gradually build up a knowledge.

Education in Governmental Schools

Of course, education, the first three or more years in subgrade schools, gives a very good knowledge of Arabic.

LITERACY (ONLY NYERTETE)

The following table shows the extent of reading and writing knowledge of Arabic among the male population in Nyertete. The men are split into two age groups:

Koran reading			Sentence reading			Writing		
yes	no	Age (rel.)	yes	no	Age (rel.)	yes	no	Age (rel.)
39	12	−35	33	18	−35	35	16	−35
25	17	36+	13	29	36+	16	26	36+

Number of men in Nyertete according to literacy and age. Chi²-tests show significances at the 0.01, 0.01 and 0.10 levels.

There is a statistically significant difference between the generations: the younger men can read and write, the older cannot. It should be noticed, however, that as much as one-third of the young men cannot read or write. The results are better when looking only at the Koran test. The schools (Koranic and state) have produced this knowledge. About half the same men can read and write on this test. Knowing the Koran does not mean that the person can read an ordinary text: the types are different and, also, it does not mean that he can correlate phones and printed types, for he cannot sort out the graphemes [11]. Furthermore, he does not necessarily know the meaning, although he can pronounce what he reads. My "can versus cannot" decision is entirely based on the ability to correlate phones and types. Prejudice against written—literary

—Arabic may have influenced the results. The informants were, however, encouraged to try hard.

The women are almost completely illiterate.

Very little printed material is obtainable in any village. To have a choice of books it is necessary to go to Nyala or El Fasher, for in the local markets only extracts from the Koran are sold. (There are no recent newspapers easily available, even in Nyala. Among the officials in Zalingei old newspapers are privately circulated.) A remedy for this situation would probably, with or without a simultaneous literacy campaign, increase not only the reading knowledge but also the spoken Arabic knowledge, at least to the point of satisfying the now unsupplied demand [12].

Thus at present any development campaign using printed material would reach only a small amount of the population. People lack experience in reading and have a weak knowledge of spoken Arabic. Moreover, I tested only the graphemic knowledge, not the understanding or comprehension of the texts. The percentage of the "reading" population that would understand literary Arabic is even smaller. No women could read anything. Using the Koran types would improve the situation among the men in the short run. In the long run this would have to be abandoned or the increase in the ability to read ordinary print would be slowed down.

THE SOCIOLECTAL FUNCTIONS OF ARABIC AND FOR

I have thus far concentrated on the amount of Arabic knowledge. Let me now examine the sociolectal obstacles to the expansion and use of Arabic.

Arabic is the language that the For consider appropriate to use to persons from other tribes. They do not expect them to know For. Outside the tribal area, Arabic is the expected language. In an agricultural campaign, for instance, the choice should not be the selection of For because of possible negative attitudes toward the use of Arabic in local contexts; the choice should be governed by the fact that not all know Arabic [13]. In the long-run promotion of Arabic, however, several facts about the usage of For and Arabic must be noted.

My discussion is based on a rank order of Arabic-For quotas, calculated from the answers given to the question Which language would you use in that (a specified) situation? This assumes that an informant does have a choice. The answers certainly indicate that it would be appropriate to use the chosen language, that it could be used, and that it is used, although, of course, the other language (For in most cases) may be used even more frequently.

Women hardly use any language other than For. The only place where they would prefer Arabic is the nonlocal market. The home and village language is For. This is a major obstacle in the spread of Arabic, of course. The men know For, so they will use the native language with the women. An outside effort would be necessary to increase the knowledge of Arabic among the women.

Some of the rankings given by the men at Nyertete are as follows, starting with more Arabic than For, ending with only For.

Mostly Arabic
> in the Zalingei or Nyala markets
> addressing an unknown person

Arabic and For
> in the local market
> talking to the shartai
> with your friend
> talking to the sheikh

For, little Arabic
> at home

Only For
> dancing

I obtained a parallel order at Fugo Kafir.

Some of the features (neither exhaustive nor mutually exclusive) that I believe explain this ranking are:

1. *Distance.* The farther away from the village, the more Arabic is spoken.

2. *Tribal.* The more "tribal" the occasion, the more For. Dancing and traditional social events are linguistically almost entirely For. The home language is For [14]. With a friend you can use any language, but For would be preferred among older men. Among the younger men this is not necessarily the case, and absolutely not if they are educated.

3. *Education.* Educated men identify themselves as a group by using Arabic. The educated also stress that they are Sudanese (i.e., *ex definitione,* Arabic speaking). This touches the next variable.

4. *National identification.* The more Sudanese the situation, the more Arabic. This could be the case in conversations with the shartai: young men would use Arabic or For to the shartai, others would use only For.

5. *Presence of Arabic speakers.* This partly explains the local market. If an Arab participates in the conversation, Arabic would be used.

For is being limited to the tribal area, and inside this area to tribal and local use. These circumstances clearly permit an active campaign to increase both the knowledge and use of Arabic. Also, it could mean that in the long run a bilingual situation develops, where For gets its permanent stronghold in local and tribal use, whereas Arabic would be used elsewhere.

CONCLUSIONS AND RECOMMENDATIONS

Locally in Turra, the school settlement (one of the Daja hamlets) now serves as a center for the spread of Arabic as well as increasing absolutely the number of Arabic speakers in that village. Not only does the service group in the school settlement know Arabic; the farmers also have a better knowledge of Arabic than elsewhere—a reflection of the contact networks formed around the Arabic speakers—for they serve as nodes in the spread of Arabic. A hierarchy of nodes might be empirically established, with an influence zone for each [15]. The areal pattern thus revealed (requiring a large-scale survey) would have a great explanatory and predictive value. Zalingei might be established as one top-level node of Arabic influence together with Nyala and El Fasher (roughly paralleling the economic hierarchical structure) in the developing Western District.

Nyertete is a node where Arabic now is being intensified and spread owing to the selection of this village for economic development purposes. The growth of any of these nodes (whether Nyala or a small village) will extend and deepen the influence zones and accelerate the acceptance of its features in the surrounding region. All these levels form an interrelated structure of dominance and influence. Zalingei is growing and becoming at the same time more and more Arabicized. Nyala is growing and with it the number of merchants traveling to and from the mountain. The better marketing conditions attract buyers and sellers from a wider area and more often. The improvement of roads and other communications have the same effects.

Within the project we found that Arabic is used in the middle and upper ranks. This serves as an example of the reinforcement of geographical and economic determinants of the spread of Arabic for social reasons: promotion in one's work requires Arabic.

Efficient language planning would take account of these determinants and might even propose, as a means of promoting language knowledge and use, the subsidizing of public transport or local products.

We must realize, however, that this may lead to an increase of Arabic knowledge only in the service group, thus reinforcing a tendency toward institutional language specialization.

The high mobility of the population—short- and long-distance traveling—contributes to the spread of Arabic once it is accepted. This should be considered in economizing with campaign resources: an intensive campaign in central villages in this network of markets and migrations would give an automatic response in the connected villages throughout their influence fields.

Even subsidies of the Gezira travels (employment agency or payments of travel and temporary accommodation) would indirectly spread Arabic: when the workers come back they are good and enthusiastic speakers, as demonstrated previously. (At the same time, the Government gets an increased and controllable—areally and maybe even in time—labor supply.)

Another example of indirect Arabic support would be the possibility of promoting the limited tourism that has begun in the foothills; were this promoted, not only would the area economically profit from it, but also the Arabic language would become a necessity.

The investment in education promotes the spread of knowledge and use of Arabic in the For society, and at the same time achieves a positive attitude toward Arabic in general. Education seems, for the moment, to be the most efficient way of spreading Arabic [16; 17; 18].

SUMMARY

The main linguistic facts to consider prior to any development campaign are the following:

1. Sex. Women generally do not know Arabic.
2. Region. Less Arabic is known in the mountains than in the foothills and lowlands.
3. Age. Younger people know more Arabic than older people.
4. Literacy. Half of the men and hardly any of the women can read or write.
5. Sociolects. Arabic is preferably not used in tribal and local contexts, but can be used in most other situations. It must be used in official, educational and religious situations and is the only wider communication language.

Education expectedly proved to be an efficient means of spreading Arabic. However, the infrastructure of the area also deserves serious attention as a possible means of promoting Arabic.

NOTES

1. W. A. Murray, "English in the Sudan: Trends and Policies: Relations with Arabic" in John Spencer (ed.), *Language in Africa*, Cambridge, 1963.

   My use of Arabic here refers to the colloquial Arabic used for wider communication purposes in this area. In the future, intensive use of written Arabic will naturally highlight the differences between colloquial and literary standards, but under the present circumstances this is only a problem for educated speakers since there is an almost complete lack of available reading material and newsprint.

2. The field study was financially supported by the Scandinavian Institute of African Studies at Uppsala University, Sandrew-stiftelsen in Stockholm, and Stockholm University. This work would not have been possible without the assistance of the Western District Council (especially there Mr. Kodi El Duma), the staff of the United Nations Jebel Marra Project, Mr. Mike Tinker of Rothman's, and the District omdas and local population, especially my three young informants AbuBaker Saif Eddin, Adam Muhammed, and Suliman Abdrakhman. The field study aimed at collecting data on the For language and describing the language situation in the For tribal area. I wish to thank Professor G. Hammarström and Dr. Jim Faris for suggestions that improved the draft paper.

3. The only description is the grammar by A. C. Beaton, former District Commissioner, Zalingei: "A Grammar of the For Language," Khartoum: Publications Bureau, 1955 (written 1937).

4. I noticed the use of written For (Arabic script) among some young men. From them I learned that it is common among school students to write letters and secret messages, and sometimes take personal notes in For.

5. Joseph H. Greenberg, *The Languages of Africa,* The Hague: Mouton, 1963.

6. The dialect map, according to speakers from, for instance, Zalingei, looks different from this one: the consciousness about dialectal differences is not the same. (Their language reference is different, the hierarchical rank of Zalingei, and thus the contact network and migration pattern are different, the sociolectal position may be different, etc.) A complete mapping of For ("Subjective") dialects would require a sampling of villages all over the tribal territory. On "subjective" dialects, see W. A. Grootaers, "La discussion autour des frontières dialectales subjectives" in *Orbis,* XIII, No. 2, 380–398, 1964; and U. G. E. Hammarström, *Linguistische Einheiten im Rahmen der modernen Sprachwissenschaft,* Berlin: Springerverlag, 1966, Chapter V:12.

7. They number 34, out of which 22 are Arabs. Out of the 17 women, 10 are Arabs. The total adult male population (during my study) was 120, the adult female 118.

8. The tables assume that only persons answering my questions and with the characteristics demonstrated by the tables are included. The findings would seem, in all cases, not to be affected by the drop out. For the same reason the absolute numbers of the tables should be taken only as a basis for general conclusions.

9. The UN Project has appointed intermediate-school graduates as translators for the higher ranks. They are mainly used by the English speakers. This English-speaking community uses marginal Arabic not only when speaking to servants but also to lower rank project personnel.

10. Merchants often come from a wider territory (usually from "higher order" markets); the permanent merchants, however, come from the "3 miles" hinterland.

11. On types and graphemes, see G. Hammarström, *op. cit.,* Chapter II:B.

12. A young man with intermediate-school education, from his own initiative, started a village school to teach Arabic to the men. He could, however, not continue his teaching because of lack of student interest: "They were drinking too much." An isolated effort of this kind does, of course, meet with far greater difficulties than a campaign on a larger scale directed by the District Council with the paid co-operation of local men.

13. Also, care has to be taken in the selection of the correct local colloquial Arabic.

14. The settled Arabs seem to acquire a fair knowledge of For; the others do not. This last category remains a foreign element, both socially and linguistically, and will probably accentuate differences in usage of Arabic versus For: the settled Arabs want to be accepted as full tribal members. Tribal events will thus be exclusively

For; other activities will be linguistically mixed: market-life, informal gatherings in the evenings, project work.

15. See T. Hägerstrand, *Innovationsförloppet ur korologisk synpunkt,* Lund, 1953; and K. W. Deutsch, *Nationalism and Social Communication,* Cambridge: MIT Press, 1953 (2nd ed. 1966).

16. State schools and Koranic schools compete for the young men. The latter type of institution is socially and economically integrated with the For traditional society. Many religious teachers depend on their group of students to make their living.

17. The teachers say that they use For, especially in the first year, "when needed," to ease the switch to Arabic only. Using For as the language of instruction in the first grade would perhaps, but not necessarily, result in a better knowledge of subject matter, but the learning of Arabic might be slowed down. An innovation of this nature could have negative effect on Arabic knowledge and subject matter, because of the present expectations and opinions among the For themselves (compare note 18). A decision on such a change would have to consider the economic benefits of the changes in Arabic *and* subject matter knowledge, on the one hand (maybe negative during the immediately following years, unless offset by intensive propaganda—which is expensive), and the changes in the costs of teacher training and production of teaching materials in For, on the other hand. The supply of teachers is scarce and with this additional restraint on recruiting or training, the expansion of the school system would be seriously hindered. Thus it would appear that education in a language other than the mother tongue is justified. This is, of course, in accordance with the Sudan Government's policy on Arabic as a national language.

18. Some informants are very language-conscious when talking about their children: "they are going to school or will go to school, therefore we use Arabic when speaking to them at home." This will, of course, contribute to the efficiency of Arabic in school.

Ali A. Mazrui

SOME SOCIOPOLITICAL FUNCTIONS OF ENGLISH LITERATURE IN AFRICA

Within the broad discipline of sociolinguistics, or intimately associated with it, is a subdiscipline which we might call *socioliterature*. A wide range of phenomena go toward making socioliterature. In Africa one relevant aspect is the sociology of creative writing in modern forms. The social context of the literature of protest in South Africa, or the colonial background of *negritude* as an intellectual movement, or the cultural implications of having to use a European language as a medium of African self-expression, are all fit subjects for a student of socioliterature. So is the study of the social context of songs, burial hymns, and versified invocation at circumcision ceremonies. In short, the study of socioliterature is an investigation into the broad sociological meaning of literary behavior in all its varied manifestations.

This essay is an exercise in socioliterature. It seeks to explore some aspects of literary acculturation in English-speaking Africa and its relationship to the politics of the area.

A useful point of departure is simply to note that poetry has important points of contact with politics. In fact, several factors help link poetry to politics. One is the phenomenon of cultural nationalism itself. Connected with this is the use of proverbs in traditional discourse. Another factor in the African experience is the impact of the Bible as a work of literature. And behind it all is the phenomenon of *emotion* as a basic element both in poetry and in certain forms of political appeal.

Among the people of Eastern Africa perhaps none have a body of indigenous poetry that is more closely linked to nationalism than the Somali. In his book about the Somali, John Drysdale mentions how Somali nationalism is fostered with "the emotional appeal of Somali poetry" [1]. And Colin Legum has examined how recent poems, in their longing for Somali reunification, have come to be "strongly tinged with ideas of 'the amputation' and 'the dismemberment' of the Somali nation" [2].

But Somalia is almost the only country in sub-Saharan Africa that is a "nation" in the Western sense of linguistic homogeneity [3]. Many have mentioned Tanzania as having Swahili for a lingua franca. But having an indigenous lingua franca, though perhaps the next best thing, is not the *same* as having only one indigenous language. In effect Tanzania has a multilingual tribal base with one intertribal language. But Somalia has, to all intents and purposes, only one indigenous language.

Tanzania is nevertheless considerably more homogeneous linguistically than almost all other sub-Saharan African states. The rule in Africa, as many have noted, is to encounter a polyglottal tribal diversity. And the tradition of songs and poetry in such countries is therefore oriented toward individual tribes. The emotional appeal of such verse operates within a universe of tribal sensibilities and associations. Under the initial impact of the English language and its detribalizing effect African nationalism therefore turned *away* from tribal songs.

In English-speaking Africa we can, in fact, say that (in the early days) cultural nationalism was an attempt to demonstrate that the African was capable of mastering the Imperial culture. As Julius Nyerere put it, "At one time it was a compliment rather than an insult to call a man who imitated the Europeans a "Black European" [4].

The different phases of nationalism occurred at different times in different African countries, although the order of stages was often remarkably similar. The highly imitative phase of African assertion in Ghana, for example, was long and went back to the middle of the nineteenth century, whereas in Kenya this tendency started in the 1930s and continued through much of the 1940s. There is of course still a good deal of imitation of Western culture all over Africa. But this early period of flamboyant and unabashed copying was in a class by itself. After all, it is no longer a compliment to call an African a "Black European"—yet Nyerere is right when he says that it once was.

Within this first imitative phase of African cultural nationalism, the English language became for an African more than merely a status symbol. The phenomenon as a whole was not of the kind normally associated with nationalist sentiments. Frederick Hartz once saw the relationship between nationalism and language in the following terms:

"National consciousness sees in the national language the principal traditional bond of the community, the means for educating the people to solidarity, and a symbol of national personality. Nationalism, moreover, regards the absolute domination of the national language in its country as a matter of prestige. . . ." [5].

But nationalism in much of Africa was not in a position to live up to these characteristics. The leaders had before them two possible methods of "educating the people to solidarity." The two were intimately related and were usually two sides of the same effort. One method of creating solidarity was to stress what the people of different tribes in an African colony had in common. Another method was to stress how *little* they had in common with the imperial race that had colonized them. At the level of language the nearest thing to a lingua franca in a polyglottal African situation was sometimes the English language. It was a common language between at least the new class of educated and semi-educated members of each tribe. To revel in the English language was indeed to stress what the political "intellectuals" had in common with one another regardless of tribal affiliation—but it was also to emphasise what they had in common with the imperial power from whom they had borrowed that language. The same language that helped the growth of solidarity between "natives" reduced the foreignness of the foreign power.

It was a choice left to nationalists to treat the English language as a necessary evil or a temporary expedient, as nationalists in India have sometimes done. The African nationalists [during the colonial period] did not think of English in those terms. For a while they took pride in their command of the English language for reasons that were, paradoxically, *nationalistic*. But would not this put these English-speaking militants in the same category as Leopold Senghor with his affectionate attachment to the French language? And yet we have to describe Senghor's pride in the French language as at best a lingustic cosmopolitanism. What makes it possible for these early English-speaking Africans to be "nationalists" in spite of revelling in the English language?

In fact, Senghor's attitude to French is different in an important way from the attitude of early English-speaking African "intellectuals" toward English. The distinction is between taking pride in a language and taking pride in one's own command of a language. Senghor once said, "If we have a choice we would choose French. . . . It is the supreme language of communication." In this eulogy to French Senghor is taking pride in the French language as a language. But the attitude of early Nigerian and Gold Coast nationalists was a matter of revelling in their own command of English, rather than in the "beauty" or any other inherent characteristic of the language itself. An individual can take pride in his own knowledge of a language without eulogizing the language itself. Indeed, there were many British administrators or missionaries in Africa who must have felt an inner satisfaction in having mastered the language of a small tribe in Africa—without necessarily investing that tribal tongue with preeminence among languages at large.

Yet this kind of pride is personal. What made the attitude of early Kenyan or Nigerian nationalists to English *nationalistic*? Two factors converge to form part of the explanation. One was the way in which English was associated with intellectual competence. The other was the way in which the Negro was regarded as incapable of attaining the heights of intellectuality. Competence in the English language was therefore a step toward contradicting the racialistic myth of the Negro's "retarded mentality." Mastering another "civilization" might not prove that Africa was capable of creating one of her own, but it should at least have proved that Africans had the mental capacity to absorb and command a "high civilization" should they decide to adopt one. The desire to prove that the African was educable in Western terms was therefore an element in the assertiveness of early African nationalism. And, in David Kimble's words, "Education to many people came to mean simply the ability to speak and write English" [6].

But education was not merely a matter of asserting racial equality; it was also a matter of establishing class differentiation. And so a knowledge of English became a factor in social stratification as well.

Out of all these factors resulted the phenomenon of extravagant linguistic exhibitionism in the early days. The extravagance was "in the misuse or overuse of long words, in the use of pompous oratory, in the ostentatious display of educational attainments" [7].

An "expert" is sometimes definable as he who knows the least known aspects of his subject. By extension, an "expert" in the English language came to be defined as he who was familiar with the least familar words of the language. Popular Nigerian literature in the English language still betrays this assumption. Donatus Nwoga of the English Department of the University at Nsukka refers us to certain characters in Nigerian literature:

"In *Veronica, My Daughter,* Chief Jombo, feeling that Veronica, his daughter, and Pauline, his wife, were trying to browbeat him with their superior knowledge of the English language, sent for Bomber Billy, reputed for the bomb words he could throw. . . . This concatenation of bombasts would be greatly effective on stage in Nigeria where big words do make an impact" [8].

Nwoga goes on to refer us to more established works in Nigerian literature. Achebe, Nigeria's leading novelist, points at his countrymen's love for big words in a speech he allocates to the President of the Omuofa Progressive Union at a reception in the novel *No Longer at Ease.* In a play by Wole Soyinka, Nigeria's leading playwright, a teacher assails the custom of paying bride price with a series of long English words—"and only stopped because he had only the *Shorter Companion Dictionary*—the longer edition which he had ordered hadn't arrived" [9].

Linked to this affection for bombast is an affection for quotations from major figures in English literature. One of the first warnings which Nnamdi Azikiwe sounded on his return to Nigeria from the United States in 1934 was a warning against what he called "the by-products of an imitative complex." He urged his countrymen to go "beyond the veneer of knowledge." And he emphasized that "ability to quote Shakespeare or Byron or Chaucer does not indicate original scholarship" [10].

Azikiwe's warning might have been pertinent if what the quotations sought to demonstrate was, indeed, "original scholarship." But what the quotations sought to display was, in any case, "scholarship" rather than "originality"—a wealth of learning rather than a brilliant turn of mind. The desire to assert Africa's intellectual capacity was indeed often present either in the speaker himself or in the audience which craved and enthused over such displays. But the intellectual capacity that was being asserted at this time was capacity to *absorb* the imperial culture at its most refined. Originality of mind as a form of intellectual nonconformity might have militated against this initial ambition of *assimilating* the imperial culture.

And yet that very love of long words and abundant utilization of literary quotations was itself a form of originality in English usage. It is said to be a prejudice of ordinary speakers of the English language that short "Anglo-Saxon" words are to be preferred over long Latinized ones. It is also said to be a prejudice of these same speakers that great literary figures who are revered precisely for the "universality" of their human sensitivities should nevertheless be cited only very rarely as authorities on some point of human interest. By ignoring both these conditions imposed by the Anglo-Saxon users of the English language, early usage in West Africa asserted a personality of its own.

It may even be argued that great figures in English literature are now subject to the laws of conversation of indigenous African languages. Conversational wit in many African languages postulates a ready command of diverse proverbs. It is assumed that there is a given number of human situations that keep on recurring. The incidentals vary, the personalities vary—but the essential elements of the situation are supposed to be recurrent themes in human experience. Westerners make a similar supposition when they attribute to great plays or great novels the quality of "universality" in the experiences they depict. The role of proverbs in African discourse is to stress the recurrence of these experiences. A set of words about "grief," used when Juma lost his first wife, when Rajabu lost his eyesight, and when Maryamu's son betrayed his ancestors, are used again—now that Singida is sent to jail for failing to pay the new poll tax. The situations vary, sometimes in important ways—but the proverb captures the recurrent nature of grief in "the human condition." The brilliant conversationalist is he who can penetrate into the fundamental similarities between types of human experience. The incidentals of each experience may tend to disguise the familiarity of the essence— but wisdom consists in the capacity to discern that essence. A ready grasp of proverbs, utilized convincingly, is therefore evidence of discernment and wisdom. As a Yoruba proverb has put it, "A wise man who knows proverbs reconciles difficulties" [11].

A similar admiration of elegant speech, and of the place of proverbs in that speech, can apparently be found among the Ibo. Donatus Nwoga tells us that the Ibos have a dictum to the effect that to make a speech without using proverbs is like trying to climb a palm tree without the climbing rope. Nwoga then goes on to suggest a connection between traditional proverbs and Shakespearean quotations in contemporary Africa. He says:

"I suggest that the tendency towards supporting one's statements with proverbs might have carried over into this market literature in the form of using quotations. In *Veronica, My Daughter,* between pages 20 and 23, there are quotations from Richard Whately, William Shakespeare, G. A. Gallock, Rudyard Kipling, Benjamin Harrison, William Ernest Henley and Henry Longfellow; and before the end of the story there are further quotations from Johann Wolfgang Von Goethe and some unknown poet" [12].

Lest it be assumed that it is only the semiliterate who use English quotations with the same abundance as they might use African proverbs, Nwoga warns that "the mania for quotations is not determined by the standard of education." On the day he started thinking about this matter he happened to pick up a Nigerian newspaper—and the lead article started its second paragraph with a quotation from Edmund Burke. Nwoga observes:

"This is impressive where breadth of knowledge of English is not only a prestige factor but also a guide to social and employment status. . . . But one has to admit that sometimes quotations are used for the genuine purposes of giving to the opinion of the speaker or writer an extra and higher authority" [13].

The capacity to adorn one's speech and to give it weight by citing great names were important factors in the process by which leadership emerged. To be able to make a good speech is an asset for a politician in almost any society, but it is even more crucial in situations where patronage as an alternative way of recruiting influential followers is as yet inadequately established. In the early days of nationalism in Africa the politicians had limited tangible rewards to offer those whose allegiance they were seeking. It was the colonial government and, in some cases, the tribal chiefs who had the more immediate powers of patronage. What the modern politicians in the colonies could best do was precisely what they were often accused of doing—the politicians worked on the vague grievances of the people and made them less vague. And in a competition between the leadership of one politician and that of another, the better speaker had an advantage which was more significant in those early African situations than the same advantage may be in Africa today. The British colonies by the 1930s were nearer to being "open societies" than are some independent African countries today. And precisely because these countries are less "open," the ability to make a good speech has depreciated in value as a qualification for political success. Nkrumah's opponents after independence were not in a position to attribute to oratorical powers the same relevance for one's political destiny that Nkrumah attributed to his own debating abilities in the colonial period. In his autobiography he tells us how he discovered quite early his talents in verbal persuasion:

"I discovered that at whatever disadvantage I began, I usually ended up winning the day, frequently converting many of my opponents to the point of view that I had conveniently supported. Although this was only a kind of game with me then, it turned out to be my most valuable discovery. Without this 'gift of the gab,' my battle would have been lost from the very beginning and the whole struggle would have been in vain" [14].

The power of verbal persuasion can sometimes be used as effectively in religion as in politics. In the earlier days of the colonial period the pulpit could be as "seductive" to a talented young man as the political platform. Nkrumah was, as it were, a "near-Jesuit." For a whole year as a young man he played with the idea of joining the Jesuit Order. But in the end his old desire to "further my education and proceed to America in order to do this, got the better of me" [15].

When he got to America he studied subjects like philosophy and sociology—but this time another old idea kept on recurring. It was theology. In 1942 he was graduated from the seminary at Lincoln University with a Bachelor of Theology degree at the head of his class. His oratorical talents were once again tested on this occasion. It fell upon him to deliver the seminary graduation oration. The subject he chose to speak on was "Ethiopia shall stretch forth her hands unto God. . . ." He was inadequately prepared and worried about how the oration was going. But when the warm congratulations ensued later he was, like a true performer, deeply gratified [16].

In fact, by that time he had already had some practice in preaching. While he was studying theology at Lincoln Seminary Nkrumah spent much of his free time preaching in Negro churches [17].

This recalls the influence of the Bible on the idiom of African rhetoric. In terms of style and language the Bible in English is, in a sense, part of the corpus of English literature. And it had an important place in the kind of literary education to which many of the African leaders were exposed in the formative years. Of Nigeria in those days James Coleman had this to say:

"In literature, Shakespeare and the Bible held the stage. Even today, it is not uncommon to find a semi-educated Nigerian working as a steward who can . . . quote the Bible, and recite Hamlet. . . ." [18].

In Ghana after independence the influence of the Bible resulted in a language of political adoration for the leader that was strikingly derived from the Holy Book. Nkrumah came to be invested with Messianic attributes and powers of "redemption" [19]. As for the idiom of his own political speeches, perhaps the most famous single sentence uttered by Nkrumah was "Seek ye first the political kingdom and all things will be added to it" [20]. In a neo-Biblical imperative Nkrumah thus asserted the primacy of politics as a basic precept of African nationalism in the struggle for independence.

Further south, religious and political sensitivities among Africans have sometimes also converged round a concept of *messianism*—but this time in a different sense from that attributed to the Osagyefo in Ghana. In an article written in 1953 Georges Balandier urged greater sociological investigation into "Neo-Christian movements" and separatist churches in Black Africa. He said:

"Neo-Christian movements must come to the attention of the sociologist insofar as they are reactions against the colonial situation. . . . These movements lead above all to the study of the origins of nationalism, and, in so doing, confront the sociologist with one of the most important problems of our time" [21].

Balandier saw these messianic movements as being mainly in South and Central Africa. But the influence of Christianity on nationalism in these parts is by no means limited to those who rise as "prophets." One of the striking aspects of nationalistic leadership in English-speaking Central Africa and in South Africa is how often it seems to bear a deep religious impact. In what is now Zambia Kenneth Kaunda is a son of an African missionary and is himself a devout Christian. Hastings Banda in Malawi is now a more controversial figure, but in his old campaigns for Nyasaland's secession from the Federation of Rhodesia and Nyasaland Banda's standing among sympathizers in Britain was helped by his position as an elder in the Church of Scotland. In Southern Rhodesia Ndabaningl Sithole, the more militant of the two leaders of African nationalism, is an actual priest. In South Africa Chief Albert Luthuli, winner of the Nobel Prize for Peace, is evidently a deeply devout Christian.

Also attributed to the influence of the Bible on their idiom, Luthuli entitled his book *Let My People Go*, echoing the Mosaic imperative to the Pharaoh. Kaunda's response to Gandhi's doctrine of nonviolence has

Christian echoes and is related to Kaunda's Christian upbringing. And the Reverend Sithole devotes part of his book *African Nationalism* to the role of Christianity in the growth of African militancy [22].

What religious fervor, nationalism, and poetry have in common is, in the ultimate analysis, the essential emotionality of the three experiences. It is to this factor of emotionality in Africa that we now turn.

Of all African leaders Leopold Senghor has perhaps gone further than anyone else in discussing with approval the place of emotion in Africa. He has asserted that a highly developed "emotive sensibility" is what distinguishes the genius of Africa from that of the Western world. "Emotion is black . . . reason is Greek," Senghor once claimed [23].

This interpretation of original Africa exposed Senghor to the charge of depriving the traditional African of the gift of rationality. Senghor defends himself with his usual ingenuity—though ultimately he insists on interpreting the African as being basically intuitive. He says:

"Young people have criticized me for reducing Negro-African knowledge to pure emotion, for denying that there is an African 'reason' or African techniques. . . . I should like to explain myself once again. . . . European reasoning is analytical, discursive by utilization; Negro-African reasoning is intuitive by participation" [24].

Senghor may be overstating his case, but his generalizations are not entirely devoid of substance. The extraemotionalism of Negro Christianity, especially in the New World, is one area of experience that affords some evidence for Senghor's assertion. Among the earliest Church services attended by the youthful Nkrumah on his arrival in the States was a Negro service at the Abyssinian Church in New York. Nkrumah tells us about the minister's "dramatization" of the story of Jesus carrying the cross to Calvary. Before long the women in the congregation were overawed and began to weep and to shout. "It is Jesus! Have mercy! Hallelujah!" The response of the audience as a whole had become loudly emotional.

Nkrumah was embarrassed. But he was embarrassed because he was accompanied by a European friend he had met on board a ship from Liverpool. With the stereotyped "stiff-upper-lip" British culture for a background, Nkrumah had apparently assumed that all Europeans despised displays of emotion. In a sense he was accepting Senghor's categories of "Greek reason" and "black emotion"—and was ashamed of that "black emotion" in the Abyssinian Church because there was a white man there to witness it. Nkrumah tells us:

"It was very embarrassing. Here was a European witnessing a most undignified Negro service. As we left the Church I tried to apologise. . . ." [25].

But the young Dutchman, who had come back to America to complete his theological studies at the Harvard Divinity School, was apparently taken aback by Nkrumah's apology. He told Nkrumah that the service at the Abyssinian Church was the most beautiful thing he had seen in any church. "It was my turn to be astonished," Nkrumah relates.

Many years later, when he was back in the Gold Coast, a hymn sung at a touching moment in his early political career made Nkrumah weep in public. He was confronted by an excited crowd which wanted him to resign as Secretary-General of the old United Gold Coast Convention, dominated by lawyers, and form a more radical party of his own. "Resign!" the crowd shouted, "resign and lead us . . . !" Nkrumah suddenly felt that they meant it. He made up his mind to resign not only the secretary-generalship but also his membership of the United Gold Coast Convention. Standing on a platform, surrounded by an expectant crowd, he asked for a pen and a piece of paper and, using somebody's back as a support, he wrote out his official resignation and read it out to the people. Their enthusiasm was deafening. Then one of the women supporters jumped up on the platform and led the singing of the hymn "Lead Kindly Light." Nkrumah relates:

"What with the strain of it all and the excitement, the singing of this hymn was as much as I felt I could take. I covered my eyes with my handkerchief, a gesture which was followed by many others. . . . The impact of all this made me suddenly humble and lonely and the tears that came were shed not from sorrow but from a deep sense of gladness and dedication" [26].

From then on that memorable hymn was sung at many a rally of the new and dynamic Convention People's Party.

Yet it was not just Christian hymns that captured the mood of the new Africa; English poetry also played its part. Senghor talks about "Greek reason." He might also have mentioned the "gravest charge against poetry" made by the most rational of the Greeks—Plato's charge that poetry had "a terrible power to corrupt even the best characters" [27].

Plato himself was in favor of submitting poetry to a censorship "designed to expunge everything unsuitable to its educational purposes" [28]. But colonial powers in Africa in the nineteenth and twentieth centuries, though sensitive to "sedition" and "subversion," underestimated the political implications of those poetically expressed ideas that were scattered in their own literary classics. Among Nyerere's earliest publications was a pamphlet entitled *Barriers to Democracy*. This was in the days when he was still trying to organize Tanganyikans to fight for greater democratization in the territory. Nyerere appealed to his countrymen in Shakespearean terms, reminding them that:

"There is a tide in the affairs of men,
Which, taken at the flood, leads on to fortune;
Omitted, all the voyage of their life
Is bound in shadows and miseries.
On such a full sea we are now afloat;
And we must take the current when it serves,
Or lose our ventures."

Very few of his countrymen could, in fact, read the pamphlet, let alone understand the Shakespearean message. But his use of the passage is a measure of at least its impact on him. Perhaps some inchoate feeling in Nyerere had suddenly found coherence on contact with Shakespeare. Before closing his appeal to his countrymen Nyerere invokes one more line from Shakespeare: "Men at some time are masters of their fates."

Chief Obafemi Awolowo, the controversial founding father of the Yoruba wing of Nigerian nationalism, has been more specific in his acknowledgments. "Some of the mighty lines of Shakespeare must have influenced my outlook on life," Awolowo confided in his autobiography [29].

For Nkrumah in his formative years it was not so much Shakespeare as Tennyson who gave an exciting expression to some longing of his. In 1934 Nkrumah applied to the Dean of Lincoln University for admission. In his application he quoted from Tennyson's *In Memoriam*:

"So many worlds, so much to do,
So little done, such things to be."

In his autobiography Nkrumah says that this verse "was to me then, and it still is today, an inspiration and a spur. It fired within me a determination to equip myself for the service of my country" [30].

But it was not with Tennyson that Nkrumah opened and concluded the longest and "in some respects the most important speech" he made before Independence. The speech was made on November 12, 1956. He was asking the National Assembly to approve his Government's Revised Constitutional Proposals for Gold Coast Independence. Nkrumah opened his speech with a reference to Edmund Burke's remark: "We are on a conspicuous stage and the world marks our demeanour." Nkrumah asserted:

"Never has this been truer than today. How we conduct ourselves when we become independent will affect not only Ghana but the whole of Africa" [31].

He concluded his speech with Wordsworth's lines about the French Revolution. Nkrumah said: "I hope that some day, somewhere, we also may be able to say with William Wordsworth:

'*Bliss was it in that dawn to be alive,*
But to be young was very heaven!' " [32].

As for the relationship between literature and political parties, it lies in the fact that the genesis of some of the African political parties is some literary or cultural organization in the early days of African political consciousness. Nkrumah's own party, the CPP, is not directly descended from a literary group, but Nkrumah's first exercise in organization on leaving school was in organizing the Nzima Literature Society and other literary societies in the Axim area [33].

Not all the literary groups that gave birth to political organizations were preoccupied with English literature as such. Sometimes the impact of Western culture gave rise to a new possessiveness about the local culture—and associations emerged to serve the interests of a tribal or linguistic heritage of some local group. Thomas Hodgkin reminds us that the Action Group in Nigeria was born out of a Yoruba cultural association, inspired and created by Awolowo. As for the Northern People's Congress, the biggest Nigerian party, it was, on attainment of Independence, a recent offspring of a predominantly Hausa cultural society, the *Jami'a* [34].

Several reasons help explain why cultural organizations were part of the origins of political parties in Africa. One major reason was that cultural nationalism was often the earliest form of nationalism in an African colony. In the face of the new and powerful culture of the imperial power, a certain cultural defensiveness afflicted some of the more politically conscious Africans. This defensiveness took the form of either trying to emulate the Western cultural model or rebelling against that model by renewed interest in local African traditions. The emulative form of African cultural defensiveness manifested itself at times in literary contacts with the British Council, the formation of play-reading groups, and the development of ornate forms of English usage. The revivalist model of African cultural defensiveness included the formation of cultural organizations preoccupied with a new idealism about African traditions. It follows therefore that since the first forms of nationalism in much of Africa were cultural, and since political parties were themselves an outgrowth of the rise of nationalism in Africa, cultural organizations in many of the colonies became parents of political parties.

Another reason for these aesthetic roots of African political parties concerned the British doctrine that civil servants should not be engaged in politics. Many of the best educated and potential nationalist leaders in much of British Africa became, in fact, civil servants. The Government was after all the biggest employer of educated African manpower. These Africans were therefore faced with the choice of having to give up their jobs and join or form nationalist parties, keeping their jobs and withdrawing altogether from politics, or finding a "nonpolitical" outlet for their growing national consciousness. There were examples of all three responses. But where the African civil servants felt impelled to find a "nonpolitical" outlet for their national consciousness, a cultural organization was one important form of outlet. It did not too seriously endanger their careers, yet it gave them a useful institution of national assertiveness. But when more risks came to be taken later, more blatant political organizations came into being.

A third factor behind the formation of cultural organizations was that, in some cases, they were calculated to challenge the monopoly of traditional elders as custodians of local customs. There were occasions when the new cultural circles staged plays to satirize the more pompous ways of customary rulers. But in any case the new clubs were often simply trying to demonstrate that, given modern conditions, the best defenders of traditions were the educated Africans. And the best way of protecting tradition was to express it in modern ways. These arguments were sometimes almost echoes of the old Japanese slogan of modernization half a century earlier—"Japanese spirit, Western techniques." How could the pride of the Yoruba or the Baganda traditions be preserved? By a selective response to the Western impact. And by the utilization of the written word, the English language, and new modes of organization in defense of the local "cultural essence." Social clubs and discussion groups were therefore not merely an expression of cultural nationalism, but also an attempt by the newly educated to challenge the protective monopoly of more traditional custodians of that "cultural essence." Political parties later took over where these social clubs left off—challenging both the imperial power and the old traditional leaders.

In conclusion, we should reiterate that either directly or by kindling a new interest in local culture the imperial culture and its literature were part of the genesis of African political consciousness. In British Africa English literature was often the most politically provocative of the high culture imported by the imperial power. It inspired a paradoxical cultural nationalism among the original "scholars" of West African self-assertion. It yielded a rhetoric for use in those early moments of aggressive intellectualism. It afforded a new version of discourse by proverbs. It merged with the Bible and the poetry of Christian hymns to provide an additional stimulant to the emotional sensibilities of the new Africa. And it sometimes provided the rationale for an exercise in organizational and oratorical wit in those early formative years of African nationalism.

But it is in the nature of nationalism to be sparing in its acknowledgement of foreign inspiration. If it be asked why nationalism should be so inhibited, the answer may perhaps best be given by the Rhodesian nationalist Ndabaningi Sithole. His answer rests on the premise that nationalism has a strong component of sheer ambition—and his answer is directly Shakespearean. Why are the origins of African nationalism not acknowledged by the nationalists? Sithole quotes:

"But 'tis a common proof,
  That lowliness is young ambition's ladder
  Whereto the climber upward turns his face;
  But when he once attains the upmost round,
  He then unto the ladder turns his back,
  Looks in the coluds, scorning the base degrees
    by which he did ascend" [35].

NOTES

1. *The Somali Dispute,* New York: Frederick A. Praeger, 1964, p. 15.
2. "Somali Liberation Songs," *J. Modern African Studies,* 1(4), 505 (December 1963).
3. "Mankind instinctively takes language as the badge of nationality," one Westerner once claimed. See Edward A. Freeman, "Race and Language," *Historical Essays,* Third Series, London: Macmillan and Co., 1879, p. 203.
4. President's Address to the Tanganyika National Assembly, December 10, 1962, special publication, p. 21.
5. *Nationality in History and Politics,* London: Routledge and Kegan Paul (first edition 1944), 1951, p. 87.
6. *A Political History of Ghana,* Oxford: Clarendon Press, 1963, p. 510.
7. See James S. Coleman, *Nigeria, Background to Nationalism,* Los Angeles: University of California Press, 1958, p. 146.
8. "Onitsha Market Literature," *Transition,* 4(19, 2 —), 28–29, (1965).
9. *Ibid.,* p. 29. Soyinka's play in question is *The Lion and the Jewel.*
10. A speech given in November 1934 in Lagos. See *Zik, A Selection From the Speeches of Nnamdi Azikiwe,* Cambridge University Press, 1961, p. 23.
11. See *African Proverbs,* compiled by Charlotte and Wolf Leslau, Mt. Vernon, New York: Peter Pauper Press, 1962. Introductory page.
12. "Onitsha Market Literature," *op. cit.,* p. 31.
13. *Ibid.,* pp. 31–32.
14. *Ghana: The Autobiography of Kwame Nkrumah,* New York and Edinburgh: Nelson, 1957, p. 19.
15. *Ibid.,* p. 21.
16. *Ibid.,* p. 32.
17. *Ibid.,* p. 41.
18. *Nigeria, op. cit.,* pp. 114–115.
19. For a sensitive sociopolitical analysis of this kind of phenomenon see David E. Apter, "Political Religion in New Nations," in Clifford Geertz (ed.), *Old Societies and New States,* New York, Free Press, 1964.
20. See, for example, Nkrumah, *I Speak of Freedom, A Statement of African Ideology,* New York: Frederick A. Praeger, 1961, pp. 90–91.
21. "Massianism and Nationalism in Black Africa," translated by Pierre L. van den Berghe from an article from *Cahiers Internationaux de Sociologie* 14, 41–65 (1953). See Van den Berghe, *Africa: Social Problems of Change and Conflict,* San Francisco, Cal.: Chandler Publishing Co., 1965, p. 460.

22. See Sithole, *African Nationalism*, London: Oxford University Press, 1959. See also Sithole's article, "African Nationalism and Christianity," *Transition*, 4(10), (September 1963).

23. L. S. Senghor, *Negritude et humanisme*, Paris: Seuil, 1964, p. 24.

24. Senghor, *On African Socialism*, London, 1964, p. 74.

25. *Autobiography, op. cit.*, p. 28.

26. *Ibid.*, pp. 107–108.

27. This rendering is from the Penguin Classics' edition of *The Republic*, Book X ("The Effects of Poetry and Drama"), London, 1963, p. 383.

28. Michael B. Foster, *Masters of Political Thought*, Vol. 1, London: George G. Harap, 1961 (reprint), p. 62.

29. "Shakespeare is my favourite. I have read all his plays, and have reread some of them—like *Julius Caesar, Hamlet, The Tempest, Anthony and Cleopatra* and *Henry V*—more than three times. Some of the mighty lines of Shakespeare must have influenced my outlook on life." See *Awo, The Autobiography of Chief Obafemi Awolowo*, Cambridge University Press, 1960, p. 70.

30. *Autobiography, op. cit.*, p. v.

31. *I Speak of Freedom, op. cit.*, p. 71.

32. *Ibid.*, The Italics are Nkrumah's.

33. "The Nzima Literature Society . . . is still functioning today," Nkrumah tells us in his autobiography two decades after he formed it. See *Autobiography, op. cit.*, p. 21.

34. See Hodgkin, *Nationalism in Colonial Africa* (first published in 1956), New York: New York University Press, 1957, esp. pp. 154–155.

35. *Julius Caesar*, II, I. Quoted by Ndabaningi Sithole in his book *African Nationalism* (first published 1959), London: Oxford University Press, 1961 (reprint), p. 57. We have referred to James Coleman's remark that in a colonial school "Shakespeare and the Bible held the stage." What Sithole was concerned with in this particular chapter was the influence of the Bible and the Church on the growth of African nationalism. This point is discussed in similar terms in my book *The Anglo-African Commonwealth* (Pergamon Press, 1967).

John N. Paden

LANGUAGE PROBLEMS OF NATIONAL INTEGRATION IN NIGERIA: THE SPECIAL POSITION OF HAUSA

Ethnolinguistic pluralism has been at the base of Nigerian political life since amalgamation in 1914. A colonial policy of indirect rule encapsulated this pluralism within administrative boundaries which, with the rise of modern politics and the achievement of independence, demarcated the internal political units of a federal and regional structure. The failure to integrate these units into a national unity may have been partly responsible for the military coup in January 1966, with its resultant experiment in centralization, and for the countercoup in July 1966, with its resultant decentralization [1].

The considerable difficulties of Nigerian national integration have overshadowed a political phenomenon, which in turn has helped to create the instability of Nigerian Federalism: the political integration of "Northern Nigeria" from a diverse collection of ethnolinguistic units to a political block able to dominate all other regions of Nigeria. The creation of a lingua franca, Hausa, has substantially aided Northern political integration. The creation of a "Northern" language area has added a new dimension to the already close relationship between political structure and linguistic units [2]. This essay [3] attempts to evaluate the role of the Hausa language as it has been functional or dysfunctional to regional and national integration in Nigeria.

The political integration of a national unit is primarily concerned with the horizontal linkage [4] of social subsystems, which in most cases are ethnic groups [5]. Ethnicity is usually regarded as a major obstacle to horizontal integration in a plural society [6]. Integration theory usually posits the primacy of political parties as the mechanism of linkage [7] and the function of a federal structure as providing checks and balances on the component subsystems of a partially integrated national system [8]. Within this context, language is usually regarded in two ways: as a major mechanism of social communication between subsystems [9], and as the

199

mechanism of expressing values, culture, and "ethnicity" within a sub-system [10]. An integrating national system requires an extension of bi-lingualism [11] or the supercession of one language by another. In most newly independent African states the language of horizontal integration has been a European language.

Northern Nigeria, with an official population of 29 million, has formed the largest integral political unit in Africa. The communication system of this political unit was significant in several respects: (a) the language of political integration was an indigenous African language (Hausa); (b) this language served as an official administrative language within the region; (c) until recently, this language served as the basis of the educational system and literacy program of the region; (d) between the various tradi-tional sectors, Hausa served as a medium of social and commercial com-munication. Hausa has proven exceptionally flexible and adaptive as a lingua franca, and it is unique among the Nigerian languages in that it serves as a major medium of communication outside of its particular area of ethnic origin.

The Hausa language is spoken by three distinct groups in Northern Nigeria: (a) the original Hausa ethnic group; (b) those who have "become Hausa" by various processes of assimilation; (c) those who are "non-Hausa" but who use Hausa as a second, third, or fourth language.

From the tenth century to the fifteenth Hausaland consisted of only seven major Habe city-states [12]. Today the boundaries of this original Hausaland are limited to the Northwest corner of Nigeria and the south-ern rim of Niger Republic stretching from Zinder in Dogonduchi. Dia-lects of Hausa developed in the various areas of Hausaland: Sakkwatanci (Sokoto), Gobirci (Gobir), Adrarci (Adrar), Kananci (Kano), Katsinanci (Katsina), and Zazzaganci (Zaria). Because of its commercial importance, the Kano dialect formed a proto-lingua franca along Sudanic trade routes even before the colonial era.

During the colonial period (1900–1960), "Hausa" became a linguistic classification rather than an ethnic classification. According to the 1952 Census: "The Hausa are simply a linguistic group consisting of those who speak the Hausa language as their mother tongue and do not claim Fulani descent, and including a wide variety of stocks and physical types" [13]. With this broadened definition, the 1952 Census listed the following ethnolinguistic distribution in Northern Nigeria: Hausa, 32.6 per cent; Fulani, 18.0 per cent; Kanuri, 7.8 per cent; Tiv, 4.6 per cent; Yoruba, 3.2 per cent; Nupe, 2.1 per cent; plus over 200 miscellaneous ethnic groups which constituted about 30 per cent of the population [14]. Many of these smaller groups have been increasingly assimilated into "Hausa" culture.

As a lingua franca outside of Northern Nigeria, Hausa is understood over a wide area. According to R. C. Abraham:

"Hausa is spoken as far north as Agades, and Hausa-speakers are met with even at Tamanrasset in the Hoggar. In the east it is well known to the Kanuri of Bornu and in Fort Lamy. Hausa is spoken in the northwest of Nigeria and beyond: in fact, many speak it in Timbuktu. . . . It is becoming more and more understood every day by the Yoruba, Ibo and other Southern Nigerians." [15].

According to A. Kirk-Greene:

". . . For the last few years it has been the turn of Hausa, the lingua franca not only of Northern Nigeria, but of some twenty million people spread across West Africa for whom it is either their mother, secondary, or communication language" [16].

Unfortunately, Nigerian census figures do not reflect the number of persons who speak or understand Hausa as a secondary language, and there have been no published studies along this line. If the 1963 Nigerian Census figure of 55 million is indicative of the total Nigerian population, those who can understand Hausa probably number 20 million in northern Nigeria, 5 million in southern Nigeria, and 10 million persons outside Nigeria, for an overall total of 35 million [17]. In two countries, Niger Republic and Nigeria, Hausa people form the major ethnolinguistic group.

Hausa seems to have several characteristics that have facilitated its use as a lingua franca in Nigeria and West Africa. Although of Chado-Hamitic origins [18] and partially influenced by neighboring vernacular languages such as Kanuri [19], the vocabulary has been heavily influenced by Arabic [20]. On matters of religion, government, trade, and law there has developed in the Hausa urban centers a "classical" Hausa in which as much as 30 per cent of the vocabulary items are direct corruptions of Arabic. Throughout the Islamic portions of West Africa, the Arabic content of Hausa would probably have aided comprehension among traders, mallams, and administrators.

Second, the Hausa language has been able to incorporate European vocabulary for "modern" sector items. This process of creating neologisms began at an earlier stage for Hausa than for many African languages because early European administrators in Northern Nigeria did much of their work in the Hausa language [21]. Consequently, Hausa is able to deal with patent medicine, "Western democracy" and nuclear devices.

In addition, the Hausa language is capable of being rendered both on a simple and on a sophisticated level. A pidgin-Hausa (or "market" Hausa) has developed, comparable to pidgin English, which may be responsible for Hausa's reputation as an "easy" language. On the other hand, the 60,000 item dictionary by Bargery [22] is now estimated to represent only about 50 per cent of the Hausa language [23]. Western linguists have long recognized the complexity of Hausa [24]. A precolonial written literature flourished in Hausa [25], adding the richness of a time dimension to contemporary writings in that language.

Finally, mechanisms have been provided for the standardization of Hausa. In the early 1930s, a Hausa Translation Bureau was established, which was superceded by the North Region Literature Agency (NORLA) and, in 1955, by the Hausa Language Board [26]. Such an early standardization of language was probably unique in both English- and French-speaking West Africa.

More recently the function of standardization and extension of the Hausa language has also been undertaken outside of Nigeria, by various Hausa broadcasting services [27] (notably the BBC-London and Radio Ghana) and by contract with the School of Oriental and African Studies, London.

Yet whatever the natural or artificial propensities of a language, the creation of an administrative lingua franca or a "national language" is ultimately a matter of political decision. In Northern Nigeria this decision was made very early by the colonial regime and was confirmed in the independence period by Northern politicians.

Colonial administration in Northern Nigeria was based on the premise of indirect rule. The linguistic concomitant of this policy was that "Native Authority" areas were administered in vernacular languages. British Residents and District Officers as "advisers" to the N.A.'s were given financial and professional incentives to learn the vernacular of their area [28]. In order to standardize procedure, Hausa administrative terminology was employed frequently even in non-Hausa areas. In the "Native Courts" throughout the north, Hausa terms also tended to supplement local vernacular. The Northern Council of Chiefs, created in 1930, was the first regional political body in Northern Nigeria. Most of the speeches were in Hausa, although summaries were printed in English. Later, with the formation of the Northern House of Assembly and Northern House of Chiefs, Hausa and English were given equal status as "official languages." There has been occasional political support for making Hausa the sole official language of Northern Nigeria [29].

Colonial policy toward education was designed to reinforce the use of vernacular languages. In this process the Hausa language received the major portion of colonial resources, and came to underlie the educational system. By 1912 textbooks on geography, arithmetic, and hygiene had been printed in Hausa [30]. In the British House of Commons this policy was defended as a unique experiment in colonial education [31]. The first Director of Education in Northern Nigeria, Hanns Vischer, declared that the purpose of the educational system was to educate:

". . . without, if possible, in any way damaging their racial feeling or separating them from their parents or their surroundings. . . . The general instruction is to be given in Hausa. . . . The technical instruction is intended to produce efficient artisans not dependent on European machinery . . ." [32].

Until the 1930s most of the education in Northern Nigeria was centered in the far north. According to D. H. Williams,

"Up to this time the pagan areas had been neglected, not for lack of desire, but mainly through difficulties of language. The pagan areas were inhabited by about 200 different tribes, nearly all of which spoke different languages, or at least different dialects. . . . The most important need [in the 1930s] was a training centre for teachers who could open schools in the pagan areas, where, having themselves been taught in Hausa, they could teach in their own tongue, and introduce Hausa as a lingua franca" [33].

A government report of 1928 had recommended the use of vernacular in schools up to the secondary level. According to D. H. Williams,

"The problem of a lingua franca for Northern Nigeria had for long been a matter of deep concern to the authorities, because in quite large areas Hausa was as much a foreign tongue as was English. The production of literature in many languages was of course financially impossible, even had written languages existed. . . . Even to produce literature in the more commonly spoken languages was not to be thought of, because of cost and the lack of staff to do the work. An excellent opportunity to make English a widely spoken second language was at this time passed over. . . . The recommendations of the Home Government laid it down that English should only be taught as a second, and in the case of Northern Nigeria, a third language. The others were to be respectively: the vernacular [which usually meant Hausa] and Arabic, with English as supplementary language for later study. This is now recognised to be a mistake" [34].

The first modification of policy was in the 1950s when English was introduced in elementary schools. Meanwhile, voluntary agency schools in the non-Muslim areas of the North were producing an increasing number of English-speaking school leavers. Yet by 1952, the percentage of population (seven years and over) with four years of elementary school was still negligible (0.9 per cent), and with only minimal variation between provinces [35]:

Adamawa	0.7%	Kano	0.5%
Bauchi	0.8	Katsina	0.5
Benue	0.9	Niger	1.0
Bornu	0.4	Plateau	2.4
Ilorin	2.9	Sokoto	0.5
Kabba	1.9	Zaria	3.0

Between 1952 and 1961 in the Middle Belt provinces the percentage of children attending elementary school increased rapidly [36], and English became the medium of instruction. In government elementary schools (until the present time), however, the first four years were taught in vernacular. In 1952, an adult literacy program (*Yaki da Jahilci*) was begun by the Northern government in vernacular languages, mainly Hausa. Meanwhile, a few schools for "sons of chiefs" [37] had produced a very small English-speaking elite from among the Hausa-Fulani populations.

Three major conclusions may be drawn from this education pattern: (a) literacy in Northern Nigeria referred primarily to literacy in Hausa (whether in Roman script or Arabic script) and not to English; (b) the number of those literate in either Hausa or English was a small fraction of the total population; (c) by the 1950s, English had begun to be used as an educational lingua franca in the Middle Belt area.

In 1950, however, "modern" politics were introduced to Northern Nigeria and political parties were created, mainly as a counterbalance to Southern-based political parties. The English-speaking Hausa-Fulani elite was coopted into this political process. Their power base lay in the Hausa-speaking areas of the far north. At first the prospect of independence stirred up ethnolinguistic separatism throughout the North, especially in the Kanuri areas of Bornu, and among the Tiv, Yoruba, and other Middle Belt groups [38]. When the British government decided in 1958 that no new regions were to be created [39], the die was cast. For various reasons Northern political power lay in the Hausa-Fulani areas. This power sought to consolidate itself in the Northern Region through a policy of "northernization," with the Hausa language as a principal medium of political communication [40], just as English was being used in the south of Nigeria.

On the federal level in 1958 and 1959 the flush of excitement preceding independence stirred discussion of an indigenous national language [41], as it had done in other colonial countries [42]. During the federal election of 1959, language became a political issue in the North. In an effort toward national unification the Northern Elements Progressive Union (NEPU) campaigned to "introduce compulsory teaching of the three principal languages of Nigeria in schools" [43]. In reply the Northern Peoples Congress (NPC) issued a statement reported as follows:

"If any of the native languages should become an official language of Nigeria, the statement went on, it was plain common sense that there was no better choice than Hausa, which is spoken and understood by the majority of the 18 million people of the Northern Region as well as in the other parts of the Federation of Nigeria and in other countries of West Africa. The Action Group, the statement continued, by proposing the three principal languages of this country was deliberately seeking to destroy the idea of oneness which the Northern Peoples Congress has been striving to foster. . . . The Action Group, the statement revealed, had accused the Northern Government during the Minority Commission at Jos, that the Northern Ministry of Education was 'forcing' school children of non-Hausa origin to learn and speak Hausa in schools. By attempting now to introduce the teaching of Hausa, Ibo and Yoruba in our school curriculum, and by recommending these languages as media of expression in the country's legislatures, the Action Group was not endeavouring to make the country's language problem any easier . . ." [44].

After independence, the debate as to a Nigerian lingua franca was submerged in regional competition for federal power, and all sides seemed to agree temporarily that there was no need to force the issue of an indigenous national language [45].

Yet in the North the most direct means to federal power lay in regional unity. On a population basis the northern region had been allocated 50 per cent of the seats in federal Parliament. This reinforced the necessity for regional consolidation and "northernization."

The premise and hope of northernization was, in the words of the Northern Premier: "The North is one. The North is an indivisible entity" [46]. As a political means of unifying the North, the full economic power of the region was geared to render preferential treatment to those whose ancestral homes were within the boundaries of the region. Only those born in the North could buy land, and certain jobs were restricted to Northerners [47]. Despite accusations from Eastern Nigerian groups [48], the impact of northernization was as great on expatriate firms as on non-Northern Nigerians. Much of the ground nut marketing industry, economic backbone of the North, was transferred from Europeans and Lebanese to Northerners, through political restrictions and licensing. On the administrative level, civil service regulations prevented both Southern Nigerians and expatriates from signing more than short-term contracts. To fill the manpower gap many persons from the Middle Belt with education in English were coopted into the better-paying positions. The Middle Belt, particularly Kabba Province, gained considerably from the northernization policy.

Yet northernization was more than a system of economic and administrative preferences. It stemmed from a deep cultural defensiveness on the part of the Hausa-Fulani north, and such matters as education and literacy were central. According to the Premier of the North, the late Alhaji Ahmadu Bello, Sardauna of Sokoto,

"One thing that I cannot lose sight of is that [persons] have called Northerners ignorant. Some people say they are tired of being ruled by ignorant people. . . . I do not like the word ignorant. An ignorant person is one who cannot understand anything. If Northerners were to discard Western knowledge and the Ibos were to discard their Western

knowledge, which of the two would be able to write in any other system?
. . . In every Division, in every corner of this Region, if you go around,
you will find people who can read and write in Arabic. This has been so
long before the British came . . ." [49].

This cultural defensiveness was partly a religious issue. In 1961 there
were 11 times as many Koranic schools in the North as there were Western elementary schools [50], and literacy in Arabic was probably higher
throughout the region than was literacy in English [51]. During the 1950s
and 1960s there was a renaissance of Islamic organizations in the North,
many of which heavily emphasized literacy in Arabic and Hausa. Northern printing presses, both public and private, began publishing bilingual
(Hausa-Arabic) books on all subjects. The various Islamic conversion
campaigns in the Middle Belt clearly linked Islamic culture with Hausa
culture, and an increasing number of villages and areas there became
assimilated into "the Northern system," of which the Hausa language was
central. Radio Kaduna broadcast more in Hausa than in English. Both
political parties (NPC and NEPU) printed most of their literature in
Hausa. Political rallies, by the time of the 1964 federal election, were usually conducted in Hausa. Middle Belt Christians, especially in the civil
service, frequently changed their "Christian" names to a Hausa equivalent [e.g., Jacob tó Yakubu, David to Daud, Solomon to Suleimanu, Isaac
to Ishaq).

Meanwhile the regional government in Kaduna had been systematically weakening the powers of the Native Authority system, always a
potential source of ethnolinguistic separatism. Legal and political power
was centralized in Kaduna [52]. The overwhelming victory, by whatever
means, of the Northern government party in the 1964 federal elections
seemed both to vindicate the policy of northernization and to demonstrate to other regions of the federation that for the next five years, and
possibly for an indefinite period, they would be dominated by the North.
Out of this frustration a Southern-inspired *coup d'état* was successfully
undertaken on January 15, 1966, in which the principal casualty was
the Premier of the Northern Region.

During the first five years of Nigerian independence the impasse of
national integration was evident to all, and it has been substantially
documented [53]. With the new military regime of General Aguiyi-Ironsi,
certain dramatic steps were undertaken to promote national integration,
including the abolition of the federal form of government. In attempting
to effectuate a unitary form of government, the most significant single
policy was the attempt at horizontal integration of the various "modern"
sectors, particularly the civil service. The premise of this policy seemed to
be that the components of a horizontally integrated civil service would
retain their vertical linkage with the various ethnolinguistic sectors. For
example, the chief civil servant (Military Governor) of the "Northern

Group of Provinces" was the son of a traditional Emir. The implicit assumption in this policy was that the language of the modern sectors was English, and that English was to be the language of horizontal integration. Given the policy of intended mobility within the civil service, Nigerians who might not have spoken Hausa could have been transferred to administrative positions in the North, which had traditionally been administered not in English but in Hausa. The language aspect of this policy was never publicly articulated, but the implications of substituting English for Hausa as the language of local government was not lost on Northern administrative cadres, many of whom would have been less competitive in English than Southern Nigerians. The countercoup of July 29, supported by Northern officers, put an end to the experiment of civil service integration. Its most notable effect was the fragmentation of the Nigerian army along ethnolinguistic lines. Subsequently, representatives of the original regions met at Lagos to consider whether any basis existed for interregional political linkage.

In the continuing constitutional deliberations language problems are likely to be submerged under more general problems of ethnic pluralism. Yet the issue remains of whether the Hausa language, as an existing lingua franca, may not still be useful as an integrative factor, even though it has become identified with the "regionalism" of the *ancien régime*. Hausa still remains the only indigenous Nigerian language that has been instrumental in effectuating political integration within a context of complex ethnic pluralism. It has done this in the nineteenth century on an emirate level and in the twentieth century on a regional level.

Yet this impressive performance of the Hausa language is complicated in that intervertical integration is not the only desired goal. In addition, an intravertical (i.e., mass-elite) integration is sought which would not only link the traditional and modern sectors but provide a channel for modernization. In this Hausa culture reflects a basic ambiguity toward modernization, although the language itself may be regarded as neutral.

In any case, the primary requisite for a transition from traditional sectors to a modern sector is social communication. It is noteworthy that in Niger Republic, after considerable effort in trying to promote mass literacy in the French language, a large-scale experiment is now underway to foster mass literacy in vernacular languages, especially Hausa [54]. What is even more apparent is that goals of modernization, such as economic development, are largely contingent upon a prior delimitation of political community. This again raises the issue of horizontal integration.

Political mechanisms of horizontal integration will depend upon the particular variables in a given state, of which the language situation is one. In Northern Nigeria a vernacular language, Hausa, was in the process of becoming the lingua franca of a community extending beyond the confines of the original ethnic group. If it is decided that Nigerian national unity requires the imposition of English as the sole language of horizontal integration, some reassessment of the special position of Hausa is in order. As a beginning, social scientists might do well to study in perspective how this indigenous language became the lingua franca, and the present extent to which social communication is conducted in that language.

NOTES

1. At present the constitutional future of Nigeria is still unclear, although it appears to be going in the direction of loose confederation.

2. *Nigeria: Report of the Commission Appointed to Inquire into the Fears of Minorities and the Means of Allaying Them,* July 1958, HMSO Cmnd. 505.

   More recently Chief Obafemi Awolowo, on his release from prison (August 1966), enunciated four principles in drawing up a constitution: (a) "If a country is unilingual and uninational the constitution must be unitary." (b) "If a country is unilingual or bilingual or multilingual, and also consists of communities which, over a period of years, have developed divergent nationalities, the constitution must be federal, and the constituent states must be organized on the dual basis of language and nationality." (c) "If a country is bilingual or multilingual the constitution must be federal, and the constituent states must be organized on linguistic basis." (d) Any experiment with a unitary constitution in a bilingual or multilingual or multinational country must fall in the long run." Excerpts from: *Thoughts on Nigerian Constitution,* London: Oxford University Press, 1966; quoted in *New Nigerian,* August 6, 1966, p. 12.

3. The interpretations of this paper are not intended to be technical in theory or in content, and have not been researched specifically for this paper. Portions of this material stem from 18 months' field research in Nigeria (1964–1965), supported by the Foreign Area Fellowship Program.

4. In this paper "vertical" and "horizontal" descriptions of social structure will be used in the manner commonly accepted by anthropologists. "Vertical" thus refers to family, clan, or ethnic solidarity: "horizontal" refers to any trans-ethnic bond of interest or loyalty, including religious, political, or economic.

5. See C. Geertz, "The Integrative Revolution: Primordial Sentiments and Civil Politics in the New States," in Geertz (ed.), *Old Societies and New States,* New York: Free Press, 1963, pp. 105–58; P. E. Jacob and J. V. Toscano, *The Integration of Political Communities,* Philadelphia, Pa.: Lippincott, 1965; J. S. Coleman, "The Problem of Political Integration in Emergent Africa," *Western Political Quarterly,* 8, 44–58 (March 1955); K. W. Deutsch, "The Growth of Nations: Some Recurrent Patterns of Political and Social Integration," *World Politics,* 5, 168–195 (Jan. 1953); M. G. Smith, "Social and Cultural Pluralism," *Annals of the New York Academy of Sciences,* 83, art. 5, 763–85 (Jan. 20, 1960); Ali A. Mazrui, "Pluralism and National Integration," 28 pp. unpublished manuscript.

6. For qualifications to this statement, see I. Wallerstein, "Ethnicity and National Integration in West Africa," *Cahiers d'Etudes Africanes,* No. 3, pp. 129–39 (Oct. 1960); R. L. Sklar, "The Contribution of Tribalism to Nationalism in Western Nigeria," *J. Human Relations,* 8, 407–415 (1960).

7. See J. S. Coleman and C. G. Rosberg (eds.), *Political Parties and National Integration in Tropical Africa,* California, 1964; R. Emerson, "Parties and National

Integration in Africa," in La Palombara and Weiner (eds.), *Political Parties and Political Development,* Princeton, N.J.: Princeton University Press, 1966, pp. 267–302; G. M. Carter (ed.), *National Unity and Regionalism in Eight African States,* Ithaca, N.Y.: Cornell University Press, 1966; K. W. Deutsch and W. Foltz, *Nation-Building,* New York, 1963; S. Rokkan, "Electoral Mobilization, Party Competition, and National Integration," La Palombara and Weiner, *op. cit.,* pp. 241–266.

8. For theoretical discussions of federalism within the Nigerian context, see B. J. Dudley, "Federalism and the Balance of Political Power in Nigeria," *J. Commonwealth Pol. Stud.,* 55, (1) 16–29 (March 1966); J. P. Mackintosh, "Federalism in Nigeria," 10 *Political Studies,* 1962; Lionel Brett (ed.), *Constitutional Problems of Federalism in Nigeria,* Times Press, Lagos, 1961; L. F. Blitz (ed.), *The Politics and Administration of Nigerian Government,* New York: Praeger, 1965; *Proposals for the Constitution of the Federal Republic of Nigeria* (adopted by the All Party Constitutional Conference held in Lagos on July 25, 26, 1963), GPL, sessional paper, no. 3, 1963; *The Constitution of Northern Nigeria Law,* GPL, 1963; E. O. Awa, *Federal Government in Nigeria,* Berkeley: University of California Press, 1964; O. I. Odumosu, *The Nigerian Constitution, History and Development,* Sweet and Maxwell, 1963. For a listing of official documents relating to the federal constitution, see Frederick Schwarz, Jr., *Nigeria, The Tribes, and Nation, or the Race,* Cambridge: M.I.T. Press, 1965, p. 299.

9. See K. W. Deutsch, *Nationalism and Social Communications: An Inquiry into the Foundations of Nationality,* New York: Wiley, 1953.

10. See W. M. Watt, *Islam and the Integration of Society,* London, 1961.

11. For preliminary discussions of bilingualism within the Nigerian context, see L. F. Brosnahan, "Bilingualism and Society in Nigeria," *Proceedings of the Third Annual Conference of the West African Institute of Social and Economic Research* (March, 1954), NISER, 1963, pp. 82–89. T. Kellaghan, "Some Implications of Bilingualism for Education in Nigeria," *Ibadan,* Number 11, pp. 31–33 (Feb. 1961).

12. See M. G. Smith, "The Beginnings of Hausa Society, A.D. 1000–1500," in J. Vansina and R. Mauny (eds.), *The Historian in Tropical Africa,* OUP, 1964, pp. 339–357. A. Kirk-Greene and J. S. Hogben, *The Emirates of Northern Nigeria,* OUP, 1965. There is a large amount of material published on Hausa history: E. J. Arnett, "A Hausa Chronicle," *JRAFS,* IX, 161–167; J. H. Greensberg, "Some Aspects of Negro-Mohammedan Culture Contact Among the Hausa," *Man. NS,* XLIII, 51–61 (1941); A. Mischlich, "Contribution to the History of the Hausa States," *J. Af. S.* 4(14), 455–457 (July 1905); D. A. Olderogge, "The Origins of the Hausa Language," paper presented at the VI International Congress of Anthropological and Ethnological Sciences. pub. Moscow, 1956, 28 pp.; C. W. Orr, "The Hausa Race," *J. Af. S.,* 7 (L907–7, PP278–283); M. G. Smith, "Field Histories Among the Hausa," *J. Af. H.,* 2 (1), 87–101 (1961). For unpublished material on Hausa history see Palmer Collection, Numbers 168 (Hausa origins), 180 (Origins of the Hausa), 179 (Bagauda-Bayaiidda); CHEAM files, 1299 (A Hausa population, The Gobirawa), 812 (The Hausa in Zinder).

13. Department of Statistics, *Population Census of the Northern Region of Nigeria, 1952,* Gaskiya Corporation, p. 13.

14. *Ibid.* Also see C. K. Meek, *Tribal Studies in Northern Nigeria,* London: Kegan Paul, Trench, Trubner, 1931, 633 pp.; C. K. Meek, *The Northern Tribes of Nigeria, An Ethnographical Account of the Northern Provinces of Nigeria,* OUP, 2, pp. 311 and 273 (1925); C. L. Temple, *Notes on the Tribes of Northern Nigeria,* Lagos, CMS, 1922.

15. R. C. Abraham, *Dictionary of the Hausa Language,* ULP 1962, p. iii.

16. A. H. M. Kirk-Greene, "The Hausa Language Board," *Africa und Übersee,* Band 47, 1964, p. 188.

17. This is an impressionistic judgment based on recent travel through most of the major towns of Nigeria, and meetings with Hausa-speaking communities in Niger Republic, Senegal, and Ghana, plus the major cities of coastal West Africa. There are, reportedly, about one million Hausa speakers in the Republic of Sudan. A basic problem in these estimates is the reliability of population statistics, and the complete lack of census data on multilingualism. An unpublished BBC (London) survey of Hausa listeners in West Africa roughly confirms the estimate given in this paper. However, with the widespread use of transistor radios, and the increasing number of Hausa broadcasting facilities, this figure is likely to increase faster than in the past.

18. See D. Westermann and M. A. Bryan, *The Languages of West Africa,* 1952. J. Greenberg, *Studies in African Linguistic Classification,* New Haven, Conn.: Yale Univ. Press, 1955. R. C. Abraham, *The Language of the Hausa People,* ULP 1959. W. Leslau, "A Prefix h in Egyptian, Modern South Arabian, and Hausa," *Africa,* **32,** No. 1 pp. 65ff. (Jan. 1962).

19. J. Greenberg, "Linguistic Evidence for the Influence of the Kanuri on the Hausa," *J. Af. Hist.,* 1(2), 2–12 (1960).

20. J. H. Greenberg, "Arabic Loan-Words in Hausa," *Word,* **3,** 85–97 (1947). Arabic has also, of course, influenced Hausa names. See A. H. M. Kirk-Greene, *A Preliminary Inquiry into Hausa Onomatology,* Zaria, 1963.

21. One of the earliest studies of neologisms was by R. M. East, "Modern Tendencies in the Languages of Northern Nigeria: The Problem of European Words." *Africa,* 10(1) (J.an 1937). East writes: "The genius of the Hausa language is, and apparently always has been, especially adapted to absorb foreign words" (p. 99). Also see A. H. M. Kirk-Greene, "Neologisms in Hausa: A Sociological Approach," *Africa,* 1963; F. W. Parsons, "Some Observations on the Contact between Hausa and English," Inter-African Committee on Linguistics (Brazzaville, 1962). For an example of neologisms, see M. J. Campbell, *A Word List of Government and Local Government Terms,* Kaduna: English-Hausa, n.d. Also, *Hausa Language Board, Alphabetical List of Words Imported into Hausa,* Kaduna: Baraka Press, n.d.

22. G. P. Bargery, *A Hausa-English Dictionary and English-Hausa Vocabulary,* 1934. For biographical sketch of Bargery, see *Nigerian Citizen,* March 28, 1959, p. 6.

23. Interview with C. Sanderson, 1964, Kano. Sanderson was Bargery's successor at the British and Foreign Bible Society, and was responsible for the revision of the Hausa translation of the New Testament. According to R. East, who established the Hausa translation bureau: "Hausa is the easiest of languages to acquire up to a point, but the final stages are so difficult that they have never yet been mastered by us." *Language Examinations,* SIM 1938, p. 118.

24. The record of European scholarship on Hausa linguistics dates from Schon's work in the 1850s. The formation of the Hausa Association by Robinson in the 1890s is the beginning of British predominance in the field of Hausa linguistic studies which has continued to the present time, especially at the School of Oriental and African Studies. Hausa has been taught and studied in the Soviet Union since 1934. (For full account of Russian Hausa studies see *Nigerian Citizen,* April 11, 1964, p. 14.) For a fuller indication of works on Hausa linguistics, see M. de Lavergne de Tressan, *Inventaire Linguistique de L'Afrique Occidentale Française et du Togo,* Ifan-Dakar, M. Ifan, No 30, pp. 59–67, (1953). (169 bibliographical entries are listed for Hausa although all of an earlier vintage).

25. See C. H. Robinson, *Specimens of Hausa Literature,* Cambridge University Press, 1896; M. Hiskett, "Song of Bagauda," *BSOAS,* **27,** part 3, 540–567 (1964); J. N. Paden, "Kano Hausa Poetry," *Kano Studies,* No. 1, 33–39 (Sept. 1965); J. N. Paden, "Kano Hausa Poetry," *Kano Studies* No. 2 (Sept. 1966); Center of Arabic Documentation, "Sifofin Shehu: An Autobiography and Character Study of Uthman

b. Fudi in Verse," (Hausa), *Research Bulletin,* 2(1), 1–38 (Jan. 1966); J. H. Green-berg, "Hausa Verse Prosody," *J. Amer. Oriental Soc.,* **69,** 125–35 (1949); R. C. Abraham, *Hausa Literature and Hausa Sound System, ULP* 1959.

26. The attempt to standardize Hausa began in 1910 with Hanns Vischer, Director of Education, Northern Nigeria: see "Rules for Hausa Spelling" *J. Royal Afr. Soc.* (April 1912). Bargery's Dictionary was a major attempt at standardizing the language; see D. Westermann, "A Standard Hausa Dictionary," *Africa,* 102, (3), 371–374 (July 1934). Also see NORLA, *Hause Spelling,* Gaskiya Corporation, 1958, according to which: "The Kano dialect is used in all cases; except (a) when a word is peculiar to Kano City, and there is another word in existence which has a wide distribution; (b) where the Kano terminations lead to ambiguity or increased difficulty of reading . . . ," p. 1. For full details of the Hausa Language Board, see Kirk-Greene, "Hausa Language Board," *loc. cit.*

27. Interviews, BBC, London, February 1964, October 1965. Interviews, Radio Ghana, September 1965. As an example of how new words are created, see *A Simple Guide to Modern Hausa Equivalents,* mimeographed by the BBC London, 1965. BBC London has a staff of about nine Hausa linguists, and Radio Ghana has had a staff of about seven Hausa linguists.

28. See R. East, *Language Examinations in the Northern Provinces of Nigeria,* S.I.M. 1938. Also, NORLA, *Government Hausa Examinations,* 1949–58, Zaria, 1958. It is not surprising that many of the outstanding contemporary Hausa linguists were former administrative officers. Most officers who took the language exams did so in Hausa. According to East (*op. cit.,* p. 9): "about 95% of the examinations in the Northern Provinces are taken in that Hausa language."

29. See Kirk-Greene, *Hausa Language Board, op. cit.,* p. 189.

30. D. H. Williams, *A Short Survey of Education in Northern Nigeria,* Ministry of Education, Northern Region of Nigeria, 1959, p. 12.

31. According to the Under-Secretary of State for the Colonies, in the British House of Commons (1917): "If honourable members look into a system of education like that of Northern Nigeria, they will find one of the most remarkable developments that has ever taken place under British rule. . . . There is an extraordinarily interesting development taking place in Northern Nigeria." Quoted, *ibid.,* p. 18.

32. Quoted *ibid.,* p. 19.

33. *Ibid.,* p. 26.

34. *Ibid.,* p. 34.

35. 1952 Census, *op. cit.,* Table 7, pp. 30–31.

36. In 1961 the percentage of children (ages 6–12) enrolled in primary schools was as follows (by Province):

Kaduna	35.4%	Adamawa	7.0%
Kabba	27.6	Niger	6.6
Ilorin	24.2	Bauchi	5.4
Plateau	18.9	Sardauna	5.1
Benue	18.0	Kano	3.7
Zaria	17.1	Katsina	3.7
		Bornu	3.3
		Sokoto	2.5

(Total average: 9.2 per cent.) Source: J. N. Eastmond and H. Adamu, *The Place of Koranic Schools in the Immediate and Long Range Planning of Northern Nigeria,* Ministry of Education, Feb. 1965 (Typescript).

37. **Primarily,** Katsina Training College, opened in 1921, which produced such notables as the late Sir Ahmadu Bello (Premier of the Northern Region), Sir Abubakar Tafawa Balawa (Prime Minister of Nigeria), Alhaji Aliyu, Makaman Bida (Minister

of Finance, Northern Region), and Alhaji Isa Kaita (Minister of Education, Northern Region).

38. See R. L. Sklar, "The Origin of Political Parties in the North" and "Party Competition in the Northern Region," *Nigerian Political Parties,* Princeton, N.J.: Princeton University Press, 1963, pp. 88–101, 321–378.
39. Cmnd. 505, *loc. cit.*
40. K. W. Post, "Modern Education and Politics in Nigeria," in H. N. Weiler (ed.), *Education and Politics in Nigeria,* Verlag Rombach, 1964, pp. 139–150. According to Post: "Hausa is also widely used as a political language in the North, and this has been a powerful contributory factor to the present gulf between North and South" (p. 146).
41. The Nigerian newspapers in 1959 frequently carried articles discussing a lingua franca, e.g., "A lingua franca is suggested: There's magic in a native language," *Nigerian Citizen,* Jan. 21, 1959, p. 5.
42. For example, see A. Spicer, "National and official languages for the Gold Coast," *Proceedings of the Fourth Annual Conference of the West African Institute of Social and Economic Research,* UCI, 1956, pp. 4–12.
43. *Nigerian Citizen,* October 3, 1959, p. 1.
44. "Hausa language should be Nigeria's lingua franca," *Nigerian Citizen,* September 30, 1959, p. 5.
45. For example, see D. C. Aligbe, "Lingua Franca for Nigeria is not Urgent," *Sunday Post,* August 23, 1964, p. 11.
46. Ahmadu Bello, speech in the Budget Session, Northern House of Assembly, March 4, 1964. Quoted in the following: Ibo State Union, *One North or One Nigeria,* Eastern Nigeria Printing Corporation, Enugu, 1965, p. 13.
47. For debates on this policy, see Northern House of Assembly proceedings, 1960–1965. For example, March 13, 1963, p. 292; March 19, 1963, p. 476. On March 12, 1963, the Northern Minister of Trade and Industry stated: "Government is most anxious to ensure that all Commercial and Industrial organizations in Northern Nigeria employ Northerners as far as is possible. With this object in view I require an assurance from sponsors of new projects that Northerners will be trained for the highest management positions in the shortest time, before supporting new ventures. Occasionally my attention is drawn to cases of alleged non-Northernization policies by commercial concerns which are then thoroughly investigated by officials in my Ministry" p. 204, H of A Debates.
48. See Ibo State Union, *Nigerian Disunity, The Guilty Ones,* Eastern Nigeria Printing Corporation, Enugu, 1964. Also, *One North or One Nigeria, loc. cit.*
49. Speech March 4, 1964, Budget Sessions. Quoted in *One North or One Nigeria, op. cit.,* p. 14.
50. Eastmond and Adamu, *op. cit.,* p. ii.
51. For various reasons, Arabic literacy in Northern Nigeria has been frequently underestimated, and never accurately established in Census data, which reflect only literacy in Arabic *script* (Ajami). In a survey of certain wards of Kano City, the author of this paper found Arabic literacy rates of up to 65 per cent among male heads of compound. The same survey found English literacy rates of about 3 per cent among male heads of compound. As a further index, the Eastmond-Adamu report shows that in 1961 there were 2777 Islamic Ilm Schools (comparable to high school) in Northern Nigeria, and only 118 post primary schools. *Op. cit.,* p. ii.
52. See R. L. Sklar and D. S. Whitaker, "Nigeria," in Coleman and Rosberg (eds.), *Political Parties and National Integration in Africa, op. cit.,* pp. 597 ff.; B. J. Dudley, "Parties and the Political Process: Aspects of Political Change in Northern Nigeria," unpublished paper presented to the West African Political Science Conference, March 1965, Ibadan. J. P. Mackintosh, "Electoral Trends and the Tendency

to a One Party System in Nigeria," *J.C.P.S.,* 1(3), 194–210 (Nov. 1962); W. H. Hudson, *Provincial Authorities,* Kaduna, 1957; J. P. Mackintosh, *Nigerian Government and Politics,* London: George Allen and Unwin, 1966. Sklar and Whitaker, "The Federal Republic of Nigeria" in G. M. Carter (ed.), *National Unity and Regionalism in Eight African States, loc. cit.;* J. J. Campbell, "The Structure of Local Government" in L. F. Blitz (ed.), *The Politics and Administration of Nigerian Government,* New York: Praeger, 1965.

53. See references listed in footnote 52.

54. See Service de l'Alphabétisation et de l'Education des Adultes, Ministère de l'Education Nationale, République du Niger, *Le Courrier de l'Alphabètisation,* nos. 1, 2, 3 (1965), Niamey.

Pierre L. van den Berghe

LANGUAGE AND "NATIONALISM" IN SOUTH AFRICA

To state that language and nationalism are closely related is a tautology, but one that needs restating in view of the loose usage of the term "nationalism" in the Third World and particularly in the African literature. In the nineteenth-century European sense of the word, "nationalism" referred to a political movement or a process of growing self-consciousness based on a feeling of common ethnicity. Of the several criteria of ethnicity, a common language has often been the paramount one, with religion coming in second place. Thus, when we speak of German or Italian nationalism, we mean primarily the growth of political consciousness by people sharing the same language.

In dealing with contemporary Africa, social scientists have greatly confused political analysis by using "nationalism" to mean broadly "anti-colonialism" [1]. If the confusion had stopped there, not too much damage would have been done, but, faced with the problem of having to use a descriptive term to refer to true nationalism in Africa, the word "tribalism" was resorted to. Apart from the invidious connotations of "tribalism," the word "tribe" and its derivatives have been used in at least half a dozen unrelated senses. A "tribe" has meant a group speaking the same language, a group inhabiting a certain area, or a traditional state, even though the three criteria often did not coincide. "Tribalism" has meant federalism as opposed to centralism, nationalism as opposed to internationalism, traditionalism as distinguished from modernism, or a rural orientation as opposed to an urban one.

I would therefore suggest that "tribe" and its derivatives be scrapped altogether. To refer to a political movement based on ethnicity, I shall use the term "nationalism" (e.g., "Yoruba nationalism," "Ewe nationalism," "Kikuyu nationalism"). To refer to political movements that use the multinational state as their defining unit, I shall speak of "territorialism" (e.g., "Nigerian territorialism," "Congolese territorialism").

Source: *Race*, **9**, No. 1, 37–46 (1967).

Only in the few cases of true African nation-states, that is, in the few instances of culturally homogeneous or nearly homogeneous states, can the term "nationalism" properly be applied at the level of the sovereign polity (e.g., Somali nationalism, Egyptian nationalism, or Rwanda nationalism). Finally, when the defining unit is larger than both the sovereign state and the ethnic group, I shall speak of "internationalism" (e.g., European internationalism, African internationalism, Pan-Islamic internationalism). However, movements aimed at uniting in a single state ethnic groups divided between several polities are properly "nationalist" (e.g., Bakongo nationalism, German nationalism before Bismarck).

Having hopefully given back to the term nationalism the reasonably clear meaning it had until my Africanist colleagues confused the issue, I shall turn to an analysis of the political role of language in the Republic of South Africa [2]. According to the preceding definitions, there is no political movement in contemporary South Africa that can properly be called "nationalist," although I confess to having loosely used the term in my previous writings about South Africa.

Whatever nationalism existed among the African nation-states of the nineteenth century (the Zulu, the Xhosa, the Sotho, the Swazi, the Ndebele) has all but disappeared by now. Although the indigenous languages are spoken by more people than ever before, and although feelings of ethnic particularism and prejudice persist between African ethnic groups, these feelings have little if any political meaning in the modern context. (They are analogous to ethnic feelings of people of Italian, Irish, or Jewish descent in the United States, for example.) What is often called "African nationalism" or "black nationalism" in South Africa is the movement aiming at the overthrow of white supremacy, and is represented by such organizations as the Pan African Congress and the African National Congress. In our terminology, this is an instance of territorialism. Similarly, "white nationalism" is simply a racist ideology for the maintenance of the *status quo*.

Of course, some scholars would argue that "Afrikaner nationalism," the political movement of people of Dutch or Boer descent, is an authentic case of nationalism as I have defined it [3]. Afrikaner nationalism does indeed have many characteristics of classical nationalism and, of all political movements in South Africa, comes closest to being truly nationalist. Yet the added element of racism complicates the picture. Speaking Afrikaans as one's mother tongue is a *necessary* condition for membership in the *Volk*. But it is not a *sufficient* condition; one must also meet the test of racial "purity." For every six "white" people who are ethnically Afrikaners, there are five "Colored" Afrikaners who are denied membership in the *Volk*. That race is an even more important criterion than ethnicity is shown by the fact that, *de jure*, a non-Afrikaans-speaking white may belong to the governing Nationalist Party (and *de facto* quite a number of German- and a few English-speaking whites *do* belong to the Party), whereas an Afrikaans-speaking Colored may not. Although there is a strong ethnic component to "Afrikaner nationalism" (probably over 95 per cent of the Nationalist Party members are Afrikaans-speaking), that movement is first and foremost racial and only secondarily nationalist. Nevertheless, the Afrikaners, of any ethnic group in South Africa, have come closest to developing a nationalist movement.

Although no South African political movement is strictly nationalist, ethnicity, next to race, has been the most important line of cleavage in South African society. More specifically, the English-Afrikaner conflict, which goes back to the first years of the nineteenth century, has an important linguistic dimension, and the official status and use of the two main European languages has long been a controversial aspect of white politics. In this essay I deal briefly with four main aspects of the political significance of language in contemporary South Africa:

TRADITIONAL AFRIKANER "NATIONALISM"

The division of the dominant white group into English and Afrikaners is based mainly on ethnicity as symbolized mostly by language [4]. The long-standing conflict between these two ethnic groups goes back to the early nineteenth century and has a long and complex history, involving many interrelated aspects. With the advent of British hegemony at the Cape in the first years of the century, the Afrikaners found themselves in a politically, economically, socially, and culturally subordinate position vis-à-vis the English, although they remained dominant in relation to the nonwhite population. In this respect their position became analogous to that of French Canadians after the British conquest, and language became much the same kind of rallying point for the development of a politico-cultural nationalism. Due to the presence of a large nonwhite majority, however, policy toward Africans, Coloreds, and Indians became a major dimension of English-Afrikaner conflicts in a somewhat analogous way to the North-South conflict over the extension of slavery in the nineteenth-century United States. Thus Afrikaner nationalism acquired a strong racial as well as ethnic component.

The feeling of ethnic and racial identity of the Afrikaners led to a growing "nationalism" which had the following characteristics:

1. An origin myth with an idealized, quasi-sacred, heroic, and epic version of Afrikaner history. The Boer fights against British imperialism and the African nations, the frontier, the Great Trek, the two Anglo-Boer Wars, and other events are glorified and legitimized in Biblical terms. The themes of the Chosen People, the flight from Egypt, the Promised Land, and Divine guidance appear frequently in Afrikaner-Calvinist historiography. This heroic conception of the *Volk's* history has its great temple (the Voortrekkers Monument near Pretoria), its demigod (Paul Kruger), its atrocity stories (the British concentration camps), its martyrs

(Piet Retief), its traitors (Jan Smuts), and its holidays (Day of the Covenant).

2. An ideology which is a complex blend of rugged individualism, egalitarianism among the Chosen People, anticapitalist agrarianism, fundamentalistic Calvinism, anticosmopolitan isolationism, white supremacy and racism, xenophobia, fear of miscegenation and cultural assimilation, anti-Communism, ascriptive exclusivism, and narrow provincialism and ethnocentrism.

3. A distinctive culture symbolized by Voortrekker costumes, diet, the Dutch Reformed Churches, and, above all, by the Afrikaans language [5]. Concern for the maintenance of this distinctive culture and for resisting anglicization has centered around the recognition of Afrikaans as a national language of equal status to English, the actual use of Afrikaans in government, and the use of that language as a medium of instruction in the racially and ethnically segregated schools. Feelings toward Afrikaner culture have often consisted of an ambivalent mixture of pride and shame *vis-à-vis* the more cosmopolitan and dynamic English culture.

4. A number of political or quasi-political organizations, the major ones being the old and the "purified" Nationalist Party, and this party's elite secret society, the Broederbond. In addition, quasi-Fascist organizations like the New Order and the Ossewa Brandwag, and splinter parties like the Afrikaner Party rose and fell in the 1930s and 1940s. Today the Nationalist Party has effectively rallied the great majority of the Afrikaners, and has ruled the country since 1948. All these political organizations have shared the aims of emancipation from Britain as a foreign power, ethnic paramountcy over English South Africans, and racial supremacy over all nonwhites, including those who are ethnically Afrikaners.

Except for the added element of racism, which is, of course, quite salient and gives Afrikaner nationalism a special character, that movement has all the main hallmarks of "classical" nationalism as defined earlier. Insofar as this is true, Afrikaner nationalism is distinctly *unlike* most political movements of independence and anticolonialism in black Africa, and is especially different from the so-called African nationalism within South Africa itself.

THE REACTION OF OTHER ETHNIC AND RACIAL GROUPS TO AFRIKANER NATIONALISM

It might be expected that militant Afrikaner nationalism would have elicited other similar movements among the other main ethnic and racial groups in South Africa. In fact, for diverse reasons, this has not been the case to any significant extent.

Of the three main nonwhite racial groups, the Coloreds have been most completely westernized, and have most aspired to social assimilation into the dominant white group. Although long frustrated in their assimilationist aspirations, most Coloreds, far from wanting to maintain a separate identity, continue to seek acceptance into the two main white ethnic groups whose culture they share.

Indians have been divided into two main religious groups, five language groups, and many more caste groups, any of which would be far too small to constitute a basis for a politically successful nationalist movement. Furthermore, South African Indians have been rapidly anglicized, and although they do not, by and large, seek assimilation to the whites, they do seek equal, nondiscriminatory acceptance into a multiracial and multiethnic South Africa. Since the days of Mahatma Gandhi, South African Indian politics have been secular, universalistic, and opposed to any ethnic or racial divisions.

English-speaking whites did develop a slight degree of nationalist feelings in response to Afrikaner nationalism. Some cultural and political organizations (including small splinter parties) did form along English ethnic lines, and, in the Province of Natal, there is a modicum of English nationalist sentiment. However, English nationalism remained a very subdued phenomenon compared to Afrikaner nationalism. There are two major reasons for this state of affairs. First, being a minority within a minority, English South Africans could only achieve power by allying themselves with non-nationalist Afrikaners, that is, by taking a racist but *antinationalist* stand in politics. The major parties in which the English have gained a share of political power (such as the South African Party and the United Party) have consistently based their appeal on all whites irrespective of ethnicity. Second, English South Africans have not developed a distinctive culture to the same extent as the Afrikaners, and, consequently, any attempt to stress English ethnicity has been stigmatized by Afrikaners as a disloyal attachment to a foreign colonial power. Local South African English has, of course, some dialectical idiosyncracies, but remains closer to standard British English than American English, and hence cannot qualify for separate language status as Afrikaans does in relation to Dutch. In addition, no single religion (comparable to the Dutch Reformed Churches for Afrikaners) unites English South Africans who are split between Anglicans, Methodists, Catholics, and Jews, not to mention many smaller Protestant denominations.

Among the various African-language groups, there still exists some degree of ethnic particularism, and the vast majority of black South Africans speak one of the Bantu tongues as their home language. Furthermore, three of these language groups are quite large, both absolutely (2 to 3 millions each) and relatively (between 14 and 20 per cent of the total population). Yet what has been called "African nationalism" has, from its inception in the first years of the twentieth century, shown few nationalist characteristics and many hallmarks of "territorialism." The African National Congress, the All-African Convention, the Pan-African Congress, and African trade unionism have all been militantly opposed to white supremacy, to racial segregation and discrimination, to ethnic particularism (which they have stigmatized as "tribalism"), and to any program of cultural distinctiveness or revivalism.

Generally, the ideology of the African political movements has stressed equality regardless of race or ethnicity, and, although tolerant of cultural pluralism, it has never based its appeal on ethnic distinctions. Faced with an acutely racist dominant group, African political movements have sometimes made a racially-based appeal to Africans or to all nonwhites but scarcely ever to specific cultural groups. European culture has rarely been disparaged (a fact which is hardly surprising since the vast majority of leaders are Western-educated, mostly in Christian mission schools), and any divisive feelings of ethnic separation between Africans have been regarded as a political liability. If anything, the black South African intelligentsia has shown a considerable drive toward westernization and attitudes of "cultural shame" toward indigenous cultures. Unlike other parts of Africa in which "nationalist" movements have adopted some traditional symbols and have sought to Africanize their ideology, the South African freedom movements have been unashamedly eclectic in ideology and organization (borrowing freely from America, Europe, and Asia) and Western, "modern," and antitraditional in both their tactics and aims. They have challenged racism and white supremacy largely in terms of Christian ethics and a Western-inspired liberal or socialist philosophy of democracy, equality, and freedom.

Thus the only group in South Africa (and one of the few in the sub-Saharan part of the continent) to have developed a nationalism based at least partly on ethnicity and language are the Afrikaners. We shall now turn to the implications of that fact for apartheid policy toward the other ethnic groups in South Africa.

THE USE OF ETHNIC REVIVALISM AND THE ATTEMPT TO REVIVE AFRICAN LINGUISTIC NATIONALISM IN THE APARTHEID PROGRAMS

The attempt by the ruling Afrikaner nationalists to impose upon the other groups a policy of rigid racial and ethnic separation is the result of complex motivations. It is partly a systematic method of dividing Africans, some two-thirds of whom have now become "detribalized," into mutually antagonistic ethnic groups. To the extent that Africans of various language groups have intermixed, intermarried, learned each other's tongues, and lived and worked side by side in the cities under identical conditions of oppression and destitution, they have developed a common consciousness which transcends ethnicity. The government policy of "retribalization" is in part a conscious effort to counteract these universalistic trends and to isolate each ethnic group in a cultural and political desert.

Beyond this rather obvious motive Pretoria-sponsored cultural revivalism for Africans arises from a confusion between race and culture on the part of the ruling Afrikaners. In spite of considerable contrary evidence in their own country, most South African whites believe that culture is in part racially determined, and hence that a given culture reflects the innate abilities and propensities of its members. Consequently, the allegedly "primitive" Bantu cultures are held to be peculiarly suited to the supposedly "primitive" mentality of Africans.

A third source of cultural revivalism arises from the projection of the Afrikaner's sense of ethnic particularism and linguistic chauvinism onto other people. Since the preservation of ethnic and racial identity has been a paramount value in Afrikaner nationalism, many Afrikaners have assumed that other ethnic groups would feel likewise.

Pretoria-sponsored revivalism vis-à-vis Africans is reflected in a number of apartheid programs. In urban areas an attempt is made to segregate Africans of different language groups from each other, as well as Africans from non-Africans. In the rural areas, the Bantustan policy consists of consolidating and reconstructing mono-ethnic areas with a semi-autonomous political structure modeled in part on traditional chieftainship. Such insignificant voting rights as Africans enjoy are based on ethnicity; for example, in the Transkei, Xhosa-speaking people vote for Xhosa candidates to the Xhosa Assembly.

Similarly, the entire educational system for Africans has been "tribalized" by the Bantu Education Department. Mother-tongue instruction is stressed at all levels of schooling despite overwhelming opposition of Africans who would prefer to be taught in English, at least beyond the lower primary grades. Ethnically segregated pseudo-universities have been created for the Zulu, Xhosa, and Sotho, and these "bush colleges" are practically the only places where Africans of a given language group can receive any form of postsecondary education. In these institutions, attempts are made to use Bantu languages as media of instruction, to modify the curriculum in line with Pretoria's conception of what is good for Africans, to create an artificial technical vocabulary in the Bantu languages, to incorporate Bantu elements into the architecture, and to instill ethnic chauvinism into the students [6].

PROBLEMS PRESENTED BY MULTILINGUALISM
IN THE FUTURE DEVELOPMENT OF SOUTH AFRICA
AS A UNITARY STATE

The significance of language in South African politics is of course not limited to the past and present. Assuming that the *status quo* is unlikely to continue for much longer and that South Africa will continue to exist as a unitary state but under a government representing the majority of the people, the use of official languages will have immediate educational and political implications. Obviously, the present situation where only the two main European languages are granted official status is unlikely to be acceptable to most South Africans under a majority government. Many Africans have developed negative feelings toward Afrikaans as the language of the oppressors, but, as the home language of more than 3 million people, nearly half of whom are nonwhites, Afrikaans cannot easily be eliminated.

Most educated Africans, who are likely to play prominent roles in the future, would probably be reluctant to substitute a Bantu language as the official tongue. To do so would revive ethnic rivalries and raise a host of other problems. No single language is spoken as a mother tongue by more than 20 per cent of the total population, and three Bantu languages are spoken by nearly equal numbers of people (i.e., between 2 and 3 millions). Some African languages (notably Zulu, Swazi, and Xhosa) are closely enough related so that they could conceivably be fused into a single official written tongue; but, even so, they would encompass only about 40 per cent of the total population.

Alternatively, to make English the only national language would also be unacceptable. Most African leaders recognize the importance and practical superiority of English as a medium of interethnic communication, of trade, of intellectual life, and of contact with the rest of Africa and of the world. Yet English is only in fifth place (after Afrikaans, Xhosa, Zulu, and Sotho) in terms of numbers of native speakers. Furthermore, English is associated with a segment of the dominant racial minority.

Another possibility would be to grant equal status to all five major languages; but this would present great practical problems which, although not insuperable, would lead to high cost and inefficiency of administration. The mere cost of translating and printing official documents in five tongues and of simultaneously translating legislative debates would be prohibitive for a none-too-affluent country. In terms of education, a five-language policy would mean one of two things. Either children of the five main groups would be taught in their mother tongue or all five languages would have to be taught in all schools. The second possibility is clearly unworkable and the first one would meet with strong African opposition because it would perpetuate *de facto* racial segregation and unequal educational opportunities.

One workable solution seems to meet pragmatic exigencies as well as to resolve at least some of the major political problems raised by language in a reconstructed South Africa of the future. English should be recognized as the national language to be taught in all schools, and used in the central legislature and in official documents. At the same time the other four main languages should also have official recognition as regional second languages. Thus, in the Western Cape, Afrikaans would be the second language; in the Eastern Cape, Xhosa; in the Orange Free State and the Transvaal, Sotho; and in Natal, Zulu. In any given area two languages (one of them English) would be used in schools and in government offices. Signs, ordinances, forms, and other written documents would be published in English and in the local second language.

*   *   *

Here is not the place to elaborate on this brief linguistic blueprint for a reconstructed South Africa. Two things, however, are certain, if one assumes that South Africa will continue to exist as a unitary multinational state, but under majority government. First, the official use of one or more languages is going to create difficult and unavoidable problems with both ethnic and racial ramifications. Second, any satisfactory solution of linguistic problems will have to take both "nonrational" and "rational" factors into account. The nonrational include such things as the demographic, educational, and other forces affecting the ethnic distribution of power, and the subjective attitudes and values of people concerning the various languages. The rational, which are likely to clash with political contingencies, involve considerations of administrative cost and efficiency of relative usefulness of tongues in various forms and fields of communication, and of the feasibility of guided linguistic change ranging from minor standardization of orthography to major fusion between existing tongues.

Clearly, South Africa offers fascinating prospects for both theoretical and applied sociolinguistics; and, equally clearly, sociolinguistics will have to assign to each set of factors its proper weight in the total equation. For such an embryonic discipline the difficulty will be as great as the opportunity.

NOTES

1. There is an abundant literature on African "nationalism." For political analyses using various definitions of nationalism, see Section VII of Pierre L. van den Berghe (ed.), *Africa, Social Problems of Change and Conflict,* San Francisco, Cal.: Chandler,

1965. This work also contains a bibliography. See also Immanuel Wallerstein (ed.), *Social Change, The Colonial Situation,* New York: Wiley, 1966.

2. The social science literature on South Africa is abundant. An extensive and recent bibliography can be found in my book *South Africa, A Study in Conflict,* Middletown, Conn.: Wesleyan University Press, 1965. Among other germane books on the subject are Gwendolen M. Carter, *The Politics of Inequality,* New York: Praeger, 1958; C. W. de Kiewiet, *A History of South Africa, Social and Economic,* Oxford: Clarendon Press, 1941; Muriel Horrell, *A Survey of Race Relations in South Africa,* Johannesburg: South African Institute of Race Relations, annual; Leo Kuper, *An African Bourgeoisie,* New Haven, Conn.: Yale University Press, 1965; Leo Marquard, *The Peoples and Policies of South Africa,* London: Oxford University Press, 1962; Sheila Patterson, *Colour and Culture in South Africa,* London: Routledge and Kegan Paul, 1953; Sheila Patterson, *The Last Trek,* London: Routledge and Kegan Paul, 1957; Michael Roberts and A. E. G. Trollip, *The South African Opposition, 1939–1945,* London: Longmans, 1947; and William Henry Vatcher, *White Laager, The Rise of Afrikaner Nationalism,* New York: Praeger, 1965.

3. In this connection Vatcher makes a twofold error when he states "Afrikaner nationalism is the classic form of all the nationalisms that now flourish on the continent of Africa." (Cf. William Henry Vatcher, *op. cit.,* p. ix.) Afrikaner "nationalism" is unlike most other African "nationalisms" in that it does have both an ethnic and a racial basis.

4. The racial breakdown of the population is as follows: Whites or "Europeans," 19.4 per cent; Africans 68.2 per cent; Indians, 3.0 per cent; and Coloreds, 9.4 per cent. Of the whites, some 57 per cent speak Afrikaans as their mother-tongue, 39 per cent English, and 4 per cent other tongues, mostly German and Dutch. The 1951 Census classified 73 per cent of the whites as bilingual, but only 2 per cent habitually speak both languages at home. Of the Coloreds, 89 per cent speak Afrikaans as their home language, and the remainder English; 46.5 per cent of the Coloreds are bilingual. The two largest language groups among Indians are Tamil and Hindi, spoken by some 40 per cent each; the remaining 20 per cent speak Telugu, Urdu, and Gugarati. In addition to those Indian languages, some 77 per cent of the Indians know English and 16 per cent Afrikaans. Among Africans, 29 per cent speak Xhosa, 26 per cent Zulu, 22 per cent Sotho, 8 per cent Tswana, 5 per cent Tsonga, 3 per cent Swazi, 3 per cent Ndebele, 2 per cent Venda, and 2 per cent a sprinkling of other Bantu languages. In addition, 15 per cent speak English and 21 per cent Afrikaans.

5. Afrikaans, originally a variety of Dutch with indigenous and Malay admixtures, gained the status of a distinct written language in the nineteenth century.

6. Leo Kuper has written a true to life satire of these bush colleges. Cf. *The College Brew,* Durban, privately printed, 1960.

III

Language Planning,
Standardization, and Policy

III

Robert G. Armstrong

LANGUAGE POLICIES AND LANGUAGE PRACTICES IN WEST AFRICA

The linguistic problems of the 14 West African nations are of immense proportions. Suffice it to say that in the great area between Yaoundé, the capital of the Cameroun Republic, and Dakar, the capital of Senegal, from 500 to 1000 different languages are spoken, and that these languages are typically divided into many different dialects. These languages are important to the people who speak them and who, speaking them, become complete human beings. So important, indeed, are their respective languages that people make them the very symbol and banner of the cultural and tribal differences that today rack Africa, as they have done and still do in other places as well. Thus it is obvious that when we discuss language problems of developing nations, we are not merely discussing cabinet and ministry decisions, the recommendations of international conferences, the statistics of examination results, and the experience of pilot teaching-projects. People kill each other over language questions, and not merely because of their failure to understand each other as they are thrust into closer contact by the conditions of modern life.

In Africa there is nothing new about the contact and conflict of people with different languages. What is new, in the modern world of school systems and bureaucracies, is the political importance of public decisions on language matters. When it is decided that language X is to be the language of instruction and examination, and not languages Y and Z, the native-speakers of language Y and Z have a corresponding disability placed on them. The West African variant of this equation is that the privileged language X is usually either French or English, and tribes that are identified as speakers of languages D, K, R, and W may for historical reasons have 10 times more educational resources for learning French or English than do tribes whose languages are Y and Z. The growth of school systems and bureaucracies also produces a great many jobs for which people compete largely in terms of their success in the educational system. In the heat of the competition, people are quick to equate privileged position with moral superiority and vice versa. If, as in Nigeria, the lagging groups have political strength, they may well use it to redress the balance.

I would argue against any theory of linguistic causation of the conflicts with which the developing world is plagued. The considerations just mentioned are economic and social ones. I suggest that languages are involved as tools and symbols. There is, however, a striking tendency for linguistic boundaries to coincide with boundaries of conflict, since great geographical areas, river valleys, climatic zones, great economic systems, and sharp class divisions are very likely to find expression in language differences. Thus a great deal of passion may be injected into what the astonished linguist might have regarded as a purely technical matter. On the other hand, wise language policy may be one of the levers available for improving a difficult political and social situation.

I have recently read with fascinated amazement a very fine report on a round-table discussion held in Peru on the subject of Quechua and Aymara monolingualism in Peruvian education. It is a measure of the generality of these problems that one could take this entire book, change the names in it appropriately, and read it as applying to any West African country. It would be an illuminating, many-sided discussion; and *nothing* of fact or argument would have to be changed [1].

As in West Africa, the discussion centers around the role of the world-language (in this case Spanish) in the school system. Spanish is the language by which the country communicates with the rest of the world and the language by which one participates in national institutions of all kinds. The great majority of the people do not speak Spanish as a native language. Many indigenous languages are heard, but most of all Quechua and Aymara. These are no closer to Spanish than is Japanese. Quechua and Aymara are languages with ancient and proud traditions; they were the languages of the Inca and other pre-Hispanic civilizations. The opening paper, by a leading linguist, proposes that the indigenous languages should be used to teach literacy for four or five months, after which Spanish would be introduced and would become in the end the language of instruction. After that Quechua or Aymara would be only one course. Spanish should be taught as a second language and not as if it were native to the students. Certain common prejudices are a problem. The *mestizos* (mixed bloods, with some Hispanic education) fear that it is proposed to substitute Quechua for Spanish. The native-speaking Quechua want their children to learn Spanish and see no reason for studying a language they already know. The discussion brings out the fact that the development of contrastive grammars would be very helpful to the teaching of Spanish. It is objected that "When we have only used

Spanish, we have not arrived at the minds, the sensitivities, the emotions of the children and adults whom we are teaching" (p. 32).

An anthropologist from Mexico says that Mexican experience suggests that Spanish and indigenous languages can be successfully taught simultaneously. Another anthropologist asks why it must be assumed that instruction in Quechua and Aymara should be limited to mere literacy: should it not go on to literature, theater, and poetry? The venerable Quechua scholar, Dr. A., laments that after 400 years of literacy and after 20 years of repeated conferences and proposals, there is still no agreed upon orthography of Quechua. He pleads for the teaching of literacy in the mother tongues so that the individual child will not learn an inferiority complex along with his Spanish (pp. 45–47). A North American anthropologist makes the point that in the confrontation between natives and mixed-bloods the knowledge of Spanish is the measure of civilization. To be a monolingual speaker of Quechua is to be subhuman, and the teachers (often *mestizos* themselves) blame their own pedagogical failures on the students' inferiority.

The most brutal comment comes from Monsignor H., who says simply that the proposal to use Quechua and Aymara during the first phase of instruction and then to pass on to Spanish

". . . is, of course, very pretty, but I think that it is not practical. The practical thing is for the teachers to know Spanish as well as Quechua and Aymara and that it be they who directly teach the children Spanish and the Spanish alphabet, using Quechua or Aymara. But that the child should first have an Aymara alphabet, or a Quechua alphabet which is still under discussion, as has just been said, would slow up the teaching, I think. One should go directly to the teaching of Spanish, and that is the usual practice in the Lima schools. . . . And this business of saying that the Castilian language is a foreign language is false. The Castilian language is completely our own, it has survived for more than four centuries among us, it is the language of all the American continent, and it is one of the most beautiful languages. . . . This is the way I think, with all due respect to the gentlemen present here" (p. 48).

In other words, the present system of using half-educated *mestizos* to teach the Indians is the right one.

The linguist answers this by spelling out in words of one syllable the distinction between teaching a pupil to write his native language and teaching him a second language. The chairman, Dr. A., himself a native-speaker of Quechua, closes the linguistic discussion by saying that the Spanish Empire did more for the languages of the Indians than the Republic has done, that very serious measures are now necessary in order to build up the self-respect of the Indians in Peru, and that the Quechua-speakers who seek to follow European ways must travel

". . . a cruel path of apprenticeship in the Spanish language and culture; that is to say that we have the case of monolingual Quechua-speakers who come down to the cities, *a la guerra,* as we say, learn Spanish during a period of martyrdom lasting many years; and once they have learned 500 or 600 words, they bury Quechua within themselves and do not wish to speak it any more: they exchange a language of limitless possibilities for a restricted language which constricts their minds and diminishes them as humans instead of exalting them" (p. 52).

I could easily quote at much greater length to the same effect. I think that anyone with experience in West African linguistic conferences and colloquia on teaching problems in West Africa will have a tremendous sense of *déjà vu*—or perhaps *déjà entendu*—on reading the report of this Andean *Mesa Redonda.* I present it as an introduction to the language problems of West Africa, which may help us to see these problems in a world setting.

I should not like to leave the impression that I think the linguistic situation is hopeless, either in Peru or in West Africa. The same growth of modern technology that has created the problem has given us many new techniques and possibilities for dealing with it. The first of these which we must mention is the development of the science of linguistics itself. Another factor is modern communication and transport. A book printed in Peru is available in Nigeria the same year. Since 1960 there have been at least a dozen international linguistic meetings in West Africa, with participants coming by plane from all over Africa as well as from Europe and America. This has meant an unprecedented mobilization of expert thought to deal with African linguistic problems. From Kinshasa in the Congo to Dakar there are now no less than 15 universities, and I can quickly count several West Africans with doctoral degrees in linguistics. Not surprisingly, our knowledge of West African languages has greatly broadened and deepened during the last 10 years. In the same period linguistics has made great strides in the Christian missions, not only through the work of the Summer Institute of Linguistics groups, led in West Africa by Dr. John Bendor-Samuel, but also in the francophone countries by the work of such persons as RP (Révérend Père) Balenghien, for Mande, RP Prost, for the Voltaic or Gur languages, RP Segurola, for Fon, and Professor M. Houis. The West African Languages Survey was founded in 1960; out of this has developed the West African Linguistic Society, and this year the Sixth West African Languages Congress, at Yaoundé. A rapidly increasing volume of technical publication has resulted from this activity, which is already having a useful effect in the improved methods of teaching English and French in the universities. For the remainder of this essay, I should like to stress some recent developments with respect to a variety of language problems.

NATIONAL LANGUAGES

When the West African countries achieved their independence, many of them were in varying degrees dissatisfied with using English or French as official languages and therefore devoted a lot of thought to finding or developing African languages that could serve as worthy vehicles for their aspirations. The Leverhulme Conference, held at Ibadan in December and January, 1961–1962, devoted a great deal of attention to this problem [2]. The working party concerned with the question produced a report on "Choice of a National Language: Factors and Consequences" (op cit, pp 129–135), which is a model of its kind and which should be available in every ministry of education in Africa. The innermost problem, which the conferees hardly dared to spell out in print, was the fact that there is not a single West African country where a given language is spoken by more than a sizable minority of the population. If one language is selected from a set as the unique national language, then the problem of examination for the schools and civil service arises, and a majority of the people resent the special advantage conferred on the native-speakers of the chosen language. If the examinations are in English or French, there is a more even start—or at least the advantage remains with those who are already in power.

To this day, not even a beginning has been made for the preparation of the teachers and pedagogic materials that would be necessary for enforcing the use of an indigenous national language in any West African country. By the time of the UNESCO Meeting of Experts on the Use of the Mother Tongue for Literacy, which was held at Ibadan in December, 1964, it was seen by all concerned that the problem is very complex indeed. Two countries, Guinea and Ghana, had adopted a policy of giving several indigenous languages the status of national languages. Guinea did this in principle for all the languages of the country. Ghana had selected nine of the 45 languages of the country for national status. The delegate said that the criterion of selection was that they be spoken in other countries as well as Ghana, and that therefore their development would be a contribution to international understanding. Given this criterion, several important Guang languages were not selected, and literacy in them was discouraged, although the Government had no objection to their being studied for scientific purposes. It is still not clear whether the overthrow of Nkrumah has affected this policy. The Ethiopian delegates pointed out that their country has a firm policy of strengthening Amharic as the national language, using the traditional alphabet for literacy. The use of other languages is actively discouraged.

The francophone countries were all firm in regarding French as their national language, but were interested in work with the African languages too. Nigeria and Sierra Leone had arrived at no stated policy.

The conference spent some time discussing whether and to what extent African governments should declare their linguistic policies. Many of the delegates took the view that the matter is so difficult politically that the governments cannot always be blamed for their hesitation. The conference closed a few days before the New Year's Weekend crisis of 1964–1965, since which time Nigeria has had little chance to think about developing an indigenous national language.

I had myself previously expressed a preference for developing as many languages as possible for literacy and conferring some sort of national status on those that have reached a defined level of importance and success (Spencer, *op. cit.*, p. 70). It seems to me that this policy would lead to a raising of the standard of instruction in English and French and would enhance their role as languages of general communication.

LITERACY

Discussions of the development of literacy in West Africa have had several dimensions. There is the problem of instruction in the schools. There is the urgency of public adult education, and there is the pattern of instruction in literacy—both in and out of school—which has developed in mission-oriented communities. Then there is the whole question of whether and to what extent literacy should mean literacy in English or French, in the anglophone and francophone countries, respectively.

To start with the last question, it has been the official, explicit policy of the governments of the francophone countries that literacy means literacy in French. Most of these countries regard this policy as the foundation of their national unity, as it undoubtedly is. It goes beyond this to a considerable nostalgia for French culture even in countries like Guinea, where relations with France have often been difficult. On the other hand, Senegal and the Cameroun Republic swallowed whatever doubts they might have had about the usefulness of linguistic study of African languages and provided two West African Languages Congresses with most excellent hospitality. And Monseigneur Gantin, the Archbishop of Cotonou, himself a Fon, has been a staunch supporter of R. P. Segurola's dictionary of Fon. The French Government itself takes the view that linguistic study of the African languages aids instruction in French in Africa. It has therefore sent strong delegations to all of the linguistic congresses in West Africa. Countries such as Guinea and Mali have also conquered their political doubts and have consistently participated in these congresses officially. Policy in the anglophone countries, both before and after independence, has in principle been friendly toward literacy in the indigenous languages and to instruction in them especially in the primary schools. The more important languages may be taken as examination subjects for the General Certificate of Education. The trouble with this policy has been that until very recently most of the languages concerned had not received anything like an adequate grammatical or phonological analysis, and therefore instruction in them has been so faulty that there has been little serious development of published literature in them. This has in effect left a clear field for English, and in practice the policy of the anglophone countries has differed little from that of the francophone countries.

There has been considerable international pressure on UNESCO to do something effective to promote literacy—especially adult literacy—in Africa, and this has been the theme of at least three international conferences: that at Ibadan in 1964, and those at Bamako and Niamey in 1966 (see the discussion of orthography following). There was also a special Committee of Experts on Problems of Linguistic Development which was organized by UNESCO and which met at Yaoundé at the same time as the Sixth West African Languages Congress. These meetings have on the whole concerned themselves with questions of instructional methods, the languages to be used for literacy, and the standardization of orthographies. They have discussed pilot projects, but have never really come to grips with the problem of how a large-scale program is to be organized. It has been assumed that a literacy program is largely a matter of adult education, and that the methods and materials to be used would also be useful in the schools. But it has never been seriously discussed whether a separate organization must be set up parallel to the schools, to concern itself with adult literacy, or whether such a program may be developed inside the school system as a part of its general activities.

On the whole, adult nonliterates want to learn English or French, as the case may be. On the other hand, linguists at these conferences emphasized the importance of literacy instruction in the mother tongue of the students, since it is only in the mother tongue that what may be called deep literacy can be quickly learned. The linguists also saw the native languages as an important bridge to literacy as such and therefore also a bridge to the study of English or French. This is true for the student, but it is also true on another level for the teacher, for whom sophistication about the students' languages greatly helps the teaching of English and French. In both the Third and the Sixth West African Languages Congresses there have been special working parties on the teaching of English and French in West Africa [3]. The linguists tend to feel that education should seize hold of and develop the ancient and widespread African habit of polyglottism.

The Commission at Yaoundé made a number of concrete technical proposals and emphasized in particular the importance of the development of typological studies of African languages and families of languages in order to facilitate their comparison with English and French.

In general, it should be said that the linguists who are active in West Africa have expressed considerable dissatisfaction with the low technical level of much of what is being done with African languages in the schools and elsewhere. This feeling was expressed quite strongly at Ibadan and finds expression in the report on that conference. The linguists were in general agreement that the complete development of a previously unwritten language for literacy purposes, including the writing of a scientific grammar, a teaching grammar, introductory books, literary texts, and a bilingual dictionary, and the training of a group of teachers capable of using these materials requires at least five years. The real costs of such an enterprise must be reckoned at $15,000.00 a year, at the prices of 1964. If a linguist involved in such an undertaking must also attend to administrative or other activities, the time required must be correspondingly lengthened. Linguists in West Africa have a strong tendency to regard projects that are not conceived on this scale as something less than serious.

ORTHOGRAPHY

There has been a serious effort, under UNESCO auspices, to unify the orthographies of languages which are spoken in both francophone and anglophone countries. Such languages as Fulani, Hausa, and Kanuri have seen the development of writing in divergent orthographic traditions. This year has seen two international conferences of specialists to deal with the question. The first, at Bamako in March 1966, produced agreed orthographies for Hausa, Fulani, Tamashek, Mande, and Kanuri. In September 1966 there was a more limited meeting at Niamey to deal with certain problems of Hausa orthography. It is the experience of many such exercises that it is no use recommending a fully elaborated, phonemic, tone-marked orthography, using an array of letters from the International Phonetic Alphabet. Such proposals produce astonishing heat and few results. What the linguists now do as a group is to produce substantially phonemic alphabets, using the letters and spelling devices of English and French as far as possible, taking care to remove the most frequent and damaging kinds of ambiguity, and being very careful that the agreed orthography is in principle expansible into a full system. This means in practice that diacritic marks are avoided which would preclude the addition of tone-marks in a scholarly edition. It also means introducing the principle of sufficient vowel letters and the principle of doubled letters. The attempt to write the seven- and nine-vowel systems of West Africa with the five vowel letters of Latin has caused enormous trouble. (It is an interesting historical question where the dogmatic insistence on writing African languages without doubled vowels and geminated consonants has come from, since the European languages make very free use of doubled letters.)

I shall not add anything to the large literature on tone-marking except to say that nearly all the linguists who have worked deeply with a West African language are persuaded of its importance. Now that we have several of these systems fairly well analyzed I have found it reasonably easy to teach young African literates to write their own languages with full and accurate tone-marking. I find that once they get the idea, they are enthusiastic about it, especially when poetic and other literary texts are involved.

ORAL LITERATURE

There has been a rapidly growing interest in the recovery and worthy publication of the enormous oral literature of West Africa. This interest has expressed itself in many places and in many forms, and quite a lot of good, professional work is in various stages of completion. There is strong UNESCO interest in the publication of oral literature, and the Fifth and Sixth West African Languages Congresses have both had working parties dedicated to this work. There is a strong feeling that this generation has a supremely important opportunity in this regard. The technological society, which has done so much to destroy oral tradition, has at the same time provided us with first-rate instruments with which it may be permanently recorded. We must use these instruments to record the great traditional artists while they are still singing and reciting [4]. Another aspect of the presentation of oral literature is that it is now possible, and I believe necessary, to publish a high-fidelity recording of the poem or the song along with the transcription. This must certainly *not* be done as a substitute for the meticulous work of transcription and translation of the text. It is done because the best of transcriptions is only an abstraction from and a guide to the work of art. Since we are now able to go much further than formerly in the representation of the whole work, it seems to me that we are honor-bound to do so. And besides that is what makes the whole process fun instead of a deadly bore.

The collection of fine performances of African oral literature and their worthy presentation is the capstone of the whole edifice of linguistic work here. It is the test and source of scientific grammars and lexicons. It is what makes literacy in the respective languages worth the trouble. It gives the native-speaking student his only guide to style that is at once reliable and alive. It is what enables Africa to make its superb contribution to world literature, and it is what enables the African student to study the literature of Europe without acquiring an inferiority complex at the same time.

NOTES

1. José Maria Arguedas (ed.), *Mesa Redonda sobre el Monolinguismo Quechua y Aymara y la Educación en el Perú,* Documentos Regionales de la Etnohistoria Andina. No. 2 (Lima: Ediciones de la Casa de la Cultura del Perú, 1966).
2. John Spencer (ed.), *Language in Africa,* Cambridge: University Press, 1963.
3. A report on this subject was prepared by the Commission on Applied Linguistics at the Yaoundé conference. Copies of this report may be obtained from the author.
4. A report on this subject was prepared by the Committee on Oral Literature at the Yaoundé conference. Copies of this report may be obtained from the author.

Haim Blanc

THE ISRAELI KOINE AS AN EMERGENT
NATIONAL STANDARD

The present essay discusses some of the sociolinguistic processes that have taken place in Hebrew since its adoption as a vernacular. These processes are, on the whole, analogous to those known from the more familiar cases of "national language formation," though this may not be entirely obvious unless the creation of Modern Hebrew is set in its proper perspective. Probably all national standard languages are "cultural artifacts" in one sense or another (cf. E. Haugen's paper in this book) so that it is not in this respect that Hebrew can lay much claim to originality. Its most unusual feature was not that it was "dead" (a much abused term) and had to be "artificially revived," but that it was no one's mother tongue, and that there were no speakers of any dialects closely related to it. The language makers thus had to rely entirely on literary and traditional sources, and to impart the new standard not to speakers with related dialect substrata, but to immigrants with foreign (chiefly European) substrata. This posed a number of special problems, but it is by no means clear whether, on balance, the non-native and heterogeneous character of the first speakers of Hebrew was a handicap or an advantage. However that may be, the following pages attempt to set the emergence and stabilization of native Israeli usage in an appropriate social and historical context.

Section 1 surveys the "koineizing" process that has led to present-day usage. Section 2 traces the emergence of native speech through four generations. Section 3 examines one result of these processes, the style differentiation. Another result, the native sound system, is examined in Section 4. Section 5 is a brief appraisal of Europeanization as a formative process. Section 6 sums up and concludes.

ORIGINS OF PRESENT USAGE

In the 1961 census, 75 per cent of Israel's Jewish population gave Hebrew as their main or sole language of daily communication. The

Jewish population was then 1,980,000, of whom 37.8 per cent were native-born, 34.8 per cent had immigrated from "Western" countries (Europe, America, etc.) and 27.4 per cent had immigrated from Asian and African countries [1]. The proportion of natives and of non-Western immigrants is, at present, on the increase, that of Western immigrants on the wane. Native speakers of Hebrew must number close to 40 per cent of the Jewish population, and together with near-native speakers, the 50 per cent mark is probably reached [2]. Other languages are in use, but none (except for Arabic in the case of the local Arabs) vie with Hebrew as the medium of intercommunal [3] communication for a sizable sector of the population.

Hebrew was adopted as a vernacular in the 1880s, largely through the activities of Eliezer Ben-Yehuda (1852–1922) and a handful of his followers. This had been preceded (a fact which is sometimes overlooked) by a secularizing literary revival that had begun over a century before the revival of speech. Hebrew had, of course, never ceased to be used for a variety of purposes, both religious and secular, throughout the centuries. The increase in its use and the broadening of its functions coincide roughly with the movement for national revival, resettlement in Palestine, and political independence. In view of the history of nation-building elsewhere in the world, it is hardly surprising that a national language was proposed, argued over, adopted first by one group and then by others, and gradually given a definitive shape by a slow "koineizing" process drawing on several pre-existing sources. Some elements of the process are specific to each particular case, others are found in most instances of national language formation.

In the case of Hebrew it should be pointed out that the literary revival of the eighteenth and nineteenth centuries had been carried out largely in Central and Eastern Europe. The prime movers of the speech revival were nearly all of East European birth; their followers, very nearly all of the Hebrew-speaking population, were of Central and East European origin for several decades after Ben-Yehuda [4]. There is thus a strong European substratum in Modern Hebrew, enhanced by the European cultural orientation of the population, and the linguistic implications of this fact have not escaped competent observers [5]. From the very outset, however, non-European factors were at work as well, whether in the heavy reliance on ancient Hebrew sources as a basic model for usage, or in the weaker influences exerted on the non-European sectors of the community by their own traditions and vernaculars. The non-European (chiefly Middle Eastern) population, once relatively insignificant, now constitutes approximately half the population, largely as a result of post-1948 immigration [6].

The forgers of the new national language, then, operated with a variety of literary dialects, several substrata, and several traditional pronunciations. As in other cases in which no dialect is naturally dominant and available for ready imitation, usage had to be established by a gradual and complex process of selection and accommodation which is, in part, still going on, but which has by now reached some degree of stabilization. Phonology and morphophonemics were anchored partly in a compromise between two major traditional pronunciations (see Section 4), partly in the phonetic habits of the first, non-Hebrew-speaking generation. Morphology was essentially Biblical, with post-Biblical features persisting in certain literary styles. Syntax was composite and showed strong European influences. The basic vocabulary was Biblical, but the total vocabulary had strong admixtures from later Hebrew and, whether as loans or loan-translations, much that was common European. There was, in all domains, a great deal of fluctuation, which the passage of time and the emergence of native speech habits has since considerably reduced. Standardizing efforts have been strong in vocabulary, moderate in grammar and phraseology, weak in orthoepy; although such efforts have contributed more directly to formal usage, some indirect influence on informal usage has also made itself felt.

Such are, basically, the antecedents of present-day usage or, more exactly, of present-day native and near-native usage. That usage is recent, not completely uniform, not yet that of a majority, but it shows unmistakable signs of becoming dominant. Older speakers grew up before the emergence of native usage; younger persons, including the new cultural and social elite, are, on the contrary, users and propagators of native speech. The relation between the generations is examined in the following section.

THE FOUR GENERATIONS

Research in the changes that have taken place since 1880 is lacking. However, taking the years 1900, 1930, and 1960 as reference points, we can attempt a brief characterization of the average, mature (about 45-year-old) speaker in the first, second, and third generation, respectively, and append a prognosis for the fourth generation, that of the present school-age children.

In 1900 the 45-year-old is Ben-Yehuda's contemporary. If he speaks Hebrew, he is not a native speaker (no one is), but speaks it as a matter of ideology. He is very likely to be of East European birth or background and to have Yiddish as his mother tongue; he has various difficulties in expressing himself in Hebrew, is constantly referring to written sources and authorities for guidance, lacks many common lexical items, uses other languages freely; he has few stylistic distinctions at his disposal (e.g., the informal versus formal difference is either nonexistent or rudimentary) and is, at all events, an oddity. Although a single pronunciation has been adopted as standard, orthoepy is weak, and communal differentiation due to vernacular substrata is strong; much the same holds true for features other than pronunciation.

By 1930 the 45-year-old is still predominantly of East European birth or background. He is not likely to be a native speaker (there are by now a handful of those, though even they grew up in an overwhelmingly non-Hebrew environment), but his Hebrew is both less of an oddity and more fluent. He may still speak Hebrew as a matter of ideology, but the younger set around him, including his own children, may be native or near-native speakers and have been raised entirely in Hebrew-language schools. Although his own contemporaries' speech is still communally marked, children of different communities brought up together begin to exhibit a certain amount of leveling. They also exhibit various deviations from both their elders' usage and the language they are taught at school; some of these deviations persist as the youngsters grow up, at least in what has become their informal style, while their formal style may be chastened by standardizing agencies that have now come into being: the Language Council, the teachers, the style editors, and so forth.

By 1960 our 45-year-old has a fifty-fifty chance of being a native or near-native speaker. Unless a recent immigrant, he was brought up in an environment in which Hebrew had greatly increased its scope, both in numbers of speakers and in diversity of functions. There is a relatively stabilized usage, variant forms having by now been selected out, some for informal use, some for formal, some neutral, some rejected. There is a marked (but not total) leveling of communal differentiation, both in pronunciation and in other domains. If he is a native, ideology plays a minor part, or no part at all, in his linguistic usage; if he is an immigrant, there is a good chance that he acquired Hebrew as much for practical as for ideological reasons. He still has one eye on normative or literary models for some features of his usage, especially in formal discourse, but his own informal usage and his pronunciation are imitated, as a matter of course, by many new speakers. It is, in fact, the language of the native and near-native speaker (in all its aspects) which most properly deserves the name of "Israeli Hebrew."

The prognosis for the fourth generation, those who will be about 45 years old in 1990 and are now going to school, should be fairly evident from what has just been said. Informal observation of such children confirms the impression of accelerated leveling, at least in communally mixed neighborhoods. More exactly, it seems likely that a leveled Israeli usage will increasingly be the common mark of native speakers who have gone through 12 years of school and two years of military service together. On the other hand, socioeconomic differentiation, especially when it entails an educational gap, may reinforce the already observable variation between less and more privileged speakers.

Some of the historical reasons for the difference between the generations should be mentioned briefly. Whereas the first and second generations grew up either before the adoption of Hebrew as a vernacular or shortly thereafter, the mature member of the third generation was born around 1915 and grew up after the establishment of the British mandate (1920–1948) over Palestine, that is, during a period of increased immigration, chiefly from Eastern Europe, and increased Hebraization. The immigrants who came during that period often knew Hebrew not as a religious language, but as a national language taught in various Zionist institutions in Europe. Hebrew was one of the official languages of mandatory Palestine, and Hebrew schools, newspapers, theaters, and books were increasing in number. Lexical expansion was rapidly closing the gap between the pre-existent vocabulary and the needs of the settlers. By 1948 there was a state apparatus, a school system, a broadcasting service, a network of public organizations, and a military apparatus using Hebrew exclusively. A population growing up under these circumstances naturally tended toward a more stabilized and more uniform usage than its predecessors. The great change that has taken place in the composition of the population since 1948, especially as a result of mass immigration from non-Western countries, will no doubt leave its mark on the linguistic situation, but at this writing the tendency of the immigrants to conform to previously established models seems stronger than influences operating in the reverse direction. Three of the results of the nativization and stabilization of usage in the third generation are discussed: differentiation of styles, leveling in phonology, and Europeanization in non-Western speakers.

EMERGENCE OF THE STYLE SCALE

First-generation speakers had, as models for their vernacular usage, a number of literary styles or dialects which, in turn, drew on a variety of ancient and medieval sources. Variant constructions with equivalent functions were thus available, and though stylistic differentiation must have had some roots in the literary dialects, the expansion of written and spoken usage accelerated the selection process in two major ways: (a) some pre-existing forms were retained in everyday conversation, and others relegated to more formal discourse; (b) the many innovations that were unavoidable under the circumstances were similarly pigeonholed, some for general use, some for formal use, and some for informal use.

If, for example, the pre-existing models offered four alternatives for the general-reference object pronoun "it" or "that," as in the phrase "I said it" ("I said that"), one variant, as in (amárti) et-zé, was retained in everyday usage; another, as in (amárti) zot, is now reserved for more formal styles, as is a third, (amárti) et-zót; the fourth, (amárti) ze, has been more or less rejected, though it can be heard from non-native speakers or read in older literary works. Since second-generation speakers, and some speakers close to the first generation, are still alive, it is still possible to hear utterances that make third-generation speakers smile, and may not be understood by the youngest of the fourth generation; an actual example: a septuagenarian asked a little girl *madúa eyné xafeycá lesaxéyk imí?* ("why don't you want to play with me?"), to which her normal equivalent, *láma at lo rocá lesaxék iti?* bears very little resemblance and, though the older speaker's words have not gone out of the language as a whole, the utterance as a whole is stylistically inappropriate in these particular circumstances for speakers of the third generation on down. In this case it was not understood.

The sentence just cited illustrates one of the commonest sources of the formal-informal differentiation, an innovation (the use of *lo* for negating the present tense) that has not yet received full right of entry into written, and hence formal spoken style. Examples could be multiplied at will, and the details of the variations are extremely complex. Many forms, of course, are neither formal nor informal in themselves, but it is hard to find a segment of discourse that is not stylistically marked. Allowing for this neutral range, then, and keeping in mind that not all speakers are equally at home in all styles, we can distinguish two major levels, "formal" and "informal," each of which can in turn be subdivided into two. The informal level has a lower or "untutored" rung, as well as a higher or "average informal" rung; the formal level has a lower or "average formal" rung and a higher or "elevated" rung [7].

A detailed description of what constitutes each of these rungs, and when or by whom each is used, is obviously out of the question here. Suffice it to say that untutored speech is the ordinary conversational style of natives with less formal education or, better, of those natives on whose speech habits formal education has had little influence, except for special occasions; that average informal speech is the ordinary conversational usage of better educated native speakers; that average formal style is common in lectures, public or official utterances, letters, and journalistic writing; and that elevated style is used in literary works. As one goes up the style scale, usage gets closer to the older literary models, and as one goes down, it is more and more permeated with recent innovations, but this is of course very far from a complete characterization. As an illustration, here is a sentence in the four style levels; optional alternatives are in parentheses. The sentence was heard in its untutored form, and I have ventured to compose the other three versions myself, though checking them with my learned friend T. Carmi to avoid mishaps. The sentence translates as "We don't think they have any in this store."

1. Untutored: *anáxnu lo xošvím še-yéš-et-ze baxanút (h)azóti.*

2. Average informal: *anáxnu lo xošvim še-zé yešnó baxanút (h)azót (hazú)*.

3. Average formal: *eyn anáxnu (ánu) svurím (xošvím) ki davár ze nimcá bexanút zu (zo)*.

4. Elevated: *eyn ánu (eynénu) svurím ki yimacé hadavár baxanút zo*.

The two informal levels negate the present with *lo*, the two formal ones with *eyn*; there is a neutral form *anáxnu* for "we," to which formal style prefers *ánu*; *yéš-et-ze* is untutored, *ze yešnó* is average, but more formal styles prefer not to use a naked *ze* in such cases; formal style also prefers various forms of *mc'* to forms of *yeš* as a *verbe d'existence*; further, *(h)azóti* is untutored, *(h)azót* neutral, *zu* without the article more formal than with, *zo* even more; the distinction *baxanút* versus *bexanút* (with versus without article) is contrary to normative grammar, which requires *buxunút* for both: the *ba-* of the less formal levels is with article, but the *ba-* of the elevated version is without; the use of *ki* as a subordinating conjunction marks an utterance as formal, whereas *še* is neutral.

Features marking the several style levels are grammatical and lexical. In phonology, most speakers have a single system for all levels; there are phonetic features associated more with rapid than with informal speech, and the two are not quite the same. On the other hand, there are distributional features and orthoepic norms which, for some speakers, are a concomitant of formal discourse, but the situation is complex; some aspects of it will be examined in the next section.

THE NATIVE SOUND SYSTEM

Before 1880, the pronunciation of Hebrew varied from community to community, both in Palestine and in the Diaspora. These pronunciations were based on a combination of two factors: (a) a set of spelling-pronunciation rules that established grapheme-to-phoneme equivalences, the graphemes being those of the Old Testament text in the Tiberian vocalization, and the phonemes being those of the language spoken by the particular community; (b) the allophonic and distributional mechanisms of the spoken vernacular, largely uncorrected by orthoepy. Since no vernacular had a phonemic stock that corresponded to the graphemic inventory of the received text, the communities varied as to the graphemic distinctions that were given oral equivalents.

The initiators of the speech revival had overwhelmingly been raised in the East European (Ashkenazic) varieties of traditional pronunciation. For various reasons, they decided to adopt the pronunciation in vogue among Mediterranean and Middle Eastern (Sephardic) communities, but which one of the several Sephardic varieties was actually used as a model is obscure. The impression is that that model was composite and somewhat vague, and that there was little concern for orthoepy, other needs being no doubt much more pressing.

It need hardly be pointed out that, under such circumstances, speakers of the first generation all spoke with a communal accent, adopting those features of the Sephardic model that did not run counter to their native phonetic habits, and rejecting (or, at best, faultily or erratically reproducing) the others [8]. Everybody had, for example, /a/, /o/, /t/ and final stress in the word "greetings," but whether one said *braxót* or *beraxót*, whether one had a uvular or apical /r/, the quality of the vowels, etc., gave one away, even though one had dropped the strictly Ashkenazic *bróxoys*, or the strictly Yemenite *bärâxöθ*, etc. Beginning with the second generation, however, and fully evident in the third and fourth, a process of leveling took place whereby the numerical and social dominance of the Ashkenazic community, coupled with the emergence of native speakers, has led to a native sound system that exists, so to speak, in two modes. One is the more generalized and communally undifferentiated "General Israeli," and the other the less generalized "Oriental Israeli," used by many (but not all) members of the Sephardic and Middle Eastern communities, but without internal communal differentiation to speak of.

The phonemic inventory of the more general of the two modes is as follows [9]:

```
p f  t s  c  č š  k x  ' h
b v  d z  -  ǧ ž  g-  --  m n r l y a e i o u
```

The /r/ is usually uvular, sometimes apical; it is the uvular version that is spreading at the moment. The /č/, /ǧ/, and /ž/ are rare and restricted to recent loanwords; the /'/ and /h/ are unstable in rapid speech. To the preceding inventory, which has a striking "common average European" air about it [10], the Oriental Israeli adds two phonemes, the pharyngeals /ḥ/ and /'/, and prefers the apical /r/. These features are also recommended by orthoepists, together with a number of others that do not constitute additions to the inventory, but modifications in distribution. Both modes have phonemic word stress.

The General Israeli mode is the common core to which new speakers (children, immigrants) tend to approximate, with some reservations to be discussed presently. It is, of course, quite similar to the non-native usage of the Ashkenazim of the first and second generations, yet clearly distinct from it. Native usage is characterized negatively by the absence of some distinctions found in non-native speech (e.g., /e/ versus /ə/ and positively by the specific allophones used and specific distributional features (e.g., which words have /e/ and which have /ey/). Briefly, the phonetics are largely a native development, the phonemics largely inherited from the non-native precursors. One phonemic feature that cannot be traced directly to the phonic habits of the East European Ashkenazim is the syllabification distinction that has led to the inclusion of /'/ in the inventory: such distinctions as *tov'ím* "drowning" (pl.) versus *tovím* "good" (pl.) are lacking in the pronunciation habits (whether in the vernaculars or in traditional Hebrew) of the East European Jews [11]. The inclusion of such a distinction in the General Israeli system could be due to orthoepic efforts, less plausibly to Sephardic influence, and is now, at any rate, a feature of the most informal General Israeli speech, including that of preliterate children, as well as of more formal styles. It is possible that it was retained from the spelling-pronunciation base because of its distinctive power, and its morphological role. Pairs such as *tov'ím-tovím* are numerous and common, and the /'/ keeps them apart not only phonemically, but also morphologically: *tovím* is merely *tov ím*, whereas *tov'ím*, is morphologically parallel to *tovlím*, "dunking," *tovxím*, "slaughtering," etc.

We now discuss some details of stylistic and social variations within the native sound system.

A few professional speakers (radio announcers, some lecturers) try to follow orthoepic prescriptions and use, as an addendum to formal discourse, the pharyngeals /ḥ/ and /'/, the apical /r/, and some other features. The pharyngeals and apical /r/ are, as has been seen, present in some types of informal discourse as well, but other features are not; for example, final stress in many words [*komunistí*, "communist," *kamá*, "(she) is getting up," etc.] for which nonprofessionals have penultimate stress. Actors, on the whole, do not use the pharyngeals, as this would have the effect of giving an elevated tone to all their lines or, in given cases, of making them sound communally marked; in fact, /ḥ/ and /'/ plus a few other devices *are* used on the stage to denote communally marked characters. The apical /r/ is, however, absolutely *de rigueur* on the stage and before the microphone, at least for professionals [12]. Imitation of this by nonprofessionals is rare, but does occur.

Some speakers who make no other concessions to orthoepy often put in a pharyngeal /'/ where it is required by the spelling even if they are not speakers of "Oriental Israeli." They do this without any other modifications, that is, as part of their ordinary speech, but with no great consistency. It is a sort of "decorative" device, but the effect it is intended to produce is hard to pinpoint. This does not apply to the replacement of /x/ by /ḥ/ as required by the spelling, which is thus more strictly a mark, *mutatis mutandis,* of either orthoepic or Oriental speech.

The native General Israeli sound system, complete with its appendages and allophonics, is used only by speakers belonging to the third and fourth generations (those born from 1915 on). Try though I have, I have never heard it in its full form in speakers born before that date. On the basis of informal observations carried out for over a dozen years and spot-checked more systematically here and there (though mostly in one communally mixed neighborhood in Jerusalem), the following points on communal differentiation (General vs. Oriental Israeli) may tentatively be hazarded.

Speakers of General Israeli who are now over 40 are exclusively, it would seem, of Ashkenazic background. Native speakers over 40 who are members of one of the Middle Eastern communities use the Oriental Israeli system. On the other hand, speakers of General Israeli from age 40 on down include members of all communities—all the Ashkenazim plus a number, hard to estimate, of persons from the Middle Eastern communities. The number of these "de-Orientalized" Sephardim, Yemenites, etc., increases visibly as age decreases, and the trend is, at the present writing, still going strong. The situation is complicated by the existence of intermediate or transitional phenomena: dropping one pharyngeal and not the other, fluctuations, and "bidialectalism," that is, using General Israeli outside the home but Oriental Israeli inside; but the trend is unmistakable. The pattern in several Sephardic families of my acquaintance is as follows: the grandparents (some native, most non-native) use the pharyngeals; the parents (natives in their forties) vary, the older ones speaking with and the younger ones without pharyngeals; the children are uniformly undistinguishable from General Israeli speakers; all live in communally mixed neighborhoods.

This trend is, however, by no means universal. A good many third- and fourth-generation speakers of Middle Eastern background stick to the pharyngeals and other hallmarks of the Oriental mode. Many of these are immigrants or children of immigrants chiefly, but not exclusively, from an Arabic-language background; they thus belong to communities whose traditional pronunciation of Hebrew includes pharyngeals and is closer to the Oriental Israeli than to the General Israeli mode. Others are natives of native stock, and it is not irrelevant to point out that Oriental features are used by persons of Sephardic extraction who belong to some of the oldest and most respected families of the country. Among these there are at least some, usually older, who would no more think of altering their pronunciation than would many a self-respecting middle-class Southerner in the United States. The degree to which General Israeli spreads at the expense of Oriental Israeli is thus controlled by a complex set of factors, too complex and too little investigated to be gone into here. It is not only commoner in younger people than in older, it also seems commoner in persons with higher income and better education.

Although the General Israeli sound system is spreading, it is not yet unequivocally "standard," in the sense of "being worthy of imitation by all educated people," at least at the level of phonemic inventory. In other matters (distribution, consonant clusters, position of stress, etc.)

that could not be discussed here, General Israeli usage *is* more or less standard in that sense, at least in the average informal and average formal discourse of nonprofessionals. This represents a *de facto* acceptance of a Europeanized sort of pronunciation. Europeanization of grammar and vocabulary have received an even greater degree of acceptance, as will be pointed out briefly now.

EUROPEANIZATION

The point to be made here is that average, educated native usage, the "emergent standard" of the title of this essay, is, without most of the qualifications that apply to the phonology, strongly marked by the dominant European substrata and adstrata in grammar and vocabulary. This seems partly due to the fact that Europeanization in these areas is tolerated or even approved by most linguistic authorities, and partly to the fact that it is not always identified as specifically "Western" as opposed to "non-Western," but often as "modern" as opposed to "old-fashioned," or simply not identified at all.

With regard to vocabulary, the story has been told too often to be repeated here [13]. European cultural orientation is accepted as a matter of course, and it makes little difference for the present discussion whether neologisms are transplanted in their European form or Hebraized, and whether the straight loan is a *pis-aller* or a deliberate choice [14]. The point is that whether a car is called *óto* or *mexonit* does not depend on the communal antecedents of the speaker. Matters are somewhat different in grammar, phraseology, and semantics. Some constructions are "General Israeli," that is, communally unmarked, whereas others are marked as "Oriental," *and* usually also (which is not the case in phonology) as less acceptable. For example, a yes-or-no question referring to future time with a first person singular subject is, in General Israeli usage, rendered by means of the infinitive: "shall I come tomorrow?" is *lavó maxár?* (literally "to come tomorrow?"); the use of the future in such cases (*avó maxár?*) marks a speaker as Oriental *and* (probably) less educated [15].

Similarly, such distinctions as *haláx*, "to go (on foot)" versus *nasá*, "to go (by vehicle)," or *yašán*, "to sleep" versus *nirdám* "to fall asleep," are communally unmarked and completely "standard." Not making the distinction—using the first member of each pair with the meaning of the second—marks a speaker as Oriental and less educated (cf. fn. 15). These and similar distinctions are lacking in the Middle Eastern substratum (notably Arabic) and, for that matter, in Biblical Hebrew; they are based on European models; for example, Yiddish *geyn* versus *forn*, *šlofn* versus *antšlofn vern* [16], but this sort of Europeanization has become part and parcel of average, educated usage.

A final example is furnished by the phrase *yotér-miday*, "too much," (literally "more than enough"). In General Israeli usage, it is an exact replica of the European "too (much)," "zu (viel)," "trop," etc. It may, again on the European model, precede the adjective (*yotér-miday gadól*, "too big"), which is contrary to older Hebrew usage; this is also true of the alternative form without *yotér*, although both *midáy gadól* and *gadól midáy* occur. The phrase does not seem to occur in Biblical Hebrew, and in later sources, if we may judge from the dictionary entries, its meaning was literally "more than (just) enough," that is, "greatly, extremely," without the necessary implication of the European model, "beyond the reasonable or desirable measure." The phrase and the Europeanized word order are now in use among all speakers irrespective of communal background, except that Middle Easterners with less education tend to use it with the meaning analogous phrases have in Arabic or Persian, which happens to be quite close to the older Hebrew usage. More precisely, such speakers tend to make no lexical differentiation between "very much" and "too much." In their usage only intonation and/or context will reveal whether *ze yotér-miday gadól* means "this is very big" or "this is too big." But this non-Europeanized usage is, as in the foregoing instances, communally marked and shunned by educated speakers.

SUMMARY AND CONCLUSION

After centuries of use in the liturgy and in various forms of literature, Hebrew was proposed for adoption as a vernacular in the 1880s in Palestine. By now it counts in the neighborhood of a million native and near-native speakers. This expansion of function triggered a number of linguistic developments and readjustments. The proposed vernacular was based on a number of literary dialects, a compromise between several traditional pronunciations, and on the linguistic habits of various immigrant communities, chiefly of East European origin. A complex "koineizing" process inevitably had to take place, and three generations later the resulting "Israeli Hebrew" has a fairly clear-cut outline.

The process of selection among alternative forms has led to the emergence of a style scale in which more formal discourse tends to follow older literary models, and more informal discourse tends to incorporate innovations more easily. But this is not the whole story; the selection processes are complex and not yet fully investigated. The style scale is most clearly in evidence among native speakers; non-native speakers either acquired Hebrew before the style scale had been formed, or are acquiring it gradually at present. At the center of the scale are the "average informal" and "average formal" levels common to most educated natives; they serve as a *de facto* double standard, roughly equivalent to the "colloquial standard" and "literary standard" (*Umgangssprache* and *Schriftsprache* or *Hochsprache*) of other national languages. At the extremities of the scale there is an "elevated" level of higher literature and an "untutored" level of popular discourse.

In phonology the outcome of the koineizing process has been a common core inventory that has a marked average European flavor to it. The native system has specific characteristics of its own, and exists in two varieties, one in which pharyngeals are absent or, at best, stylistic appendages, and another that includes them as regular phonemes. The first, "General Israeli," is spreading and is communally undifferentiated and thus approximates a *de facto* standard; the second, "Oriental Israeli," is communally marked and is receding.

Europeanization of vocabulary and grammar has gone a long way and has, to a very large degree, become part and parcel of the national standard: as education increases, speakers of non-Western background adopt the Europeanized forms as a matter of course.

NOTES

1. Figures are from *Pirsumey,* p. 29, and *šnaton,* p. 46. Estimates for 1964 (*šnaton, ibid.*) are: total Jewish population, 2,239,000; natives, 39.4 per cent; Western immigrants, 31.0 per cent; non-Western immigrants, 28.7 per cent.
2. A good many natives, especially persons over 60, are not native speakers of Hebrew, but on the other hand a good many persons listed as immigrants arrived in infancy and are undistinguishable from native speakers; my guess is that the number of the latter exceeds that of the former, hence the rough 40 per cent estimate. I would not like to be pressed on what constitutes a "near-native" speaker and how I know how many there are, but an added 10 per cent seems a fair guess.
3. The terms "communal" and "community" refer to the so-called *eydót,* sing. *eydá,* which are more or less homogeneous groups of immigrants sharing an area of origin and a cultural and linguistic tradition. Some of these are grouped together under a loose common label (e.g., *Aškenazim* for all or nearly all Europeans), some continue their group cohesion in varying degrees for generations after immigration. In Israel, their role is in many ways analogous to the regional groupings of old, settled territories, not least in matters of national language formation.
4. For details on the background of the revival of Hebrew, cf. Ben-Hayyim; Chomsky, pp. 178–226; Kutscher. For an analysis of the demographic factors and their role in the expansion of Hebrew down to 1954, cf. Bachi. Studies in recent Israeli Hebrew usage are listed in Blanc, 1964, Weinberg, 1966, and most completely and with useful annotations in Weinberg, 1965.
5. Cf. Bergstraesser's acute (if somewhat one-sided) observations, p. 47; and Plessner. A thorough review of the problem, based largely on written sources, may be found in Garbell. Cf. also Tubielewicz; Blanc, 1965; Zand; Chomsky, *ibid.;* Ben-Hayyim.
6. In 1948 the ratios were as follows: natives, 35.4 per cent; Western immigrants, 54.8 per cent; non-Western immigrants, 9.8 per cent; for comparison, see note 1. For figures preceding 1948, see Bachi, pp. 181–182, figs. 2 and 3.
7. The existence of an *Umgangssprache* in Hebrew, as opposed to the *Literatursprache,* was noted by Garbell, *passim;* Ben-Hayyim, pp. 30 ff., distinguishes between *lešón hatarbút,* "the language of culture," (more or less my "formal") and *lešón hadibúr,* "the colloquial" (roughly my "informal"); Rosén, 1953a, p. 8, distinguishes between

sub-standard (roughly my "untutored"), standard (roughly my two "average" levels), and super-standard (roughly my "elevated"). Rabin, 1958, 1959, distinguishes between colloquial (my "informal"), a "modern literary" (my "average formal"), and an "elevated language." Cf. also Blanc, 1965.

8. Garbell; Morag; Rosén, 1958; Blanc, 1965.
9. For more details on phonemics and phonetics, see Rosén, 1955; Blanc, 1964; Weinberg, 1966, gives a catalogue of differences (mainly distributional) between present usage and traditional spelling pronunciation rules.
10. It is not entirely accidental that this phoneme inventory is practically identical with that proposed by Zamenhof for Esperanto, the sole differences being the presence of /w/ and the absence of /'/ in Esperanto. Some varieties of Israeli Hebrew even seem to have a /w/–/u/ contrast here and there. Distribution and frequency, of course, differ widely.
11. Some non-natives of East European background and many of German background, however, do make such distinctions, the former more erratically (as a feature of careful enunciation only), the latter more consistently. German speech has had little influence on Israeli phonetics, but this might conceivably be one.
12. In the Hebrew version of *My Fair Lady* (the musical play based on G. B. Shaw's *Pygmalion*), Professor Higgins makes Eliza Doolittle switch from a uvular to an apical /r/, so that instead of "the rain in Spain stays mainly in the plain," she sings *barád yarád bidróm sfarád haérev*, "hail came down in Southern Spain this evening." The lower-class versus upper-class contrast is thus replaced by an off-stage versus on-stage contrast, or a plain versus orthoepic contrast, which is no doubt the best the ingenious translator could do. It is, of course, somewhat ambiguous, and to a literal-minded 11-year-old (my own daughter) it looked like "just the other way around," for she hears the uvular from her middle-class friends and the apical /r/ mostly, though not exclusively, from the plumber and the carpenter.
13. Cf. Chomsky, *loc. cit.*; Morag; Rosén, 1958; Garbell; Ben-Hayyim.
14. The name akadémya (or, by the Academy's ruling, *akademyá*) rather than some Hebraized substitute, was, for example, deliberately chosen for itself by the Hebrew Language Academy in 1953. Such choices are, no doubt, dictated by a desire to underscore, through the similarity in name, a similarity to the Western model of the institution or concept named.
15. In this and in the following examples, the reference is, of course, to native and near-native speakers. Non-native speakers might use forms based on their personal substratum, for example, an English speaking person might also say *avó* for "shall I come" rather than *lavó*, etc.
16. For details, see Blanc, 1965.

REFERENCES

Bachi, R. 1956. A Statistical Analysis of the Revival of Hebrew in Israel. *Scripta Hierosolymitana*, **3**, 179–247.

Ben-Hayyim, Z. 1953. *Lašon atika bimciut xadaša* = (*Lešonenu la-Am*, nos. 35–37).

Bergstraesser, G. 1927. *Einführung in die Semitischen Sprachen*, Munich.

Blanc, H. 1964. Israeli Hebrew Texts. *Studies in Egyptology and Linguistics in Honour of H. J. Polotsky*, Jerusalem.

———. 1964. Some Yiddish Influences in Israeli Hebrew. *The Field of Yiddish*, 2:185–201 (New York).

Chomsky, W. 1957. *Hebrew—The Eternal Language*, Philadelphia.

Garbell (Chanoch), I. 1930. *Fremdsprachliche Einflüsse im Modernen Hebräisch*, Berlin.

Kutscher, E. J. 1956. Modern Hebrew and Israeli Hebrew, *Conservative Judaism*, pp. 28–45.

Morag, S. 1959. Planned and Unplanned Development in Modern Hebrew, *Lingua* 8:247–263

Pirsumey mifkad hauxlusin vehadiyur. 1961. No. 15, Jerusalem, 1963.

Plessner, M. 1931. Modernes Hebräisch, *OLZ* 34:803–808.

Rabin, C. 1958. Lexeker haivrit hasifrutit haxadaša, *Lešonenu* 22, 246–257.

———. 1959. Hanaxot yesod lexeker lešono šel Š. Y. Agnon, *Š. Y. Agnon Jubilee Volume*, Jerusalem, pp. 217–236.

Rosén, H. B. 1953. Al standard venorma, al tahalixim ušgiot, *Lešonenu la-Am*, 38, 3–8, 39:3–7, 40/41, 3–11.

———. 1955/56. *Haivrit šelanu*, Tel Aviv.

———. 1958. "L'hébreu israélien," *REJ*, 17, 59–90.

Šnaton statisti le-Yisrael. 1965. Jerusalem.

Tubielewicz, W. 1956. Vom Einflusse Europäischer Sprachen auf die Gestaltung des Modernen Hebräisch, *Rocznik Orientalistyczny*, 20, 337–350.

Weinberg, W. 1965. A Bibliography of Spoken Israeli Hebrew, *Hebrew Abstracts*, 10, 3–16.

———. 1966. Spoken Israeli Hebrew: Trends in the Departures from Classical Phonology, *JSS*, 11, 40–68.

Zand, M. 1965. Idiš kak substrat sovremennogo ivrita, *Semitskie Jazyki*, 2(1), 221–246 (Moscow).

Charles A. Ferguson

ST. STEFAN OF PERM AND APPLIED LINGUISTICS

The fourteenth-century Russian Orthodox bishop of Perm, St. Stefan, "Apostle of the Zyrians," is almost completely unknown today among both hagiographers and specialists in applied linguistics [1]. Yet this unusual man dealt with all the major problems of linguistic development in a nonliterate society and devised solutions well worth consideration today by workers in applied linguistics facing the same problems in the developing countries of Asia, Africa, and Latin America. Similarly, his missionary strategy deserves study by church historians and theologians of Christian mission, not only in terms of success and failure but also in terms of the religious background from which it sprang and its subsequent fate.

Culture change related to socioeconomic development is often tied to the spread of religious systems, and in the case of two major world religions, Buddhism and Christianity, the use of local languages and the invention of new alphabets have sometimes received explicit ideological approval as a policy in missionary expansion [2]. St. Stefan's efforts will be examined here as a case study in the general area of language aspects of national development [3].

St. Stefan [4]

Stefan was born about the year 1335 in Ustjug, a town in the area of the Zyrians, or Komi [5], where there had been a settlement of Russians as early as 1212. He was apparently Russian in origin and culture, but from early childhood he was familiar with the living conditions, character, and language of the Komi who lived around him. In 1365 he entered a monastery at Rostov, where he spent 13 years in study and training, including the study of Greek. He was strongly influenced by the great Sergius of Radonezh, probably the most loved of the Russian saints, and is accounted one of his important disciples. Among his fellow

---

This paper is dedicated to Roman Jakobson.

monks Stefan was admired for the unusual holiness of his personal life and his sensitivity to the feelings and wants of others. Finally, he was ordained to the priesthood and returned home to proclaim the gospel to the Komi. As he began this task he found great resistance among the Komi, stemming partly from their loyalty to their own customs and the traditional shamanistic religion of the people and partly from the growing opposition to the Russians, who had begun to settle in the region as early as the eleventh century but were now beginning to take a position of economic and political dominance.

Stefan's attitude toward the Komi form of paganism was uncompromising: he fought the resistance movement led by Pam, the chief shaman, and he steadily replaced the local shrines and their pagan decorations by Christian churches with images of saints. On the other hand, he sympathized with the Komi in their opposition to the Russians: he made extensive use of the Komi language and he often took the side of the Komi in controversies with the Russians. He invented an alphabet for the Komi language and translated major parts of the liturgy into Komi, thus giving Komi the oldest literary monuments of any Uralic language except Hungarian, and he introduced the use of Komi in public worship and in the schools he established [6].

Whether by virtue of these policies or by his demonstrated bravery and his model Christian life—contrasting sharply with that of many of his fellow Russians—Stefan was remarkably successful in his missionary work, and during his lifetime he saw the majority of the Komi baptized into the Orthodox Church. In 1383 he was made the first Bishop of Perm, whose seat is in Ust'vym. Stefan visited Moscow on a number of occasions, and he died there in 1396. He is commemorated in Orthodox Churches on April 26, presumably the date of his death, and his sainthood has also been recognized by the Roman Catholic Church, even though he lived after the great schism between East and West.

After St. Stefan [7]

With the death of Stefan the Komi people began their history of five centuries of loyalty to the Orthodox Church, love and reverence for the name of St. Stefan, and pride in the early possession of a literary language of their own. Stefan's successors, however, were not of his caliber, and neither Russians nor Komi carried his linguistic work further [8]. The history of Old Permian literature is mostly the copying and recopying of translations made by Stefan himself or made shortly after his time. The next burst of literary activity did not occur until the nineteenth century, when Komi nationalist stirrings gave rise to some new works; because of the czarist prohibition of any written use of the Komi language for all but religious purposes, the existing works are all devotional materials, new translations from the Gospels, and the like. A knowledge of the script remained alive for three centuries, perhaps more among Moscow copyists of manuscripts than among the Komi people themselves. Gradually, however, the script was abandoned and the language was transliterated in Old Church Slavonic characters. Then the use of the language in written form or even for the celebration of the liturgy also disappeared and the church became Russified.

The Russian Orthodox Church, in spite of the success of St. Stefan's work and the use of national languages elsewhere in Eastern Orthodoxy, apparently did not again try the use of local languages until the nineteenth century, when, with the missionary work of such men as Makary Glucharev, Innokenty Veniaminov, and Nikolai Kasatkin, the liturgy was translated into Tatar, Chuvash, Finnish, Japanese, Chinese, Aleut, and other languages [9].

With the revolution of 1917 and the sociopolitical changes it brought, a new government language policy was instituted. Although the goals of the intended culture change were different, the Lenin policy of using national languages [10] represented a return to Stefan's ideas. By 1925 the territory of the northern Komi had been made an Autonomous Region (later an Autonomous Republic) and the territory in the south a National District. A writing system for Komi was devised, based on the Russian Cyrillic alphabet, each political entity was given a literary language based on the Komi spoken in it, and the two official literary languages were adopted for use in the educational system and the "mass media" (books, press, radio, and so on). The previously existing parish schools, which had been conducted in Russian, were abolished. Information is not readily available on the present use of Komi in the work of the Orthodox Church.

LINGUISTIC CHOICES

The basic linguistic question to be answered by the agent of culture change is: What language shall be chosen as the principal means of communication (hereafter PMC [11]) in the process of change? Various answers to this question have been given, and arguments on their relative merits are still heard among contemporary specialists on education in developing countries. If, as in the case of Stefan, the answer is the choice of a previously unwritten local language, three additional questions must be answered: What variety of the language shall be chosen as the standard? What kind of writing system shall be used? What kind of literature shall be produced? These more technical questions have also received different answers, but it may be hoped that modern workers in applied linguistics will develop a body of knowledge and experience that can serve as the basis for more rational decisions than have been possible in the past.

Choice of Language

Regardless of the initial means of communication, whether by interpreter, the use of a common second language, or gestures and the learning of the local language, sooner or later the decision on the language to use as the PMC must be made.

The easiest choice for the missionary [12] is to use his own language, teaching it to the people he is dealing with and then proclaiming or explaining his message through it. This choice has often been made, and indeed it has many practical advantages, the chief of which are the immediate utility of written and recorded materials in the missionary's language which do not require translation, the possibility of using additional missionaries without special language training, and the possibility of more advanced study by promising local individuals at the institutions of the missionary's home country. If the missionary's language also happens to be a major world language, other advantages are also apparent. A variant of this choice is the use of a language the missionary knows as a second language but which is not his native language. This is most commonly the choice either (a) when the missionary is the agent of a group that uses a different language, or (b) when a particular language is closely tied to the religion the missionary is bringing or is the regular medium of education in his home society.

A possible example of (a) is the use of English by the German clergymen sent by the missionary societies of the Church of England in the eighteenth century to such places as India and East Africa [13]. The best known case of (b) is the expansion of Western Christianity to northern Europe in the fifth to eleventh centuries, when the individual missionaries often learned the local language for initial contacts and preaching, but chose Latin as the PMC. This use of Latin regardless of the local language has remained typical of the Western Church up to the Reformation and of the Roman Catholic since then, with few exceptions. The Eastern Churches, on the other hand, have generally assumed that when the gospel was taken to a new people the local language would be chosen [14].

The second possible choice is that of a local language, either the native language of the community or a local lingua franca. If the society in question already has a written language with some degree of standardization, the missionary's problem is one of mastering this form of the language, possibly with adaptations for the new uses to which the language will be put. As an example of this we may cite the work of the Baptist missionary to Bengal, William Carey, and his associates, whose use of the Bengali language for prose works for education and instruction was the beginning of modern Bengali literature. Written Bengali at that time was used chiefly for certain kinds of poetry and when used at all for prose was in a heavily Sanskritized form far removed from the spoken language. Here the missionaries' choice of neither Sanskrit nor English as the PMC was decisive for the future of the Bengali language and the Bengali speech community [15].

In regions of extreme multilingualism the missionary may find it advisable to choose one local language out of many to serve as the PMC. At times this choice has been for an existing local lingua franca—a language that is already learned as a second language and used for intercommunication among speakers of different languages, typically for purposes of trade. A good example of the choice of a local lingua franca is the policy of the Spanish friars to use Nahuatl as the PMC in the evangelization of highly multilingual Mexico [16]. Sometimes, however, the choice has been based on the simple accident of the location of the initial missionary activity in the area. An example of language choice in a multilingual situation is the decision by Lutheran missionaries in New Guinea. The missionaries were faced with a large number of languages, each with a small number of speakers, and after some years of consideration and the production of materials in about a dozen languages, the three languages of Kate, Yabem, and Graged were chosen as PMCs for several dozen speech communities [17]. This process of reduction of PMCs will probably proceed further in New Guinea with the increasing use of Neo-Melanesian (Pidgin English) as a lingua franca and the recent government emphasis on English. Some missionary-linguists object to the choice of lingua francas and insist that every speech community, no matter how small, should have the gospel presented in its own language, and this has become the general policy of the Wycliffe Bible Translators and the Summer Institutes of Linguistics, which constitute the largest single group of workers using applied linguistics for religious purposes [18].

In closing the discussion of this point it is worth noting that in recent years many specialists in education in developing countries have expressed strong preference for the use of the vernacular, that is, the local primary language, as the medium of instruction, at least at the lower levels. A number of reservations have been expressed, however, and it seems clear that further experimentation and comparative case studies are needed to determine the critical factors to be considered in making this kind of choice [19].

Choice of Standard

The choice of a previously unwritten language to serve as a PMC involves the choice of one particular variety of the language in preference to others. If the language in question is relatively homogeneous, that is, if dialect variation is at a minimum, this problem is unimportant, but it often happens that the dialectal variation is considerable and the choice of a particular variety as the norm may have repercussions on a number of levels. The two policies most often adopted are (a) to choose the dialect most highly regarded by the whole speech community (an incipient standard), or (b) to choose the dialect at the point of entry of the outside influence in the community as representing the dialect that will naturally tend to be the one used by bilingual and bicultural individuals. It must be noted in connection with (a) that an incipient standard may not be the variety informants assert is the "purest" or the "best" but one that is spreading rapidly by the processes of migration and urbanization; an example is the urban Wolof of Senegal.

Stefan seems to have adopted the second policy, basing his language mostly on the variety of Komi spoken along the lower course of the Vyčegda River. This was essentially the kind he himself had learned in his childhood in the Russian settlement, and incidentally is not far geographically from the present-day political center of the Komi Autonomous Republic. The linguistic evidence seems to show, however, that the Komi language was more nearly uniform at that time than it is now and that the lines of dialect difference did not coincide very closely with modern boundaries [20]. The various examples of texts in Old Permian show slight dialect variations among themselves, suggesting that there was no rigidly codified norm or true standard at that time, and the religious publications of the nineteenth century also show some dialect variation.

When the two literary languages were created after the Revolution, one was based on the Komi of Syktyvkar, the capital of the Komi ASSR, and the other on that of Kudymkar, the capital of the Permyak National District. The first is called Zyrian-Komi, or simply Komi, the latter Permyak-Komi. These two literary languages are very close together and it is hard to see any linguistic reason for keeping them separate, although there may be political or cultural justification for doing so not apparent to the outsider [21].

In many speech communities the question of choice of a preferred variety is a much more complex question, and at times missionaries have adopted a third policy, the creation of a common language which is not based on any one dialect and minimizes the features that separate the dialects. Although something of this sort happens to some extent in the formation of any standard language, its conscious adoption as a policy has usually led to many difficulties. One of the most often cited examples of this kind of policy is the attempt to create a standard Ibo in the face of complex dialect variation [22].

Choice of Writing System

One of the basic issues involved in language planning in a nonliterate society is the nature of the writing system to be introduced. Beyond the fundamental choice between syllabary and alphabet, there is the choice between the use of an existing system and one specially invented for the language. Within these major choices there are a host of details, such as the use of symbol sequences and diacritics, the degree of morphophonemic information to be incorporated, and features of punctuation. This whole issue has been examined somewhat more systematically than other linguistic questions in national development, and many of the relevant sociolinguistic factors have at least been identified [23].

The typical view of missionaries today seems to be that one should choose the alphabet that is used for the national language of the country and the spelling conventions should be such that they would provide an easy transition to the national language. This also seems to be the considered judgment of Soviet linguists, who have preferred modified versions of the Cyrillic alphabet for minority languages in the USSR. In the language planning activity after the Revolution and on into the twenties Arabic script was sometimes used and a number of Roman alphabet orthographies were devised, but these were all replaced by Cyrillic orthographies in the forties. One difference between Soviet and SIL practice has been in the spelling of loanwords from the national language: the Soviets have generally preferred to have Russian loanwords spelled in the minority language just as they are in Russian regardless of the discrepancies in pronunciation or orthographic conventions, whereas the SIL workers generally prefer a spelling of Spanish or Portuguese loans consistent with the pronunciation and orthographic conventions of the borrowing language. Russian practice in this respect has now shifted, but the earlier practice was like that followed in the language development activity associated with the spread of Islam. In most languages written with the Arabic script, Arabic loanwords, including proper names, are spelled as they are in Arabic regardless of their pronunciation in the borrowing language, a procedure that facilitates the study of Arabic or other Islamic languages but causes trouble for the monolingual person learning to read his own language.

Stefan's choice of writing system is of special interest. He invented an alphabet, called Abur, which was clearly based on his knowledge of Greek and Church Slavonic, but he deliberately made the forms of the letters sufficiently different from either so that the Komi could regard the writing system as distinctively theirs and not an alphabet used for another language. It even seems likely that he gave some of the letters an appearance suggestive of the Tamga signs in use among the Komi as property markers and decorations.

In the creation of new writing systems in the early centuries of the Church's expansion to new peoples in the East, the usual pattern was to use the letters of the Greek alphabet as a base and add new letters as required by sounds not present in Greek. This was, for example, the procedure followed in the creation of the Coptic alphabet, Bishop Wulfilas' invention of the Gothic writing system, and in the creation of an

alphabet for Slavic by St. Cyril and St. Methodius, although this last was
perhaps made especially distinctive. In some cases, however, the origina-
tor of the new alphabet had reasons for wanting to emphasize the distinctiveness of the new writing system. A good example of this is the creation
of the Armenian alphabet by St. Mesrop in the fifth century. St. Mesrop
clearly felt that the Armenian people needed an alphabet that would
not only be adequate to represent the sounds of their language but would
also be distinctly different from the Greek and Syriac alphabets in use by
the surrounding peoples.

In all these cases the invention of the new alphabet has been based on
some kind of phonological analysis of the language to be served, as indeed
the original invention of the alphabetic system of writing in the Eastern
Mediterranean in the second millennium B.C. may be regarded as the first
attempt at phonemic analysis and notation; for some practitioners of
modern linguistics the procedures of "phonemics" are still primarily an
attempt to provide a consistent and natural notation for languages [24].
The chief limitation on the phonemic principle in the later alphabet
inventions has been the orthographic conventions of the source alphabet.
St. Stefan's, for example, provided two letters for the phonemically distinct o's of Komi but failed to do so for the e's, and this reflects the existence of two o's in the Greek alphabet (omicron and omega, pronounced
alike at that time) and only one e (epsilon; the eta was then pronounced
i).

When the inventor of a new alphabet is a religious figure it is to be
expected that some reference will be made to supernatural elements in
the process. Among Christian linguist-saints this has generally been limited in contemporary reports to an acknowledgment of the help of
prayer, but later generations have often found a miracle in the achievement and have added details of divine intervention and revelation. A
good example is the work of St. Mesrop. The earliest biography of the
saint recounts his study with Greek and Syrian scholars, a two-year period
of experimentation with children using a preliminary form of the alphabet, and the final designing of all the variant forms of the letters with the
aid of a Greek scribe. In the account of the Armenian historian Movses
of Khoren who lived at a somewhat later period, although his dates are
uncertain, ". . . to the eyes of his soul was revealed a right hand writing
on a stone so that the stone kept the trace of the lines as on snow. . . .
And rising from prayer he created our letters" [25]. Although St. Stefan
was much revered, no such accretions of legend about his invention of
the Abur seem to have developed.

Choice of Literature

When the missionary has chosen the language, decided on the standard
variety, and devised the writing system, his final question is what kind of

material to produce in the language. Christian missionaries have generally produced primers for teaching the alphabet, and then the books that they felt were most important for the spread of the Christian faith, regardless of what other needs or desires of the people may have been. It is interesting to compare in this connection the somewhat different priorities assigned by different branches of Christendom. The Orthodox Churches typically issue first translations of basic parts of the Divine Liturgy, including, of course, selections from the Bible which are found in it. Roman Catholic missionaries usually produce first devotional materials and catechisms, and Protestant missionaries tend to turn their attention first to translation of the Bible, especially the New Testament and Psalms [26]. The Lutheran linguist-reformers of the sixteenth century who started new orthographies and standard languages in Europe in connection with the spread of the Reformation, such as Michael Agricola for Finnish and Primož Trubar for Slovenian, typically worked first on the New Testament and Luther's Small Catechism, then the Psalms, the liturgy, and the Augsburg Confession [27].

Stefan's choice of literature seems to have been in accordance with the tendencies of Eastern Orthodoxy. Almost all the extant documents of Old Permian are translations of the liturgy, and the major exception is the existence of inscriptions on icons, which in the Orthodox tradition are essential elements of public worship. After giving the briefest introduction to the writing system—a number of lists of the letters and even letter names are extant—Stefan apparently felt that the most important task of the written language was to enable the Komi to follow the Orthodox pattern of public worship. It is reasonable to assume that Stefan was also interested in questions of doctrinal instruction, private prayer, and practical ethics, but these were related to the liturgy, with its treasury of Scripture readings and ancient hymns and prayers.

CONCLUSION

In the fourteenth century St. Stefan of Perm undertook to convert to Christianity a nonliterate society of some thousands of people. In meeting the language problems involved in this undertaking he made the following decisions. He chose the local language as the principal means of communication. He chose as the basis for its standard the dialect whose speakers had the greatest contact with the Christianizing culture. He invented a writing system that was essentially phonemic and distinctively different in the shape of its letters from any other known system. He chose as the first publication in the language the books most necessary for conducting the proper rites of the Church.

In all these decisions the good saint acted without benefit of a sociolinguistic theory or frame of reference, and without any recorded body of previous sociolinguistic experience he could consult. One must admire St. Stefan's clear-cut decisions and successful implementations of them, but equally one must bewail the fact that a present-day agent of culture change faced with language problems in a nonliterate society still has no sociolinguistic theory and very little in the way of recorded and analyzed case histories to give guidance. We have not progressed much beyond St. Stefan's competence of five centuries ago.

Without attempting to chart any of the future courses of sociolinguistic inquiry related to national development, it seems only reasonable to suggest that an immediate step of considerable practical value and—one might hope—ultimately of significance for the growth of sociolinguistic theory would be the preparation of an inventory of the several hundred documentable examples of linguistic innovation of the kind described here. Such an inventory should include not only information on the questions of linguistic choice discussed here but also information on such relevant questions as the size of the speech community and its attitude toward language; it could also include some crude measures of success or failure such as time elapsed before first major literary figure or first indigenous periodical. One feels that Stefan would have welcomed the existence of such a collection of information, and it even seems likely that such strange professional colleagues as Soviet linguists implementing Lenin's policies and SIL workers intent on spreading Christianity could cooperate in the compilation and use of the inventory. If it were not for the fact that Soviet scholars and evangelical missionaries would equally reject the formulation, although for different reasons, one would be tempted to see St. Stefan of Perm as the patron saint of workers in the applied linguistics of national development and ask his blessing on their research and its application.

NOTES

1. Roman Jakobson, in his important article, "The Beginning of National Self-Determination in Europe," *The Review of Politics* (1945), pp. 29–45, referred to the work of St. Stefan as part of the East European heritage of linguistic nationalism. In Constantin de Grunwald's *Saints of Russia* (London, 1960), however, Stefan rates only three lines, on p. 83. In the interesting survey by W. Wonderly and E. Nida, "Linguistics and Christian Missions," *Anthrop. Lings.*, 5, 1 (January, 1963), pp. 104–144, his name does not even appear. The most convenient account of him available in English is probably Alban Butler's *Lives of the Saints* (2nd ed., London, 1956), Vol. 2, p. 167.

2. For example, Theodore Balsamon, Patriarch of Antioch in the twelfth century, wrote, "Those who are wholly orthodox, but who are altogether ignorant of the Greek tongue, shall celebrate in their own language; provided only that they have exact versions of the customary prayers translated on to rolls and well written in Greek characters." Quoted in Cyril Korolevsky, *Living Languages in Catholic Worship,* translated by Donald Attwater (London, 1957), p. 15.

3. Cf. C. A. Ferguson, "The Language Factor in National Development," *Anthrop. Lings.*, 4, 1 (January, 1962), pp. 23–27, reprinted in Frank A. Rice, editor, *Study of the Role of Second Languages* . . . (Washington, 1962), pp. 8–14. On the need for case histories, see Alfred S. Hayes (ed.), *Recommendations of the Work Conference on Literacy* (Washington, 1965), p. 14.

4. The chief source for information on the life of Stefan is the biography written by his contemporary, the monk Epiphanius the Wise. The nineteenth-century Russian edition of V. G. Družinin, *Žitie Svjatogo Stefana Episkopa Permskogo Napisannoe Epifaniem Premudrym* (St. Petersburg, 1897) has been reprinted photomechanically, with an English introduction by Dmitrij Čiževskij on the literary position of Epiphanius (The Hague, Mouton, 1959). There seems to be no English translation except for a small part that appears under the title the "Panegyric to St. Stefan of Perm," in S. A. Zenkovsky (ed.), *Medieval Russia's Epics, Chronicles, and Tales* (New York, 1963), pp. 206–208.

5. The general name for the whole people and their language is Komi, and this will be used throughout the paper, but the name Zyrian or Zyrvenian has also been used, especially to refer to the northern population and their speech. The name Permian is used especially to refer to Stefan's literary language (Old Permian) and as an inclusive term for Komi and Udmurt, which constitute a branch of the Finno-Ugric language family.

6. The best account of Old Komi (= Old Permian) is that of the prominent Komi linguist V. I. Lytkin, *Drevnepermskij jazyk; čtenie tekstov, grammatika, slovar'* (Moscow, 1952). There is a lengthy, informative review of this in German in *Acta Linguistica (Hung.)* 4 (1954), pp. 225–249 by D. Fokos-Fuchs.

7. No comprehensive work on the history of the Komi people has been available to me. The account here is based on scraps of information from a variety of sources. Doubtless it can be corrected in detail, but I hope it is reliable in its general outline.

8. One name stands out among his successors: Jona, who was bishop from 1456 to 1470. Jona carried the Christianizing of the Komi to the southern population in what was then called Great Permia, baptizing the prince, who took the name Michael. With the subjugation of Prince Michael by the forces of Moscow the whole Komi people came formally into the political structure of the Moscow state, and the bishops came to live more in Russian Vologda than in Komi Ust'vym.

9. For a convenient account in English of these three missionaries, see Stephen Neill, *A History of Christian Missions* (Penguin Books, 1964), pp. 440–449. Glucharev, whose life's work was among the Kalmucks in the Altai plateau of Central Asia, wrote a penetrating book, *Thoughts on the Methods to be Followed for a Successful Dissemination of the Faith,* in which he advocated the use of local languages and the development of popular education on the widest scale, but his views were generally ignored by his contemporaries.

10. Cf. V. I. Lenin, *O Prave Nacij na Samoopredelenie,* numerous editions and translations.

11. The expression "principal means of communication" is used here to refer to the language used for formal instruction, for meetings related to culture change (planning and implementation of change, carrying on of new institutions), and for publication. The possibilities are, of course, more complex than this phrasing of the question suggests. For example, the choice may be made to use one language for early years of primary school and another as the medium for secondary and higher education. Possibilities of this kind will be ignored here partly for simplicity of presentation and partly because not so many alternatives are likely to have been considered in the Permian situation.

12. Hereafter the term "missionary" will be used as the most appropriate term for the

present study, but it must be remembered that the missionary is only a special case of the conscious agent of culture change, which includes conquerors, colonizers, technical assistance personnel, and even social science experimenters.

13. Cf. J. Richter, *Allgemeine evangelische Missionsgeschichte*, Vol. 1. *Indische Missionsgeschichte*, 2nd ed., 1924.

14. Cf. Christine Mohrmann, "Linguistic Problems in the Early Christian Church," *Vigiliae Christianae*, 11 (1957), pp. 11–36, esp. pp. 17–19, and Koralevsky, *op. cit.*, Chapter I.

15. Cf. Edward C. Dimock, "Literary and Colloquial Bengali in Modern Bengali Prose," in Charles A. Ferguson and John J. Gumperz (eds.), *Linguistic Diversity in South East Asia* (Bloomington, 1960), esp. pp. 51–58.

16. Cf. Robert Ricard, *The Spiritual Conquest of Mexico*, translated by Lesley Byrd Simpson (Berkeley and Los Angeles, 1966), pp. 45–60, for discussion of the language problem; the use of Nahuatl is treated on pp. 45–51 and p. 290.

17. Cf. A. C. Frerichs, *Anutu Conquers in New Guinea* (Columbus, Ohio, 1957), Chapter 10, "Language and Literature," esp. p. 163. For further discussion of the New Guinea language situation, see S. A. Wurm, "Papua-New Guinea Nationhood: The Problem of a National Language," *J. Papua New Guinea Soc.* (1966).

18. For an impassioned statement of this view see Kenneth L. Pike, "We Will Tell Them, But in What Language," *His* (October 1951), pp. 8–11, 14; reprinted in Kenneth L. Pike, *With Heart and Mind* (Grand Rapids, Mich., 1964), pp. 124–130.

19. For a persuasive statement of the preference for the vernaculars, see *The Use of Vernacular Languages in Education* (UNESCO Monograph on Fundamental Education No. 8, Paris, 1953), and for some of the reservations, see the thoughtful review of this book by William Bull, *International Journal of American Linguistics*, 21 (1955), pp. 228–294; reprinted with added bibliography in Dell Hymes (ed.), *Language in Culture and Society* (New York, 1965), pp. 527–533. For a thorough discussion of the alternatives and a set of definite recommendations for the New Guinea area, see S. A. Wurm, "Language and Literacy" in E. K. Fisk (ed.), *New Guinea on the Threshold* (Canberra, 1966), pp. 135–148.

20. "In any case, the old Komi (Old Permian) literary language, created in the fourteenth century by the missionary Stefan on the basis of the Lower Vyčegda dialect, was still equally close to the Vyčegda and Kama Komi, and it was not by chance that the Permian (Ust'vym) bishops spread Christianity by this language also among the Kama Komi." V. I. Lytkin (ed.), *Komi-Permyackij Jazyk* (Kudymkar, 1962), p. 26.

21. "The Permyak-Komi and Zyrian-Komi languages are particularly close to each other; therefore in scientific literature they are not counted as two languages, but as the two main dialects of the one Komi language." *Ibid.*, p. 5.

22. For a detailed discussion of the linguistic problems in Ibo, see Ida C. Ward, *Ibo Dialects and the Development of a Common Language* (Cambridge, 1941). An example of the creation of a standard based on careful analysis of dialects and a kind of reconstruction of a logical ancestor to them is reported by Einar Haugen, "Construction and Reconstruction in Language Planning: Ivar Aasen's Grammar," *Word*, 21 (1965), pp. 188–207; see also his "Linguistics and Language Planning," in William Bright (ed.), *Sociolinguistics* (The Hague, 1966), pp. 50–72.

23. The best general account of the factors involved in the creation and change of orthographies is Jack Berry, "The Making of Alphabets," in *Proceedings of the Eighth International Congress of Linguists* (Oslo, 1957), pp. 752–764. See also Sarah C. Gudshinsky, *Handbook of Literacy* (Glendale, California, 1957); Andrée F. Sjoberg, "Socio-Cultural and Linguistic Factors in the Development of Writing Systems for Preliterate Peoples," in William Bright (ed.), pp. 260–276; William A. Smalley et al., *Orthography Studies* (London, 1964). An instructive case study is provided by Paul Garvin, "Literacy as a Problem in Language and Culture," in *Report of*

the Fifth Annual Round Table Meeting on Linguistics and Language Teaching (Georgetown University Monograph Series on Language and Linguistics No. 7, Washington, 1954), pp. 117–129.

24. Cf. Kenneth L. Pike, *Phonemics; A Technique for Reducing Language to Writing* (Ann Arbor, Mich., 1947).

25. Cf. Korium, *The Life of Mashtots* [Mesrop], translated by Bedros Norehad (New York, 1964). Here is a very informative introduction translated from the modern Armenian introduction to Korium by a Soviet scholar, the late Manouk Abeghian. The quotation from Movses of Khoren is from his *History of the Armenians*, translated [into modern Armenian] by Stephan Malkastian (Erevan, 1961), pp. 325–326.

26. In the choice between "practical" books of instruction for everyday behavior and ideological documents that attempt a conversion to new viewpoints, the modern Russian linguists seem to have been more like the Protestants in preferring the ideological, since translations of the works of Marx, Lenin, etc., are often among the early publications for newly literate communities.

27. Cf. Jaakko Gummerus, *Michael Agricola, der Reformator Finnlands* (Helsinki, 1941), pp. 40–67.

Einar Haugen

THE SCANDINAVIAN LANGUAGES
AS CULTURAL ARTIFACTS

In the Early Modern period following the Reformation, the Scandinavian countries were developing nations, and the creation of national languages was a significant part of their development. It appears to me that the history of these languages offers a valuable opportunity to study the elaboration (what Kloss calls the *"Ausbau"*) of standard languages in a region of minimal language distance (*"Abstand"*) (Kloss 1952). Scandinavia is a single dialect area with gradual rather than sharp transitions from country to country (we are disregarding here the Finno-Ugric languages of the area, Finnish and Lappish). Yet within this area there are six standard languages, each with a respectable literary tradition and a group of enthusiastic users: Danish, Swedish, Dano-Norwegian, New Norwegian, Faroese, and Icelandic.

PROBLEM

Our study will be devoted primarily to the initial problem of standardization, the *selection* of a norm, and secondarily to its *acceptance* (for these terms see Haugen, 1966a, in greater detail 1966c). There are two rival hypotheses concerning selection: (a) that an SL (standard language) is (or should be) based on a single dialect, that is, someone's vernacular; (b) that an SL is (or should be) a composite of dialects (the nature of the composition being left unspecified). We may call the first the *unitary* thesis and the second the *compositional* thesis. This problem was much debated in Renaissance Italy, where some writers maintained that Italian should be based on Tuscan, whereas others (e.g., Dante) held that it should be a supralocal norm based on all the dialects. Both theses have been argued in Scandinavia as well, with inconclusive results. It will be suggested here that both theses are true—and false—in varying degrees according to time and place. However, by the time a norm has been codified and elaborated by its users, it has become virtually impossible to identify its base. It has become an independent artifact in the culture, one of the devices by means of which a particular group, usually a power elite, manages to maintain or assert its identity and, when possible, its power.[1]

The acceptance of a norm is also a problem of power and identity. Language distance is not the only factor in identification. Unless it agrees with other cultural norms, it may easily be overridden. But when it is allied with a whole complex of traditional differences, it becomes a high-level symbol of that complex. I shall trace in a quite informal and anecdotal way some of the political constellations that have determined the rise of new SLs in Scandinavia, suggesting what the reasons may have been for the differential reactions to the establishment of these. In the Early Modern Period Norway accepted Danish, Iceland did not; Northern Jutland accepted Danish, Southern Jutland did not; Scania accepted Swedish, Finland did not.

If we think of the spread of languages and their gradual differentiation through time as a "natural" or "inevitable" phenomenon, we still need to account for the tremendously convergent linguistic trends that have led to the spread of SLs. From the point of view of the comparative linguist, this is a disturbing and unpredictable factor, which is likely to throw his reconstructions off. If we adopt the metaphor of the traditional family tree for languages, SLs are artifacts that result either from pruning or grafting the tree. The gardeners are a special priesthood of taste and learning, who are entrusted by society with the codification and elaboration of a code that is part of the conscious heritage of the social establishment.

Although it has been asserted that standardization can take place without writing (Stewart 1962, p. 24), the evidence for this is slender. Languages can obviously spread over large areas without writing and can achieve a relatively homogeneous norm (Eskimo, Indo-European). Non-literate tribes have various types of formalized discourse as well as standards of correctness. Unless the rules are explicitly formulated, however, it is questionable that this should be regarded as standardization. All the known standards have had the technical support of writing; even the Greek *koine* is known to us primarily as a written language. It is clear that before the spread of writing through the printing of books and newspapers and the common school, the influence of writing made itself

---

[1] Cf. M. M. Guxman (1960), Conclusion (tr. p. 25): "The common national norm embodied in the literary language is never the result of a spontaneous process of language development, but to a certain degree the result of artificial selection and interference with this spontaneous process." *Ibid.*, p. 27: "In Germany, the literary norm of the national language is by no means a codification of the system of characteristics of the Eastern Middle German dialects, generally considered to be the basis of literary German."

felt only within very restricted circles of literate elites. I shall therefore distinguish between a *writing tradition,* which is passed on by hand, and a *standard language,* with explicit codification of its orthography, grammar, and lexicon. Only Iceland among the Scandinavian countries has a medieval grammatical literature, so that its writing tradition may also be regarded as a standard language.

SURVEY

Scandinavia is here understood to include the present-day nations of Denmark, Finland, Iceland, Norway, and Sweden; my chief interest here is Danish. A history of the Scandinavian languages may well be called "The Rejection of Danish." Danish is the ugly duckling of Scandinavia, with humble beginnings under the shadow of Latin and Low German, with tremendous potentialities for becoming the SL of all Scandinavia, and with the most brilliant development in modern times as the language of Hans Christian Andersen and Søren Kierkegaard. In spite of this it has suffered a continual restriction of area and rejection by its neighbors, which has made it the least Scandinavian, although in some ways the most developed of the Scandinavian languages (Haugen 1966b). At least Danish has one advantage over the others for our purposes: it is the only one to have received full historical treatment not only of its internal development but also of its changing social context (Skautrup 1944–1953).[2]

The writing traditions of Scandinavia fall into three distinct historical periods, which we may name "ancient" (third to tenth centuries), "medi-

TABLE 1. *Scandinavian History: A Sociolinguistic Aperçu*

	Periods		
	Ancient (*third to tenth centuries*)	*Medieval* (*eleventh to fifteenth centuries*)	*Modern* (*sixteenth to twentieth centuries*)
Society	Tribal	Monarchic	National
Religion	Pagan Norse	Roman Catholic	Lutheran
Writing	Epigraphic	Epigraphic Manuscript	Printed
Script	Runic	Runic Roman	Roman
Language	Unified ("Common Norse")	Dialectal ("Old Norse")	Standardized (in six varieties)

[2] I am deeply indebted to the work of Peter Skautrup, whose monumental three-volume history discusses these problems at some length and will be quoted frequently in the following pages.

eval" (eleventh to fifteenth centuries), and "modern" (sixteenth to twentieth centuries). As Table 1 indicates, the ancient and medieval periods include an epigraphic tradition of runic writing. We shall here disregard this tradition, in spite of its value for linguistic history, because there is no significant relationship between the runes and the development of the modern SLs. The history of the SLs is closely linked to that of the Latin alphabet, which came to Scandinavia with the Roman Catholic church in the tenth century. Although the foundations of the medieval monarchies were laid in the ancient period, even the Middle Ages did not see the rise of nations in our sense of that word. The kings were often weak, the nobility unruly, and the people untouched by national affairs. Borders were still fluid, but there was a clear trend toward the centralization of power throughout the area. This seemed to have achieved its historical goal in 1397, when the kingdoms of Norway (including Iceland, the Faroes, and Greenland) and Sweden (including Finland) joined in a dynastic union with Denmark (including Schleswig-Holstein) under the leadership of the Danish monarch, Queen Margaret. Denmark was by far the strongest of the Scandinavian countries, having under its immediate rule the greater part of Scandinavia's arable soil, from the Eider River just north of Hamburg and Bremen to the border of Småland in what is today central Sweden. All of Scania (plus the shires of Halland and Blekinge and the island of Gotland) were Danish. Since archeological times, Denmark had been the wealthiest Scandinavian country, the closest both geographically and culturally to the European continent.

THE MIDDLE AGES

The nature of manuscript writing was substantially the same in all western countries in the Middle Ages. Latin as the universal tongue of religion and learning was the language of wider communication used by the clergy and the royal houses, and eventually by all men of learning. Within Scandinavia the Latin tradition was strongest in Denmark, the last country to adopt the native language in legal documents issued by the royal chancery. This adoption occurred in 1371 under Queen Margaret, 30 years later than in Sweden and nearly two centuries later than in Norway (Seip, 1955, p. 96). The native tradition was stronger in Norway and Iceland, no doubt because of their having been converted from England where (thanks to Irish influence) the native language had long been used in writing. It is characteristic that the Icelander Snorri Sturluson wrote his *History of the Kings of Norway* in Icelandic, whereas his Danish contemporary Saxo Grammaticus wrote his *History of Denmark* in Latin (*Gesta Danorum*).

In all these countries the oldest preserved monuments of the native languages are laws, which were transcribed from oral recitation. Since these were only superficially changed at the time of conversion, their language is formulaic and archaic, but thoroughly native. Their style is in marked contrast to that found in the flood of translations with which the clergy supplied Scandinavians for edification and enlightenment, occasionally even for entertainment. Favorite types were saints' legends, Bible paraphrases, homilies, leech books, tax lists, rhymed historical chronicles, and romances of the order of *Tristan and Isolde* or *Flores and Blanchefleur.*

Translations and original documents alike were written and copied in scriptoria attached to important centers of church and state. In Denmark there were such centers in Jutland, at Copenhagen, and at the archbishop's seat in Lund, in Scania. In Sweden there were centers in Western Guthnia, in Eastern Guthnia (at Vadstena Monastery, seat of St. Birgitta), at the archbishop's seat in Uppsala and the royal chancery in Stockholm. In Norway there were centers at the archbishop's seat in Trondheim, the older royal residence in Bergen, and the younger royal residence in Oslo. In Iceland there were centers at the bishop's seats in Holar and Skálholt and at the chief's estate of Oddi. Each of these centers wrote without much regard for the practices of others, and there were marked changes from century to century. It is clear that the spoken dialects were diverging, but it is extremely difficult to recover these from the written traditions. The last century of the Middle Ages, the period of political union, is particularly confusing, since Swedish, Norwegian, and Danish forms appear to be almost inextricably mingled. The order founded by the Swedish St. Birgitta at Vadstena Monastery spread a great number of writings in a kind of inter-Scandinavian language. The Danish administration in Copenhagen sent out documents having marked Danish characteristics to all three countries.

The writing traditions were slowly changing in response to a rapid development of local variations in speech. A strong wave of linguistic change was rolling from south to north, beginning in Jutland, spreading across Fyen and Zealand into Scania, and from here into Sweden and Norway. The wave ebbed as it moved and for the most part it never got to Iceland. It left Danish most strongly affected: all unstressed vowels fell together as schwa, the tonal distinction was replaced by glottalization, short postvocalic stops joined the spirants, and the system of cases and persons was reduced even beyond that of modern English. Swedish was more conservative, Norwegian still more so, and only Icelandic resisted almost completely this transformation of structure.

Danish was also most directly exposed to the pervasive influence from the south exerted by the speakers of Low German. In this case the influence did not enter through writing only, as did Latin, but through innumerable personal contacts on every level of society. In Holstein and southern Schleswig Low German was the folk speech, which slowly but surely pushed the Danish-speaking border northwards. The cities of Hamburg, Bremen, and Lübeck formed the powerful trading cartel known as the Hanseatic League, which early established quasi-permanent quarters in such prominent Scandinavian cities as Bergen, Copenhagen, Stockholm, and Visby. Several of the Danish monarchs in the Union Period and later were Germans, who spoke Low German at home and at court (Skautrup, Vol. 2, pp. 31–35). Great numbers of Germans immigrated to Scandinavia as tradesmen, craftsmen, and officials. The result was that all Scandinavians of any status had to learn Low German; the whole new world of bourgeois enterprise that sprang up in the late Middle Ages came to Scandinavia by way of Low German. The inevitable result was that these languages were infused with German loans to almost the same extent that English is infused with French.

At the turn from the Middle to the Modern Age it is therefore not just facetious to speak of these countries as underdeveloped. Their populations were predominantly rural and agrarian, their industries extractive, and their commerce in the hands of foreign entrepreneurs. Their literary and religious life was largely conducted either in Latin or Low German, except in remote Iceland. Even in dominant Denmark the position of Danish was weak, though still potentially stronger than that of the other Scandinavian languages.

THE REFORMATION

In the first two decades of the sixteenth century a sharp break occurred in the whole intellectual life of northern Europe; this quickly altered the language situation in Scandinavia. The art of printing, which reached Denmark and Sweden from Germany shortly before 1500, proved to be a tremendous factor in establishing the new religious ideas that also proceeded from that country. In 1521 the Pope excommunicated Martin Luther for heresy, but instead of executing the Pope's orders, the German princes, including the powerful Elector of Saxony, supported his adversary. They saw many advantages—including the possibility of gaining full control over the Church and its property—in setting up their own churches, which would not be subject to a foreign potentate. The Evangelical Church, which Luther established, was to lay great stress on popular education and the use of the native tongue. Luther translated the New Testament into High German in 1522 and completed the whole Bible by 1532.

In the year of Luther's excommunication a Swedish nobleman named Gustavus Vasa succeeded in defeating the Danish troops in Sweden and having himself declared king of Sweden. He was quick to follow the example of the German princes, and with the aid of his advisers, the

brothers Olaus and Laurentius Petri, he succeeded in establishing a
Swedish Lutheran church. His advisers were able to get out a New
Testament in Swedish by 1526, and eventually a complete Bible in 1541.
In Denmark the royal power was paralyzed by internal dissension and
revolt, until the accession of Frederik I in 1523. An official New Testament translated by Christiern Pedersen appeared in 1529, even before
the organization of a Danish Lutheran church in 1536. The complete
Bible followed in 1550. Although both of these versions were strongly
influenced by Luther's, they were worthy representatives of their respective languages and remained central in the religious life of these
countries until well into the nineteenth and twentieth centuries. Even
though the complete Bibles were found in every church, they had their
chief influence through printed books based on them, such as Bible
stories, catechisms, sermons, and other devotional literature spread
among the populace. But from our point of view the main result was
to establish once and for all that there would be at least two SLs in
Scandinavia: Danish and Swedish.[3]

The printing of Bibles in a relatively unified language form did not
at once command complete agreement. Handwritten documents continued to be important in all administrative work, and these were often
highly deviant. The printed norm was more unified, thanks to the need
for orthographic consistency in books that reached a wider public and
were often to be used for teaching.

DANISH

The Danish norm was based on the writing tradition of Copenhagen,
as modified by Christiern Pedersen. There was great confusion in the
tradition because of the extensive changes in Danish pronunciation,
especially of the postvocalic consonants. Historical *p t k* were sometimes
retained alongside various attempts to represent the new spirant or
semivocalic pronunciations: *b d g, bh dh gh, v w j.* Pedersen usually wrote
b d g, a definitely archaizing spelling which was at least clear and phonemically if not phonetically accurate for the new entities that had arisen
from the confusion of stops and spirants (Skautrup, Vol. 2, pp. 180–186).
Even so, the application of the rule was not historically consistent, for
some words escaped their etymology and were spelled more like their
current pronunciation: so *møje,* "exertion," compared with *føde,* "food"
(both had ð in Old Danish), *lave,* "make," compared with *drage,* "draw"
(from spirant *g*), *bie,* "wait," compared with *stride,* "fight" (both from ð)
(Wessén 1944, p. 60).

---

[3] The Finnish SL, which will not be treated further here, was established in a similar
way at the time of the Reformation, breaking with Swedish (Gummerus, 1941).

The spellings thus partly concealed and partly revealed pronunciations and could not have corresponded to anyone's speech at the time of the normalization. Dialect speech was virtually universal and the great present-day divergences between the major Danish dialects were already present. A supralocal norm might have been developing, but it was strongly dependent on a group of people whose daily activity brought them into close contact with the written word. Denmark's first phonetician, Jacob Madsen Århus, writing in 1589, gave budding orators the same advice as had Cicero, to "learn from politicians and learned men, who have long held public office, preachers who have long practice, and sensible and respected women" (Skautrup, Vol. 2, p. 191). In discussing the rise of a spoken norm, Skautrup notes that "it is not possible on the basis of materials so far advanced to determine the exact point of origin nor to what extent this speech already was distinguished from the dialect as an independent language limited to certain higher circles" (Skautrup, *ibid.*). Letters written in 1523–1524 by the Danish Queen Elizabeth, who seems to have escaped the need of learning Danish orthography, show that she used a number of forms which would today stamp her as a vulgar speaker [e.g., *tave* (tawə), "lose," for *tabe,* Old Danish *tapæ*].

During the ensuing centuries the orthography has had a growing influence on cultivated speech, no doubt due to the spelling pronunciations encouraged in formal reading at church services, in schoolrooms, in courts, and at public ceremonies (Skautrup, Vol. 2, p. 333). In the seventeenth and eighteenth centuries a flourishing grammatical literature developed the doctrine of correctness to the same extent as in other European countries. The mid-eighteenth century saw a mild purism develop, in which some of the Romance loanwords were replaced by native formations. In this way was begun a gradual reduction of the gap between the speech of the elite and the speech of the people, which has been one of the tasks of the common public school. The spread of the standard to new layers of the population has led to a marked abandonment of local dialects by many speakers, often in favor of regional forms of the standard. At the same time the strengthening of national feeling in the nineteenth century led to the complete dominance of Danish in the public life of the nation. Danish became the language for all occasions in the domestic lives of the Danes; other modern languages taught in the schools, such as German, English, or French, were for external communication only.

At the same time that Danish was developing into a fully articulated standard, its domain was being restricted century by century. The new Swedish government went to work systematically to reduce Danish power. In 1645 the island of Gotland and the province of Halland were taken from Denmark, Härjedalen and Jämtland from Norway. In 1658 the conquest of Scania and Blekinge followed; of the former East Danish dialect area only Bornholm was destined to remain Danish. In 1678 King Karl I of Sweden instituted a policy of "uniformity," which assimilated the inhabitants of the former Danish provinces to Swedish ecclesiastical and juridical practices, including language. (Skautrup, Vol. 2, pp. 294–296; Fabricius, 1958, p. 21). This did not immediately affect anyone's speech (and in any case the dialects were intermediate between Danish and Swedish), so that it was largely a question of official written usage. Before the end of the century, in the words of a recent Danish historian, "the Swedish government had succeeded in instilling in the Scanians the belief that Swedish was the standard language that naturally corresponded to their folk speech" (Fabricius, 1958, p. 297). In the Duchies of Schleswig-Holstein between Germany and Denmark the area of Danish was steadily encroached on by Low German. By 1864, when Prussia took them away from Denmark, only a northern section of Schleswig still spoke Danish; this was the area returned to Denmark by plebiscite in 1918. In 1814 Denmark lost Norway to Sweden, but the Norwegians succeeded in gaining home rule from the Swedes and in 1905 independence. Denmark had to grant Iceland home rule in 1918, and Iceland declared her independence in 1944. The only linguistically unassimilated part of Denmark that still remains (aside from the Eskimo of Greenland) are the Faroe Islands, which won home rule in 1948.

SWEDISH

The development of the Swedish norm from the time of the Reformation was in many ways parallel to that of Danish. Linguistically, as we have seen, they were very similar, except for the greater conservatism of Swedish. As late as 1506 the Swedish Councillors of State could write to the Danes that they were all "of one language" (Skautrup, Vol. 2, p. 36). But in 1510 a Swedish agitator named Heming Gadh drew up a scathing indictment of the Danes, including some uncomplimentary remarks about their language: "In addition, they do not trouble to speak like other people, but press their words out as if they want to cough, and seem almost on purpose to twist their words in the throat before they come out. . . . The German tongue they delight in talking even if they do not know it very well, but the language of the Goths and the Swedes they hold in contempt . . ." (Gadh, 1871; see Skautrup, Vol. 2, p. 36). During the Swedish revolt the phrase *hvit hest i korngulf* was used by the Swedish armies as a shibboleth to detect Danes. The hastily compiled New Testament of 1526 still contains some Danish traits, but in Gustav Vasa's Bible of 1541 these have been systematically removed. As an example of the kind of deliberate differentiation established by Swedish at this time we may note the symbols for the three extra vowels of Scandinavian. In Danish these were established as *æ, ø,* and *aa,* in Swedish as *ä, ö,* and *å*—purely graphic differences stemming from various writing traditions.

This definitive bifurcation of Scandinavian, which some might regret, is described as follows by a Swedish linguist, writing on the language of the New Testament: "The mainstream [of Swedish], after having been lost in the swamps of the Union Period, once more broke forth into the light of day, fed by new tributaries from medieval sources" (Lindqvist, 1928, p. 260). In less picturesque language: the translators leaned heavily on the writing tradition of Vadstena Monastery. Again the norm they established did not correspond precisely to anyone's speech (Wessén, 1944, p. 75). The three chief translators were from the central Swedish area around Stockholm and Uppsala, whereas Vadstena was southwest in East Guthnia. As in the case of Danish, it is easy to point out features in the norm that differ from the dialects of central Sweden such as the writing of final *t* and *d* in forms like *huset,* "the house," or *kastad,* "thrown"; yet these once silent consonants are now regularly pronounced. It was an archaic, etymologizing norm, even at the time of its establishment. Lindqvist describes Laurentius Petri as Sweden's "first conscious and consistent language reformer," noting that he adopted words not only from older Swedish, but also from West Scandinavian and from Swedish dialects (Lindqvist, 1928, p. 258).

The course thus initiated in Swedish was continued in later years, with a definite puristic trend; the church ordinance of 1575 provided that printed books be examined by the authorities before printing "in order that we may keep our Swedish tongue correct and pure, unmixed with other, foreign tongues, whether they be Latin or German" (Wessén 1944, p. 77). The seventeenth and eighteenth centuries were rife with grammatical studies aiming to support this policy. In 1677 Professor Olof Rudbeck began lecturing in Swedish at Uppsala University, 10 years before Christian Thomasius did the same for German at Leipzig (Wessén, *ibid.;* Blackall, 1959, p. 12). In 1786 King Gustav III, a great patron of the arts, established the Swedish Academy to promote the "purity, strength, and sublimity" of the Swedish language. Not until the nineteenth century, however, did the mother tongue become the sole instrument of national life and a regular subject of academic instruction, after its establishment in the common public school.

As we see, the sociolinguistic situation we have sketched here for Denmark and Sweden conforms very closely to the description of a "national language" by the Russian scholar M. M. Guxman (Guxman, 1960, Introduction, p. 6): "a complex system of language types" including "not only a literary language with its oral and written varieties, but also colloquial folk speech, semidialects, urban vernaculars, and regional dialects." If I may suggest a metaphor: the national language is a socially stratified peak rising from a broad plain of rural vernaculars crisscrossed by isoglosses. The peak loses itself in the clouds of "correctness," but its sides are adorned by the cold aloofness of the "best society" of Copenhagen and Stockholm, tempered by "provincial" standards a cut below those of the capitals. The Middle Class is struggling to climb the magic mountain, while Labor is contentedly and comfortably talking its substandard and virtually subterranean "cockney-like" urban vernacular.

ICELANDIC

At the end of the Middle Ages the Danish standard spread out over the areas that were firmly under Danish control, specifically Norway and her former colonies, the Faroes, Iceland, and Greenland. In this area there was one firm projection that Danish could not absorb. This was the hyperborean Iceland, where certain circumstances conspired to create resistance. In spite of its small population, Iceland had three factors in its favor: the physical remoteness, which saved its popular speech from participating in the extensive changes of the continental vernaculars; an extraordinary medieval tradition of literary production, which was revered and diligently studied until it was familiar to nearly everyone; and a type of fishing-ranching economy, which promoted mobility and inhibited the formation of local dialects. The resistance to Danish was supported by the language gap between Danish and Icelandic, the two dialectal extremes of Scandinavia. Here there was an *Abstand* that made a separate language inevitable, and the Danish government recognized this by permitting and encouraging a translation of the New Testament into Icelandic, produced in 1540 by Oddr Gottskalkson (Helgason, 1929, 1931). The whole Bible followed in 1584 (Bandle, 1956). This ensured the continuous use of Icelandic in the churches, although the Danish and Danicized officials who ruled the island used Danish in all governmental affairs down into the nineteenth century.

The orthography of Icelandic used in the Bible was largely that of the manuscripts and reflected the changing pronunciation reasonably well (Jónsson, 1959). This meant a considerable deviation from the earliest Icelandic spelling; but the grammar was intact. In the Early Modern period the lexicon was heavily infused with Danish loanwords. Not until the end of the eighteenth century was a policy initiated of deliberate exclusion of loanwords and the return to classical Old Icelandic spelling. A pioneer was Eggert Ólafsson, who began urging reform shortly after 1760. In 1772 the first book appeared in which the old symbol ð was restored; in 1779 a learned society was established to promote a reform of Icelandic. The movement won its point through the enthusiasm of the Danish linguist Rasmus Christian Rask, who "discovered" Icelandic and went to Iceland in 1813 to study the language. His grammatical and orthographic

writings not only established a new, classical form of Icelandic for the
Icelanders themselves to use, but also made Icelandic the classic language
of all Scandinavia. This was in part promoted by a confusion of Rask's
to which he clung throughout his brief life, in spite of criticism from
Jakob Grimm: he identified modern Icelandic as the common mother
tongue of all Scandinavians. The title of his grammar of Icelandic (1811)
was: *Vejledning til det Islandske eller gamle Nordiske Sprog (Guide to
the Icelandic or Old Scandinavian Language).* Whatever the weakness of
this position, it helped to turn the attention of patriotic grammarians
and scholars in all Scandinavia to Icelandic as the model of what a Scandinavian tongue ought to be. Its relative purity, which was increased
throughout the nineteenth and twentieth centuries by diligent elimination of Danish and German loans, was promoted in the schools and borne
by a great wave of political opposition to Denmark. The Old Icelandic
literature inspired translations, from which ancient words and proper
names flowed into the other Scandinavian tongues in a small, but characteristic trickle. The events of World War II, when Iceland was cut off
from Denmark by the fortunes of war and occupied by British and
American forces, completed the disjunction of Icelandic from Danish.
Although Danish continues to be taught even after Icelandic independence, its position as the obvious second language for Icelanders is being
rapidly usurped by English.

The development here sketched has given Iceland an entirely different
sociolinguistic profile from those of Denmark and Sweden. The SL is
based on a classical form of the language, and since the country has no
marked dialect differences, no traditional aristocracy, and only a shallow
urban tradition, the prestige speakers are the rural speakers, whose "un-
spoiled" language conforms most closely to the standard (Benediktsson,
1961–1962). In practice the most influential speech may be that of Rey-
kjavík, the capital; but teachers of Icelandic firmly oppose its occasional
deviations in pronunciation and lexicon from the norm (Groenke, 1966).

FAROESE

Some of the same scholars who restored Icelandic to its pristine form
were also actively interested in the language of the Faroe Islands, a
former Norwegian colony, which in modern times remained with Denmark after the separation of Norway in 1814. The Faroes consist of 17
inhabited islands midway between Iceland and Norway, directly north
of Great Britain. Contrary to Icelandic, Faroese is deeply divided dialec-
tally. There is no medieval writing tradition to speak of. The earliest
modern texts are medieval ballads written down in the late eighteenth
century in a phonemic orthography based on Danish conventions. The
language is less archaic than Icelandic but more than Norwegian and

has altered its phonemic structure markedly from that of Old Norwegian (e.g., ON long i and $y > ui$, lengthened $o > oa$, $a > æa$; postvocalic $ð$ and g were lost and replaced by j before i and v before u, etc.). It was not used in serious writing until the nineteenth century; Danish was the sole language of church and government, so that spoken Faroese has a large percentage of Danish loanwords for all cultural vocabulary (Djupedal, 1964).

Rasmus Rask brought Faroese to the attention of the learned world by including a short grammar of the language in his Icelandic Grammar of 1811 (Rask, 1811, pp. 262–282). Rask described Faroese as a dialect of Icelandic, the "Old Scandinavian language," which naturally stirred the interest of connoisseurs among the native speakers of the language (Skårup, p. 3). Some years later he advised the editors of *Færeyinga Saga* (1832) on the orthography to be used in their Faroese version of this Icelandic document. Rask did not himself draw the logical consequences of Faroese as a dialect of Icelandic, for his own views on spelling were phonetic rather than etymological. This was done by others, who were caught up by the wave of Romantic thinking in the scholarship of the day, above all the Danish writer N. M. Petersen. In 1846 a Faroese orthography was created by V. U. Hammershaimb along lines proposed by Petersen. This went about as far as humanly possible in uniforming Faroese according to the classic model of Icelandic. In effect, the orthography was a historical reconstruction based on the newly discovered methods of comparative linguistics. It was called forth by the need for a school orthography to be used in the introductory grades, for pupils who had not yet learned to understand Danish (Djupedal, 1964, pp. 162–163). The etymological spelling solved the problem of dialect differences by concealing them in a common, nonphonetic, "starred" form (e.g., variations in the diphthongization of the vowel ew/ow are concealed by the spelling $ó$, corresponding to Icelandic).

In spite of the difficulties this orthography created for Faroese children by introducing many unphonetic spellings (e.g., *kvæði* for *kveaji*, "poem"), it has proved impregnable to all later attacks by phonetically minded reformers. This may be due also to its conformity with the underlying system of Faroese morphology (O'Neill 1965), to its similarity to the spellings of the other Scandinavian languages, and to the very air of dignity contributed by its difference from colloquial speech. Hammershaimb wrote in his *Færøsk Sproglære* (1854): "The orthography of Faroese is here adapted to that of the ancient language, which the Faroese themselves once used, wherever the present pronunciation does not make it impossible: the true peculiarities of Faroese are carefully retained" (e.g., he did not reintroduce *þ*, for which Faroese has either t or h). In this orthography Faroese has gradually won its way to official recognition, in spite of sharp opposition from dissident Faroese scholars and from the

Danish government. Puristic efforts to imitate Icelandic style have only partially succeeded; but the written language has substituted many Faroese words (or Icelandic-type creations) for Danish words which are still used in speech. Faroese was first taught in the schools in 1912; in 1937 a Faroese New Testament appeared; in 1938 the language was required to be taught alongside Danish, and since home rule was established in 1948, it is the main language taught. Textbooks have been written in a number of elementary subjects; there is an extensive native literature, and in 1965 a scientific academy was established in Torshavn with Chr. Matras as the first resident professor of Faroese. Today the language is easily available to foreigners through the grammar of W. B. Lockwood (1955).

NORWEGIAN

Closely related developments were taking place at the same time in Norway, the motherland of Icelandic and Faroese. It will not be possible here to give a complete statement of the complex situation in that country; readers are referred to my *Language Conflict and Language Planning* (Haugen, 1966a). The political separation of Norway from Denmark in 1814 led to widespread discussion in Norway of the linguistic consequences which this separation ought to have. Since the introduction of the Reformation, Norway, while retaining its name as a partner in the united kingdom of Denmark-Norway, had in fact been treated as a province of Denmark. All the printed literature of the Reformation, including the Bible, was introduced into Norway in the same form as in Denmark, and there was no longer, as in Sweden or Iceland, a tradition of writing that could provide models for a national standard norm. As in other parts of the kingdom, the ruling class of bourgeois and bureaucrats spoke a local version of the written standard on official occasions, a local urban or rural dialect otherwise. By the time of Norway's independence a fairly uniform "cultivated" speech norm had sprung up; this was the only form of supralocal Norwegian in existence. Its characteristics distinguished it sharply from the corresponding Danish speech norm by retaining Norwegian pronunciations for everyday words (e.g., *sag*, "case," was pronounced as *sak*, *tabe*, "lose," as *tape*; *ud*, "out," as *ut*), while adopting spelling pronunciations of bookish words (e.g., *sagfører*, "lawyer," *håbe*, "hope," *udmerket*, "excellent," all as spelled). The sound system was far closer to that of Swedish than of Danish, but the grammar was distinctively Norwegian and the lexicon strongly Danicized. As in the other countries (except Iceland), rural speakers were split into local dialects. The sociolinguistic profile was therefore the same as that of Denmark and Sweden, except for the fact that the written norm was identical with Denmark's; after some three centuries of successful use, the Norwegians were persuaded (as were the Danes in Skåne concerning Swedish) that Danish was the "standard language that naturally corresponded to their folk speech."

It became the mission of a young self-taught linguist of rural stock, Ivar Aasen, to prove that this was not true. In 1836, only 23 years old, he set himself the task of recovering the lost Norwegian language from its daughter dialects. The inspiration from Icelandic, which was thought of as the common Scandinavian mother tongue, is clear; in 1841 he wrote a grammar of his native dialect in which he compared it directly with Icelandic (Indrebø 1951, p. 427). He went on to make the first field studies of Norwegian dialects, and on the basis of these researches he created a norm which step by step departed from the individual dialects and became an overarching reconstructed norm for all the dialects. He was closely familiar with developments in Icelandic and Faroese, and in his definitive grammar of 1864 he established a norm that was less archaic than Faroese, closer in many respects to the spoken dialects, especially in western and midland Norway. Like the Icelanders and the Faroese he rejected Danish, in whatever form, as a guide or even as a source of borrowing for his new language (Haugen, 1965).

Aasen therefore rejected also the form of Danish spoken by the upper classes in Norway. Since this was already well-established and prestigious, however, other reformers preferred to take a more moderate course whereby the Danish orthography should be gradually adapted to the norms of upper-class speech. This line of "reform" rather than "revolution" has so far proved to be the most widely acceptable. It became an absolute necessity after the official recognition of Aasen's norm in 1885 as a potential school language under the name of Landsmåal, or Nynorsk. The goal of achieving a distinctive Norwegian language by building on cultivated speech was pursued in successive major reforms adopted in 1907 and 1917. These radically altered the appearance of Norwegian Danish, by spelling it according to the orthographic conventions of Aasen's norm while maintaining the grammar and lexicon of urban, upper-class speech. Under the name of Riksmål or Bokmål this new Norwegian norm dominates the literary life of Norway to the extent of 90 per cent of the literary production and 80 per cent of the school population. Attempts were initiated in 1917 and vigorously pursued in reforms of 1938 and 1959 to bring the two norms still closer together by homogenizing their grammars. So far these efforts have enjoyed only a limited success. Of all the norms so far discussed in Scandinavia it may seem as if the Riksmål norm of Norwegian is closest to actual speech. This is only because it has been deliberately shaped by a policy of bringing the writing into line with a speech norm felt to be more national than the Danish orthography. In practice it retains many etymological and unphonemic traits derived from its dual tradition of Danish and New Norwegian (e.g., *mann,* "man," rhyming with *land,* "land," and *kan,* "can," or *væte,* "moisture," homophonous with *hvete,* "wheat").

The two Norwegian languages illustrate opposite but complementary ideals in their approach to the problem of a standard norm: the folk ideal versus the elite ideal. The New Norwegian language, like Icelandic and Faroese, finds its prestigious speakers in the rural population and the principles of its normalization in a classic language. Dano-Norwegian, like Danish and Swedish, finds its prestigious speakers in the urban, upper-class population and the principles of its normalization in a traditional language. In neither case is anyone seriously trying to conform to anyone's speech; if anything, it is assumed that speech will be molded by writing, which gives writing an importance beyond its due.

CONCLUSION

The divergent manuscript traditions of the Middle Ages were standard languages in embryo, but were of limited influence and subject to extinction and radical alteration according to the often unstable political and religious constellations of the period. The trend toward political unification of Scandinavia under the scepter of Denmark was beginning to have a corresponding linguistic effect at the end of the fifteenth century. The revolt and eventual military predominance of Sweden over Denmark upset this trend and assured the fragmentation of Scandinavia. The invention of printing and the establishment of the Reformation in Germany gave each of the two Scandinavian states the technical means for setting up similar but distinct norms of writing and subsequently spreading them through the church, the schools, and the courts to every part of the realm controlled by each state. Eventually these were accepted as instruments of communication and symbols of identity, except where language distance or political self-assertion led to their rejection (as Swedish was rejected in Finland, which we have to disregard here; or as Danish in Scania, Schleswig, Iceland, the Faroes, and Norway).

In each case the norms selected correspond only in the most general sense to any particular vernacular as spoken then or later. Latin rules were adopted to create the first writing traditions and reflect the gross features of each writer's structure. But the codified norms of the present day are complex creations from various dialects resulting in large part from conscious regularization by generations of grammarians and rhetoricians. The relation of each written tradition to speech is that of providing a guide for certain types of formal discourse, but generally the written tradition is an ideal norm which sensible people follow only insofar as suits their personal convenience and permits them to demonstrate a decent respect for the opinions of their fellows.

REFERENCES

Aasen, Ivar. 1965. *Norsk Grammatik*. Christiania, 1864. (Reprinted, Oslo: Universitetsforlaget.)

Bandle, Oskar. 1956. *Die Sprache der Guðbrandsbiblia*. Bibliotheca Arnamagnæana, XVII; Hafniæ.

Benediktsson, Hreinn. 1961–1962. Icelandic Dialectology: Methods and Results. *Íslenzk tunga* 3, 72–113.

Blackall, Eric. 1959. *The Emergence of German as a Literary Language*. Cambridge: University Press.

Brun, Auguste. 1946. *Parlers régionaux: France dialectale et unité française*. Paris-Toulouse: Didier.

Djupedal, Reidar. 1964. Litt om framvoksteren av det færøyske skriftmålet. In Alf Hellevik and Einar Lundeby (eds.), *Skriftspråk i utvikling*, Oslo: Cappelen, pp. 144–186.

Fabricius, Knud. 1958. *Skaanes overgang fra Danmark til Sverige. Fjerde Del*. Copenhagen.

Gadh, Heming. 1871. *Scriptores Rerum Svecicarum Medii Aevi*, Vol. III, 1. Stockholm. 49 pp.

Groenke, Ulrich. 1966. On Standard, Substandard, and Slang in Icelandic. *Scandinavian Studies*, **38**, 217–230.

Gummerus, Jaakko. 1941. *Michael Agricola, der Reformation Finnlands*. Helsinki.

Guxman, M. M. 1960. *Voprosy formirovanija i razvitija nacional'nyx jazyhov* [Problems of the Formation and Development of National Languages], Moscow. (Here cited from preliminary translation prepared by Center for Applied Linguistics.)

Hammershaimb, V. U. 1854. Færøisk Sproglære. *Annaler for nordisk Oldhyndighed*, pp. 233–316.

Haugen, Einar. 1965. Construction and Reconstruction in Language Planning: Ivar Aasen's Grammar. *Word*, **21**, 188–207.

Haugen, Einar. 1966. Linguistics and Language Planning. In William Bright (ed.), *Sociolinguistics*. The Hague: Mouton, pp. 50–71.

Haugen, Einar. 1966a. *Language Conflict and Language Planning: The Case of Modern Norwegian*. Cambridge, Mass.: Harvard University Press.

Haugen, Einar. 1966b. Semicommunication: The Language Gap in Scandinavia. *Sociological Inquiry*, **36**, 280–297.

Haugen, Einar. 1966c. Dialect, Language, Nation. *Amer. Anthrop.*, **68**, 922–935.

Helgason, Jón. 1929. *Málið á Nýja testamenti Odds Gottskálkssonar*, *Safn Fræðafjelagsins*, VII, Copenhagen.

Helgason, Jón. 1931. Från Oddur Gottskálksson til Fjölnir. Tre hundra års isländsk språkutveckling. *Island: Bilder från gammal och ny tid*, Uppsala, 1931, pp. 36–50.

Indrebø, Gustav. 1951. *Norsk målsoga*, Per Hovda and Per Thorson (eds.). Bergen: John Grieg.

Jónsson, Jón Aðalsteinn. 1959. Ágrip af sögu íslenzkrar stafsetningar. *Íslenzk tunga*, **1**, 71–119.

Kloss, Heinz. 1952. *Die Entwicklung neuer germanischer Kultursprachen von 1800 bis 1950*. München: Pohl.

Lindqvist, Natan. 1928. Bibelsvenskans medeltida ursprung. *Nysvenska Studier*, **8**, 165–260.

Lockwood, W. B. 1955. *An Introduction to Modern Faroese*. Copenhagen: Munksgaard.

O'Neil, Wayne. The Morphophonemics of Faroese (Unpub. paper).

Rask, Rasmus. 1811. *Vejledning til det Islandske eller gamle Nordiske Sprog.* Copenhagen.

Seip, Didrik Arup. 1955. *Norsk språkhistorie til omkring 1370,* 2 ed. Oslo: Aschehoug.

Skårup, Povl. 1964. *Rasmus Rask og færøsk.* Copenhagen: Munksgaard.

Skautrup, Peter. 1944, 1947, 1953. *Det danske sprogs historie,* 3 Vols. Copenhagen: Gyldendal.

Stewart, William A. 1962. Linguistic Typology. Study of the Role of Second Languages in Asia, Africa, and Latin America (Washington, D.C.: Center for Applied Linguistics), pp. 14–25.

Wessén, Elias. 1937. Vårt riksspråk, några huvudpunkter av dess historiska utveckling. *Årsskrift för Modersmålslärarnas förening,* pp. 289–305.

Wessén, Elias. 1944. *De nordiska språken.* Stockholm: Filologiska Föreningen vid Stockholms Högskola.

Wessén, Elias. 1955. *Svensk språkhistoria. I Ljudlära och ordböjningslära,* 4th ed. Stockholm: Filologiska Föreningen vid Stockholms Högskola.

Jiri V. Neustupný

SOME GENERAL ASPECTS OF "LANGUAGE" PROBLEMS AND "LANGUAGE" POLICY IN DEVELOPING SOCIETIES

THE NEED FOR A GENERAL THEORY OF LANGUAGE PROBLEMS AND LANGUAGE POLICY

Language problems and language policy have been widely discussed with regard to individual languages. Yet very few attempts have been made either to give a *full* and systematic account of problems and policies in one language, or to go beyond the boundaries of a single language and find *cross-cultural constants*. No doubt, every speech community presents quite irrecursive problems and policies. The idea of considering language problems of developing nations more generally presupposes the existence of one or more constants recurring in all included specific cases.

The absence of systematic analyses of language problems and language policy in individual languages and the failure to identify explicitly constants across the boundaries of individual languages are connected with the absence of attempts to formulate a *general theory* in the field. Difficulties begin with the concepts of "problems," "policy," and "language." The descriptive level is confused with the prescriptive one. There is no model on which a systematic description may be passed. And prescriptions far more frequently belong to the sphere of actual politics than to the sphere of political science.

If we claim that the general theory should begin by elucidating the concept of "language problems," this does not mean that it would be expedient to offer a narrow and necessarily arbitrary definition including some and excluding other clearly related phenomena. On the contrary, we should try to map the area as extensively and intensively as possible. For example, along with the group of well known "language problems" like the relationship between different languages within a nation (especially the relationship between the national language and other languages), literacy, orthography, etc., which may be called conscious problems, there should be enough room in our theoretical system for "language problems" of which the speech community is not fully aware, which have not become a target of language policy, and which are still capable of contributing largely to the tensions within the society. I am referring to such problems as language patterns connected with a certain type of family—problems that reinforce that type of family—language patterns connected with nonindividualistic social psychology, etc. Such problems are probably not given adequate attention at present; to exclude these problems from our field because they are unconscious would lead to arbitrary cuts, first, because the boundary between conscious and unconscious is not clear, and second, because there is permanent fluctuation between the two types. A guide to sound prescription for language policy should, of course, start with language problems that are important political issues, but it should also include consideration of problems society is not paying attention to, but that are relevant in any respect. Another necessary task for the general theory of language problems and language policy is to encompass previous approaches that used different terminology but dealt basically with the same material: "language culture" of the Prague School [1], the first structural contribution in this field, can serve as one example, and "language situation" [2] can serve as another one.

This essay attempts a sketch of some basic concepts with special reference to constants within developing societies. The discussion is based on the experience of a linguist. A similar attempt by a political scientist would be welcome, for political science alone can be responsible for illuminating the use of the previously mentioned concepts of "problems," "policy," and other important pillars of the theory, such as a model for the actual process of implementation of a language policy. Only cooperation between linguistics and political science, which still leaves much to be desired, can save the field from the vulgarization of laymen, and what is perhaps still more harmful, the quasi-expert, but actually naïve judgments of "pure" linguists and "pure" political scientists.

LANGUAGE PROBLEMS
AND COMMUNICATION PROBLEMS

Any general consideration of language problems and language policy can hardly evade the fundamental problem of the notion "language" and its place in the overall structure of culture and society. Famous as this problem is, after de Saussure, it would be difficult for professional linguists to maintain that it has ever acquired wider comprehension and sympathy among representatives of related social sciences. Even for linguists, of course, much remains to be elucidated, as the constant reiteration of the language/parole problem in the pages of linguistic literature suggests. Nevertheless, some relatively final conclusions may be drawn, and among them are (a) the necessity to distinguish between *patterns* (systems) and *processes* in which these patterns are manifested (realized), and (b) the necessity to distinguish, within the sphere of patterns, between "la langue" or the *"language code"* and the *neighboring social patterns*.

A theory of "language" problems should, of course, follow these conclusions rather than be influenced by the general meaning of the word "language," which either includes, without differentiation, verbal processes as well as the language code and perhaps even other patterns manifested in the verbal processes, or excludes everything except the language code. A theory of "language" problems should differentiate between the different patterns manifested in verbal processes—as far as this is possible [3]—but on the other hand, as has been stressed several times (e.g., by Skalička and Hymes [4]), it should not exclude any of them from its perspective. Moreover, they should always be considered in connection with the wider class of communication. COMMUNICATION PROBLEMS may then be divided into VERBAL (or "LANGUAGE") and NONVERBAL communication problems; verbal include LANGUAGE CODE PROBLEMS and SPEECH PROBLEMS. This scheme probably still needs substantial correction and amplification, but even in this form it may be fruitful in showing the inner complexity of the sphere of "language" problems. At this point I would especially like to stress that preoccupation with language code problems such as the relationship of different codes within the same language block [5], problems of the standard or official language, problems of orthography, of the choice between variants within the same code, of honorifics, or vocabulary, etc., at the expense of speech problems and nonverbal communication problems—is especially dangerous. History can supply dozens of examples of reforms of language codes that failed because they did not comply with the problems of other communication patterns and were not accompanied by corresponding policies. Hence the first thesis of this paper is: *There is a necessity to think of "language" problems in the broad context of communication problems, and to include in "language" problems besides language code problems also the problems of speech* [6].

EVALUATION OF "LANGUAGE" PATTERNS: THE PROBLEM OF MOTIVATION

A conscious solution of a "language" problem, the "language" policy, cannot have any starting point but the comparison of two or more states of "language" patterns, one real, and the others potential. One of the patterns is evaluated as "better," or preferable in comparison to all other patterns. Thus it is clear that the evaluation of "language" patterns is an inherent and inevitable part of the process of any "language" policy.

It is perhaps not an exaggeration to claim that theoretical linguistics, at present, pays but slight attention to the problems of evaluation of even those communication patterns that are its traditional constituents [7]. It is true that the language code, the center of traditional linguistics, is most difficult, though not impossible, to evaluate among all communication patterns, and that older linguistics has not always had a happy hand in this respect (cf. so-called primitive languages, the evaluation of language types, etc.). As a consequence, value judgments are at present virtually tabooed in linguistics. On the one hand, there is surely no doubt that no evaluation is possible in the abstract, without regard to other patterns. The necessity to oppose irresponsible judgments based on nationalism or the feeling of real or supposed economic or cultural superiority still exists. On the other hand, it would be foolish not to recognize the fact that certain features of "language" patterns in relation to other patterns can be, and often really are, evaluated.

While evaluating the "language" patterns, it is expedient to distinguish between *arbitrary* (unmotivated, undetermined) and *motivated* (imposed, determined) features [8]. An absolutely arbitrary feature, because it has no relation to features of other patterns, is not subject to evaluation and is equivalent to any other arbitrary feature. Some parts of the language code and, to a lesser degree, of other communication patterns are surely arbitrary. Mostly, however, even the language code, perhaps much more than has been assumed, is affected by motivational relations and thus comprises motivated features that can be evaluated. Features of communication patterns may either be motivated or motivating, or both at the same time. They can be motivated either by another feature of "language" patterns (e.g., parallelism in a speech pattern motivates parallelism in a code pattern), by a feature of the social pattern (e.g., the structure of the family motivates speech patterns within a family), by biological and other conditions of verbal communication (e.g., language universals motivated by the technical problems of transmission of signals), or, in the majority of cases, by several features of different order simultaneously. *Primarily motivated* communication features may *secondarily motivate* the primary feature (e.g., the honorific system, primarily motivated by social structure, may secondarily influence the retention of that part of the social structure). Besides this, it is possible to conceive, at least in theory, of a relation in which it is difficult or impossible to state which of the two motivational directions is primary and which secondary. This is a frequent case within the language code (cf. my remarks on typology in "First Steps . . . ," 1965, passim) but a full description of this phenomenon is still missing.

Of paramount importance in this context is whether any features of the language code exist that motivate primarily features of other patterns. Often we are forced to meet a very general assumption that the language code has a basic position within the whole social structure and widely motivates other social patterns. This assumption seems to be a consequence of all kinds of Whorfian theories that exert important influence on nonlinguists. If these theories were true, such motivational relations might become a basis for a far-reaching evaluation of the language code and a starting point for extensive language policy.

Attention has, however, often been drawn to contrary evidence, from which three points are of special importance. First, there is the question of the direction of the motivation: is it the code pattern that is primary? Second, the relation of the motivation can be assumed only where there is a congruity of two independently detectable features in two different patterns. For example, the existence of singular and plural should first be proved independently for both language and culture, before the relation is proclaimed to exist. Third *it should be questioned whether in many cases it is not features of speech rather than language code patterns that are to be considered as the motivating elements.*

The whole complicated mechanism of the motivational relations which are the basic premise for any evaluation has, however, not yet been fully described. Hence it is most difficult to make relevant judgments about the evaluation itself *and it is necessary to call for wider attention to these problems before any prescriptive approach to the "language" problem can be accepted.*

I would like to indicate only one warning here. It concerns the evaluability of so-called *petrified* features [9]. For instance, at *first* there normally exists a motivational relation [foreign cultural elements] → [foreign language code elements]; with the assimilation of the cultural elements, the relation, however, weakens or entirely disappears, even though the "foreign" elements within the language code may preserve their special position and thus become petrified features. A fully petrified feature becomes, of course, arbitrary and cannot be subject to evaluation. The language code and also speech patterns are especially full of weakened (partly petrified) motivational relations and the *degree of petrification* should therefore be carefully studied before any evaluative judgment is made.

THE CONCEPT OF DEVELOPING COMMUNICATION

Let us diverge, for a moment, from the conceptual line PROBLEM—EVALUATION (ATTITUDES)—POLICY IMPLEMENTATION to consider the degree of uniformity of this line in different developing societies. Is it possible to find any constants occurring nonaccidentally in the languages of developing nations? In other words, are there any language problems peculiar to developing societies? This question might be answered on a purely *empirical* basis affirmatively, but the meaning of our question is whether the obvious coincidences are in connection with the fact that the societies in question are *developing* societies.

I have tried to show, in a paper entitled "First Steps toward the Conception of 'Oriental Languages'," that there are some features of languages spoken in the developing societies that are connected with other nonlinguistic features of these societies. The obvious fact of complex "dialectal" stratification which can hardly be taken out of the context of a highly segmented society with low social mobility may be quoted as an example. This fact deeply affects the whole structure of developing languages (a term which I have proposed for such languages), commencing with their phonology (coexistent phonological systems, etc.) and stretching over to their morphology (high degree of morphological synonymity), vocabulary, and syntax. No doubt, the highly developed synonymity, which is different from *functional*, meaningful synonymity, presents important language problems in the process of standardization alone. This is only one example of a typical problem for developing languages. It shows clearly that the question of cross-cultural constants in language problems is a valid one.

However a few mere examples will not suffice. The task of the day is the compilation of a complete list of problems in the developing languages, and this presupposes a complete list of all features of these languages which are connected, that is, in a nonpetrified motivation relation in the sense of the preceding section of this paper, with other developing features of the corresponding social structures, because all such features are likely to fulfill some function outside the language itself. This shows the special importance of the theory of developing languages for the theory of language problems.

In the previously mentioned paper I was mainly concerned with the language code. Now, from Section 2 of this paper it follows that, as with language code, this approach may be applied to speech and communication patterns in general. If any features of the communication patterns can be found that are motivated by developing features of the social structure, they will be called *developing features of communication* and we can therefore speak of developing communication.

Since I intend to pay special attention to the developing features of communication elsewhere, let us limit ourselves to the following examples. It is the underdevelopment of *dialogue* that has important social connections and thus constitutes, in my opinion, a major language problem. There is, of course, dialogue in any society, but its distribution in certain situations is connected with features of the social structure. Dialogue as a form of verbal entertainment in developed societies corresponds to monologue in developing societies; a "party" where all individuals are equal and take the same part in verbal behavior corresponds to a gathering with one narrator and his audience. It is not difficult to discover the older (developing) pattern in nineteenth-century Europe, especially in her less developed parts, and follow its change, as in the family dialogue, during the first half of this century. It is probably obvious that the lesser proportion of dialogue is connected with a lower degree of individualization in developing societies, and it can present important problems, for instance in the sphere of administration (democratic discussion, etc.).

A few other examples may be helpful to illustrate the idea of developing communication. It will probably be agreed that certain features of communication patterns within a developing family, such as *one-directional communication* and patterns of *distribution of silence* are connected with developing features of family structure. Some of these patterns, in turn, frequently motivate language code patterns, such as systems of family terminology, and are supported by them. Other examples are *speech particularism,* underdevelopment or absence of certain *speech styles,* formalized speech, and a high degree of arbitrary patterning in general.

From Section 3 of this paper it follows that all developing features of communication are subject to evaluation. Their evaluation will be dependent upon the evaluation of the motivating features—the developing features of the social structure. This, of course, is neither to claim that any developing feature of communication becomes, or, seen prescriptively, should become, a "language" problem, nor to try to evaluate any such feature negatively [10]. The concrete evaluation depends on principles (criteria) of evaluation (see Section 5). I hope that *the concept of developing communication will be accepted as one having a basic significance for the solution of "language" problems.* Prior to making decisions concerning communication policy in developing societies one should try to describe as many developing features of communication as possible and evaluate them. If this condition remains unfulfilled, we run the risk that the set of problems treated in the prescriptive part of our considerations will be deficient, and important problems may escape our attention.

EVALUATION OF "LANGUAGE" PATTERNS: THE PROBLEM OF CRITERIA

After the discovery of the motivational network consisting of connecting links between communication and other social patterns (cf. Section 3) the whole network is subject to scrutiny according to a limited number of principles (criteria), and the final attitude is determined.

It is interesting to observe that the application of criteria and the resulting attitudes are often really analogous, if not identical, in the case of "language" and other policies within the same society. The general character, for instance, of "language" policy in postwar Japan presents, in its stress on democratization, features analogous to the general trend in other spheres of Japanese society. On the other hand, as stressed by Shibata [11], the sphere of "language" policy is often partly independent of other policies: the distribution of progressivism and conservatism in postwar Japan's "language" policy does not fully coincide with the distribution in other spheres. This means that different principles are applied in different areas of the network of social structure, and this phenomenon also deserves our full attention since it seems to be specific not only for "language" policy in Japan.

The full typology of principles (criteria) for "language" policy is one of the foremost tasks for future research in this field. At present we are able to quote only four general principles:

1. *Development.* (Does the feature contribute to the development of the society? Of course, not only the economic development is to be considered.)
2. *Democratization.* (Is the feature favorable to the creation of equal opportunities for all members of the society?)
3. *Unity.* (Does the feature reinforce the unity of the society in question?)
4. *Foreign relations.* (Is the feature an obstacle to communication with other specific communities?)

These principles seem to possess different degrees of importance to different social groups pursuing the policy. For example, the most traditional social groups of developing societies will probably not care about development. It may be typical for the attitude of former colonial administrators that the necessity of communication with other communities (i.e., the problem of retention of the former colonial language) is excessively stressed. An authoritative political group in a multilingual country is likely to think about unity first, whereas a party looking for support would prefer democratization. In general, however, democratization and its possible implications for development rarely seem to be favored, because it too often seems undesirable from the point of view of the present economic organization. It will be necessary to obtain a thorough analysis of the attitudes of various social groups with regard to the different criteria implied. R. F. Amonoo [12], who has already correctly identified the four criteria quoted above, also stressed the fact that ". . . some of these needs run counter to each other." This is undoubtedly an important aspect of the problem: the establishment of dialects of a language as standard languages may serve democratization (all local groups have linguistically equal opportunities) but it may also be undersirable in respect of unity. This fact should be fully realized before any prescriptive work is undertaken. But it is only one aspect of the problem of criteria for "language" policy, the bulk of which still awaits a systematic treatment within a theory of "language" problems and "language" policy.

CONCLUSIONS

Several conclusions may be drawn on the basis of the preceding discussion.

1. There is an urgent necessity to develop a general theory of "language" problems and "language" policy.

2. The theory, both descriptive and prescriptive, should be developed not only with regard to language code but, more broadly, with due inclusion of the system of speech and communication in general.

3. As long as "language" policy presupposes a conscious selection from several possibilities, it requires the evaluation of "language" patterns.

4. The evaluation should consider motivational links of communication patterns with other social phenomena, followed by the application of the policy criteria. The attitude formed in this process is materialized in the execution of the policy.

5. The communication systems of developing societies share "language" problems that define them as a special field in the theory.

Some of our conclusions are schematized in Table 1.

TABLE 1

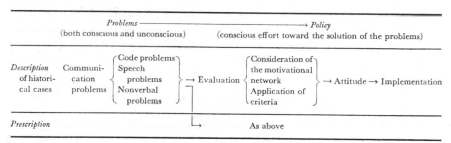

There are implications of these conclusions for the systematic descriptions of "language" problems and policies in individual communities: it will be necessary to widen the range of problems, to consider the whole sphere of links between the communication patterns and other social patterns, and to describe the functioning of the criteria as well as the mechanisms for the execution of the policy. The main implication for the theory of developing "language" problems is the need for a fuller description of the shared features, the constants in the developing communication systems. At the same time, our conclusions show the necessity for further elaboration of the theory: many particular problems (e.g., the question of the execution of the policy, which presents complicated but recursive mechanisms, involves a number of legal problems, etc.)

still need to be inserted or added. The theory will undoubtedly be enriched by concurrent work in individual languages, but such work will, in turn, never be valid until the theory is reinforced.

NOTES

1. Thèses présentées au Premier Congres des philologues slaves, originally in *TCLP*, 1 (1929), p. 27, reprinted in J. Vachek's *A Prague School Reader in Linguistics*, p. 56. Cf. also B. Havránek, *Studie o spisovném jazyce*, Praha, 1963.
2. *Materialy k diskussii "Problemy izučenija jazykovoj situacii v stranax Azii i Afriki."* Moscow, 1965.
3. It is not always possible to keep *"la langue"* and *"la parole"* apart. Cf. our remarks on vagueness of the opposition in Neustupný, "On the Analysis of Linguistic Vagueness." *Travaux linguistiques de Prague, 2* (1966), p. 49.
4. V. Skalička, The Need for a Linguistics of *"la parole."* Originally in *Recueil linguistique de Bratislava* 1, 1948, reprinted in J. Vachek (ed.), *A Prague School Reader in Linguistics*, 1964. D. Hymes, The Ethnography of Speaking. In *Anthropology and Human Behavior*, 1962.
5. For this term see J. V. Neustupný, First Steps Toward the Conception of "Oriental Languages," *Archiv orientálni, 33* (1965), p. 85 *et sequ.*
6. To my knowledge D. Hymes' recent work "The Ethnography of Speaking" and his Introduction to *The Ethnography of Communication,* offer the best foundations for further development in this field and the reader will also recognize how much my own approach owes to him. Future research should perhaps include still more of the classical *membra disiecta* relevant to the theme, to say nothing of such contributions as those of P. Trost, "Bemerkungen zum Sprachtabu," originally in *TCLP, 6* (1936), reprinted in Vachek's *Reader;* Trubetzkoy's chapter "Phonologie und Lautstilistik" in his *Grundzüge* (1939); and Skalička's already cited "The Need for a Linguistics of *la parole.*" Two Prague discussions on style (1941 and 1955) and their continuation (cf. K. Hausenblas, on the Characterisation and Classification of Discourses, *Travaux linguistiques de Prague,* 1964, p. 67–83) are equally stimulating.
7. There are interesting exceptions; cf. Punya Sloka Ray, *Language Standardization,* 1963.
8. Trubetzkoy in 1939 in the chapter cited calls this opposition "konventionell" versus "naturgegeben." I have called it, in a more concrete context, "dialect" versus "style" (cf. Neustupný 1965, fn. 6, p. 86).
9. This term was coined in Neustupný 1965.
10. The wide distribution of the talent of narrative, though often clearly a developing feature, will probably never be evaluated as undesirable.
11. Takeshi Shibata, Kokuji ronsō no shinpoha to hoshuha, *Asahi shinbun (yūkan)* (February 4, 1966).
12. R. F. Amonoo, Problems of Ghanian lingue francae, in J. Spencer (ed.), *Language in Africa,* 1963, p. 80. The same conclusion is inherent in the second part of the Third Report of the Leverhulme Conference (cf. *Language in Africa,* pp. 133–135), 240–248.

Edgar Polomé

THE CHOICE OF OFFICIAL LANGUAGES
IN THE DEMOCRATIC REPUBLIC OF THE CONGO

In the brief outline on the Democratic Republic of the Congo distributed by the Information and Public Relations Service of the Embassy in Washington the language situation in the Congo is described as follows:

"There are more than 200 dialects but only four of the vernacular languages have official status:

"1. Kiswahili or Kingwana is spoken mostly in the area between Kivu (north), Katanga (south), Lualaba (west), and the Great Lakes (east).

"2. Tshiluba or Kiluba is spoken in the area between Angola and Lake Mwero.

"3. Kikongo, the language of Lower Congo and of Kwango.

"4. Lingala, or language of the river, is spoken in the area between Stanleypool and Ubangi-Uele."

"BUT French remains the Congo's official language."

This statement agrees with the factual situation with regard to the use of languages by the Belgian administration at the end of the colonial regime.

Belgium's linguistic policy in the Congo was, indeed, essentially pragmatic and attuned to the practical purposes pursued by the colonial power in the various areas of its activity. To rule a territory more than 80 times the size of its own, Belgium had to organize an efficient system of local government requiring a limited number of European personnel. This was achieved by integrating the African political institutions—small tribal communities with traditional chiefs—as units of local government into the framework of the colonial administration. This measure was actually a continuation of the policy of the pioneers establishing the political power of King Leopold's Congo Free State by concluding agreements with local chiefs. The *chefferies* recognized since 1891 by the Free

State administration were too small and too numerous, and in 1920, the constitution of larger administrative units—*secteurs,* grouping small rural units—was recommended. Gradually the number of *chefferies* was reduced from 6095 in 1917 to 2496 in 1935 and 432 in 1955, while the *secteurs,* first established in the Oriental Province in 1922, increased in number, from 57 in 1937 to 517 in 1950. By the time of independence, the number of local government units was about 900 for a rural population of about 10.5 million, each possessing the complete infrastructure of a modern administrative unit. Whereas local business was transacted orally in the local vernacular, it stands to reason that the keeping of the records and the maintenance of close relations with the central government could not be carried out in the more than 200 distinct vernaculars currently used in the country.

Although Article 3 of the Colonial Charter, which served as the fundamental law of the country during the colonial regime, made the use of all languages optional, this rule was applied only to direct relationship with the local population, but not to the various levels of government—general, provincial, district, and territorial. The first paragraph of Article 3 provided for the promulgation of decrees insuring the rights of the Africans with regard to the use of languages in justice, but since most disputes were settled by customary law before the tribunal of the *chefferie,* no major problem ever developed from the multiplicity of African languages and vernaculars, at least in the rural areas. In the absence of special legislation, the administration merely applied the ordinance of May 14, 1886, considering as official the language sanctioned by tradition. As a consequence, since 1877, French has been *the* language of administration and justice in the Congo. However, during the colonial regime, special provisions were made to guarantee the linguistic rights of the Flemish-speaking Belgians: Article 3 of the Charter stipulates: "All decrees and regulations of a general bearing will be written and published in French and Dutch. Both texts are official." Moreover, the right of the same Belgians to be defended and tried in their own language was explicitly recognized by the tribunal of Elizabethville on January 9, 1952. This decision was rescinded, however, by a court of appeal which stated that French was the only legal language in the Congo. A decree issued in 1957 finally settled the question in favor of the use of Dutch, along with French, in matters of law. But these were matters with political connotations which did not concern the Africans.

While using French in all its official documents applying to the African population, the central government and the administration of the provinces and their subdivisions (districts and territories) were concerned with finding adequate contact vernaculars to communicate with their subordinates. In territories with languages of wider expansion such as Mangbetu, which is used in the Uele and Aruwimi basins, it would have been possible to adopt the language of the area to translate all official documents in the territory under reference. However, even the number of such languages was too high for an administration with rather limited resources. Furthermore, if there were many cases of vast expanses appearing as linguistically coherent areas (such as that of the Mongo, e.g.), dialect differences within them would be of such importance that they would have required linguistic unification, either by choosing a definite dialect as the common standard or by creating a dialanguage on the basis of the characteristics shared by the majority of the dialects. During the difficult period of implantation of the colonial administration, such an activity was obviously out of the question. Accordingly, the administration resorted to the immediately available practical solution—the use of the lingua francas.

Typical, in this respect, is the case of the southwest Congo where the first Bantu language known to Europeans—kiKongo—was spoken. Early European penetration in this area had led to the development of a simplified trade language, which became known under the name of Fiote. In the Kwilu-Kwango area, where an extremely complex ethnic and linguistic situation made the use of a contact vernacular unavoidable, the influence and penetration of kiKongo as early as the sixteenth century entailed the development of a simplified form of a kiKongo dialect —kiMpaangu, according to Father Swartenbroeck—whose lexicon was renewed by numerous borrowings from other contact vernaculars. Often called kiKongo ya Leta because of its use by Belgian civil servants, it soon spread widely throughout the commercial centers of the former province of Leopoldville and beyond the Congo River in the area of Brazzaville, where it was called Monokutuba. It has now become the main means of communication between the lower-river tribes speaking primarily dialects of kiKongo and the up-river Congolese using liNgala. It is currently used under the name of kiKongo (véhiculaire) by Radio-Kinshasa (formerly Leopoldville) and Radio-Brazzaville, though the missions as well as linguists, such as H. W. Fehderau and L. B. Swift, prefer to call it kiTuba to distinguish it from tribal kiKongo. It is now the second language of about a million and a half people, but has become the first language of a limited number of young people as a consequence of intertribal marriage. The present expansion of kiTuba, which is partly responsible for the failure to develop a unified literary kiKongo, illustrates the far-reaching effects of the choice of a lingua franca by the colonial power to communicate with its African subjects.

One of the immediate consequences of colonization was the development of cities in Central Africa, a phenomenon that resulted in the creation of a type of society previously unknown in this part of Africa. Flocks of people left their traditional environment to cluster in the urban centers mushrooming in the vicinity of newly developed industry.

In 1959, this urban population represented 22 per cent of the total population of the Congo. Before 1957, it was organized either in *cités indigènes*—"native cities," with a chief and council—or *centres extra-coutumiers*—self-contained administrative units not ruled by customary law. Later, these were replaced by incorporated municipalities—*communes*—with wider African participation in political and administrative life. Since the populations of these urban units were of widely different tribal and linguistic background, the only language suitable for the needs of communication among them was often the local lingua franca—a situation that, in turn, favored its expansion and partial creolization.

A typical example of urban development is Lubumbashi (formerly Elizabethville). This town, situated in the middle of the wooded savanna, owes its origin and growth to the working of the mines in the rich copper-ore deposits of Upper Katanga. The building of the Lubumbashi processing plant and the arrival of the railway linking the community with the big commercial and industrial centers of South Africa were the decisive steps in its development. Before this, in April 1910, there were only about 20 Europeans in the area, but afterwards the town experienced a real boom; by 1912 the resident population amounted to about 8000 people, 15 per cent European. Numerous Africans from the neighboring areas flocked to the mushrooming town. They were speaking dialects of Bemba, Luba, Lunda, and other languages, but for intertribal communication, they resorted to the simplified Swahili that had already spread in the Garengaze kingdom of Msiri before the coming of the Europeans. As the copper production soared, the African personnel of the *Union Minière du Haut-Katanga* rose—to 21,107 units by 1928. Though a large portion of the personnel were transient workers, recruited mainly in Rhodesia, a considerable number settled in Elizabethville with their families, while more joined them to work in the smaller industries that were developing steadily or to perform household tasks for the European population. Besides, the rural population, which amounted to barely a few hundred in the area at the beginning of the century, also increased in number as agricultural colonization was organized and as Africans from various regions were lured by the call for unskilled labor.

In all these situations Swahili appeared to be the only adequate means of communication between Europeans and Africans as well as among Africans of different ethnic and tribal backgrounds. No wonder therefore that the government resorted to this same lingua franca to communicate with its subjects—the more so since it had been used as a trade language all over the east of the country since the penetration of the slavers and elephant hunters from East Africa in the nineteenth century.

Similar situations occurred elsewhere. Before the arrival of the Europeans there was already quite an active trade carried on between the ethnically related tribes living along the Congo River from Lolango to

Mobeka, as well as along the Lower Ubangi and in the Ngiri marshes. The vernacular used around 1890 for these intertribal contacts seems to have developed on the basis of the local language—boBangi (or rather boLoki?)—with borrowings from the kiKongo dialects of the Lower Congo and the Swahili of the *askari* of the Free State. When Leopoldville was established, a considerable part of the early African population came from the areas where this trade language was used, and liNgala (as it was called) normally became the main language of communication in the African township as well as for contact with the European. It was, accordingly, used by the administration in its relations with the local population and became the language of elementary education in the schools as well.

In the meantime, liNgala was spread in modified forms by the European penetration along the tributaries of the Congo, as far as the Uele basin. There, as well as in the Equator province, the government resorted to liNgala for its relations with its subjects, and this situation was practically maintained until Independence in spite of the strenuous efforts of the missions to have loMongo-loNkundo recognized as *the* African language used for administrative purposes in the larger Mongo area.

In the Kasayi, however, the situation was different, because there ciLuba had enjoyed considerable prestige among the neighboring tribes ever since the days of Kalamba Mukenge, when Wissmann founded Luluaburg (1884). It was currently used by the baKuba, the baTetela, and others, and was therefore immediately adopted for teaching purposes when the first Catholic mission was established in Luba territory in 1892. It has spread ever since as the cultural and administrative language of the area, though most Europeans never mastered ciLuba sufficiently to communicate properly with the local population. Accordingly, in the urban centers of the Kasayi and South-Senkuru, they resorted for such purpose to a form of kiTuba borrowing heavily from the ciLuba lexicon.

To sum up, the colonial administration of the early days, being too much concerned with other urgent problems to devote any attention to consistent linguistic planning, deliberately resorted to a practical language policy adapted to the situations which the development of intertribal trade had created in Central Africa. Taking over the existing lingua francas, it contributed to their expansion. In one case, however, the language of an ethnic group had started imposing itself sufficiently as a language of wider communication over a vast territory to make the administration adopt it for its own needs. This use of **Luba** was also promoted by its own speakers, who proved particularly prone to serve the interests of the Europeans and who consequently acquired a rather privileged position in colonial society. This situation was also brought about by the greater opportunities for education provided to the baLuba at an early date by the establishment of very active missions on their territory. As a result, the proportion of baLuba in the civil service, in the teaching profession, and in the economy exceeded by far their numerical importance.

On the other hand, the limitation of the number of African languages in administrative usage to four, beside French and Dutch, advantageously simplified the training of the European personnel. Future ranking administrators were thoroughly prepared for the complex duties they would have to fulfill in Central Africa in the *Institut Universitaire des Territoires d'Outre-Mer* in Antwerp, where they were taught Swahili and liNgala with a view to achieving an oral command of these languages. Later, courses providing a reading knowledge of ciLuba and kiKongo were added, as well as an introduction to the structure of Bantu languages. Similarly, other civil servants and leading administrative personnel in private enterprise were trained in liNgala and Swahili in a special school at the Ministry of Colonies in Brussels. However, after the Second World War, more emphasis was laid on surveying the grammatical features of the main Bantu languages used in the Congo, giving particular attention to cultural languages such as ciLuba and loMongo-loNkundo beside the two main lingua francas, Swahili and liNgala. From the start of the colonial regime, the mobility of the civil servants prevented them from getting a thorough command of local vernaculars and encouraged them to concentrate on a practical knowledge of the contact vernaculars, which would be useful to them throughout their career. The limitation of the training of lower rank civil servants and other personnel to a grammatical introduction to a set of Bantu languages in the fifties, however, entailed a considerable drop in the command of African languages by European administrators.[1]

To maintain the armed forces, the Congo Free State initially recruited mercenaries in various parts of Africa, and such languages as Hausa and Swahili were used with the troops, especially in the northeastern territories. Later an effort was made to standardize the use of languages in the *Force Publique,* as the army was called. Until World War I, Swahili was still used as language of instruction for the troops in the Oriental Province and in Katanga, but it was eliminated later in favor of liNgala, which became *the* language of the armed forces, making the relations between the soldiers recruited all over the territory of the colony and their African NCO's and Belgian officers much easier. The use of *one* language of command was actually consciously imposed as a means of promoting *esprit de corps* in the army. Because of the multiple tasks the

[1] This reduced training actually resulted from a lack of motivation to study African languages, because so many Congolese in the lower administrative ranks, as well as among the current domestic staff, had acquired a sufficient grasp of French to cope with most situations arising from their contacts with their Belgian bosses.

Force Publique was called upon to perform in the country, its consistent use of liNgala also contributed to the spread of this lingua franca.

The problem of the use of languages in education is much more complex. The policy of the Congo Free State toward the missions was essentially to grant them the greatest possible freedom of action in educational matters. As a consequence, the missions resorted to the local vernaculars for the purpose of teaching as well as evangelizing. This led to the publication of a series of grammars and vocabularies in the 1880s and 1890s. As the missionary penetration went upstream along the Aruwimi, the Itimbiri, the Ubangi and the Ngiri, new contacts were established with the riverside tribes and growing attention was given to the language of the paddlers. As early as 1903, Rev. W. H. Stapleton of the Baptist Missionary Society established at Yakusu, near the Stanley Falls, published there his *Comparative Handbook of Congo Languages Spoken Along the Banks of the Congo River from the West Coast of Africa to Stanley Falls . . . and of Swahili, the Lingua Franca, Stretching Thence to the East Coast,* together with his *Suggestions pour une Grammaire du Bangala, la "lingua franca" du Haut-Congo.*

The Fathers of Scheut, established in New Antwerp, favored liNgala, and so did the newly founded *vicariats apostoliques* in Ubangi and in Uele-Ituri, so that liNgala was taught even in the heart of Zande territory until the arrival of the Dominicans. Only kiKongo in the lower Congo, ciLuba in Kasayi, and loMongo-loNkundo preserved their position in missionary education, while Swahili was favored in the East by the White Fathers. Although keeping a lively interest in the local vernaculars, they indeed adopted Swahili as the language of evangelization and of instruction, even in the southeast, preventing the expansion of Luba into this area and probably also preventing the possible adoption of Bemba as contact-vernacular in the Upper-Katanga mining district, parallel to its spread in this function in the Zambian Copperbelt. It appears that the missions initially adopted to a large extent the contact vernaculars on grounds of expediency, but by doing so, they definitely favored the expansion and increased the prestige of the existing lingua francas.

The first State intervention in the problem of the use of languages in education is evidenced by Article 3 of the 1906 convention between the Congo Free State and the Vatican. It stipulates that "the teaching of the Belgian national languages is an essential part of the curriculum"; but the 1924 report of the Commission established by Minister Franck to coordinate the curricula of the missions stresses that "teaching must be done in a native language. Only the Africans of the urban centers, bound to be living in close contact with the Europeans, will be taught French." The 1926 unified curriculum, based on the conclusions of this report, provided that French should become the language of the curriculum in the upper forms. This curriculum was revised in 1929 and 1938, but the same principle prevailed: "The pupils who will leave junior high school (*école moyenne*) will usually be called upon to work in contact with Europeans. . . . They must accordingly be Europeanized to a degree." To achieve that purpose, French was introduced as a subject in primary schools from the third year on, and in the secondary schools became the language of the curriculum, the formerly used African language being taught as a subject.

In 1948 a new curriculum was made compulsory for the mission schools. In primary education the language of the curriculum was to be the mother tongue or, if possible (and preferably), the lingua franca, which had to be taught as a subject at any rate. In rural schools, no European language was to be taught, but French was optional as a second language in urban centers in lower grade schools, whereas it was compulsory in schools that provided for continuation beyond the lower grade. French was the language of the curriculum in all secondary schools, but in the *écoles de moniteurs,* training first grade teachers mainly for rural schools, the lingua franca remained the language of the curriculum, with French as compulsory second language. In girls' schools, however, the teaching of French as second language was compulsory only from the second grade on in major towns and in the last (sixth) form of primary education elsewhere, as well as in the lower grade teacher training schools (*écoles de monitrices*) and the schools for home economics (*écoles ménagères*).

A few years later the creation of metropolitan-type schools introduced French as the language of the curriculum from the start and the lingua franca was taught only as a subject on the primary level. This was part of an effort to upgrade education for Africans by establishing a complete equivalence with Belgian metropolitan degrees. All instruction being given in French, the teaching personnel was entirely European and submitted to the same requirements with regard to training and qualifications as their colleagues in Belgium. However, since a great number of these schools were interracial, this entailed compliance with the requirements of the Belgian linguistic policy concerning respect for the rights of the Flemings. Consequently, Dutch was taught beside French as second language, just as it was in Belgian bilingual communities like Brussels, though, in a few cases, English was taught as second language in secondary schools in departure from this rule.

At the universities, French was the language of the curriculum. However, in the first year of college, Dutch was a compulsory subject in the Faculty of Arts at the State University at Elizabethville, where parallel sections with Dutch as the language of the curriculum existed in certain fields until independence. Lovanium University and the State University both organized a comprehensive program in African linguistics, and the curriculum of the School of Education at Elizabethville included a set of compulsory courses in African linguistics including the intensive study of an African language.

In 1959, a Commission was established in Leopoldville to draft a course plan for the study of African culture and linguistics as part of the curriculum of secondary schools. The submitted proposal provided for the teaching of an African language in junior high school to serve as a basis for the teaching of African linguistics in senior high schools. Furthermore, this language teaching was to be closely coordinated with the part of the course giving an introduction to African culture. The languages to be taught had to have an adequate literary form and their choice would depend on local situations. The following languages were proposed:

1. Bantu. kiKongo, Luba, loMongo, oTetela, liNgombe, kiNande, loKela, kiLega, Lunda, Ciokwe, ciBemba, maShi.
2. non-Bantu: Zande, Ngbandi, Ngbaka, Mangbetu, Alur, Lugbara.

The program was to have been introduced in all secondary schools in September 1959, but owing to strong political pressure, it was never enacted, so that at the time of independence, African languages had practically been ousted from all the schools where the future Congolese *élite* was being trained, and were being maintained only on the primary level, often merely as a rather poorly treated subject.

This does not mean that there has never been any deliberate effort of linguistic planning in the Congo. The most decisive step taken in this direction by the Belgian authorities probably was the creation in the late 1940s of the advisory Commission on African linguistics. Eager to coordinate the efforts toward organized linguistic development in the Congo, this body of specialists tried to promote the careful study of complex local situations in various parts of the colony and to evaluate the progress made in the unification of languages of major expansion to be able to give competent advice to the Minister of Colonies on steps to be taken to solve the pending linguistic problems in Belgian Africa. Its activity resulted in the production of a series of well-documented reports with many useful suggestions, which unfortunately appear not to have been followed very often. The Commission seems to have been essentially in favor of maintaining linguistic pluralism by promoting the development of African cultural languages. The success attained in establishing loMongo-loNkundo as a recognized literary language was indeed a striking example of what could be achieved through doggedness of purpose and consistent strenuous activity by well-organized groups of devoted educators. However, the solution of its linguistic situation toward which the Congo appears to tend is not a pluralism based on the multiplicity of tribal languages. The latter would imply having, for example, in the vicariate of the Kivu alone at least three cultural languages—maShi, kiRega, and kinvaRwanda—other than the Swahili lingua franca, already introduced in precolonial days and alone able to solve satisfactorily the problems of intertribal relationship in communities where economic factors had brought important groups of immigrants.

For years the question of the advisability of adopting a definite national language for the whole territory of the Congo has been brought up by competent authorities. However, the proposed solutions to this problem have too often been biased. Emphasizing the superiority of Western culture, some people would advocate the exclusive use of French, unconditionally rejecting all African languages as inadequate to express the refined concepts of modern civilization—a highly prejudiced attitude that has been utterly disproved by recent developments in languages such as Swahili! Others would insist on the necessity for giving the Congolese an African national language they could really consider their own, because it would help preserve the genuine values of African culture. The question was debated for the first time in a constructive proposal by E. De Jonghe in his article, "Les langues communes du Congo Belge" in the journal *Congo* in November 1933, and it was reiterated with further precision and increased conviction in a paper read before the Institut Royal Colonial Belge and published in its *Bulletin des Séances* [Vol. 6 (1935), pp. 340–51] under the title, "Vers une langue nationale congolaise." In these studies De Jonghe stressed that the multiplicity of languages was a direct obstacle to the advancement of the African masses. Since it was a pedagogical heresy to impose a European language, it was advisable to develop an African language into an adequate tool for the promotion of cultural and social progress through education throughout the Congo. Since four "common languages" (kiKongo, liNgala, Swahili, ciLuba) were apparently expanding toward covering the whole territory of the colony, De Jonghe recommended that the government encourage their harmonious development as a preparatory step to the adoption of one of them as *the* national language, and he decidedly proposed that ciLuba be chosen for that purpose since it was the only genuine Congolese language of culture to have become a language of wider expansion.

This proposal started a rather lively controversy, especially because the authority and position of its author—a professor at the University of Louvain and internationally known ethnologist, director-general at the Ministry of Colonies and secretary-general to the Royal Colonial Institute—conferred a special weight on this pronouncement. Most of those who became involved in the debate agreed that the efforts of the government had not been successful in stabilizing liNgala, whose use as mother tongue remained restricted to an insignificant minority of Africans. It indeed required a thorough grammatical and lexical unification with a systematic re-Bantuization to be raised to the level of a genuine cultural language. On the other hand, many people reproached De Jonghe with leaving aside the Mongo group, which constituted a coherent ethnic entity covering a continuous territory stretching from the Lulonga-Lopori in the north to Lake Leopold II and even beyond the Lukenie into the Kasayi in the south, reaching the border and the Congo River in the west and even crossing the Lomami in the east and penetrating into the Sankuru in the southwest. The linguistic differentiation within this area did not create any difficulty that could not be easily overcome in an effort toward its unification, and the speakers of Mongo dialects ranked at least second in number among the Congolese. Father Hulstaert's argument against the choice of only one national language was particularly conclusive:

1. Education must be given in the mother tongue; trying to substitute a foreign language for the mother tongue, even if this foreign language is Congolese, constitutes a complete reversal of values.

2. Teaching in a language other than the mother tongue will help widen the gap between the elite and the masses (though the situation would probably have been less disturbing with ciLuba than it is with French).

3. Favoring one Congolese cultural language at the expense of the others will undoubtedly entail violent reaction from the elite of the neglected languages, especially among the baKongo and the Mongo, as well as in the large cities, where liNgala and Swahili are solidly established.

4. Will the chosen African language carry enough prestige among the Congolese elite to prevent their being more attracted by the European language used by the administration and the major economic powers in the country?

5. Where will the thousands of instructors required for the introduction of ciLuba as national language be found?

Adding to these points some pertinent remarks about the necessity of preserving the mother tongue as a language of evangelization, Father Hulstaert concluded in favor of pluralism, hoping that the territorial organization of the State and the Church would ultimately be revised to correspond to ethnic and linguistic subdivisions.

Nevertheless, at the eve of the entry of Belgium into World War II, Father Liesenborghs proposed once more to make ciLuba the national language of the Congo, after reexamining the problem of the lingua francas which the government essentially went on using. Fully aware of the involved problems, he brought forward a motion at the Fifteenth Congress of Philologists in Ghent in March 1940 requesting that the government create a commission with the explicit task of studying the linguistic situation in the Congo and drawing up practical proposals in order to regulate by law the use of African languages in administration, justice, and education.

A few months before the Liberation of Belgium, the discussion was resumed with renewed vigor, when the linguistic problem in the Congo was put on the agenda of the Royal Colonial Institute. This debate provided the contributors with an opportunity to display their persuasiveness in promoting with forcible arguments the language they particularly favored but, at the same time, betrayed the prejudices which biased the judgment of the participants. Thus kiKongo, proposed with lukewarm conviction by Mgr. J. Cuvelier, was rejected by E. De Jonghe because it had "the disadvantage of being the mother tongue of populations which belonged to three different colonies," whereas Swahili, fervently defended by J. Tanghe, G. van der Kerken, and V. Gelders on account of its international importance, was dismissed by the same De Jonghe as "a language which is absolutely foreign to the Congo." He, indeed, decided in favor of ciLuba because it had "the advantage of being a very widespread language in the Kasayi, spoken by a solid nucleus of homogenous Congolese populations endowed with a very high vitality." Though he explicitly denied that any "imperialistic or exaggerated nationalistic bias" was affecting his choice, De Jonghe thought that "the colonial government must have all the control levers at its disposal with regard to the evolution of the national language," which would obviously not be the case if Swahili were chosen, since the Congo would then be integrated into a linguistic area stretching far beyond the boundaries artificially established by the colonial powers during the partition of Africa.

As a matter of fact, by that time the debate was purely academic. In spite of the repeated assertion that contact vernaculars were not cultural languages and the claim that literary forms of languages of wider expansion should be developed, stronger forces than the limited influence of the promotors of such and such a language were at work, and even those who, like Father Stappers, devoted the best of their time and effort to molding ciLuba into a cultural language with an original living literature, had to acknowledge that, among other things, it would be necessary to oust Swahili from the large towns of Katanga to have the slightest chance of success in expanding the presently developed Luba cultural language outside the Kasayi. Such a move would indeed encounter tremendous difficulties, in spite of the sizeable emigration of baLuba from the Kasayi to Kantanga, in spite of the presence in northern Katanga of linguistically closely related Luba populations with whom the Sanga, further south, are also connected, and even in spite of the fact that a majority of the African schoolteachers in the Katangese mining district were baLuba from the Kasayi. A close examination of the facts shows that the evolution of the linguistic situation in Katanga works in favor of Swahili as the African language of wider expansion. Its only serious rival is French, but the prevalence of either of them will depend on the effect the spread of education has on language usage in urban communities.

An enquiry conducted in June 1963 with a group of 484 students of the E. Wangermée Secondary School and Teachers' Training College at Katuba, near Elizabethville, shows that out of 174 Luba students, 151 remain loyal to their tribal language in the narrower family circle and 19 claim to use French, and 42 use Swahili as the first or second language at home. Socially, these young men belong to families of lower and middle level civil servants and clerks working in banks and offices of local plants and commercial organizations. Quite interesting is the fact that the languages they resort to in their social relations outside the family circle are essentially Swahili (128) and French (109); only nine state that they address their friends in Luba. This situation clearly indicates that their social relations are essentially intertribal, and the relative importance of the use of French points to their preference for associating with people with the same level of education. When addressing strangers, only four of them think it fit to resort to Luba dialects; the vast majority obviously find it natural to use either Swahili (101) or preferably French (118), perhaps purposely to display the command they have achieved in this language of higher prestige. By way of comparison, let us briefly examine the corresponding figures for a group of 86 Lunda students from the same school: 63 remain loyal to their tribal language, but 32 use either exclusively Swahili or Swahili in addition to Lunda in the family circle, whereas only 9 resort to French either as a first or as a second language at home. With friends, only 6 usually speak Lunda, whereas the vast majority use either French (63) or Swahili (53); with strangers, they similarly resort either to French (60) or to Swahili (54). Like their baLuba fellow students, all these Lunda speakers are actually trilingual.

Considering the composition of the population of Elizabethville/ *Lubumbashi,* it is probable that this new generation will loosen its ties with the tribal community to a much larger extent than their parents ever did, and that intertribal marriages will undoubtedly increase the number of those whose mother-tongue is Katanga Swahili. If this creolized Swahili is in many respects different from kiUnguja, the Zanzibar dialect of Swahili adopted as standard language, and shows several of the features of kiNgwana combined with local peculiarities, essentially due to the influence of Luba and probably also of Bemba, it is in no way so far from the kiSwahili cha Kitabu taught in the schools that a child raised in Katanga Swahili would have any more trouble studying the standard language than a child speaking a rather divergent dialect of a western language would experience in being taught that language. Furthermore, except for numerous French loanwords, the written form of Katanga Swahili as it appears in the local press, for example, in *Uhaki,* differs only from the current language used, for example, in *Taifa Leo* in Nairobi, by a set of morphological and syntactic peculiarities that are rather easily identifiable. This is mainly because as far as it is used in education, the Swahili taught in the schools is essentially the East African standard language. Considering the prestige now enjoyed by Swahili in Africa, the Katangese elite can be expected to cling to it, together with French, and to use it with growing correctness and accuracy, at least in its written form.

More complex is the situation in Leopoldville/Kinshasa owing to the tremendous rate at which its population has increased. In 1923, only 16,701 Africans were living in the capital of the Congo. Thirty years later there were more than a quarter of a million of them there and their number increased at a rate of 30,000 a year, reaching over 400,000 inhabitants on the eve of independence. Since then, the flow of immigrants has only increased and Kinshasa has become the largest city in Central Africa. If, in the beginning, the majority of the immigrants came from the north and the east along the major waterways of the Congo and the Kasayi, whereas only notably less would come upstream from the west, the population growth of the capital after 1939 changed this situation. From 1880 until that date, the baKongo formed only a minority of little influence compared to the masses of immigrants from other regions. The contact vernacular that prevailed in Leopoldville under the pressure of the circumstances was liNgala, which was soon also introduced as the language of the curriculum in African schools, so that even the baKongo who had settled in town had to resort to liNgala outside their family circle and strictly tribal contacts. Furthermore, the detribalization of many immigrants produced a generation of townspeople whose mother-tongue was liNgala. At the eve of World War II, liNgala accordingly appeared to stand a fair chance of becoming *the* language of Leopoldville. The following years of prosperity, however, lured tremendous numbers of baKongo to the booming town right at the border of their tribal territory. From a minority, they became the majority of the town population, increasing to the point of 75 per cent of the population in the early 1950s, while the speakers of liNgala as first language no longer represented more than 10 per cent of the townspeople. Nevertheless, the government stuck to its policy of imposing liNgala as the language of the curriculum in primary education, and soon numerous protests were raised against this improper treatment of the new baKongo majority which prevented them from having their children educated in their mother-tongue.[2] The main objection against the introduction of kiKongo beside liNgala was the absence of a generally accepted kiKongo standard, as the efforts toward

[2] The protest against liNgala was actually more a matter of form; the real target was colonial policy. As a matter of fact, the baKongo of Kinshasa have gone on using liNgala to the present day when associating with friends and strangers in town.

unification of the widely divergent kiKongo dialects had failed in the 1930s. However, the problem of linguistic unification was taken up again, but it now appeared to be further complicated by political involvements. The question of the choice of the language of the curriculum was settled finally by the decision of the colonial authorities to impose French at all levels, a measure which became applicable to the whole territory in 1959.

This decision probably constitutes the most radical intervention of the government in matters of linguistic policy. Though practicing linguistic pluralism from a purely practical point of view in its relations with the local population, the colonial government never went any further than using the contact vernaculars which economic factors had already started developing and spreading before it moved in. In the promotion of African cultural languages, its policy was essentially characterized by a prudent expectant attitude: it gave the missions a free hand to try and perform this difficult task—sometimes quite successfully as in the case of loMongo—but, obviously, except when strictly practical necessities were involved, the Belgian authorities carefully abstained from any direct intervention in the touchy matters of regional planning of definite linguistic policies. The only language whose expansion they ever actively encouraged through direct use of their executive powers was French, as is evident when one follows step by step the growing prevalence of this language in the curriculum until its eventual use as the only language of education. Their support of liNgala remained limited and restrained, except in the case of the *Force Publique*, where again practical considerations prevailed to unify the language of command.

The outcome of this policy is the situation described at the beginning of this paper. To be sure, "there is an urgent need for a *single Congolese language*," as Yvon Nsuka recently pointed out in his survey of the linguistic problem in the Congo, published in the July 1964 issue of *Documents pour l'Action* in Leopoldville, but it is probable that for many years to come Article 89 of the Constitution of the Democratic Republic of the Congo of August 1964: "French is the official language of the Parliament. However, each of the Houses can also accept other working languages" will remain applicable, not only to the legislature, but also to the whole administration of the country.

SELECT BIBLIOGRAPHY

Anon. *Belgian Congo*. Vol. 1. Brussels: Belgian Congo and Ruanda-Urundi Information and Public Relations Office, 1959.
Anon. *Comité Spécial du Katanga 1900–1950*. Brussels: L. Cupyers, s.a.
Boelaert, E. 1936. Naar een nationale inlandsche taal in Kongo?, in *Kongo-Overzee*, **2**, 240–248.

Boelaert, E. 1958. Afrikaanse talen in het onderwijs in Belgisch-Kongo. In *Bulletin des séanus de l'Académie Royale des Sciences Coloniales*, Vol. 4, pp. 861–76. (Note: pp. 877–945 report the debate which followed the presentation of Boelaert's paper.)

Brausch, G. 1961. *Belgian Administration in the Congo*. London: Oxford University Press (Institute of Race Relations).

Burssens, A. 1954. *Inleiding tot de studie van de Kongolese Bantoetalen*. Antwerp: De Sikkel (Kongo-Overzee Bibliotheek, Vol. VIII).

Cleire, R. 1951. Talen en Taalunificatie in het Vicariaat Kivu, *Kongo-Overzee*, 17, 32–37.

Cuvelier, J. 1944. Note sur la langue Kongo (kiKongo). *Bulletin des Séances de l'Institut Royal Colonial Belge*, 15, 25–26.

Cuvelier, J. 1944. La "lingua franca" du Bas-Congo. *Bulletin des Séances de l'Institut Royal Colonial Belge*, 15, 73–75.

De Boeck, L.-B. 1949. *Taalkunde en de Talenkwestie in Belgisch-Kongo*. Brussels: G. Van Campenhout (Institut Royal Colonial Belge. Section des Sciences Morales et Politiques. Mémoires. Collection in-80. Vol. 17, part 1).

De Boeck, L.-B. 1952. Het Lingala op de weegschaal, *Zaïre*, 6, 115–153.

De Boeck, L.-B. 1953. Taaltoestand te Leopoldstad, *Kongo-Overzee*, 19, 1–7.

De Clercq, A. 1937. Hoe het Tshiluba zich in Kasai verspreidde, *Kongo-Overzee*, 3, 241–244.

De Jonghe, E. 1935. Vers une langue nationale congolaise, *Bulletin des Séances de l'Institut Royal Colonial Belge*, 6, 340–351.

De Jonghe, E. 1944. L'unification des langues congolaises, *Bulletin des Séances de l'Institut Royal Colonial Belge*, 15, 61–71.

De Koster, L. 1951. Problèmes linguistiques et culturals au Congo Belge, *Problèmes d'Afrique Centrale*, 1, 7–31.

Denis, J. 1958. *Le phénomène urbain en Afrique centrale*. Brussels (Académie Royale des Sciences coloniales. Classe des Sciences Morales et Politiques. Mémoires in-80 N.S., vol. 19, part 1).

De Pauw, W. 1957. *Het Talenproblem in het Onderwijs van Belgisch-Kongo*. Ghent: Julius Vuylsteke-Fonds.

De Rop, A. 1953. De Bakongo on het Lingala, *Kongo-Overzee*, 19, 170–174.

De Rop, A. 1960. Les langues du Congo, *Aequatoria*, 23, 1–24.

Fehderau, H. 1962. The place of the Kituba language in Congo, *Congo Mission News*, 196, 9–10.

Gelders, V. 1944. La langue commune au Congo, *Bulletin des Séances de l'Institut Royal Colonial Belge*, 15, 77–104.

Guilbert, D. 1952. Civilisation occidentale et langage au Congo Belge, *Zaïre*, 6, 899–928.

Harries, L. 1956. Le Swahili au Congo Belge, *Kongo-Overzee*, 22, 395–400.

Heyse, Th. 1952–1959. *Congo Belge et Ruanda-Urundi. Notes de Droit Public et Commentaires de la Charte Coloniale*, 2 vols. Brussels; G. Van Campenhout.

Hulstaert, G. 1937. Het talenvraagstuk in Belgisch-Kongo, *Kongo-Overzee*, 3, 49–68.

Hulstaert, G. 1950. Taaleenmaking in het Mongo-gebied, *Kongo-Overzee*, 16, 292–298.

Hulstaert, G. 1950. Les langues indigènes peuvent-elles servir dans l'enseignement?, *Bulletin des Séances de l'Institut Royal Colonial Belge*, 21, 316–340.

Larochette, J. 1952. Le problème des langues dans l'enseignement aux indigènes du Congo Belge, *Problèmes d'Afrique Centrale*, 2, 72–78.

Lemarchand, R. 1961. The bases of nationalism among the Bakongo, *Africa*, 31, 344–354.

Liesenborghs, O. 1941–1942. Beschouwingen over wezen, nut en toekomst der zogenaade "linguae francae" van Belgisch-Kongo, *Kongo-Overzee*, 7–8, 87–99.

Malengreau, G. 1953. De l'emploi des langues en justice au Congo, *Journal des Tribunaux d'Outremer*, 15, 3–6.

Nsuka, Y. 1964. Le problème linguistique au Congo, *Documents pour l'Action*, 4(27), 207–216.

Ntahokaja, J. 1957. La place des langues Bantu dans la culture africaine, *Kongo-Oversee*, **23**, 232–241.

Polomé, E. 1963. Cultural Languages and Contact Vernaculars in the Republic of the Congo, *Texas Studies in Literature and Language*, **4**, 499–511.

Slade, R. 1962. *King Leopold's Congo*. London: Oxford University Press.

Stappers, L. 1952. Het Tshiluba als omgangstaal, of unificatie van de Luba-dialecten?, *Kongo-Overzee*, **18**, 50–65.

Tanghe, J. 1930. Le Lingala, la langue du Fleuve, *Congo*, **9**, 341–358.

Tanghe, J. 1944. Le Swahili, langue de grande expansion, *Bulletin des Séances de l'Institut Royal Colonial Belge*, **15**, 1–24.

Van Bulck, G. 1948. *Les Recherches Linguistiques au Congo Belge*. Brussels: G. Van Campenhout (Institut Royal Colonial Belge. Section des Sciences Morales et Politiques Mémoires. Collection in-8o. Vol. 16).

Van Bulck, G. 1950. Le problème linguistique dans les Missions de l'Afrique Centrale, *Zaïre*, **4**, 49–65.

Van Bulck, G. 1953. Het taalprobleen in het Kongolees universitair onderuija, *Kongo-Overzee*, **19**, 343–356.

Van Caeneghen, R. 1950. Les langues indigènes dans l'enseignement, *Zaïre*, **4**, 707–720.

Van der Kerken, G. 1944. Le Swahili, langue de grande expansion, *Bulletin des Séances de l'Institut Royal Colonial Belge*, **15**, 27–60.

Van Wing, J. 1951. Nota over de "Commissie voor unificatie van het Kikongo" (1935–1936), *Kongo Overzee*, **17**, 38–10.

Van Wing, J. 1953. Het Kikongo en het Lingala te Lespoldstad, *Kongo-Overzee*, **19**, 175–178.

Vorblicher, A. 1964. Das Spachenproblem in Kongo (Léo), *Neues Afrika*, **6**, 167–169.

Albert Valdman

LANGUAGE STANDARDIZATION
IN A DIGLOSSIA SITUATION: HAITI

DIGLOSSIA IN HAITI

Haiti is one of several nations characterized by an interesting type of multilingualism, diglossia [1]. Haitian diglossia differs from other well-known cases of the phenomenon (in the Arabic-speaking world, Greece, and the German-speaking cantons of Switzerland) in that the two forms of speech that coexist—Haitian Creole and French, the primary or "low" and superposed or "high" speech forms, respectively—are probably different languages rather than different varieties of the same language. Also, the fact that Haitian Creole (Creole) arose as a pidginized form of some French dialect or group of dialects under the special conditions of the slave trade and the colonial plantation economy has considerable sociolinguistic import [2].

In Haiti Creole and the local variety of Standard French, Haitian French (French)—which shows few divergences from the prestige Parisian variety—functions in the discourse of bilinguals very much as do the various style levels of Standard French in the discourse of educated Parisian speakers. The two forms of speech have well-defined domains, which William A. Stewart described in terms of two intersecting sets of sociolinguistic variables: (a) *public* (impersonal or representative) behavior versus *private* (personal or nonrepresentative) behavior, and (b) *formal* (formally prescribed) behavior versus *informal* (not formally prescribed) behavior [3]. Creole is used nearly exclusively in private informal situations, such as in a conversation between two siblings at home, and French is used exclusively in formalized public circumstances, such as in the courts, at school, in dealing with officials. Both languages are used interchangeably in public-informal situations (in shops, radio broadcasts, sermons) or private-formal situations (receptions, conversations with acquaintances, conversations with friends in the presence of outsiders):

	Formal	*Informal*
Public	French	French or Creole
Private	French or Creole	Creole (French)

The choice of Creole or French in public-informal and private-formal situations is no doubt indicative of the speaker's degree of association with native Haitian culture, his nationalism, his race consciousness (*négritude*), and thus is of high sociological significance. Haitian bilinguals may shift from French to Creole within a sentence, for instance, "Alors il se met à tempêter jusqu'à ce que *u vini uvri pòt la ba li*": "Then he begins to carry on until you (ya) open the door for him (for 'im)"[4]. Such shifts constitute a sensitive stylistic device, for they signal subtle changes of roles and attitudes among interlocutors.

Diglossia characterizes the speech behavior of only a small minority of Haitians, precisely the segment of the population that is literate and educated and that aspires to economic and social prestige [5]. Monolingual Haitians, who constitute approximately 90 per cent of the population of the country, are totally excluded from participation in public-formal situations, including administrative and legal procedures, for these are the situations that require a control of French. On the other hand, the outsider who cannot understand and speak Creole will fail to have entry in many aspects of the nation's culture: "Creole incorporates the entire history of the indigenous people of the island. Consciousness of this history is achieved through Creole, as the language is the depository of the folklore of the people. . . . Creole is, therefore, expressive of what is called the 'soul' of the people" [6]. Although these comments were made by Alleyne with reference to the British protectorate of Saint-Lucia, an island where a Creole French dialect mutually intelligible with Haitian Creole coexists with English, they apply equally well to Haiti. Clearly, in Haiti an individual can participate fully in the total life of the community only if he speaks the vernacular (Creole) and both speaks *and* reads the superposed official language (French); and there cannot be any significant development—economic, political, social—unless a significant proportion of the Creole monolinguals become diglossic.

The acquisition by all of Haiti's citizens of diglossia and biculturism within the limitations indicated by the respective domains of Creole and French requires a mobilization of resources on the part of all segments of the population, which this economically feeble country will find difficult if not impossible. It will also require a complete change of attitude on the part of the diglossic, educated elite toward Creole and the role it is to play in the development of the country. Although the Haitian elite have come to accept the diglossia relationship between French and Creole, many still consider Creole a corruption of French, an ill-formed and primitive tool to which they deny the status of language; and some, in their hearts if not openly, still advocate its eradication through the exclusive study of French in the schools and a massive literacy campaign in French. This is obviously utopian in a country where fewer than 30 per cent of school-age children are provided with two or three years of schooling [7]. Better communication between the government and the people, and between the educated urban segments of the population and the rural masses, would be effected by the extension of the use of the vernacular in public-formal situations until such times as the rural masses have been taught to use the official language for limited purposes.

The recent visitor to Haiti cannot fail to be impressed by the displacement of French by Creole in all except public-formal circumstances and to note that all persons involved in language planning are reaching the consensus that Creole rather than French is the country's national language [8]. Although these same persons are unwilling to challenge the position of French as the official language, and although they have not completely cast away denigrating clichés about Creole, Ferguson was quite right in predicting that Haitian diglossia will give way to a slow development toward the adoption of a unified standard based on the Port-au-Prince variety of Creole [9]. It is precisely the problems that the elaboration of a standard dialect of Haitian Creole entails and the relationship between standardization and the devising of a suitable orthography that we should like to discuss in this paper.

VARIATION IN HAITIAN CREOLE

It is widely held that Creole languages have no fixed usage, that indeed they have no grammar, and that consequently it would be difficult to isolate a fixed set of pronunciation habits, forms, and constructions that could constitute a standard. This state of affairs does in fact properly characterize Jamaican vernacular speech, which constitutes a continuum ranging from the "bongo talk" of the Maroon country to the local variety of standard English spoken in the residential suburbs of Kingston:

"A given speaker is likely to shift back and forth from Creole to English within a single utterance, without ever being conscious of this shift. Most observers of language in Jamaica have encountered extreme difficulty in distinguishing between the various layers of the language structure, and indeed the lines of demarcation are very hard to draw . . ." [10].

Creolists who are familiar with the linguistic situation in both Jamaica and Haiti are quick to point out that in Haiti it is easy to draw the line between the vernacular and the official language and that any utterance produced by a diglossic speaker can be unambiguously assigned to French or to Creole. This accurately describes the speech behavior of the educated literate elite whose control of French is usually flawless, but the speech of semiliterate or illiterate urban quasi-diglossics will contain numerous utterances that may be interpreted as either inaccurate renditions of French or gallicized renditions of Creole. And while past denigrators have exaggerated the amount of variation within Creole, considerable variation does exist and goes far beyond the well-known instances of geographical lexical variants such as *kanistè, mamit,* or *fèblã* for "tin can" [11]. Descriptions of Creole, both structurally oriented and traditional, have merely noted variants in anecdotal or haphazard fashion without distinguishing between, for instance, geographical or social variants and forms that alternate freely within a single geographical and social dialect. If a Haitian Creole standard is to be developed, some objective and consistent basis must be evolved to establish one of several variants as the "normal" form. Before we consider this problem, let us rapidly survey the types of linguistic variation to be found in Creole.

In Creole, variation manifests itself primarily at the phonological, morphophonemic, and lexical levels. Significantly, except at the morphophonemic level, variation results from what appears to be extensive borrowing from French. The phonological systems of French and Creole differ primarily in their vowel inventories.

	Haitian French			*Haitian Creole*		
Oral	i	ü	u	i		u
	é	œ́	ó	é		ó
	è	œ̀	ò	è		ò
		a	â		a	
Nasal	œ̃		o			
				ẽ	ã	õ
	ẽ		ã			

Creole lacks the entire front rounded series (/ü/ as in *jus,* /œ́/ as in *jeu,* /œ̀/ as in *jeune*) as well as the contrast between front /a/ and back /â/ (*là* versus *las*) and the contrast /ẽ/ versus /œ̃/ (*brin* versus *brun*). There are also differences in the distribution and allophonic range of near-equivalent phonemes, but these need not occupy us here [12]. Although it is posited by all analysts, the vowel system listed above for Haitian Creole describes accurately only certain rural varieties of Creole referred to by urban Haitians as *gros créole,* "rough Creole," or *créole natif-natal,* "homespun Creole." Creole speakers in the larger urban centers (Port-au-Prince, Cap Haïtien, Gonaïves, etc.)—speakers who, it should be noted, are usually unable to construct French sentences and have difficulty understanding French utterances—will produce front rounded vowels both in words that are clearly part of the native Creole stock (e.g., *plüm,* "pen," *dǽ*, "two," *lǽ*, "when") and in apparent loans from French (e.g., *lüté*, "to struggle," versus *gumẽ*, *tübèkülǽ*, "person stricken by tuberculosis" versus *pwatrimẽ*).

Another striking difference between the phonological systems of French and of rural varieties of Creole is the absence of postvocalic /r/. However, I have observed clearly articulated postvocalic /r/ in the speech of urban Cap-Haïtien Creole monolinguals, and Michelson Hyppolite, among many others, notes the following instances in his transcription of folk tales collected in the Cap-Haïtien region: *pèr ~ pè*, "father"; *pèrdu ~ pèrdi ~ pèdu*, "lost"; *Mardi*, "Mr. Tuesday" [13].

Both French and Creole have nasal vowel phonemes, but the function and distribution of nasalization differ markedly in the two languages. In French, nasal vowels occur in utterance- or syllable-final position and before consonants except the nasal consonants /m n ñ/. In Creole, nasal vowels occur before all types of consonants including the nasal consonants /m n ñ/, and nasal vowels alternate freely with corresponding oral vowels in the environment of nasal consonants. The occurrence of nasality with vowels is best accounted for by establishing three types of vowels: (a) "inherently nasal" vowels, which are always nasalized (*pãt*, "slope," *pẽs*, "pliers"); (b) "long" vowels, which are never nasalized even when they occur before a nasal consonant (*ša:m*, "room," *bò:n*, "boundary marker"; *pa:n*, "breakdown"); (c) plain vowels, which are optionally nasalized in the vicinity of a nasal segment—contiguous or discontinuous (*šèn ~ šẽn*, "chain," *lamè ~ lãmè, ~ lãmẽ*, "sea," *avã ~ ãvã*, "before." One might hazard the observation that plain vowels that occur in the vicinity of nasal segments are generally nasalized in rural varieties of Creole and that denasalization in this environment is a feature of gallicization.

MORPHOPHONEMIC VARIATION

As is well known, French exhibits wide-scale sandhi variation subsumed by the traditional labels of liaison and elision. Creole also is characterized by extensive sandhi variation of the elision type only, but to a much greater degree than is French [14]. All verbal particles and pronouns optionally lose their final vowel or vowels (including semivowels when proclitic or enclitic to a verb form, for example, *mwe té alé ~ m t alé*, "I went," *yó apé mãzé ~ y ap mãzé*, "they're eating," *mwe wẽ li ~ m wè l*, "I see him (it, her)." Morphophonemic alteration is often compounded by dialect variation. The forms of the third-person singular pronoun will be discussed to show the extent of morphophonemic alteration in Creole.

Descriptions of Creole list the basic shape of the third person singular pronoun as *li;* application of the optional elision rule produces the shortened form *l*, which occurs more frequently in normal speed utterances. The Cap-Haïtien variety of Creole shows, in addition to *li* and *l*, reflexes of an underlying *"yi"* form realized as *yi*, *i*, and *y*. Table 1 pre-

TABLE 1. *Frequency of Occurrence of Variants of the Third-Person Singular Pronoun*

	li	*l*	*"li"*	*yi*	*i*	*y*	*"yi"*
Proclitic (Subject)	32	5	37	11	47	2	60
Verbal particle	2	4	6	3	14	1	18
Verb	27	0	28	8	25	0	33
Others	3	0	3	0	8	1	9
Enclitic	4	3	7	67	5	0	67
Direct object	2	2	4	17	22	0	19
Object of preposition	2	0	2	39	3	0	42
Possessive	0	1	1	6	0	0	6

sents the frequency of occurrence of the five phonemically distinct forms of the third person singular pronoun in one of the folk tales transcribed by Hyppolite [15]. While we may discount *l* and *y* because of their relatively low frequency, we are left with three other forms whose occurrence cannot be fully predicted in terms of the syntactic environment.

In addition to morphophonemic alternation Creole exhibits variations in form no doubt dialectal in nature, for example, *lè ~ lò*, "when, hour, time," *vwazinaž ~ vwazinaj*, "neighbor," *püi ~ pli*, "rain," *jũn ~ jũ ~ õ ~ ũ*, "indefinite article," *bay ~ ba*, "to give."

LEXICAL BORROWING

The speech of urban Creole speakers contains numerous lexical borrowings from French. These lexical borrowings may consist of isolated words or phrases, many of them cliché expressions. Although borrowing from French may be very heavy within a single discourse, particularly in the case of semiliterate speakers with a faulty command of French who wish to impress others with their knowledge of the official language, it seldom affects the grammatical structure of the sentence within which it is incorporated. Consider, for example, the following utterances produced by the monitor of a literacy class exhorting his monolingual Creole charges with the obvious intent of impressing a French-speaking visitor.

1. *ou kapab fèr fas*   "you're able to face"   *vous serez capable de faire face*

2. *plü ēbü dǽ konésãs pa l*   "more imbued with his knowledge"
   plus imbu de ses connaissances
3. *ǽ ptit pǽ òrgœjǽ*   "a little conceited"   *un petit peu orgueil-
   leux* (/ǽ pti pǽ orgœjǽ/)

Note that all four utterances contain phonological features that are
absent from rural varieties of Creole: the rounded vowels /ü œ œ/, postvocalic /r/, and the nasal vowel /œ/. That in sentence (1) the speaker
simply borrowed the complete phrase *faire face* is demonstrated by the
use of *fèr*, although the equivalent form *fè* is part of the stock of native
Creole words. Note, too, that in the same sentence the speaker used the
full form *kapab,* "to be able," rather than the more frequent reduced
forms *kab, kap,* or *ka.* In (2) the emphatic possessive construction
pa + personal pronoun is used instead of the preposed French possessive
determiner *ses.* Sentence (3) contains *ptit,* a form that is neither correct
French /pti/ nor authentic Creole *ti.* In a Creole whose authenticity is
less suspect, sentences (1) and (3) would be rendered as follows [16]:

1. *ou kapab (kab) gumē avèk l (ak li; avè l)*
3. *yūn žã tròp pu kò l*

My informant was stumped by sentence (2), and the closest interpretive
translation he could come up with was: *li kwa li té gē (yē) ãpil kónésãs nã
kalbas tèt li,* literally, "he thinks he has a lot of knowledge in that cala-
bash head of his."

   Urban monolingual Creole speakers have frequent contacts with persons with varying proficiency in French, and, since prestige and economic
and social advantages accrue to one in direct proportion to his control
of the official language, they will replace native Creole words by French
synonyms. Thus, for example, *gumē,* "to fight, to struggle," is replaced by
lüté (lité) or *kõbat; maladi kaj* or *maladi tusé,* "tuberculosis," is replaced
by *tübèkülóz* (or *tibèkilóz* in a more creolized version). In the case of the
last item, when we take into account the fact that a person stricken by
tuberculosis is called *mun pwatrinè* or, more metaphorically, *mun ki bõ
pu l al(é) nã tébé,* "a person who should go to a sanatorium," we more
fully appreciate the difficulty and the magnitude of the task the standardization of Creole entails.

ORTHOGRAPHY AND STANDARDIZATION

   Language planners in Haiti have limited themselves to the question of
the preparation of an orthography for Creole or, more accurately, to the
devising of a suitable alphabet. First attempts to write down Creole
utterances made use of widely varying etymological spellings, and it was
not until 1941 that Ormonde McConnell, a Methodist minister from

Northern Ireland who was acquainted with the literacy work of Frank Laubach, proposed an alphabet for Creole that deliberately rejected French spelling conventions. The McConnell-Laubach orthography was an adaptation of the IPA alphabet designed to provide one grapheme for each phoneme of the language, and therefore it received the unqualified blessing of American structural linguists such as Robert A. Hall, Jr. But it needlessly departed from some of the conventions of French spelling that would not have destroyed bidirectional correspondence between phonemes and graphemic units. Predictably, the McConnell-Laubach orthography provoked violent reactions on the part of the segment of the diglossic Haitian elite that opposed any attempt to give Creole status as a language, and it was also rejected by those Haitian intellectuals who shared with McConnell, Laubach, and Hall the desire to provide Haitian monolinguals with access to the written word but who had deeper insights into the diglossia relationship between the two speech forms of the country and who understood the necessity of some accommodation of the "low" form to the "high" form. Thus Charles-Fernand Pressoir devised a counterproposal to the McConnell-Laubach orthography that, although it maintained on the whole bidirectional correspondence between graphemes and phonemes, adopted some of the conventions and symbols of French spelling [17]; for instance, nasal vowels were represented by combinations of vowel letters plus *n* instead of vowel letters plus the circumflex accent. Table 2 compares various forms.

TABLE 2

Phonemic Transcription	McConnell	Pressoir	French Cognate
mãmã	mâmâ	manman	maman
swẽ	swê	souin	soin
sõžé	sôjé	sonjé	songer

The Pressoir (or Faublas-Pressoir) orthography has now been adopted essentially unchanged by the official agency for development (ONEC, the Office National d'Education Communautaire) and all Protestant and Catholic literacy programs.

Pressoir also correctly diagnosed the principal weakness of the McConnell-Laubach "phonetic" orthography, the choice of an inappropriate variety of Creole:

"Ne connaissant pas assez notre idiome pour en saisir les nuances, (McConnell) ne s'appliqua à rendre que les voyelles du 'gros créole,' sans tenir compte des double en usage, non seulement dans le parler des haïtiens cultivés mais encore dans la langue d'un nombre considérable de prolétaires mêlés à la masse de ceux qui parlent le 'gros créole' " [18].

The choice of rural Creole forms as standard resulted from the faulty assumption that such features of urban Creole as the front rounded series are acquired directly from French by individual speakers. It would appear that these features are more deeply rooted. Too often analysts attribute aberrant features of languages existing in a contact situation to bilingual interference and fail to consider the alternative possibility of retention of features from an older stage of the language. Certainly the presence of /ü œ̃œ/ and of postvocalic /r/ in the speech of Cap Haïtien monolinguals suggests that these features may be survivals from more conservative dialects of Creole or, more correctly, perhaps, from an earlier layer of gallicization of the Creole spoken in Northern Haiti in the late seventeenth or early eighteenth century. Even for Creole speakers who consistently fail to distinguish /ü/ from /i/, /œ́/ from /é/, or /œ/ from /è/, front rounded vowels must be assumed, at least as part of their passive inventory. Stated differently, the possibility of realization with /ü œ̃œ/ as well as /i é è/ is a feature of certain Creole vowels; accordingly, they must be given separate status at the underlying level and provisions must be made for their representation in the orthography.

More important, the selection of a rural variety of Creole as a standard conflicts with sociolinguistic realities. As Stewart points out, the Port-au-Prince variety of Creole has much higher social prestige than the rural variety "because among other things it, and not rural Creole, is the variety of Creole which is the normal co-participant in Haitian diglossia" [19].

Rural Creole speakers who migrate to urban centers strive to cast off marked nonurban features to avoid being exposed to ridicule, or, as it is expressed in Creole, *pu yó pa pasé-yo lã bètiz,* "so that people don't take them for stupid dolts." Thus a boy from a village in the southern part of Haiti who had been placed in a Port-au-Prince family declared to me that the goal of his sojourn in the capital was *šašé bjẽ palé,* "trying to learn to speak well," by which he was not referring to learning French but Port-au-Prince Creole usage. Even rural Creole speakers who have remained in their native area but who have had brief exposure to French at school or who have come in contact with city dwellers are able to *fè ti buš pwẽtü,* "to make their mouths a little bit rounded," that is, to produce front rounded vowels and to shift, for example, from *nã la ri* to *nã la rü,* "in the street," *blé-a* to *blœ́-a,* "the blue," or *sè-m* to *sœ̀-m,* "my sister." Finally, the large number of denigrating expressions referring to rural inhabitants and their linguistic habits should lead one to suspect that rural Creole could hardly be an appropriate model for imitation. Note, for instance: *li gró sulyé,* "he's like a big shoes"; *li uvri bwat kréòl li,* "and he opens up that big Creole mug of his."

That normalization of morphophonemic and lexical form was a prerequisite to the launching of a literacy campaign does not seem to have

been considered fully by the authors of primers and reading materials
addressed to Creole speakers or of courses designed to teach foreign learners Creole. McConnell, as we have seen, elected to choose rural forms as
standard, and materials prepared under his aegis consistently represented
forms that contained underlying front rounded vowel with the corresponding front unrounded vowel letter; for example, *lari ~ larü → lari*.
Materials written in the Faublas-Pressoir orthography represent underlying "ü" by the letter *u*. For instance, in the health and hygiene reader
Konésans sé richès [20] we find such graphs as *kru, légum, kokluch, duré,
sui*, but the normalization is not always consistent, for we find both
tubèkuloz and *tibèkiloz* and underlying "*œ́*" and "*œ̀*" are not differentiated from "*é*" and "*è*," respectively. In a more completely normalized
orthography these vowels would be indicated by the graphs *éu* versus *é*
and *eù* versus *è*, as in *sèkeùy* instead of attested *sèkèy* and *eskéu* instead
of attested *eské*. In all extant materials written in the McConnell-Laubach
or in the Faublas-Pressoir orthographies there has been no attempt to
normalize the representation of clitics (personal pronouns, verb particles,
determiners, auxiliaries), for instance, to represent the five variant forms
of the third person singular by a single underlying standard form.

This failure to normalize the written representation of Creole forms
is due ultimately to the confusion on the part of structural linguists and
many literacy experts between *transcription* and *orthography*. The function of a transcription is to fix the phonic features of an utterance spoken
by a single speaker at a single moment in time, whereas writing attempts
to provide a more enduring, abstract, and generalizable record of an
utterance. Stated differently, transcription merely notes surface representation, whereas writing attempts to note underlying form. In both
French and Creole underlying form and surface structure are not isomorphic and, since the conventional French spelling economically and
elegantly maps underlying form into surface structure, pioneers in the
elaboration of an orthography for Creole erred in rejecting French spelling conventions outright. The normalization of variant forms of individual Creole morphemes and the selection of a single written form for
each morpheme is the least difficult of the steps toward the development
of a Creole standard. If we take the speech of monolingual or quasi-
monolingual Port-au-Prince Creole speakers as standard, we posit underlying *ü* and write *u* if we observe alternations /i/~/ü/, we posit an
underlying *r* and we write *r* if we observe alternations / /~/r/, etc.
Undoubtedly, underlying Creole forms will be highly similar to but not
identical with French forms; for example, William A. Stewart claims
that "pen" has the underlying form *plüm* (i.e., it is pronounced *plüm* or
plim) whereas "feather" has the underlying form *plim* and is always
pronounced *plim* [21]; in French, both words have an underlying *ü*.
Clitics would be assigned underlying forms with structure CV or CVCV

and written accordingly (e.g., *té*, "past verb particle" → *té ~ t*; *vini*, "to have just" → *vini ~ vin*). More complicated cases of mixed sandhi alternation and dialect variation such as that of the third person singular pronoun would require standardization in addition to normalization of spelling; forms and lexical items that occur in peripheral dialect would be eliminated in favor of forms and lexical items that are found in Port-au-Prince. Of course this presupposes extensive descriptive studies of dialects, both social and geographical.

More troublesome will be the establishment of a line of demarcation between enrichment of Standard Haitian Creole by individual loans from French and wholesale incorporation of phrase-long items such as those contained in sentences (1)–(3) above. It is likely that Haitian diglossics who tend to idealize the "pure" Creole of rural areas would advocate elimination from Standard Haitian Creole of French loans synonymous to native Creole words (e.g., *lüté* versus *gumẽ*, "fight") and of cliché phrases, very much as many educated metropolitan French speakers wage a quixotic war against Anglicisms and English loans. If the natural forces of language are allowed to operate freely, ultimately those French lexical items and phrases that prove to be redundant would gradually be eliminated. The presence in Creole of French cliché phrases would probably be of short duration or they would be reinterpreted as freely recombinable elements in the same way as French *ma tante*, "my aunt," was fused into Creole *matãt*, "aunt" ("my aunt" in Creole is *matãt-mwẽ*) or *la mer*, "the sea," was transformed to *lamè*, "sea" ("the sea" is *lamè-a*).

One notes in the speech of diglossic Haitians a complementary convergence between French and Creole. Creole is borrowing heavily from French lexical resources and, as a consequence, its phonological system and lexicon are nearly identical with those of French. On the other hand, the grammatical system of French, in particular its system of verbal categories, is partially affected by interference from the Creole morphological and syntactic patterns that differ widely from its own. But since grammatical systems are more resistant to change than phonological systems and lexis, we may hazard the prediction that in the long run French and Standard Haitian Creole will exhibit shared phonological systems and lexis and will differ significantly only with regard to their grammatical features.

The interests of the Creole-speaking majority of Haiti can be advanced and the development of the country enhanced only if the vernacular is raised in prestige and dignity. Now that linguists, by detailed analysis of its structure, have demonstrated that Creole is indeed a full-fledged language, and now that a workable orthography that does not jar the sensitivities of the literate elite has been given official recognition and is widely employed, there remains the task of codifying the language so that its speakers are given a set of conventions dealing with pronunciation (really, morphophonemic) norms, orthography, and lexical usage. Though there is hardly any risk that Haiti will turn its back on its French cultural heritage, and though it is difficult to see how Creole could dislodge French as the official language, raising the prestige of the vernacular through the process of standardization will more highly motivate the monolingual masses to learn to read it and will open up new channels of communication for them. Before Creole can be standardized many descriptive and normative studies will need to be undertaken, and in particular a dictionary and a normative grammar will need to be compiled, ideally by a "Creole Academy." That more than 25 years after Creole was reduced to writing, no start toward standardization has been made may be attributed in part to the failure on the part of linguists and language planners to pay close attention to Leonard Bloomfield when he wrote:

"Just as there are no 'primitive' languages without grammar, so there are no 'primitive' speech communities without socially recognized standards of speech . . . contrary to views sometimes held, speech variation and evaluation are universal, and no groups can be excused from receiving fresh and careful attention in the greatly needed work of constructing an empirically adequate taxonomy of speech communities or types of communication structure" [22].

NOTES

1. Charles A. Ferguson ["Diglossia," *Word*, 15, 325–340 (1959), p. 336] defines diglossia as follows:
   ". . . a relatively stable language situation, in which in addition to the primary dialects of the language, which may include a standard or regional standards, there is a very divergent, highly codified, often grammatically more complex, superposed variety, the vehicle of a large and respected body of written literature, heir of an earlier period or in another speech community, which is learned largely by formal education and is used for most written and formal spoken purposes, but is not used by any sector of the community for ordinary conversation."
2. For a discussion of the geographical distribution and genesis of Creole French dialects see Douglas Taylor, "Language Shift as Changing Relationships," *International Journal of American Linguistics*, 26, 155–161 (1960) ; William A. Stewart, "Creole Languages in the Caribbean," in Frank A. Rice (ed.), *Study of the Role of Second Languages in Asia, Africa, and Latin America*, Washington: Center for Applied Linguistics, 1962; Morris F. Goodman, *A Comparative Study of Creole French Dialects*, The Hague: Mouton, 1964. I am inclined to view Haitian Creole as a reflex of some dialect of Northern (Francian) French with some admixture of features from various African languages and an Afro-Portuguese contact language. No doubt, linguistic convergence played an important role in the incorporation of non-French features.
3. William A. Stewart, "The Functional Distribution of Creole and French in Haiti,"

in E. E. Woodworth (ed.), *Linguistics and Language Study*, Georgetown University Monograph Series on Languages and Linguistics, No. 15, 1963, pp. 149–162. I have replaced Stewart's formalized and unformalized by formal and informal, respectively.

4. This example is cited by Pradel Pompilus, *La langue française en Haïti*, Paris: Institut des Hautes Etudes de l'Amérique Latine, 1961, p. 137. In this article Creole utterances will be transcribed in a notation which differs from IPA as follows:

/š/ = /ʃ/,　/ž/ = /ʒ/,　/ñ/ = /ɲ/,　/ü/ = /y/,　/é/ = /e/,　/è/ = /ɛ/,　/ǽ/ = /ø/,　/œ̀/ = /œ/,　/ó/ = /o/,　/ò/ = /ɔ/,　/â/ = /ɑ/,　/ẽ/ = /ɛ̃/,　/ã/ = /õ/,　/o/ = /ɔ̃/.

5. The last official census taken in 1950 lists the total population of Haiti as approximately 3,500,000. The most authoritative demographic projections assume a 1965 population of 4,500,000 to 4,750,000; see Jacques Saint-Surin, *Indices démographiques et perspectives de la population d' Haïti de 1950 à 1980*. Port-au-Prince: Imprimerie de l'Etat, 1962.

6. Mervin C. Alleyne, "Language and Society in Saint-Lucia," *Caribbean Studies*, I, 1–10 (1961), p. 8.

7. It appears even more utopian if we consider the fact that the rural proportion of school-age children enrolled is only 13.5 per cent compared to an urban proportion of approximately 75 per cent. Of the 123,000 rural children attending school in 1961, 60,000 were in first-year classes, 17,000 in second-year classes, and only 700 in last-year classes; see Edouard C. Paul, *L'Alphabétisation en Haïti*, Port-au-Prince: Imprimerie des Antilles, 1965, p. 113.

8. Some Haitian observers even claim that Creole is assuming some public-formal functions: ". . . la langue créole domine sans conteste les conversations des fonctionaires de l'administration," Odnell David, *Le Créole, langue nationale du peuple haïtien*, cited by Jacques-J. Zéphir, "Situation de la langue française en Haïti," *Revue de l'Université Laval*, 19, 1–15 (1965), p. 9.

9. *Op. cit.*, p. 34.

10. Beryl L. Bailey, *Jamaican Creole Syntax*, London: Cambridge University Press, 1965, p. 1.

11. Michelson P. Hyppolite, *Les origines des variations du créole haïtien*, Port-au-Prince, 1950.

12. For a detailed contrastive analysis of Creole and Haitian French, see Albert Valdman, "Du créole au français en Haïti," *Linguistics*, 8, 84–94 (1964).

13. Michelson P. Hyppolite, *Contes dramatiques haïtiens*, Port-au-Prince: Musée du peuple haïtien, 1956. Volume II.

14. The most rigorous and comprehensive grammar of Creole is Robert A. Hall, Jr., *Haitian Creole; Grammar, Texts, Vocabulary*. Menasha, Wisconsin, 1953 (Memoir 74, American Anthropological Association and Memoir 43, American Folklore Society). Hall deems morphophonemic alternation extensive enough to treat it under a separate rubric; some alternations we consider also morphophonemic in nature are taken up by him under the rubric phonemic effects of close juncture and disjuncture.

15. *Op. cit.*, pp. 1–19.

16. These translations were given out of context, and many other alternations are possible depending on the context.

17. Charles-Fernand Pressoir, *Débats sur le créole et le folklore*, Port-au-Prince: Imprimerie de l'Etat, 1947, especially pp. 64–75.

18. *Op. cit.*, p. 67.

19. "The Functional Distribution of Creole and French in Haiti," p. 154. The choice by McConnell and other pioneers of literacy work in Haiti of rural Creole was

determined in great part by pedagogical considerations. Since the objective of a literacy campaign in Haiti is to provide Creole monolinguals access to written communication, the most efficient strategy would be to teach them to read their native language by the use of the simplest alphabet. Proponents of gallicizing orthographies have argued that these allow diglossic speakers and Creole monolingual speakers who have been taught to read French to transfer their reading skills to Creole. Conversely, they also make it possible for newly literate Creole monolinguals to learn to read French. The number of graduates of first-stage literacy programs who set out to learn French is so small that the question of positive transfer of orthographic habits is not highly significant. Proponents of both the McConnell-Laubach and Faublas-Pressoir orthographies have claimed that the system they advocate is learned more quickly by Creole monolinguals. No controlled experiment has ever been conducted to substantiate claims; and this writer is of the opinion that should rigorous experimentation be undertaken, the two orthographies will probably prove to be comparable from a pedagogical point of view. In the final analysis, the Faublas-Pressoir orthography carried the day because it was less offensive to educated diglossic speakers.

20. *Konésans sé richès*. Port-au-Prince: Comité Protestant d'Alphabétisation et de Littérature (no date).
21. Personal communication.
22. Leonard Bloomfield, "Literate and Illiterate Speech," in Dell Hymes (ed.), *Language in Culture and Society,* New York: Harper and Row, 1964, p. 388 [also in *American Speech,* 2, 432–439 (1927)].

W. H. Whiteley

IDEAL AND REALITY
IN NATIONAL LANGUAGE POLICY:
A CASE STUDY FROM TANZANIA

In this essay I want to consider the present position of Swahili as Tanzania's national language, some of the ways in which its status is being
enhanced, and the possible long-term implications of this. As a national
language Swahili has an extremely short history, dating back only to the
attainment of independence in December, 1961; as a standard language
its history reaches back only to the 1930s; and as the second language of
large populations its popularity goes back no further than the middle of
the nineteenth century. For most of its history Swahili has designated a
geographical area and those who live in it rather than a specific linguistic
entity; probably less than 10 percent of Tanzania's population speak
Swahili as a first language. Some consideration of its remarkable expansion must therefore be given here, though a number of accounts are
readily available elsewhere [1].
    At the time of the first missionary contact with East Africa in the
middle of the last century [2], different closely related varieties of this
Bantu language were spoken by widely scattered communities from Brava
on the Somalia coast down to the northern coast of Mozambique, including the off-shore islands of Pemba, Zanzibar, Mafia, Kilwa, and the
Comoros. Those varieties that were most closely related to one another
were, on the whole, spoken in generally contiguous areas, and the
following dialect clusters may be recognized: a northern cluster including
the dialects of Brava (Ci-Miini), Lamu, and the vicinity (Ki-Amu, Ki-
Shela, Ki-Siu, etc.); a central cluster including the dialects of Pemba,
rural Zanzibar (Ki-Hadimu, Ki-Tumbatu), the dialects of the Kenya
coast around Vanga (Ki-Vumba), and the adjoining areas of Tanganyika
(Ki-Mtang'ata); and a southern cluster including the dialects of Zanzibar
town and the closely related dialects of the southern Tanganyika coast,
including Mafia and Kilwa. The dialects of the Comoro Islands (Ki-

Nzwani, Ki-Ngazija,) and of the Congo (e.g., Ki-Ngwana) form special
clusters. A group of dialects with some of the characteristics of both
northern and central dialects occurs on the Kenya coast and includes
that of Mombasa (Ki-Mvita) and the surrounding area of the mainland
(Ki-Ngare, Chi-Jomvu, Chi-Chifundi). The earliest literary traditions
from the eighteenth century are in the dialect of Lamu, and this tradition extended southwards to Mombasa and Pemba during the nineteenth
century.

The most important early agent of expansion was undoubtedly the
trading caravans of the mid-nineteenth century, and the fact that a majority of their personnel spoke a southern variety of the language meant
that it was this form of the language which penetrated most quickly
throughout what is now Tanzania and the Congo Republic. When the
waves of this expansion receded, small Swahili-speaking enclaves remained as far west as the Congo River (e.g., Kindu) and as far south as
northern Zambia. Some of these centers (Ujiji, Tabora, Bujumbura, etc.)
have continued to flourish up to the present time. Missionary activities
tended to reinforce this pattern in Tanzania, but in Kenya and Uganda
the diffusion was less intense and apart from some settlements like
Mumias permanent effects were relatively slight.

THE PREINDEPENDENCE PERIOD

With the establishment in Tanzania (then German East Africa) of a
settled administration under the Germans, Swahili, of a predominantly
southern variety, was an obvious choice for the language of administration and education in a country of more than 100 languages. For the
early British administrators in Kenya and Uganda there was no such
obvious choice and attitudes to the language have on the whole been
ambivalent in Kenya and hostile in Uganda. In the post-1918 period of
intensified administration and education it became increasingly clear
that some kind of standardization of orthography and grammar was
needed, and the choice lay between the southern variety (exemplified by
Zanzibar town), with its advocates the University Mission to Central
Africa, and the Mombasa variety sponsored by the Church Missionary
Society. While Tanganyika was using the Southern type, the Mombasa
was used in parts of Kenya, but this was generally unacceptable to a
majority of up-country Kenya speakers, many of whom spoke non-Bantu
languages anyway. At a series of meetings in the late 1920s at which the
distinguished scholar of Bantu languages Dr. Carl Meinhof was present,
it was decided to adopt the southern variety of Swahili as spoken in Zanzibar town rather than of Mombasa for the standard form of the language. Henceforth books accepted for use in schools would have to have
the Imprimatur of a special Committee [3] and during the next decade

this was the form of the language chosen for the writing of grammars, dictionaries, and textbooks generally. Choice of this southern variety of Swahili piqued the advocates of the Mombasa dialect, with their literary and historical claims, and the dialect has, from that date, been associated with separatism and conservatism. In many ways this has been unfortunate: the interior of Kenya might well have been more willing to accept a variety of Swahili that was not so obviously nor so closely tied to Islam and a historical tradition with little relevance to the rest of the country, and a genuine standard form of the language might then have emerged. Furthermore, such literary and historical traditions constitute a background that is very largely lacking further south, and their absence from school syllabuses in both Kenya and Tanganyika until very recently certainly impoverished the Swahili courses of several generations of students. Against this, however, the adoption of a variety closely similar to varieties of the language already spoken over large areas of inland Tanganyika contributed powerfully to its rapid acceptance, even though it has from time to time been labeled a European product and accordingly out of touch with the "real spirit of the language," whatever that may be [4]. It is certainly true that many of the tireless and devoted adherents of Standard Swahili were somewhat rigid in applying its precepts, and some Swahili writers could complain with justice that when standardized —not always judiciously—their Swahili seemed stilted and artificial. On the other hand it is surprising how quickly the members of one generation have adopted the standpoint contended by their elders. When in recent times writers have been given an opportunity—indeed encouraged —to write with greater freedom, and to shake off the artificiality of the standard form, critics have been quick to condemn them for lowering standards. In a country where so many speakers claim to be "experts" it is difficult to decide on a standard which can hope for wide acceptance [5].

During the period 1930–1955 there was a general, if gradual, extension in the use of Swahili as a second language, but generally it is probably true to say that its popularity with any given speaker was in inverse proportion to his education. There were a number of reasons for this. Swahili was used throughout the District Administration as the means of communication between administrators and administered where this was the only possible means of communication but also, in some cases, where English could have been used. The language was thus a mark, if only secondarily, of social distance; a means of reaching down to the people, rather than of enabling people to reach up to the administration. Swahili was also used as the medium of instruction in the primary schools and as a subject up to the Cambridge School Certificate (taken after 12 years of schooling), but the medium of instruction in secondary schools and schools of higher education was English. The differences in the quality and quantity of secondary school teachers and materials was clear evidence to pupils, if to no one else, of the inferior status of the language. In this connection it is worth noting that institutions of higher education in East Africa designed primarily for East Africans made no provision for the study of the language, whereas such institutions in Europe and elsewhere had been providing courses of various kinds for many years, since their major concern was not with the training of East Africans but with that of training Europeans to do their jobs with greater efficiency during their period of service in East Africa [6]. One may lament the failure of the School of Oriental and African Studies to turn out trained teachers of Swahili, but one needs to remember that this was not their concern nor, so long as the language of the administering authority was English, could one expect East Africans to be greatly interested in this. Although the language of the Lower Courts was Swahili, that of the Higher Courts was English. Although Swahili newspapers proliferated, the attractive, glossy magazines were in English, and when, in 1954, the weekly *Tazama* attempted to raise its circulation by emulating English-style weeklies there were immediate outcries against the lowering of moral standards. Although Swahili records have always been plentiful—at least since the 1930s—there has been a falling off of interest in Swahili traditional songs in favor of those modeled on current British or American "pop" styles and in these the language element—as in English—is minimal. There has never been a Swahili film industry because it is simply too expensive to undertake. Although Swahili programs were available on the local radio, they were directed primarily to those who could not listen to the English programs, that is, the less educated sections of the community.

It must be recognized that Tanzania and East Africa generally have been linguistically trifocal [7] throughout the period under consideration. The local language was a mark of membership in a local community and wherever such local ties need stressing this would be the language of discourse, even where, as might happen in Dar es Salaam, the participants are also Swahili- and English-speaking. On the other hand, ability to control only the local language marked one as a person of limited education and restricted opportunities. Swahili was the means of communication between the outside world, representing opportunity, and East Africa: speakers of Swahili could therefore be cognizant of what these opportunities represented yet be unable to participate in them [8]. Control of English therefore symbolized participation in the outside world and, by extension, control of those opportunities which it offered. Under these circumstances one is not surprised to find Swahili occupying an inferior position [9].

However, with the onset of the struggle for independence under the leadership of TANU in the mid-1950s, certain changes of attitude became noticeable. Although negotiations for independence had to be carried on in English, the mobilization of resources within the country was effected through Swahili, and this was something for which the language was peculiarly well suited; it was not the language of any one local group and could therefore serve as an effective rallying point in establishing national unity. Kenya and Uganda during these years cast envious eyes across the border at the ease with which a political campaign could be mounted in a single African language. There was no perceptible shift in educational or general cultural attitudes to the language, but in political terms it was now recognized as the language of national unity.

THE POSTINDEPENDENCE PERIOD

In the period since independence there has been no dramatic shift in the status of Swahili, indeed in some spheres there has simply been a logical and gradual extension of the areas in which the language was used. What is new is a growing recognition that Swahili is the proper language to use on numerous occasions when English would formerly have been used. This is not to minimize the formidable difficulties in- volved in any major extension in the use of Swahili, but it is now part of Government and Party policy to see that the language is invested with the status it formerly lacked. Tanzania is still, and is likely to remain, linguistically trifocal, though the importance of French for contact with francophone Africa adds a new element in the search for opportunities among the elite. There is, however, a rather subtle shift in emphasis between the three major areas of language focus. First, English is still the mark of membership in a wider political and economic unit than the State, and with more people enjoying secondary and higher education, more English is used. In just what contexts of everyday life English is used in preference to Swahili can only be the subject of guesswork at the present time, but it is clear that it is still the dominant language of the elite. Ability to operate only a local language is decreasing with the in- crease in educational opportunity, but there is an increasing, if transient, concern on the part of those who are themselves linguistically trifocal that ties with the local community and especially their local culture should not be lost; thus it is not uncommon to find parents who spend much of their time speaking Swahili or English nevertheless teaching their children their own local language. This seems most marked among Haya, Chaga, and Nyakyusa speakers, but is by no means restricted to them. Where parents belong to different language groups there is no clear propensity to select either the language of the mother or the father. Ability to operate Swahili, however, is now a mark of national pride, even though it may not mean that one operates it any more efficiently than previously, and the choice of Swahili as the national language is partly recognition of the part played by the language during the achievement of independence [10]. On the other hand it is not easy to say in what specific respects such national pride has contributed to the use of Swahili. There are more frequent letters to the local press praising the language, perhaps one per two weeks, and there are more poems, perhaps one per month. The following verses are typical of the type of praise-poems occurring:

> Mapambo ya Kiswahili, kwa lugha yetu huvuma
> Kwa vingi vitandawili, na mashairi kusoma,
> Nakutumia methali, na nyimbo za Lelemama
> Kiswahili lugha njema, lugha yetu asilia [11].

(The riches of Swahili, are widely known for our language, there are plenty of riddles, and poems to recite; I send you proverbs and songs of the Lelemama dance, Swahili is a good language, our original language.)

> Tukitumie kwa haki, karani na wakulima
> Na kama hamsadiki, Kingereza kitahama,
> Lugha ngeni hatutaki, twaona zina lawama,
> Kiswahili lugha njema, lugha yetu asilia.

(Let us use it as a right, clerks and farmers, and though you may not believe it, English will move out, we don't want foreign languages, we feel they are a reproach, Swahili is a good language, our original language [12].)

At the same time there has been an increase in societies devoted to the spread and development of the language; informative articles have appeared in the press, very often concerned with lexical problems and with comparing unfavorably the work of expatriate lexicographers and grammarians with that now being done—in such articles. Yet Swahili has been very widely used for the last 20 years and what one is witnessing now is really a continuing public demonstration of independence, and sentiments such as the following, from a speech by the present Minister for Community Development and National Culture are as much statements of faith as they are programs for action:

"Mr. Mgonja said that the language heritage and the study of Kiswahili as a national language was part of the cultural revival. He told the members that Kiswahili was a great national heritage and all was being done to enrich and spread it. He called on people to study the language diligently" [13].

One of the most difficult problems posed by the use of Swahili as a national language is this relationship to the national cultural revival. The great strength of the language in the pre-independence period was the fact that it was associated with no single tribal unit. The culture associated with Swahili where it does occur as a mother tongue is generally that of an Islamic coastal community, by no means characteristic of the country as a whole. The national culture of Tanzania is, in a sense, the sum of its regional cultures, expressed in local languages—more than 100 of them—and tied to local custom and situation. Against this background such coastal features as the *taarabu* and *magungu* songs are neither more nor less a part of the national culture than is Makonde stilt-dancing. Bold, far-sighted, and imaginative experiments will need to be made if we are to witness the transformation of regional cultures using local languages into a national culture using Swahili, which can command the loyalty, affection, and respect of young Tanzanians.

SWAHILI AND GOVERNMENT POLICY

The two Ministries most closely involved with the development of the language are those of Education and of Community Development and National Culture. The Ministry of Education has for the past few years been paying close attention to the teaching of Swahili at all levels of the educational system [14]. Not only have workshops (in mathematics and science as well as specifically in Swahili) been organized to produce teaching materials at the primary level, but subcommittees have been studying ways of revising the secondary school syllabus, the form of the school certificate examination itself, and, most recently, the possibility of extending the teaching of the language up to university entrance level. Not only will pupils entering secondary schools have to satisfy the authorities of their competence in the language but during their four years of courses leading to the school certificate Swahili will be a compulsory subject. Mention should also be made of the fact that courses in Swahili were introduced at the University College, Dar es Salaam, in 1964 in association with courses given in descriptive linguistics.

The biggest problems to be faced here are the shortages of trained teachers and teaching materials. This is least acute in the primary schools and most acute at the higher forms of the secondary schools. At this level the teaching of Swahili has suffered from a situation inherited from the pre-independence period when the teaching of the language was often in the hands of expatriates, or teachers who, though trained in another subject, were held for one reason or another to be capable of teaching Swahili. Although it is the second language of the great majority of Tanzanians, it still receives a much smaller weekly allocation of time than does English (3 hours as against 8–9 hours), and the disparity between the variety of teaching materials available encourages the view that the language is somehow inferior, and for many years it constituted an easy option in the school certificate. For every book available for general reading, 10 were forthcoming in English, whose content and variety stimulated students eager to progress to higher education. Too often such Swahili books as have been available have been inherited from lists prescribed for primary schools. While there are at present quite a number of people writing various kinds of material suitable for the primary school, there is virtually no one writing material for secondary schools. This is partly because the elite of the country, who know what is needed at that level, are largely committed to English, and partly because those who have both the ability and enthusiasm have not the time. There is, furthermore, very little conception of what is involved in "grading"; it is widely assumed that what is more difficult is that which contains more difficult words.

There is an additional problem at the primary level, where the medium of instruction is Swahili, of translating the technical terms used in scientific subjects. There is no doubt that, given time and resources, this can perfectly adequately be done [15]; the real question is not whether it is possible but, given available resources, whether it is practicable. The possibility of extending the use of Swahili as a medium of instruction into the secondary schools is a somewhat controversial question, but again there is no doubt that it could be done if it were felt that resources could be diverted to it.

From its inception the Ministry of Community Development and National Culture has been concerned with the development of Swahili as an expression of the national culture, and at various times during the past few years plans have been put forward for the establishment of additional organizations to carry out the general task of "developing the language," though these have usually had to be shelved for lack of funds [16]. With the recent appointment of a "Promoter for Swahili" new attempts are being made to set up cultural committees throughout the country which shall have as one of their aims the task of encouraging people to use Swahili more. A useful summary of the Ministry's views was recently given by the Swahili Promoter, Mr. S. Mushi, and they are, on the whole, typical of much that has been said, both officially and unofficially, during the past few years:

"The role played by Swahili language in Tanzania is immense. Almost everybody in Tanzania can speak the language: and, therefore, it has become a useful medium of communication. Since the language has now become the national language, we feel we must do something to widen its scope so that it may be sufficiently useful in all Government activities, in schools and commercial circles. We want to rid the language of bad influences and to guide it to grow along the proper road. We want to standardize its orthography and usage, and to encourage all our people to learn to speak and write properly grammatical Swahili" [17].

One may applaud the sentiments of such a statement, but it leaves many points of policy unresolved and gives no hint as to how such ideals may be translated into reality. What, for example, is meant by "sufficiently useful"? Does it mean that all Government business will be carried out in Swahili, as is being attempted in Zanzibar? Does it mean that instruction in secondary schools should be carried out in Swahili? One must distinguish here between long-term and short-term aims. It seems likely that in the long term it is hoped that ultimately Swahili will be used for all internal State business [18] and that it may even be used as a medium of instruction in secondary schools where this can be shown to be practicable; but in the short term all that is intended is that efforts should be made to extend the use of the language wherever possible. To this end, for example, the Ministry is trying to compile a list of suitable terms for use within the various ministries, and it is likely that other lists will be compiled in other fields. However, the only serious work in this field so far has been the attempt to provide a legal dictionary for translating the country's laws. A subcommittee was set up in 1963 by the Minister, the late Sheikh Amri Abedi, under the Chairmanship of Professor A. B. Weston [19], Dean of the Faculty of Law, University College, Dar es Salaam. This met regularly between 1963 and 1965 and a preliminary version of the projected dictionary has now been prepared in a cyclostyled form [20]. This represents a selection of appropriate legal terms culled from various legal dictionaries and initially based on a list prepared by the Minister, from an English-Urdu law dictionary. This material is now being revised and will then require checking against the legal terms that are actually in use in the lower courts. This project has raised many important questions; should a legal terminology be esoteric and used only by specialists, in which case one may only require of it that lawyers be satisfied as to its definitions and linguists as to the relation between the legal definitions provided and those others which may be in nonspecialized use. If, however, one asks that a legal terminology be accessible to all, then one must assess the implications for various terminologies already in use in the courts of additional requirements embodied in such a dictionary. Refinement of terminology necessarily involves a redefinition of terms within the system under consideration.

Again, what is meant by the reference to "bad influences" and the desire to guide the language to grow along the "proper road"? We do, in this case, know something about people's views on "bad influences." Late in 1964 the Second Vice-President sent a circular to civil servants and others urging them to "desist from the habit of mixing Swahili and English." By this is meant particularly the habit of code-switching within a given sentence; for example, "Halafu tulirudi ofisini tukakutana na Bwana X. and had a very fruitful discussion. Then we returned to the office, met Mr. X. . . ." [21]. Criticism was also leveled at the inordinate use of English terms, and civil servants were urged to remedy the weakness of "being unable to express themselves elegantly in Swahili." Another such influence is that of inefficient translation, in which the material is either carelessly handled or translated literally from English. A good example of this was cited recently by a correspondent in the daily *Uhuru* (March 3, 1966) from a radio news bulletin:

"Mnasikiliza radio Tanzania kutoka Dar es Salaam. Na sasa mtasomewa hutuba ya Bwana Waziri alio wahutubia wafanya kazi wa pwani *akiwa yeye ni kama Waziri wa Leba.*"

Translation: "You are listening to Radio Tanzania from Dar es Salaam. And now you will have read to you the speech of the Minister addressing workers on the coast, *in his capacity of Minister of Labor/as though he were the Minister of Labor.*"

The correspondent only draws attention to the final phrase, which he finds meaningless, but the rest of the citation also bears the mark of literal translation. Another habit which has received widespread criticism is the extensive use of loanwords, especially where suitable terms in Swahili already exist. Thus a Mr. K. Z. Kidasi, writing in *Uhuru* (March 14, 1966) complains of the use of a word like *kuinjoi* (enjoy) when perfectly adequate nonloans occur. Criticism of colloquialisms seems to be the import of the Minister of Community Development and National Culture's reference (1964) to "lugha isiyo na asili". He urged all Swahili newspapers to appoint a language expert to screen all articles—this remark was greeted by cheers—so that they should appear in a manner fit for bequeathing to the next generation [22]. In similar vein Mr. J. K. Kiimbila writing in *Kiongozi* urges that Swahili should not be "destroyed" by the inordinate use of Arabic loans, though his evidence is not really representative [23]. To sum up, then, bad influences appear to comprise code-switching, inordinate use of loans, colloquialisms, and literal translations.

The call to standardize orthography and usage raises still other problems: first, it must be pointed out that a very considerable degree of standardization of orthography has already been achieved, particularly in school textbooks and books generally, though it must be admitted that standardization is much less in evidence in some newspapers [24]. On the other hand it is difficult to know what is meant by a standardization of usage, and there is little guidance from Swahili speakers themselves, who would probably agree that over an area as large as that in which Swahili's spoken, variation of dialect, register, style, and mode [25] are likely to be considerable and, further, as inevitable as they are desirable. It is worth remarking at this point that although there are a considerable number of studies of Swahili dialect, there is virtually nothing on register, style, or mode.

The suggestion that everyone should "speak and write properly grammatical Swahili" raises a number of questions. First of these is the fact that Swahili is a second language for perhaps 90 percent of Tanzanians so that while it is operated with facility by such speakers there is considerable local variation at all levels. Furthermore, there is, at present, a wide divergence of opinion among those who regard themselves as experts, not only as to what is or is not acceptable but also regarding those whose views on "acceptability" can be accepted. It is worth considering in some detail the views of one such expert, Sh. Mohamed Ally. Writing in the local *Nchi Yetu* (December 1964) [26], he distinguishes three groups of Swahili speakers. The first group comprises those for whom Swahili is a first language and who therefore " understand Swahili words by recognizing all their meanings from within," and are able to differentiate between words of closely similar meaning [27]. Such speakers are, however, not familiar with modern educational and scientific usage. The second group—one might almost say second grade—of speakers are also first-language speakers, but whereas they speak with fluency, there are limits to the range of their competency particularly when faced with unaccustomed patterns such as epigrammatic sayings in dialect [28]. The third group are those for whom Swahili is a second language, and they are subdivided into three:

1. Those who learned some Swahili at school [29] and then went on to higher education in English. While some members of this subgroup make efforts to improve their Swahili, others boast of their skill and try to substitute their own "rotten" variety of Swahili for others' "good" Swahili.

2. Those who have neither learned Swahili at school nor are interested in knowing "proper" Swahili [30].

3. Those who despite the handicap of having to learn it as a second language nevertheless apply themselves to the task with diligence, and even write books. The *hubris* of such speakers is in their assumption of omniscience and their attempts to bend the language according to the logic of their own thoughts without paying complete attention to its "original" form [31].

The view put forward here that language competence is somehow bound up with the knowledge of an extensive vocabulary is very widely held and occurs in many discussions on the language, whether one is talking about the need to upgrade examination papers or to raise people's language competence generally. It is perhaps bound up with traditions in Swahili versification where a premium is put on the poet's ability to use such a vocabulary to outwit a poetic rival. One of the objectives of the characteristic Swahili verse-contests, avers a leading Swahili poet, is to "dive into the sea of the poet's thoughts" so that "very few of those who are not poets can understand these contests" [32].

THE INSTITUTE OF SWAHILI RESEARCH

The Institute of Swahili Research was established as a Research Unit of the University College, Dar es Salaam in 1964 [33] with the initial help of a three-year grant from the Ministry of Overseas Development in London and the Galouste Gulbenkian Foundation. It thereby absorbed and transformed the East African Swahili Committee who preceded it. The old Committee had started in Dar es Salaam in 1930 with annual subventions from the three East African countries: starting at about £600 per annum they had risen to £800 when the Institute was established. At this point Uganda decided that Swahili was not sufficiently important in Uganda [34] for her to continue making the subventions, so the Institute is now financed by an annual subvention of £800 from Kenya and the United Republic of Tanzania, a smaller grant of £175 from Zanzibar, and the Foundation Grant.

The Institute is primarily concerned with basic research into language, literature, and lexicography, and the project to which most of its resources will be devoted over the next few years is a new Swahili-English dictionary. This is fitting, since the present Standard Swahili dictionary was largely the work of the East African Swahili Committee's first Secretary, and the Committee maintained a close interest in lexicography throughout its life. Indeed from the many lists of terms which the Committee discussed, drew up, and published, was learned the important lesson that you may tell people what they should say, but you cannot effectively persuade them to say it unless you have really massive resources at your disposal. For most of the past 15 years the Committee had very slender resources, and these were always stretched to the utmost. From the continuing work of the dictionary, which is a long-term project, it is hoped to produce lists of new terms, words not in the present dictionary, etc., with each issue of the Journal, and the Institute is also collaborating with the Ministry of Community Development and National Culture. It is also proposed to produce two small dictionaries for schools, one at primary level and one at secondary level. In the field of literature the Institute is interested in facilitating the collection of literary and historical material and, where possible, assisting in the editing of any material that can be made available to the general public. A large collection, both of manuscripts and microfilm, has now been deposited in the Library of the University College thanks largely to the energies of Dr. J. Knappert and Mr. J. W. T. Allen and the generosity of the supporting Foundations. It must be stressed, however, that much of the collection is of religious material, and that all of it needs careful and detailed annotation and editing before it can do anything to remedy the acute shortage of books in schools. Language research has been carried on as and when staff became available: Dr. E. Closs of the University College, in collaboration with the Institute's two Research Assistants, made a detailed study of the copula in Swahili; and the Director, with similar collaboration, is making an equally detailed study of transitivity and verbal extensions.

NONOFFICIAL ORGANIZATIONS DEVOTED TO SWAHILI

During the 1961–66 period of independence, two nonofficial organizations devoted to Swahili have come into existence, the first representing a continuation of a similar society founded some 10 years before in Tanga. Both have operated fitfully and their activities are at present suspended while plans are being worked out for their amalgamation.

The Jumuiya ya kustawisha Kiswahili (Association for the Advancement of Swahili) was founded in 1963 and set out its main objectives at the end of 1964 [35]. They may be summarized as follows:

1. To discover the origins of Swahili words, in the belief that understanding the origin of something is to understand its quality, and indeed is the basis for loving and respecting it [36].
2. To cherish Swahili, by correcting the misleading use of words.
3. To cooperate with similar-minded bodies.
4. To promulgate preferred usage.
5. To increase the word-stock of the language.
6. To correct existing grammatical descriptions.
7. To translate and write books.

These objectives have, as far as possible, been pursued mainly by weekly articles in the press and talks on the radio. The newspaper articles appearing in *Ngurumo* under the title of *"Tengeneza Kiswahili* (See to Swahili) are primarily concerned with common errors, such as the confusion between "kh" and "h," or the tendency for some speakers to reproduce "r" for "l," or for speakers to use a word with a meaning different from its original meaning [37]. They have also chastized the Institute of Swahili Research for using "katika" in its title instead of "wa," apparently forgetting that they had themselves scrutinized the title before it was used. More recently they have been drawing attention to errors in the existing dictionaries.

It is worth pointing out that no one—least of all the authors—is complacent about the serious lacunae in existing grammatical and lexical studies, and it is a pity that societies such as this do not do more in the way of constructive criticism.

The Chama cha usanifu wa Kiswahili na Ushairi (Society for the

Enhancement of the Swahili Language and Verse), under the leadership
of the leading poet Mr. M. E. Mnyampala, has five main objectives:

1. To preserve the language, encourage its poetry, and also purity of
form and style; to develop the language in Bantu terms and encourage
poetry as a special study that contributes to a knowledge of Swahili
for the national benefit.

2. To awaken and stimulate people who wish to be experts in the
language and poetry.

3. To awaken the efforts of those who wish to write books on various
subjects in Swahili, and in verse, and to find ways of publishing their
work.

4. To set about compiling a dictionary and grammar more adequate
than the present ones.

5. To encourage dramatic performances and other cultural features.

The society charges a membership fee of shs.5/-per year and is said to
have several hundred members, mainly in Dar es Salaam, but since it
does not receive any financial support from Government its activities
have been somewhat limited. Like the Jumuiya, it has contributed a
series of weekly articles, from time to time, in *Uhuru*, entitled "Taaluma
ya Kiswahili," which have been mainly concerned with examining words
commonly confused, or which are closely similar in meaning, but it has
recently branched out into discussing dialectal variants, names for children's games, birds, animals, and proverbial utterances.

CONCLUSIONS

There are, it seems to me, at least two important aspects to a national
language policy: the ideological and the technical. The ideological aspect
is concerned with mobilizing the nation's sentiments and with ensuring
that the image of the language is polished on every suitable occasion; the
technical aspect deals with the practical problems of implementing such an
ideology—with the working out, for example, of new courses throughout
the educational system, and with devising terminologies for such contexts
of the national life as are thought to require them and where they have
previously been lacking. The ideological aspect may cost relatively little
and can sometimes achieve quite startling results, though these are likely to
be ephemeral unless they are quickly and effectively reinforced by technological implementation. As with Hebrew in the nineteenth and Turkish
in the twentieth centuries such ideology commonly derives its impetus,
and ultimately also its effective implementation, from the efforts of small
groups of dedicated chauvinists. The technical aspect is likely to cost
much more, depending as it does on the work of specialists in many
fields who may have to be specially recruited or diverted from other

activities. Tanzania is not yet fully committed to the technical aspects of her national language policy and her three greatest needs are summarized now.

First, in the educational field there are the acute shortage of reading materials, which becomes more acute the higher one proceeds up the educational system, and the lack of teachers trained not only in teaching the language but in the general principles and objectives of second-language teaching as applied to Swahili. The shortage of reading material can only be alleviated, in the short run, by a massive program of book production undertaken by people with the necessary qualifications. The possibility of seconding people on full salary is a difficult one, partly because there is a widespread shortage of skilled staff generally, and partly because of the expense involved. While it may not be possible to allocate sums of the order of the £30,000 per year that Turkey put into her language program during the period 1946–1949 [38], it is important to remember that the effective implementation of a national language policy costs money, and that where reseources are scarce this means delicate decisions as to whether and which resources should be switched. Some increase in the allocation of resources seems essential in the present situation [39].

Greater use of the language in daily life and in Government requires the compilation of adequate, standard word-lists, and this again is a task that requires time, skills, and money. There is also the question of the extent to which technical terms should be translated, and this requires the setting up not only of technically qualified subcommittees but the services of a linguist to advise on patterns of assimilation [40].

Finally, there is still no sign of any prose literature to match the rise of local writers in English: anthologies of East African writing in English have already appeared, but nothing comparable is in sight for Swahili. The East African writer seeks the widest possible horizons for his work. A large quantity of verse is being written, but there is a marked reluctance to experiment, and young poets need guidance. The importance for the future of Swahili of capturing and holding the allegiance of secondary and postsecondary pupils cannot in my view be overestimated: encouragement to ordinary people to perfect their knowledge will be largely nullified if such people cannot be given guidance and an example from those fortunate enough to reap the benefits of higher education.

NOTES

1. I have discussed various aspects of the use of Swahili in East Africa in a series of articles, on which I have drawn here. The most useful general statements are probably: "The Changing Position of Swahili in East Africa," *Africa*, **26** (1956); "Language and Politics in East Africa," *Tanganyika Notes*, **47/8** (1957); and "Swahili

as a lingua franca in East Africa," *Multilingualism,* CSA/CCTA (1964). More detailed studies of particular features are "Swahili and the Classical Tradition," *Tanganyika Notes,* 53 (1959); "Political Concepts and Connotations," *St. Antony's Papers X,* Chatto and Windus, 1961; "Problems of a lingua franca; Swahili and the Trade Unions," *JAL,* 3, 111 (1964); "Priorities of Linguistic Research in East Africa," *Research and Development in East Africa,* East African Academy, Nairobi, 1966; "The Future of Swahili Literature," *East Africa's Cultural Heritage,* Contemporary African Monograph Series No. 4., E.A. Institute of Social and Cultural Affairs, 1966. (Subsequently referred to as *EACH*). See also "Language Situation in E. Africa," Ruth E. Sutherlin, *Study of the Role of Second Languages in Asia, Africa and Latin America,* Frank Rice (ed.), Washington 1962; "Le Swahili, langue de grande expansion," J. Tanghe, *Bull. I.R.C.B.,* XV (1944); and "Le Swahili, langue de grande expansion," G. Van der Kerken, *Bull. I.R.C.B., XV* (1944).

2. I am leaving out of account here the earlier contact with the Portuguese since this seems to have had little lasting effect on the language beyond a small residue of "culture" words.

3. The East African Inter-Territorial Language (Swahili) Committee. I have discussed the history of this in "The Work of the East African Swahili Committee," *Kongo-Overzee,* 23 (1957).

4. See below, and also "Maendelezo ya Maandishi ya Kishwahili," Mohamed Ali, in the Catholic newspaper *Kiongozi* (April 4, 1966).

5. There is a sense in which a standard form imposed by outsiders, say, Europeans, has a greater chance of acceptance than one put forward by citizens, who may well be suspected of furthering sectional interests. Compare the Chaga situation of the mid-fifties cited in Whiteley, *op. cit.* (1957) and the views put forward by the participants in the protracted debate on Swahili in the newspaper *Kiongozi* during 1964.

6. It is interesting in this connection to note the comments of Tanzanians at the present time with respect to the learning of Swahili by other nationals. They are apt to point proudly at the anxiety of Cubans, Ghanaians, Chinese, Czechs, and Poles to learn the language as evidence of its importance, and ignore the possibility that such people are primarily interested in doing a particular job as efficiently as possible.

7. By linguistically trifocal I mean that language choices are focused on three planes: English, Swahili, and a local language (Asian or African).

8. Compare in this respect the role of a language like Luganda in Uganda during this period, for which see Whiteley, *op. cit.,* 1957.

9. For some details of this see Whiteley, *op. cit.* (1965), especially p. 346 (evidence given before the Joint Select Committee on Closer Union in East Africa in 1931), and pp. 350–351 (on contemporary objections to Swahili).

10. "While we may expect that English will remain the language of our international relations, and for a considerable time to come the language of higher instruction, there can be no doubt that Swahili is the more important language. It has proved our greatest asset in our pre-independence struggle as the instrument of uniting the people of the nation's different tribes." Leading article in the *Nationalist* (January 8, 1966).

11. It is worth comparing this with the well known poem of the late Shaaban Robert written nearly 20 years ago:
"Swahili is rich, in its elegance and proverbs, and I think that in the near future, it will be possible to translate many fields of education, and render a service to mankind both with insight and beauty, mother's breast is sweet, no other satisfies."
—*Pambo la Lugha,* Witwatersrand, 1948.

12. "Kiswahili lugha njema" by Juma Shamte Makuka. *Uhuru* (July 16, 1966).

13. Reported in the *Nationalist* (June 27, 1966). I do not, in general, wish to make comparisons with other national language programs, but it is perhaps worth drawing attention to that of Turkey in the period 1920–1950, which in some ways paralleled that of Tanzania. Note the characteristic tone in the statutes of the constitution of the Turkish Linguistic Society (1932) that the aim of the Society was "to bring out the genuine beauty and richness of the Turkish language and to elevate it to the high rank it deserves among world languages." *Language Reform in Modern Turkey.* U. Heyd, Oriental Notes and Studies No. 5, Jerusalem, 1954 pp. 25–26.

14. See, for example, the speech of the Minister of Education presenting his estimates for 1963–1964 (Hansard, 7th Meeting, Government Printer, 1963), pp. 710–735.

15. Some idea of what can be done in this field is provided by Mohamed Hyder in his "Swahili in a Technical Age," *EACH,* pp. 78–87.

16. Such as that for establishing a special magazine to serve as a means of presenting models of Swahili prose and verse and of disseminating results of research. This was mentioned in the Estimates of the Ministry of National Culture and Youth for 1963–1964 (Hansard, 7th Meeting, Government Printer, 1963, p. 946) and again in the estimates of the Ministry of Community Development and National Culture of 1964–1965 (Hansard, 13th Meeting Government Printer, 1964, p. 874) but still not implemented. See a similar proposal put forward by the Chama cha Usanifu wa Kiswahili in *Uhuru* (February 22, 1966).

17. "The Role of the Ministry of Culture in National Development," presented to a seminar on African Culture and new writing held in Nairobi, December 2–7, 1965, and subsequently published in *EACH,* p. 18.

18. A circular from the Second Vice-President of 1964 refers to a time when 'kazi zetu zote na za kila namna zitaendeshwa kwa Kiswahili, and since this article was written (September, 1966), a further statement from the second Vice-President has directed (January 4, 1967) that Swahili be used for all Government business, and that the use of English or any other foreign languages unnecessarily is to cease forthwith. All Ministries, District Councils, Co-Operative Unions, and parastatal organizations are therefore obliged to use Swahili in their day-to-day business.

19. A useful statement of the problems involved is Professor A. B. Weston's "Law in Swahili—Problems in Developing the National Language," *East African Law Journal* **1,** 1 (1965).

20. At the same time a small translation unit in the Ministry of Justice has been working on the Penal Code and other projects. It would be wrong, however, to imagine that this is the first time that legal translation has been instituted. Ordinances and Rules have appeared since the 1950s; e.g., The Local Courts Handbook, *Baraza za Wenyeji,* and the Explosives Ordinance, *Sheria na Kanuni ya vitu vya kulipuka,* Government Printer, 1959, and these have continued to come out in the early 1960s; e.g., *Sheria za Mahakama za Mahakimu* (1963) Government Printer, 1963, and the *Maelezo ya Mahakama za Mwanzo,* 1964. The most recent publication is the Standing Rules for the National Assembly, *Kanuni za Bunge la Taifa,* 1966.

21. I have discussed this and similar phenomena in my "Loan-words in Linguistic description; a Case Study from Tanzania" *Approaches in Linguistic Methodology,* I. Rauch and C. T. Scott (eds.), University of Wisconsin Press, 1966.

22. Hansard, 13th Meeting (1964, pp. 874–5). "Ingefaa magazeti yote ya Kiswahili yaweke fundi wa lugha ambaye atasahihisha makala zote ili—(makofi)—zitokee kwa lugha safi itakayofaa kurithiwa na watoto wetu."

23. Neither he nor other opponents of the use of Arabic loans reach the extremes of the early Turkish linguistic nationalists: ". . . even the most uncouth Turkish word . . . is to us more pleasing than the most harmonious foreign word." However, Tanzanians do not always recognize the truth of the position later adopted by the Turkish Linguistic Society in 1945: "We have no right to impose words. We

make them and the Government and the writers use them if they want to." Heyd, *op. cit.,* pp. 30 and 53.

24. A reminder of the rules originally agreed on in 1926, together with some recent comments appears, in *Swahili,* **36,** 1 (1966), pp. 11–14.

25. I am following here the terminology of J. C. Catford in his *A Linguistic Theory of Translation,* OUP, 1965.

26. His views are challenged by J. K. Kiimbila and others in a series of articles in *Kiongozi* during May and June 1966 entitled "Kiswahili si lugha ya kabila fulani."

27. He cites as evidence the following series of words which all might be translated by the English term "fool": *zuzu,* a "greenhorn"; *zebe,* a "half-wit"; *mpumbavu,* a stupid person; *bahau,* a "bullish," unintelligent person; *duwazi,* a "simpleton"; and *mjinga,* an ignorant, really stupid person.

28. He selects for this "ndimiye mzushi mabaa. Kwambawe si mtambuzi wa lo ndimi mjulishawe."

29. ". . . limekujua kiswahili mitaani tu au limepata kujua kiswahili katika shule kwa kuparuza tu."

30. ". . . hawajishughulishi na kutaka kukijua kiswahili kama ipasavyo."

31. "Ubaya wao ni kuwa hujaribu sana kukiviringa Kiswahili mujibu wa fikira zao bila kuangalia kwa utimilifu umbile lake la asili." In this article as in the correspondence mentioned above Sh.Mohamed Ally shows himself to be a Platonist, e.g., "maneno ya lugha yo yote huwa kila neno lina maana yake maalum iliyowekewa neno hilo toka kuanzishwa kwake," *Kiongozi,* June 1, 1964), p. 12, while Mr. Kiimbila, perhaps as a result of his year's course in linguistics in the United States, maintains a more Aristotelian view of the meaning of words and change of meaning; thus, note his criticism of Sh.Mohamed Ally and others who ". . . hufikiri kuwa maadam neno fulani lilikuwa na maana fulani wakati wa miaka nenda na miaka rudi, basi maana yake hubakia ile ile" *Kiongozi* (March 15, 1964).

32. *Mashairi ya hekima na malumbano ya ushairi,* M. E. Mnyampala, Dar es Salaam, p. 15.

33. For further details see *Linguistic Reporter,* **8,** 3 (June, 1966) .

34. Confirmation of this would seem to be provided in M. B. Nsimbi's "The Future of Vernacular Literature in Uganda," *EACH,* pp. 95–102, where there is no reference to Swahili at all.

35. Jumuiya ya kustawisha Kiswahili, *KIONGOZI,* 1.10.64.

36. "Wanachama wanaamini kabisa kwamba kufahamu asili ya kitu ndio hasa kuelewa ubora wa kitu hicho na ndio msingi wa kukipenda na kukiheshimu," *Kiongozi* (October 1, 1964).

37. As, for example, in "Tengeneza Kiswahili," *Ngurumo* (January 8, 1966).

38. Heyd, *op. cit.,* p. 51.

39. It is encouraging to note the financial help recently given by the Ministry of Education to the second workshop on Primary Courses in Swahili, however modest this appears when compared to the resources made available by outside agencies to workshops in other subjects, e.g., science.

40. Heyd, *op. cit.,* pp. 80–86.

Stephen A. Wurm

PAPUA-NEW GUINEA NATIONHOOD:
THE PROBLEM OF A NATIONAL LANGUAGE

It is a well-known fact that a difficult problem confronting the native population of Papua-New Guinea on its way to nationhood lies in the enormous multiplicity of the languages spoken in the area, and in the resulting complexity and vexedness of the linguistic situation.

A short review of the exact nature of this linguistic situation may be of use here:

The precise number of distinct languages located in the Territory is not known. The reasons for this are twofold: in the first place, our knowledge of the linguistic picture in very considerable parts of the area can be described as even less than extremely superficial and sketchy in spite of the large amount of linguistic work carried out in the Territory in recent years, and in quite a few parts it is simply nonexistent. In the second place, it is extremely difficult in many cases to draw an exact borderline between languages and dialects, and according to the manner of interpretation, the number of distinct "languages" encountered in a given area in the Territory can vary greatly. So, for instance, the author has found that in an area encompassing the greater part of the three Highlands Districts, the number of distinct languages encountered there could be said to be 48 or 26 according to what linguistic criteria were applied to distinguish between languages and dialects (Wurm and Laycock 1961).

If one is to hazard a guess, it may seem justifiable to assume the existence of around 500 distinct languages in the Territory. There may be more, or there may be less—the exact figure will not be known until an adequate survey has been carried out of the entire area of Papua-New Guinea, and until the same criteria for distinguishing languages

Reprinted from *The Journal of the Papua and New Guinea Society*, Vol. 1, No. 1, Summer 1966, pp. 7–19, by permission of the author and the publisher.

and dialects have been applied to all forms of speech[1] encountered there. Even then the figures arrived at could well be regarded as somewhat arbitrary because it seems difficult to find absolutely objective criteria for distinguishing between languages and dialects, and a set of criteria employed by linguists in such an approach could well be questioned by other linguists disagreeing with them in one or several points. Also, even if full agreement could be reached regarding the criteria to be employed, it must be borne in mind that the border between a "language" and a "dialect" is not a sharp, thin line, but rather a broad band representing a gradual transition, and in this transition zone lying between clear-cut languages and dialects, there may be quite a number of forms of speech—i.e., communalects—whose assignment to "language" or "dialect" status remains arbitrary.

Whatever the precise outcome of such a survey and assessment may be, there can be no possible doubt already at this stage of our imperfect knowledge that the number of distinct languages in the Territory is very large. In fact, when considering the comparative smallness of the geographical expanse of Papua-New Guinea, it can only be described as enormous. It is obvious that under these circumstances the average number of speakers per language can only be very small—in fact, New Guinea languages with comparatively large numbers of speakers—(though approaching 100,000 in only a very few instances) have only been discovered during the last 10 or 15 years. Most languages in the Territory have only a few thousand speakers each, and many of them only a few hundred or even less.

The languages in Papua-New Guinea belong to two different kinds: along portions of the coast of the mainland and in some hinterland sections, as well as on most of the smaller islands, in the greater part of New Britain and New Ireland, and in parts of Bougainville Island, and on most of the Admiralty Islands languages traditionally called Melanesian languages are found. These languages are related to other languages in the Pacific which constitute the geographically most extended group of interrelated languages in the world, and are known as Malayo-Polynesian or Austronesian languages. There has been a great deal of diversity of opinion amongst linguists as to whether the Malayo-Polynesian—i.e., Melanesian—languages located in the Territory are in fact genetically related to the other Malayo-Polynesian languages, or whether the obvious links they have with them are due to some other linguistic phenomenon like Pidginization of the Malayo-Polynesian languages of an immigrant population by autochthonous speakers of entirely different, i.e., Papuan languages (see below for a definition of the term "Papuan" in this connection). Whichever of these two possibilities may be correct

---

[1] Linguists use the term "communalect" to designate a form of speech without committing themselves to calling it either a language or a dialect.

is of no relevance to the discussion put forward in this article—the fact remains that these Melanesian languages show close links with each other, and obvious links with other Malayo-Polynesian languages, and as a language type, differ very markedly from the other type of languages located in Papua-New Guinea.

These other languages are known as non-Melanesian or Papuan languages. They occupy the bulk of the mainland, including the entire interior, as well as the greater part of Bougainville Island. Several Papuan languages are located on New Britain, New Ireland and on some of the smaller islands. It may be mentioned in passing that there are some Papuan languages further east in the Solomon Islands and the Santa Cruz Archipelago, but the bulk of the languages there is of the Melanesian type. At the same time, the bulk of the languages in West Irian is also Papuan, with Melanesian languages located only in some coastal and hinterland areas, and on offshore islands.

In contrast to the Melanesian languages, the Papuan languages do not display close links with each other, and until a few years ago it had been thought that most of them were completely unrelated to each other, and that only a few of them could be linked together linquistically to constitute small groups of interrelated languages. Research carried out during the last few years has, however, shown that a considerable number of Papuan languages can be included in several large groups and families of interrelated languages. Within the Territory, nine such groups have so far been established, and they comprise around 100 languages. If the 200-odd Melanesian languages located in Papua-New Guinea are also taken into account, it results that around 300 languages are members of 10 large groups of interrelated languages, which simplifies the linguistic picture of the Territory considerably. Furthermore, many of the languages belonging to these groups have numbers of speakers far above the Papua-New Guinea average, which leads to the fact that the total number of speakers of languages belonging to large groups in the Territory is in the vicinity of 1.2 million, which enhances the importance of these groups of interrelated languages for practical purposes. If at the same time the Melanesian languages are disregarded in thinking of the languages belonging to large groups, it is apparent that the speakers of around 100 languages belonging to 9 groups, number around 1 million i.e., comprise approximately one-half of the entire population of the Territory.

It is true that the discovery of these large language groups in recent years, and the likelihood of the presence of further, as yet unknown, such groups in the Territory has brought about a considerable simplification of the linguistic picture of Papua-New Guinea, and may perhaps have some practical importance with regard to the use of languages belonging to such groups for administrative and educational purposes.

However, this discovery does in no way constitute a significant step toward the solution of the problem of finding a native language in the Territory that could possibly be thought of in terms of a future national language of the emerging Papua-New Guinean nation.

This remark leads up to the main theme of this article. It seems to be an inevitable fact of history that nations, upon arriving at nationhood, are striving to find a language that they can justly regard as their national language and can call their own and that characterizes the nation as such.

Such a language is easily found if most members of such a new nation, or at least the majority, speak one language. In the case of communities speaking a variety of languages constituting a new nation, a language will become the national language that, even if spoken by a minority, carries prestige recognized by all or at least the majority of the population. Such prestige may be based on economic or cultural factors such as the language being that of an economically or politically powerful group, and used by this group in its dealings with other communities now comprised in the same nation. The prestige language may have its prestige for religious reasons, or it may simply be a trade language understood and used by a large portion of the different communities in their dealings with each other.

None of the tribal languages in the Territory can be said to qualify as the future national language of the emerging Papua-New Guinean nation in the light of what has been said above. Only a few of them are spoken and understood outside their tribal territory to a significant degree: in spite of the extreme prevalence of bi- and multilingualism observable in New Guinea that is so common that it can be described as one of the characteristic features of the linguistic picture of the Territory, this phenomenon does not contribute to bringing any of the tribal languages significantly closer to universal acceptability. All it does is to widen the geographical extent of the individual languages, but they nevertheless remain very strictly regional. The fact that several or even quite a few of such languages are more or less closely interrelated, and each one of them is spoken by a sizeable speech community, does in no way improve the situation: the fact that a neighboring large language happens to be genetically related, and in some ways quite similar, to the language spoken by a given speech community, does not make this neighboring large language any more acceptable as a national language to the latter speech community—i.e., as a language to be regarded as superior to their own—if there are not special prestige factors like the ones mentioned above giving that language a special standing. None among the interrelated languages in the groups established so far can lay much claim to this—though there may be some minor exceptions that will be discussed below. In the absence of such prestige attached to another language, even if it may be closely related to that of a given speech community, the members of the latter community have no more reason or inclination to recognize that other language as culturally superior to their own than English speakers may have to admit to the cultural superiority of Dutch or German, which are closely related to English. If Dutch and German speakers are inclined to grant English the status of an international—i.e., supernational—language this is not because it happens to be the closely related language of a large neighboring nation, but because of economic, cultural and political factors that have given English a special prestige position among the languages of the world.

Some linguists have considered the possibility of creating semi-artificial "unified" languages by combining lexical and grammatical elements of several closely related languages so as to increase the geographical and numerical range of one kind of linguistic currency. Such an attempt could theoretically be thought of in a few areas of Papua-New Guinea, but the maximum number of speakers that could within reason be encompassed by such an attempt would be below 300,000 in one given restricted area of the Territory, which would still leave this semi-artificial language very much in the state of a strictly regional language. Strictly regional languages however have no universal currency by definition, irrespective of the number of their speakers: Mandarin Chinese, the largest single language in the world, is still very much a regional language from the international point of view in spite of its 470 million speakers, and in this respect ranks far below the numerically much less significant French that has wide currency in many parts of the world.

Apart from this consideration, resistance to such a semi-artificial language would be likely to be practically universal among all those speakers whom the creators of such a language would expect to accept it as a language superior to their own—unless it could be given some special prestige. If however such an endowment with prestige could be achieved, there would be no need whatever in the first place to create such a semi-artificial language by blending several closely related languages: if a prestige language is accepted it is because of its being a prestige language, and not because it may be related or similar to the language spoken by the speech community recognizing and accepting it as culturally superior to their own.

Much the same can be said about any attempt to spread one large local language artificially over a much wider area, optimally making it the national language of a new nation. If the sole merit of such a language is that the number of its speakers is somewhat larger than that of languages spoken by other speech communities in the nation, though its speakers constitute still no more than a smallish fraction of the total population of that nation, such an attempt cannot be expected to be successful unless backed by very considerable force and sanctions that

would of course give it a sort of prestige. If it could be given a good deal
of prestige of this or any other kind, it could succeed—but the number
of its speakers would then be irrelevant, only the prestige factor would
count. The number of native speakers of Latin in mediaeval Europe
was zero, but because of its great cultural prestige it persisted for centuries as the international language recognized by all, and even came
close to being regarded as the national language in some countries, like
Hungary for instance, for short periods.

This brings us to those tribal languages in the Territory that for some
reason carry special prestige. Such a prestige is in most cases religious in
nature, i.e., the languages have been adopted as official church languages
by various Missions, religious literature has been published in them, and
the languages have been employed in teaching and education. At the
same time, knowledge of such a language on the part of a native has
served to identify him as belonging to a certain cultural group characterized by a number of features such as the possession of a certain religion
and the right of access to certain institutions and privileges like educational establishments for instance.

The difficulty with one of these languages being a potential national
language is twofold:

In the first place, there are a number of rival missions in the Territory,
each of them with its very definite identity that marks it off from the
other missions, and in only a single instance has the same language been
adopted by two rival mission groups as their official church language.
This language is the Tolai language, which is used as the church language of the Methodist Mission throughout the New Britain-New Ireland
area, while it is also used by the Catholic Mission, but only in the Tolai
area itself. At the same time, the two missions had, until a few years
ago, been using different spellings in writing the language.

The fact that each of these languages—with the exception of Tolai—
is a distinguishing feature of a particular mission gives these languages
a very clear-cut sectional importance, their sectionality being culturally
determined, and makes them just as alien to natives who are outside
the cultural orbit that they represent, as a different tribal language
is alien to natives belonging to a given tribe. Worse still, natives belonging to any particular one of these religiously oriented cultural orbits
may regard the language identifying one of the rival cultural orbits
with even greater suspicion, and sometimes hostility, than tribal natives
may feel for the language of another tribe.

The second difficulty is that the distribution of missions belonging to
various denominations is largely geographically restricted in Papua-New
Guinea, so that any one particular church language has not only culturally but also regionally restricted currency, though the areas covered by

the individual church languages vary very considerably in size. It may be argued that with further expansion of the geographical areas covered by missions belonging to certain denominations the regional restriction of the currency of their church languages may diminish, but the cultural restriction of their validity will largely remain.

It is true that in several instances, the currency of given church languages has spread beyond their cultural limits, and that they have to a limited extent been adopted as lingua franca by natives standing outside their immediate religion-oriented cultural orbits. One of the main reasons for this phenomenon is the fact that the tribe whose language has been adopted by the mission as the church language has thereby risen in prestige in the eyes of natives who are not committed to another mission, and who at the same time look towards this tribe and its language as the source of possible economic and other advantages. Such a spread of a church language beyond its cultural orbit is however only likely to take place in the immediate geographical neighborhood of the tribe whose language has become the church language, even if the church language itself is used over a much larger area in missionary matters and is at least understood by natives regarding themselves as Christians of the denomination represented by the mission. A good example to illustrate the foregoing is the Kâte language, one of the three church languages used by the New Guinea Lutheran Mission. The Kâte tribe itself, numbering around 8000, is located inland from Finschhafen on the Huon Peninsula, but its language is believed to be spoken and understood by around 60,000 natives throughout the Huon Peninsula and around a number of Lutheran Mission Stations in the Highlands Districts where the native population contains Lutheran converts. At the same time, this number includes a considerable number of non-Christian natives in the Huon Peninsula, i.e., in areas close to the Kâte tribe but there are hardly any non-Lutheran and non-Christian Kâte speakers in the Highlands Districts.

There is at least one tribal prestige language in the Territory whose prestige is not predominantly religious, though the fact that it has been the church language of a Mission has greatly contributed to its gaining importance. This is the Motu language in and around Port Moresby, which is the mother tongue of approximately 10,000 natives, but is spoken and understood by many others in the Central District. Its prestige stems from the fact that it is the language of the tribe living in and around the administrative and cultural center of the Territory, and also from the important role the Motuans play in the cultural and educational advance of at least a part of Papua. Nevertheless, it cannot well be considered as having a chance to become the national language of Papua-New Guinea because of its very strictly defined regional currency, and the comparatively very small impact that Motuans have made upon the cultural and economic life of other parts of the Territory. Even if such an impact may have been felt in some parts as a result of the presence of educated Motuans, this impact was dissociated from the Motu language.

At this stage, mention may be made of the Chimbu people of the Eastern Highlands whose language could theoretically have had a chance to become the most important tribal lingua franca in the Territory, but failed to achieve any importance beyond being one of the largest regional tribal languages of the Territory and of all New Guinea (it is spoken by over 60,000 natives, and around 40,000 more speak language forms so closely related to it that they can be regarded as Chimbu dialects). The Chimbu, or at least many individuals among them, are economically enterprising and progressive people, and the majority of the natives engaged in independent economic ventures like running trade stores or transport services, etc., or employing other natives for gold digging purposes in areas where the yield is too low to attract the interest of white gold miners, are Chimbu, especially so in the Highlands Districts. Cases are known from other parts of the world where the languages spoken by traders operating outside their sometimes quite small tribal or native regions have spread over wide areas, and have become important lingua francas. Kiswahili of East Africa is a good example. However, in all such cases the important factor has been that the traders insisted on using their own language, and speakers of other languages who wanted to have dealings with them had to learn to speak them. At the same time, there was a strong stimulus for outsiders to enter into dealings with the traders—the service that they provided was an important and desirable one. The same can be said of the services provided by the Chimbu referred to above, but in no case is the Chimbu language used by them in their dealings with non-Chimbu: the language used by them in such situations is exclusively Pidgin, and the Pidgin spoken by Chimbu can well be accepted as the standard form of Highlands Pidgin because it is a widespread Highlands dialect of Pidgin—in that respect at least the Chimbu have contributed to the spread and standardization of an important lingua franca, though the language that they have been spreading is not their own tribal language.

In view of the foregoing it seems unlikely that any tribal language found in the Territory will have a chance ever to be considered as the potential national language of the emerging Papua-New Guinea nation. There are however three more languages spoken in Papua-New Guinea each of which deserves consideration in this connection. They are Pidgin, Police Motu, and English.

Of these, Police Motu is perhaps least likely to be seriously considered as the potential national language of the emerging Papua-New Guinea nation. This can perhaps be regarded as somewhat ironical, because it is the only one of these three languages whose origin and development is wholly native Papua-New Guinean. It came into being as a trade language employed by Motuans on their annual maritime trading expeditions to the west, to the present Kerema coastal area in the Gulf District, where they bartered earthenware vessels for garden produce. The language, a simplified Motu that, under the influence of the Papuan languages spoken by the tribes visited, had in addition undergone a few structural modifications bringing it a little more in line with some features of those languages, was later adopted as the official language of the native police force, the Royal Papuan and New Guinea Constabulary, and hence given the name Police Motu. It has, over the years, become the lingua franca of Papua, and is spoken and understood by approximately 60,000 natives in many parts of it, but it is almost unknown in the Territory of New Guinea, and is more or less rapidly giving up ground to Pidgin in parts of Papua itself. It has, to a certain extent, the quality of identifying its speakers as belonging to the Territory of Papua as opposed to the Territory of New Guinea, much like the knowledge of a certain church language on the part of a native identifies him as belonging to a certain cultural orbit. Conversely, the knowledge of Pidgin used to identify a native as belonging to the Territory of New Guinea as opposed to the Territory of Papua, but this identification is becoming a thing of the past with the rapid inroads Pidgin is making in Papua at the expense of Police Motu. The latter remains therefore a lingua franca of regional currency only, at the same time giving its speaker an air reminiscent of a certain amount of parochialism, whereas Pidgin is gaining in universality at its expense. Outside Papua, and in part even within it, Police Motu tends to be identified with the Motuans and their language, though paradoxically enough speakers of Motu proper of the Port Moresby area cannot readily understand Police Motu if they have not been previously exposed to it (Wurm 1964), though they can learn to understand and speak it in a very short time.

This brings us to Pidgin, undoubtedly the most controversial language among the three mentioned above. Rarely has a language been maligned as much as this idiom, and at the same time been found so useful or, more correctly, indispensable.

Pidgin is the lingua franca of the Territory of New Guinea and is moving towards becoming a lingua franca in Papua as well. It is spoken and understood by certainly more than 300,000 natives in the Territory, very probably by even many more, and the number of its speakers and the extent of its geographical currency are rapidly expanding.

The language came into being on the sugar cane fields of North Queensland in the 1870s when large numbers of natives, predominantly from the Blanche Bay area of northern New Britain, were more or less forcibly brought to Australia as workers in those fields. The language of the majority of these natives was the Tolai language, also known as Kuanua or (Tinata) Tuna, a Melanesian language that is at present the mother tongue of approximately 25,000 natives. In the attempt at communication between these native laborers, and their English-speaking employers and overseers, a rudimentary language developed whose grammatical structure was largely Melanesian, whereas its vocabulary was composed of prevalent English elements (many of them with modified meanings as a result of misunderstandings on the part of the natives, and all of them with drastically altered, i.e., Melanesianized, pronunciation) and a fair percentage of words from the Tolai language. This rudimentary language became fuller and more elaborate over the years, and underwent a certain amount of standardization. The English speaking employers and overseers made more or less conscious efforts to learn at least enough of it to allow them to engage in elementary communication with the native workers, and the natives themselves began to employ it as a general means of intercommunication among themselves, allowing them to cut across the language barrier separating the non-Tolai speaking native workers from the Tolai speakers.

Many of these native workers returned home to New Britain after years in Australia, taking this language with them, and showing off their knowledge of what they believed to be the white man's language. Other natives who had not been away in Australia became eager to learn it, and it soon started spreading as a useful medium of intercommunication between natives speaking different languages. The German administration of Kaiser Wilhelms Land, which subsequently became the Trust Territory of New Guinea, adopted this language as the official language for administrative purposes in dealing with the native population, and it spread rapidly to many parts of the area. It must however be kept in mind that this spread of the language, though encouraged by the administration, was predominantly due to the natives' interest in it, in the first place as a means of overcoming the communication barriers that existed between members of different tribes because of the multiplicity of the languages, and in the second place as a means of communicating with the then numerically very small white population that contributed a limited number of German words to its vocabulary. There was very little active effort on the part of the white population to teach this language to the natives—they were learning it rapidly from each other. The language was named "Pidgin English," after the "Pidgin English" employed in Chinese seaside cities by Chinese in their dealings with Europeans—"Pidgin" being derived from "business"—although the two forms of speech have only little in common.

The spread of Pidgin English through parts of the Territory under German rule accelerated when the Australian administration took over after World War I. More and more of the area was being brought under administrative control, with the subsequent penetration of Pidgin English—or simply "Pidgin"—into the newly opened up areas. Frequently the spread of Pidgin into such areas actually antedated the extension of administrative control into them, with natives from such areas coming into areas already under control, learning Pidgin there, and returning home—often teaching at least some Pidgin to their fellow tribesmen.

The Australian administration did not adopt Pidgin officially as the administrative language of the Territory of New Guinea, but unofficially, this language has been, and in virtually every respect still is, *the* language of the administration in almost all of its dealings with the native population, and it is the plain truth to say that without Pidgin, the administration of the Territory of New Guinea, or even the Papua—New Guinea House of Representatives, could simply not function.

The basic original reason for the spread of Pidgin was that it was a prestige language of the highest order: it gave natives familiar with it an important position in view of the fact that they could communicate with white men and speak for their fellow tribesmen who were ignorant of the language; it also enabled such natives to obtain coveted employment with white employers that was barred to natives not knowing Pidgin. Last but not least, it put such natives into a position to communicate with their Pidgin-speaking counterparts in other tribes, which became increasingly important with the spread of pacification and the consequent replacement of hostilities between tribes by friendlier relations. In addition, Pidgin, being essentially a native language in its structure and mode of expression, and created as a means of expressing native ways of thinking, could be learned by natives with great ease and in a relatively short time. At the same time, Pidgin is deceptively easy looking to speakers of English who in consequence are quite willing to try to use it, which has again given the language a prestige boost in the eyes of the natives, even though the "Pidgin" spoken by the majority of the white population in the Territory constitutes a very poor effort indeed.

In addition to this, many natives have in recent years begun to develop what may well be termed a nationalistic pride in Pidgin. With increasing frequency, one hears natives refer to Pidgin as "our language" ("tok bilong mipela") in contrast to the white man's language, i.e., English, and they are greatly impressed when hearing a white man speak Pidgin native fashion, and are proud and flattered at hearing him speak "their language" so well.

It appears therefore that Pidgin has all the makings of being the obvious choice for becoming the national language of the emerging Papua-New Guinean nation. However, Pidgin has for a long time been the target of criticism and objections and even defamation and abuse, both in the Territory and, even more, outside it, and the idea of its becoming the national language of a Papua-New Guinean nation may appear quite monstrous to a good many of such objectors.

Before dealing with the nature of these objections in detail, it may be pointed out that they come, inside the Territory, from the English-speaking white population, to a very great extent, and only to a comparatively very small extent from sections of the native population with a vested interest in the importance of their own language, like the Motu for instance. A few native leaders may, at the same time, share the white population's contempt for Pidgin for reasons similar to those prompting non-white members of the United Nations to look upon Pidgin with disfavor (see below, the third of the major criticisms of Pidgin).

It has to be borne in mind that the choice of its national language is most certainly a matter for the nation in question itself to decide upon —i.e., in the case of the Papua-New Guinean nation, of the native population of the Territory that will constitute this nation. If, therefore, criticisms of and objections to a language that seems to fulfil all the requirements necessary for making a language a suitable candidate for becoming the national language are made and raised largely by members of the nonnative alien population that is ruling the Territory at present, and not by the native population itself, these criticisms and objections seem to be intrinsically inapplicable and unsuited for being regarded as arguments of validity. At the same time, it appears that even if the situational inapplicably of these criticisms and objections is disregarded, they are in their substance largely incorrect and based on erroneous views, prejudice and biased attitudes.

These criticisms are of three kinds, and will be discussed in what follows:

1. Pidgin is regarded by the critics as a revolting and debased corruption of English, full of insulting words, and sounding ridiculous and extremely funny to listeners.

None of these criticisms have objective validity. Pidgin is not English, not any more than English is French because of its containing an abundance of words of French origin. In its structure and functional principles, Pidgin is a Melanesian language, and in this respect quite different from English, just as English is structurally different from French. It is true that the percentage of the English-derived content of the vocabulary of Pidgin is considerably greater than that of the French-derived vocabulary of English, but it is not greater than the Latin-derived vocabulary content of French and Italian. But nevertheless, nobody will call present-day French or Italian corruptions of Latin, though they owe their historical origin to exactly that, just like Pidgin owed its birth to such a corruption of English, but in its present-day form, constitutes an established language when judged from the linguistic point of view.

To describe Pidgin as revolting and debased, as being full of insulting words, and sounding ridiculous and extremely funny to listeners, is the result of looking at it with an outside yardstick of values that is based on the nature and content of a different language, i.e., English. In such a manner any language closely related to another in part of its vocabulary, or in both structure and vocabulary, could, when looked at from the point of view of this other language, be described as being revolting, debased, full of insulting words, and as sounding ridiculous and extremely funny to listeners—i.e., to listeners speaking this other language, and not the language in question itself. Dutch people and Germans, Spaniards and Portuguese, members of the various Slavic nations and others can potentially find themselves in such situations quite frequently —quite a few of the words in such closely related languages are quite similar in form and to speakers of one such language, they appear to be easily recognizable when uttered by speakers of the other language, but their meanings may in fact be rather different, and a quite harmless word in one language may be a highly insulting one in the other, though it may sound nearly the same. Spanish and Portuguese and Slavic languages provide good examples of this. Educated members of two such speech communities who are aware of this problem do not blandly describe each others' languages as being full of insulting words. Why then, one may wonder, do speakers of English describe Pidgin as being full of insulting words; though they ought to be aware of the fact that these words, which bear formal resemblance to insulting words in English, have perfectly harmless meanings in Pidgin? It may be taken into account, as a partial explanation for this seemingly unreasonable attitude, that some English speakers are, as a result of their continued adherence to a Victorian heritage, perhaps more sensitive to and emotional about what they regard as insulting words than members of most other speech communities. Also it has to be considered that English is not a member of a pair of very closely related major languages like those mentioned above so that most English speakers have never been exposed to a language sounding much like theirs in many respects, though curiously, and sometimes revoltingly or funnily, differing from it in many instances (that is if the cases of minor dialectal differences like those between British and Australian English, or British and American English are disregarded, though these cases provide a few examples similar to those referred to above, like the basically harmless British English word "cock" when viewed from the Australian English point of view). It seems that if Pidgin is taken into account, English can be said to be a member of just such a pair of languages that are closely related in some respects—i.e., vocabulary. At the same time, only a very small proportion of the speakers of English ever come into contact with, or is aware of the exact nature of, Pidgin, which helps explain the exaggerated reaction of the majority of English speakers on first contact with this, to them, unfamiliar and strange sounding idiom. Characteristically, the most ardent, emotional, and vociferous critics of Pidgin are largely persons who know very little about it, whereas many of the established Territorials who have a good knowledge of the language are prepared to either regard it impartially and dispassionately or have a lot to say in its favor.

One last word about the argument that Pidgin sounds ridiculous and extremely funny to listeners, i.e., speakers of English unfamiliar or only a little familiar with it: one cannot help wondering if it has ever occurred to people holding this view how ridiculous and extremely funny much of English sounds to a French speaker who hears hundreds of corrupted French words tumbling from the mouth of an English speaker in what to a Frenchman appears as a jumble of either largely incoherent references, or worse still as an occasional sequence of, to him, extremely funny connotations. To help an English speaker realize this, he may be advised to consider his own reactions to a Frenchman's using corrupted English words derived from "camping," "weekend," etc., when speaking French, or, to the English listener, "mispronouncing" scores of familiar words like "repetition," "miserable," "original," and so forth. But of course, familiarity with these facts has traditionally blunted the Englishman's and Frenchman's reaction to these "ridiculous" matters that are under the dictations of their cultures, so that they are no longer regarded as ridiculous by members of the two speech communities. On the other hand, it is culturally in order for the speakers of English to think of Pidgin as a ridiculous and extremely funny language, and at the same time, to regard it as nothing more than a revolting and debased corruption of English.

2. The second argument frequently leveled against Pidgin is that it is an inadequate, restricted language unsuited for the expression of thoughts on an advanced level.

Before this argument is taken up on the specific level, it must be pointed out that the question as to whether a language is "adequate" or "inadequate" is in itself quite unsound. If "adequacy" is to mean the suitability or otherwise of a given language for the expression of, and reference to, cultural concepts, it has to be considered that a question concerning this adequacy of a language is only meaningful if the culture is named for whose expression the language is being thought of. Since every natural language constitutes a reference system for the culture within which it has been developed, it stands to reason that every language is adequate for the expression of, and reference to, the sum total of the cultural concepts making up the culture to which it belongs, and undergoes changes in accordance with changes of this culture. It stands equally to reason that any language is inadequate for the expression of a culture to which it does not belong, this inadequacy increasing in direct proportion with the degree of difference between the culture to which the language belongs, and the one which it is expected to express.

Turning to Pidgin in this connection, it must first be examined whether Pidgin is a fully adequate medium for the expression of the cultural concepts of the people of Papua-New Guinea who have been using it as their lingua franca. This examination is necessary: it is true that Pidgin is resorted to by natives in multilanguage situations as the almost exclusive means of intercommunication between them in all situations concerning the multilanguage group as a whole, or at least a multilanguage section of it. However, there are numerous culture situations involving members of one tribe only in which the language of intercommunication is never Pidgin, but always the tribal language, and for which Pidgin is definitely inadequate—understandably so, because it has no connection with that specific part of tribal culture that is often ritual in nature. One must add, at the same time, that a language other than Pidgin would also be inadequate, English probably more so than Pidgin because of the alienness of the culture to which English belongs, to the cultures of the native population of the Territory.

The cultures of the native population of Papua-New Guinea are rapidly changing, much of them getting lost and being replaced by something that is approaching uniformity. It seems clear that the language serving as a reference system for this new growing uniform element in the cultures of the population is Pidgin. Being the means of expression of this new set of cultural concepts, it is naturally adequate for this task. The most obvious proof for the adequacy of Pidgin as a means of expression for this modern Papua-New Guinean culture is the existence of thousands of natives in the Territory whose mother tongue, i.e., first language, is Pidgin, and who certainly find Pidgin fully adequate for the expression of all aspects of their culture.

It may well be argued that Pidgin is not adequate for the expression of the concepts constituting a sophisticated western culture like the Australian toward an approximation of which the Papua-New Guinean culture is believed to be heading. The first part of this argument is undoubtedly correct for the present moment—no native language can a priori be adequate for the expression of a western culture, and Pidgin has to be regarded as a native language. However, it is unlikely that the basic culture of the emerging Papua-New Guinea nation will ever become just a copy of the Australian—it will most certainly become something with a character decidedly its own, and what will have been absorbed into it from the Australian culture will only be a component element that will have undergone drastic changes and adaptations making it rather different from the original. As this basic culture will develop and become richer and more complex, the language serving it as a means of expression will develop with it and become richer and more complex, in step with the culture to which it belongs. Assuming that this language is Pidgin it can draw without limit on the word-stock of English, just like English used to draw profusely on the word-stock of French and Latin many centuries ago when the Anglo-Saxon language proved inadequate for the expression of a culture that was moving toward greater complexity and refinement. These French and Latin words were adapted to the sound-structure of English—one expects new English loan words in Pidgin to be adapted to the—totally un-English—sound-structure of native Pidgin. The suggestion that, if such a large-scale adoption of English words into Pidgin becomes necessary, Pidgin might just as well be replaced by English, seems about as justified as the argument that, centuries ago, the Anglo-Saxon speakers would have done better to adopt French wholesale rather than filling their language with French loan words, or that the Japanese who during the westernization of much of their culture had hundreds of English loan words entering their language, might have done better to switch to English entirely instead. This suggestion concerning Pidgin is of course largely caused by the erroneous assumption held by so many that New Guinea Pidgin is not a language in its own right, but just a sort of incorrect English.

There is a good present-day example of a Pidgin-type language being successfully adopted as the national language of a newly emerged nation: Indonesian. A type of low Malay had become the lingua franca in a good part of what constitutes present-day Indonesian, although it came from outside the area. It had been, in a simplified form, used by the Dutch during their rule, and it spread through most of the area now occupied by the new country. After independence, this language was adopted as the basis of the new national language, Bahasa Indonesia, in spite of the fact that there was a large regional language, Javanese, in the new country that was spoken by almost one-half of its entire population. It has undergone a steady process of enrichment and enlargement of vocabulary and form to remain adequate for the expression of the Indonesian culture that is growing in complexity with the absorption of new ideas and technical and other features from outside cultures.

The Indonesian example may be considerably different in detail from the Pidgin situation in the Territory, but it demonstrates that it is perfectly feasible for a Pidginized language to become a national language. It may also be taken into account in this comparison that the resistance to Indonesian on the part of the native population in Indonesia has been much greater than that of the native population of the Territory to Pidgin.

3. The third criticism of Pidgin is that it constitutes a sorry heritage from the days of colonial oppression, and that it has been used as a language accentuating, emphasizing and perpetuating social and racial distinctions, i.e., it has been used by the white masters in speaking to members of the native population to keep them in their place.

Parts of this argument are true as far as the bygone past is concerned, though the fact is overlooked in it that by far the greater portion of the use of Pidgin as a means of intercommunication has been from native to native, and not from white man to native.

The views outlined above are largely held by some white and quite a few non-white members of the United Nations Assembly, and also by a few white persons, as well as by some very few native leaders, in the Territory itself. However, it appears unrealistic, to say the very least, to hold such a view for the present or the future and its only justification may lie in the fact that it constitutes a topical and convenient political slogan. Many languages that in the past used to be characterized by just those social features ascribed to Pidgin in the above argument, have become the national languages of nations. Indonesian again is the classical example: it may be remembered that until the middle of the last century, natives in the then Dutch East Indies were forbidden by law even to learn Dutch so they could be kept linguistically, and in consequence socially, clearly separated from the white rulers. Nevertheless, the linguistic tool of this separation has become the national language of the new Indonesian nation.

Concerning Pidgin it must be noted that, as has been pointed out above, many of the natives in the Territory, including some of the members of the House of Assembly, are beginning to develop something akin to a nationalistic pride in Pidgin, and do not regard it as a means of social suppression, but rather as a means of self-identification. This attitude can safely be expected to spread further, and clearly demonstrates that the third criticism of Pidgin mentioned above is no longer applicable.

The foregoing rather lengthy discussion of Pidgin should not be taken as meaning that the author strongly recommends the choice of Pidgin as the future national language of the emerging Papua-New Guinean nation. The choice of its national language will be made by the new nation itself, and it is not to be expected that a recommendation by the author, even if he was to make one, would have the weight to influence their decision in the slightest. However, the author feels that because he is a professional anthropological linguist, it may be his task and duty to give the reader an opportunity to hear the opinion of a politically disinterested outside expert on the suitability or otherwise of Pidgin as a potential national language of the future Papua-New Guinean nation, and his views of the validity or otherwise, of the main criticisms leveled against this language by so many.

The third language that may be regarded as a candidate for becoming the future Papua-New Guinean national language is English. There is no doubt that this language has at present the highest prestige value of all the languages in the Territory, and many of the natives are very keen indeed to learn it. This interest is very largely motivated by practical considerations: English constitutes in their eyes the key to advancement and betterment of their positions, something with the help of which they hope to advance to the level of the white rulers. Although there may be a measure of truth in these assumptions, one cannot help wondering if these natives are not tending to overrate the advantages and benefits they are expecting to derive from a successful mastery of English on their part, and one is left wondering what their reaction may be once they arrive at the realization that the knowledge of English alone is only one, though an important, step towards the fulfillment of their hopes. There is no doubt that for years to come, English will constitute the sole key for Papua-New Guineans to higher education that in turn is the sole means for them for a successful handling of their and their country's problems after independence. Also, English will be the obvious language for them with the help of which they can get easy access to the outside world and its accumulated knowledge and experience, and make themselves heard and understood by the outside world. Again, English seems the most adequate tool for them to build up and conduct the complex administrative and legal principles that form the backbone of a modern nation.

Much of this seems to speak greatly in favor of English. However these are all solely practical considerations, and may not have enough weight in the collective mind of a newly emerging nation whose nationalistic feelings are on the verge of awakening to counterbalance the very important fact that English is the language of its present day alien rulers who belong to a different race.

It has been argued above that the fact that Pidgin may have been a language marking social differentiation at some time in the past cannot be regarded as a reason for it not being considered as a good candidate for becoming the future national language of Papua-New Guinea. The reader may therefore ask in the light of this as to why the fact that English is the language of the alien white rulers, i.e., also indicative of social distinction, should be of consequence. The answer seems obvious, and is borne out by historical evidence: if colonially or otherwise suppressed or ruled people who are identified by speaking a caste language gain independence, there seems no emotional reason on their part for not adopting their linguistic identification, i.e., their former caste language, as their new national language. However, they may have quite powerful emotional reasons for not adopting the high-caste language of their former masters as their national language, even if practical considerations may prompt them to do so. The examples set by India and Samoa for instance in recent years bear out this argument. In the face of necessity, such nations, if possessing leaders given to rational thinking even in highly emotional matters, may reluctantly adopt the language of their former masters as the *official* language, as distinct from a *national* language, for a limited period, but will strive hard in this period to develop what they would like to adopt as their national language with a view to its replacing the temporary official language as soon as possible, except perhaps in some special fields like that of higher, in particular tertiary, education. India's recent attempt to do this will be remembered by many of the readers—it failed because of the unsuitability of the language chosen and proposed as the national language: it was largely a regional language spoken by what, in spite of the spectacular number of its speakers, constituted a minority, could not be described as a lingua franca, and lacked prestige in the eyes of a large portion of the population.

It is by no means unlikely that the emerging Papua-New Guinean nation may choose a course similar to that followed by India in first adopting English as its official language, and will gradually prepare itself for replacing it in an ever-increasing sphere by a language that they can regard as a nationalistically acceptable means of self-identification, and can rightly describe as their own. English will of course remain as an important official language in several orbits of activity like higher education and relations with the outside world, but in matters concerning the new nation in its internal aspects the national language will undoubtedly take over. Papua New Guinea is in this respect in an almost uniquely favorable position in having, in addition to its numerous tribal languages and the language of the present-day white rulers, a lingua franca that is moving towards universality and general acceptability on the part of the native population, and that is more and more being regarded by it as a means of nationalistic self-identification. The author for one would not be suprised in the least if the new Papua-New Guinean nation will at some time in the future decide to adopt this language, Pidgin, as their national language—perhaps giving it a better sounding name, free from the heritage of the past, in the process.

REFERENCES

Wurm, S. A. 1964. Motu and Police Motu, A Study in Typological Contrasts. In Papers in New Guinea Linguistics No. 2, *Linguistic Circle of Canberra Publications, Series A: Occasional Papers*, No. 4, 1964, pp. 19–41.

Wurm, S. A., and D. C. Laycock. 1961. The Question of Language and Dialect in New Guinea, *Oceania*, **32**, 128–143.

Petr Zima

HAUSA IN WEST AFRICA:
REMARKS ON CONTEMPORARY ROLE
AND FUNCTIONS

There has been little or no disagreement among the older authors characterizing the area where the Hausa language is used in communication and attempting to describe its functions. Robinson [1] Mischlich [2], and even Weydling [3], Westermann [4], and Taylor [5] stressed in different words three main basic functions of Hausa:

1. As a medium of communication for native [6] Hausas in Hausaland "proper," the area covered by the territory of the historical Hausa states (and later Fulani-dominated emirates).
2. As a medium of communication for native Hausas living in the diaspora of Hausa colonies, scattered throughout large parts of West Africa, and extending, according to some authors, far to the North and to the East. Such important centers of the Mediterranean trade as Cairo and Tripoli as well as large agglomerations in the Sudan on the way to Mecca are also reported to have more or less cohesive Hausa settlements.
3. As a medium of communication for nonnative Hausa speakers, who use Hausa as a lingua franca. West Africa, or at least large areas of West Africa, are mentioned in this connection, but comments on the use of Hausa in this function in other areas of the African continent have also appeared.

The existence of an important tradition of writing Hausa in Ajami (Arabic) script has also been stressed on several occasions, and many documents of this type of written Hausa have been collected and published [7].

These basic facts seem to present a true picture of the areas where Hausa was used for communication and of its functions in these areas at the period when first systematic linguistic investigations were started and efforts to describe the structure of Hausa began. Description of the structure of the Hausa language has progressed considerably since this time [8] but curiously enough, little or nothing has changed in the descriptions of the role and functions of Hausa.

The last six decades have, in fact, considerably modified the functions and the role of Hausa; it is also quite possible that even the territory of the Hausa language community has changed, at least in some areas. Since almost nothing is known about the present state of Hausa diaspora settlements in North Africa and Arabia and only marginally interesting notes can be found about the situation in the Sudan [9], we intend to limit our observations to the areas of West Africa, where we were either able to investigate the situation on the spot during our field research, or where considerable sources of materials are at our disposal [10]. In this essay we therefore want to present a contemporary picture of the role and functions of Hausa in the area covered at present by the territories of Nigeria, Ghana, and their French-speaking neighbors, mainly Niger, Togo, and Dahomey, which represent the main Hausa-speaking territory of Africa.

Two new factors are characteristic of the condition in which communication in Hausa has occurred in this area during the last decades. The whole area was divided into two zones of different European administration. Although the European administrations presented even from the linguistic point of view some common features, they differed fundamentally in their attitude toward *language* policies. In addition, they further subdivided for various extralinguistic reasons their respective zones into smaller administrative entities. These two basic facts—the existence of two different language policies on the territory of one language community and the inclusion of different parts of this territory into different administrative units with a varying proportion of Hausa speakers in the total population—seem to be basically new in the development of the Hausa language community. They obviously influenced the role of Hausa in communication and its functions within the different parts of the whole territory.

The basic differences between the language policies of the former British and French administrations are well known [11]. The British language policy usually introduced at least in a facultative way the major vernaculars into public life, administrative procedures, education, etc. Serious efforts were made to create (where necessary) a written form of speech based on the Latin script and the publication of printed literature was sponsored and supported [12]. The French policy was different, stressing the basic function of French at all levels of administration, public life, and education [13]. Because of this, no written form of the vernaculars was created and practically no printed literature exists [14]. These general rules of language policy obviously influenced the conditions of contact of the Hausa language with the two officially introduced European languages, English and French.

The area under investigation was not only divided into two different spheres of administration, but different administrative entities were created within the two spheres. In Northern Nigeria and Niger—the former belonging to the sphere of a British type of language policy and the latter to the French one—the Hausa speakers, both native and non-native, happened to be included in an administrative unit where they constituted the main bulk of the total population. On the other hand in Ghana—formerly Gold Coast—as well as in Togo, Dahomey, and possibly also Upper Volta, they happened to be included in units where they constituted a minority either of native Hausa settlers in small colonies of the diaspora or of nonnative speakers using Hausa as a lingua franca. Just as the general rules of language policy obviously influenced the conditions of contact of the Hausa language with the official European language, the inclusion of different parts of the Hausa area in different administrative units with new frontiers influenced the conditions of its contact with other vernaculars.

So from the point of view of new language policies and language contacts, the whole area must be divided into not only two but four different zones, limited and characterized by two mutually intersecting factors: the general style of the language policy on the one hand and the particular functions of Hausa within the newly created administrative units on the other. The following table illustrates this.

	A. Hausa a majority or the main bulk of population	B. Hausa a minority and/or lingua franca
I. Zones of former British language policy	Northern Nigeria	Ghana (Gold Coast)
II. Zones of former French language policy	Niger	Other small French-speaking territories (Dahomey, Togo, Upper Volta)

This partition did not go too far, however. The arbitrary nature of these new frontiers and the more or less liberal attitude toward the frequent traffic across the frontiers facilitated easy and intensive social and language contacts between Hausa speakers from different zones. Not the frontiers but the different conditions of development behind the frontiers have brought some new, interesting features. These mostly concern the mutual relation of spoken and written forms of the language, the vocabulary, and some aspects of the formation of a norm in grammar. Let us now treat them in greater detail.

The problem of the written form of a language is very often treated as an exclusive problem of creation or adaptation of a system of a script (or orthography) for the given language. But in the case of Hausa, where not only one but several scripts and orthographies exist, the question is far from being so simple. As shown a long time ago by scholars of the Prague school [15], both the spoken and the written forms of language have their specific functions and are to be considered as specially related to a single language norm. Usually the correlation of the spoken and written form of the language is studied by comparing one written form to the spoken form. Cases of language communities that used—or are using—two or more written forms of a language are also known but in traditional linguistic areas they are not so frequent. The case of Hausa is further complicated by the partition of the main language areas into zones with different language policies, the attitude toward written Hausa being one of the key differences of these two language policies.

When the European administration of different parts of the Hausa-speaking territory in West Africa started to function, there always existed, as is well known, both a spoken and written form of this language. Not even the most skeptical voices about the age of the Hausa literature using the Ajami type of Arabic script question the existence of this literature in the second half of the nineteenth century [16]. Although this was not a frequent case in West African language communities, the European influence did not interfere too greatly with the traditional culture at this stage, and so this form of written Hausa continued to spread throughout the whole of Hausa territory and surrounding areas, probably even in some areas to the nonnative speakers of Hausa. In zones labeled I in our diagram—former British territories—and especially in zone IA, in the area of present Northern Nigeria, the European influence established and introduced a new form of written Hausa, using the Latin characters as a basis, with some minor modifications. Three special graphemes have been gradually introduced, the ɓ, ɗ, ƙ letters. Some phonetic symbols, taken over from the so-called Memorandum [17], have been dropped. Orthographically, however, this type of written Hausa is closely tied to the rules of English orthography. The transcription of vowel sounds, far from being phonemis or phonetic, omits totally the prosodic factors, and several consonantal features are simply taken over from the orthography of English. Thus j is used for $d_ʒ$, the digraph *sh* for ʃ, etc. Another digraph, *ch*, which was previously used for *tʃ*, recently has been replaced by simple c. After several official and unofficial attempts to reform orthography (not the script), there seems to be a system that is more or less recognized at least by official and semi-official publications. This written Hausa is usually called Gaskiya-literature [18]. It is true that the present Gaskiya system is far from being phonemically accurate and consistent, but it is also true that a considerable literature has been written, printed, and distributed in it.

In other zones there were, and occasionally still are, spontaneous attempts to use this type of written Hausa, based on Latin characters. Some educated native Hausa speakers in zone IB (Ghana) also use it occasionally, although instruction is not usually given in Gaskiya orthography. Most probably the knowledge of the rules of English orthography facilitates for native Hausas at least a basic decoding of written Gaskiya publications. Some influence of Hausa from Nigeria cannot, of course, be excluded. The existence of written (or printed) Hausa communications based on Latin characters is otherwise limited in this zone to occasional publications (sections of some periodicals, etc.) using different forms of orthography that may be characterized as more or less spontaneous transcription. Some rules of English orthography as well as some distant knowledge of Gaskiya publications may have had an influence here [19].

In zone IIB, and with some restrictions also in zone IIA, practically no written form of Hausa based on Latin characters is in use. The only written forms of language existing here are either Hausa written in Ajami characters and French written in Latin characters. The situation in zone IIA is, however, characterized by a strong, very recent additional tendency to introduce some kind of written Hausa based on Latin characters [20]. The most extensive of these experiments was an attempt to distribute mechanically in this zone Hausa literature printed in Gaskiya orthography in Northern Nigeria. Although two centers [21] of distribution of these publications were created, there was surprisingly little interest in these Hausa publications in this zone, where Hausa speakers are the substantial proportion of the whole population. In view of the basic facts of the language policy prevailing in this zone, this result is not so surprising. French was the only language written and read in Latin characters by Hausa readers in this zone. Those who could write and read French were not accustomed to any other language in the functions of written language. And even those who could recognize characters by the relation between the written and spoken forms of language had considerable difficulty in decoding the written form of their own native (or second) language presented in Gaskiya orthography, owing to its links with English orthography. The only rules of correlation between the Latin alphabet and sounds they had been taught were those of French orthography, which are obviously very different from those of English. Those who were accustomed to read or write Hausa in this zone did it in Ajami and for the most part did not know Latin characters at all.

The position of Hausa written in the Ajami form of Arabic script might well seem unchanged and unaffected by the partition of the whole area into zones with different official languages and different language policies. Some recent papers confirm, indeed, that this tradition of writing Hausa is still living even in some more remote areas and in the diaspora [22]. If we study, however, the role and functions of Hausa written in Ajami in relation to the parallel existence or nonexistence of other, more recently created forms of written Hausa, the result is different. We may say that in the zones IIA and IIB and to a lesser extent in zone IB, Hausa communications written in Ajami represent the only form of written Hausa. All possible functions of written language must be fullfilled by this form of written Hausa, if the communication is realized in Hausa (and not in French or Arabic). We may speak therefore in these zones about the exclusive (or predominant) occurrence of Hausa written in Ajami, to the exclusion of foreign languages.

In zone IA (Northern Nigeria) and to a lesser extent in zone IB (Ghana) the Ajami type of written Hausa coexists with another type of written Hausa based on Latin script (Gaskiya system and other occasional variants). At least theoretically the Hausa speaker has the choice of writing and reading Hausa either in the written form based on Ajami or on Latin characters. We can therefore speak about the alternation of the two types of written Hausa.

For most Hausa speakers, however, this option remains, at least for the present, purely theoretical, because the use of the one or the other form of written Hausa still remains one of the characteristic symbols of general education (Islamic or modern). Nevertheless, the very existence of people who can use both types of written Hausa presents two alternatives. In some styles the choice is still largely free and linguistically totally unpredictable. Thus a recent contribution on Hausa poetry [23] shows the important fact that a group of contemporary poets exists, writing in both forms of written Hausa. In some areas of communication and in some styles and subjects, however, the alternative forms seem to show at least a tendency toward complementary occurrence; that is, Hausa communications on some topics are most probably using a particular form of written language. This seems valid especially as far as printed communciations are concerned. Thus written (or printed) communications on modern administration, technical development, science, and all aspects of European-imported elements of public life are usually written in Gaskiya form. Religious (Islamic) topics as well as moralities, subjects from traditional history and customs are usually—if not exclusively—written in Ajami. The same seems to be valid for traditional law as opposed to modern law [24]. The existence (even sometimes only theoretical) of complementary occurrences of the two types of written Hausa in zone IA confronted with exclusivity of occurrence of one type of written Hausa in other zones (with marginal overlapping) seems to be one of the basic new features of the divided Hausa language community. It is interesting that the exclusivity of occurrence of Hausa written in Ajami leads to some quite unusual types of written communications (public Ajami inscription on the road in North Togo, Ajami Hausa inscriptions on old banknotes in Ghana, etc.).

The more or less homogeneous Hausa-speaking community therefore corresponds to a split in the Hausa writing (and reading) community, which is divided at least into four subcommunities, dissimilar in size, education, and cultural orientation:

1. The community of those Hausa speakers who use only the Ajami form of written Hausa (or use it in alternation with French, which is a comparatively rare situation, or with Arabic, which is a quite common situation).

2. The community of those who use Gaskiya or any other written form of Hausa based on Latin characters. (Some of those people use written English also.)

3. The community of those Hausa speakers who use both types of written Hausa. The alternation of the two types might be either complementary or free.

4. The community of those who do not use any type of written Hausa. Some of them use, if certain of the basic functions of written language are to be fullfilled, a written form of a foreign language (French, Arabic, or English).

Although the basic lines of this division are territorial, frequent overlapping from one community to another gives way to speculations as to possible further development of a single Hausa reading and writing community.

Generally, we may say that the division and the dividing factors had little or no effect on the grammatical structure of the Hausa language. Neither administrative frontiers nor the existence of several zones with different language policies could have influenced the structure of any language after only a few decades. They had, however, some influence on the process of establishing a standard norm in Hausa, both in its spoken and written form.

Traditionally it has been assumed that the Kano dialect (the eastern dialectal complex) can be taken as the basis of some kind of standard norm in Hausa. Although there are some tendencies to stress the function of the Sokoto dialect (western dialectal complex) in this respect as well, nevertheless in the spoken form of the language at least, the position of the forms of the Kano dialect is very important. Recent investigation shows that Kano forms are penetrating even into idiolects of speakers in areas where other dialectal forms were supposed to exist in the past [25]. Thus Kano forms are now being used in some Hausa settlements where earlier Sokoto forms were reported. They are even sometimes coexistent with other dialectal forms that occur alternatively in the speech of the same speakers. Their frequency of occurrence is higher in the idiolects of speakers of the younger generations of native Hausas and they are also more frequent in bigger urban agglomerations. Non-Kano forms are reported to be more frequent in the speech of older generations of Hausa speakers and, in more remote areas, of the investigated non-Kano dialectal areas. This may be one of the symptoms of further progress of the Kano dialectal forms in the function of some kind of standard, or at least interdialectal (or supradialectal) link.

In written Hausa, however, the position of Kano dialectal forms is far from being as important as in the spoken form of Hausa. The norm in the Ajami written form is inconsistent and it is open to discussion whether we may speak about any standard norm in this connection at all. The influence and the importance of Sokoto dialectal forms seem to be decisive in many Ajami written communications. As far as the Gaskiya form of written Hausa is concerned, the influence of Kano forms seems to be stronger, at least a tendency to use them as a standard norm obviously exists. But even the best Gaskiya authors occasionally use Sokoto and other dialectal forms.

Most probably the dividing factors had, at least in an indirect form, some influence, especially in the written form of Hausa and its norm. Both Kano and Sokoto had already lost much of their prestige in economy, administration, and to some extent even in culture during the period preceding the partition of the Hausa-speaking territory. This fact very likely weakened the process of establishing either of the dialects in the function of a standard norm. After the partition, both the two main centers, Kano and Sokoto, happened to be included in one zone (IA). They could conserve some basic influence in this zone and most probably in spoken form of the language the influence of Kano dialect continued to be felt even outside zone IA. Owing to the particular problems of the written form of Hausa, which was mostly affected by the problems arising from the establishment of four different zones of language policies, the establishment of a standard norm in the divided writing and reading community is much more complicated. Language contacts between Hausas of zone IA and Hausa-speakers of other zones are much more frequent in the spoken form of Hausa than in the written form, and even the media of mass communication from this zone have a much broader acceptance in their spoken form than in their written form (many more people from other zones listen to Kaduna broadcasting than read *Gaskiya ta fi kwabo*) [26].

New attempts at standardization in other zones (except IA), and especially in zone IIA, are facing serious difficulties as far as the problem of choice of standard norm is concerned, because the recognition of either the Kano or Sokoto dialect as a basis of the standard norm puts the standard area outside the given zone or state. Certain tendencies toward dialectal particularism seem to be emerging and it is interesting to notice that other dialects are being proposed as a basis for regional standards. The dialect of Gobir, for example, was proposed as the basis of a planned alphabetization in Niger [27].

The question of a spoken and written standard norm in all zones is also complicated by the existence of nonnative Hausa. On the one hand the use of Hausa as a lingua franca by non-Hausas seems to some extent to have simplified Hausa structure in marginal areas and the possibility cannot be excluded that the contact of native Hausas with the simplified structure of non-native Hausa might have had some destructive reverse influence on the process of establishing a standard norm in spoken and written Hausa. It seems to me, however, that the complex interdependence of native and non-native Hausa cannot be limited to only such a destructive and simplifying influence. The fact that the main source of diffusion of non-native Hausa in the function of a lingua franca was obviously trade seems to be important, because large proportions of the Hausa tradesmen come from the main areas in what is contemporary Northern Nigeria, that is, from Kano and Sokoto dialectal areas. They were obviously a major primary influence in the formation of non-native Hausa usage in West Africa, and this non-native usage of Hausa has, even in its simplified and unstable structure, some features of clear Kano (and to some extent also Sokoto) dialectal origin. Since the influence of the nonnative Hausa usage, though limited by the competition with the languages of administration, still persists, it also may help to maintain the position of Kano forms in spoken Hausa, especially in zones IB and IIB (Ghana and small French-speaking countries with the exception of Niger). But many other factors may, perhaps, influence this process and direct it elsewhere.

The Hausa vocabulary could not fail to have been affected by the division of the Hausa-speaking community in West Africa into several zones with different language policies and different language contacts. Although the two IE languages that came into contact with Hausa are by historical chance members of the same big language family and have—by another historical and linguistic chance—very much in common lexically, the contact with them has been decidedly a strong dividing factor. Here we would like to stress the general characteristics of this contact and of the resulting process of borrowing, the details being given elsewhere [28].

Borrowing from English took place in the spirit of the language policy of zones I. There were at least two types of borrowing, spontaneous and organized. Organized borrowing was a part of a more or less coordinated effort by different instruments of language policy to adapt the Hausa vocabulary to its new functions. In zone IA this process is particularly remarkable, since the instruments of language policy in this zone are oriented mainly on Hausa [29]. In zone IB (Ghana) the results of the efforts from zone IA were moderately put into practice in limited areas, the main attention of the language policy in this zone being oriented toward other languages. Borrowing, or at least its organized section, was a part of a much broader process of rebuilding the Hausa vocabulary. In zone IA the process of borrowing was accompanied therefore by the formation of new words from older roots (or construction) and occasional semantic shifts [30]. Besides this officially sponsored process there was obviously an unofficial spontaneous borrowing resulting from the nature of contact of Hausa and English.

The result of these types of borrowing is characterized by a relatively high degree of assimilation of English loanwords into the Hausa structure at all levels, phonemic, morphemic, and syntactic as well. It seems to me that the process of borrowing from English to Hausa was relatively easy not only because of the direct influence of the instruments of language policy and its institutions, but most probably also because both languages were and to a large extent still are coexistent in so many different functions and styles, and at different levels. This contact is realized in both the spoken and written form of languages, so that there is generally little or no difference between loanwords in spoken and written usage in the Gaskiya type of written Hausa.

The process of borrowing from French, however, obviously occurred under different conditions. No organized borrowing occurred and no institutional help was established, and even the contact itself occurred under completely different conditions. It occurred only in the spoken form of the languages and in certain styles and functions. The contact of Hausa with French was therefore limited to certain parts of the vocabulary only, because in many styles and functions French was the only possible language of communication. The result, when compared with the borrowing from English, is very interesting: there are also many loanwords from French (even if they seem generally to be less numerous than those from English), but they are less assimilated into the Hausa phonemic and grammatical structure. They are much more "Fremdwörter" (foreign words) than "Lehnwörter" (loanwords), to use the German linguistic terminology.

The overlapping of loanwords, as well as of some new words from on zone to another, was limited by two important factors:

1. The mutual competition of loanwords. There are cases of what I call elsewhere "parallel" borrowing, that is, two loanwords of different origin existing with the same meaning in different zones.

2. By differences of realities, given by different administrative and cultural structures, borrowed from different administrations.

Nevertheless this overlapping of loanwords from different zones does occur and it is sometimes the basis of further important changes in the Hausa vocabulary.

In view of the peculiar situation of written Hausa it is important to note that most loanwords from English and French penetrate very rarely into the written form of Hausa using the Ajami script, but Arabic loanwords [39], borrowed through the process of contact with Arabic, do penetrate into the written Hausa texts using the Latin characters. They are, however, not so frequent in this type of written Hausa as they are in Hausa using the Ajami script. It is highly probable that the frequency of occurrence of the loanwords from arabic in Gaskiya texts is about the same as in spoken Hausa.

Although there are many other possible effects of the division of the West African Hausa-speaking community into several zones with different language contacts and different language policies, we shall limit our observations to what has been said above. What is most interesting are not the dividing factors themselves, but the reactions of the language and its users. Daily social and language communication of Hausa-speakers from different zones brings frequent overlapping of all features, previously characteristic of one zone, or only of some zones. Nobody can foresee the result of this whole process, and many possible factors, both linguistic and nonlinguistic (social), will influence it. Although from the practical point of view this makes the problem of the development and standardization of Hausa more difficult, from the point of view of theoretical and sociolinguistic analysis it can perhaps contribute to the understanding of many general language problems of the developing nations.

NOTES

1. C. H. Robinson, *Hausa Grammar*, London, 1923, pp. 1–2.
2. A. Mischlich, *Wörterbuch der Hausasprache* I, Berlin, 1906, p. ix.
3. G. Weydling, *Einführung ins Hausa*, Leipzig, 1942, p. vii.
4. In his introductory paper to G. P. Bargery's *Dictionary of the Hausa Language*.
5. F. W. Taylor, *Hausa Grammar*, London, 1923, p. v.

6. The terms non-native Hausa (i.e., Hausa used as a lingua franca) and native Hausa (i.e., Hausa of those whose mother tongue it is) are taken over, in principle, from C. T. Hodge's contribution on "Non-native Hausa" (Georgetown Univ. Mon. Ser. on Lang. and Linguistics, No. 11, 1958, pp. 57–64).

7. See, e.g., C. H. Robinson, *Specimens of Hausa Literature*, Cambridge, 1896. Recently D. A. Olderogge has published some of the specimen of this literature, collected by older German authors in a critical edition in the publication *Zapadnyj Sudan*, Trudy inst. etn. AN SSSR, t. 53, Moskva-Leningrad 1960. See also M. Hiskett's edition of "Song of Bagauda" in *BSOAS*, **27** (1964), and **28** (1965). A well done bibliography of the older German editions is to be found in Olderogge's publication.

8. Thanks to well-known contributions by such authors as F. W. Parsons, C. T. Hodge, Cl. Gouffé, D. A. Olderogge and his pupils, and many others.

9. Some very interesting remarks about the present situation of Hausa colonies in the Republic of Sudan are in P. F. McLoughlin, *Language Switching as an Index to Socialization in the Republic of the Sudan*, Los Angeles, 1964; see also marginal notes in "English in the Sudan" by W. A. Murray, in *Language in Africa*, J. Spencer (ed.) Cambridge, 1963, pp. 86–96.

10. During our field trip to West Africa in 1962–1963 and recently during our activity at the Department of Linguistics, University of Ghana.

11. See, e.g., in N. Denny's survey, *Language and Education in Africa*, "Language in Africa," pp. 47–48 f.

12. A very good survey of such a literature is given by R. M. East, *A Vernacular Bibliography for the Languages of Nigeria*, Zaria, 1941.

13. See, e.g., P. Alexandre, Les problemes linguistiques africains vus de Paris, in *Language in Africa*, pp. 53 f.

14. With the exception of missionary literature.

15. See J. Vachek, "Zum Problem der Geschriebenen Sprache," *TCLP*, **8** (1939), p. 94, id. "Written and Printed Language," *Recueil Linguistique de Bratislava*, **1** (1948), pp. 67–75.

16. See a recent judgment by M. Hiskett, "The Historical Background to the Naturalization of Arabic Loanwords in Hausa," *ALS*, **6** (1965), p. 24.

17. Practical Orthography of African Languages (Intern. Afr. Inst., Memorandum, I., London 1927), a sample of Hausa text is given on p. 15.

18. Gaskiya (= truth in Hausa) is the name of a company publishing Hausa books and periodicals in Zaria, N. Nigeria.

19. A typical example of such a type of written Hausa in this zone was the occasional Hausa page (or section) in the Accra weekly *The African Spectator*.

20. A new orthography for Hausa was proposed by the French linguist Cl. Gouffe in 1962 to the Niger authorities. A recent (1965) *UNESCO* conference on alphabetization also considered, as far as I know, the problems of Hausa orthography for Niger.

21. In Niamey and Zinder, according to news brought by the Hausa journal published in Nigeria (*Gaskiya ta fi kwabo*) in 1962.

22. See, e.g., a report on collection of "Arabic" manuscripts, including also many Hausa texts in Ajami in *Research Review*, Inst. Afr. Studies, Univ. of Ghana, Vol. 1, 1965, pp. 15 et panum.

23. John N. Paden, "A Survey of Kano Hausa Poetry," *Kano Studies*, **1** (1965), pp. 33–39.

24. Cf. the edition of new Hausa translation of the Penal Code of N. Nigeria in 1959, supervised by F. W. Parsons.

25. See my contribution on Hausa in Ghana and Togo in "Some Remarks on West African Languages in Diaspora," Papers presented to the Vth WALC, Accra 1965.

26. The best Hausa newspaper, published by Gaskiya Corporation in Zaria, Northern Nigeria.

27. This is the case of Cl. Gouffé's proposals mentioned here in footnote 20.

28. See my paper, "Some Remarks on Loanwords in Modern Hausa," *Archiv Orientalni*, **32** (1964), 522–528; A. H. M. Kirk-Green, "Neologisms in Hausa—A Sociological Approach," *Africa*, **23** (1963), pp. 24–44 [with some notes by T. G. Brierly in *Africa*, **23** (1963), p. 269].

29. A special Hausa Language Board has been created here. Previously there were other instruments of language policy, such as the so-called Translation Bureau, later Literature Bureau.

30. A bibliography of wordlists and lists of terms published by various institutions for Hausa is in my article on loanwords, p. 522.

31. On Arabic loanwords see J. H. Greenberg's "Arabic Loan-words in Hausa," *Word*, **3** (1947), pp. 85–97; see also Hiskett's article mentioned in footnote 15.

IV

Literature
and Education

IV

John Bowers

LANGUAGE PROBLEMS AND LITERACY

DEFINITIONS

Literacy is a relative term. A definition generally used for census pur
poses is: "a person is considered literate who can read and write with
understanding a simple statement on his everyday life." Such elementary
literacy is, however, of very limited value, and the "intensive" strategy
adopted by UNESCO for the World Literacy Program sets the target at
functional literacy. This is described as follows in the report of the World
Conference of Ministers of Education on the Eradication of Illiteracy,
held in Teheran in October, 1965 [1]:

"Rather than an end in itself, literacy should be regarded as a way
of preparing man for a social, civic and economic role that goes far
beyond the limits of rudimentary literacy training, consisting merely in
the teaching of reading and writing. The very process of learning to
read and write should be made an opportunity for acquiring information that can immediately be used to improve living standards; reading
and writing should lead not only to elementary general knowledge but
to training for work, increased productivity, a greater participation in
civil life and a better understanding of the surrounding world, and
should ultimately open the way to basic human culture.

"Literacy teaching should be resolutely oriented towards development, and should be an integral part not only of any national education
plans but also of plans and projects for development in all sectors of
the national life."

This paper is therefore concerned with functional literacy as a component of adult education and training in the developing countries.

RELATIONSHIP OF ILLITERACY
AND LANGUAGE PROBLEMS

It is natural that the problem of illiteracy should be most acute in
multilingual societies, and especially where the spoken languages have

not been transcribed. Information and statistics are, however, so deficient
in this field that the relationship between illiteracy and language distribution is largely a matter of conjecture.

A meeting of experts on Language Development Problems convened
by UNESCO in Yaounde, Cameroun March 17–22, 1966 [2] proposed
a study of the language situation, linguistic problems, and current linguistic research and needs for the continent of Africa. For the world as a
whole the situation should be improved by closer collaboration between
linguists, anthropologists, statisticians, and census authorities.

NEED FOR LINGUISTIC POLICY

Literacy is related to linguistics in the sense that an attack on illiteracy in a multilingual society must generally be preceded by decisions of
language policy and the solution of linguistic problems. This action may
involve the following:

1. Choice of the language or languages to be used.
2. Choice of script.
3. Analysis and transcription of unwritten languages.
4. Revision of orthography and vocabulary of written languages.
5. Second-language teaching.

CHOICE OF LANGUAGES

Language policy is relevant to educational activities of various kinds
and at all levels; among them we may distinguish:

1. The school and university system.
2. Adult literacy.
3. Adult education:
   a. By direct oral communication.
   b. Using the written word and therefore involving literacy.
   c. Through the media of mass communication (especially radio and
      television).

LANGUAGE POLICY IN THE SCHOOL
AND UNIVERSITY SYSTEM

Although this paper is essentially concerned with *adult* literacy, it
may be well to consider the question of language policy in schools and
universities as a background to the main subject.

Language policy in the educational systems of multilingual societies
varies widely, being generally a compromise, influenced by many—and
often conflicting—factors:

1. The psychological advantages of teaching in the mother tongue.

2. The "literary status" of the languages spoken—whether they have been satisfactorily transcribed and to what extent they possess a literature.

3. The demands of particular culture groups for recognition of their languages and the influence or status of such groups within the nation.

4. The cost of multiplying the number of languages used in the education system.

5. The availability of teachers who can handle the local and the national language.

6. Lack of textbooks in many languages and consequent problems of writing, translation, and publication.

7. The problem of organizing comparable examination systems in several languages.

8. The difficulty in conducting secondary and higher education in any language that lacks a literature or is deficient as a medium for the expression of modern concepts.

9. The supposedly unifying effect of using a single national or official language.

The problem often presents itself as a conflict between the first and last of these factors—between the claims of the mother tongue and of the national language to be the medium of education. This is not, however, an either-or choice, and the mother tongue may be used as the initial medium of instruction, leading, where necessary and when appropriate, to the learning of a second and even a third language.

Higher education is generally imparted in the national language, or in a world language that is not the official national language, and this, of course, influences language policy in the primary and secondary schools that feed students into the universities.

CHOICE OF LANGUAGES FOR ADULT LITERACY

Different factors operate in the choice of languages for adult literacy programs—or the same factors operate in different ways—and in situations that vary between one social group and another.

Where the Choice Lies

Governments are assuming increasing responsibility for adult literacy and therefore are, and should be, establishing policy in regard to the languages to be used. This should, of course be flexible, allowing for local variations in culture, and for local needs and preferences. It should also be periodically reviewed and revised, in the light of progress in linguistic studies, new teaching techniques, and social and cultural change.

Adult literacy programs may be organized by provincial and local authorities, and by nongovernmental or quasi-governmental agencies—voluntary organizations, churches, and religious bodies, industrial concerns, the armed forces, and even by small local groups of illiterates engaging their own teacher. Thus policy is likely to be less standardized than in the school system and a measure of choice in the matter of language may well be left to the local or subsidiary organizing agency.

Adult literacy, unlike schooling, is generally a voluntary and spare-time activity. How does this affect the choice of language? Should it, like the activity itself, be subject to the wishes of the "consumers"—the illiterates themselves? This would certainly be in line with modern trends in favor of adult study-groups—involving the students as active partners in learning—as opposed to traditional literacy classes, where they were simply given instruction. If, however, the choice of language is to be left to the illiterates themselves, they must be given the data on which to base a rational choice. This should include a clear indication of facilities available, guidance on the potential usefulness of the alternatives open to them, and an assessment of the time and effort needed to achieve each of these.

The Nature of the Choice

For the government of a multilingual country, the choice is generally between providing, or encouraging the provision of, facilities for adult literacy in (a) the official national language only; (b) all languages spoken by sizeable groups of the population; or (c) some of these.

A local organizing agency may then provide for literacy in any one or more languages that illiterates in its area speak or need to learn, subject to any limitations laid upon it by national policy and by the various psychological and material factors considered next.

The illiterate adult in a multilingual country may thus be confronted, by choice or necessity, with any of the following possibilities:

1. Learning to read and write in his mother tongue alone.
2. Where he belongs to a small language group situated in the territory of a larger group, learning in the language of the larger group, which is neither his mother tongue nor the official national language.
3. Where he is living away from his native area, learning in the language of his new residence.
4. Becoming literate both in his mother tongue and in a second language, which will most probably be the official national language.
5. Becoming literate directly in the official national language (this may be the only course open to him if his mother tongue is not a written language or is not used for literacy).

In a complex language situation therefore government policy, the facilities available to the organizing agency, and the needs and wishes of the illiterate adults themselves should, as far as possible, be harmonized. What then are the factors controlling and influencing the choice of languages?

Psychological Factors

Psychological and educational considerations clearly favor the learning of reading and writing in the mother tongue. It is naturally quicker and easier to relate written symbols to known sounds and concepts than to those of an unknown or foreign language. Moreover, a person who has to speak, read, write, learn, and think in a language with which he is not familiar is at a disadvantage: his capacity to express himself is handicapped; communication is slowed down; and misunderstandings cause frustration and tension. These factors may, however, be offset where the knowledge of a second language enhances prestige and widens the scope of communication, or where the illiterate already speaks the second language. (More or less bilingual illiterates are by no means uncommon in multilingual societies.)

Adults, unlike schoolchildren, must often learn at night when they are tired. They are also likely to be preoccupied with problems, undernourished, and weakened by disease. Incentives are needed to bring them to study, and unless progress is demonstrable and study not too difficult classes will dwindle. These considerations again favor the easier and speedier course of literacy in the mother tongue, unless there is a special incentive to learn another language.

Literary Status of the Language

These psychological considerations are subject to others of a more material kind. The most crucial is whether the language has an accepted alphabet, grammar, texts, and word lists that establish the spelling of at least the common words of the language in a standard form (where there are differing dialects), and preferably also a dictionary. A language can be chosen if it does not fulfill these criteria, but its use for literacy will have to be deferred for months or even years until preparatory work has been done.

If the lack of an alphabet and texts is a bar to the use of a language, their inadequacy, even where they exist, may still be a serious handicap. Where, for example, a language has been endowed by amateur linguists with an unsatisfactory alphabet, or more than one alphabet, or where there are various dialects and no accepted standard form of the language, it is unwise to launch a literacy program until language reform has been undertaken.

Availability of Teachers

Various types of teachers are employed for adult literacy work, including full-time adult literacy teachers, schoolteachers, social workers, and others who are expected to give part of their time to literacy work, and volunteers. It is generally agreed that all categories of teachers require special training for working with adults. Certainly they should not be called upon to teach literacy in a language they do not speak, read, and write fluently and correctly.

The availability of teachers capable of handling a particular language is therefore a factor that may influence policy. This may sometimes operate against the mother tongue; for example, in a highly illiterate community there are hardly any literate persons who speak the local language. More generally it operates in favor of the mother tongue, for there is usually a lack of teachers able to handle any other language. However, where an established school system is teaching a national language that is not the mother tongue of the locality, the emergence of a bilingual "élite" will make it possible to find teachers capable of handling two languages, and to set up adult literacy programs which aim at literacy in a second language.

Teaching and Reading Materials

Another important factor in the choice of language for literacy is the existence of teaching and reading materials specially adapted to the needs and interests of adults, and no literacy program should be launched until the necessary supply is available. Assuming that the study and transcription of the language is satisfactorily completed, the preparation, testing, revision, and publication of teaching materials will generally take a specialist team of three or four persons from six months upwards. A year is perhaps a reasonable period to allow for the basic teaching kit (say a primer in two parts and from three to six graded readers). Thereafter the production of reading matter is a continuous need.

Costs and Returns

These material requirements can be expressed in terms of manpower, time, and money, so that the decision to use a new language for literacy is essentially a question of costs and returns—costs of linguistic study and transcription (to be discussed later), of the preparation and printing of materials, and the training and employment of teachers—returns in the form of more effective and functional literacy.

Language and the Aims of Literacy

The choice of language should certainly be influenced by the aims set for literacy in any given situation. If literacy is to be functional, in what language will it be most functional?

Where literacy programs are designed to bring adults who have had little or no schooling into the educational circuit they must be conducted in, or give command of, the language used in the school system. In a number of countries deferred primary schooling enables illiterate adults to work for certificates and diplomas equivalent to those currently awarded in the schools.

In any case, literacy should lead to further education and this may be shared between adults emerging from a literacy program and young people leaving the schools—another reason for adults to learn the language used in the school system.

Where adult literacy is to be interlocked with technical and vocational training the choice of language may be conditioned by the language used in the training courses or spoken by the instructors. This will more usually be the case in urban and industrial communities, and here also the existence of a multilingual and perhaps multiracial labor force may indicate the need for a common language that will not be the mother tongue of all students.

In rural areas the written word should serve as a medium for agricultural extension and community development. Except where migratory labor is involved, rural communities are likely to be linguistically more homogeneous. Literacy is therefore generally imparted in a local language that is the mother tongue of the majority and the current language of communication.

Population movements from rural to urban areas, which are a common phenomenon in developing countries, demand training in rural areas for prospective emigrants and in urban areas for new immigrants. Occasionally a reverse movement—back to the land—is engendered. In both situations adult literacy programs may be called upon to give language instruction, and to make people literate, in the language of the area to which they are moving. Literacy programs for immigrants coming from outside the country may also aim at teaching the national or local language.

Where young people are getting their school education in a language other than their mother tongue there may be a case for giving the parents literacy in the same language as the children. This may help to bridge the gulf between generations and enable parents to prepare their children for school.

A general aim of literacy programs is to create a literate society. It is obviously easier to do this—and to foster social cohesion—in one language than in several, and, if national cohesion is the aim, it is arguable that this can best be achieved through a national language.

Subjective Factors

Apart from the objective factors (psychological and material) there are generally—and perhaps regrettably—also subjective, and often political, influences that bear upon the choice of language for literacy. At their best these may take the form of honest beliefs, for example, that the exclusive use of the national language will break down tribalism and communal discord and unify the country, or, on the contrary, that the use of local languages will maintain a valuable cultural diversity. At their worst such influences may be seen as the tendency of power groups or individuals to suppress minority languages and cultures, or to undermine the influence of a particular language. Such tendencies may be related to political and religious rivalries. The time is not long past—perhaps not quite past—when certain great powers exerted political pressure to influence the language policy of smaller nations in directions that seemed to favor their cultural, economic, or political interests.

Conclusion

These factors will, of course, be weighted differently in each particular situation, but three of them may be considered dominant, for a language cannot be used for literacy until:

1. It possesses an accepted alphabet and texts.
2. Basic teaching and reading materials have been prepared.
3. Teachers who speak, read, and write it can be found, trained, and deployed.

If the learners' mother tongue satisfies these criteria it is the natural choice, either as the sole medium of literacy or as a "bridge" to literacy in a second language—generally the official national language. A policy of teaching literacy directly in the national language may, however, be preferred, in spite of its obvious difficulty, where it will be more functional, where there is strong motivation to learn it, and especially where the school system has established it as a second language of communication.

Insofar as international policy exists on the choice of languages for literacy, it is summed up in Recommendation 2.45 of the World Congress of Ministers of Education on the Eradication of Illiteracy:

"The desirable objective of teaching adults to read and write in their mother tongue first is endorsed, but it is recognised that a multiplicity of languages within one country may oblige that country to base its literacy programme on a single language or on a limited selection of languages."

CHOICE OF LANGUAGES FOR VARIOUS FORMS OF ADULT EDUCATION

There is often a variety of activities and services in developing countries that aim to provide general education and special training for adults. They are described by various names, including "adults," "further," "mass," and "community" education, "extension," "training" (of various kinds), and "community development," which has been described as "both an educational and an organizational process."

From the point of view of language policy we may distinguish three types of programs: (a) preliteracy programs; (b) postliteracy programs; and (c) mass media programs. These may, of course, overlap and mix in a single area.

Preliteracy Programs

In areas of high illiteracy, adult education and training must make use of oral communication, supported perhaps by audiovisual aids. The mother tongue of the people or occasionally a local lingua franca is used. Where the local language is unwritten and no lingua franca is operative, adult education will require bilingual teachers and field workers who can be trained and guided in a language of wider communication, generally the national language, and can then train local teachers and leaders and speak to the illiterate population in their mother tongue. Manuals and other written material may be given to the bilingual teachers and workers in the national language. Where bilingual teachers are not available a program may have to be set up to teach the local language to "foreign" teachers and workers. This may run concurrently with, and be gradually replaced by, the reverse program of teaching a second language to selected local people and training them as teachers and field workers. Happily such situations exist only in remote tribal areas, since some education has generally been available to at least a few children in most of the world's smaller language groups, thus forming nuclei of bilingual literates within the group.

Postliteracy Programs

The term postliteracy is perhaps a little out of date, since the modern strategy for adult literacy programs envisages a simultaneous amalgamation of adult education and training with literacy teaching. The term is, however, convenient to describe programs designed for populations that are at least partly literate and can therefore make use of the written word in combination with other media. One of the crucial requirements of such a program is a continuing, increasing, and varied provision of reading matter, specially designed for adults at different levels of reading ability. (UNESCO has published a useful booklet on this subject entitled *Simple Reading Materials for Adults* [3]). The provision of such reading matter is generally regarded as a vital part of any adult literacy program and the languages used are normally and naturally those used in the literacy program itself. It must, of course, be related to a whole range of adult education and training activities, which may also use oral and visual approaches.

Mass-media Programs

Where the media of mass communication, especially radio and television, are at the disposal of adult education their use extends the range of the program but at the same time raises many problems. Some of these are educational and organizational and not essentially related to language policy; for example:

1. The distribution and maintenance of receivers.
2. The organization of listening groups.
3. The planning and production of programs that carry the desired information and hold the attention of noncaptive audiences.

The last demands close teamwork between educators, various subject-matter specialists, and broadcasters.

Should the media be used:

1. For literacy teaching?
2. For language teaching?
3. For general adult education?
4. For training and guidance of teachers?
5. For technical and vocational training?

In what languages—even in what dialects—should the programs be broadcast?

Should there be a more or less independent program for each selected language, with its own staff and possibly its own local station and transmittee? Or should there be facilities within a national broadcasting system for the translation and adaptation of prototype programs into the chosen language?

The answers to these questions and others like them will vary with each individual situation and will depend on such factors as:

1. The nature of the broadcasting network.
2. What agencies control its policy.
3. The availability of specialist staff, including educators and translators, who can handle various languages.
4. Above all, the budget.

It is also possible that the choice of languages for radio and television broadcasting will be subject to political pressures.

The use of films for adult education in multilingual areas presents fewer problems than broadcasting, since the addition of sound-tracks in several languages, the use of magnetic stripe film or of a live commentary are comparatively easy operations and effectively adapt the film for different language groups. There remains, however, the cost and difficulty of making films that convey the intended message to uneducated audiences irrespective of their language.

The press—essentially the mass medium of the printed word—can play an important part in postliteracy programs and adult education, especially in areas that lack efficient publishing and book-selling facilities. Existing newspapers can carry educational columns or special pages for new literates in the appropriate language or languages, and low-cost periodicals designed for new literates can be produced, published, and distributed. UNESCO has published a useful monograph on this subject [4].

There are those who believe that radio and television can replace literacy; a more rational view is that they should supplement and complement it. If this is the aim, then programs of adult education through these media should be closely related to adult literacy in the same areas, and particularly in the same language groups. This means teamwork and coordination in the production of media and materials and a consequent economy in scarce specialist staff.

THE IDEAL: A COMPREHENSIVE ADULT EDUCATION PROGRAM

Perhaps the eventual ideal is a comprehensive program of adult literacy, adult education and training, making the fullest possible use of current languages, speaking to the people in their mother tongues, helping them to learn other languages they need to know—especially their national language—and conveying essential information and knowledge through all appropriate channels, oral, written, and audiovisual.

The program must have not only an efficient administration and coordinating machinery, making optimal use of various agencies, but also technical supporting services:

1. For research and evaluation.
2. For production of teaching media and reading materials.
3. For training of specialists and teachers.

These three should be related through collaborative arrangements between different agencies, or in a single center, or both. Wherever language problems occur, linguists must be involved in the program—employed in the study and research service, or associated with it.

CHOICE OF SCRIPT

Related to the choice of a language for literacy is the choice of the script—the type of alphabet—to be used in writing it. This again is related to the adaptation that may be needed to fit an alphabet that has grown up with one language to the phonemic structure of another.

There are two principal situations in which a choice of script is relevant:

1. Where a previously unwritten language is to be used for literacy.
2. Where a script actually in use is considered unsuitable and a change is proposed.

Through historical time scripts have grown, evolved and sometimes died, as languages came to be written and went out of use. They have been adopted for, and adapted to, other languages, generally by cultural affinity, peaceful penetration, conquest, or colonization. Nowadays the element of conscious choice is increasingly apparent—a choice that is generally, and probably should be, made by Government, with the technical advice of linguists and educators.

There are undoubtedly objective factors that should influence this choice. Certain writing systems are more—or less—suited to the structure of particular languages; or we may go further and say that certain writing systems are intrinsically superior or inferior. It is even tenable that the human race would benefit from a single accepted alphabetic system, just as it might benefit from a single common language, but such utopian thinking would not even reach the stage of a UNESCO resolution. It is therefore likely that the choice of scripts will continue to operate by cultural affinity—one hopes they will be increasingly influenced by the advice of linguists.

The process of cultural affinity is well illustrated by the following extract from a report [5] prepared by Professor G. Serdyuchenko of the Moscow Academy of Sciences for a UNESCO Seminar on the Planning and Organisation of Adult Literacy Programs in Africa (Tashkent, Uzbek SSR, May 1966):

"New alphabets for Soviet nationalities at first were compiled on the basis of the Latin alphabet. At the end of the 30s the interest in the study of Russian had grown in all the Soviet Republics. At their native language lessons the students studied Latin alphabet while at the Russian language lessons they studied Russian alphabet. It was often the case when they had to spell the same words differently at their native language lessons. This hindered their progress in learning both languages. That is why at the end of the 30s almost all the nationalities of the Soviet Union changed their alphabets on the basis of the Russian alphabet which immediately made it easier for the students to learn their native and Russian languages.

"However, Georgians and Armenians, who had their own ancient alphabets, have preserved them until now. The alphabets of the Baltic area nationalities, Letts, Lithuanians and Estonians, as well as Karelians are at present based on the Latin alphabet."

It is interesting to note that the Uzbek language was written originally in Arabic script, subsequently in Latin, and in Cyrillic.

An interesting recent example of the choice of script for an unwritten language is that of Somalia, whose government requested that UNESCO send a mission of specialists to advise them on the script to be adopted for the Somali language. UNESCO made it clear that the decision must rest with the government and that the international mission of experts would limit itself to reporting on the technical aspects of the question. The report [6] has been submitted to the government and it is expected that a decision will soon be taken as to which script is to be used.

Analysis and Transcription

Where it has been decided to use an unwritten language for literacy there arises the need for analysis and transcription. This task is essentially one for trained linguists; but it is a task in which they must collaborate with educators, publishers, and politicians and must keep in touch with public opinion, since the end product must be a written language that can be used by educators, conveniently typewritten and printed, is endorsed by government, and enjoys wide popular acceptance.

A LANGUAGE COMMITTEE

An effective device to foster this collaboration may be a national or local language committee (or both), appointed by government, including representatives of government, of interested nongovernmental agencies, of religious bodies and, of appropriate institutes and universities, as well as qualified individuals. Among qualified individuals should be educators, literacy specialists, and someone, at least, who knows about the techniques and costs of printing and publishing. It should be an advisory committee, working with the linguist, helping him to obtain support for his proposals or to modify them where necessary, but not diminishing his right and duty to submit an objective technical report to the government, nor the government's right and duty to determine language policy.

BASIC STUDY OF THE LANGUAGE AND DIALECTS

The basic study of the language will include phonetic and phonemic analysis, a description of the grammar, and the preparation of word lists and eventually a dictionary. It will often involve the study of dialects. Mme. Genevieve Calame-Griaule of the National Center for Scientific Research, Paris, comments as follows on this point [7]:

"Given the multiplicity of dialects in most African languages the problem of choice presents itself at the start. Two methods are actually possible:

- to explore in depth one of the dialects in question, chosen for various reasons (e.g., numerical, geographical or cultural importance), while making checks in other dialects, or
- to study all the dialects at once in the same way with the aid of word lists.

"In the present state of the knowledge on African languages, and with the particular objective set by literacy, the second method is preferable. One will not then try to improve one dialect artificially at the expense of others, but to give value to all possible variants which will also allow linguistic unity to emerge from diversity."

Proposals that give preference to any one dialect in establishing the standard form of language are certainly likely to generate a high emotional charge and, where necessary, a language committee may render useful service in gaining their acceptance by politicians and public.

Professor P. F. Lacroix in a document prepared for the Bamako meeting gives valuable advice on the "Study of Basic Vocabulary through Lexical Lists" [8]. In this connection it may also be of help to those who eventually have to prepare graded literacy materials if word frequency is counted—or the most common words are listed—from the recorded speech of the local population.

ORTHOGRAPHY

Perhaps the most crucial stage in the preparation of a language for literacy is the development of an orthography for literacy and general use. Dr. Hans Wolff wrote in "Nigerian Orthography" [9]:

"A good orthography is a writing system which not only is a faithful representation of the spoken language but also a system that can be learned easily. It should have the following characteristics:

"(a) accuracy: no significant sound should remain, without representation in writing;
"(b) economy: only the phonemically significant sounds should be written;
"(c) consistency: every letter or letter combination should stand for the same sound or sounds throughout the system;
"(d) similarity to other orthographies.

"This last criterion applies only when the languages to be transcribed have a very similar phonemic structure."

The Meeting of Experts on the Use of the Mother Tongue for Literacy (Bamako, February 28–March 5, 1966) agreed: "that a balance had to be struck between too much scientific detail and what was humanly consumable" [10]. One criterion for "human consumability" may be that the alphabet should be capable of being typed conveniently (without too much back-spacing for diacritical marks) on a standard typewriter suitably adapted, and of being printed at reasonable cost. A valuable paper on this aspect was presented by M. Jean-Louis Ferru to the Bamako meeting under the title "Possible Repercussions of a Technical and Economic Nature of the Adoption of Particular Letters for the Standardised Transcription of West African Languages" [11]. The Bamako meeting proposed that "factors such as similarity to the alphabet of an international language such as English or French should be kept in mind" and that "symbols should have a similar value in the alphabets of several languages in a country," . . . "such considerations being applied carefully so that they do not violate the basic sound system of the language" [12]. Ideally it would seem preferable that symbols should have "a similar value" in the alphabets of all newly written languages using the same script, irrespective of the country they are in. Is not an approach to universal consistency of greater long-term importance than that new alphabets should be assimilated to the orthographic peculiarities of a particular "international" language on grounds of cultural affinity?

When the government of Niger decided to use Hausa for literacy the National Language Committee adopted a new orthography assimilated to French (the national language). A French specialist, sent by UNESCO at the invitation of the Government to advise them on this problem, proposed a revision of this orthography, which differed only slightly from that used for Hausa in Nigeria. There is thus a hope that a unified Hausa script will soon be attainable. It is in this sense that UNESCO's project for the standardization of African alphabets is now proceeding.

TIMING AND COST OF ANALYSIS
AND TRANSCRIPTION

A factor that gravely affects the choice and use of previously unwritten languages for literacy is the time and money needed for analysis and transcription. The Bamako meeting set this at three to five years' work by a qualified linguist, with specialist assistants, equipment, secretarial help, informants, transcribing staff, and travel, at a minimum cost of $14,500 a year. This is certainly a minimum cost and may well have to be doubled. Fortunately many languages not yet endowed with a working alphabet have been more or less thoroughly studied—or are related to languages that have been studied and written. In such cases the Bamako meeting agreed "that a competent linguist could . . . suggest emergency measures, including a provisional orthography, in a three month period," but that this must be regarded as only a preliminary to further study and essential revision. Some of these costs may be financed from multilateral and bilateral technical assistance, but some will inevitably be the responsibility of the government of the country concerned. In any case the problem of time and cost remains where linguists very properly demand several years for the study of an unwritten language, while literacy planners, under pressure to launch their programs rapidly and on limited budgets, cry out for quicker and cheaper results or decide against the choice of unwritten languages for literacy.

REVISION OF ORTHOGRAPHIES

Very few of the world's languages can be said to possess satisfactory orthographies. The older world languages are generally the worst—English with its chaotic vowel system, French not much better, and Arabic with three forms for every consonant and a rash of diacritical signs. Of the languages that have been written more recently, especially in Africa, few seem to have wholly satisfactory alphabets, and some have more than one alphabet in current use. The case for orthography revision on a world scale seems incontestable, and yet the difficulties of changing one iota of an established orthography are such that governments must be very cautious of embarking even on local language reforms. A radical change such as the adoption of a new script may even be more easily accepted than smaller improvements.

Perhaps the case for revision is strongest:

1. Where there is more than one alphabet in current use in one language.

2. Where a new alphabet is developed in one country for a language that is inconsistently or differently written in another (in the case of Hausa cited previously, the new alphabet adopted in Niger might appropriately lead to minor changes in Nigeria and thus to a standard alphabet for the Hausa language).

3. At times of political, social, cultural, or educational revolution or reform, when change appears more acceptable and even desirable (perhaps there is "a tide in the affair of alphabets" . . .).

Revision naturally demands scientific language study, which not only analyzes the flaws in an existing orthography but provides the basis for proposed changes.

VOCABULARY EXPANSION

Many languages that are still unwritten, or have not been used for educational purposes beyond elementary literacy, are rich in vocabulary relevant to the traditional life and environment of the people who speak them, but deficient in technical terms and terms for modern and abstract concepts. If these languages are to be used for literacy and for further education and training, their vocabulary must be expanded by borrowing foreign terms or adapting indigenous ones. The first alternative presents particular problems where a local language overlaps frontiers and has cultural affinities with two or more national or world languages from which borrowing may take place. The expansion of vocabulary, with the related problem of deciding upon the spelling of adopted words, is another area in which linguists should be called upon to work with educators—and, of course, with indigenous speakers of the language concerned. Here, too, an advisory language committee may have an important role to play.

LITERACY AND SECOND-LANGUAGE TEACHING

A World Literacy Program is being launched to make several hundred million adults literate in several hundred languages. Many of these people will have to become literate in a second language, either because their mother tongue is unwritten or not used for literacy, or because they need to communicate in the second language.

Several possible approaches are open:

1. Teaching people to read and write in the mother tongue and in the second language:

   a. Simultaneously (e.g., using bilingual texts); or
   b. Consecutively (introducing the second language at a later stage).

2. Going direct to the second language, and teaching people to speak, read and write it, either:
   a. By the direct method; or
   b. Using the mother tongue as an oral medium.

Where the mother tongue is an unwritten language there is no choice but (2); where the mother tongue is written but the objective is literacy in another (e.g., national) language, it is by no means proven which of the procedures listed is the most efficient in any given circumstances. Research is badly needed to throw further light on these questions.

The inconsistent orthographies of some languages, such as English, add to the difficulties of teaching them as second languages, especially to illiterate adults. It may be found useful to design an initial teaching alphabet for the second language, which is as far as possible consistent with the learner's mother tongue, and will serve as a bridge to literacy in the standard (inconsistent) form of the second language. Working along these lines, the organizers of a teacher-training project at the University

of Witwatersrand designed a phonetic English orthography to teach
English pronunciation to Bantu teachers.

The difficulties of making adults literate in a second language, even
under favorable conditions, must not be underestimated. In Algeria,
working with highly motivated and disciplined Arabic-speaking workers
in the oil wells, where French is a current working language, it needed
135 half-days of teaching in small groups of 12–15 students, with teachers
trained for 3 months and equipped with voluminous manuals, to achieve
literacy in French with a working vocabulary of 750 words and an acceptable but scarcely correct pronunciation. This indicates what might
be the cost and difficulty of achieving second-language literacy in less
favorable circumstances. Nevertheless, often this must be the aim and
special measures should be taken to expand and improve second-language teaching for adults. These may include:

1. Research to test and develop the most effective methods for various
circumstances.
2. Improved training of teachers.
3. Development of a whole range of graded and programed materials
and audiovisual media especially designed to help speakers of particular
local languages to learn, and become literate in, their national languages,
or any other second language they may need.

The collaboration of linguists will be vital in this field, to advise educational planners and media specialists and to carry out comparative and
contrastive analyses of the languages in question, in order to discover the
difficulties that face speakers of one language in learning another and to
suggest ways of overcoming them.

GENERAL CONCLUSIONS

The main conclusion to be drawn from this generalized survey of language problems and literacy in developing countries is that any national
or local plan for functional literacy and adult education in any multilingual area must have, built into it, a sound language policy and adequate provision for applied linguistics.

At its simplest this policy may take the form of a decision to use only
one official national language for literacy, on grounds of either cultural
unity or economy, though it may be a matter of doubt whether either
of these aims will be truly served. In such a case, various forms of adult
education will probably be provided, using oral communication in the
local languages. Linguists may then be called upon to assist educators,
for example, in preparing materials for teaching the official national
language to those who do not speak it, and perhaps in training teachers

and preparing recorded material and radio programs for oral education and training in local languages.

A more complex, probably more effective, and possibly more costly policy would be to work progressively toward the teaching of literacy in all local languages, except perhaps those of small tribal groups, and the teaching of the official national language as a second language to those who need and want to learn it. Here linguists should be associated with the program at many stages, perhaps as part of a literacy research service and in collaboration with a national language committee. They may be involved in the following:

1. A survey of the extent and distribution of languages and dialects in the country, related to the extent and distribution of illiteracy.

2. A review of linguistic research already done, of the status of each language (existence and quality of its orthography, grammar, word lists, etc.), and its use or usability for literacy.

On the basis of the preceding studies a phased language policy should be embodied in the literacy plan, involving any or all of the following elements:

1. Choice of languages to be used for literacy and adult education, immediately and in the future; indicating when and for what specific purposes such use is proposed.

2. Choice of scripts, where necessary.

3. Linguistic analysis and research on unwritten languages.

4. Proposals for any necessary or desirable revision of existing orthographies and expansion of vocabulary.

5. Proposals for the development and improvement of second-language teaching methods and media where these are needed.

The last three elements would involve specific plans and budgets with provision for (a) the employment of qualified linguists; and probably (b) the training of nationals of the country as linguists and field workers.

The continuing advice of linguists will also be needed in:

1. The preparation of literacy teaching materials in previously unwritten languages.

2. Contrastive analyses and other studies leading to the preparation of programs and materials for second-language teaching.

3. The continuing evaluation of the literacy program, wherever language problems intervene and applied linguistics can improve its efficiency and achievements.

The World Literacy Program will thus call for a very considerable contribution from linguists wherever language problems handicap the progress of literacy in the developing countries. At conferences and meetings, such as those of Ibadan, Bamako, and Yaounde, linguists have accepted the responsibility of applying their science to literacy. Moreover, educators and administrators are increasingly recognizing the need for linguistic support. In May 1966, for example, 40 African literacy specialists at the Tashkent Literacy Seminar adopted a report on African language and literacy that closely follows the recommendations of the meetings in Ibadan and Bamako. Of wider significance again is the text of Recommendation 8 adopted by the International Conference on Public Education at its 28th session in Geneva in July 1965 [13]:

"In countries where a number of different languages are spoken by the population, the government, before launching or extending a literacy programme, may have to decide what language or languages are to be used for literacy in the country as a whole or in particular areas or groups of population; furthermore, where it is decided to use an unwritten language or a language with a deficient orthography or lacking written texts, the important task of studying and transcribing the language and preparing basic word lists, grammar and literacy texts must be entrusted to specialised linguists and educators, who must be given sufficient time to carry out this task before the teaching can begin."

It is important that these ideas should reach literacy workers at all levels and a suggestion is made that a manual on language problems and literacy should be prepared and published for organizers of adult literacy programs, setting out in clear and simple style the requirements and processes of linguistic analysis and transcription and indicating what linguists can and should do for them in the various stages of a literacy program.

NOTES

1. UNESCO (ED/217). World Conference of Ministers of Education on the Eradication of Illiteracy: Final Report. Paris, 1965, 89 pp.
2. UNESCO Document YALING/3 (August 24, 1966).
3. UNESCO. Manuals on Adult and Youth Education. Simple Reading Materials for Adults. Paris, 1963.
4. "Rural Mimeo Newspapers," UNESCO. Reports and Papers on Mass Communication No. 46. Paris, 1965, 42 pp.
5. Prof G. Serdyuchenko, "Elimination of Illiteracy among the People Who Had no Alphabets." U.S.S.R. Commission for UNESCO. Ministry of Education RSFSR. Moscow, 1965, 16 pp.
6. UNESCO Document PP/Consultant. "Somalia: The Writing of Somali." Paris, 1966, 19 pp. (distribution limited).
7. This quotation is from a paper entitled "Problems of Lexicography" (unofficial translation from the original French document UNESCO/CLT/BALING/11, Feb-

ruary 1966, p. 1). The paper was prepared for The Group of Experts on the Standardization of African Alphabets organized by UNESCO at Bamako, Mali, February 28–March 5, 1966.

8. UNESCO CLT/BALING/10.
9. Gaskiya-Zaria, 1954. (Quoted in a Report on the Use of the Mother Tongue for Literacy. UNESCO/MELIT/5 12th December 1964.)
10. UNESCO/CLT/BALING/5.
11. Unnumbered.
12. UNESCO/BALING/.
13. UNESCO Document Minedlit 6. Literacy and Adult Education (recommendation adapted by the International Conference on Public Education, Geneva, July, 1965.). Paris, 1965, 13 pp.

Donald H. Burns

BILINGUAL EDUCATION IN THE ANDES OF PERU [1]

In the Peruvian highland Quechua area [2] of the Sierra States of Ayacucho, Huancavelica, and Apurimac, an extensive though incalculable percentage of the rural population are monolingual Quechua speakers [3]. The area is obviously heavily populated with Quechua monolinguals, with monolingual Spanish speakers limited to a few immigrants from areas other than the one involved in this study. Bilingual Spanish-Quechuas are limited to the urban areas in the zone and there is a very small percentage in rural areas who periodically migrate to the coast or have been educated in the urban areas within the zone. The isolation of these monolingual Quechua speakers, the result of a complicated sociolinguistic picture, constitutes a problem of great concern for cultural, political, and scientific institutions within the country whose desire seems to be the immediate incorporation of this extensive population into the Peruvian national culture [4].

For the linguist, incorporation does not signify the eradication of the campesino's culture patterns and a forced adoption of the Western European standards and patterns, but rather the opening of lines of communication between two sectors of the Peruvian population. The chief concern of this essay is a program that anticipates opening a medium of communication for the Quechua-speaking population on the level of primary education, which is expected to produce a spontaneous and voluntary adoption of new patterns and norms that are considered to be national and Peruvian. The mechanism for this communication is intended to be basically indigenous inasmuch as educational materials are designed in the vernacular, and specially trained teachers, native to the area, are the human medium for their application. The University training program and orientation courses for Normal School teachers hope to contribute somewhat to opening the lines of communication toward the Quechua-speaking cultures.

The area with which this report is concerned boasts a total population of 1,098,200, according to the 1960 census, brought up to date by subsequent bulletins [5]. Approximately 27 percent of the total population of the zone, 296,000 people are of primary-school age. However the total enrollment of children in primary schools, private and public, in this entire zone is 96,093, which means that only approximately 36 percent of the primary-school age children are matriculated in a primary school somewhere in the area. In addition, it is frequently found that the matriculation figure is much higher than the actual number of students in attendance. Since the percentage of primary age children enrolled in school is much higher for the urban area, this means that well over 70 percent of the rural, Quechua-speaking population never even enroll in school. It is to this tragically inadequate educational situation that the program we describe in this report is directed.

It is obvious that the greatest need is to provide schools for rural, Quechua-speaking children, yet even the existing rural schools in the area are often found unable to cope with the sociolinguistic obstacles that prevent them from carrying out what might otherwise be the very important role as a medium for the education and incorporation of this large sector of the country's population. The rural school system is, at least in theory, a Spanish-speaking institution, yet it is ministering to a virtually monolingual Quechua population. Although a high percentage of the teachers of these rural schools are bilingual Quechua-Spanish speakers, the lack of any adequate didactic materials in the vernacular, or a methodology for the teaching of Spanish as a second language, and a certain negative attitude toward the employment of the vernacular language neutralize whatever advantage this factor might be.

THE PROGRAM

In view of this situation the Ministry of Public Education of Peru put into operation in August 1964 an experimental education program based on the use of the vernacular language in the education of monolingual Quechua-speaking children [6]. The program considers two years of special instruction in Quechua (called "Transición Bilingüe") to effect the academic and sociological adaption of the child toward his incorporation in the first year of common primary school. This includes the teaching of reading and writing, the basic concepts and processes of mathematics, oral Spanish, and moral and religious education.

Bilingual teachers are chosen from among candidates of the Quechua-speaking communities who have, to a better degree than their neighbors, overcome the problems of isolation and education. In addition, the program anticipates a special orientation of rural Normal School teachers who will inherit the bilingual educated children and continue their education from the first year of primary school on. During the two-year period of bilingual transition, Quechua is the language of the classroom and Spanish is one of the courses taught. From the first year of primary school on, Spanish will become the language of the classroom and the student will continue reading bilingual materials, possibly for three years more.

In cooperation with the National University of San Cristobal de Huamanga, the Summer Institute of Linguistics assigned the author of this paper to occupy the Chair of Linguistics at the University of Huamanga in 1962 in preparation for the involvement of Peruvian University-trained personnel in the technical and administrative part of the bilingual education program [7]. The graduate students now included in the program were given general linguistics with a structural orientation and seminars in the field of Quechua and in linguistics applied to the problems of education. This personnel, all Quechua speakers, have cooperated in co-authoring most of the materials now being used in the program.

At the present time the bilingual system described in this report is being used in 16 indigenous communities in 3 provinces of the State of Ayacucho with approximately 700 monolingual Quechua-speaking students enrolled. Nineteen bilingual teachers in three different categories of teachers, promotors, and alphabetizers, according to their own educational training and experience, are carrying out the experiment in the communities mentioned.

Didactic Materials

Materials designed, tried, and now revised and published or in the process of being published include a series of four graduated primers in Quechua and two bilingual Quechua-Spanish reading books; a series of four writing and independent reading-builder books; a manual for the teaching of oral Spanish; a text for teaching mathematics using the Cuisenaire-Gattegno method of numbers by colored rods; and a teacher's manual for moral and religious education, not to mention several smaller manuals that establish the programs and step-by-step procedures of teaching these materials.

The primers are based on the psychophonemic method [8], which establishes the principal of understanding what is read by starting from the word and working through syllables to the letters without teaching either of the latter two in isolation or without meaningful context. In Primers 1–3 all of the letters of the phonemic alphabet of Quechua, as well as the resultant syllables, including all possible distribution of these letters, are introduced. In Primer 4 the letters of Spanish, which differ from or are additional to the letters of Quechua, are introduced within the Spanish loans used in Quechua and are written with Spanish orthography in accordance with the custom of the zone. These Spanish loans are first introduced as Spanish words as in a Spanish primer. The following page is dedicated to Quechua text at a level already achieved by the student in the previous three primers, incorporating the Spanish words that are used as Quechua-Spanish loanwords in the speech of the rural Quechua community. Although this type of book contains a heavy load of new letters, it is found that the child has by now overcome the problems of basic reading and because of the very light addition of anything new in the Quechua reading section, the student is able to focus his attention on the mastery of these new letters and syllables. Care is taken in this primer that the Spanish pages are read with Spanish pronunciations. Of course, no such care is observed on the Quechua pages where the Spanish loans are used within the phonological and semantic scope of Quechua.

First and second bilingual readers are designed to amplify the reader's capability of manipulating the heavy load of suffixes, characteristic of Quechua, in a natural and interesting Quechua text. Each page is bilingual, the upper part dedicated to Quechua and the lower part to Spanish. The alternative of making every other page Quechua and Spanish has not yet been experimented with. The Spanish text is a culturally equivalent translation of the Quechua text and a small bilingual dictionary, Spanish-Quechua, is found at the end of each reading book.

The themes chosen and developed within the readers are autochthonous to the monolingual Quechua-speaking communities of this zone, and special care has been taken to avoid unpleasant and vulgar double-meaning words, which are prevalent in Quechua. Review for the reader is built into the series of primers and readers so that they can become as autodidactic as possible. Suffix substitution drill has proved both interesting and helpful to the children in learning to manipulate the hundreds of thousands of possibilities for each verb and substantive form.

These materials are beautifully illustrated by Peru's famed mural artist, Dr. Teodoro Núñez Ureta.

Writing books are composed of two sections: the first part segments the words into syllables by the visual contrast between words the student has read in the primers. This permits the introduction of the syllable, not in isolation, but as a part of a meaningful unit which the student pulls out of words arranged according to the syllables they have in common. The second part consists of writing exercises starting from the simple stroke to cursive writing of all of the letters of the Quechua and Spanish orthographies for children who have never before held a piece of chalk or pencil in their hand.

The text or manual for the teaching of oral Spanish, the most difficult course by far, is designed to substitute to some degree for the lack of Spanish-speaking environment that is the rural, monolingual, Quechua-speaking child's lot. Eight units of dialogues and grammatical exercises have been developed in an attempt to cover the vocabulary of Grade 1 of the urban primary school level and to acquaint the student with the Spanish pronunciation and meanings of the Spanish vocabulary introduced in Primer 4 and ensuing readers. Exercises that must be presented only orally have proved the most difficult part of this course both in designing the materials and in teaching the course.

Because Quechua uses a rigidly decimal numerical system, the Cuisenaire-Gattegno method for teaching mathematics by colored rods was found to be very applicable [9]. The children need only to learn 10 numbers, a word for hundred, and a word for thousand and they have all the number system necessary for learning basic mathematics. Eleven is "ten-possessing-one," 20 is "two-tens," and there are no exceptions to the system. The children identify the rods first by color and then by numbers and learn the concepts and processes of addition, subtraction, division, and multiplication, later transferring that knowledge to the written figures that correspond so beautifully to the numerical system in Quechua. The flannelgraph and flash cards are used to introduce the printed numbers and to relate them to the colored rods. The use of the colored rods bridges very nicely the lack of number-concept experiences for children in communities where there is neither money nor clocks and takes them to the abstraction of mathematical processes and symbolization with a minimum of effort. The children after two years of bilingual education have had no difficulty in advancing well beyond the math achievement requirements for Grade 1 in common primary school.

The teacher's manual for the course of moral and religious education consists of a bilingual rendering of the Scripture portions of the Old and New Testaments called for in the official Plans and Programs for the level of transition. The Spanish portion appearing in the manual and on which the Quechua translation is based is the modern Roman Catholic Version of Nacar and Colunga. The first chapter, on the theme of creation, coordinates with the teaching of basic astronomy concepts related to the sun, earth, and moon and the meaning of day and night, month, year, and the eclipses.

The Communities Selected for Experimentation

With the exception of one community on the periphery of the city of Ayacucho, all of the communities participating in the experiment have the following common characteristics: (a) they have never before had a school in the history of the community; (b) they are composed of illiterate, monolingual Quechua speakers, (c) they have manifested some concrete interest in the establishment of a school by either having constructed the locale or adapted for the school existing buildings within the community, and (d) they presented a formal request for the establishment of the school to the office of bilingual education. To avoid as much as possible misunderstanding as to the nature of this program, the program team visits the community prior to responding to a formal request. These requests frequently come to the office with nothing more than index fingerprints for signatures, both by the authorities of the community and by the parents. During this visit the special system of education is explained to the parents. The drive the Quechua campesino has toward the acquisition of Spanish for his children makes it difficult for him to understand why Quechua should be used in the schools. The "different" nature of the bilingual school system needs to be thoroughly explained since there exists a clear image in the mind of the campesino of *how* a rural school should function and just *what* it should teach. A demonstration of the psychophonemic method is given; this always ends in enthusiastic participation by the men and women of the community as they realize that in just a few moments with the use of illustrated flash cards and flannelgraph they are able to actually begin to read.

The Bilingual Teacher

The teachers chosen for the experiment, who are often suggested by the communities themselves, are of varied backgrounds and levels of academic preparation. However, all of them have the following traits: (a) they are Quechua speakers with Spanish as a learned, second language, (b) they have primary education, (c) they have given some evidence of their capacity for teaching, and (d) they are intimately associated in some practical way with a rural community and have received its approval and recommendation. The training of these teachers is carried on at a special six-weeks course, "Curso de Capacitación para Maestros Bilingües de la Sierra," which is held in a rural community with all of the teacher candidates living in. Courses both morning and afternoon and special study and discussion periods in the evening keep the teacher fully occupied during the entire six weeks. Teaching is done primarily by practicing rather than by theoretical presentation, and the course curriculum includes the teaching of reading, writing, mathematics, oral Spanish, moral and religious education, school administration, and Spanish. In the first five courses mentioned, the teacher candidates learn to manipulate the didactic materials, and in the school administration course they learn to fill in the forms and manipulate the controls that are used to maintain an adequate supervision of individual student progress and the teacher's capabilities and success. In the final course mentioned, the candidates are taught the outline and vocabularies for documents and official communications which teachers must prepare on behalf of their communities and in correspondence with the office of bilingual education and other official entities of the country. Attention is also given to the improvement of the candidates' command of spoken and written Spanish.

MEASURABLE RESULTS

Graphs and charts that have been prepared showing the individual progress of the student demonstrate that the average and slower-than-average students have very little problem in completing the first four primers and respective writing books and the first four units of the oral Spanish course in the first year of training.

The older and more alert students are able to cover considerably more than the requirements of the first year of bilingual transition, and it is possible that some would be capable of moving into the first year of primary with only one year of bilingual transition. This possibility, however, has not been pressed, since once the older students are pushed on into the higher grades it is anticipated that only six-year-olds will be matriculated in the bilingual courses and hence attention is primarily focused on this age level.

In 1967 the first group of bilingually prepared children were confronted with the first grade of primary- and normal school-trained teachers. It is considered premature to judge the effectiveness of this aspect of adaptation, although the enthusiasm and ease with which the bilingual students both absorb instruction and express themselves is felt to be markedly superior to the ordinary rural school transition levels in which Spanish is virtually the only medium of instruction. The program has begun a study of the actual achievement at the transition level, both in the urban area of Ayacucho and in three rural villages to establish an accurate point of reference.

Absenteeism, naturally increasing during the periods of planting and harvesting, has been considerably less than what is observed to be the norm of this almost exclusively agricultural zone. Difficulty in obtaining adequate statistics on this factor, of course, is due to the status of the rural schoolteacher and the security of his job. It should be noted that attempts to adjust the school calendar to a more realistic distribution of study and vacation were totally rejected by parents because of the rural school image they possess. Vacation periods, both in summer and winter, correspond to those periods of greatest inactivity in the community and hence greatest possibility of taking advantage of the student's presence in the school. Harvest and planting correspond to the beginning and ending of the school year, critical times for establishing correct attitudes toward the school and completing the children's education. At the present time it is not considered possible, however, to alter this picture until the distribution of the bilingual schools is much greater and a new image can be established.

As the second year of bilingual education draws to a close it can be established that in this period of time a very adequate level of achievement in reading, writing, and arithmetic can be achieved through the use of the vernacular and that an adequate mastery of Spanish for use in the classroom at the first grade level can be achieved, making the normal school-trained teacher's task of incorporating the child into the plans and programs of public primary education to be less arduous, though somewhat different. The primary-school teacher will only need to cement the child's capacities and control of reading, writing, and arithmetic and will need to focus the principal part of his preparation of the student in the field of expanding the child's control of spoken Spanish. Social science studies will need to be introduced in this first year of primary with bilingual materials which are now in preparation.

Until social, political, and economic circumstances change the isolation of the rural, monolingual Quechua speaker, the instruction of a second language will necessarily be limited in its success. The substitution of a Spanish-speaking environment will be difficult until roads are opened and commerce begins in direct contact with the campesino.

PROBLEMS

Some problems not anticipated included the duplication of the creation of schools in some of the communities selected for the experiment. In some cases, duplicate teachers, one a bilingual teacher and the other a common primary school teacher, were assigned to the same community, creating conflicts of varying sorts. Ample cooperation, however, was achieved from other departments of the Ministry of Education, eliminating this duplication but not without, in some cases, affecting the general functioning of the bilingual school. Again, the image of the rural school predominates in the mind of the campesino and he is leary and suspicious of anything that varies from this image.

The primary school system in which most of the bilingual teachers received their training has been a very rigid memory-by-rote, writing-on-the-blackboard, copying-in-notebooks affair. To alter this concept to one of communication between the teacher and the student and independent thinking has not been thoroughly established in all cases.

Preliminary orientation of the community has, in some cases, proven inadequate. This is especially true where the community of the bilingual school is less isolated than others, and the image of the functioning of a school is more clearly established. It is found that greater success is assured when a greater number of the factors mentioned as requirements for communities and teachers are met.

THE FUTURE

The Ministry of Education, under the able and progressive leadership of Ministers of Education of the present and previous administrations, has demonstrated a determination to cope with the special sociolinguistic problems facing the education system of Peru by means of special programs. In the budget for 1967, the nation considered expanding the bilingual experiment to 25 communities with a resultant increase in the number of teachers. A special pay-rate schedule was considered by the Ministry to incorporate these bilingual teachers into an adequate official relationship with the Ministry reflecting their education and experience. With the obvious need for an increase in rural schools to cope with the lamentable statistics cited early in this essay, it is probably no exaggeration to anticipate the hundredfold expansion of the program in the Department of Ayacucho alone. Materials prepared for this dialect will be applicable in the states of Huancavelica and Apurimac with a minimum of dialectal adjustments necessary.

The incorporation of bilingual transition into the existing framework of primary education within the country and within the area affected will no doubt take years and a good deal of careful effort. A course "Specialization in Bilingual Education" is being prepared and it is hoped this will help prepare normal school-trained teachers to be oriented to the basic problems of language and culture that affect their work in rural Quechua-speaking areas. The University of San Marcos, in cooperation with Cornell University and with financing through the Ford Foundation's program of linguistic promotion, "Fomento Lingüístico," is carrying out a special program for the development of techniques for rural education and rural teachers, which it is hoped will complement on a level higher than transition the work of the bilingual experiment.

More adequate attitudes of government agencies toward both the Indian problems in Peru and the linguistic obstacles facing education have been seen in the establishment of these programs and in the officialization of the Quechua language by the Ministry of Education and the assertion repeated by the Ministry in several recent official documents of the advisability of the use of the vernacular languages in the primary phases of education. There also exists a sizable group of "Quechualogos" who faithfully beset official entities advocating officializing and promoting the use of Quechua and Aymara in educational and national programs.

It is anticipated that when the experiment in Ayacucho is completed, if the results referred to here can be established as adequate and desirable, the bilingual system for the levels of transition will be incorporated in a general way for the Puno, Cuzco, Junín, Huánuco, and Ancash dialects as well. At the present time linguistic teams have been assigned to two other dialect areas for the preparation both of analytical work and didactic materials.

NOTES

1. For bilingual education in the lowland tribes of Peru see Gamaniel Arroyo and Donald H. Burns, *Educación Bilingüe y Desarollo de La Communidad en el Perú*, paper presented at the V Congreso de Indigenistas Interamericano, Quito, October, 1965. A preliminary sketch of this report was presented at the Congreso Interamericano de Lingüística Filología y Enseñanza de Idioma in Montevideo, January, 1966.

2. This area composes one common dialect of Quechua which is usually called the dialect of Ayacucho, and which is only one of seven existing "dialects" of the Quechua trunk in Peru. To some extent the sociolinguistic picture described in this paper reflects the other areas of the Sierra dialects of Ancash, Huánuco, Junín, Cuzco, and Puno.

3. Census data, based on the national census of 1959 and 1960, contain very scanty details regarding the linguistic picture in the zone. Even so, the number of Quechua speakers is listed as 500,000 + for the three states.

4. See *Informe del Plan Nacional de Integración de la Población Aborigen—Planteamiento del Problema Indígena, Realizaci ones Enero 1962–Junio 1963*, Ministerio de Trabajo y Asuntos Indígenas, October 1963, Lima, Peru; *Plan Nacional de Integración de la Población Aborigen* and subsequent reports for 1963–1964; Gonzalo Aguirre, B., *Integración Regional*, Manuales Técnicos No. 3, *Plan Nacional de Integración de la Población Aborigen*, Ministerio de Trabajo y Asuntos Indígenas, 1964, Lima, Peru; *Desarrollo de la Communidad y Servicios Conexos*, Manuales Técnicos No. 2, *Plan Nacional de Integración de la Población Aborigen*, Ministerio de Trabajos y Asuntos Indígenas, Lima, Peru, 1964; Carlos, Monje M., *La Vida en los Altiplanisias Andinas: Procesos Ecológicos*, Lima, Peru, 1963. In these materials, the Peruvian national culture is defined as urban, Criollan, Spanish-speaking culture ("Euro-American"), typified by Lima. Other Peruvian culture groups are referred to as marginal, although they admittedly compose some 50 percent of the country's population. For a unique treatise on this subject see Luis Lumbreras, *Clases Sociales en el Perú*, Universidad Nacional de San Cristobal de Huamanga, Ayacucho, Perú, 1966.

5. See Boletines de Estadística Peruana, Ministerio de Hacienda y Comercio, Dirección Nacional de Estadística y Censos, 1960–1964, Lima, Peru.

6. Ministerial Resolution of August 1, 1964.

7. At that time we were more interested in the investigation rather than the application aspect of the problem. However, the Ministry would not permit us to postpone the applied program as we requested because of the urgency felt by the then Minister of Education, Dr. Francisco Miro Quesada.

8. See W. Cameron Townsend, *Psycho-Phonemic Method of Primer Construction*, Summer Institute of Linguistics; Sara Gudschinsky, *Handbook on Literacy*, Summer Institute of Linguistics, University of Oklahoma, 1960; and Sara Gudschinsky, *Recent Trends in Primer Construction*, Vol. XI (1959) No. 2 (UNESCO). Flannelgraph and flash cards are used during the first two weeks of reading class to introduce the concepts of idea-to-figure, figure-to-word, word-matching and finally reading by matching word to figure.

9. See C. Gattegno, *Arithmetic, A Teachers Introduction to Cuisenaire-Gattegno Methods*. Cuisenaire Company of America, New York, 1961, 75 pp.; and John V. Trivett, *Mathematical Awareness*, Part I, Revised Edition, Cuisenaire Company of America, New York, 1962. Cuisenaire and Gattegno, *Numbers in Colors*, Cuisenaire

Company of America, New York, and Gattegno, Pupil's Books (ABCD78910) also referred to in Trivett's text, were not available at the writing of this paper. Also Donald H. Burns, *Runasimi y la Enseñanza de Matemáticas*, Revista Ayacucho, Agosto 1965.

Lyndon Harries

SWAHILI IN MODERN EAST AFRICA

This essay discusses the role of the Swahili language in providing African linguistic expression for East Africans in the modern context. The status of Swahili in contrast to English in East Africa is considered. Reference is made to the earlier expansion of Swahili under influences from Southern Arabia and the Persian Gulf, an expansion comparable in some measure to the modern expansion under influences from the West. Some of the problems occurring in the process of modern linguistic adaptation and change are indicated, especially with reference to the need for resolving the status of Swahili on a long-term basis.

THE GENERAL SITUATION

The term *Swahili* properly applies not to an ethnic group but to a cultural group, a stratified society belonging to the coastal civilization of East Africa, following an Islamic way of life. In the modern context Swahili is usually a linguistic term applying to the lingua franca spoken by perhaps as many as 25 million people all over East Africa from Somalia to Mozambique and as far west in the Republic of the Congo as the townships of Lubumbashi (Elisabethville) and Kisangani (Stanley-ville). In its extended use the term Swahili has only secondary reference to the Swahili culture and language of the coast, since the lingua franca today is orientated toward the Western world rather than toward its traditional centers of origin.

The language is spoken on many different levels, but we shall consider standardized Swahili developed first from the dialect of Zanzibar township (the Unguja dialect) and now strongly influenced by speech forms in Dar es Salaam (the Mrima dialect), the capital city of Tanzania. The language enjoys great status in East Africa, not least because of the multiplicity of other languages. In Tanganyika alone there are more than 100 languages. In Kenya, although Swahili is spoken as a first language along the coast and many Kenyans know and speak a form of

Swahili, individual languages like Kikuyu and Luo are spoken by many more people than are tribal languages in Tanzania, and the majority are influenced by their mother tongue and by English more than by Swahili.

The language has been subject to many differing judgments in the past, even by those who wished for its promotion, chiefly because of its association with Islam and the slave trade. For example, the Lutheran missions from 1890 on were strongly opposed to the use of Swahili, because they believed that the African must be reached first emotionally, through his tribal existence. "Tribal languages were the key to this evangelism and the enemies were the detribalizing influences and subversive religious ideas tied up with Swahili" [1]. In 1956, the then Secretary of the East Africa Swahili Committee wrote: "The language has none of the advantages of being able to appeal to sentiment and national pride" [2]. This was a reasonable point of view at that time, but with the coming of political independence African leaders saw in the Swahili language a unifying factor, and its use was encouraged by official action as being first and foremost an African language capable of strengthening the cause of nationalism. Swahili was adopted fervently as the national language of Tanzania and received added prestige not only as an African language capable of overcoming the linguistic diversification of East African countries, but also as a language capable of world status. Subsequent broadcast programs in Swahili from Washington, London, Moscow, Peking, and New Delhi were evidence of the East African presence in world affairs.

Since independence, controversy has continued as to the relative merits of Swahili and English in East Africa, and it may be true to say that the status of both languages has been strengthened. The enthusiasm for Swahili has not diminished the use of English in East Africa, chiefly because in the higher levels of education English still has precedence, and the influence of this language tends to spread downward from the top. On the other hand, the adoption of Swahili as the national language of Tanzania has undoubtedly increased the prestige of the language, though official support in favor of its extended use does not in every case correspond with its actual extension in current usage. Perhaps the most important factor in the development of Swahili is its new orientation toward the West and the consequent diminishing linguistic influence of Arabic.

THE RETREAT FROM ARABIC

Swahili has sometimes been described as "a compromise between Arabic and Bantu" [3]. There is ample evidence that previously mainland Africans regarded Swahili as something of a foreign language, and the Swahilis were in no haste to disillusion them in this respect, because they were proud of the Arabian connection. The Islamic content gave prestige to Swahili in the regard of mainland Africans, and for the Swahili people themselves repudiation of the Arabic linguistic connection was tantamount to a repudiation of Islam. For political reasons relating to the expulsion of the Sultan of Zanzibar in 1964, modern East Africans tend to resent the suggestion of any kind of compromise with the Arabs. It is not surprising to find statements that play down the Arabic linguistic connection, and such statements come even from Swahilis who under different circumstances could legitimately claim some Arab descent. The Shirazi, who opposed the Omani Sultan, have always regarded themselves as distinct from the *soi-distant* Arab Swahili, but as their name suggests they have been known to claim an early *emigre* Perso-Arabian descent. With the rebellion of Zanzibar the Shirazi identified themselves with the African cause, dissociating themselves from the Arabian connection. On the Kenya coast the desire to be classified as Arabs under the colonial regime was much stronger, due to British favoritism, than in Tanganyika, so it is of special interest to find a modern Swahili from Mombasa, one of the northern Shirazi, writing to emphasize the essentially African character of Swahili. The writer, a zoologist, explains that Arabic words were merely superimposed on the matrix of Bantu structure. "In biological terminology, one would say that the so-called hybridization is not and never has been a genetic process affecting the form and structure of the language, but a phenotypic manifestation related to function" [4].

Modern Africans, whether Swahilis or not, are right in rejecting the idea that Swahili is a compromise between Arabic and Bantu because the evidence shows that the language is basically Bantu in structure, although heavily weighted with words of Arabic origin. With the end of Arabian influence in East Africa, there was a marked change of attitude toward this Arabic content of Swahili. Whereas previously it had been a matter of prestige for mainland Africans to use words of Arabic origin, now such words were to be eschewed. The late Sheikh Amri Abedi, Minister of Justice in Tanzania and a leading mainland Swahili translator, told this writer that if a word was needed for translational purposes they would prefer to adopt a Bantu word from up-country rather than go to Zanzibar to find a word of Arabic derivation. The African character of Swahili must now be emphasized, but as in other countries—Iran, for instance—the attempt to replace Arabic words by indigenous equivalents coincided with the complete, and in some instances unknowing acceptance of words of Arabic origin. Ironically, East Africans eagerly adopted the word *Uhuru*, "Freedom," as a slogan in the struggle for independence, unmindful that the word derived from Arabic, the language of those who had enslaved their forefathers.

The complete Bantuization of Swahili vocabulary is, of course, an impossible task because in most instances the Arabic borrowings filled a lexical gap in the original Bantu languages of the coast. If the lexical gap has been filled in East African mainland languages, it is usually by a secondary borrowing from Swahili. There is no East African Bantu language that does not owe at least some debt to Swahili vocabulary, a debt that can be fully acknowledged only by reference to the original borrowing into Swahili from Arabic. But the urge to Africanize the Swahili language corresponded with the desire to Africanize the political administration after independence. It may not have been generally understood that for many years before the achievement of independence the process of Africanization had been going on in the Swahili language. For instance, Swahili poetry created by the Seyyid families from the Hadramawt in the seventeenth and eighteenth centuries became Africanized in the nineteenth century. The early poets were mostly Hadramis who would have preferred to retain their Arabic verses, but who had to come to terms with the stronger Bantu environment in East Africa by providing at first interlinear versions of the same poem in both Arabic and Swahili. Gradually the Arabic versions were discarded, because so few people could speak Arabic. As in so many other parts of the world the religion of Islam extended farther than its spoken language. In the nineteenth century the subject matter of the poetry was no longer exclusively Islamic propaganda but embraced many aspects of African contemporary life. The majority of Muslims who were Africans showed little interest in Arabic as a possible medium of daily communication, but they continued to show great interest in Swahili as an African Islamic language.

The fall of the Zanzibar sultanate marked the end of Arabic-inspired Swahili for East Africa, at least as a continuing process. But even before this on the mainland the Swahili promoted and used by Western educators had less Arabic content than in the coastal centers of Islam. The application of Islamic law to every aspect of African life on the coast meant a far richer legal vocabulary from Arabic than was ever needed, for example, by the Christian missions. The general influence of the missions, even in places like Zanzibar, was to diminish, at least for their converts, the use of borrowings from Arabic, though the converts, mostly of tribal origin, felt that they were being introduced to a wider vocabulary than that of their tribal language. Furthermore, the missions were orientated toward the tribal, non-Muslim peoples of the mainland. In the schools a simplified Swahili was taught and used, and for general purposes the trend was toward a simplified, standardized language reflecting more or less the current usage of Swahili-speaking Africans not living in a Muslim area.

Reference to Sacleux's valuable Swahili-French dictionary [5] shows the richness of Swahili vocabulary in its coastal, Islamic setting where Swahili is the mother tongue. This vocabulary is largely dependent for its continuation upon the survival of the traditional Swahili way of life, and since that way of life, with its emphasis upon contacts with southern Arabia, is inimicable to the changes in modern East Africa, much of the vocabulary suitable to earlier conditions must be discarded. Already some Swahili translators, engaged in translational projects but schooled in deep Swahili, are fighting a rear-guard action by claiming that "Swahili already has a word for it," usually a word of Arabic derivation familiar enough to people at the Islamic coast, but unfamiliar to non-Muslims who may prefer a borrowing from English.

SWAHILI OR ENGLISH?

The decision to make Swahili the national language of Tanzania was more a decision of intention than of fulfillment. Obviously the choice between Swahili and English was not a choice between two languages of equal status in the modern context. The decision implied that Swahili was potentially capable of becoming a national language in the fullest sense, but not that it already could fulfill its new role in every sector of national activity. Professor Weston, Dean of the Law School at Dar es Salaam University College, has written:

"In the month of Tanganyika's independence, December 1961, the Minister of Education called together a committee of Swahili experts, which also included expatriates experienced in law and administration, to report on the measures necessary for making Swahili the national language in a modern, rapidly developing state.

The problem was a sizeable and complex one, for Swahili was, until independence, relegated to a very lowly position. Its teaching in schools was left in the main to second-rate teachers working with third-rate materials, and not a single important aspect of national life was carried on in Swahili. And yet all the leaders and the great mass of the population were far more able to express themselves in Swahili than in English. In order to reverse the disabilities and to unite the people under a single language tied in with their common culture, it was essential that Swahili should become the national language in every aspect of national life" [6].

In contrast to the lowly position of Swahili, the English language was being used in all of the higher levels of national activity. The idea of Swahili being "tied in with their (the Africans') common culture" is to be interpreted in its broadest sense of African culture in its modern setting, and bears no relation to any particular African culture, least of all Swahili culture. This "common culture" is itself a modern phenomenon which, so far as I am aware, has never been much discussed by East Africans themselves, and has certainly never been described or identified. The wider context of national politics and administration made it necessary to think and speak in broad generalizations, and one of the most popular African generalizations after independence was that Swahili was an African language, but that English was the language of the colonial rulers. If at all possible, preference would be given to Swahili. If at all possible—and the government of Tanzania would set out to make it possible—Swahili would replace the English language. It remained to be seen how far this would come about.

In Tanzania the general assumption is that Swahili is in fact the national language; for this reason debate on the relative merits of Swahili and English is regarded by many as a retrograde step. In Kenya, however, where the question of a national language is still an open issue, though in fact English is generally preferred, the debate has continued in the national press. The arguments for and against the use of Swahili in higher education, in preference to English, have been well set out by Dr. Mohamed Hyder in his article already quoted in this paper. While accepting the relevance of the viewpoint that the immediate introduction of Swahili as a medium for instruction in the higher levels would be impracticable, he maintains that "it has never been our aim that the situation should be perpetuated." He writes:

"By passively accepting English as the medium of intellectual activity, we are unwittingly placing a barrier to the intellectual development of our peoples. We are unconsciously inflicting the same malady that the great bulk of the so-called intellectual elite of East Africa suffers from— namely, of being almost completely incapacitated to undertake any serious thinking in our own languages. This kind of mental and spiritual stagnation is a direct, but long-lasting effect of colonialism.

"Another thing which is wrong with the perpetuation of the present set-up is that by having English as a medium of thought and Swahili as a medium of the masses, we are encouraging the development of class on the strict basis of the English-speaking intellectuals and the Swahili-speaking workers and peasants. This development is a negation of almost consistently all the species [sic] of African socialism that have been pronounced" [7].

It can be seen that the statement about the incapacity of the African elite to undertake any serious thinking in their own languages is some-what at variance with the statement in the quotation from Professor Weston's article that all the leaders and the great mass of the population were far more able to express themselves in Swahili than in English. These are generalities which need to be broken down if they are to be made valid. What, for example, is meant by "serious thinking" in this context? But from the published literature in Swahili it would seem clear that Dr. Hyder is right—even though this spoils his general argument, for it is plain that the cultural status of progressive East Africans is not reflected in what has been written in Swahili.

Dr. Hyder attributes this to the effect of colonialism, and he may be partly right about this, but there are more cogent reasons why East Africans do not undertake any mature writing in their own languages. Although Swahili is rightly considered to have a much wider contextual range in the written word than any other East African language, it is typically lacking in serious creative writing by individuals. This is a feature of African vernacular literature anywhere south of the Sahara. Apart from the practical difficulty of finding a publisher for work in a tribal language, a factor not applying so much to Swahili, the simple truth is that African writers have failed to dissociate their vernacular writing from the immediate African sociological background. The best-known writers in the vernaculars naturally write about what appeals to their own people, and although they may claim that this does not prevent them from expressing general human values, the foreign reader who knows the vernacular is more likely to find literary features characteristic of folk literature than of creative writing by individuals.

This is true of Swahili literature where Swahili is the first language. With a few exceptions, creative writing in the vernacular by African writers for whom Swahili is a second language simply does not exist. Even during the colonial period various agencies encouraged creative writing in Swahili, but the response was most unsatisfactory. The reasons for this literary barrenness were sociological, not linguistic. Under the colonial system of indirect rule, East African societies to a large extent remained closed societies, and the art of writing was never an African cultural activity. The unique literary tradition of Swahili poetry was introduced by the Arabs, and even to the present day this art retains stylized conventions which make it quite distinct from free creative writing in the Western sense.

Since the reading matter available to the vast majority of East Africans remains limited to religious tracts, simple school texts, folk tales, proverbs, and the occasional thriller, the literary outlook in the vernaculars is not very encouraging. At the same time we find in East Africa a desperate shortage of educational opportunity combined with a pressing urge to develop at express speed. This has meant an enormous increase in the appetite for reading material. In Tanzania there is a national language without a national literature. It is not surprising therefore that the educated elite do most of their serious thinking and reading in English. Some may not wish to perpetuate this situation, but it is difficult to see how in the foreseeable future they can change it. The President of Tanzania translates Shakespeare's *Julius Caesar* into Swahili, and this is rightly claimed as evidence of the linguistic capacity of Swahili; but so many more works still remain to be translated, and so many more, with a creative African context, still remain to be written.

At the time of independence it was widely believed that the East

African countries Tanzania, Kenya and Uganda would form a political federation, in which case the value of a common language, Swahili, would be greatly enhanced. Since independence, however, the prospect of federation has receded further and further. This affects the status of Swahili in all three countries, and not least in Tanzania. It becomes increasingly unrealistic for Tanzania to take official unilateral action for promoting Swahili at the highest level so long as Kenya and Uganda act differently on the matter. It seems unlikely that Uganda will ever take official action to make Swahili the national language. With federation, this might possibly have happened, but Uganda is no doubt the chief opponent of federation. In Kenya the matter is in abeyance, for although the use of Swahili is encouraged, English is becoming more deeply entrenched in education and government. Allowing for tribal differences within Kenya and Tanzania, the two countries have much in common. The common heritage provides a reason for a common decision on the linguistic issue, but it also makes the Tanzanian decision more difficult to fulfill in practice.

The East Africa Common Services Organization operating from Nairobi is retained in spite of the growing divergence between the three countries, and its extensive and important business is conducted in English. The common ties between Kenya and Tanzania cannot altogether be severed, and so long as they remain the decision by Tanzania to make Swahili the national language cannot be only a domestic issue.

The Tanzanian decision to make Swahili the national language implies the rejection of English for the same purpose, but in fact English is not so rejected, except perhaps in name. It has been suggested that the tenacity with which the British and Americans hold to their own language has been a factor in the spread of the English language. "For if the English-speaking peoples would not learn a foreign language, it is evident that foreigners, to trade with them, had to learn English" [8]. But foreigners do not have to learn Swahili in order to do business with Tanzania. The Russians and the Chinese normally use English in their dealings with Tanzanian leaders and businessmen. This is something for which the British colonial administration cannot be blamed, for in the absence of English speakers trained by the British to speak English—a lack for which the British would most certainly have been blamed—Tanzanians would perhaps be in a better position to insist that only Swahili should be employed. The most that the Tanzanian leaders can do is to Swahilize certain sectors of national activity which hitherto have been conducted in English and which are part of the domestic scene. Inevitably Swahili has to be made internally a truly national language before it can be meaningfully promoted as such to the outside world.

THE WORK OF TRANSLATION

For mass media, the work of translation into Swahili has greatly increased since independence. This applies especially to Kenya and Tanzania, besides the foreign agencies concerned with the dissemination of information and propaganda in Swahili. In this work of translation, linguistic invention often has precedence over the normal process of linguistic usage, since the imperative need is for the immediate adaptation of foreign terms and concepts. The question has been asked: does Swahili possess a sufficiently large vocabulary for it to be capable of the degree of specificity required of a language by cultural and intellectual people? The answer is that if Swahili-speaking people have the opportunity to assimilate a culture different from their own, their language is capable of any degree of specificity required. The problem is that for the general population no such cultural assimilation has yet taken place. Only the people at the top can claim to have assimilated, and in some instances in practice this means not assimilation but emancipation from African cultural ties. For the people at the top, however much assimilated, to make linguistic decisions without regard to the general linguistic situation outside national boundaries is as unwise as for them to make political decisions without regard to the general political situation.

Take, for example, the project initiated by the late Sheikh Amri Abedi, Minister of Justice in Tanzania, who formed a committee in August 1963 to compile "a law dictionary" in Swahili. The project has been described by Professor Weston, and a member of the committee, in his article already mentioned in this paper [9]. The first function of the Swahili legal terms ratified by the committee is to enable the existing statutes, which are all English-law oriented, to be translated into the national language. When the missions adopted new words or put new meanings into old words, they had the time and the opportunity to teach the meanings, but when the modern journeyman translator is faced with the immediate necessity of translating, say, some article dealing with a foreign activity like ice hockey or television production, he usually has neither the time nor the opportunity to explain what his newly coined terms (coined by himself) really mean, nor can he wait until the people have understood what he is writing about and made their own linguistic adaptation. With reference to the "law dictionary," however, the legal people would follow missionary example. It is intended that the Faculty of Law at the University in Dar will have the responsibility of introducing those students who will be practicing in Swahili to the Swahili legal vocabulary prepared by the committee, and "there is a certain amount of rote learning to be done when the vocabulary is introduced." This means rote learning of the meanings attributed by the committee to Swahili words and phrases in a legal context.

If the committee is agreed as to what the Swahili equivalents should be, it may be thought that people in the legal profession in East Africa would be grateful for their suggestions and automatically accept them, but certainly some will have doubts about the interpretation of some of the Swahili terms listed. For example, Professor Weston states that the most common solution for coining a new word was "the logical development in Swahili from an appropriate verb stem." He means here the use of extra separable extensions of the radical to modify its meaning, for example, passive, reciprocal, reversive. But this is by no means "a logical" development in Swahili or in any other Bantu language. The modification of meaning, although for any given extension generally the same, is not "logically" predictable, so that it may not be true, as Professor Weston states, that all of the words "logically developed" by the committee are "abundantly clear" in meaning to any Swahili "as soon as he hears them." Professor Weston is careful to state that this process of "logical development" is not regarded by Swahilis as "coining words," but rather as "the natural functioning of language." However, it is reasonable to doubt if the purposeful application of a so-called "logical development" by a committee who already know the English form can be legitimately described as a natural linguistic function.

Professor Weston writes: "To expect the courts, in interpreting a particular Swahili word or expression, to turn to English precedents, would be to reduce the language to the second-rate position of having no separate existence independent of its English equivalents, and to assume that the draftsman's mental processes must inevitably start in English and then translate into Swahili." But since the mental processes of the committee itself have largely followed this direction, and since it will be necessary to teach by rote the meanings attributed by the committee, it is only to be expected that the courts must for some time to come turn to the English precedents. Not only legal textbooks dealing with English common law but textbooks dealing with East African customary law continue to be published in English. The plain fact is that for the majority of legal terms borrowing is inevitable, either from Arabic or English, and since the mental processes of most modern East Africans have easier reference to English than to Arabic, English has the advantage in this respect.

Although the intention of the committee is to use simple, modern language to popularize an understanding of the law, they admit, or at least Professor Weston does, that a complete understanding by the layman is impossible, not least because of the definite limit of connotation of terms in the legal context. The committee's intention is to strip the law of "its occult science garb," but this is unlikely to happen, for in any language the meaning of many legal terms is not self-evident but is interpreted by legal experts. It therefore may not matter very much whether the Swahili terms are adequate equivalents as long as the legal experts are satisfied that they know what the Swahili terms are meant to represent. Legal terminology in any language is something of a closed shop, even more so when it is made up by a committee.

As Sapir wrote: "Language is a complex inventory of all the ideas, interests and occupations that take up the attention of the community" [10]. The attention of the East African community is not at this time greatly drawn to such ideas as *fee tail, primogeniture,* or *dower,* but if a committee at the Ministry of Justice decides to invent Swahili equivalents in order to be able to say that the particular concept does not exist in East African law, no one is going to object. The main problem at the Ministry is that "East African law" has its source in English common law and is not yet Africanized. It is distinct from "Swahili law," which is based on the Islamic legal system and for which there is a fully adequate Swahili vocabulary with many Arabic borrowings. The translators of East African law are ready enough to borrow words of Arabic origin from the Swahili law, but they prefer to limit English borrowings to the minimum, a limitation that is not matched in current usage by the Swahilis themselves.

MODERN TRENDS IN SWAHILI

The ideas, interests, and occupations of many in East Africa have reference to the world in which English is the chief medium of communication. It is a commonplace that they live in two worlds. Educated East Africans may often be heard switching from one language to another, Swahili and English, when conversing among themselves. There are some things they feel can be properly expressed only by using one language or the other. English borrowings are made at almost every level of Swahili speech. Popular literature in the press, short stories in *Kiswahili cha kihuni,* "the Swahili of the bums," with modern themes of crime, sex, and booze, are full of English words and phrases. Wherever people are sure of their Swahili, they are not afraid to borrow. The committee on legal translation has references to "English, the language of the administration of the colonial government." Professor Weston writes that English "has bastardised the Swahili language with a whole host of terms for which adequate Swahili words exist or could readily be developed." It is the old story of the purists at a time of linguistic expansion. The common people, and especially those with an ample vocabulary of adequate Swahili words, love to expand their language by assimilating English borrowings. This is history repeating itself, but now many Arabic borrowings have to give way to English borrowings. This is linguistic history in the making, for after the retreat from Arabic comes the advance toward English. In neither case need the basic African structure of the language be affected adversely—at least not as long as the advance toward English is made from where Swahili is best represented.

Lexical expansion by incorporating English borrowings proceeds apace in the mass media and in Swahili speech, two fronts mutually related. Even in the modern setting it is still true that coastal Swahili acts as a check, or as a standard for the more off-beat Swahili occurring away from the coast. It is generally considered that in comparison with many tribal languages Swahili is an easy language. What Swahili lacks on a comparative basis, however—such as grammatical or lexical tone, vowel-length— it makes up for by its deceptively simple syntactical structure and by its extended vocabulary. Swahili syntax is far more regular and complex than would at first seem to be the case. It has been suggested by some European Bantuists that it is impossible to categorize Swahili syntax, because for anything that may be said the opposite may be cited as conflicting evidence. If this were really so, then surely the situation would be quite unique. But this judgment is superficial and may result from the fact that often linguistic informants, even in Dar, are people for whom Swahili is a second language. Even this qualification has to be qualified further, because it does not mean the same thing for all such informants. For some, like the Bondei and the Shambala, Swahili, though technically a second language, is like a first language, for they speak it almost exclusively and they speak it well. For others, like the Yao or the Chaga, Swahili is further removed. The higher the status of the first language, the more unlikely it is that the speaker will use Swahili validly. American research students have returned home with material that vitiates many of their findings, because their informants have convinced both the students and themselves that their Swahili is valid, whereas it departs from forms acceptable to those for whom Swahili is the mother tongue.

This confusion of linguistic usage is the consequence of linguistic expansion, and, of course, something can be said for claiming a validity for departures from the norm, but only when these have common acceptance within a group or community. So often the variants are idiolects. Experience in marking Swahili examination papers written by Africans has shown that it is possible to associate particular areas, as in parts of Kenya, with particular variants, but otherwise in the changing situation it is not always possible to identify a particular variant as characteristic of speech practice within a group. This leads to the view held by some that in Swahili "anything goes." The question is even asked: What is Swahili? The answer is: The mother-tongue of the Swahili people, and in its modern expanded usage it has its foundation still on the East African coast, particularly in the townships of Zanzibar, Dar es Salaam, and Tanga. There, as further north, the basic Bantu structure was strong enough to maintain itself against the powerful influence of Arabic, and it will do the same against the modern influence of English.

It may be that we overemphasise the importance of foreign influence upon the basic language. The missionary Binns who lived for 40 years on the East African coast and who in 1925 published a revision of Krapf's Swahili dictionary, wrote in the preface to his revised edition: "In doing this work I have been astonished at the number of words which one never hears used, and it is a marvel how Dr. Krapf got hold of so many of these. I should think that nearly half of the words in this dictionary one hardly ever hears." The same would probably be true of any good dictionary, because current speech may reflect only a fraction of the complete lexis of the language. More important perhaps is the basic structure of the language, and so long as Swahili has reference to its proper environment it seems unlikely that the variation from normal syntactical patterns, influenced often by English patterns as found in modern journalese, will have any lasting adverse effect upon the language. Some observers have doubts about this. As a lingua franca, particularly in Nairobi, they see Swahili away from its moorings, but the most that can happen is the evolution of recognized departures from the norm, and these will be of equal interest to the linguist and will not affect the speech of monolinguals on the coast.

It is readily accepted that these considerations involve value judgments concerning grammaticality. The tendency among American research workers in the Swahili field to prefer the synchronic method of analysis leads to the exclusion of value judgments, since it is taken for granted that all utterances have, at least for the scholar, the same validity. But it is not necessary even on the synchronic level to seek confirmation of the grammaticality of a Swahili utterance by depending on the value judgment of the native speaker, for there are other points of reference. A Swahili utterance may be appropriate outside the Swahili coastal community, although the same utterance may be inappropriate within that community. Reference only to the first community has only a limited significance within the general Swahili field, and the limitation should be, but sometimes is not, clearly indicated.

When Stigand wrote his book on dialect changes in Swahili [11] in 1915 the range of variation he recorded from the coastal dialects was hardly any more extensive than what could be observed today in the Swahili of some rural communities on the mainland in Kenya. Since Stigand's time, much more has been recorded of speech behavior in Swahili coastal dialects showing the wide divergence from standard Swahili. The Makunduchi and Tumbatu dialects on Zanzibar island are widely different from standard Swahili in grammatical forms and in lexis. The same standards of reference have to be adopted whether our concern is with a coastal dialect or with a type of up-country dialect, but except for the more obvious divergent speech-types like Kisetla (the Swahili of the European settlers) or Kingwana (the Swahili of parts of the eastern Congo), the various types of mainland usage of the lingua franca have all been dignified by the name *Swahili*. This gives an authority to divergent types, whether in speech or the written word, which reference to standard Swahili would at least place into perspective and make comparative.

We recognize that standard Swahili is in some degree an artificial dialect of the Swahili language, influenced strongly by the written word, but at least it is rooted in identifiable forms of coastal speech. Mainland Africans learn their Swahili at school from standard forms. In describing the lingua franca in its different main types, or even in describing coastal dialects, reference has to be made to standard Swahili. In the article "Sociolinguistic Research in Africa" reporting the conference sponsored by the Africa Research Committee held in January 1966 at Palo Alto, California [12], the welcome suggestion is made of a research project in the Swahili-speaking areas of Africa, and a detailed description of the subjects for inquiry is provided. Some of the subjects suggested for inquiry have been adequately dealt with in the literature on Swahili, but there is much scope for inquiry into Swahili linguistic repertoires in the urban areas, on linguistic interference by a first language—this would involve intimate knowledge of both languages—and psycholinguistic aspects, particularly in Dar es Salaam. The report states: "The project would involve a detailed dialectal survey of Swahili itself, contrasting the indigenous coastal varieties with the secondarily developed up-country varieties." Such a contrast would serve no useful purpose. Any contrast should be with standard Swahili, or between coastal dialects and standard, or between up-country varieties and standard. There are important sociological reasons for not contrasting coastal dialects with up-country dialects, quite apart from the linguistic gulf which can be bridged only through standard Swahili.

In the past many statements about the future of Swahili have proved to be wrong, so one hesitates about prophesying the scope of its future development. Certainly the future of the language was never so full of promise as at the time of achieving political independence, but since that time political events in East Africa have not brought about any significant official boosting of the language outside Tanzania. Since all three countries are developing in the same general Western direction, it may become increasingly difficult for Tanzania to maintain its intention to make Swahili a national language at every level. A common language would have helped to unite the three countries, but a separate language, even when it is an African language, may only serve to emphasize political separation. However, as a lingua franca on the domestic level there can be no doubt that modern developments have expanded considerably the range of Swahili in all three countries.

NOTES

1. Marcia Wright, "Swahili Language Policy," *Swahili, J. Inst. of Swahili Research,* **35, 2** (1965).
2. W. H. Whiteley, "The Changing Position of Swahili in East Africa," *Africa,* **26** (1956), p. 343.
3. A. B. Hellier, "Swahili Prose Literature," *Bantu Studies,* Vol. XIV, No. 3 (1940).
4. Mohammed Hyder, "Swahili in the Technical Age," *East Africa Journal,* **11,** 9 (February 1966).
5. Ch. Sacleux, *Dictionnaire Suahili-Francais,* Paris, 1939.
6. A. B. Weston, "Law in Swahili—Problems in Developing a National Language,' *Swahili, JISR,* 95, 2 (September 1965).
7. Mohammed Hyder, *ibid.,* p. 9.
8. Stuart Robertson and Fred Cassidy, "World English," pp. 73–81 in John Rycenga and Jos. Swartz, *Perspectives on Language: An Anthology,* 1963.
9. A. B. Weston, *ibid.*
10. Edward Sapir, "Language and Environment," *American Anthropologist,* 14(1912), 228. Reprinted in *Selected Writings of Edward Sapir,* Berkeley, Cal., 1949, pp. 90–91.
11. Stigand, *Dialect Changes in Swahili,* Cambridge, England, 1915.
12. *African Studies Bulletin,* Vol. IX, No. 2 (1966).

Robert B. Le Page

PROBLEMS TO BE FACED IN THE USE OF ENGLISH AS THE MEDIUM OF EDUCATION IN FOUR WEST INDIAN TERRITORIES

This essay is concerned primarily with certain fairly specific language problems that beset the educational systems of the former British West Indian territories of Jamaica, British Honduras, Guyana (formerly British Guiana), and Trinidad and Tobago. It is concerned secondarily with relating these problems to the wider interlocking complex of demographic, economic, political, and cultural matters that affect them.

The political expectations aroused by independence have not all been fulfilled; what is particularly noticeable in Jamaica, and may become more of a factor in the future in the other territories, is that the expectation of greatly increased social mobility through education has been frustrated and that frustration may well lead—as in the case of the Ras

---

A fuller version of this report was addressed to the British Council, at whose invitation I undertook a seven-week tour of schools and colleges in Jamaica, British Honduras, Trinidad, and British Guyana in March and April 1966. The report is, however, not based solely on the observations of this tour, but rather on 10 years' teaching and research in the field of English language and linguistics as a member of the University (College) of the West Indies from 1950–1960, on the work of the Linguistic Survey of the British West Indies, which I directed during that period, and of the work of the friends and colleagues who collaborated with me in that work: F. G. Cassidy of the University of Wisconsin; Louise McLoskey; Beryl Loftman Bailey now of Yeshiva University, New York; David De Camp of the University of Texas; Jan Voorhoeve of the Bureau of Linguistic Research of the University of Amsterdam; Jack Berry, now of Northwestern University and his colleagues then at the school of Oriental and African Studies in London; Robert A. Hall, Jr., of Cornell; Douglas Taylor of Dominica; Morris Goodman now of UCLA; R. Wallace Thompson now of La Trobe University, Melbourne; and former students now on the staff of the University of the West Indies or teaching in West Indian schools, notably Miss Jean Creary and Dr. Mervyn Alleyne.

Tafari[1]—to energies being diverted into less productive channels than those the educational process could, and ought to, provide.

In several of the territories the starting point or impetus for a renewed inquiry into the language problem in education was the concern felt at the very high failure rate in the English-language paper, which is taken at the ordinary level of the General Certificate of Education as set by the University of London, or at the equivalent examination of the Cambridge Overseas Examination Syndicate. Passing one of these or an equivalent examination is in most cases the passport to a Civil Service job, entry to a training college or to the University, entry into one of the professions or into technical training courses. In short it acts rather like a sluice gate controlling the flow of manpower into the educated roles that should provide the dynamism for the economic and cultural growth of the countries concerned.

The reason for the failure rate will be examined shortly, but we should first consider why these territories continue to rely for such an important function on examinations set and marked in an overseas country such as Great Britain. The answer to this question is partly administrative and partly psychological. The suggestion has been made many times since the establishment of the University College of the West Indies in 1947 that it or some allied body should take over from the English universities the role of chief examiner for the schools, just as in West and East Africa local examination syndicates have been or are being formed to take over this role. I understand that exploratory discussions are still going forward as to the establishment of a Caribbean Examinations Syndicate. Certainly it seems to me that such a step is essential if the problems we are concerned with are to be dealt with. However, the establishment of machinery to run such examinations is costly both in clerical and secretarial resources and in terms of recruiting a body of well-qualified examiners. No single territory feels very happy about handling the problem on its own, although in Jamaica there has been for many years a local examinations board. Unless the Caribbean examinations syndicate were set up under the aegis of a body such as the University of the West Indies there would, I think, be a good deal of suspicion on the part of the people of one territory that examiners from another territory were almost as remote from them as those in England, but without the virtues that detachment brings.

The Cambridge Overseas Examinations Syndicate, like its London counterpart, is from an administrative point of view a highly efficient body with many years of experience in this work. There is a kind of certainty about its operation that many West Indians would be unhappy to sacrifice. *What it does not have is examiners with experience of the*

[1] A "back-to-Africa" sect in Jamaica which proclaims the Emperor Haile Selassie as its (unwitting) leader.

*linguistic differences between West Indian speech and English speech,
West Indian accepted usage and English accepted usage.*

TABLE 1. *Achievement in London G.C.E. "0"-Level in Various Subjects, 1962*

Subject	Barbados Entry	Per-cent Pass	Guyana Entry	Per-cent Pass	British Honduras Entry	Per-cent Pass	Cyprus Entry	Per-cent Pass	Jamaica Entry	Per-cent Pass	Trinidad Entry	Per-cent Pass
English language	150	10.7	2483	19.6	24	21.0	286	21.3	661	19.4	1521	23.1
English literature	91	24.2	1245	21.5	1	0	79	43.1	46	13.0	349	12.3
Geography	34	0	409	39.8	0	0	129	45.0	51	13.7	366	14.2
History	77	29.9	1167	34.4	3	0	118	33.1	41	4.9	145	23.4
French	52	15.4	113	19.5	0	0	24	75.0	16	25.0	229	11.4
Pure maths (syll. A)	45	8.9	898	24.6	5	60.0	179	43.0	135	7.4	659	17.3
Biology	13	23.1	344	20.3	0	0	93	25.8	103	14.6	140	12.9
Physics	5	60.0	90	31.1	0	0	63	49.2	38	18.4	97	20.6
Chemistry	8	37.5	119	27.7	0	0	63	33.3	52	7.7	107	20.6

Taken from *Germanacos Report on Trinidad*, Appendix H, Table IVb, p. 107; British Honduras Department of Education Statistics supplied by that Department.

Table 1 shows the comparative success achieved in five West Indian territories as against those for Cyprus, in a range of subjects taken at the London General Certificate of Education Ordinary level examination in 1962. I do not think that a scrutiny of these figures, however minute, will yield any valid general conclusions. I know very well from experience in the West Indies and in Southeast Asia that the presence of just one outstanding teacher in a school may make a quite disproportionate statistical difference in the academic record of that school, and that when the good teacher leaves the record may slump in an equally disproportionate way. The examinations referred to are those toward which the secondary schools concentrate their efforts; the language problem here is at least measurable. In the field of technical education it is not measurable, but I believe it to be far more acute. First, those same attitudes which lead to concentration on an academic role for the schools, and to overseas examinations as the gateway to a white-collar job, lead also to contempt for the sociocultural environment and language of the potential artisan and technician. Second, they inhibit any kind of rational study of the language barrier that is in the way of producing the technicians so urgently needed in the West Indies.

The result of their settlement history, coupled with the contact situa-

tions in each territory, has been that the four territories share a sociolinguistic situation in which a Creole version of English is spoken at
one end of the social scale and an educated variety of English with distinctive regional characteristics at the other end. A high proportion of
the inhabitants in each case are bidialectal in that they have a command
both of broad dialect and of the educated dialect. Within the West Indies we can make a tentative division among the Creole-English-speak-
ing territories between those whose dialects are most closely related to
Jamaican Creole—and this includes British Honduras—and those whose
dialects are most closely related to Bajan[2]—and this includes Trinidad.
The second group must be subdivided between those islands where Creole French has been spoken until replaced by English and those where
this was never the case. Where Creole French has been replaced by English
—the Windward Islands and Trinidad—to a large extent the people
learned their English from Barbadian schoolmasters. For complex historical and sociological reasons Creole French has been retained much
longer in some islands than in others—it has virtually disappeared in
St. Vincent, is rapidly disappearing in Trinidad and Granada, but is
still widely spoken in St. Lucia and Dominica. In the case of Guyana
it is possible to distinguish pockets of Jamaican settlement from the
areas under predominantly Bajan influence.

In British Honduras the problem of Creole is complicated by the
"Black Carib" (a Creolized version of Island Carib)[3] spoken along the
coast from Stann Creek to Punta Gorda, by the Maya and Kekchi of
the Amerindians, and by the Spanish infiltrating steadily from Guatemala and Mexico. In Trinidad, Spanish is a small item in the inventory
of complication; the Creole French patios of previous generations is now
giving way to Creole English, which in turn is full of Creole French
loanwords and has also been influenced by the Tamil and Urdu of East
Indian estate laborers. In Guyana again, Tamil and Urdu are only just
disappearing on the estates, to be replaced by a Creole English slightly
influenced by Dutch. Characteristically the Creole vernacular may be
described in terms of interference between West African linguistic structures and those of seventeenth century English, with continuing subsequent influence from the English of the day as a model language, and
from other languages of the region through contact.

The problem for most West Indian children in the Creole-English-
speaking islands is not that of foreign-language learners of English or
native speakers. Their Creole speech has no *literary* norm other than
that of standard English; but as a spoken language it has its own phono-

[2] The Creole speech of Barbados.
[3] See Douglas Taylor, *The Black Carib of British Honduras*. New York: Viking Fund,
1951.

logical, grammatical, lexical, and semantic structures, which differ, often quite sharply, from those of the spoken dialects that underlie the standard usage of the textbooks and of the examiners. But neither the teachers nor the children are equipped to recognize the differences. Instead of being able to keep the two systems separate, therefore, the children try to make one composite system out of the vernacular they know in their homes and the model language they are supposedly taught in school; the result naturally satisfies nobody—not even the children themselves, for whom it remains an artificial construct. The problem is greatly intensified by the fact that so many of the teachers are untrained, unsure of their own command of the model language, and therefore poor teachers of it.

The agency that should form a bridge between the research being carried out at the University of the West Indies and the teacher training colleges, which are themselves the bridge to the primary schools, is the University's Institute of Education. The University's Department of Education, through its postgraduate training of teachers and its contact with secondary schools, should be the bridge between the research workers and the secondary schools. But there have to date been very considerable psychological barriers to overcome in making effective use of the linguistic research so far produced. It is necessary next to have a look at the situation in the schools and at these psychological barriers.

The demographic information relevant to the school situation in the four territories under consideration may be briefly summarized. The population is increasing very rapidly in each case although there are signs that in Trinidad and Tobago at least the rate of increase is beginning to lessen. Each territory has a very high proportion of young people in its population and the demand for school places increases year by year. The school-age population projections are fallible but at least serve to give an indication of the size of the problem. If it were not for large-scale absenteeism, which itself leads to loss of continuity and a wasteful use of teaching resources, many classes in Jamaica would be completely swamped. Not only are the territories faced with the problem of providing very large numbers of additional primary school places— when in some cases, as in Jamaica, they have not even enough places for the existing children—but in addition they are committed to educational programs which rest on the concept of equality of opportunity and they must therefore try to provide secondary education for a very much higher proportion of their primary school children than achieved it in the past. Formerly the bulk of secondary education in the West Indies had been provided by church schools of one denomination or another and was fee-paying; this meant that children from middle-class homes benefited, whereas very few from poor homes did. Today in each territory the Gov-

ernment offers scholarships or free secondary education based on a
selection process at 11, with the following results:

1. If the selection process is based on language skills—even if only
incidentally—it is biased in favor of middle-class and urban children.

2. If, as in Trinidad, a very determined effort is made to avoid dependence on language skills in the selection, children from poorer homes
may enter the secondary schools with a very poor command of that
dialect of English in which they are taught and examined. Trinidadian
primary teachers have complained to me that they "no longer have any
incentive to teach good English because it's not in the examination";
other teachers, however, as was intended, see the new process of selection
as an opportunity for genuine educational reform.

3. Some secondary teachers blame the primary-school teachers for
sending them children with a poor command of English. There is a
grain of truth in this criticism, since in the West Indies as in other parts
of the world the rate of wastage and turnover in the teaching profession
is much higher than it used to be. Some primary-school teachers blame
the secondary-school teachers, saying in effect "In the past we only sent
them a handful of pupils, highly selected for their verbal skills, so that
they have never had to teach English as a language and are not equipped
by their training to do it." This is on the whole a fair statement. Many
of the older teachers in both the primary and secondary schools blame
the "decline in standards" (although they are not comparing like with
like in assessing this decline) on the loss of the old-style "rule-and-birch"
teaching of "grammar." Again, there is a grain of truth in what they
say, since the reaction against this style of teaching on the part of the
linguistically-naive educationists led too often to the total abandonment
of all attempts to teach "grammar," and to the idea that one could in
some mysterious way learn a language without learning the grammar.
The educationists themselves—indigenous and imported "experts" alike
—have lacked the basic training in linguistics that would have enabled
them to assess the situation correctly.

A great many of the older generation of primary school teachers—and
this category necessarily includes a high proportion of head teachers—
stubbornly refuse to recognize the problem as a linguistic problem at all.
With many this takes the form of insisting that, "though of course there
is the Creole or Patois, that's not what we use in the school, which is as
good English English as you'll find anywhere." They display many of
the attitudes satirized by H. L. Mencken in *The American Language*:

"[Pickering's] theory is still entertained by multitudes of American
pedagogues. They believe as he did that the natural growth of the language is wild and wicked, and that it should be regulated according to

the rules formulated in England. To this end they undertake periodical crusades against 'bad grammar,' the American scheme of pronunciation, and the general body of Americanisms. . . ." [4]

I was assured on my recent visit by at least one headmaster in Jamaica, one in Trinidad, and a Training College lecturer in Guyana that the teachers all used "English English" in the classroom and as their natural speech. To those who know the true situation this statement may well sound incredible. It is nevertheless to be understood against the whole background of the emotional and psychological capital which such teachers (and others of their generation) have themselves invested in the acquisition of "the best English" by copybook and rule-of-thumb methods as the road to middle-class status in a colonial society in which in the past gradations of "color," social class, and dialect have tended to be covariant. One middle-aged woman has told me that her own father, intent on raising his children in a respectable, middle-class way, lost no opportunity of making them recite in mnemonic form the rules of grammar and the relevant examples—if she woke up in the night this exercise took the place of counting sheep to get to sleep again. She is still able to recite the rules today. Very often the teachers are themselves unaware of the extent to which and the ways in which educated and acceptable West Indian usage differs from English usage. I tried out on most of my school-teacher audiences this sentence:

If you let your house, the tenants don't care the garden as you would yourself.

I very rarely received a correct answer to the question: How does this differ from English usage? In most cases, the only admission of difference was in "accent."

The teachers *are* in most cases aware of the fact that the vernacular of the lower-middle-class and working-class homes is different from the language they are supposed to use in the classroom, but they are not able to formulate in any methodical way where the differences lie or what they are due to—they describe the vernacular as "bad talk" or "patois." Understanding the structure of the vernacular means giving a dignity to something you have been taught to regard as the essence of the undignifiable. The tendency to fall back on narrowly prescriptive "rules" as a means of teaching English is reinforced by the fact that most of the younger primary-school teachers are very unsure of their own command of the language and really use a good deal of vernacular in the classroom. One very specious headmaster, in a large, modern, comprehensive school in a very poor part of Jamaica, introduced me to his teachers as follows:

[4] *The American Language* (Fourth Edition), New York: Alfred Knopf, 1960, p. 51.

"Ladies, there is no doubt that we must *eradicate* the *bad talk* of our children, and the answer to this problem is more and more attention to the *grammar*—they *must learn* the *grammar,* there is *no substitute* for the *grammar,* and Professor Le Page is here to say something to us about this."

But as I spoke of the need for studying the grammar of the Creole vernacular his face dropped and his manner toward me at the end of my talk was remarkably cool. It has long been stated in the West Indies that Creoles have no grammar; they have just "bad talk."

For the children, the psychological results of these attitudes are very bad. In the first place, children from urban or better-class homes start with an even greater advantage than otherwise, and children from rural or poorer homes have even more of a defeatist attitude than otherwise because of obvious linguistic discrepancies. This is of course almost universally so. Second, an excessive amount of time tends to be devoted to the development of language skills. Third, this is done in a very prescriptive and stereotyped way and is largely unproductive. Fourth, as a result two things happen: many children are inhibited from any kind of creative expression at all; and the prizes go to the best mimics rather than to the most talented, *so that in any sample of secondary-school children who have come up from primary schools, or in any sample of undergraduates at the University of the West Indies, there is far too high a proportion of mimics who lack real creative and critical ability.* These results are common in situations where children are being educated in a language other than their own first language.

Physical difficulties in West Indian schools stem from overlarge primary classes (120 on the roll in one class of one school in Jamaica) mitigated only by large-scale absenteeism; old and unsuitable school-buildings, many of which lack any partitions whatever between classes (it is not at all uncommon to find many hundreds of children in one huge room, the classes separated only by a blackboard); a great lack of readers and reading material; and an acute shortage of trained teachers. It must be remembered that the untrained teachers frequently used are most often pupil teachers with no formal training at all, although a small proportion may have received a crash training course, which in Jamaica, at Caledonia College, currently lasts only three months. As to books, in most cases the children have to pay for them, and the small sum involved—perhaps £3 a year—is beyond the means of many poor parents, so that frequently only one child in three has a reader. Where books are made available on a hiring system far more children have copies.

The Minister of Education in each territory must be able to convince his Treasury colleagues and his Prime Minister that investment in education is essential to the economic future of the country. If he cannot do so, or if he lacks political prestige, vote-getting power, or status in the Cabinet, then Education's share of very limited resources will be less than it should be. The reports of the UNESCO Educational Planning Missions under the chairmanship of Dr. C. L. Germanacos in 1964 and 1965 have resulted in Educational Planning Units being set up in the four territories and should in time result in the available resources being spent more rationally than hitherto, but all too often the civil service cannot provide adequate staff for the Ministry of Education, for the Inspectorate, or for the Planning Unit itself. Only in British Honduras, where the problems are comparatively small scale, did I have the impression that the civil servants I met were, by and large, competent to cope with the job that needed to be done. In both Trinidad and Jamaica the teaching profession in general seemed to be in despair at the failure of the Ministry of Education to respond competently to communications—from schools, training colleges, parents, or teachers.

It is no exaggeration to say that a sizable portion of the money at present being spent on education in the West Indies is being wasted through failure to appreciate and to deal with the basic problem of communication. *If the primary-school teachers can be helped to use the available time more efficiently—by understanding the true nature of the situation, by devising teaching methods to cope with it, by being sympathetic and encouraging to children from vernacular-speaking homes —more time will become available for extended reading and for creative writing, and the whole educative process in West Indian primary schools will benefit.*

The linguist as such can do nothing to help with most of the physical difficulties mentioned. All he can do is help the teachers make the most efficient use of the resources that are available to them and point out the likely results of neglecting his advice. These are, in short, the progressive divergence of the *medium* of instruction in West Indian primary schools from any educated *model* dialect of English—whether this is educated southern English English, or educated midwestern American English, or educated West Indian English of the kind now fairly uniformly used and understood throughout the former British West Indies. In other words the former elite—trained and taught by expatriate speakers of English and finishing their education in American or Canadian or British colleges while the indigenous secondary educational system left 95 per cent of West Indian children untouched—will be swamped by the new situation. Much larger numbers of teachers will be required, will themselves start their training as native speakers of a more divergent dialect, will be trained by West Indians instead of expatriates, and will stay in the West Indies for their training instead of going overseas. Unless the resources for the teaching of English are more rationally and intensively used, the gap between what is supposed to be happening in the schools and what is actually happening will get steadily wider. The problem must be tackled in the primary schools, and *it is through improving the training of primary-school teachers that the greatest impact can be made with limited resources.*

It will be difficult, but I am convinced it is necessary, to persuade the respective Governments that a specialist post in English language teacher-training should be established for each training college and that *these posts should carry terms and conditions of employment comparable with those of a university lectureship.*

It is essential that these specialists have a thorough basic training in linguistics, psychological and sociological aspects of linguistic behavior, the psychology of language learning, the processes of creolization, the principles of contrastive analysis, and the structure of the languages involved in their situation (e.g., Creole English, Creole French, English, Spanish, Maya). They must also be trained in the general principles of education, in the preparation of teaching materials, and in the use of audio-visual aids, radio, and television.

In addition to training primary school teachers to understand and cope with the language problems of their pupils, such specialists should be given further tasks, and the means to carry them out:

1. To improve the trainee-teacher's own command of and confidence in educated English usage. For this purpose, language laboratories should be provided in the training colleges.

2. To prepare teaching materials closely related to the West Indian environment, graded relative to the child's ability, and making use of contrastive analysis to help the child overcome interference and to keep the systems of educated usage separate from those of his native language —Creole, Patois, Spanish, Hindi, or Maya. The use of the Initial Teaching Alphabet should be explored further.

3. To retrain existing teachers, by means of refresher courses or vacation courses, to bring them into sympathy with new ideas wherever possible.

4. To cooperate in setting up the most effective radio and television language teaching for schools.

I mentioned earlier that continuity was essential in any remedial program. The specialists who are trained should be bonded to serve their Government for at least three and preferably five years *in the job for which they have been trained.* (I understand that one of the ablest West Indian graduate linguists, currently working on St. Lucian patois, is to be assigned to the Trinidad Diplomatic Service on completion of his doctorate!)

Only by providing continuity in enlightened teacher training courses, so that two or three generations of teachers imbued with the new outlook are to be found in the schools, can one guard against a relapse caused by the reaction of older generations of teachers and head teachers to new ideas.

It is probably unreasonable to expect any real change of outlook on the part of the older teachers, although the retraining suggested may at least make them more tolerant of ideas that can only really be put into effect by a younger generation free from the psychological conditioning the older ones have suffered. But my experience in the past has been that where one of my former students was on his own in a school, the pressure upon him to conform to the ideas of the Headmaster and older members of staff was too great to resist; where two or more were together, they gave each other moral support and were able to achieve a great deal more.

The syllabus in the Teacher Training Colleges and in the schools also will need to be changed. The Institute of Education of the University of the West Indies has a very heavy responsibility in this respect; it can only be discharged by staff of the highest calibre.

SUMMARY

1. In the West Indian territories under discussion (Jamaica, British Honduras, Guyana, and Trinidad and Tobago) the lingua franca, and native language of the vast majority of the population ["the vernacular"] is a creolized form of English. The usage of educated West Indians, and of West Indian schoolteachers ["the medium"] retains many features of this Creole particularly at the phonological and lexical levels, although many educated West Indians are unwilling to admit that their dialect differs at all from "English English" ["the model language"].

2. The education system of each territory lays great stress upon a command of the model language, and the main avenue of advancement for West Indian children is by passing the Cambridge Overseas School Certificate or London General Certificate of Education at Ordinary level, with English language as a compulsory paper. The failure rate in this paper, however, is between 70 and 90 per cent. The reasons for the failures arise to a large extent out of the failure to recognize the problem posed for the vernacular-speaking child.

3. Among those who pass what is essentially an examination in an alien dialect here is too high a proportion of "clever but uncritical noncreative mimics." Among those who fail are many whose talents are desperately needed in the West Indies but wasted by the failure to get further training.

4. The situation has other unfortunate side-effects which restrict social mobility and lead to political discontent.

5. For complex psychological reasons there is a certain unwillingness, among the older generation at least, to recognize the linguistic element in the problem. It is in any case greatly exacerbated by the economic and political problems of the region.

6. The process of description of the Creoles is under way and must be encouraged to continue, but already enough has been done to be applied in the training of schoolteachers. The best help that can now be given is in the training of language specialists who should be attached to the Teacher Training Colleges under the aegis of the Institutes of Education of the University of the West Indies and the University of Guyana. Concurrently, the examination structure for West Indian schools and the syllabuses of the Teacher Training Colleges must be reorganized.

Herbert Passin

WRITER AND JOURNALIST
IN THE TRANSITIONAL SOCIETY

Each nation that enters the cycle of modernization must at some point break through in three fields: political and social reform, language, and journalism. The break-throughs may take place simultaneously or at sep-arate times within a broad historical period. In China the May 4th movement of 1919 was a simultaneous climax of literary, philosophical, and political ideas seeking to burst free of the restraints of the half-eman-cipation of the 1911 Revolution. But in India the Bengal renaissance of the late 19th and early 20th century—that outpouring of creative energy in literature, the arts, music, and philosophy led by Tagore—came first; the modern developments in politics led by Gandhi followed by several decades. The Japanese cultural renaissance, insofar as this is the correct label, started about twenty years after the Meiji Restoration in 1868, when political and administrative reforms were well under way.

The relations among these three elements are governed not only by the stage of development of the society but also by its traditions and its specific historic experiences. Underdeveloped countries are not *tabulae rasae* waiting virginally for Western ideas to be inscribed. Each has a long history, a set of predispositions which select out, under specific his-toric conditions, the particular Western influences to which they will respond. There is obviously a great difference between a country like Japan, which enters the modern world with an already established tradi-tion of secular literature, a well-developed script, a relatively well-edu-cated population, and a differentiated class of writers, scribes, scholars, publicists, and users of the written word [1], and a country like the Congo, with no unified national language, a multiplicity of tongues, high

Reprinted from *Communication and Political Development,* Lucian W. Pye (ed.), Princeton: Princeton University Press, 1963, pp. 82–97. Reprinted by permission of Princeton University Press and the author.

illiteracy, and only an indigenous oral literary tradition. The problem of the writer in the advanced non-Western civilizations, like Japan, China, Korea, India, and the Arab states, is therefore fundamentally different from what it is in countries without a powerful secular literary tradition. When the former enter the modernization process, they bring with them a literary tradition and a model of the writer as artist. The problem we have to explore with them is how an older pre-existent literary tradition is gradually transformed in response to new needs, ideas, and literary models. With the societies lacking this literate tradition the problem must start at a more primitive level: how does literature itself, as a creative pursuit and as a profession, emerge?

The relations among these elements also vary with the particular historical situation that is being faced. By now Japan is into her fifth modern generation since the Meiji Restoration. Most of the new French African states are only at the start of their pioneer modernizing generation. It is not only that the particular problems faced are different, but also that each country faces the challenge posed by the West at different times. In effect it is a different challenge and in some senses even a different West. Japan first faced these problems in an age of expansive imperialism and capitalism, when the literary models immediately available to her in the English language were those current in late Victorian England. A flood of novels in the early Meiji period took their inspiration from such secondary literary figures as Bulwer-Lytton and Disraeli. It was only at a later point that real contact was made with the great models of West European and Russian literature. The French African writers, who have given birth to a remarkable, if somewhat limited, literature, had their point of departure in later phases of French literature, so that the influence of symbolism and other modern literary trends has entrenched itself centrally among them. A distinguished Japanese composer, whose son, still in his twenties, is also a composer, once said to me: "I am the Shostakovich of Japan [actually he was much more like César Franck], and my son is the Schoenberg." The father, who was educated in the early 1920's, encountered Western music largely in its late 19th-century romantic form; his models were the late classical tradition. His son, on the other hand, came into musical consciousness of the West in the period of neo-classical and atonalist ascendance, the age of Schoenberg, Bartók (almost passé), Webern, and Berg. "Western music" meant something different to each one.

Moreover, each generation in the course of ongoing modernization faces different problems, and the accumulation of its experience gives the succeeding generation a new starting point. The "struggle generation," with its heroes and renaissance men, gives way to the bureaucrats, engineers, and politicians. In India, which is still only midway through its independence generation, there are already long and loud complaints that the post-independence bureaucrats are betraying the ideals of the Gandhi generation. But in Japan, which is still "modernizing" and "Westernizing," the fifth modern generation is so far from its heroic forebears that the Meiji Era has now entered the realm of historical study and romance. At this point the changes going on in Japan are to be described more accurately as the development of a Japanese version of advanced industrial civilization than as "modernization." Each generation, then, creates a new tradition for its successor. The first modernizing generation faces Western literature from an immediate background of the traditional literature. But for the next generation the past, or tradition, already includes a considerable admixture of Western literature. Contemporary Japanese literature today therefore takes its point of departure not from the pure Japanese past, nor in direct response to Western influences, but from its own tradition, which by now is a melding of both elements that has gone through several stages of achieving its own form.

In this chapter I shall analyze the relations between writers and journalists in the transitional societies. My examples will be drawn mainly from Asia, but occasional reference will be made to other areas as seems appropriate. Inevitably I draw heavily on the Japanese experience, in spite of her uniqueness in certain respects, not only because it is the case I know best but also because I am persuaded it has unique illustrative value.

On the surface there would appear to be no greater contrast than between modern Japan, with her highly developed industrial economy, her near-universal literacy, her 700,000 university students whose number grows yearly, her newspapers reaching millions of readers, her thousands of professional writers, and some newly launched French African state with near-universal illiteracy, an overwhelmingly primitive economy, and a limited intellectual class that is too busy to deal with anything except politics and that has still to establish a regular newspaper. Yet to some extent the difference is one only of degree. Japan, having started on the road of resolute modernization first, has already in one form or another had to face up to the problems others have faced or still have to face. Her history, then, provides us with a preview, as it were, of the choice points, the problems, and the alternatives that lie along the way. The outcomes will very likely be different, but there is much to learn from seeing how different peoples with their own particular traditions and historical experiences have dealt with these problems.

It would be as well at the outset to make clear what we mean by the "writer" and the "journalist." If we look to the extremes, we can define them fairly clearly. At one pole we have the creative artist with a vision, a *vocation*, represented, let us say, by someone like Henry James. At the other we have the technician of words, the scribbler preoccupied with the immediate, the evanescent, the surface; the image that comes to mind is the hot-shot police reporter on the big city daily. But the reality is much more like a continuum. The moment we leave the extremes, the distinctions become blurred. At the higher ranges of journalism the journalist stops being a mere reporter and becomes a commentator, essayist, propagandist—a "writer." The writer who leaves pure fiction becomes a commentator or essayist, thus meeting the journalist moving in the other direction. Even at lower journalistic levels the writer and journalist meet: the human interest of feature reporter is often not clearly distinguishable from the light essayist or short-story writer. If we take the full range of periodical publications, we shall find daily journalism at one end and the literary journal at the other. Yet even these extremes may not be absolutely pure. The press may be an important outlet for creative writing, essays, commentary, and criticism (social, literary, and artistic); and in these activities the professional journalist may take as much part as the professional writer. Between these extremes we find a whole range of weeklies, monthlies, and specialized journals that combine news, commentary, philosophy, politics, literature, aesthetic theory, and literary criticism. Here the journalist becomes a writer, even if not a creative writer, and the writer, as commentator with views on philosophy, aesthetics, politics, and social reform, becomes a journalist. In fact, in the central areas it is hard to separate them out.

I. LANGUAGE AND MODERNIZATION

By now even the casual student of the underdeveloped countries knows about economic growth, political modernization, and national unity. But for some reason the problem of language, which is so central to the development of a modern outlook, has received very little attention [2]. This problem has two principal aspects: first, the need for a modern language capable of expressing new ideas; second, the relation of language to the unified nation-state. The first will be discussed in Part I, and the second, more briefly, in Part II.

In the course of its transition to modernity every non-Western country finds itself at one time or another confronting the problem of language. One reason is simply that in the early stages the content of modernity comes to them in some foreign language, usually a European one. (In Korea, Japanese was the "metropolitan language.") Modern educated people must often therefore actually think their modern thoughts and express their modern sensibilities in a foreign language. Just recently, for example, an Indian friend of mine, a professor of philosophy, commented that he has never, to the best of his recollection, thought in Hindi about philosophical problems. My friend was not educated abroad, and he speaks and writes Hindi very well; but when it comes to the modern philosophical problems that preoccupy him, which he has studied only in English, he feels at a loss to formulate them in Hindi.

This will not surprise us as it applies in the advanced ranges of Western thought that have no counterpart in the traditional languages. For many decades the Japanese medical student was required to write his thesis in German, with the result that he could properly express his medical ideas only in that language; today the vocabulary of Japanese medicine has developed to the point where it is possible to write textbooks and to carry on medical education in Japanese. Nor should we be surprised to discover an African physicist working in some European language rather than in his native dialect. This is quite common in culture contact that involves much borrowing. When the Japanese started to take over Chinese Buddhism, from the 6th century on, they had in the first instance to take it over entirely in the Chinese language. Their own relatively simple language and religion had no counterparts for the complex elaborated *corpus* of Buddhist theology, metaphysics, and philosophy. For several centuries the Japanese sat on this indigestible heap, expressing Buddhist thoughts in mispronounced Chinese, and only gradually domesticating the vocabulary. Some words and ideas became sufficiently current so that they could pass as perfectly good Japanese; others had to be encapsulated and swallowed whole (just as, for example, the Greek word "hubris" becomes a standard part of the vocabulary of philosophers and literary critics; we know that it is not English, but it occupies a place in thought that cannot be exactly filled by any English word); for still others, Japanese equivalents were found or invented. But even after 1,200 years a proper reading of Buddhist texts in Japanese requires special training; the vocabulary has still not been completely digested.

Thus technical language, whether of science, philosophy, or religion, may, we can well understand, have to be expressed for a period at least in a foreign language. But the modern sensibility goes much farther. A good example is the Japanese difficulty in finding a satisfactory generic term for "the people." There are of course many Japanese terms that refer to people in particular capacities or statuses or as biological organisms. But none of these can quite convey the modern notion of people as "citizens," endowed with "rights." Traditionally the people, or the common people (*shomin*), were subjects (*tami*) bearing obligations to their superiors. A wise ruler was enjoined to treat them well and look out for their needs, but this was not a matter of right. Therefore the development of a modern political vocabulary presented unique problems. In the earliest documents of Meiji Japan the term *heimin* (ordinary people) was used, but this had the sense of the "lower orders" as distinguished from the "higher orders." Later words were equally unsatisfactory in one way or another. *Kokumin,* one of the most commonly used, is made up of two elements: *koku*—which means country, or nation, but rather in the sense of state or government; and *min*—which has the sense of subject, rather than people. *Minzoku* (*min* = subject, or people; *zoku* = family, group), which is often used in the Japanese word for "nationalism" (*minzoku-shugi*), emphasizes the national or ethnic group character of the people. *Minshu* (*min* = subject, people; *shu* = type) implies the notion of the people as a racial group. Attempts have been made to use the term *shimin* (*shi* = city; *min* = subject, people), but this cannot have the same connotation as in the West, where the word "citizen" has come from the specific experience of the mediaeval city, with its corporate rights as against the king or the feudal power. More recently Japanese left-wingers have turned to the word *jinmin* (*jin* = person, human; *min* = subject, person) as a closer approximation to their concept as it used in the "people's democracies" [3].

The problem therefore is not simply one of substantive words but of concepts, notions of process, inherent perceptions of logic and order—the expression of ideas and sensibilities perhaps never before expressed in the language [4]. A recent court case in Japan illustrates this dramatically. A prominent politician, Arita Hachiro, has sued the novelist Mishima Yukio [5] for "invasion of privacy." Now, apart from the novelty this presents in Japanese law, the interesting thing is that there is no word in Japanese for "privacy" [6]; the legal brief must use the English word (pronounced *puraibashii*). Arita is charging Mishima with a violation, that cannot be formulated in traditional Japanese, of a law that does not clearly exist on the Japanese lawbooks. The result is the type of anomaly familiar to all observers of the underdeveloped countries.

Here are a few other examples that come to my mind (I am sure that others will have their own pet examples): a group of Korean professors, huddled around a fireless pot-belly stove one freezing February day in 1947 at the University of Seoul, who confessed that they could express themselves much more accurately and freely in Japanese than in Korean; an Indian couple, the wife from the north, the husband from the south, who carry on their ordinary communication in Hindi but in their tender moments express their feelings to each other only in English; or Gabriel D'Arboussier, one of French West Africa's greatest political leaders, energetically campaigning in his elegant French in Kaolack, a Woloff-speaking back district of Senegal, through an interpreter.

These are not, in my view, idle paradoxes. They point to the problem of the modern educated classes, particularly of the writer and the user of words, and to major national problems. How uncomfortable it is to live in an uncertain language medium we perhaps cannot even comprehend. For many modern educated people there is often a sharp separation between the language of thought and the language of emotion or of daily life. An Indian may be raised at home speaking Malayalam and then have his education in English. This means that his early experiences, emotions, and affective relations are carried on in one language and his contact with ideas, modern life, and modern institutions in another. If he then has a traditional family life after he is married, the discontinuity can become very extreme indeed. Or take the case of a Filipino who may have been raised at home speaking Ilocano, then started his education in Spanish and finished it in English; now that Tagalog is being made the national language, in what language will he be able to express himself well? [7] In many countries we find that writers are uncertain of themselves in whatever language they use.

Their uncertainty may not be entirely a disadvantage. At its best it brings a differentiated sensitivity. The writer's words and experiences have a different echo, which may give a shadow and a perspective that the unilingual writer cannot achieve. Thus the non-Westerner writing in a Western language often brings to it a distinctive flavor, as we can see in the poetry of Senghor and other French Africans or in some contemporary Filipino writing. By knowing words in a slightly different way, or by knowing other words for the same experience or for part of the same experience, the experience itself becomes something different. The Indian writer Raja Rao has even argued that this situation offers the possibilities of a new and fresh language. "Indian English," he holds, is not simply an imperfect form of standard English but a distinct language or dialect of its own [8]. In the same vein, a Filipino critic argues that a distinctive Filipino-English, just like Irish, Australian, or American (as distinct from British) English, is in the making: "It is a living language . . . on the lips and minds of an ever growing number of users, with a modified vocabulary and diction, idiom, and sentence structure, and a new cadence. . . . (It) has all the promise of a new way of thought and talk. Upon this new, or rather newest, English, Filipino writers will 'erect' the literary language" [9].

But apart from its implications for the quality of writing and the plight of the writer this linguistic schizophrenia accentuates the separation of the modern educated person from his fellow-nationals who still live a more or less traditional life and carry on their daily existence and thoughts in the traditional language. The alienation of the modern elite from "the masses" has one of its sources right here. The modern educated person often finds that he cannot discuss with the "masses" many of the problems that preoccupy him because they present themselves to him in a foreign language or in words for which the popular language has no counterpart. In some instances he may not even speak the indigenous language well. And since he may be strongly motivated by nationalist and populist-democratic sentiments, his inability to feel himself in real communication with "the people" produces guilt and frustration. In the colonial countries this split between the traditional and the modern sensibility becomes institutionalized in the social structure, and the language becomes one of the important defining elements in the distinction between the traditional elite and the modern elite, between the elite and the masses.

The form in which the modernizing elite takes shape is decisive for this general process. Japan, for example, had the good fortune to be able to carry on her modern development in her own language. She had, of course, to absorb other languages, but these could be taken as objects of study rather than as the languages of thought itself. Undoubtedly she started out with certain advantages, not the least of which—by comparison with many other new states—were a compact geographic area whose borders were more or less clearly defined both by the sea and by virtually unchallenged historical sanction [10]; a population relatively homogeneous in race, language, religion, and custom; and a centralized national state, although not of a modern type. She already had, in spite of dialectical variations, a single well-developed national language that was adaptable to new ideas, or from which new ideas could be constructed. A standardized version of the Tokyo dialect was made the national language and diffused through the schools and all national institutions [11]. Since Japan had resolved on universal compulsory education as early as 1872—well before many Western countries—the national language soon became very nearly universal. Therefore it was completely usable for much of the work of modernization. By 1886 [12] the form of the solution to the colloquial-classical problem became clear, and the new *gembun-itchi* (unification of the spoken and the literary style) provided the basis for the development of a modern literary style based upon a refined and elaborated colloquial. There was always of course a contact with foreign languages, but Japanese were by and large able to think and write in their own language. Foreign languages played an important role in the early stages of the modern educational system through foreign teachers and professors [13] and through foreign-sponsored (usually missionary) schools, but it was not long before the main bulk of foreign teachers were replaced by nationals and the foreign-sponsored schools turned to Japanese. Textbooks were written in Japanese, scientific vocabularies were developed and domesticated, and, although new ideas and concepts continue to come from foreign languages, Japanese is able to absorb them in its own idiom and at its own pace. It is therefore possible for a Japanese to acquire a complete modern, even Western, education in his own language. There is no currently underdeveloped country of which this can be said.

One unique advantage of Japanese—as of several other languages—is its possession of a "classical" language. Japanese has an open-channel relationship with Chinese, drawing upon it for new concepts and vocabulary, much as we do with Latin and Greek, or the Indians with Sanskrit, or the Arabs with classical Arabic. Not all classical languages are equally usable, of course, but most of them have such a long tradition of literature and speculative philosophy, as in the case of Sanskrit, that they offer at least the same resources as Latin for the construction of new words. The question is a highly technical one, but we may put it very briefly: confronted with new ideas and objects, a language has fundamentally two alternatives—to generate new words from its own resources, or to incorporate foreign words *in toto*. The Japanese, for example, when trying to express the notion of a "motor" could create a neo-Japanese term derived from Chinese root-words, *hatsudōki* (generating-motion-machine), or simply take over the foreign word, which they pronounced as *mōtā*. All languages do both—and in the example given the Japanese did both at the same time—but there is a great variation in their inherent capacity to generate a modern vocabulary and style from their own resources. Fashion, and the vagaries of nationalistic sensitivity, may also have something to do with the final decision. Many new nations seem to be wasting an inordinate amount of time trying to create words for Western objects and ideas when they might more conveniently take over a Western word. During the war, for example, Japanese ultranationalism required the purging of the language of Anglicisms, so that *beisubōru* (baseball), a perfectly acceptable and understandable word for Japan's national sport, had to be rendered in a Sino-Japanese neologism as *yakyū* (field ball). (It has now become *beisubōru* again.)

A Japanese type of development seems possible to some extent for certain other countries that have either escaped colonialism or have an adequate linguistic basis for the growth of a modern language. It would take us too far afield to discuss them in detail here, but we might mention Hebrew, Korean, Thai, Chinese, Vietnamese, Burmese, Arabic, and Bahasa Indonesian. Whether they will in fact succeed, and how long they will take, is quite another matter. All we can say is that they show the possibility of developing into a modern unified national language.

How different is the situation in countries that have experienced a long period of colonial domination, or that have either no usable literate language or no single language with an unambiguous claim to priority, we can see in India, the Philippines and most of Africa. None of these were historically nations in the Western sense, and in none had there ever been a sovereign political state which covered exactly the same territory as the present governments. In India, for example, there are dozens of separate "national" groups speaking fourteen major languages and hundreds of dialects. Under British rule English became the common language of the educated classes, and even of the semi-educated, since it was the language of administration and of education. The attempt to make Hindi the national language runs into the opposition of entrenched institutions and also of the other language groups, jealous of their status and convinced that Hindi is inferior to their own languages. The Bengali and Marathi are able to argue with some justice that they have a much more developed literature than Hindi. The speakers of the southern, Dravidian languages, which are not even genetically related to Hindi, have additional objections. The establishment of Hindi, they feel, will impose an enormous burden on them. Every person will have to speak his native language at home and in his own province, and in addition he will have to learn the national language. Beyond that, however, educated southerners feel that they will have to know English as an international language, so that at the very least they will have to know three languages, all of them unrelated. If in addition the speaker comes from some dialect area in the south, he may very well have to dominate a minimum of four languages in order to operate: his native dialect, the standard language of his region, Hindi, and English. The Philippines have similar and perhaps even more difficult problems; because the indigenous languages all lack an important literate tradition [14], there is serious question whether they provide within the foreseeable future a sufficient basis for a modern language. The many tribes of which the Philippines are made up speak dozens of distinct languages, such as Tagalog, Visayan, Ilocano, Bicol, Pampango, and Moro. None has an unchallengeable claim to priority; Tagalog, which has become the national language, apparently provides the best groundwork for a national language, but Visayan can claim more indigenous speakers [15]. The problem is complicated by the fact that the first national modern language was Spanish. Although it is slowly dying out, it still lives on, especially among the upper classes and older educated people. Since the American occupation, English has become the true national language of the educated and administrative classes. Whether it can really be displaced by Tagalog is a major cultural and political problem [16]. In most of the new African states the situation is even more difficult; there is no language for which even the slightest claim to status as a national language can be made. The result is that all of the new African nations must carry on the business of modernization —administration, economic development, public enlightenment, education, and intellectual development—in the metropolitan language, either English or French.

In all of these cases the problem has not been the "recovery" of independence, or the "restoration" of a previously existing sovereign nationhood, but rather the creation *de novo* of a common national sentiment among all the people living in a given geographic area: in other words, the creation of a nation where none existed before. If we allow ourselves to speculate on the future, there would appear to be three models to which these new nations can approximate: first, a strictly federated form, such as the Swiss, where each local language would remain in full force and with no single national language. Many people, however, would be likely to learn at least one of the other regional languages. Second, the complete dominance of one national language and the reduction of the others to dialect status for purely domestic or local use, as in the case of a number of European countries. In France, for example, Provençal, Breton, and Basque carry on a feeble local existence while French is the effective language of national communication, literature, thought, administration, and education. A less extreme case might be Spain, where Catalan, Basque, and Gallego still manage to carry on a minor literature in spite of the overwhelming domination of Spanish. The third possible model is that of the Soviet Union: the vigorous existence of certain local languages along with the complete penetration of Russian as the national language. In most of the new African states the "national" language is most likely to be foreign, either English or French.

II. LANGUAGE AND POLITICS

Let us now look at the relations of language to politics in the narrower sense. Most of the new states come into existence without that unity of sentiment, geography, administrative organization, language, and cultural tradition that is taken for granted as the basis of nationhood in the more settled states. Japan and Korea, with their relatively homogeneous populations sharing the same language, culture, and tradition, come closest to the Western conception of the nation state. But even an enduring historic entity like China was not so much a nation-state in the modern sense as a multi-national empire with a central core of Han people and a periphery of tributary states. The rest, as we have seen, are to a great extent creations of the colonial powers. Their geographical limits have been determined by extremely complex historical considerations, and when we come to the newly formed African states it is apparent that the present limits cannot be assumed to be permanently fixed. A common national language becomes an urgent necessity for the promotion of the sense of nationhood and, therewith, national unity.

It is not surprising therefore that in many of the new states the problem of language penetrates into the very heart of national politics in a way that it no longer does, except peripherally, in the more settled states [17]. A few examples will illustrate this linkage of language and politics. The reform of the Turkish script was, we may recall, a basic part of Ataturk's political program. In India the attempt to establish Hindi as the national language presents the country with some of its most pressing current issues. It has aroused the provincial nationalism of the non-Hindi language groups; stirred deep regional, communal, and cultural divisions; and forced the reorganization of state boundaries to the accompaniment of vast civil violence running into tens of thousands of deaths [18]. The ramifications of the language problem reach into the inmost problems of the country—in literature, the arts, journalism, education, and public life. In Ceylon the problems of the national language, of the recognition of the minority language, and of the relations between the speakers of Sinhalese and Tamil are central to an understanding of what is happening today. The very basis of pan-Arab nationalism, Albert Hourani has argued eloquently, lies in the community bounded by a common language rather than by religion or by traditional law. ". . . [language] emerged as the common good of the Near-Eastern people, just as law had been their common good in the past" [19]. In China language reform is an old political issue; the struggle for the ascendance of *pai-hua*—the vernacular, spoken language—as against the stilted classical, official language, which played such an important part in the May 4th Movement, has been well won, but the Chinese Communists have raised new issues by their radical plan of replacing the traditional system of ideographic writing with a fully alphabetic script. For thirty-five years the Japanese virtually suppressed the use of Korean as a public language [20], much as the Russians did with Polish; the result is that the Koreans today have among their most urgent tasks to bring their language up to date and to develop a body of materials that can be used for study in the schools and universities. At the end of World War II, when Korea became independent, Seoul National University (formerly the Japanese Keijō Imperial University) had a library of several hundred thousand volumes in Japanese but virtually none in Korean except for some of the classics. A whole modern literature and journalism, not to speak of textbooks, had to be developed in the Korean language, and to a great extent by a generation whose modern education and modern sensibilities were expressed in Japanese, just as so many Indians today can properly express their (modern) [21] ideas only in English. In black Africa there is virtually no new or prospective state (with the possible exception of Somalia) that does not have built into the very center of its problems that of language; their modern development must be carried on in the metropolitan language they have inherited in their schools, public institutions, and administrative structure. Some of the more ardent pan-Africans of the Présence Africaine have proposed the development of Swahili as a pan-African language, but so far none of the African languages has a realistic and enforceable claim to the status of national language. The tenuous and fragile unity of the new states, most explosively illustrated in the Congo, is constantly menaced by divisive groups based primarily on linguistic allegiance.

Since writers and journalists are by definition professional users of language, we can expect a priori that their work, even without explicit intent, is often more political in implication than it would be in countries with a more settled relation between language and politics.

NOTES

1. Almost two hundred years before the opening of Japan there was a distinctively modern flavor in her literary life. The Genroku period (1688–1704) saw a modest renaissance in literature and the popular arts based upon the rising strength of the cities and the urban classes. (This was the period of the *ukiyo-e,* the "pictures of the floating world," perhaps the form of Japanese art best known in the Western world.) From Genroku on, a lively publishing industry developed, with large commercial publishing houses and professional writers and book illustrators. Large editions, running into the thousands, were published, using an improved version of the traditional wood-block prints, to satisfy the vastly increased audiences created by the growing prosperity and aggressiveness of the urban population. Commercial lending libraries distributed these to even larger audiences. Sansom describes a publisher's party of the early 19th century that has the solid ring of Madison Avenue: ". . . over eight hundred guests, including the elegant and the vulgar . . . more than two hundred who had not been invited. Meals were served for 1,284 persons." Among the guests were "Confucian scholars; academic painters . . . ; three renowned calligraphers; leading colour-print men . . . ; comic prose writers and poets . . . ; and distinguished officials and scholars as well as a number of publishers, book sellers, paper-merchants and wood block makers. Glamour was added to the occasion by the presence of important military personages from the shogun's court." (*The Western World and Japan,* London, The Cresset Press, 1950, pp. 232–233.) The best account of the Genroku renaissance will be found in Howard Hibbett, *The Floating World in Japanese Fiction,* New York, Oxford University Press, 1959.
2. One of the few full-length treatments of language problems in a transitional society is John De Francis' interesting, if somewhat biased, analysis of the language issue in China, *Nationalism and Language Reform in China,* Princeton, Princeton University Press, 1950.
3. This term is used in the official name of Communist China, as translated into Japanese, *Chūgoku Jinmin Kyowakoku* (Chinese People's Republic).
4. See Edward Sapir (chapter on "Language," in *Culture, Language and Personality,* selected essays edited by David G. Mandelbaum, Berkeley, University of California Press, 1958): "It would be difficult in some languages, for instance, to express the distinction which we feel between 'to kill' and 'to murder,' for the simple reason that the underlying legal philosophy which determines our use of these words does not seem natural to all societies. Abstract terms, which are so necessary to our thinking, may be infrequent in a language whose speakers formulate their behaviour on more pragmatic lines. On the other hand, the question of presence or absence of abstract nouns may be bound up with the fundamental form of the language; and there exist a large number of primitive languages whose structure allows of the very ready creation and use of abstract nouns of quality or action" (p. 36).
5. The reader may recognize him from some of his novels translated into English: *Five Noh Plays, Temple of the Golden Pavilion, Confessions of a Mask,* and *The Sound of Waves.*
6. Other languages also seem to lack a generic word for "privacy." The reader might have an interesting time trying to formulate a sentence using the word in French, Spanish, or Italian. In Spanish one can use *privado* as an adjective, but there is no noun counterpart; all the possible words imply solitude, retirement, isolation,

secrecy, reserve, etc. The same is true in French. What this implies for "national character," I would not presume to say.

7. "One cannot write completely in a language in which one does not think," Leopoldo Yabes reminds us in his "Fifty Years of Filipino Writing in English," *Literary Apprentice,* 1951, p. 97. "The earlier writers thought in Spanish or perhaps in the vernacular; while the younger writers, at least the more able among them, think in English."

8. In the preface to his collection of short stories, *The Cow on the Barricades,* Bombay, Oxford University Press.

9. Cristino Jamías, "Our Literature in English," *Literary Apprentice,* 1951, p. 107.

10. There were marginal problems with the Russians in the north and with the Chinese over the Ryukyu Islands.

11. This was done energetically from 1882, with the publication of a plan by Yatabe Ryōkichi.

12. With the publication of Mozume Takami's *Gembun Itchi* in that year.

13. At the peak of foreign influence, in the late 1870's, there were over 5,000 foreign teachers in Japanese schools, particularly in the sciences and technology. (Hugh Borton, *Japan's Modern Century,* New York, Ronald Press, 1955, p. 176.)

14. I am aware that there were some pre-Spanish scripts in the Philippines, perhaps syllabaries related to those of Malay. But these completely disappeared under Spanish rule to the point that no effective indigenous literate tradition remains for modern Filipinos. The effective starting point of their own literate tradition is Spanish and English.

15. According to the 1939 *Census of the Philippines,* the three divisions of Visayan (Cebuan, Hiligaynon, and Samar-Leyte together) tallied 6,491,699 speakers, while Tagalog tallied 4,068,565. For the considerations that went into the selection of Tagalog as the national language, see Ernest J. Frei, "The Historical Development of the Philippine National Language—III," *Philippine Social Sciences and Humanities Review,* Vol. xv, No. 2, June 1950.

16. The rancorous debate on this issue in Filipino intellectual life is linked with a new wave of Filipino nationalism, part of the search for disengagement from American "cultural domination" and for a new "Asian personality" for the Filipinos. For the feeling of this argument, see the recent article by Jose Villa Panganiban, Director of the Institute of the National Language, "Language and Nationalism," *Comment, Second Quarter,* 1960.

17. In Spain, for example, where Basque, Catalan, and Galician separatism still remain latent political issues.

18. At the moment of writing (August 1961), India is going through another language struggle. Master Tara Singh, leader of the Sikh community, is in the midst of a fast "unto the death" to force the establishment of Sikh as the official language of the Punjab. Sikh is already, it should be noted, one of the two official languages, along with Hindi. Moreover, the only difference between Sikh and Punjabi—the vernacular of the Punjab State—is the script: Punjabi is written in the Devanagari script, as is Hindi, while Sikh is written in Gurumukhi; otherwise the two "languages" are identical. This is a good example of how passionately people feel about language allegiances. For the first time in Indian history, however, a political fast has been challenged: two Hindi leaders have concurrently entered a fast "unto the death" to prevent the government from giving in to Master Tara Singh's demands.

19. Albert Hourani, "The Regulative Principle of Society," in *Democracy in the New States—Rhodes Seminar Papers,* New Delhi, Office for Asian Affairs, Congress for Cultural Freedom, 1959.

20. The use of Korean was not forbidden outright, but it was discouraged, and

Japanese was deeply entrenched as the official, public language. Immediately after the annexation of Korea in 1910, the Korean language was permitted in the inferior schools for Koreans but not in the superior institutions. All Korean language newspapers were abolished except for one, the *Mei Ilbo*, which was under government control. After the independence demonstrations of 1919, the policy was eased somewhat, so that two vernacular newspapers as well as magazines could be published. In higher education, although the main channel for advance, the Keijō (Seoul) Imperial University, carried on in Japanese, several mission colleges were allowed to offer Korean as an elective. But in 1940, with the intensification of the war crisis, the use of Korean was almost completely prohibited.

21. There is a Yoruba proverb which seems appropriate here: "Modern traps are extremely good for catching modern rabbits."

Clifford H. Prator

THE BRITISH HERESY IN TESL

As the title indicates, this is frankly a polemic paper. It deals with a doctrine regarding the teaching of English as a second language (TESL) which I believe to be unjustifiable intellectually and not conducive to the best possible results in practice. Though the line of thinking here opposed is heard from non-British sources, and in spite of the fact that some British specialists in TESL appear not to subscribe to it, to label it the British heresy is perhaps not too great an exaggeration. In recent years it has repeatedly been championed, all too ably and persuasively, by some of the most prestigious methodologists and linguists of the United Kingdom, and I have yet to see it challenged in print by a British authority [1]. On the other hand, the French and the Americans, who share with the British a major interest in fostering the teaching of their national language in many parts of the world, seem to reject the doctrine in question with near-unanimity.

In a nutshell, the heretical tenet I feel I must take exception to is the idea that it is best, in a country where English is not spoken natively but is widely used as the medium of instruction, to set up the local variety of English as the ultimate model to be imitated by those learning the language. The plan of this paper calls for exploring the ramifications of the doctrine, stating the case that is usually made in favor of it, attempting to point out the fallacies in that case, contrasting the British with the typically French and American points of view, seeking the reasons for the contrast in the differences among national psychologies and social structures, and finally indicating the apparent practical effects on language teaching of the application of the doctrine.

THE DOCTRINE OF ESTABLISHING
LOCAL MODELS FOR TESL

It would be manifestly untrue to suggest that the British originated the idea that there is a special Indian variety of English that should be

459

taught in the schools of India, a Ghanaian variety that should be the model for young Ghanaians, an Egyptian variety for Egyptians, etc. The same proposal has at times been made by Filipinos with regard to the English taught in the schools of their own country, an area in which American influence has been strong and British influence correspondingly slight. In fact, such proposals seem to arise spontaneously and inevitably in every formerly colonial area where English has been the principal medium of instruction long enough for the people to begin to feel somewhat possessive about the language.

The doctrine of establishing local models for TESL thus appears to be a natural outgrowth of the much deplored colonial mentality. It is met with sporadically almost everywhere in formerly colonial countries but is particularly prevalent, for reasons that I shall attempt to explain later, in formerly British possessions such as India, Pakistan, Ceylon, Ghana, and Nigeria. It does not seem to flourish in countries that have little or no recent history as colonies. English is very widely used as a medium of instruction in Ethiopia, yet I have never heard of an Ethiopian proposing that an Ethiopian variety of the language be taught in his country's schools. An Afghan will probably be greatly pleased if you tell him he speaks English like an Englishman or an American; an Indian may be quite disconcerted by the same remark.

Perhaps as colonial memories fade and new generations grow up under independent regimes, the doctrine will die a natural death and the practical problems that it entails will thus be solved. On the other hand, if it is allowed to make its way unopposed in the meantime, it could harden into pedagogical dogma and become very nearly ineradicable. In its least sophisticated form the argument in favor of the doctrine is often stated in some such terms as these: "The Americans don't speak like Englishmen; they have their own kind of English. The Scotch, the Australians, the South Africans each speak their own particular brand of English. Why shouldn't we have our own variety too? We have studied the language in our schools for many years now and shall probably continue to do so. Many educated citizens of this country speak English better than some Americans and Englishmen. We prefer to learn to speak the language as our educated countrymen do rather than as you speak it. It's much more important for us to understand one another well than to understand outsiders" [2].

The objections to foreign models usually single out the element of pronunciation; there is little tendency consciously to reject traditional grammatical structures or lexical items. There is a bland assumption that no essential difference exists between a mother-tongue variety of English and a second-language variety. It is also assumed without proof or evidence of any kind that an Indian, for example, will necessarily understand Indian English more easily than any other type.

THE BRITISH METHODOLOGISTS'
CASE IN FAVOR OF THE DOCTRINE

In the last decade this line of thinking has been accepted and developed by many of those to whom English teachers in areas formerly controlled by the British look for professional guidance—the linguistics and methodologists in the universities of the United Kingdom and the TESL specialists sent out by various British agencies to help strengthen English instruction overseas. It seems reasonable, then, to see more than a coincidence in the fact that indigenous models for English instruction have generally been most enthusiastically approved at centers where the influence of these expatriate specialists has been particularly strong: at the Central Institute of English in Hyderabad and the University of Malaya in Kuala Lumpur, for example.

A typical formulation of the case in favor of the doctrine—and the version in which it is perhaps most likely to come to the attention of teachers of ESL around the world—is to be found in the recently published work on *The Linguistic Sciences and Language Teaching* by Halliday, McIntosh, and Strevens. The authors hail the emergence of varieties of English that are identified with and specific to particular countries from among the former British colonies. They argue that:

"In West Africa, in the West Indies, and in Pakistan and India . . . it is no longer accepted by the majority that the English of England, with R P as its accent, are the only possible models of English to be set before the young. These countries are now independent yet retain English as an administrative and official language. Many of the new professional and political leaders, however, speak English very differently from the way Englishmen speak it. Their grammar remains that of standard English, with few important variations; their lexis, too, differs little from the normal usage; but the accent is noticeably and identifiably local.

"One need be neither surprised nor upset by such developments, which are part of a normal pattern of sociological and political evolution. They provide these countries with their own 'model' of English and permit the school generation to orient their learning towards a home-grown product rather than an imported one. It seems to be in general true that, if the people of these countries identified the English language with colonial rule and lack of independence, this was very largely through the social and educational accent-markers of the professional and governmental Englishmen they were accustomed to meeting; English without these markers, and a fortiori English with local markers, is quite neutral and can the more readily become a tool for communication, to be used or discarded according to practical considerations" [3].

The authors admit that not all the kinds of variant English heard in a country such as India are suitable as instructional models.

"It is possible to suggest two basic criteria to determine whether a variety of English is acceptable for use as an educational model. First, it must be a variety actually used by a reasonably large body of the population, in particular by a proportion of those whose level of education makes them in other respects desirable models. This means that we would exclude forms of English which have been invented or imported and bear no relation to the professional and educational standards of the country. Second, it must be mutually intelligible with other varieties of English used by similar professional and educated groups in other countries. . . . It follows from this that the extent of deviation from Standard English grammar and lexis must be small. It also follows, as far as phonology is concerned, that while the actual quality of vowels and consonants may vary a great deal between one accent and another, the number of contrasts, the number of phonological units, and the number of systems being operated must also remain fairly close to those of other 'educated accents', since otherwise speakers of one would have great difficulty in understanding speakers of another" [4].

Halliday, McIntosh, and Strevens seem to believe that suitable varieties of English, meeting their two criteria, actually do exist in the countries in question and that there will thus be no need to "invent" one. Others incline to think that much language engineering will be necessary in order to create a variety that will meet each country's needs. In the case of India, for example, "it would seem to be most efficient and economical to tolerate a good deal of common interference from Indian languages" [5]. "It is not worth while spending an equal amount of time trying to eradicate each kind of interference. It is necessary to decide first what uses the English language will be put to, at what levels and in what dimensions intercomprehensibility is desired, and what resources are available to tackle the problem. It is then necessary to discover, partly by linguistic analysis and prediction and partly by experiment, which interference factors do cause real trouble at the levels and dimensions under discussion. It is necessary to investigate not only the contrastive features themselves of the languages involved in the contact situation but also the functional load carried by these features" [6].

Advocates of the doctrine appear to agree in expecting that, if a local variety of English gains acceptance as the instructional model in a given country, the chances that the language will continue to play a significant role in the life of that country will thereby be considerably increased. Halliday, McIntosh, and Strevens see this role as that of "a tool for communication, to be used or discarded according to practical considerations." Others go further and avow the hope that such acceptance will be accompanied by the emergence of English as one of the indigenous languages of the country [7]. It will then be possible for a Malayan, say, to use Malayan English as a means of identifying himself with his own national culture [8]. However, unless an "educated standard variety of English" can be identified or created "in those countries where English is not the native language of an indigenous white population," the only alternatives may be "some form of Pidgin as an indigenous lingua franca which may flourish or English spoken simply as a foreign language by fewer and fewer of the population" [9].

FALLACIES IN THE CASE

It is not easy to understand how men who have always been counted among the faithful can have fallen into so ill-buttressed a heresy. The fallacies in their strange doctrine seem to cry out for enumeration and denunciation.

Second-Language Varieties of English Can Legitimately Be Equated with Mother-Tongue Varieties

The British, American, and other mother-tongue types of English are each the unique linguistic component of the culture that produced them and are inseparable from the rest of that culture. They are the languages by means of which all members of the culture, with negligible exceptions, live their entire lives, formulate their thoughts, communicate with one another. They have sprung from a common linguistic stock and have evolved at a relatively slow rate over the decades since they achieved their separate identities. Such changes as have occurred in them have been largely the result of little-understood processes of internal evolution and have kept pace with other elements of social change; even after many years of semi-independent development these types of English are still characterized by a high degree of intercomprehensibility, especially as spoken by the well educated.

Second-language varieties of English, on the other hand, are usually mastered by no more than a small minority of the population in the countries where they are spoken. Most speakers of them have a very imperfect command of only a limited portion of the language. They may be used often or very rarely, but almost no one has recourse to them to fulfill all his needs for communication; typically they are reserved for use with specific individuals in a narrowly restricted range of situations. The more intimate and meaningful parts of life are lived in a different and more congenial tongue, one which—in contrast to English—seems to abound in the nuances of expression needed for social intercourse and to provide the *mot juste* with unfailing ease. In a second-language situation English usually has bookish associations and connotations; the mother tongue smacks of the realities of daily existence. Infinitely more than a few concessions regarding English pronunciation, graciously granted by schoolteachers, would be needed to accomplish the miracle of making English as suitable a medium as the vernacular or vernaculars for expressing the national culture.

Furthermore, whereas mother-tongue varieties of English are relatively stable, second-language varieties are never free from the strongest sort of pressures impelling them toward rapid and radical change. Powerful countervailing influences must constantly be brought to bear if the linguistic interference stemming from the vernaculars is to be held within bounds. Inherently, a second-language variety of English is a tongue caught up in a process that tends to transform it swiftly and quite predictably into an utterly dissimilar tongue.

Second-Language Varieties of English Really Exist as Coherent, Homogeneous Linguistic Systems, Describable in the Usual Way as the Speech of an Identifiable Social Group

There is no doubt of the existence of a certain linguistic phenomenon that is often popularly and impressionistically labeled "Indian English." Among the prominent features whereby it can be recognized are tendencies toward equalizing the four or more degrees of phonemic stress notable in mother-tongue types and toward using retroflex consonants for /t/, /d/, /n/, and /l/. Some of these features are shared by a great many speakers, but the rub is that very few speakers limit their aberrancies to the widely shared features: each individual typically adds in his own speech a large and idosyncratic collection of features reflecting his particular native language, educational background, and personal temperament. To be sure, mother-tongue varieties of English also lack complete consistency, and even idiolects vary with circumstances. The great difference lies in the fact that the amount and range of individual linguistic variation is much greater among an otherwise homogeneous group of speakers using a second-language type of English than among a similar group of Britons or Americans.

Although there is variation within all types of natural languages, the amount of variation itself may be said to vary along a sort of continuum. Mother-tongue and second-language types appear to be separated by so wide a distance along the continuum as to justify speaking of a difference in kind rather than a mere difference in degree. In any given second-language-speaking group the task of determining the system of *la langue* by listening to *la parole* of many different individuals is probably impossible to achieve through the use of the descriptive techniques usually employed by linguistic scientists [10].

It is likely that the only way to define Indian English clearly enough to set it up as an instructional model would be by arbitrary decision and prescription. Such a definition as "Indian English is the English spoken by educated Indians" would have no scientific meaning; there are undoubtedly some educated Indians who distinguish nine vowel phonemes, others who distinguish eleven. The only recourse would be to decree that Educated Indian English has, say, 11 vowel phonemes; at least the speakers of the language could then be easily determined, but they would not constitute a natural social group.

A Few Minor Concessions in the Type of English Taught in Schools Would Tend to or Suffice to Stabilize the Language

Second languages, like mother tongues, are learned primarily by the imitation of a model. However, in second-language learning the imitation is generally quite imperfect, for reasons that are obvious. An imitation of the imitation is normally still less like the original model, and the deviation becomes progressively more marked with each new link in the chain of imitation. The ultimate original model for all the learning of English that takes place in a second-language situation was indubitably a mother-tongue variety of English.

It would seem that the only possibility of halting or reversing the process of change through progressive deviation would be to find some way of moving the model in the direction opposite to that of the deviation. To allow or even encourage the model to follow the deviation could only accelerate the process of change; one concession would simply become a justification for calling for further concessions. The end product would be, in the case we are considering, a pidgin or jargon, defined by Bloomfield as "nobody's language but only a compromise between a foreign speaker's version, and so on, in which each party imperfectly reproduces the other's reproduction" [11].

"Intelligibility" Could Serve as a Practical Guideline in Setting Up Limits Beyond Which no Concessions Would Be Allowed

"A little deviation will do no harm as long as intelligibility is maintained and we continue to understand one another," is the tenor of the argument. But intelligibility is a relative rather than an absolute quality. It may approach 100 percent in the case of a speaker and hearer who always use the same variety of the same language, know each other well, and are close to each other in a quiet room; it may be near zero when two perfect strangers attempt to converse, separated by some distance in a noisy street and neither at all familiar with the language spoken by the other. And of course it may fall anywhere between the two extremes. What percentage of intelligibility shall we content ourselves with? Between whom and whom? Under what circumstances? How is a percentage of intelligibility calculated?

The "-emic/-etic" distinction, unfortunately, does not supply an an-

swer. There is ample evidence that a great deal of variation at the phonetic level, even when all phonemic distinctions are preserved, can reduce intelligibility to a point at which no reliable communication takes
place [12]. It seems to be a fact that at present we simply do not know
what types of deviation from the phonetic norms of a language contribute
most to unintelligibility. Until more accurate information becomes available, a language teacher would be well advised to regard unintelligibility
not as the result of phonemic substitution, but as the cumulative effect
of many little departures from the phonetic norms. Under certain circumstances, *any* abnormality of speech can contribute to unintelligibility.

A Second-Language Variety of English is Necessarily More
Intelligible to a Native of the Country Where That Variety Is
Spoken Than Is a Mother-Tongue Type of English

What little objective evidence I have seen is inconclusive but points
rather in the other direction. Ladefoged, in an informal experiment with
Filipino students at UCLA, tested their ability to identify English mono-
syllables as pronounced by a speaker of Received Pronunciation, by an
American from the Middle West, and by other Filipinos. The Filipinos
understood both the American and the Englishman much more often
than they did their own compatriots. Similar results were reported by
Strevens from a more formal experiment he conducted some years ago
in Ghana:

"Taking first the recordings made by the Received Pronunciation
speaker, the average score of Received Pronunciation-speaking subjects
was 84%, while the average score of Type 2-speaking subjects [speakers
of that type of English used in Southern Nigeria and Southern Ghana]
was 62%. When it came to the recordings made by the speakers of Type
2 pronunciation, the averages were 27% by Received Pronunciation-
speaking subjects, and 35% by Type 2-speaking subjects. Even allowing
for imperfections in the design and conduct of the tests, it seems an in-
escapable conclusion, on the basis of these figures, that Type 2 pronunciation is a less efficient means of communication" [13].

One Level of a Language, Its Phonology, can Be Allowed to
Change Without Entailing Corresponding Changes at Other Levels

When the case endings of Old English ceased to be distinctive through
phonological change, the position in the sentence of the direct object,
which had formerly shown considerable variation, came to be fixed after
the verb. In almost any language with a known history it is easy to find
similar examples of grammatical changes triggered by phonological
changes.

It so happens that English has a considerably larger number of vocalic phonemes than do most of the tongues native to countries where English is widely used as a second language. A general characteristic of second-language varieties of English, then, seems to be fewer vowel contrasts than are heard in mother-tongue varieties. Sometimes the reduction is extreme; many Filipinos, including college graduates who have received practically all their education through English, regularly replace the 11 to 14 vowels of American English by the three vowels (/i/, /a/, /u/) that constitute the entire inventory of most Philippine languages. The effects of this phonological reduction are quite sweeping at the lexical level. Even to reduce the number of vowel contrasts to five or seven, in a largely mono-syllabic tongue such as English, is to produce literally thousands of new homonyms and thus to decrease drastically the amount of redundancy in the language.

If there is any level at which change in second-language varieties of English might well be encouraged, it would seem to be the lexical level rather than the phonological. New words are certainly needed to identify things and processes for which there is no name in British or American society. But is there really any need for new phonological and grammatical structures?

*It Would Be a Simple Matter to Establish a Second-Language
Variety of English as an Effective Instructional Model Once
It Had Been Clearly Identified and Described*

If linguists actually did succeed in describing or agree on prescribing a national brand of English for, say, Indian students to learn, there is every indication that it would still have to be taught not only to the students but also to the great majority of their teachers as well as to the teachers of teachers. And anyone familiar with TESL should realize what a tremendous expenditure of time and effort is required to produce even a slight change in pronunciation habits of adults who have known English for most of their lifetime. Is it realistic to expect that the Indian government would provide, on behalf of any language other than perhaps Hindi, the massive financing to pay for all the special workshops, the scholarships, the language laboratories that would be needed? It appears that such funds as could be made available might effect a more notable change in the quality of the English spoken if the instructional model were set up at a respectable distance than if aim were myopically taken at a target found close at hand.

*Students Would Long Be Content to Study English
in a Situation in Which, as a Matter of Policy, They
Were Denied Access to a Mother-Tongue Model*

Apparently a policy of this sort is already in effect in the Union of South Africa and is justified by phoneticians at the University of the

Witwatersrand. In the materials produced at Witwatersrand for upgrading the pronunciation of nonwhite teachers of English, the aim is definitely not to equip these teachers with South African English (SAE) but with a slightly modified version of African English in southern Africa (SAAE). "In spite of the zeal which Africans of all ages bring to the learning of English and their desire for 'proper' English, the pressures behind the maintenance of aberrant African English must be reckoned with." It is explained that one of these pressures is the "undesirable social connotations connected with young Africans using British English or SAE pronunciation" [14].

To imagine the effect that such a policy would have if made official in Nigeria or India, one has only to explain the South African situation to a Nigerian or an Indian and then await the inevitable reaction. The speaker of a second-language variety that has been thrust on him, he indignantly rejects the idea that this language should be deliberately withheld from him if he wishes to acquire it.

*Granting a Second-Language Variety of English Official
Status in a Country's Schools Would Lead to Its
Widespread Adoption as a Mother Tongue*

If two centuries of British colonial rule in India were insufficient to make English the mother tongue of a significant proportion of the population, it seems quite unlikely, to say the least, that this result will now be achieved by incomparably less potent means.

THE FRENCH AND AMERICAN POINT OF VIEW

French and American methodologists and linguists have not often expressed themselves in writing regarding the doctrine of establishing local models for instruction in French or English. Perhaps this is because the possibility that such a step could be seriously considered has never occurred to many of them. It would not be easy to find discussants to present both sides of the question at a regional conference in Chicago or Lyons. In the United States, where language teaching is strongly influenced by linguistics at present and the "audiolingual" approach has the support of almost all theorists, there is little tendency to question the prime importance of teaching pronunciation or to challenge the widely accepted dogma that the aim of such instruction should normally be to enable students to approximate as nearly as possible the pronunciation of one who speaks the language as his mother tongue. In France, where it is a duty of the government to define and describe the national language and where the attraction of Parisian speech is unrivaled, any deviant pronunciation of the language is likely to be quickly dismissed as dialectal.

There is mutual agreement that the types of English and French generally spoken in formerly colonial areas are recognizably different from the metropolitan variety or varieties of the language, but there is little inclination to view types that practically nobody speaks natively as comparable in stability, homogeneity, or usefulness to established mothertongue varieties. The Americans perhaps incline slightly more than the French to accept the appearance of second-language varieties of their mother tongue as a quite natural, even inevitable phenomenon. If a second-language variety should actually come to be spoken natively by a majority or a sizable minority of the population of a given area, Americans would certainly feel strongly that that variety should be given every recognition and encouragement. Barring such an eventuality, however, few Americans or French can see the wisdom of setting up, say, Philippine English or Senegalese French, as the official and ultimate model for school instruction.

Probably the strongest argument in favor of maintaining a mothertongue variety of the language as the model, in the eyes of both the French and the Americans, is that if teachers in many different parts of the world aim at the same stable, well documented model, the general effect of their instruction will be convergent: the speech of their pupils will become more and more similar to that of pupils in many other regions, and the area within which communication is possible will grow progressively larger. If many diverse models are chosen, however, and one concession to regionalism leads to ever further concessions, the overall effect is bound to be divergent. Widespread intercomprehensibility will be lost with no guaranteed corresponding gain in local intelligibility. In the Philippines the most widely understood Filipino speakers of English (the radio announcers, the actors, the distinguished orators) attain their effectiveness in communication by approximating American pronunciation.

In one developing country after another the government is making strenuous efforts to establish an indigenous language (Filipino, Bahasa Indonesia, Malay, Hindi, Sinhalese, Arabic, Swahili, etc.) as the preferred medium of communication within the national boundaries. As more and more of these attempts are successful, the importance of English and French will increasingly reside in their usefulness as channels to the outside world. The shift in the role of the latter two languages is accelerated by the internationalization of economic development programs, the vastly augmented dependence of men everywhere on science and technology, and the oft-cited shrinkage of the world. The present moment in history appears to be a singularly inappropriate time to set about the deliberate cultivation of varieties of French and English that would have less international viability than the currently taught varieties.

The British cite the gradual elimination of expatriate teachers in formerly colonial countries as a reason for taking a pessimistic view of the possibility of maintaining present standards of pronunciation (though in many countries the number of such expatriates is actually greater today than ever before as a result of the efforts of the Peace Corps and other similar agencies). The French and Americans tend rather to look to newly developed electronic teaching equipment as a reason for optimism. Americans also note that, perhaps for the first time in history, local dialects of the standard languages spoken in such advanced areas as France, the United States—and the United Kingdom—are beginning to converge rather than continuing on their divergent ways. It seems reasonable to believe that the same forces that are changing the direction of the evolution of the mother-tongue varieties of English and French—greater mobility, new media of communication, urbanization, mass education—will eventually make their homogenizing influence felt on second-language varieties as well.

POSSIBLE REASONS FOR THE CONTRASTING VIEWS

Though a polemic among academicians and educators about the teaching of pronunciation may on the surface seem to be a very insubstantial matter, we can be sure that its roots run deep. For reasons already alluded to in this paper, pronunciation is almost always a sensitive point. If my general thesis here is correct, the neuralgic pain that normally results when the point is touched is less acute for the British than for the French and Americans. Whether one approves or not of the greater tolerance of deviations from their mother tongue which the British appear to show, it is instructive to try to explain how they came to develop it.

One part of the explanation must certainly lie in differences in the linguistic model that the three countries have to offer to the rest of the world.

The British model is Received Pronunciation (RP), as described by Daniel Jones, Ida Ward, and a series of other distinguished phoneticians. RP is the pronunciation "very usually heard in everyday speech in the families of Southern English people who have been educated at the public schools (in the English sense). This pronunciation is also used (sometimes with modifications) by those who do not come from Southern England, but who have been educated at these schools" [15]. It is essentially, then, a variety based on a social class rather than a geographical region. In recent years, as opposition to the class system has grown stronger in the United Kingdom, more social approval has been extended to a somewhat wider range of pronunciation types, and the model is now often referred to as "B.B.C. English" or "intellectual middle-class city dwellers" [16]. But RP appears to have lost little of its former prestige, and certain doors to social and professional advancement are still quite slow to open to one who does not show himself a master of it.

As the Englishman hopes that his speech labels him as a gentleman, so the Frenchman hopes that his pronunciation identifies him with Paris. A few purists would prefer the more conservative accent of Tours or Orleans, but the choice seldom wanders far from the Ile de France and is normally expressed in geographical terms. The forces of officialdom, education, the communication media, wealth, and intellectual life are all arrayed on the side of the language of the capital to an extent that is equalled in few other countries.

The American would usually find it difficult to say what kind of English he prefers, provided only that it be a variety that makes a person sound very much like everybody else. Bostonian English has long since lost any prestige it may once have enjoyed throughout the rest of the country, New York speech is widely regarded as part of a comedian's stock in trade, and a distinct educated Washington accent is probably indefinable. Social classes are difficult to distinguish in the United States, and social dialects show relatively little systematic variation. The best that American phoneticians have been able to come up with in their efforts to describe an acceptable national model has been the General American English on which the Kenyon and Knott *Pronouncing Dictionary of American English* is based. General American is a form of Midwestern speech and, though recent research has shown that it does not have the widespread range it was once thought to have, it is probably the variety that strikes the largest number of Americans as least strange.

At least one well known British linguist believes that many of his countrymen have a deep-seated mistrust of the African who presumes to speak English too well [17]. The mistrust of French and Americans seems rather to be directed toward the outsider who does *not* speak French or English well. A man who consciously regards language as a symbol of social status is naturally suspicious of one who appropriates the symbol but clearly does not belong to the social group that it typifies. If an Englishman is himself a proud speaker of RP, he may find each encounter with a person who obviously does not speak his language well a pleasantly reassuring reminder of the exclusiveness of his own social group. On the other hand, the American's greater experience with large numbers of immigrants, whose presence in his country he has felt as an economic threat and a social problem, undoubtedly helps to explain his greater antipathy toward foreign accents. In France the tourist and the expatriate may have contributed to a similar attitude.

Another important part of the explanation for the contrasting national points of view must reside in the quite dissimilar history of the three countries as colonizing powers. Great Britain has been a fertile mother of commonwealths peopled by settlers of predominantly British stock, a powerfully formative experience that France and the United States have not shared. As the early English colonies gradually evolved into independent nations, Britons became inured to the idea that the colonials would relinquish none of their legitimate rights to their mother tongue, that the English language could no longer be regarded as the exclusive property of Great Britain, and that in time new national varieties of English would have to be recognized. Recognition has been followed by a growing pride that the mother tongue has given birth to a whole family of new Englishes. It would be nice to have the family a little larger, even if that should mean confusing mother-tongue and second-language varieties.

A dominant theme of French colonial policy has always been the gradual assimilation of the indigenous population into the life and the civilization of France: marriage between Frenchmen and colonials has been encouraged officially; when possible, territories have been thought of as overseas *départments* of France with representation in the national legislative assembly. When applied to language teaching in the schools, this policy has led to the use of French as the universal medium of instruction from the first grade on and to the general exclusion of the vernaculars from any role in education. The Chairman of the *Comité Interafricain de Linguistique* of the *Conseil Scientifique pour l'Afrique* notes: "The French language is normally regarded, by those responsible for teaching it, as part of a complex which may be termed, the French way of life. This to an outside observer also appears to be generally accepted by French speakers as a quite proper attitude" [18]. Within the framework of such a policy, only one answer is possible to the question of the type of pronunciation that should be taught.

The observer cited above goes on to state: "English on the other hand is very frequently regarded [by the British] as a tool to be acquired, without which it is impossible to make progress in other fields of knowledge. Put in its most crude form the difference between French and English in this respect would seem to be that the acquisition of French is normally regarded as an end in itself with certain valuable by-products, but the learning of English as a means to an end." He attributes this attitude of the British toward the use of their mother tongue by outsiders to a quality inherent in the language itself: "it *can* operate in a cultural void . . . cultural factors do not appear to be an essential characteristic of the operation of the English language." I would prefer to attribute the concept of English as a tool or instrument to the Briton's great interest in and respect for cultures other than his own coupled with his tendency to keep people of other races and nationalities at arm's length, and to the generally pragmatic nature of British colonial policy.

The one great experiment of the United States in direct colonialism was carried out in the Philippines. Though there were waverings from time to time, the constantly proclaimed aim of the Americans in replacing the Spaniards as occupiers was, from the very beginning, to prepare the islanders for independence. Certainly most Americans believed this to be the primary aim. Since Filipinos were seldom if ever regarded as potential Americans, it might be thought that the language policy developed for the schools by the American colonial administrators would have resembled the British policy. But there was actually more resemblance to the French: the Philippine languages were allowed no place in education, English was made the universal medium of instruction, pupils were subject to punishment if they were heard speaking their mother tongue during school hours. The administrators explained their decisions in terms of sheer practical necessity. A widespread system of mass public instruction was to be created almost overnight with little or no foundation to build on. American teachers and textbooks had to be imported by the shipload since both Filipino teachers and texts in any Philippine language were quite unavailable [19]. However, the American's conviction that his own language—American English—possesses unequaled virtues, a conviction as unshakable as the similar conviction of the Frenchman, doubtless had something to do with the matter too. By the time American theorists got around to answering the Filipinos' question "What kind of English pronunciation shall we teach?" it was easy to answer "Whatever mother-tongue variety will be most useful to you" in full confidence that the decision would turn out to be in favor of General American English.

PRACTICAL EFFECTS OF THE APPLICATION OF THE DOCTRINE

After 20 years of testing the English of hundreds of incoming foreign students semester after semester at the University of California, I am firmly convinced that for the rest of the English-speaking world the most unintelligible educated variety is Indian English. The national group that profits least from the University's efforts to improve their intelligibility by classroom instruction also seems to be the Indians; they can almost never be brought to believe that there is any reason for trying to change their pronunciation. It is hard to doubt that there is a direct connection between these conclusions and the fact that the doctrine of local models of English is championed more often and more vehemently in India than anywhere else.

At the Brazzaville Symposium on Multilingualism in 1962, the Chairman conceded, as have other British observers before and after him, that "in areas where French or English has been the language of education, the standard of achievement in French is in general clearly superior to that in English in comparable situations" [20]. This is exactly the result that would have been predicted by research carried out over the last eight years on the effects of various types of motivation on achievement in language learning by Lambert of McGill University. "The orientation [toward learning a second language] is 'instrumental' in form if the purposes of language study reflect the more utilitarian value of linguistic achievement, such as getting ahead in one's occupation, and is 'integrative' if the student is oriented to learn more about the other cultural community as if he desired to become a potential member of the other group" [21]. The clearest conclusion to be drawn from Lambert's experiments, which were repeated under several different sets of circumstances, was that "students with an integrative orientation were the more successful in language learning in contrast to those instrumentally oriented" [22]. It was also demonstrated a number of times that "the learner must want to identify with members of the other linguistic-cultural group and be willing to take on very subtle aspects of their behavior such as their language *or even their style of speech*" (italics mine) [23]. It appears obvious that Lambert's "instrumental orientation" corresponds to the typically British attitude toward the teaching of English, and that his "integrative orientation"—of which insistence on aiming toward a mother-tongue type of pronunciation is an essential part—is exemplified by the French approach to instruction in French.

The limitation of objectives implied in the doctrine of establishing local models for TESL seems to lead inevitably in practice to a deliberate lowering of instructional standards. In the minds of many students it becomes a convenient, officially sanctioned justification for avoiding the strenuous effort entailed in upgrading their own pronunciation. It weakens any sense of obligation a teacher may feel to improve his own speech and makes it impossible for him to put any real conviction into his attempts to encourage or impel his students in the same direction. It has no doubt contributed to the reluctance of many authors of elementary English texts to include in them an effective treatment of pronunciation problems; the French and American texts are in general notably superior in this regard. It may have something to do with the relative lack of interest shown until quite recently by the British in the development of language laboratories, which can offer the great advantage of providing an authentic mother-tongue model of English almost anywhere in the world.

The total British effort on behalf of the teaching of English as a second language is too intelligently planned, too well executed, too crucial to the successful development of the emerging countries to allow for an indefinite prolongation of this flirtation with a pernicious heresy.

NOTES

1. Peter Strevens of the University of Essex describes the difference between the British and American points of view as follows: "One of the most important changes that took place in the period between 1950 and 1960 was the acceptance that 'to speak like an Englishman' was not the obvious and only aim in teaching English to overseas learners (as far as speaking ability was imparted at all): in this respect British acceptance of variations of accent in English used overseas has run ahead of American views. Although linguistic theory was applied to language teaching by American workers long before it became a widespread practice to do so in Britain, the linguistic consequences of social and political changes, and especially of newly won political independence, have been recognized and accepted by the British while many American language teachers remained troubled but unconvinced. Some American language teachers accept only American forms of English, but in the eyes of the British language teaching profession one or other of the varieties of English that are growing up may in specific cases be of a kind more appropriate to the local educational systems than any form current in the British Isles. This acceptance is accorded to varieties of English such as those labeled 'Educated Indian English', 'Educated West African English' and so on; and obviously such acceptance makes a difference to the inventory of language-teaching items." M. A. K. Halliday, A. McIntosh, and P. Strevens, *The Linguistic Sciences and Language Teaching*, London, Longmans, 1964, pp. 203–204.

2. Cf. *Linguistics and English Language Teaching*, P. B. Pandit (ed.), Deccan College, Poona, 1965.

3. *Op. cit.* (fn. 1), p. 294.

4. *Ibid.*, p. 296.

5. R. B. Le Page, *Intercomprehensibility between English-Language-Using Communities: a Preliminary Study* (mimeographed), 1966, p. 14.

6. *Ibid.*, pp. 17–18.

7. "It seems possible therefore that by the time any really effective changes [in the language policy in the schools] can be made, English will be too strongly entrenched for the change to be possible. If my forecasts are correct, therefore, English will then begin to emerge as one of the indigenous languages of Malaya instead of one of the foreign languages being learned in Malaya." R. B. Le Page, "Multilingualism in Malaya," in *Colloque sur le Multilinguisme*, Brazzaville, CCTA/CSA, 1962, p. 145.

8. R. B. Le Page, *op. cit.* (fn. 5), p. 20.

9. *Ibid.*, p. 38.

10. It seems significant—no mere coincidence—that no reasonably complete analysis of a second-language variety of English which meets Halliday, McIntosh, and Strevens' two criteria has as yet, to the best of my knowledge, been published. Though some methodologists have been insistently calling for such analyses for more than a decade now, one still only hears of their existence as unpublished master's theses at such universities as Edinburgh and Malaya. It would indeed be interesting to know how many informants were used in these studies and how the informant group was selected.

11. L. Bloomfield, *Language*, New York, Holt, 1933, p. 473.

12. Cf. C. H. Prator, *Manual of American English Pronunciation*, New York, Rinehart, 1957, pp. xii-xiv.

13. P. D. Strevens, "Pronunciations of English in West Africa" (a paper delivered at the Conference of the West African Institute for Social and Economic Research, 1955), in *Papers in Language and Language Teaching*, London, Oxford University Press, 1965, p. 120.
14. L. W. Lanham, "Teaching English Pronunciation in Southern Africa," in *Language Learning*, Vol. XIII, Nos. 3 and 4 (1963), p. 159.
15. D. Jones, *An English Pronouncing Dictionary*, London, Dent, 1956, p. xv.
16. D. R. Powell, "American vs. British English," in *Language Learning*, Vol. XVI, Nos. 1 and 2 (1966), p. 32.
17. I. Richardson, "Linguistic Change in Africa with Special Reference to the Demba-Speaking Area of Northern Rhodesia," in *Colloque sur le Multi-linguisme*, Brazzaville, p. 190.
18. M. Guthrie, "Multilingualism and Cultural Factors," in *Colloque sur le Multi-linguisme*, p. 107.
19. Cf. C. H. Prator, *Language Teaching in the Philippines*, Manila, U.S. Educational Foundation, 1950, pp. 6–8.
20. M. Guthrie, *op. cit.*, fn. 19, p. 107.
21. W. Lambert, "Psychological Approaches to the Study of Language," in *Teaching English as a Second Language*, H. Allen (ed.), McGraw-Hill, New York, 1965, p. 39.
22. *Ibid.*, p. 41.
23. *Ibid.*, p. 40.

Joan Rubin

LANGUAGE AND EDUCATION IN PARAGUAY

THE LANGUAGE SITUATION

According to the figures of the official census of 1950, Paraguay is the most bilingual nation in Latin America and one of the most bilingual nations in the world. In the nation as a whole in 1950, some 52 per cent of the population (three years and older) claimed to be bilingual in Spanish and the aboriginal language Guarani. In the capital itself, some 76 per cent of the population claimed to be bilingual (*Anuario Estadistico* . . . , 1955) [1]. This bilingual character results in large part in the areas outside of the major cities of Asunción, Villarica, Concepción, and Encarnación from the superimposition of Spanish in the school system. The large majority of rural Paraguayans have Guarani as their first language and are first exposed to Spanish in the classroom. Whereas one could live in the rural areas today without ever speaking Spanish, lack of knowledge of Guarani would be a real handicap. Although the reverse is true for the major cities, there are numerous occasions when lack of knowledge of Guarani would isolate a person from casual speech —for example, at even the most formal dinners after-dinner jokes are usually told in Guarani.

In this paper we shall examine how Paraguay has achieved this bilingual character and at what cost. Because the large majority of the rural popu-

The research for this paper was carried out in Paraguay in 1960–61 and during the summer of 1965 and was made possible by the National Institutes of Mental Health Grant MF-11,528, The National Science Foundation Grant GS-872, and a grant from the Wenner-Gren Foundation. The author is indebted to Dr. Efraím Cardozo for calling her attention to certain historical information on language policy; she is also grateful to Ruth Krulfeld and Bernarda Erwin for editorial comments and criticism. The author worked principally in two areas, the town of Luque (population 11,000) and the rural farming area of Itapuamí (population 1,350). In addition, some research was carried out in the cities of Asunción and Concepción, and visits were made to other rural towns and farming areas.

lation is first, and often most concentratedly, exposed to Spanish in the school system, the school system would seem to be of primary importance as a source of language learning. We shall consider how effectively the schools have performed their task.

In Paraguay, sound educational policy concerning the language of instruction would seem to be easy to establish and to implement. There are only two languages, Spanish and Guarani; everyone seems to agree that one of the major goals of the schools should be the learning of Spanish. Yet we suggest that the assumption by school authorities that students are bilingual has prevented teachers from effectively teaching the Spanish language and the rest of the curriculum.

It is unique in Latin America to find the aboriginal language given so much importance. Elsewhere in Latin America the Indian language has a secondary position; city people do not speak it at all or if they do, they may deny their linguistic ability or the aboriginal language's importance [2]. Indeed, one of the major criteria for becoming socially "white" in most Hispanic America is fluency in Spanish [3]. Insofar as we can tell, bilingualism in the rest of Latin America is a transitional stage in the process of changing from a monolingual aboriginal speaker to a monolingual Spanish or Portuguese speaker. This is in strong contrast to Paraguay where we feel bilingualism has been and still is a permanent feature of the society. Such bilingualism presupposes that people continue to use the aboriginal language after learning Spanish. This is indeed the case. In Paraguay, the aboriginal language is spoken by almost everyone. For the country as a whole some 92 per cent of the population (three years and older) was reported to know Guarani; in Asunción, the capital, 86 per cent claimed to speak Guarani (*Anuario Estadístico* . . . , 1955) [4].

While Spanish has probably always been important for communication and business purposes in Asunción, Guarani has also played a striking role as an urban and national language. As far back as 1555 (30 years after the discovery of Paraguay) we find that the colonists had learned Guarani to such an extent that when a small group of Spanish women arrived in Asunción, the frustrated conquerors found that their habitual use of Guarani had inhibited their "speaking in Spanish to real ladies dressed in the manner God expected" (translated from Gandía, 1939, p. 132) [5]. The continuing importance of Guarani during the colonial period is indicated by a report of the Governor of Paraguay who complained in a 1777 report to the Spanish crown of the difficulties the authorities had in communicating with the populace because of its monolingual character (Fernando, 1777, p. 49). Again, in 1791, Peramás noted that even from the pulpit in Asunción, the mysteries of the Catholic religion by popular preference were explained in Guarani, although he reports the audience was largely bilingual (Peramás, 1946, p. 74). The

British traveler Robertson also indicated that in 1815 distinguished Paraguayans visiting him in Corrientes spoke first in Spanish but as soon as they relaxed they turned to speaking in Guarani (Robertson, 1920, p. 104).

The foregoing examples indicate that Guarani served as an important communication medium throughout the early history of Paraguay, not only for those living in the rural areas but also for the most sophisticated citizens of the capital. The importance of Guarani in the post-colonial period of the nineteenth and twentieth centuries is seen in the literature produced in Guarani by prominent Paraguayans. Among the best-known were two by Narciso Colman: *Ocara Poty*, a collection of poems, and *Our Ancestors*, and a well-known epic poem *Ñande Ypycuera*. The success of the major dramatist, Julio Correa, who wrote some 20 plays in Guarani, caused the Mayor of Asunción to write a congratulatory letter noting the value of his work and its contribution to the national theater. Guarani is cited by many as the symbol of Paraguayan uniqueness. Its national function is illustrated by its use as the only language of the army during two major wars—The War of the Triple Alliance, 1865–1870, and the Chaco War, 1932–1935.

However, in spite of its continuing importance and the positive value given it by many citizens, Guarani is and has been the object of considerable disdain. Many urban Paraguayans feel that Paraguay's progress is impeded by the widespread lack of knowledge of Spanish and by the continuing use of Guarani. Monolingual speakers of Guarani are often the object of a series of pejoratives. The man who controls only Guarani is called a *Guarango* (country-bumpkin, boor), he is thought to be *menos inteligente* (less intelligent), *menos desarrollado* (less cultured), and *no tiene principios* (without principles). Monolingual speakers of Guarani even refer to themselves as *tavi* (stupid) because they are unable to speak Spanish. The continuing use of Guarani is often seen by literary scholars as an important factor in the dearth of Paraguayan Spanish literature. Guarani is said to *entorpecer la lengua* (dull the tongue). This fact then serves to explain Paraguayan inability to speak or write effectively in Spanish.

These negative feelings toward Guarani underlie its total rejection by the Constitutional Congress of 1870. When the representative from Paraguari, a small town in the interior, moved that Congress members be permitted to use Guarani if they so desired, the response was a "general hilarity" and the motion ". . . was fought energetically by the deputies . . . who requested not only that it be rejected, but also that in the future the making of such motions be forbidden. The Assembly by a two-thirds vote rejected the motion" (translated from Decoud, 1934, p. 179).

LANGUAGE IN EDUCATION

We have suggested that throughout Paraguayan history Guarani had an important role as a means of communication for all Paraguayans and often served as a source of group identity once independence was gained. At the same time, Spanish served as the language of government and as a vehicle for communication with other countries. Through these functions, Spanish gained prestige. Thus, although Guarani seems to have been in greater use, it was often viewed with disdain as the more primitive language. As a result educational policy has always prescribed Spanish as the only possible medium of instruction.

In establishing the school curriculum, little or no account was taken of the greater importance of Guarani as the main means of communication. The Ministry of Education seems to have assumed that Spanish was to be the official language of instruction. No concern seems to have ever been expressed for the many school children to whom Spanish was almost a foreign language. Many teachers today feel that since in most towns some people speak Spanish, the children will have an opportunity to hear it and will automatically understand it when they hear it in school. This is, of course, an unfortunate fallacy. As we have indicated, one can get along quite successfully in the rural areas without Spanish.

Over the years the Ministry of Education has ignored the discrepancy between educational policy and linguistic reality. Teachers have tried to teach monolingual Guarani speakers to read, write, and do arithmetic in Spanish without first giving them language lessons. The Ministry has expected teachers to use Spanish in the classroom as early as possible. At the same time, all of the teachers we interviewed indicated they had been given no special instruction in their normal school preparation on how to cope with the language problem.

In 1812 the governmental junta advised schoolteachers to make sure that Spanish was the language of the classroom and to banish Guarani from school usage (*Instrucciones* . . . , 1812). That this was indeed a difficult problem can be seen from the memoirs of the writer Juan Crisóstomo Centurión, born in 1840. "In school the use of Guarani in class hours was prohibited. To enforce this rule, teachers distributed to monitors bronze rings which were given to anyone found conversing in Guarani. . . . on Saturday, return of the rings was requested and each one caught with a ring was punished with four or five lashes" (translated from J. C. Centurión, 1894, p. 62). In 1894 Manuel Dominguez, head of the Ministry of Education and a man known for his interest in the progress of the school system, referred to Guarani "as a great enemy of the cultural progress of Paraguay" (Cardozo, 1959, p. 82). Whereas Dominguez clearly recognized the problem posed by the monolingual

Guarani speakers, he did not recognize the discrepancy between the requirement for the Spanish instruction and the language ability of the pupils.

Even today the discrepancy goes largely unrecognized. The normal schools do not deal with the problem in their training of teachers. On the other hand, rural teachers in interviews expressed awareness of the difficulties created by monolingualism, but they did not feel it was particularly serious. Instead they indicated that the difficulty encountered was a "normal" part of teaching. In the rural areas we visited, teachers stated that although their students could not speak Spanish, almost all of them could understand it. Our classroom visits usually indicated the opposite. On a couple of occasions, we requested that a class be given in Guarani. The difference in student response was appreciable. Instead of students evidencing the apathy and lack of understanding obvious in the classes given in Spanish, student participation and interest were extremely high when the class was in Guarani.

One principal we met was aware of the language problem. She told us that she had discovered that the best student in Grade 1 of a school on the edge of town was a monolingual Guarani speaker. The child's teacher had been unaware of his ability and had discovered it only when the principal had quizzed the student.

Most teachers blame the student's inability to speak Spanish on a lack of desire to do so. Yet this hardly seems to be the case. Most students who go to school want to learn Spanish and indeed seem eager to learn everything. To test their general learning ability we spent two hours teaching 60 second-grade children three English sentences: *This is chalk. This is a pencil. This is an eraser.* On our return four years later we found children who still remembered these equivalents. Yet the very same students could not give us the Spanish equivalents of these common school utensils.

In the first few grades, many teachers begin by using a limited amount of Spanish, which is gradually increased as the year progresses. Translation into Guarani is the most frequent technique used to convey the meaning of Spanish. The teacher says the sentence in Spanish, translates it into Guarani, and then asks the student to repeat in Spanish. Another technique is the memorization of poems and stories in Spanish. For many children these exercises remain completely rote during the first months or years of their education. In one rural school we found, for example, that when the first-grade teacher asked the students a question, they replied by repeating the question instead of answering it. We also found that, in order to avoid the silences which resulted from the monolinguals' lack of comprehension, the teacher called more frequently on the bilingual students, thus showing awareness of a communication problem without fully understanding it.

In addition to reliance on the translation-repetition method, some teachers forbid the use of Guarani in the classroom and at times also on the playground. This procedure, which used to be more common, has been considerably discouraged recently. Teachers have been requested to encourage use of Spanish but not to exercise sanctions against those using Guarani. In some schools teachers put monolingual and bilingual students together in the hope that the exposure will aid the monolinguals. A third procedure is to encourage the use of Spanish in the homes of students. Parents often talk about the need to use Spanish, and many make the effort when they remember. However, for many monolingual parents this is impossible, and of those who do try to speak Spanish to their children, many continue to speak Guarani to their spouses and friends, so that the exposure to Spanish is often limited.

A byproduct of the insistence on Spanish in the classroom is the widespread conviction that Spanish alone is appropriate there, even among students who speak only Guarani. So strong is this feeling that when we requested the use of Guarani both teachers and students broke into laughter. Parents who are incipient or subordinate bilinguals are often inhibited in their conversations with others because they feel Spanish is the appropriate language for such a meeting.

Although there is a greater need for a good Spanish model in the rural areas than elsewhere, it is unfortunately true that rural teachers are often limited in their ability to speak Spanish and their general academic preparation. The result is that rural students are less skilled in Spanish and in their school subjects than their co-equals in town.

The lack of attention to the language problem resulting from the fiction that Spanish is heard by all has many serious repercussions. To mention one, students acquire Spanish very slowly. High-school teachers reported that students in the seventh grade level were often so deficient in Spanish that they could not understand instruction in that language adequately.

Most rural speakers who have had only second- or third-grade education are not very proficient speakers of Spanish. In fact, there is a high correlation between the degree of proficiency in Spanish and the number of school years completed. The number of years of school completed is the major determinant of the linguistic skill of rural inhabitants and, indeed, a major determinant of the skill of many townspeople as well. Tables 1 and 2 use our data to illustrate this point for the rural area of Itapuamí and the rural town of Luque [6].

Several observations can be made from Table 1.

1. A large proportion (77 per cent) of monolingual Guarani speakers had never passed a single school grade. Almost all (92 per cent) of our monolingual speakers had passed no more than first grade.

TABLE 1. *Degree of Proficiency and Number of School Years Completed for 817 Itapuamí Speakers, 10 Years and Above (in raw scores)*

	School Years Passed								
	None	*1*	*2*	*3*	*4*	*5*	*6*	*7 plus*	*Total*
Monolingual[a]	143	27	13	2	—	—	—	—	185
Incipient	45	44	58	23	3	—	—	—	173
Subordinate	12	13	86	102	42	2	2	—	259
Coordinate	4	5	19	40	51	38	30	13	200

[a] The categorization of an individual's linguistic proficiency was based on subjective observation and judgment of the skill of an informant. This impressionistic information was then fitted into Diebold's (1961) useful tripartite scale of bilingualism resulting in the following categories:

1. Coordinate bilinguals—only those individuals who spoke *and* understood both languages well. Persons were included who were fluent but who had some "accent" in the second language, as well as individuals who were fluent but who made the standard sort of lexical interference error of loan translation.

2. Subordinate bilinguals—those individuals who were scored "so-so" in speaking (able to speak but not fluently) and were "good" or "so-so" in understanding.

3. Incipient bilinguals—those individuals who could not speak one of the languages but who in understanding the second language scored "so-so" or "good."

2. Of those whose bilingual ability was considered incipient, the largest proportion (85 per cent) had never gone to school or had passed only the first or second grade.

3. Of those having subordinate bilingual ability, the largest proportion (88.8 per cent) had passed only the second, third, or fourth grades.

4. Of those whose bilingual ability was considered coordinate, the largest proportion (86 per cent) had passed the third grade or more in school.

TABLE 2. *Degree of Proficiency and Number of School Years Completed for 272 Luque Speakers, 10 Years and Above (in raw scores)*

	School Years Passed								
	None	*1*	*2*	*3*	*4*	*5*	*6*	*7 plus*	*Total*
Monolingual	3	—	—	—	1[a]	—	1[a]	3[a]	8
Incipient	4	6	2	—	—	—	—	—	12
Subordinate	5	7	5	10	3	1	1	2	34
Coordinate	5	6	25	31	20	31	49	51	218

[a] Foreigners whose only language was Spanish.

Several observations can be made from Table 2:

1. The number of monolinguals does not correlate to school grade passed because in Luque, five of the eight monolinguals were Spanish speakers.

2. Of those who were incipient bilinguals, the great majority (83.3 per cent) had either not passed a single grade or had passed only the first grade.

3. Of those who were classified as subordinate bilinguals, a small majority (64.7 per cent) had passed the first, second, or third grade. It is interesting that a larger majority had passed only the first, second, and third grades than had passed the second, third, and fourth grades (52.9 per cent). This differs from the finding for Itapuamí where the amount of schooling relates directly to bilingual proficiency.

4. Of those who were coordinate bilinguals the large percentage (83.4 per cent) had had third grade or above education.

5. The opportunities for informal exposure to Spanish in Luque are much greater and would tend to make the direct effect of schooling less than in the rural areas where informal exposure is much less.

It should be noted that other factors do play some part in the acquisition of Spanish proficiency for those whose first language was not Spanish. We found in our study that opportunities to learn Spanish outside the school were sometimes available to rural and urban inhabitants through their jobs and their army service. These opportunities usually occur in adulthood and the amount of Spanish required depends on the particular job or particular post (for example, a man stationed in Asunción would be more likely to learn Spanish than one stationed at an outpost; army officers usually address their men in Guarani).

In Paraguay, a tremendous number of schoolchildren repeat grades several times. In part, of course, such repetition is due to illness or poor attendance, or intellectual deficiency. However, we are convinced that a great part of it results from the student's inability to understand instruction given in Spanish without first having mastered that language. We feel strongly that if greater recognition were given to the student's need to learn Spanish as a foreign language and if more successful language-teaching procedures were followed, the number of grade repetitions would be drastically reduced. To illustrate the extent of this wasteful process of repetition, in Table 3 data collected at a remote rural school are compared with data from two schools in Luque.

It should not come as a surprise that Paraguay has not dealt with this problem. The choice of language to be used in a school system and the individual, social, and practical factors to be taken into account have been the subject of several seminars and studies [7], but the issue is still to be resolved and remains a complex problem. Most educators would probably agree, however, that the child profits from having his first experience in class in his mother tongue, if at all possible [8]. In Paraguay this suggestion has been made repeatedly by the Guarani scholar and educator Francisco Decoud. He has long tried to promote the use of

TABLE 3

Grade	Class Total			Per cent Repeating		
	School 1[a]	School 2[b]	School 3[c]	School 1	School 2	School 3
1	185	210	177	53%	29%	19%
2	150	175	185	61	24	14
3	75	138	129	41	18	9
4	38[d]	140	173	34	19	13
5	20	65	129	20	20	10
6	25	55	89	8	9	0

[a] School 1 in Itakyry (remote rural town).
[b] School 2 in Luque (town close to Asunción). School attracts a great many rural children.
[c] School 3 in Luque (town close to Asunción). Considered to attract the better students in town.
[d] Rural schoolchildren may transfer to town for the fourth grade because many rural schools stop at the third grade.

Guarani as a medium of instruction in the schools and has recommended in numerous speeches that the early grades be taught in Guarani and that the later grades be in Spanish. It is our impression that his efforts have not met with much success. Many people in Paraguay use the arguments often cited in the literature about other countries that one of the important goals of the school curriculum, the widening of the intellectual scope of the child, could not be achieved by instruction in Guarani because of its nonintellectual nature. Even those who understand Decoud's reasoning seem to feel it would be expensive and therefore impractical to create Guarani texts for the classroom.

Another solution that has often been suggested in the literature on this subject is to teach the world language (in this case Spanish) as a foreign language before beginning the regular curriculum. Some scholars argue (Bull, 1955; Le Page, 1964) that the social needs of the community should supersede those of the individual and that the teaching of the language of wider communication should begin as soon as possible. This has only recently been recognized in Paraguay as a possible solution. Recently the UNESCO office in Paraguay has been trying to teach Spanish as a foreign language in the first grade along with other school subjects. When we visited the program in 1965, however, it seemed to be at an impasse because of the teachers' and supervisors' lack of experience in materials preparation and the methodology of foreign language teaching.

SUMMARY

We have tried to present some of the educational problems of Paraguay that seem to arise from the language situation in the country. Paraguay is basically a Guarani-speaking nation with a heavy incidence of Spanish-Guarani bilingualism in which each language tends to fulfill distinct functions. The roles of the two languages are such that Spanish is the language of the schools. We have suggested that such educational problems as the high rate of dropout, frequent repetition of grades, and widespread failure to achieve adequate mastery of Spanish could be dealt with more effectively if administrators and teachers would plan curriculum, instructional materials, teaching methods, and teacher training in explicit recognition of the fact that a large segment of the population is not bilingual and that many schools, especially in rural areas, must therefore teach the children Guarani.

NOTES

1. The 1962 census figures for Asunción (those for the whole country have not yet been released) seem to indicate no major change in this percentage. Of those three years and older, some 79 per cent claimed they *habitually* spoke Spanish and Guarani (República de Paraguay. *Censo . . . 1962, 1965*). This figure is probably somewhat higher since it can be assumed that of those who said they habitually spoke only Spanish or Guarani, some must also be able to speak Guarani or Spanish, respectively. It should be noted that exact comparability is lost because the 1950 census question asked about language ability and the 1962 census question asked about habitual language usage (Cf: Lieberson, 1966, for a discussion of the need for gathering comparable linguistic data in censuses).

2. According to the Mexican census of 1950, approximately 2 per cent of the population of Mexico City spoke Spanish and an aboriginal language; according to the 1960 Mexican census this percentage was reduced to 1.1 per cent; according to the Peruvian census of 1940 (none was available for 1950 and the 1961 census figures for language ability are not yet in print), approximately 10 per cent of the population of Lima spoke Spanish and the aboriginal language.

3. The conflict presented in "passing" from "Indian" to "white" is illustrated by the often-cited dilemma of a Peruvian Indian who went to the coast to "pass," learned Spanish, and married a chola girl (Spanish-speaking lower-class person). Much later, some Indian friends of his appeared and to tease him insulted his wife in Quechua. He was faced with the alternative of protecting his wife and his manhood by defending himself in Quechua, and thus admitting his Indian origin, or keeping silent and maintaining his "white" character.

4. The 1962 census figures for Asunción (República de Paraguay. *Censo . . . 1962, 1965*) indicated that these figures do not seem to have changed substantially. In Asunción, 84 per cent said they habitually spoke Guarani; in addition, some of those who habitually spoke Spanish also probably know Guarani and their ability should be added to the above percentage. See footnote 1 for the difficulties encountered in comparing the figures from these two censuses.

5. The rather complex social and political reasons for the initial and continuing importance of Guarani are taken up in Rubin, *National Bilingualism in Paraguay*, Chapter 2, in press.

6. Tables 1 and 2 and the comments following are from Rubin, in press.

7. International Seminar on Bilingualism in Education . . . , 1965; UNESCO, *African Languages and English in Education*, 1953; UNESCO, *The Use of Vernacular*

Languages . . . , 1953; John MacNamara, 1966; UNESCO, *Foreign Languages* . . . , 1963; Eugene A. Nida, 1949; Peter Wingard, 1963; John Bowers, 1966; and Robert Le Page, 1966).
8. Eugene A. Nida, 1949; UNESCO, *The Use of Vernacular Languages* . . . , 1953; UNESCO, *African Languages and English in Education,* 1953.

REFERENCES

Anuario Estadístico de la República del Paraguay 1948–1953. 1955. Asunción: Ministerio de Hacienda Dirección General de Estadística y Censos.
Bowers, John. 1966. "Language Problems and Literacy," Conference on Language Problems in Developing Nations, Nov. 1–3.
Bull, William E. 1955. "Review of: The Use of Vernacular Languages in Education," *International Journal of American Linguistics,* 21, 288–294.
Cardozo, Efraím. 1959. *Historiografía Paraguaya.* Mexico: Instituto Panamericano de Geografía e Historia—Comisión de Historia.
Censo Nacional de Población y Ocupación 1940. 1942. Lima.
Centurión, Juan Crisóstomo. 1894. *Memorias del Coronel Juan Crisóstomo Centurión ó sea Reminiscencias históricas sobre la guerra del Paraguay.* Buenos Aires: J. A. Berra.
Decoud, Hector Francisco. 1934. *La Convención Nacional Constituyente y La Carta Magna de la República.* Buenos Aires: Talleres Gráficos Argentinos L. J. Rosso.
Diebold, A. Richard. 1961. "Incipient Bilingualism," *Language,* XXXVII, 97–112.
Fernando de Pinedo, Agustín. 1777. Unpublished "Informe del Gobernador del Paraguay, Agustín Fernando de Pinedo, al Rey de España Sobre la Provincia del Paraguay." Asunción: January 29, 1777. [Published in *Revista del Instituto Paraguayo,* 52 (1905)].
Gandía, Enrique de. 1939. *Francisco de Alfaro y la Condición Social de los Indios.* Buenos Aires: El Ateneo.
Garvin, Paul L., and Madeleine Mathiot. 1960. The Urbanization of the Guarani Language—A Problem in Language and Culture. In Anthony F. C. Wallace (ed.), *Men and Cultures.* Philadelphia: University of Pennsylvania Press, pp. 783–790.
Gokak, V. K. 1964. *English in India: Its Present and Future.* Madras: Asia Publishing House.
Instrucciones para los maestros de Escuelas por la Junta Superior Gubernativa. 1812. Asunción: February 15.
International Seminar on Bilingualism in Education, Aberstwyth, 1960. 1965. *Report.* London: H. M. Stationery Office.
Le Page, Robert B. 1964. *The National Language Question.* London: Oxford University Press.
———. 1966. "Problems to be Faced in the Use of English as the Medium of Education in Four West Indian Territories." This volume, pp. 431–442.
Lieberson, Stanley. 1966. "Language Questions in Censuses," *Sociological Inquiry,* 36, 262–279.
MacNamara, John. 1966. *Bilingualism and Primary Education: A Study of the Irish Experience.* Edinburgh: Edinburgh University Press.
Nida, Eugene A. 1949. "Approaching Reading Through the Native Language," *Language Learning,* 2, 16–20.
Octavo Censo General de Población, 8 de junio de 1960: Resumen general. Mexico City: Dirección General de Estadística.

Osterberg, Tore. 1961. *Bilingualism and the First School Language. An Educational Problem Illustrated by Results from a Swedish Dialect Area.* Umea.

Peramás, José Manuel. 1946. *La República de Platón y los Guaraníes.* Buenos Aires: Emece, Editores, s. a. (1st edition, 1791).

República de Paraguay. 1965. *Censo de Población y Vivienda 1962 Asunción.* Asunción: Ministerio de Hacienda.

Robertson, John P. 1920. *La Argentina en la Epoca de la Revolución. Cartas sobre el Paraguay: Comprendiendo la Relación de Una Residencia de Cuatro Anos en esa República, Bajo el Gobierno del Dictador Francia.* Buenos Aires: Administración General Vaccaro.

Rona, Jose Pedro. 1966. The Cultural and Social Status of Guarani in Paraguay. In William Bright (ed.), *Sociolinguistics.* The Hague: Mouton, pp. 277–293.

Rubin, Joan. *National Bilingualism in Paraguay.* The Hague: Mouton (in press).

Séptimo Censo General de Población, 6 de junio de 1950: Resumen. 1953. Mexico City: Dirección General de Estadística.

UNESCO. 1953. *The Use of Vernacular Languages in Education.* Paris: UNESCO. (Monographs on Fundamental Education, 8.)

UNESCO, Educational Clearing House. 1953. *African Languages and English in Education:* A Report of a Meeting of Experts on the Use in Education of African Languages in Relation to English, where English is the Accepted Second Language, Held at Jos, Nigeria, November, 1952. Paris: UNESCO. (Educational Studies and Documents, number 11.)

UNESCO, International Studies in Education. 1963. *Foreign Languages in Primary Education: The Teaching of Foreign or Second Languages to Younger Children.* Paris: UNESCO.

Wingard, Peter. 1963. Problems of The Media of Instruction in Some Uganda School Classes: A Preliminary Survey. In John Spencer (ed.), *Language in Africa.* London: The Cambridge University Press.

V

Integrative Summary

Joshua A. Fishman

LANGUAGE PROBLEMS AND TYPES OF POLITICAL AND SOCIOCULTURAL INTEGRATION: A CONCEPTUAL POSTSCRIPT

All nations face the task of finding or defining a usable past in such a way as to contribute to a more viable future. Some developing nations already have attained a substantial degree of consensus and must now struggle with its assets and debits insofar as modern purposes and problems are concerned. Other developing nations have not yet achieved such consensus and must also create a past out of their present rather than merely seek to fashion a better future out of their past. There are difficulties to be faced and language involvements to be pondered in both connections.

THE NEW DEVELOPING NATIONS

The problems of the literally "new nation" are easily recognizable. Its urgent need to attain greater national integration can draw upon precious little, either in terms of a usable sociocultural past or in terms of a usable political past, in relation to its current territorial limits. The recent past is particularly useless to the "new nation." If it is to avoid a federational compromise with national integration (or even greater fractionization) it must pursue both the unification that derives from modern technology and modern life styles and that which derives from current (or from far distant) supraregional myths and symbols. Unfortunately, the resources needed for either (let alone both) of these pursuits are substantial and most frequently lacking. The procedures arrived at have usually and quickly focused upon a Western language and a Western-trained elite as most congruent with the needs of current national efficiency and current national mythology, since the available past is both relatively divisive and archaic (archaic in the sense that the "Little Traditions" of essentially "new nations" are inevitably even less integrative at the national level than are the pre-industrial Great Traditions of "old developing nations"). From the point of view of participation in the nation, regional and local languages are recognized for transitional or short-term purposes only, rather than for more long range integrative purposes—cultural or political. The transition from tradition to modernity and from localized ethnicity to larger scale nationalism (and no nation is *entirely* at one end or the other of these two interrelated continua) will require the acquisition of a foreign tongue, with all of the additional guilt and incongruity, insight and contrast, that is always required when the foreign must be transmuted into the "own." It is out of the long-term process of living with and transmuting a modern foreign technology and a modern foreign language (and the modern foreign life style to which both are anchored) that the future sociocultural integration of the "new nation" will come.

The language problems of the ethnically fragmented "new nation" reflect its relatively greater emphasis on political integration and on the efficient *nationism* on which it initially depends. Language selection is a relatively short-lived problem[1] since the linguistic tie to technological and political modernity is usually unambiguous. Problems of language development, codification, and acceptance are also minimal as long as these processes are seen as emanating justifiably and primarily from the "metropolitan country." The entire panoply of language institutes and language associations is lacking (at least until such time as indigenous norms arise and find favor in the eyes of a newly rising elite). Although some attention may be given to the pedagogic demands of initial literacy (or transitional literacy) for *young* people and to terminal literacy for *old* people in as few local vernaculars or contact languages as is immediately unavoidable, the lion's share of literacy effort and resources is placed at the disposal of spreading the adopted Western tongue of current political (and, it is hoped, of ultimate sociocultural) integration. When fully implemented these efforts include the preparation of teaching and learning materials that take into explicit account the linguistic repertoires of the prospective students and therefore the contrastive learning difficulties that they can be expected to face in the realms of phonology, lexicon, morphology-syntax, and meaning systems. In order to accomplish this goal it may be necessary to provide detailed accounts of the structures of particular languages where these have not hitherto received analytic attention. Such efforts should not be confused with language development per se, although they can be altered and expanded in that direction given proper sociocultural and political redirection.

---

[1] This will not always tend to be the case in those few "new nations" whose sociocultural integration is substantial as a result of the presence of large numbers (or proportions) of speakers of a particular native or contact language. This factor may counterbalance ethnic diversity and lead to developments more akin to those of the "old" or "intermediate" developing societies, discussed later.

The transitional nature of the language efforts and language goals of the essentially "new nations" [i.e., of nations whose political frontiers are quite recent and/or quite unrelated to the sociocultural (dis)unity of their populaces, none of which boasts a widely accepted and indigenized Great Tradition] is both a result of and a contributor to the transitional nature of the sociocultural goals of these nations. Just as language shift toward the adopted Western tongue is the overt or covert goal of nation-oriented language policy, so sociocultural shift toward technologically based modernity (urban, industrial, and postethnic at its base) is the goal of nation-oriented social policy. Just as bilingualism [which inevitably obtains as populations add the language of government, school and modern technology to their initial language(s) of home, immediate region, and indigenous tradition] is expected to be transitional (rather than stable and diglossic), that is, it is expected to be "bilingualism en route to monolingualism" in the new generations, so biculturism (the combination of traditional and modern behaviors in food, dress, religion, amusements, etc.) is also expected to be transitional. The model of the "new national" is primarily that of his "metropolitan" counterparts, with obvious differences only in terms of nation-loyalty, and with less obviously meaningful differences in terms of long-distant primordial, or still to be evolved supranational myths and symbols (Negritude, Pan Africanism, etc.).

The intellectuals of the essentially "new nations" carry the scars of great personal and societal discontinuity but they do not (by and large) carry the burden of creating and rationalizing a new synthesis of old and new. Having broken with the past or having been separated from it, as the case may be, they may literally be among the most modern and most pan-Western in sentiment and in life style on the face of the globe. Their more ordinary compatriots may show greater transitional pangs and "imperfections" but, in general, their traditional patterns cannot be ideologized by them to serve at the *national* level. Barring brief episodes of revitalization (reactions to the dislocation of so much for so many) the essentially "new nations" must be viewed as having embarked on the creation of a new sociocultural-political order rather than on the adaptation or modernization of an old one that still commands widespread loyalty and admiration.

THE OLD DEVELOPING NATIONS

Far different, in all of these respects, is the situation of those developing nations that constitute old sociocultural entities as well as old polities. Their pasts are very much with them and part of them today. Their great religions provide direction for the daily lives of millions, for they are not primarily belief systems (as is the case for Western Christendom

ever since it distinguished between the sacred and the secular, on the
one hand, and between being a Christian and being a national on the
other) but rather systems that are inextricably interwoven with the cultural, economic, and political existence of their adherents. Their ancient
literatures and legal codes command admiration, study, and obedience
to this very day, representing as they do some of the very pinnacles of
human groping toward a definition of the good and the worthwhile.
Their great heroes and leaders of the past cannot be dismissed today,
and their national borders have been hallowed by centuries of common
practice, common sacrifice, and general recognition. The problem of
such newly developing societies is not that of achieving or even maintaining sociocultural or political *integration,* but rather of modernizing
the integration already attained on the basis of untold centuries. As hard
as it may be to create the new out of almost nothing, it may be harder
yet to create it out of the old and the hallowed.

The language problems of the "old developing nations" are quite
different from those of the "new developing nations." Their classical
standard languages usually differ substantially from the current vernaculars of the masses that must be mobilized if national development and
modernization are to be attained. In addition, these languages themselves
must be developed to cope with Western technology and procedure, and
simplified to hasten widespread literacy and participation. The direction
that language development must take is not unambiguous, however.
Just as national integration can alternatively stress ethnic authenticity
or modern efficiency, so can language development proceed in either or
both of these directions. The carriers of modern ideas and modern goals
are themselves most likely to be Westernized or "internationalized" in
language and education. Their tendency may be to import a Western
language *in toto,* if possible, for the purposes of modernity. Since the
availability of a classical great tradition makes this much harder to do
on a broad scale than is the case in the essentially "new nations," the obvious compromise is to use Western loanwords or translation loans to attain
lexical expansion. However, this too is resisted by the guardians of the
classical tradition (writers, teachers, grammarians and priests) and a concerted effort is usually made to utilize traditional lexical and syntactic resources, for conveying modern concepts. As a result, even the modern
educated elites may encounter hardships in extracting precise and appropriate meanings from technical communications that have been rendered
or rerendered in traditional garb.

Language institutes, language agencies, and language associations frequently adopt differing *positions* and proceed at differing *rates* with
respect to the development (modernization) and the simplification (ver-
nacularization) of the traditional language of education and government
that every old-but-developing-national-society possesses. Whereas the "new

nations" frequently employ indigenous languages for transitional purposes en route to (more) widespread adoption of a Western tongue, the "old developing nations" frequently recognize a Western language for transitional purposes en route to (more) widespread adoption of a modernized and simplified indigenous one. Whereas language politics is either a very early or a very ominous phenomenon in the "new nations," it can become a more common, class-related (rather than ethnically polarized) phenomenon in the "old developing nations." Whereas successful language policy in the "new nations" leads to bilingualism en route to monolingualism (i.e., bilingualism without diglossia), successful language policy in the "old developing nations" need aim at nothing more than rendering bilingual each successive monolingual generation. Thus, in the latter case, as each generation arrives at the modern school and in the modern work-arena with its home and neighborhood language variety (and, less commonly, with that variety *as well as* with the unmodernized classical variety obtained through traditional religious and educational exposure), its language repertoire is *expanded* by the addition of the modernized variety without any intended displacement. While interpenetration ("interference") and switching between varieties certainly occurs in the everyday speech of common folk and in the excited or intimate speech of even the more educated, the undeniably greater appropriateness of each variety for specific contexts and functions, and the availability of purity guardians for one or more of these varieties, safeguard their coexistence, barring excessively rapid and disruptive social change.

The stable and widespread coexistence of separate varieties (and even separate languages) in "old developing societies" that have not lost contact with their Great Traditions is indicative of the continued viability of those traditions in the very face of development and modernization. The model national is a bicultural rather than a "metropolitan" or international man. He participates in and contributes to national integration on both the authenticity and the efficiency levels and in both the traditional and modern veins. By combining in himself both the "old wisdom" and the "new skills" he can (in popular belief, at least) help defend the former and civilize (or humanize) the latter. Nevertheless, just as forces on the language front are not entirely in agreement with respect to questions of direction or degree, so is the sociocultural front marked by both extremes of traditionalism and modernity as well as by many intermediate and highly personalized positions. However, whether the coexistence between old and new is symbiotic or compartmentalized, evolving or static, political integration is rarely in danger from internal forces (as is, at times, the case in the essentially "new nations"), since the ethnic origins of all concerned provide an authentic unity that none will deny. As a result, old developing nations can withstand much greater political diversity and unrest as a result of sociocultural change. The centripetal forces set in motion by many centuries of shared tradition more than counterbalance the centrifugal forces that are generated by the modernization and development process per se (as long as these are largely internally directed).

INTERMEDIATE TYPES

If several of the nations of sub-Saharan and East Africa are characterized by the lines of sociocultural, political, and language development previously ascribed to the "new developing nations," and if some of the nations of North Africa, the Near East, and Southeast Asia are characterized by the lines of sociocultural, political, and language development previously ascribed to the "old developing nations," there also remains a third category of developing nations (such as India and Pakistan) that undeniably reveals characteristics of *both* camps. On the one hand their political boundaries are arbitrary from the point of view of perceived authenticity of sociocultural integration. On the other hand several of their sociocultural *components* have strong and uninterrupted links with truly Great Traditions (none of which has had any counterpart at the level of political integration during the past century or more). Countries with such intermediate characteristics seem to present the difficulties of both camps without benefiting from their counterbalancing advantages. The several Great Traditions militate against the development of a single sociocultural authenticity at the national level, perhaps even more so than does the absence of any such Traditions in the truly "new nations." The political boundaries, however, have existed for an appreciable period or have come to represent such considerable political and economic efficiency as not to be easily dismissed. These cases seem to present the makings of federalism, a solution which may initially be resorted to frequently but which may ultimately be as atypical for the developing nations as that of Switzerland, Belgium, and Canada is for the more developed portion of the globe.

The rival Great Traditions in the "intermediate type" developing nations do not permit an early bicultural adjustment to obtain between them. As a result neither a single indigenous national language nor a stable pattern of bilingualism with diglossia on the basis of indigenous languages alone seems to be feasible at a functional level. Nor does it seem probable that a Western language alone can be the basis for political or sociocultural integration, as a sort of "sweet lemons" compromise, as it is in the new nations. Finally, it does not seem that a Western language can serve as a purely and avowedly transitional integrator, since the major problem facing the indigenous languages is not merely that of modernization or simplification for national purposes (both attainable goals) but, rather, that of the "unfair" politico-economic and sociocultural advantage that may come from honorific status for any one national indigenous language at any foreseeable time whatsoever. Thus the "intermediate type" developing nations seem destined to an intermediate type of solution to their language problems. Like the "new nations" they may require the more permanent utilization of a Western language for the purposes of political and economic modernization and national integration. Like the "old developing nations" they may require the development and modernization of several indigenous traditional languages for local and for regional sociocultural modernization and integration. The pretense may be made that one and only one indigenous language is the national tongue but, in actuality, the most common governmental language at the *national* level is a Western one, whereas the language of *regional* integration officially varies from one locality to the next. Thus diglossia and biculturism (to the extent that either will become stabilized in the future) will long tend to involve a *local* Great Tradition language plus the Western ("auxiliary" or "working") language, rather than two indigenous languages or varieties (one local and traditional, the other national and modern) as in countries of the "old developing nations" type.

It is in the case of the "intermediate type" developing countries that

National Languages and Languages of Wider Communication in the Developing Nations

Factors	*Cluster A Nations*	*Cluster B Nations*	*Cluster C Nations*
1. *Prior sociocultural integration*	*No* integrating *Great Tradition* at the national level	*One Great Tradition* at the national level	*Several Great Traditions* seeking separate socio-political recognition
2. *Selection of national language* (= *N*)	Governed by considerations of political integration: nationism	Governed by considerations of sociocultural authenticity: nationalism	Governed by need to compromise between polit. integ. and separate authenticities
3. *Adoption of LWC*	Yes, as permanent, national tool and symbol	Often transitionally: for modern functions	Yes, as unifying compromise (working lang. = W)
4. *Language planning concerns*	Minor: exonormative standardization of LWC	Modernization of traditional lang. H or L?	Modernization of several traditional languages
5. *Bilingualism goals*	Local, regional; transitional to LWC	National; transitional to indigenous monolingualism	Regional bilingualism (H and L, W and N) and national bilingualism (W and N)
6. *Biculturism goals*	Transitional to modernity	Traditional plus modern spheres	Traditional plus modern spheres
	New Developing Nations	*Old Developing Nations*	*Intermediate Developing Nations*

language problems may well be most intense and diversified, at least until the noncontending stage of federalism is reached. As in the case of the "new nations," there will be serious problems of spreading and improving mastery of a single Western language that can serve the immediate purposes of political and economic integration. As in the "old developing nations," there will be differences of opinion as to the rate and the extent of desired modernization of the languages of classical scholarship and Great Tradition. An additional danger is a possible strife-ridden "period of adjustment" in which various groups, primarily larger ones, strive to establish their tongue as *the* (or as *a*) national language, while other groups, primarily smaller ones, agitate to obtain for their tongue the perquisites of previously recognized local languages. These struggles are, on occasion, only minimally politicized, that is, they are not always seen as subject to political bargaining and political compromise. It often takes considerable time until language claims, intertwined as they are with convictions concerning authenticity and primordial righteousness, can be rationalized, politicized, and adjudicated. Once that stage is reached, and not before, the relatively stabilized Swiss Federational model (rather than the less stabilized Belgian or Canadian ones) can begin to serve as an appropriate beacon for developing nations of the "intermediate type." It is only then that the claims of *national* political and economic integration can receive separate attention, without seeming to threaten or to be threatened by the authenticity of *local* Great Traditions and their relative modernity or traditionalism.

Author Index

A lower-case n before a number indicates footnote (100 n2 = page 100, footnote 2).

Subject Index

A lower-case n before a number indicates footnote (100 n2 = page 100, footnote 2).

Abur (Komi) alphabet, 254, 259, 260
Adamawa province, Nigeria, 203, 211 n36
Admiralty Islands, 346
Adrar, Nigeria, and adrarci, 200
Afghanistan, 89, 460
Africa, ix, 8, 54, 89
  English literature and, 102, 183–197, 421
  European development modes, 6, 18, 48 n8, 49 n12, 108–118, 119, 122
  Israel immigration, 238, 241
  multilingual nations of, 44, 45, 46, 50 n17, 51 n21, 61, 69, 85 n7, 8, 92–93, 102, 117, 119–120, 121, 184, 394, 415–516, 452, 454
  nationalisms of, 48 n8, 11, 215–217
  territorialist movements in, 215, 216
  urbanization of, 111–113
African National Congress, 216, 220
Afrikaans, 223
  nationalism, 6, 216–217, 218, 219
Afrikaners, 216–219
  apartheid policies, 220–221
Agades, Nigeria, 201
Age, and Arabic language skills, 135, 142, 171, 172, 175, 177, 179
  British West Indians school-age population, 435–436, 438
  and Hebrew language styles, 239–241, 242, 245, 246, 249 n2
  and migration, 111, 112, 114–115
  Peruvian school-age population, 404, 409
Agriculture:
  Arab, 132, 133
  Belgian Congo, 298
  France, 113, 114

linguistic homogeneity, 56, 110, 114–115, 387
Peru, 409
slave labor, 88–89
Sudan, 167, 170–171, 173, 174, 176, 178
see also Rural areas
Aleut, 255
Algeria, 62(tab), 95(tab), 99(tab), 105 n3
  Arabic spread in, 100(tab), 134(tab), 135, 137–139
  educational goals in, 133, 136 139, 143, 148 n7–9, 150 n18, 398
  French domination of, 88, 130, 131, 133
Alphabets, 253, 454
  Amharic, 231
  Cyrillic, 255, 259, 260, 392–393
  Haiti Creole, 319–320, 325 n19
  Komi, 254, 259, 260
  Latin, 270, 366, 368, 369–370, 375, 392, 393
  literacy programs and, 385, 388, 391–393, 395, 396, 397
  Quechua, 229, 405
  tone marks, 234–235, 395
  and unstandardized languages, 75, 78, 82, 83, 85 n18–19
Alsace, France, 108
  Alsatian dialect, 110–111, 112–113
Alur, 303
Amerindians, 434
Amhara, 72
Amharic, 82, 85 n8, 231
Ancash, 411, 412 n2
Angola, 96(tab), 120, 295
Apartheid, 216–221
Arabic, 73, 259, 398, 454, 469

505